Library and Information Center Management

Recent Titles in Library and Information Science Text Series

LIBRARY AND INFORMATION CENTER MANAGEMENT

Seventh Edition

Robert D. Stueart and Barbara B. Moran

Library and Information Science Text Series

U N L I M I T E D

A Member of the Greenwood Publishing Group

Westport, Connecticut • London

Library of Congress Cataloging-in-Publication Data

Stueart, Robert D.
  Library and information center management / Robert D. Stueart and
Barbara B. Moran. — 7th ed.
      p. cm. — (Library and information science text series)
  Includes bibliographical references and index.
  ISBN 978–1–59158–408–7 (alk. paper)
  ISBN 978–1–59158–406–3 (pbk. : alk. paper)
  1. Library administration—United States. 2. Information services—
United States—Management.   I. Moran, Barbara B. II. Title.
  Z678.S799 2007
  025.1—dc22   2007007922

British Library Cataloguing in Publication Data is available.

Library of Congress Catalog Card Number: 2007007922
ISBN: 978–1–59158–408–7
        978–1–59158–406–3 (pbk.)

First published in 2007

Libraries Unlimited, 88 Post Road West, Westport, CT 06881
A Member of the Greenwood Publishing Group, Inc.
www.lu.com

Printed in the United States of America

The paper used in this book complies with the
Permanent Paper Standard issued by the National
Information Standards Organization (Z39.48-1984).

10 9 8 7 6 5 4 3

To our grandchildren
Annika, Jacob, Katherine, Madison, Magnus, and Molly

Contents

Section 1: Introduction

Section 3: Organizing

Section 4: Human Resources

Section 5: Leading

Section 6: Coordinating

Section 7: Managing in the Twenty-First Century

Illustrations

FIGURES

TABLES

Preface

Thirty years ago, when the first edition of this book was published, little had been written about the management of libraries and information centers. Those seeking advice, examples, and information about how to manage libraries were forced to search for answers in the literature of public administration or business management. Since then, there has been a growing interest in the topic reflected in the large number of articles and monographs published on all aspects of management of library and information centers.

The first edition of *Library Management*, written by colleagues Robert D. Stueart and John T. Eastlick, was conceived as a basic text for library and information science curriculum, primarily in North America, because the authors were both faculty members in schools on that continent. Many students in programs for which the textbook was intended had work experience in libraries or other types of information centers before entering graduate school, but they had little understanding of the theories and philosophies that impact the environments in which they worked or would be working in the future. They simply accepted patterns of library and information center organization, personnel procedures, budgetary controls, and planning processes, with their mission and goals—if they were even stated—as a given, without understanding why processes and procedures were followed. They were subjected to the "what" and "how" without understanding the "why." Even when examples and forms, such as budgetary and personnel evaluation forms, were available, these were mostly regional or type-of-center specific and did not reflect a broad cross-section of libraries and information centers in the United States, not to mention the rest of the world. The second edition was broader in scope. While maintaining its usefulness as a basic text, it also served as a primary source of information and contemplation for lower- and middle-management personnel. Its geographic scope broadened to be more representative of practices throughout North America. The third edition, published in 1987, had a new coauthor, Barbara B. Moran. This edition brought additional insight, expertise, and depth to the discussions. With the fourth edition, published in 1993, the two authors expanded the coverage to include themes of importance for an international audience. Over that 15-year period, the previous editions had been translated into several languages—some without prior knowledge of the authors and publisher. That edition also changed its title to *Library and Information Center Management* to more accurately reflect a broader focus and to incorporate a deeper discussion on each topical chapter, with new materials, features, topics, examples, and insights. The fifth edition identified trends, updated discussion of research and theories, and was greatly expanded to include many more examples of practice in modern libraries and information centers. The sixth edition updated and expanded the materials contained in the previous five editions and discussed new thoughts and techniques as well as reemphasized those that had stood the test of time.

This seventh edition uses contemporary examples to illustrate discussions on such themes as strategic planning, marketing, measurements, and human resources management. Thought-provoking minicases and other activities have been incorporated to elicit discussion of points being made. The volume has been rethought, reworked, and reedited, indeed renewed, to reflect recent changes and new issues in the information services environment. Citations and examples have been updated and the Web site expanded as a valuable aid for teaching and learning as well as managing information services. New examples of library and information service practice are included. The edition incorporates more international materials; some provide direct application for those seeking to establish new processes and procedures, and others provide useful guidelines for establishing standards throughout the world. Concepts covered in the earlier editions in 7 chapters now are covered in greater depth in 20 chapters. New chapters added to the seventh edition cover marketing, team building, and ethics.

The volume covers all of the important functions involved in library management and development. Although these functions are presented and discussed separately, it is important to remember that they are carried out simultaneously and concurrently. The actual operation of a library or information center follows no precise linear pattern. Most managerial functions progress simultaneously; they do not exist in a hierarchical relationship. For instance, budgeting is not likely to be reflective of the enterprise's success without some measure of planning in which goals and objectives are established. Therefore, management cannot be viewed as a rigid system, and the concepts discussed in this text must be viewed as a whole. In this volume, each concept discussed is related to or builds upon others and each relates to all levels of management and supervision in information service organizations.

The Web site accommodates those and many other relevant sources. Feedback from faculty of library and information services management courses and practitioners have expressed appreciation of the comprehensive coverage in both the textbook and the Web site.

Since publication of the first edition of *Library Management,* libraries and information services have changed dramatically. This change has been precipitated by both the internal and the external environment. This continuous process requires a more systematic approach to reviewing functions and developing strategies in the organization's setting. Political, economic, technological, and social environments (PEST) are powerful forces that influence the planning and development of information services today. New knowledge, skills, and techniques are required by diverse staff at every level of an information service enterprise's operations. Different organizational structures, communications processes, measurement techniques, and budgeting strategies are required in the information age, in which the focus is upon strategic initiatives for services necessary to connect the customer with the information being sought—whether for cultural, education, entertainment, or information purposes. Even while established theories and practices of management have been modified and expanded, new theories, concepts, and practices have been developed. For example, the relatively new knowledge management concept is essential for the planned growth and viability of an institution in the current world is social and technological climate. The virtual library concept, accompanied by changing demographics, ethical issues, social responsibilities, and other forces, requires reexamination of how effectively and efficiently resources of a human, material, and technological nature are used.

With all of these new features, the basic theme of the book remains unchanged. The book focuses upon the complex and interrelated functions common to all organizations and is intended specifically for managers and future managers of services and staffs. The purpose of separating and individually discussing the functions that make up the management process is to examine the various threads in the fabric of what managers actually do.

This book was not written in a vacuum, nor is it intended for use in one. In-basket exercises, case studies, action mazes, and other simulation techniques can complement, supplement, and magnify the principles discussed. Case studies can be helpful. Anderson's[1] volume, although somewhat dated, was specifically developed as a companion piece for earlier editions of this text. The most applicable cases from Anderson are available on the Web site for this volume. In addition, each chapter is introduced by a minicase to set the discussion of the principles to be discussed. In preparing the revision, the authors have drawn freely from writings and research in cognate fields, including business management, public administration, and the social sciences.

Finally, it is particularly important to point out that anyone who is supervising another person is involved in the management process. Further, anyone involved in an organizational setting that requires interaction between individuals should understand the dynamics that relate to managing situations and organizations. Therefore, the principles discussed in this volume have relevance for each person whose job involves interacting with others to achieve the common goals and objectives of their organization.

NOTE

1. A. J. Anderson, *Problems in Library Management* (Littleton, CO: Libraries Unlimited, 1981).

Acknowledgments

As with previous editions, many people have contributed to the seventh edition of *Library and Information Center Management*. Readers of previous editions, including students, faculty, and practitioners, have made useful suggestions, and many have been incorporated into this latest edition. Colleagues throughout the world have indicated the value and use of this textbook. To them we are grateful for their encouragement and hope they will be pleased with the changes made in this edition.

The authors would especially like to thank those who read and made comments on the content of various chapters. We would especially like to thank Dr. A. J. Anderson, a colleague and friend, who supplied several of the case studies that are on the Web site and wrote a companion case studies volume several years ago. Our appreciation also goes to Linda Watkins, the GSLIS librarian at Simmons College, and Rebecca Vargha, the SILS librarian at the University of North Carolina at Chapel Hill, who are two of the best librarians we have ever known, for their help in this latest edition. We are also grateful to colleagues who helped in the preparation of the manuscript, especially Dana Hanson-Baldauf, Eric Werthmann, and Scott Adams. Our editor at Libraries Unlimited, Sue Easun, provided us with assistance throughout. Grateful acknowledgment is also due to other colleagues at Libraries Unlimited—Ron Maas and his very capable staff—for their efficiency and continuing encouragement to write yet another edition of this successful textbook.

Many libraries and information center managers permitted us to reproduce documents that are used as examples in the book, and we thank them. Their management practices and procedures make our discussions and illustrations of the issues and challenges more relevant and effective.

Finally, and once again, we thank our spouses, Marlies and Joe, and our families for their help and support during the writing of this manuscript.

Robert D. Stueart
Wellesley, Massachusetts

Barbara B. Moran
Chapel Hill, North Carolina

The Web Site

Library and Information Center Management has a companion Web site that has been expanded and updated for the seventh edition. The redesigned Web site contains four categories of material:

- **Examples:** Many specific examples of documents such as strategic plans, organizational charts, and job descriptions that were included in the appendixes of earlier editions of the textbook have been moved to the Web site. These examples provide help for students, faculty, and practitioners seeking to understand or establish processes, policies, or procedures. Many examples have international appeal and application as librarians across the world continue to explore issues important to international information service.

- **Case Studies:** Case studies are invaluable adjuncts to most management classes. This section of the Web site contains case studies related to library management written by A. J. Anderson and others that can be used in or outside of class to further learning.

- **Exercises:** This section contains some exercises and simulations that we have used successfully in our own management teaching. These activities are designed to help students learn by doing and then reflecting on the experience.

- **Useful Web Sites:** In addition to providing additional material for every section of the book, the Web site provides links that direct students and instructors to other Web resources that give examples or explain processes in greater detail. Because of the rapid changes in librarianship, Web sites can be very important both for classroom activities and as guides for information specialists trying to keep abreast of current trends.

This Web site can be accessed at http://www.lu.com/management/. Obviously, one of the major advantages of a Web site over a printed text is that it can be updated and expanded. We welcome suggestions from readers and users of the textbook for new items to be added to the site. And, if you have exercises or case studies of your own that you think would be useful, we invite you to share them with your colleagues through this Web site. Of course, credit would be given to anyone who submits materials that are used.

1

Introduction

Library and information centers are experiencing change in almost every area of responsibility and activity. The only constant in today's library and information services organizations is change. Recognizing that change is inevitable, coping with its effects, and embracing its outcome are vital steps in those organizations. External factors—those political, economic, social, and technological factors—reinforce the need to examine not only what is done and why it is done, but also the way it is done. One aim is to more effectively implement new methods and systems in an ongoing organization. The change factor requires consideration of models, methods and techniques, tools, skills, and other forms of knowledge that go into making up the practice of information services. How this goal is accomplished depends upon how organizations address those questions in a planned, systematic fashion. A vision of the future of information services is required. Managing that change is the primary characteristic of future-focused, knowledge-based information services organizations as they pursue a mission of creating, organizing, analyzing, preserving, and providing access to information in whatever format in order for seekers to meet their knowledge needs.

Today's turbulent environment requires that a holistic view be taken, identifying techniques, skills, and knowledge to accomplish priorities and initiatives in order to satisfy customer needs. Tolerating ambiguity and risk taking are factors in organizational change and are reflected in every element of a structured work environment. The practice of managing in such a dynamic environment requires awareness of strengths, weaknesses, opportunities, and threats—internal and external—that influence the development of information services.

Theories that are identified, applied, and reinterpreted as well as new ones that are constantly being posed also change or are augmented. What seems right and proper at one point in an organization's development may not be totally appropriate at a different stage as an organization morphs into a more sophisticated organism or has decided to take a completely different direction. Some theories may no longer have relevance for the organization in this new century.

Many of the principles developed over the past century continue to provide a framework for modern organizations, however, even if only for a historical perspective, allowing a retrospective view of where we have been. Those components of evolution and the change it brings are the basis for this first section of the textbook.

Managing in Today's Libraries and Information Centers

 Overview

You are the library director at a state university in a medium-size city. A decision has been made to combine your library and the city's public library in a new building that will provide services for both sets of users. You and your public library counterpart must plan how to merge the collections of the two libraries and manage the services and staff in a shared facility.[1]

You are the director of the information center in a multinational corporation in which employees are rarely in their offices. You have just been asked to make plans to transform the library into a virtual library with information available by telephone and Internet [2]

You are a school librarian just hired by a city planning a new high school. Suddenly you find that you are the administrator of a million-dollar operation and need to be skilled as a facilities planner, designer, technology consultant, and budget authority.[3]

You work in a public library that is in the midst of changing from one organized by departments to one organized by teams. You have been put on the steering committee that will decide what needs to be done to make a transition between these two types of managing.[4]

Imagine that you are a manager in a library facing challenging problems such as the real ones described previously. Today's libraries are complex organizations located in rapidly changing environments. Being a manager in such a setting requires both managerial skills and hard work, but it also can be extremely rewarding. Individuals who become managers have an opportunity to make a real difference in their organizations. Top managers set the tone for the entire organization and make the difference between one that is mediocre and one that is outstanding. Lower-level managers allow the people they supervise to accomplish their work more efficiently. In today's flatter organizations, management responsibility is found at all levels, and most librarians have at least some managerial responsibilities.

Management is one of the most essential skills in ensuring the effective functioning of any type of organization. This chapter will provide an overview of management, managers, and managerial functions focusing specifically on library management.

Many great libraries flourished in ancient times, and these institutions continue their importance in the modern information age. Although libraries have been developed by various nations and cultures, they all share one overriding feature: They provide access to information recorded on some type of medium. Over the years, the form of the medium has changed, from stone to clay tablets, from papyrus and palm leaf to vellum, from scrolls to hand-copied books, and, most recently, from print on paper to interactive electronic and multimedia resources.

It is likely that there was as much concern among information professionals working in libraries at the time that books replaced scrolls as there is today in modern hybrid libraries where print resources are being supplemented, and in some cases replaced, by electronic ones. For librarians, however, the format in which the information is recorded is not their primary concern. Instead, what is far more important to them is the ability of patrons to retrieve and access this information in an efficient and effective manner. To make that retrieval and access possible, managers need to employ successful management processes in order to create appropriate work environments.

From the agrarian age to the information age, the science—or some would call it an art—of management has changed as dramatically as have libraries and information services. But in all that long history, it has never before been so important for organizations of all types to be responsive to changes in what their customers want and need and to be creative and innovative in delivering a product or service to meet those needs.

THE IMPORTANCE OF MANAGEMENT

Libraries and other information-intense enterprises have, over the years, adopted and adapted many management principles from business, industry, and government. In some cases, as part of a government structure or other larger organization, libraries and information centers have been required to do so. In all cases, however, library managers have attempted to adopt proven principles from the nonlibrary world that they think will contribute to the successful operation of their organizations.

There is, of course, a major difference between most libraries and businesses, because almost all libraries are nonprofit organizations. Nevertheless, whatever the nature of the enterprise, whether profit making or nonprofit, it must operate to provide a product to customers or clients, to give the employees and employers a sense of well-being and self-esteem, to maintain an attractive and healthy environment, and to provide consistent and efficient services. A well-managed library or information center accomplishes all of these objectives better than one that is poorly managed.

Effective organizations cannot rest on past success. Instead, they must focus on quality and customer satisfaction, must respond quickly to changes in the external environment, must be creative and innovative, and must be committed to continuous learning. Libraries will need to continue to change in order to succeed in the future as they face a redefined world of information provision. A well-managed library or information center accomplishes all of these objectives better than one that is poorly managed.

Because of their long history, libraries often have tended to perpetuate practices that have worked effectively in the past. There is a natural tendency in mature organizations to become disinclined to innovate. Mature organizations often are marked by inflexibility and inability to compete and respond to the needs of customers. Libraries have changed tremendously over the past few decades, but the changes must continue, and libraries need to remain open to new methods and techniques. If libraries and information centers are to remain viable entities in the future, they must be able to compete with the burgeoning and often aggressive information industry, and this will require flexibility and adaptability to change.

 Try This!

Think a bit about a job you held in the past or have now. First, consider your supervisor and his or her general behavior, managerial style, and attitude. Then think about your fellow employees and your perception of their competence and of their attitudes toward their work, the organization, and you. Finally, reflect upon the organization itself and its policies, procedures, and practices.

What were the good things about this job? What were its negative features? How much did the managers, both your immediate supervisor and those at a higher level, contribute to what you liked or disliked about the job? What did you learn about management from this job?

The importance of management to librarians has grown over the years as libraries have become larger—larger in terms of budgets, collections, and staff. There is an obvious need for management skills at the level of library director, especially in large libraries. Library directors in major national, public, and academic libraries face enormous challenges in managing organizations that are in many ways the equivalent of large for-profit corporations. In fact, library directors are necessarily becoming more like chief executive officers (CEOs) of large corporations than the scholars they used to be. Directors of large libraries are responsible for very large budgets. The Library of Congress has a budget of more than $600 million. The British Library has a budget of over £135 million or about $260 million. Of course, we would expect these large national libraries to have large budgets, but it is very common for library managers in all types of libraries to be dealing with multimillion-dollar budgets. Even in those libraries with smaller budgets, knowing how to secure and manage funding is critical for the institution's success. Library managers are also in charge of many employees and large physical plants, and managing people and physical resources is often more difficult than managing money.

But it is not just library directors who need to have these managerial skills. The demands on every librarian's managerial ability have become larger and more complex in recent years. Most librarians in modern libraries are managers, and they, too, need to know how to manage. Today, librarians are facing greater challenges than ever before, resulting from increased competition, growing globalization, ever-changing technology, and the pace of change. The only constant in today's organizations is change. Although all change is challenging, that occurring at the present presents particular problems, for as the British management expert Charles Handy has stated, it is not change as we have known it in the past, but discontinuous change, which is particularly disturbing and confusing.[5] Libraries will need good managers at all levels to manage the change as they face the redefined world of information provision.

WHAT IS MANAGEMENT?

Management has been defined in many ways, but the basic essence of management is using organizational resources to achieve objectives through planning, organizing, staffing, leading, and controlling. Managers are those individuals within an organization who are in a position to make the decisions that allow an organization to reach its objectives. They work to ensure that these objectives are reached both effectively and efficiently. Early in the twentieth century, Mary Follett defined management as "the art of getting things done through people." This definition is still relevant because one of the things we know about management is that it is impossible for anyone to manage alone. Managers have to use the skills and labor of others to succeed, and thus, for them, interpersonal skills are extremely important. Regardless of the type of organization or the level of management, the functions of planning, organizing, human resources, leading, and controlling are essential to all managers. Each of these functions will be discussed in more depth later in this chapter.

WHO ARE MANAGERS?

Managers are individuals within an organization who are responsible for, and support the work of, other individuals. Managers can be categorized in a number of ways. One of the most common is to think about managers within a vertical hierarchy. Managers occur at all levels of the organization, but the ones nearer the top have broader responsibilities and authority than those at lower levels. In most typical organizations, including libraries, management can be divided into three levels:

- Top management, which in libraries usually means the director and the assistant and associate directors, is responsible for the overall functioning of the entire organization. In most organizations, managers at the highest levels have the power to establish organization-wide policy and are influential in setting the leadership style throughout the organization.

- Middle management is in charge of specific subunits or functions of the organization. In libraries and information centers, department heads are middle managers. Their management responsibilities are concentrated on the successful functioning of individual areas of the library. Middle managers, in addition to leading their specific subunits or functions, also serve as liaisons between top management and supervisors.

- The managers in the lowest position of the management hierarchy are supervisors, sometimes called first-line managers. First-line managers or supervisors lead the day-to-day activities of individual employees as they work to accomplish the desired organizational objectives, and they are responsible for the production of goods or services. These managers implement procedures and processes that allow their units to work effectively and efficiently.

It is important to point out that anyone who is supervising another person is involved in the management process. Many new graduates from library and information science programs become managers in their first professional position. The traditional management hierarchy can be seen in figure 1.1.

Figure 1.1—Levels of Management in Libraries

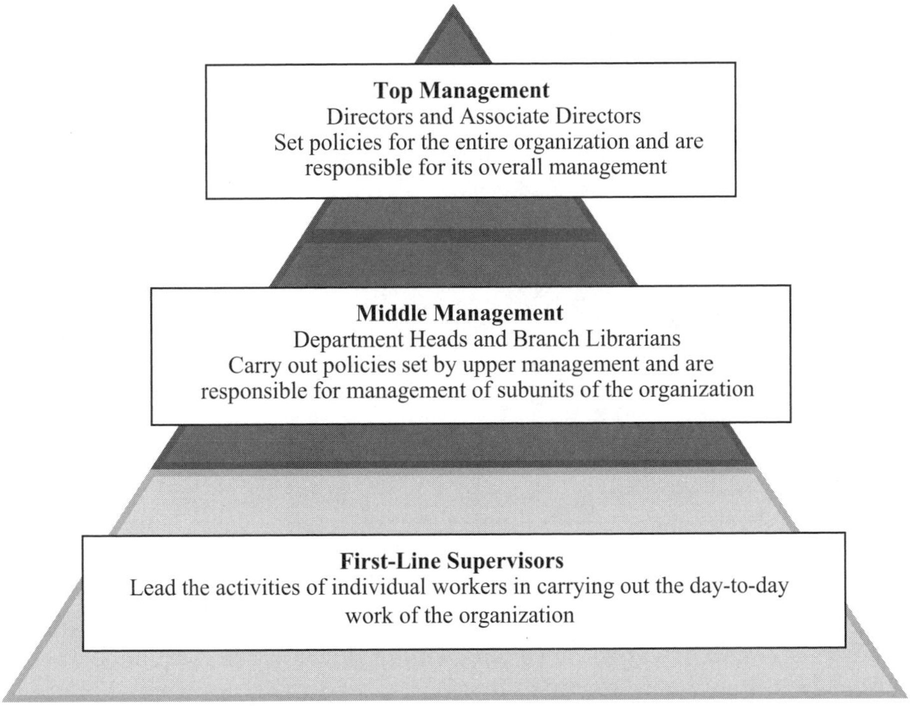

Top Management
Directors and Associate Directors
Set policies for the entire organization and are
responsible for its overall management

Middle Management
Department Heads and Branch Librarians
Carry out policies set by upper management and are
responsible for management of subunits of the organization

First-Line Supervisors
Lead the activities of individual workers in carrying out the day-to-day
work of the organization

As will be discussed later in this book, this traditional managerial hierarchy is being affected by many of the changes in today's workplace, including the increasing popularity of team-based organizations, which has led to a flattening of the pyramid and the elimination of some middle-management positions. In most of today's organizations, including libraries, management responsibility is being distributed more widely throughout the organization than ever before.

WHAT DO MANAGERS DO?

Managers are usually very busy people who have a number of responsibilities and duties.

The duties associated with a managerial position are carried out simultaneously and concurrently. Managers are often multitasking, and their work is frequently interrupted and done in a fragmented fashion. Many managers seem to be juggling a number of responsibilities, almost at the same time. Some managerial functions are engaged in almost daily, whereas others are performed on a more irregular basis. For these reasons, it is sometimes difficult to tease out the actual strands of the fabric of managerial life. The two most common ways of looking at what managers do are by considering the functions that managers perform and by describing the roles managers play.

 What Do You Think?

Henry Mintzberg wrote:

> The manager can never be free to forget the job, and never has the pleasure of knowing, even temporarily, that there is nothing else to do.... Managers always carry the nagging suspicion that they might be able to contribute just a little bit more. Hence they assume an unrelenting pace in their work.

Managers are almost always paid more than nonmanagers, but they have more responsibilities and often seem to work harder. Do you think that they deserve to be paid more? Would being a manager appeal to you?

Henry Mintzberg, *The Nature of Managerial Work* (New York: Harper and Row, 1973), 36.

MANAGERIAL FUNCTIONS

One very common way to view management is as a set of common processes or functions that, when properly carried out, lead to organizational efficiency and effectiveness. The managerial functions are those tasks that managers perform as part of their managerial positions. These functions can be classified in various ways,[6] but, regardless of the terminology used, it is generally agreed that managers perform five main functions: planning, organizing, staffing, leading, and controlling. The five functions of management are depicted graphically in figure 1.2. Anyone who has experience with management will be familiar with all of these functions.

Planning is the first function carried out by all managers. Planning allows managers to think ahead to the things that need to be done and to the methods for getting them done, in order to accomplish the organizations goals. Planning defines where the organization wants to be in the future and allows an organization to make the transition from today to tomorrow.

Organizing is the second function of management. Managers must establish the formal structure of authority through which work subdivisions are arranged. They must first decide how to match individuals and their talents with the kinds of functions and structures that are needed to get the job done and then how to structure the organization so that there is easy communication between the units.

Figure 1.2—The Functions of Management

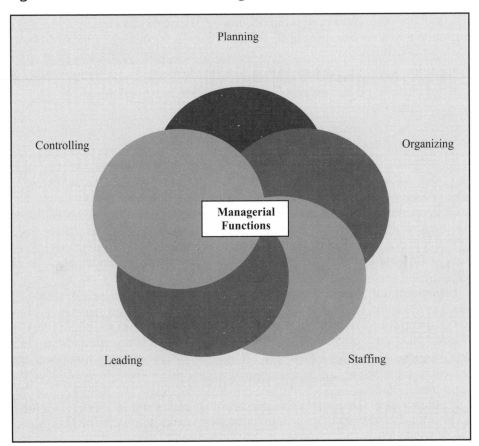

Human resources is the third managerial function. This function is often called *staffing* or *personnel* and involves hiring, training, compensating, and retaining the people necessary to achieve the organizational objectives. Organizations usually state that the people who work there are their most valuable resource; good work in the human resource function ensures that the employees will be strong contributors to the organization's purpose.

Leading involves creating a shared culture and values, communicating goals to employees, and motivating employees at all levels of the organization. All of the subfunctions encompassed under the category of "leading" focus on the human element in the organization. This human element is very important, because employees' attitudes, personality attributes, and perceptions affect the way they work.

Controlling means monitoring the activities of an organization to be sure it is on the right path to meet its goals. Controlling involves first analyzing the way in which the organization is operating and then feeding information back into the planning process so that the organization has a way of continually examining and correcting its goals in light of current information. Controlling is the mirror image of planning. In planning, managers establish where the organization is going, and in controlling, they decide whether they are on target to reach these goals. If planning allows an organization to decide where it is going, controlling allows it to know if it has gotten there.

All managers engage in performing these five functions, although managers at different levels and in different parts of an organization differ in the time they devote to them and the depth at which they perform them. Like most other management textbooks, *Library and Information Center Management* is organized around these five major managerial functions, with a section devoted to each.

MANAGERIAL ROLES

Another way is to think about what managers do is to consider the roles they play while performing their work. A role can be defined as an expected set of behaviors and activities. Henry Mintzberg observed the activities of a number of managers over a period of time and, from his observations, drew conclusions about what managers actually do. According to Mintzberg, managers play a number of roles, and these roles can be grouped into three broad categories: interpersonal roles, information roles, and decisional roles.[7] These roles can be seen in figure 1.3.

Interpersonal Roles. The first category of managerial roles are those related to working with people—the interpersonal roles. Top managers often serve as figureheads. Although the term sounds a bit pejorative, managers, especially higher-level managers, spend a great deal of time representing their organizations to the outside world. They perform ceremonial functions and entertain on behalf of the organization. Top managers serve as symbols of the organization itself.

Managers also play a role as leaders. As part of this role, they perform functions such as motivating, communicating with, and inspiring the individuals who work for them.

Figure 1.3—Mintzberg's Managerial Roles

Interpersonal Roles	Informational Roles	Decisional Roles
Figurehead	Monitor	Disturbance handler
Leader	Disseminator	Resource allocator
Liaison	Spokesperson	Negotiator
		Entrepreneur

Managers often serve as liaisons between groups of employees or between employees and customers. Liaisons link information sources both inside and outside the organization. We often say that managers need to be good networkers; when they are serving as liaisons they are building essential networks between parts of the organization or between the organization and the outside world.

Information Roles. The second set of roles is related to information. In today's information-based organizations, these roles are more important than ever before. Mintzberg says that managers play the role of monitor. Monitors are always seeking information, both from outside the organization and from inside. They develop systems that keep track of the progress of the overall performance of their unit. They oversee the use of resources.

Another informational role played by managers is that of disseminator. Managers not only gather information, but they also share it with others. This information dissemination can take place in person or by means of e-mail or other types of communication media. As organizations have become more participatory, information is shared much more broadly than it was in the past.

The final informational role played by a manager is that of spokesperson. Managers transmit official information about an organization to the outside by means of memos, speeches, newsletters, and other methods of communication.

Decision-Making Roles. The last set of roles is related to decision making. Managers often have to serve as disturbance handlers. Conflict resolution and crisis response are often among the more challenging aspects of a manager's job.

One of a manager's most important roles is that of resource allocator. Managers spend a great deal of time making decisions about how resources such as time, money, and people are distributed within an organization.

Managers often have to play the role of negotiator. Here they represent their organization or subunit in situations in which bargaining for resources such as money, equipment, or other forms of support is taking place. Sometime managers are involved in other types of negotiations such as collective bargaining.

Finally, managers play the role of entrepreneur when they work to introduce innovation into the organization. Managers are responsible for bringing new ideas into an organization and for ensuring that the organization makes the necessary changes to keep it competitive in a fast-changing environment.

Mintzberg's concept of managerial roles has been built upon by other researchers,[8] and it offers an interesting and useful alternative to the traditional view of managerial functions. Some of the roles that Mintzberg describes, such as acting as a figurehead or serving as a spokesperson for the organization, are performed primarily by top-level managers; however, all managers perform many of these roles as part of their managerial activities.

 Try This!

Think about the managers who work in any organization with which you are familiar. Have you seen them playing the roles that Mintzberg describes? How did they play them? Have you ever played any of these roles yourself?

WHAT RESOURCES DO MANAGERS USE?

One definition of a manager is someone who holds the authority to commit organizational resources, and managers do, in fact, spend a large amount of time managing a number of diverse resources. As was discussed previously, one of Mintzberg's managerial roles was that of resource allocator; a manager decides how best to distribute resources throughout an organization. The resources controlled by managers are of four main types:

Human resources are all the employees who work in an organization. These employees have varying levels of skill, experience, and education, but they all should be considered an essential part of the organization. In libraries, there are many different classifications of employees, including professional librarians, paraprofessionals, clerical workers, technical specialists, and, in many libraries, part-time workers such as student assistants and pages. Managers are in charge of the distribution of all of the human resources throughout an organization.

Financial resources are the sources of funding used to operate an organization. In the for-profit world, the funding sources are usually the customers who purchase goods or services. In not-for-profit organizations, funding typically comes from donations; federal, state, or city governments; grants; or other sources. Managers in all types of organizations are increasingly held accountable for the financial resources of those organizations. Even in nonprofit organizations, there is now often an expectation that managers will play a role in increasing resources by securing grants or by fund-raising.

Physical resources are the tangible or material parts of an organization. They consist of assets ranging from supplies to the actual building where an organization functions. Often libraries are located in spaces that are provided by other entities, such as cities or universities, but library managers are still accountable for the proper management of all physical resources. Control of some physical resources (such as supplies) is usually delegated to lower-level managers. Management of physical resources can be a time-consuming function, because it includes acquisition, maintenance, and eventual replacement of a large number of physical resources. Many large libraries have individuals designated as facilities managers, but top-level managers typically make the decisions about expensive resources.

Information resources are an increasingly important part of all organizations, including libraries. One of the prime functions of libraries has always been to provide information resources, but the particular information resources that managers control are those that relate to the functioning of the organization itself. At one time these resources were largely on paper and were kept in file cabinets in one central location in the organization. With the advent of computers, organizations of all types have constructed databases of information relating to employees, resources, and other aspects of management, and much of this information is now available to many employees throughout the organization, typically through an intranet connection. All of these information resources must be managed as valuable assets and leveraged for strategic advantage. In addition, an increasingly important role of management is ensuring the privacy and confidentiality of the material that is contained in information resources, especially those that are available electronically.

WHAT SKILLS ARE NEEDED BY TODAY'S MANAGERS?

What managerial skills do librarians need? Obviously, they need different sets of skills at different levels of management. Robert Katz identified three managerial skills essential to successful management: technical, human, and conceptual skills.[9] Technical skills, those skills that relate to specific functions and tasks, are most important at the first-line level. To be an effective first-line manager or supervisor, an individual has to understand the process that is being carried out. It would be very difficult for a library manager to supervise a group of copy catalogers without knowing about cataloging and classification. On the other hand, the library director may have had such technical knowledge at one time, but because the director now does no cataloging or classification, he or she may not still possess such skills, especially in newer competencies such as producing metadata records. Because top-level managers are often in charge of many diverse units, they often have either never known or have lost proficiency in many of the technical skills that are so important for lower-level managers and supervisors.

 ## What Would You Do?

There was great rejoicing at the Fawville Public Library. Sam Grillo, the director, was leaving. The staff had been hoping—praying—for this announcement since he arrived six months ago.

Why this rejoicing? Put to a direct question, the staff would have answered, "Because the man has serious psychological problems that interfere with his and our ability to do our jobs." Asked to elucidate, they would have said that he was timid, supersensitive, and morbidly self-conscious.

This shyness robbed him of all spontaneity and naturalness. He appeared cold, reserved, and stiff.

The Fawville library staff needs help. They have been asked by the trustees what characteristics, abilities, and talents a public library director should possess. They also have been told that they will be permitted to be present at the interview for the new director. They have a chance to have input in this hiring decision and need help with both deciding what qualities the director should have and with how to find out during an interview whether a candidate for the position has them. (For the rest of this case study, see http://www.lu.com/management.)

At the upper level, managers need to have more conceptual skills and be able to look at the so-called big picture of the organization. The human skill, the ability to interact effectively with people, is important at all levels. Katz uses a broad brush in terms of identifying managerial skills. Other management experts have attempted to identify specific management skills that are crucial, and some studies have looked specifically at the skills necessary for library managers. A few years ago, for instance, G. Edward Evans proposed a universal core of managerial knowledge for librarians, archivists, and information managers. His list includes 12 areas: planning, staffing, fiscal management, innovation, motivation, communication, leadership, quantitative methods, ethics, decision making, delegation, and marketing.[10] It is difficult to define the exact competencies needed by managers because they differ according to position and location. It is even more difficult to define these skills globally because of the different social, cultural, and economic conditions in varying countries. Nonetheless, the following skills are essential to most contemporary managers:

- **Political Skills.** Libraries and information agencies are intensely political organizations, and awareness of this is vital to survival in today's climate. Managers need to create a vision and inspire others to believe in that vision. They must create a climate conducive to strategic thinking and action. Organizations are often hotly and intensely political, both internally and in their relationship to forces outside the organization. Flexibility is required to maintain equilibrium for the organization in the political arena. Being willing to be a risk taker is often a vital skill.

- **Analytical Skills.** Managers serve as change agents and thus must be good at analysis. Insight is useful, but decisions based on insight or intuition are almost impossible to defend. A lucid, rational, well-argued analysis is what is needed to support the actions of managers. Critical thinking is key to effective management.

- **Problem-Solving Skills.** Problem solving is arguably the most important day-to-day activity of a manager. Managers need to develop a positive attitude toward change management, because flexibility is often the key to success in modern organizations.

- **People Skills.** People are the heart of every organization. They possess many different dimensions, and a manager has to deal with all of these dimensions. The skills most needed in this area are those that typically fall under the categories of communication, conflict resolution, and interpersonal skills. In more and more organizations, managers are responsible for the coordination of team-based initiatives. Managers need to know the best techniques for managing teams as well as how to coach and mentor their subordinates. A sense of humor is always useful. Seeing things through the eyes of others in the organization can facilitate cooperation and reduce conflict among disparate points of view. It helps if managers convey a concern and interest in the people they manage.

- **Financial Skills.** All managers need a sound grounding in financial skills, including where funding comes from, where it goes, and how to get it. These skills include knowledge of marketing because marketing of organizations or service often results in funding for them. Additionally, in more and more libraries, as governmental funding has decreased, the need for private fund-raising has become a primary responsibility, especially for top managers. Fund-raising is time-consuming, but it often provides the additional support needed for the extras in a library's budget.

- **System Skills.** There is much more to this than learning about computers, although all library managers need to be familiar with computer-based information systems. A system is not only a technological one but also an arrangement of resources and routines intended to produce specified results. Today's library is usually part of a larger system, and managers need to be aware of the place of their organization within the larger system.

 ## What Do You Think?

A recent job advertisement for a director of public services at a large urban public library describes the responsibilities and requirements for the position:

> Your focus will be on leading the management teams at a main library, 20 branch libraries, and a "virtual" branch to successfully implement innovative public service initiatives, while continuing excellence in customer service in a community of avid library users and supporters. Reporting to the executive director, you will manage a budget of $24 million and a staff of 800. You will work with other executive leadership team members to develop strategy and assist with the achievement of the library's vision. 2007 challenges include implementation of a new marketing plan and brand image, revision of the public services programs, identifying and mentoring staff as a part of succession planning and development of a long-

range facilities plan. Key characteristics of the successful candidate will include demonstrated presentation skills, strategic agility, and a quick grasp of process management and systems thinking.

Using the vertical hierarchy of management levels, what level of manager is this? What skills are required for this position? How could a librarian who wished to become qualified for such a position acquire those skills?

A manager's job is complex and multidimensional, and managers need to have a number of skills to succeed. Managers need to possess both so-called hard skills, which include the technical and specific business skills, and soft skills, which include the interpersonal skills described previously. No manager is a complete master of all of the skills that might be useful to him or her. But good managers know that their success is dependent upon their skills and knowledge, and they never stop learning or developing skills throughout the course of their careers.

WHAT ARE THE DIFFERENCES IN MANAGING IN FOR-PROFIT AND NOT-FOR-PROFIT ORGANIZATIONS?

Although some library and information centers are located in for-profit organizations, the vast majority are not. Most libraries are either funded by state or local taxes or are located in not-for-profit organizations such as private colleges and universities. Not-for-profit organizations are unique entities created to provide a public service rather than to generate profit. Most management literature often seems to be geared to the for-profit sector, with a heavy emphasis on making money for the business owners or stockholders. The emphasis in most libraries is not on creating profit; instead, libraries exist to contribute to the public good. Because not-for-profits do not typically generate their own budgets, they usually use different forms of financial controls and accounting. Often, they are not permitted to have either deficits in their budgets or large reserves. The difference in the bottom line is the most significant difference in managing in the not-for-profit sphere.

Management in the not-for-profit world sometime seems comparatively complicated because the goals of these organizations are often difficult to articulate. The goal of the for-profit organization is to make money for its owners, and this goal is fairly straightforward. Contrast it with the "serving society" or "doing good" goal of a not-for-profit; that goal could be interpreted in many different ways. Not only do managers in not-for-profits sometimes have more trouble setting goals, but it can be equally hard to assess whether the organization has achieved these goals.[11] Also, some aspects of human resources management can differ if the not-for-profit's employees are government workers or if they have the special benefits, such as tenure, often found in college and university libraries.

Nonetheless, the majority of what managers do in the for-profit and the not-for-profit spheres is the same. The well-known management expert Peter

Drucker turned his attention to the nonprofit world a few years before his death. He stressed the similarities between for-profit and nonprofit organizations. He advocated the need for not-for-profit organizations to focus on mission, demonstrate accountability, and achieve results.[12] Drucker suggested that the managers in every nonprofit ask themselves five essential questions: What is our mission? Who is our customer? What does the customer value? What are our results? and What is our plan?[13] This type of self-assessment is just as necessary in the not-for-profit world as in the profit-making one, and sometime more so, because not-for-profits have to produce results if they want to retain the confidence and trust of those entities from which they get their funding.

So there are some differences in management between these two types of organizations, but managers in both still engage in the five managerial functions of planning, organizing, human resources, leading, and controlling. Both types of managers also play the managerial roles described by Mintzberg. A good manager in one type of organization could fairly easily transfer to one in the other sphere, because there are more similarities than differences between managing for-profit and not-for-profit organizations. Regardless of how organizations are structured, they all need good managers to help accomplish their mission and goals.

CONCLUSION

This textbook provides an introduction to the principles of management, but it should serve only as a foundation. Management really cannot be taught; the principles can be imparted, but management also must be learned through experience. This book will acquaint you with the basic principles, concepts, and techniques of management. It also will teach you its vocabulary. If you are interested in becoming a manager, you will need to continue to learn. But it is hoped that this book will get you interested in the possibility of becoming a manager, because good management is critical to the success of all organizations.

It is clear that librarians of the future will be working in environments that will continue to be turbulent and fast changing. Peter Vaill provides a compelling metaphor to describe this turbulent future. He states that managers need to be prepared to confront a period of chaotic change, or what he calls permanent "white water." In his view, management of organizations used to be like a pleasant boat ride down a calm, quiet river, but the future will be different. It will be full of rapids, whirlpools, eddies, and endless white water.[14] Libraries need to have experienced managers to take the helm as libraries continue their exhilarating journey into the future.

Today's managers face a number of challenges, but, although management is sometimes a difficult undertaking, it also presents great opportunities and allows one to make changes in organizations. We are badly in need of people who are both willing and able to serve as managers in order to ensure the success of libraries and information centers in the future.

This first chapter of *Library and Information Center Management* has provided an overview of what managers do and of the skills needed by modern managers. The next chapter looks at the evolution of management thought over the centuries. This section will then conclude with a third chapter, which focuses on the need for change and change management in today's fast-moving library environment.

NOTES

1. Ilene Rockman, "Joint Use Facilities: The View from San Jose," *Library Administration and Management* 13 (1999): 64–67.

2. Doris Small Helfer, "Lessons from PricewaterhouseCoopers," *Searcher* 7, no. 1 (January 1999): 16–17

3. Lisa Wilson, "Bringing Vision to Practice: Planning and Provisioning the New Library Resource Center," *Teacher Librarian* 32, no. 1 (October 2004): 23–27.

4. Betsy A. Bernfeld, "Developing a Team Management Structure in a Public Library," *Library Trends* 53, no. 1 (Summer 2004): 112–28.

5. Charles Handy, *The Age of Unreason* (Boston: Harvard Business School Press, 1989), 8.

6. One of the first attempts to codify the functions of management was proposed by Gulick and Urwick, who proposed the acronym POSDCORB (planning, organizing, staffing, directing, coordinating, reporting, and budgeting) to describe the functions of a manager.

7. Henry Mintzberg, *The Nature of Managerial Work* (New York: Harper & Row, 1980).

8. See, for instance, Jeffrey S. Shippman, Eric Prien, and Gary L. Hughes, "The Content of Management Work," *Journal of Business and Psychology* 5 (March 1991): 325–54.

9. Robert Katz, "Skills of an Effective Administrator," *Harvard Business Review* 52 (September–October 1974): 90–102.

10. G. Edward Evans, "Management Education for Archivists, Information Managers and Librarians: Is There a Global Core?" *Education for Information* 2 (December 1984): 295–307.

11. Thomas Wolf and Barbara Carter, *Managing a Non-Profit Organization in the 21st Century* (New York: Fireside, 1999), 19.

12. Peter Drucker, *Managing the Non-Profit Organization: Principles and Practices* (New York: Harper Collins, 1990).

13. Information about Drucker's self-assessment for nonprofits and much other useful information about managing in the not-for-profit sphere can be found at the Leader to Leader Institute, http://www.leadertoleader.org/knowledgecenter/sat/index.html.

14. Peter Vaill, *Managing as a Performance Art: New Ideas for a World of Chaotic Change* (San Francisco: Jossey-Bass, 1989).

The Evolution of Management Thought

 Overview

The vast majority of workers are employed by some sort of an organization. They travel to work each morning and put in a certain number of hours on the job, and then they go home. They usually work with a number of other people, and there is a separation between their work and the rest of their lives. It is hard for modern-day workers to realize how much the nature of work has changed from what existed not too long ago. Over the past 200 years, almost all nations have evolved from societies in which most workers were self-employed, either as farmers or as independent craftsmen, into ones in which almost all workers are employed by organizations. A little more than 100 years ago, farmers still constituted more than one-third of the total U.S. workforce. Many other people worked as skilled craftsmen for themselves or in small shops. In 1849, the largest factory in the United States was run by Chicago Harvester and employed 123 workers. The number of people working in manufacturing in the United States quintupled from 1860 to 1890. By 1913, there were more than 12,000 people employed in a single Ford factory in Michigan. This growth in the number of people working in organizations was accompanied by a growth in interest in management. Management techniques had not been very important when most organizations were small, but suddenly there was a real need for knowledge about the best way to manage large numbers of employees and complex organizations.

Management theory has expanded greatly over recent decades, fueled by new ideas that have helped countless cohorts of professional managers become successful. There has been a proliferation of management theories

> and a development of various schools of management, each purporting to provide the best approach to management.
>
> This chapter will present a history of management and management thought from prehistory to the present. The chapter will end with a brief look at how librarians have used and adapted general management principles in libraries.

A hundred years ago, most organizations were relatively small, and their focus was upon productivity and techniques, with little analysis of the underlying principles of management. Since then, organizations have grown in size and multiplied in numbers.

Today's management has evolved from earlier practices, principles, and research. An examination of the history of management provides context and background for current management thought. Being familiar with the history of management is a good way to learn what has worked in the past and to avoid repeating mistakes from the past. No student of management thought can afford to be unfamiliar with the contributions of the major pioneer thinkers in the field. Although we have moved away from some of the practices they once advocated, their ideas are still the basis for the development of many management techniques currently in practice, and their contributions also provide insight into the theories that are the essence of management today.

Although management as a formal field of study is less than 150 years old, there was a need for managing long before its principles were studied and codified. From the time of the earliest civilizations, management techniques were being employed widely.

MANAGEMENT IN ANCIENT HISTORY

As early as 3000 B.C.E., the Sumerians kept records on clay tablets; many of those records applied to the management practices of the priests of Ur. Early Babylonia implemented very strict control of business enterprises with its Codes of Akkadian and Hammurabi. The Hebrews' understanding of hierarchy and of the importance of delegation is reflected in the Old Testament, particularly in Exodus 18:25–26, in which Moses, "chose able men out of all Israel and made them heads over the people, rulers of thousands, rulers of hundreds, rulers of fifties, and rulers of tens. And they judged the people at all seasons; the hard cases they brought unto Moses, but every small matter they judged themselves."

Construction of one pyramid in Egypt around 5000 B.C.E. was accomplished by about 100,000 people working for 20 years. It is obvious that such a feat could not have been completed without extensive planning, organizing, and controlling. Around 2000 B.C.E., the principle of decentralized control was introduced, by a vesting of control in the individual states of Egypt; it was only later that the pharaoh established central control over all.[1] There is also evidence that Egyptians employed long-range planning techniques and staff advisers. Similar records exist for activities in ancient China. In the China of 3,000 years ago, there were "concepts that have a contemporary managerial ring: organization, functions, cooperation, procedures to bring efficiency, and various control techniques."[2] The staff principle, later perfected by military organizations, was used very effectively by Chinese dynasties as far back as 2250 B.C.E.

 What Do You Think?

Many of the things that we think of as modern and cutting edge have been used in the past. An article in a recent issue of *Harvard Magazine* dealt a serious blow to the Hollywood version of pyramid building, with Charlton Heston as Moses commanding the pharaoh to "Let my people go!" Mark Lehner, an archeologist, has been studying the building of the pyramids and has found evidence that pyramid workers were not slaves at all, at least not in the modern sense of the word. Lehner believes that the pyramids were built by "a rotating labor force in a modular, team-based kind of organization."

Lehner's discovery provides a good example of how many approaches or techniques that we think are very modern are really much older. Can you think of any other instances of seemingly new developments that have really been taken from the past?

Jonathan Shaw, "Who Built the Pyramids?" *Harvard Magazine*, July–August 2003, 42–49, 99.

Although the records of early Greece offer little insight into the principles of management, the very existence of the Athenian commonwealth, with its councils, popular courts, administrative officials, and board of generals, indicates an appreciation of various managerial functions. Socrates' definition of management as a skill separate from technical knowledge and experience is remarkably close to our current understanding of it. The Greek influence on scientific management is revealed in their writings; for example, Plato wrote about specialization, and Socrates described management issues.[3] In ancient Rome, the complexity of a huge empire demanded the use of management techniques. In fact, much of the secret of the Roman Empire's success lay in the ability of the Romans to organize work and people for the cause.

Many ancient leaders were not only charismatic individuals but skillful organizers as well. Hannibal's crossing of the Alps in 218 B.C.E., with his Carthaginian troops and equipment, was a remarkable organizational feat. At about the same time, Qin Shi Huang Di, the first emperor of China, was able to organize hundreds of thousands of slaves and convicts to create his burial complex at Xian and to connect portions of the Great Wall. He also unified warring factions and standardized weights and measures as part of his centralization initiative. Thus, the origins of many of the techniques that are employed today in modern organizations can be traced to ancient times and civilizations.

THE EFFECTS OF THE INDUSTRIAL AGE ON MANAGEMENT

As society became less agrarian, there was an increasing interest in management. The development of technology during the Industrial Revolution, at the end of the nineteenth and the beginning of the twentieth centuries, produced a factory system that brought workers into a central location and into contact with other workers. It was during the development of effective and efficient management control of these newly founded organizations that many management concepts began to emerge. Adam Smith, in his writing, particularly in *The Wealth of Nations,* described division of work and time-and-motion studies as they should be employed in organizations. Other writers of the period, including Robert Owen, Charles Babbage, and Charles Dupin, wrote about the problems of management in factories.[4] Many of the principles that were later reemphasized and further refined in the scientific management approach and the human relations approach were first developed during the eighteenth and nineteenth centuries.

Widespread interest in management grew in the late nineteenth and early twentieth centuries as the factory system increased in size and complexity. The number of people employed as managers grew tremendously, and there was a rising demand for solutions to problems encountered in the workplace. At this time, the study of management became more systematized and formal, and various approaches or so-called schools of management began to be developed. These schools are theoretical frameworks that are based on different assumptions about people and organizations. Each of them reflects the problems and the best solutions of the time in which they were developed.

A discussion of the various schools is always a bit confusing, because some writers place a particular idea, theory, or observation into one school, whereas others might place it in a different, though still aligned, school. There is also no agreement about the number of schools of management, because experts divide and subdivide the schools in different ways. The complexity of the interrelationships between the many schools was once characterized as "The Management Theory Jungle,"[5] and, indeed, sometimes the descriptions of the schools seem to be as impenetrable as a jungle. The next section of this chapter will provide a brief discussion of the most important of these schools of thought. To simplify the discussion, not every school, nor all of their subdivisions, will be covered. This section will cover only the six major ways of thinking about management: the classical perspective, the humanistic approach, the quantitative perspective, the systems approach, contingency management, and learning organizations. These schools and their approximate dates are displayed in figure 2.1.

CLASSICAL PERSPECTIVES

The earliest management schools are often categorized as being classical perspectives. These schools all arose in response to the growth in size and number of organizations, and each sought to make organizations more efficient by applying a systematic, more scientific approach to management.

Figure 2.1—The Major Schools of Management Thought

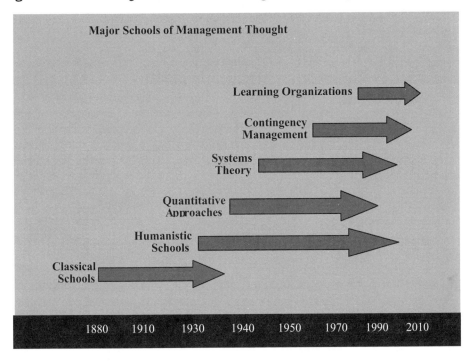

Before the advent of the classical perspectives on management, most managerial decisions could be described as "seat-of-the-pants." Every manager drew on past experience in managing, but there was no attempt to find out if one way of doing a job was better than another. Workers were hired with little thought about matching their skills to the jobs that needed to be done, and new workers usually were not given any systematic training. There was no standardization of tools or processes. The writers of the classical perspectives attempted to bring a more systematic approach to management by proposing more efficient and effective ways to manage. Although these schools were developed in different places, they share many common characteristics. The most important of these schools are the scientific management, the bureaucratic, and the administrative principles schools. Each of these schools will be described separately.

Scientific Management Movement

Frederick Winslow Taylor (1856–1915), an American, is considered to be the father of scientific management. The basic assumption of this school of management is that workers are primarily economically motivated and that they will put forth their best efforts if they are rewarded financially. The emphasis is on maximum output and on eliminating waste and inefficiency. Planning and standardization of efforts and techniques are viewed as important factors in creating a more efficient organization. Taylor thought managers should:

Figure 2.2—Major Schools Contained in the Classical Perspective on Management

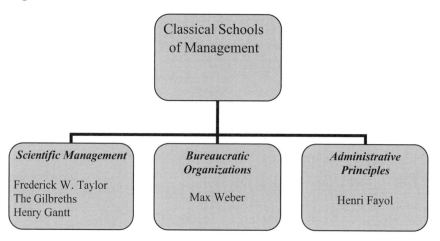

- Develop a series of rules and routines to help workers in their daily work.
- Replace the rule-of-thumb method by finding the most efficient way.
- Select scientifically, and then train, teach, and develop the worker.
- Provide wage incentives to workers for increased output.[6]

Efficiency was Taylor's central theme. As a steelworks manager in Philadelphia, Pennsylvania, in the United States, he was interested in knowing how to get more work out of workers whom he considered to be naturally lazy. This attitude, he speculated, was fostered by poor management. He observed "when a naturally energetic man works for a few days beside a lazy one, the logic of the situation is unanswerable. 'Why should I work hard when the lazy fellow gets the same pay that I do and does only half as much work?'"[7] Taylor proposed using scientific research methods to discover the one best way to perform a job. He felt that faster work could be assured only through enforced standardization of methods; enforced adaptation of the best instruments available for the work; adoption of good, hygienic working conditions; and enforced cooperation.

Even though Taylor was the most important advocate of the scientific management movement, others contributed to the growth of the scientific method, including Frank (1868–1924) and Lillian (1878–1972) Gilbreth. Frank, an engineer, and Lillian, who held a doctorate in psychology, were concerned with the human aspects of managing, and they expanded the concepts of time-and-motion studies. They tried to identify the one best way to perform a task in the most comfortable and time-efficient manner. (The Gilbreths are also famous for being the efficiency-expert parents in *Cheaper by the Dozen*, a book written by two of their children.)

Henry L. Gantt (1861–1919), experimenting at about the same time, developed the task-and-bonus system, which was similar to Taylor's awards incentive. Gantt's system set rates of output; if those rates were exceeded, bonuses were paid. In some cases, when his system was adopted, production more than doubled. The Gantt Chart is still widely used in production schedules and is used in many libraries and information systems to chart and calculate work schedules. Along the horizontal axis of the chart, Gantt placed the time, work schedule, and work-completed aspects; along the vertical axis, he placed the individuals and machines assigned to those schedules. In this way, the path to completion could be easily calculated.

In its early development, scientific management had little concern for the external environment of the organization and was almost exclusively concerned with internal operations. It also placed little emphasis on the needs of the workers; instead it focused on producing better results.

 Try This!

Imagine that you are a director in a large, urban public library in the early twentieth century and are interested in all of that newfangled management theory that is being propounded by your contemporaries, Frederick W. Taylor, the Gilbreths, and Henry Gantt. What impact do you think their ideas might have had upon your way of managing? Which of their principles might you have used in your own management? Would some of these principles be harder to implement in a library than in a factory setting?

Bureaucratic School

At about the same time that scientific management was developing in the United States, the concept of bureaucracy was taking form in Europe. Max Weber (1864–1920), a German sociologist, introduced many of the theories of the bureaucratic school. He was the first to articulate a theory of the structure of authority in organizations and to distinguish between power and authority and between compelling action and voluntary response. He was more concerned with the structure of the organization than with the individual. Most of his writings and research related to the importance of specialization in labor, of regulations and procedures, and of the advantages of a hierarchical system in making informed decisions. Weber characterized a bureaucratic organization as an ideal type of organization, in which:

- Labor is divided with a clear indication of authority and responsibility.
- The principle of hierarchy exists.
- Personnel are selected and promoted based on qualifications.
- Rules are written down and impersonally and uniformly applied.
- Promotion into management is only through demonstrated technical competence.
- Rules and procedures ensure reliable and predictable behavior.[8]

Although the term *bureaucracy* is sometimes used pejoratively, and is often associated with mindless rules and red tape, Weber's concept of the ideal structure has been extremely powerful. Bureaucracies work well under many conditions, especially in stable organizations in stable environments. Many large organizations, including many libraries, have been structured to reflect Weber's bureaucratic principles.

Administrative Principles

Another movement also began to develop in France about the same time as Taylor's experiments in the United States. Using some of the same scientific management methods, it sought to establish a conceptual framework for, as well as to identify principles and build a theory of, management. The father of the administrative principles (also sometimes called the classical or generalist) movement was a Frenchman, Henri Fayol (1841–1925). Fayol took a scientific approach, but unlike Taylor, who began by looking at the workers on the job, Fayol looked at administration from the top down. As an industrialist, he concentrated on the roles that managers should perform as planners, organizers, and controllers. He believed that managers needed guidelines, or basic principles upon which to operate, and he emphasized the need to teach administration at all levels. He was the first to write about the functions of management, including planning, organization, command, coordination, and control. He devised a set of principles, which can be seen in table 2.1.

TABLE 2.1 Fayol's 14 Principles of Management

Division of work	There should be a clear division of duties. Breaking jobs into smaller pieces will result in specialization. Management should be separate and distinct.
Authority	The authority that individuals possess should be equal to their responsibility. Anyone responsible for the results of a task should be given the authority to take the actions necessary to ensure its success.
Discipline	There should be clear rules and complete obedience to behavior in the best interest of the organization.
Unity of command	An employee should receive orders from only one superior, in order to avoid confusion and conflict.
Unity of direction	There should be one head and one plan, in order to ensure a coordinated effort.
Subordination of individual interest to the general interest	Employees should place the organization's concerns before their own.
Remuneration of personnel	Pay should be fair.
Centralization	Centralization is the most desirable arrangement within an organization.

(continued)

TABLE 2.1 *(continued)*

Scalar chain	Each position is part of a vertical chain of authority (the scalar chain). Communication should move up and down this chain of command.
Order	To avoid conflicts, there should be a right place for everything and everyone in the organization.
Equity	Equality of treatment must be taken into account in dealing with employees. Justice should be tempered with kindness.
Stability of tenure of personnel	Long-term stability for workers is good for an organization.
Initiative	Incentive rewards must be provided to stimulate production.
Esprit de corps	Develop a strong sense of morale and unity. Communication is the key to a satisfied working group.

Source: Henri Fayol, *General and Industrial Management,* trans. Constance Storrs (New York: Pitman, 1949), 22.

Like Taylor, Fayol believed that workers were naturally lazy, resisted work more effectively when working in groups, must be subjected to discipline, could be best motivated by the incentive of higher wages, could work better when properly instructed, and differed markedly in native ability and capacity.

All three of these schools of the classical perspective emphasized consistency, efficiency, and clear rules, and they all subordinated the needs of the worker to that of the organization. They paid little or no attention to outside environmental factors. The greatest criticism of these early schools is that they place undue emphasis on the formal aspects of organization and neglect entirely the effects of individual personalities, informal groups, intraorganizational conflicts, and the decision-making process on the formal structure. They also have been criticized as leading to rigidity and resistance to change. Yet the theories of these three schools provided a way to efficiently organize and manage the large organizations that were developing at the same time that they were being formulated. There is little doubt that many organizations, including libraries and other information agencies, still depend heavily on these classic theories.

 What Would You Do?

The time is 1883, the place New York City. Melvil Dewey has just been appointed librarian at Columbia College. Although Columbia has a progressive president, it has a very conservative faculty who view new ideas as a threat to what they teach and a Board of Trustees that also prefers the status quo. Dewey has ambitious plans for the library and recommends that Columbia consolidate its collections into a single library, create a shelf list, construct a complete catalog in one alphabet, and build a subject catalog. Dewey wants to increase the hours the library is open from 15 per week to 14 per day.

"It will," Dewey states, "require more employees to carry out these reforms." He estimates that the consolidation will eliminate two positions but that the recataloging and extended hours will require about eleven additional workers. Except for one employee whom he inherited from his predecessor, Dewey has been able to choose all of the new personnel. He has hired seven women on a campus described as "almost as hermetically sealed to women as a monastery." As Dewey explains, hiring college-educated women allows him to recruit a talented workforce for low cost. These new workers come with good character, and because they are college graduates, they arrive with knowledge of books and reading. In addition, because there are few other professional opportunities for women available, they will work for less money.

Dewey is not interested in just the large issues but is equally attentive to the small. He is concerned about noise and has had rubber tips placed on all chairs and table legs and rubber wheels put on book trucks and has ordered all the pages to wear slippers. New readers have been handed cards requesting them to step lightly and not to talk, even in low tones. They also have been told that they may not use tobacco, wear hats, or put their feet on the chairs or tables. Mr. Dewey came in yesterday with new cards that he just had printed. He plans to hand one to anyone he sees littering. The cards read: "I picked these pieces in the hall and infer that you threw them on the floor. My time and that of my assistants is too valuable for this work. Still we prefer to do it rather than have the building disfigured." Principle above diplomacy is always his approach.

Dewey has begun the library consolidation with a move into a new library building containing 50,000 volumes previously located in nine different locations. He is beginning the reclassification and recataloging of the collections. Dewey is considering innovative ways to increase the size of the book collection. Dewey is also engaged in a number of so-called larger interests. He is considering beginning a new reference service for students. He has established a new series of bibliographic lectures. He recently invited 72 New York City librarians to a meeting at Columbia where they voted to form a New York Library Club whose "object will be by consultation and cooperation to increase the usefulness and promote the interests of the libraries of New York." Dewey also has been talking about starting a new school for library education at Columbia and is planning to advertise for female students, even though Columbia admits only men as students.

Because Dewey has pressed so hard and so relentlessly for his interests, it was only a matter of time before dissatisfaction with his administration began to appear. The costs of his reforms and his larger interests have been criticized by a number of faculty and alumni. In an attempt to reduce costs, he recently decided to fire the only employee he had inherited, a move that badly backfired when the faculty demanded that he reinstate "their librarian." Dewey is now scheduled to appear before the Columbia College trustees to defend his administration to a group who think that his larger interests do not fit the narrower needs of the college and that he is making too many changes too quickly.

What are the major issues that have led to the conflict between Melvil Dewey and the Board of Trustees? Imagine you are a member of the Board of Trustees. What will you plan to say to Mr. Dewey? Now switch roles and imagine that you are Melvil Dewey. How would you justify your actions to the board?

The information for this case was taken from Wayne A. Wiegand, *Irrepressible Reformer: A Biography of Melvil Dewey* (Chicago: American Library Association, 1996), chap. 4.

THE HUMANISTIC APPROACH

During the 1930s, management studies began to give more attention to the concerns of individuals working in organizations. No longer were workers considered cogs in the machinery of industry. The main emphasis of observation and study became the individual and the informal group in the formal organization; the primary concern was with integrating people into the work environment. This movement had two major schools: the human relations and the self-actualization schools.

Human Relations Movement

This movement focused on the behavior of the individual and his or her quality of life in the organization, as well as on the needs, aspirations, and motivations of this individual and on those of the group and the organization. The major assumption was that if management can make employees happy, maximum performance will be the result. One of the early writers in this movement was Chester Barnard (1886–1961), who dwelled on the contribution-satisfaction equilibrium as he examined the organization as a social system. He was the first to introduce the issue of the social responsibility of management, including fair wages, security, and the creation of an atmosphere conducive to work.[9] Mary Parker Follett (1868–1933) was also an early pioneer who recognized the interdependencies between the individual, the work, and the environment. She emphasized worker participation and the importance of shared goals. Follett also advocated so-called constructive conflict; she saw conflict within an organization as inevitable and wanted to provide ways to make that conflict work for the organization. Although her contributions to management theory were initially overlooked by management scholars, they are now being rediscovered and reapplied in modern organizations.[10]

The proponents of this school drew many of their ideas from research conducted by Elton Mayo (1880–1949) and a group of industrial psychologists at the Western Electric Hawthorne Plant in Chicago, Illinois. The Hawthorne studies in the late 1920s were among the first studies that demonstrated the importance of the human side of organizations.[11] Interestingly, the studies were begun as a result of scientific management and were designed to attempt to find a way of increasing efficiency and effectiveness by varying the level of illumination for workers in the organization.

As efficiency engineers at the Hawthorne plant were experimenting with various forms of illumination, they noted an unexpected reaction from employees. When illumination was increased, so was productivity. What was really surprising, however, was that when illumination was decreased, production continued to increase. This same increase in production also occurred when the illumination was not changed at all. Mayo was asked to examine this paradox. He found that the explanation to the increased production lay not in the changes in the working conditions, but in the changes in the way the workers felt about themselves. By lavishing attention on the workers, the experimenters had made them feel as though they were an important part of the company. These previously indifferent employees had coalesced into congenial, cohesive groups with a great deal of group pride. Their needs for affiliation, competency, and achievement had been fulfilled, and their productivity had thus increased. The Hawthorne studies are important because they demonstrated that:

1. Workers are more motivated by social rewards and sanctions than by economic incentives.
2. Workers' actions are influenced by the group.
3. Whenever formal organizations exist, both formal and informal norms exist.

In short, the Hawthorne studies are a landmark in management research because they were the first studies to recognize that organizations are social systems and that the productivity of workers is a result not of just physical factors but of interpersonal ones as well.

Mayo's conclusions were different from those of Taylor who thought that workers were motivated only by money. Mayo maintained that workers are primarily motivated by togetherness and crave individual recognition within the group. In general, the human behavior movement maintained that if the organization makes employees happy, it will gain their full cooperation and effort and therefore reach optimum efficiency.

Self-Actualizing Movement

The self-actualization movement was closely related to the human relations movement and is often confused or intertwined with it. It differed from the human relations school, however, in that its emphasis was not primarily on managers recognizing the importance of workers and trying to make them happy; instead it emphasized designing jobs that would allow workers to satisfy higher-level needs and utilize more of their potential. Abraham Maslow was one of the early proponents of this school. Maslow's needs theory is built upon the concept that humans have a hierarchy of needs, starting with the basic physical necessities of food, shelter, and clothing and ascending five steps to the intangible needs of self-actualization and fulfillment, with the emphasis on self-actualization.[12] Maslow's theory will be described in greater depth in chapter 13.

Douglas McGregor (1906–1964) was another powerful influence from this school. In the 1950s, McGregor put forth two influential set of assumptions about workers; he called these sets of assumptions Theory X and Theory Y.[13] These assumptions can be seen in table 2.2. The first set of assumptions, Theory X, reflects what McGregor saw as the traditional, autocratic, managerial perception of workers. McGregor questioned whether a Theory X perception of workers was adequate in a democratic society in which the workforce enjoys a rising standard of living and has an increasing level of education. He argued that the intellectual potential of the average human being was only partly utilized in most workplaces. He then put forth an alternative set of generalizations about human nature and the management of human resources, which he called Theory Y.

Theory Y presents a much more positive picture of people, but the assumptions that constitute this theory are more challenging to managers. These assumptions imply that human nature is dynamic, not static. They indicate that human beings have the capacity to grow and develop. Most important, Theory Y makes managers responsible for creating an environment that promotes positive development of individual employees. Theory Y managers do not try to impose external control and direction over employees; instead managers allow them self-direction and control. McGregor's assumptions made many managers aware that they had overlooked the potential of individual workers.

TABLE 2.2 The Assumptions of McGregor's Theory X and Theory Y

Assumptions of Theory X	Assumptions of Theory Y
Average human beings have an inherent dislike of work and will avoid it if they can.	The expenditure of physical and mental effort in work is as natural as play or rest.
People must be coerced, controlled, directed, and threatened with punishment to get them to work	Individuals will exercise self-direction and self-control in the service of objectives to which they are committed.
People prefer to be directed, wish to avoid responsibility, have relatively little ambition, and, above all, want security.	People learn, under proper conditions, not only to accept but also to seek responsibility.
People are self-centered and do not like change.	Imagination, ingenuity, and creativity are widely distributed among workers.

Source: Douglas McGregor, *The Human Side of Enterprise* (New york: McGraw-Hill, 1960).

> ### ❓ What Do You Think?
>
> John Doe, the supervisor of the mail room in a very large library, is a micromanager. He stands over the shoulders of workers while they are performing tasks and makes "helpful" comments. He insists on checking and double-checking every piece of work that is produced by his employees. He arranges all of the schedules and makes all of the decisions. Workers are required to sign in and sign out of the workplace and are allowed no flexibility in scheduling. McGregor has given us a theory to explain this manager. Using McGregor's theories, how would you classify John Doe, and what characteristics cause you to place him in that category?

Peter Drucker (1919–2005), who in the 1950s introduced management by objectives, an approach that advocates substituting a more participative approach for that of authoritarianism, was another proponent of this school. So was Chris Argyris, who suggested that organizational structure can curtail self-fulfillment.[14] Other disciples of this approach include Rensis Likert, Warren G. Bennis, and Robert Blake and Jane Mouton. More about these theorists can be found in later chapters in this book.

The writers of the humanistic school challenged the view of employees as so-called tools, a view that had been the basis of much of the classical perspective. They forced managers to think about the interpersonal processes in organizations and to consider workers as valuable resources. Although some of these writers have been accused of being overly simplistic about the nature of workers and the complexity of individuals in the workforce, the ideas that they advanced about workers and their talents and needs are still very influential.

THE QUANTITATIVE APPROACH

After World War II, there was a movement in the United States and a number of other countries to develop better and more sophisticated tools to use in management. Scientists, mathematicians, and statisticians had been used extensively in the war effort to solve problems and to improve the efforts of the countries involved. When the fighting was finished, there was a move to use these same techniques in civilian life. This gave rise to a movement that is referred to as the quantitative (or the management science) approach to management. Thinkers in this school wanted to improve managerial decision making by using sophisticated mathematical and statistical methods. Mathematics, statistics, and economics were used to contribute to management through the use of mathematical models for decision making and prediction. In many ways, the quantitative perspective is similar to the earlier scientific management approach. As Herbert Simon points out, "no meaningful line can be drawn anymore to demarcate operations research from scientific management or scientific management from management science."[15]

Subfields within this perspective include areas such as management science, decision theory, and operations research. Management scientists share common characteristics, namely the application of scientific analysis to managerial problems, the goal of improving the manager's decision-making ability, high regard for economic effectiveness criteria, reliance on mathematical models, and the use of computers.[16] The decision theory movement uses techniques such as game theory, simulation, and linear programming in presenting alternatives for decision makers to consider. The decision theory movement is primarily concerned with the study of rational decision-making procedures and the way managers actually reach decisions. The implication is that mathematical models and quantitative processes can serve as the basis for all management decisions. Many of the researchers in this movement have concentrated on describing the decision-making process, drawing on psychology and economics,[17] or on prescribing how decisions should be made.[18] The mathematical branch of the decision theory movement is concerned with both what to measure and why, the goal being to indicate how best to improve a system or solve a problem. Operations research is an applied form of management science that helps organizations develop techniques to produce their products and services more efficiently. Operations research uses techniques such as cost-benefit analyses, linear programming, systems analysis, simulation, Monte Carlo techniques, and game theory.

Managing information for timely decision making has become a major focus of some research efforts. Management information systems (MIS) developed as a sophisticated technique for systematically gathering relevant information for decision makers. Recent advances in technology have greatly aided researchers in the development of MIS and have allowed them to test theories more quickly using simulation models. Researchers in the quantitative school have advanced managers' awareness of how models and quantitative techniques can be used in the planning, controlling, and decision-making processes of managing.

THE SYSTEMS APPROACH

One of the most widely accepted theoretical bases for modern management is called the systems approach. This movement integrates knowledge gleaned from the biological, physical, and behavioral sciences. Organizations are regarded as systems that function as a whole. Ludwig von Bertalanffy (1901–1972) was one of the first people to write about the "system theory of the organism."[19] He defined a system as "a set of elements standing in interrelation among themselves and with the environment. The really important aspect is the interaction among the elements to create a whole, dynamic system. This system, if it is an open one, interacts with its environment."[20] The system is influenced by the environment and in turn influences the environment. If the system is dissected, it becomes evident that it comprises a number of subsystems; likewise, the organization is but one subsystem of a larger environment. The older schools of management envisioned organizations as closed systems, ones in which the outside environment did not interact with the system. The systems approach to management differs from these older classical perspectives because it acknowledges the impact of the outside environment on everything that happens within an organization. System theory envisions organizations as porous entities that are greatly affected by the outside environment.

Writers in this school view organizations as a part of a larger system. Each organization has inputs that enter the organization, that are then processed in some way, and that finally emerge from the system as outputs. The environment influences all of the elements of the system and provides feedback that allows the organization to assess whether its outputs are successful or not. The elements of the system theory can be seen in figure 2.3.

The inputs and the outputs vary according to the type of organization. In a library, the inputs could be considered to be things such as funding coming to the library from the city to support services, unprocessed books and journals being received, users looking for information and reading material, or children coming for a story hour. All of these inputs are received from the outside environment and taken into the library, where they are processed or transformed in some way. Then the library produces outputs. These can be elements as diverse as books going home with patrons, adults who have had their information needs satisfied at the reference desk, or children who go home talking about the story they heard at the library that morning. Systems theory also has given managers the concept of synergy; that is, the concept that the whole is greater than the sum of its parts. When an organization is working well, each subunit can accomplish more than it could if it were working alone. Systems theory has moved organizations away from thinking about themselves in isolation. Using this approach, managers are reminded of the importance of the environment on any organization and of the interdependence of the subsystems and the larger system.

Figure 2.3—The Systems Approach to Management

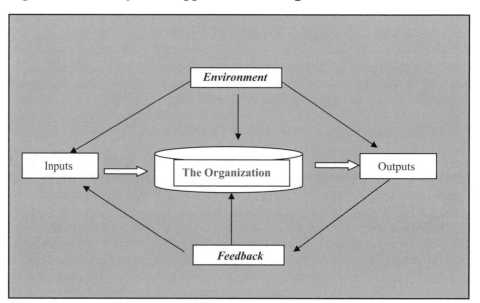

 **Try This!**

Think about an organization you know well, either a library or another type of organization, and view it from the systems perspective. What are the inputs and the outputs of the system? What is done in the system to transform the inputs into outputs? How does the environment influence the system, and how is feedback received? Do you think that the organization is synergistic?

THE CONTINGENCY APPROACH

Beginning in the 1970s, the contingency approach became one of the most influential ways of thinking about management. Frederick W. Taylor was trying to find the "best way" to manage; contingency theory says that there is no one best way. This concept takes the situational approach. It considers the circumstances of each situation and then decides which response has the greatest chance of success.[21] The contingency or situational approach asserts that:

- There is no best management technique.
- There is no best way to manage.
- No technique or managerial principle is effective all of the time.
- Should the question be posed as to what works best, the simple response is, "It all depends on the situation."[22]

Technological impact, size, and outside influences, among other factors, play a role in determining the structure of the organization. The challenges of the contingency approach are in perceiving organizational situations as they actually exist, choosing the management tactic best suited to those situations, and competently implementing those tactics.[23] It argues that universal principles cannot be applied in organizations because each one is unique. Contingency theory tells managers that there is no so-called silver bullet—no one-size-fits-all approach. Instead, a manager has to look at the organization, its goals and objectives, the technology it uses, the people who work there, the outside environment, and a number of other factors before deciding how to manage.

THE LEARNING ORGANIZATION

In the 1990s, another influential approach to management became popular. The learning organization approach was first put forth by Peter Senge as a way to help organizations meet the challenges of a rapidly changing environment.[24] As its name implies, a learning organization is one in which all employees are constantly learning. People at all levels of the organization are focusing on identifying and solving the problems confronting it. The learning organization maintains open communications, decentralized decision making, and a flattened organization. It is an organization that can overcome limitations, understand the pressures against it, and seize opportunities when they present themselves. The basic principles of this approach are made up of five core areas:

1. **Personal mastery,** with people identifying what is important in the process.
2. **Mental models,** with the organization continuously challenging members in order to improve their mental models.
3. **Shared vision,** requiring an imagining of what the organization should be.
4. **Team learning,** through cooperation, communication, and compatibility.
5. **Systems thinking,** recognizing the organization as a whole.

Leaders assume various roles—innovator, broker, director, producer, coordinator, monitor, facilitator,[25] teacher, steward, or designer of learning processes—serving the staff rather than controlling it.[26] The learning organization approach seems to be a good fit as more organizations are making "the shift from the command-and-control organization, the organization of departments and divisions, to the information-based organization, the organization of knowledge specialists."[27]

SUMMARY

This general overview does not permit detailed discussions of these concepts or theories. Instead, these brief discussions are intended to provide the basic background necessary for a student or other interested professional to place into perspective the observed theories as they apply to today's libraries and information centers. Applications of many of the theories mentioned are discussed in later chapters of this book.

Perhaps the best way of viewing the maze that is management theory is to consider each movement as a subsystem that contributes to the overall system of people working together in organizations that are changing. Each theory brings new means of examining these organizations. The current political, economic, social, and technological climate is forcing a reevaluation of systems and structures and a reexamination of some of the early management theories. Modern managers are still using some parts of all of the theoretical frameworks discussed. Modern management often needs to use a pastiche of approaches to fashion the best way to manage in any one particular organization.

LIBRARY AND INFORMATION CENTER MANAGEMENT: THE HISTORICAL PERSPECTIVE

The rest of this chapter will look at how libraries and information centers have used these general management approaches. From its beginning, library management, as might be expected, showed no identifiable characteristics that set it apart from other types of organizational management. Trends, theories, and techniques discussed in management literature easily found their way into library practice, and, over the years, they have been adapted with varying degrees of success. Libraries often adopted the managerial approaches later than they were adopted in the for-profit world, but almost every managerial approach introduced into the corporate sector was eventually tried in libraries. The integration of those theories and techniques into library operations has been extensively reported in library literature for well over a hundred years.

In 1887, F. M. Cruden, then librarian of the St. Louis Public Library, stated that "the duties of a chief executive of a library differ in no essential way from those of a manager of a stock company.... The librarian may profit by the methods of the businessman."[28] Arthur E. Bostwick, addressing the New Zealand Library Association in 1891, advocated the adoption of the methods of business efficiency in the operation of libraries [29] Other early library leaders, including Charles C. Williamson, emphasized the value to libraries of industrial methods, pointing out that "no one has attempted yet to treat comprehensively the principles and philosophy of library service or library management."[30] This was stated at the time of the development of the scientific management school, whose theories already had been applied to a number of industrial situations but not yet to libraries. It was not until the 1930s that particular attention was paid to the application of scientific management to libraries. Donald Coney emphasized this "new" approach by stating that "scientific management furnishes library administrators with a useful instrument for orientating their activities."[31] Ralph R. Shaw began his landmark studies of the scientific management of library operations in the late 1940s and early 1950s.[32]

The influence of the human relations school on library and information services also became particularly evident in the early 1930s; issues relating to people working in libraries began to receive attention, and preparation for library administrators emphasized the personnel relations approach. An article by J. Periam Danton emphasized the trend toward analyzing the human side of management, in which personnel administration became paramount to the democratization of the library organization.[33] This was further expounded in Clara W. Herbert's 1939 volume on personnel administration.[34] Among Herbert's recommendations were greater attention to personnel administration, greater consideration of basic organization directed toward the simplification and coordination of activities, greater staff development, and better working conditions.[35]

It is also important to look at the quantitative, or mathematical, school and the influence it has had on library operations. From the late 1960s onward, managers of libraries have used applied operations research in decision making.[36] In the 1960s, an innovative group of researchers, led by Philip Morse at MIT, and a later group, headed by Ferdinand Leimkuhler at Purdue, studied library problems using operations research. Two reports from other sources illustrate this trend. In 1972, the Wharton School at the University of Pennsylvania finished a study that had been supported by a federal grant to design and develop a model for management of information systems in universities and large public libraries.[37]

What Do You Think?

Many libraries are trying to make the transition to becoming learning organizations. One of these is the library at the University of Nebraska at Lincoln. Two librarians from there recently wrote:

> To advance, libraries need to move away from being knowing organizations that emphasize one best way to do things by following rules and regulations. They need to move past being understanding organizations where organizational culture and values dominate decision making so that change is unlikely to occur. They need to advance past thinking organizations that emphasize fixing and solving problems without questioning why the system broke. Instead, they must become organizations that create a climate that fosters learning, experimenting, and risk taking.

Why is it often hard to make the transition to a learning organization? What would you think would be the first steps in making such a transition? Should it be easier to make the transition in a library than in many other types of organizations?

Joan Giesecke and Beth McNeil, "Transitioning to the Learning Organization," *Library Trends* 52, no. 1 (Summer 2004): 54.

As management theory continued to evolve, libraries continued to take the precepts and principles being developed and apply them to libraries. Just as they had with the scientific and the humanistic schools of management, libraries also adopted the concepts of the systems, the contingency management, and the learning theory perspectives. Libraries now are seen as open systems that are influenced by, and that need to be responsive to, the larger environment. The library management literature over the past few decades shows that contingency management also has been widely accepted, and library managers are trying to find the specific management approach that will best suit the needs of their own unique setting. It is not surprising that so many libraries have enthusiastically adopted the precepts of the learning organization theory. Many articles have been published recently that have described libraries of various types adopting Senge's concept of the learning organization.[38]

How the systems, the contingency and the learning organization approach are applied in libraries will be discussed in greater depth later in this book, because these approaches are the foundation of much that is going on in contemporary library management.

CONCLUSION

It is evident that the various management theories developed in the past 150 years—scientific management, human relations, quantitative, open system, contingency, and learning environment—are being applied to library and information center operations today. The continued use, development, and refinement of those thoughts and techniques will result in more efficient and effective library and information service. The remaining chapters of this textbook discuss factors necessary to consider as change is instituted in knowledge-based library and information services organizations.

NOTES

1. J. H. Breasted, *Ancient Records* (Chicago: University of Chicago Press, 1906), 150–250.

2. Claude S. George Jr., *The History of Management Thought*, 2nd ed. (Englewood Cliffs, NJ: Prentice-Hall, 1972), 12.

3. Daniel Wren, *The Evolution of Management Theory*, 3rd ed. (New York: Wiley, 1987).

4. Larry N. Killough, "Management and the Industrial Revolution," *Advanced Management Journal* 7 (July 1970): 67–70.

5. Harold Koontz, "The Management Theory Jungle," *Academy of Management Journal* 4 (December 1961): 174–75.

6. Frederick W. Taylor, *Principles of Scientific Management* (New York: Harper & Row, 1941), 36–37.

7. Ibid., 31.

8. Max Weber, *The Theory of Social and Economic Organizations*, ed. and trans. A. M. Henderson and T. Parsons (Oxford: Oxford University Press, 1947).

9. Chester I. Barnard, *The Functions of the Executive* (Cambridge, MA: Harvard University Press, 1938).

10. Mary Parker Follett, *Mary Parker Follett: A Prophet of Management: A Celebration of Writings from the 1920s*, ed. P Graham (Boston: Harvard Business School Press, 1995).

11. Saul W. Gellerman, *The Management of Human Relations* (New York: Holt, Rinehart & Winston, 1966), 27.

12. Abraham Maslow, *Toward a Psychology of Being* (Princeton, NJ: Van Nostrand, 1964).

13. Douglas McGregor, *The Human Side of Enterprise* (New York: McGraw-Hill, 1960), chaps. 3, 4.

14. Chris Argyris, *Integrating the Individual and the Organization* (New York: Wiley, 1964).

15. Herbert A. Simon, *The Shape of Automation for Men and Management* (New York: Harper & Row, 1965), 69.

16. Richard M. Hodgetts, *Management: Theory, Process and Practice* (Philadelphia: Saunders, 1975), 113.

17. James G. March and Herbert A. Simon, *Organizations* (New York: Wiley, 1958).

18. Sheen Kassouf, *Normative Decision Making* (Englewood Cliffs, NJ: Prentice-Hall, 1970).

19. Ludwig von Bertalanffy, "The History and Status of General Systems Theory," *Academy of Management Journal* 15 (December 1972): 407.

20. Ibid., 417.

21. Don Helbriegel, J. S. Slocum, and R. W. Woodman, *Organizational Behavior* (St. Paul, MN: West, 1986), 22.

22. Chimezie A. B. Osigweh, *Professional Management: An Evolutionary Perspective* (Dubuque, IA: Kendall/Hunt, 1985), 160.

23. Samuel C. Certo, *Modern Management,* 5th ed. (Boston: Allyn & Bacon, 1992), 48.

24. Peter M. Senge, *The Fifth Discipline: The Art and Practice of the Learning Organization* (New York: Doubleday/Currency, 1990).

25. Sue R. Faerman, "Organizational Change and Leadership Styles," *Journal of Library Administration* 19 (1993): 62.

26. Diane Worrell, "The Learning Organization: Management Theory for the Information Age or New Age Fad?" *Journal of Academic Librarianship* 21 (September 1995): 356.

27. Peter F. Drucker, *The Coming of the New Organization; Harvard Business Review 66* (January–February 1988): 45.

28. Gertrude G. Drury, *The Library and Its Organization* (New York: Wilson, 1924), 83–84.

29. Arthur E. Bostwick, "Two Tendencies of American Library Work," *Library Journal* 36 (January 1911): 275–78.

30. Charles C. Williamson, "Efficiency in Library Management," *Library Journal* 44 (February 1919): 76.

31. Donald Coney, "Scientific Management in University Libraries," in *Management Problems,* ed. G. T. Schwennig (Chapel Hill: University of North Carolina Press, 1930), 173.

32. Ralph R. Shaw, "Scientific Management," *Library Trends* 2 (January 1954): 359–483.

33. J. Periam Danton, "Our Libraries—The Trend toward Democracy," *Library Quarterly* 4 (January 1934): 16–27.

34. Clara W. Herbert, *Personnel Administration in Public Libraries* (Chicago: American Library Association, 1939).

35. Ibid., xiii–xiv.

36. Don R. Swanson and Abraham Bookstein, eds., *Operations Research: Implications for Libraries* (Chicago: University of Chicago Press, 1972).

37. Morris Hamburg, Richard C. Clelland, Michael R. W. Bommer, Leonard E. Ramist, and Ronald M. Whitfield. *Library Planning and Decision Making Systems* (Cambridge, MA: MIT Press, 1974).

38. Sue Baughman and Bette Anne Hubbard, "Becoming a Learning Organization" (University of Maryland Libraries Working Paper No. 3, 2001), http://www.lib.umd.edu/PUB/working_paper_3.html; L. J. Bender, "Team Organization—Learning Organization: The University of Arizona Four Years into It," *Information Outlook* 1, no. 9 (1997): 19–22; J. Hayes, M. Sullivan, and I Baaske, "Choosing the Road Less Traveled: The North Suburban Library System Creates a Learning Organization," *Public Libraries* 38, no. 2 (1999): 110–14.

3

Change—The Innovative Process

 Overview

The management of a large public library in a midwestern state has come to the realization that, for the survival of good information services in this dynamic, demanding community of users, it is necessary to change in order for the organization to survive and prosper. Among other things, this may mean empowering all levels of responsible workers in the library system to participate fully in a change process that might be initiated. This would probably mean that old ways of looking at things may need to be discarded and a culture of empowerment developed to address issues and enhance quality of services.

The popular concept of a paradigm shift, in order for major changes to occur, most often means changing the culture into a new organizational structure with a realignment between what customers need and the requirements that would place on the workplace and workforce. It requires reviewing individual worker efforts with revised organizational goals.

This, then, can be viewed as the important role that change could play in developing information services in all types of libraries and other information centers. This chapter presents an introduction to the topic of change and its affects and effects on information services organizations in a universally changing global environment.

FACTORS PROMOTING CHANGE

The old cliché that "the future isn't what it used to be" holds true today more than ever before in the provision of good knowledge-based information services in which the focus is no longer primarily on processes and procedures and particularly not on the physical entity called the library, but more specifically on users, those seekers and their information needs. Lively, sometimes heated, discussions center not on whether there should be change, but how to identify what should be done differently and how best to do it. In information services circles, just as in most areas of society today, one can hear various proposed, sometimes conflicting, alternatives to the status quo. Many change strategies are expressed, at least initially, in the form of a "how" question: "How do we get people to be more open or to assume more responsibility or to be more creative or be more productive?"—all questions and issues focusing on the means of doing things. Intertwined is the question of "what?": "What changes are necessary, what measures should be in place to ensure performance, what standards need to be applied, what do we want to accomplish with change?" The primary and most basic question of all must be addressed before either of them can legitimately be addressed, however, and that is one of "why?" "Why do we do what we do? Why can't or why should we identify a better way of doing what we do?" All of this questioning leads to an underlying question of "What does doing something differently really require? What indicators can be used to predict success? What new or different standards should be applied? What measures of performance are we trying to affect?"

A successful outcome of that questioning of change requires a review of the culture of the organization and a questioning of the mindset necessary to accept the need for change, combined with a basic understanding of change and how to manage it. Understanding reduces uncertainty and promotes openness, good communications, and a clear vision. Effective leadership and empowerment are additional components in a positive end result. Strategic change, even reengineering, is the outcome of this questioning and learning process.

 ## Some Definitions

Change: Those situations in which performance of job functions requires most people throughout the organization to learn new behaviors and skills.

Empowerment: Encouraging and authorizing workers to take the initiative to improve operations, reduce costs, and improve product quality and customer service.

Reengineering: Examination and alteration of a system to reconstitute it in a new form and the subsequent implementation of that new form.

Paradigm shift: Significant change from one fundamental view to another, which often includes a discontinuity.

The most difficult change-driven task, however, is that of implementing new methods and systems into an already long-established organization. That effort is not easy because it requires a delicate balance and a deliberate progression toward renewing the organization through a series of time-consuming initiatives that demands questioning the status quo.

What Do You Think?

Change is the law of life. And those who look only to the past or present are certain to miss the future.

John Fitzgerald Kennedy offered this sage advice almost fifty years ago. Has the information services community been able to live up to that pronouncement? If so, how? If not, what first steps must be taken?

Many outside factors serve as primary agents for change in information services. Those so-called environmental pressures, outside the organization, are most often ones over which the organization can exercise little control—such as legislation—or no control at all—such as economic trends. Faced with such external forces, the information services organization is challenged in its effort to develop a successful outcome. One of the most important external factors is the development of new information technologies as an ongoing phenomenon. Historically, the introduction of new technology—from the electric typewriter to the duplicating machine, and from the fax machine to the computer, with all of the peripheral developments—has been a driving force and has resulted in major change in the organization of information work. Most recently, the impact of technology has become ubiquitous, sparked by the Internet and powered by telecommunications technologies that have enabled major changes, not only in what is done, but also in the way it is done. This development has both encouraged and enabled partnerships, consortia, and collaborative alliances that are now transforming theories and principles of organizational development into systems and services in a faster and more comprehensive manner as information webs link information workers with users of information and seekers of knowledge. Those technological structures are making a comparable impact on the global information village as did the invention of printing more than five hundred years ago. This universal revolution affects library and information services perhaps more than any other profession. This technological impact has focused efforts of libraries and other information services organizations on what can be described as amorphous relationship areas of organizational culture and people within the organization.

In addition, several global changes have affected knowledge-based libraries and information centers. Primary among them are:

- The emergence of a global complex that enables information services centers, as a part of the information economy, to offer a greater variety of services—in-house, online, consortial, and virtual access projects.

- The development of a changing political and social matrix that enables seekers of information to express disenchantment with the status quo and to demand alternatives.

- The creation of a so-called knowledge economy in which greater effort is spent on procuring ideas and information in a global society in which knowledge has become an important central factor in development.

These initiatives present new challenges because, although information services organizations cannot control much of the changing world around them, they can control how they respond in the area of information services and can choose whether to anticipate and embrace change or to resist it. Organizations can choose to view change as a cause or a condition and thereby become reactive or proactive.

What Do You Think?

When the only tool available is a hammer, everything looks like a nail.

Do you think Mark Twain's tongue-in-cheek admonition has any relevance to the use of technology in providing information services? If so, how does it apply?

For knowledge-based organizations, the ongoing revolution already has launched a gigantic wave of change. How customers seek, access, use, and value information have forced new physical and intellectual structures to meet those needs. Immediate decisions are made to effectively organize and commit resources in support of the future of technology, employee development, and other ongoing or new priorities or initiatives. The information services organization should be managed, or more appropriately guided, in a way that effective decisions can be made. However, the framework for identifying and implementing change continues to be shortened. This requires managers and staff at every level to be immediately accountable for their performance as a result of present decisions about the future of their primary information services initiatives, based upon best-guess assumptions about the future.

In some extreme scenarios, management theorists and consultants have advocated redesigning organizations through such popular techniques as that of reengineering,[1] a term that has become synonymous with redundancy and downsizing. However, such a process of radical change requires reinventing the structure, systems, and services of libraries and information centers to achieve projected improvement and to present a value-added profile. Other theorists and consultants encourage more fundamental restructuring, whereas a few take it one thought farther, forecasting the need to cope with what has been called an "age of unreason." With few dissenting opinions, it is accepted that the present time of discontinuity and ferment—what some have called chaos[2]—demands reevaluation, renewal, revamping, even redesign of previously rather stable library and information service organizations. In that process, futurists, trying to predict outcomes, are making forecasts concerning the importance of various forces that have been growing for some time. To coin an alliterative phrase, "confusion about comprehensive change complicates compliance with contemporary conditions" in library and information service.

What Do You Think?

As new discoveries are made, new truths discovered and manners and opinions change, with the change of circumstances, institutions must advance and also to keep pace with the times.

Does Thomas Jefferson's statement ring true today? If yes, can you cite specific examples? What new "truths" have been discovered and what "manners" have changed in information services?

At the same time, information services organizations have felt dramatic internal change pressures, precipitated by such factors as ethics and social responsibility and the desire for team building and empowerment. Other change factors can be discussed in relation to values and attitudes toward work life, organizational structures, and even application of different management theories and practices in library and information service organizations. All of this activity can be viewed as focusing information services within the organization primarily on providing information to customers. This philosophy of knowledge management, a relatively recent concept for libraries and information centers, is proving to be a catalyst for change—creating an atmosphere in which focus is no longer upon processes taking place in buildings called libraries, but upon knowledge workers as information intermediaries and upon organizing systems to capture that knowledge embedded therein and then transmitting it to those customers who seek answers.

This process is spawning a new set of information-to-knowledge management vocabulary terms: knowledge work, knowledge workers, knowledge management, and the all-encompassing concept of a knowledge society. Knowledge now is the primary resource, and the dynamics of knowledge impose change in the very structure of knowledge-based organizations.

Figure 3.1—Hierarchy of Data to Enlightenment

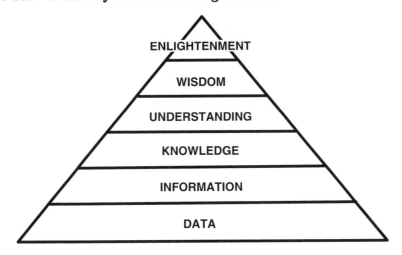

Links between information, the services and systems to access it, and the application of knowledge, with the conversion to wisdom being the desirable outcome, affect every transaction in a library and information service organization's development, management, and successful performance. However, this change activity phenomenon produces a paradox because an organization's success depends upon its ability to maintain stability while managing change. A delicate balance between the concept of control and the need to inspire on the part of management requires planning, development, and maintenance. Knowing what to change and how to change are imperative for the process, and this requires an understanding of how a knowledge-based organization's direction of change and innovation can shape the level of knowledge transfer because implementing that transfer requires self-direction and teamwork.

Library and information services organizations today require knowledge workers whose chief resource is their ability to think conceptually and act logically on what they know. This also demands combining energies and talents of groups of people with an open, two-way communication strategy—with all members taking responsibility for actions—versus the so-called grapevine approach, which in the past prevented organizing to achieve desired results. Individuals working in such a proactive organizational setting view change not as happening to them but as an opportunity to create what they have agreed upon as a viable future.

Both deliberate planning and directional change, then, are required, because without the order that planned change provides, an organization is crippled, and without change, a knowledge-based organization is no longer viable, becomes obsolete, and is quickly superseded by other entities willing and ready to take the risk, unfortunately oftentimes with a profit motive.

EMPOWERMENT—AN AGENT OF CHANGE

There is a tendency for individuals to discount change as a force in an organization's life, while at the same time embracing it in their own personal lives. As an example, research has shown that almost a third of all U.S. workers are so-called discounters, who routinely reject the significance of potential future change; another 40 percent are so-called extrapolators, who believe that the trends of the recent past will continue into the foreseeable future. However, 40 percent of the discounters and extrapolators indicate that they are currently going through a major, self-initiated change in their own lives or careers, and another 40 percent are actively planning to undertake such a change.[3] How can this variance of attitude toward acceptance of change in personal lives but resistance to change in the organizational life be explained? Perhaps the answer lies in an organizational culture and value system that traditionally would present barriers to change. Those barriers can be identified as:

- Failure to create a sense of urgency for change.
- Lack of a clear vision.

- Not removing the obstacles to change.
- Failure to anchor changes into the organization's culture.
- Failure to follow through with plans.[4]

When libraries and information centers are confident of their success and believe that they are necessary, complacency easily becomes a trap. Although historic success has been built on innovative ideas, there is a common tendency to rest upon those past laurels. But a continuation of that success requires a reawakening and renewal in today's competitive environment, and this is an active and deliberate process. From the human side, barriers to that success are both psychological and institutional, with most being in the minds of knowledge workers rather than on organization charts.[5] Predictably, this requires a reorientation and recommitment of all people, managers and nonmanagers, professional and support staff, working in knowledge-based organizations. It also requires a marketing program that informs both customers and potential customers that their information and knowledge needs can be met. It is obvious that without due preparation, change can place any organization on a confrontation course because it is a threatening process and change can easily get out of control. To address that resistance, one must look at what is happening in knowledge-based libraries and information centers.

Information services organizations are now finding it beneficial to embrace change. Initially, some have reevaluated the types of knowledge and skills needed by the workforce in anticipation of future needs. They have developed concerted efforts to form alliances with educators of information professionals to identify core subjects and values necessary for current and future services. With this knowledge and ethical approach has come empowerment of professionals with increased authority and more freedom to be creative. This also enables the ability to diffuse ideas that encourage change and improvement across information services boundaries. A common aspiration, the vision, which will be discussed in more detail under strategic planning, can form the basis for a vision of information services in the organization. Those human resources—complemented by materials and methods, techniques and tools, those components to which long-established management principles traditionally have been applied—remain the core of a changing knowledge-based organization's life, and its success depends upon their knowledge and commitment.

Various other factors also drive strategic initiatives for change in library and information services, including costs of services, speed of delivery, changing values and expectations of customers, entrepreneurial activities, and quality of the value-added service, all enhanced by the technological climate and those global communication systems that promote the reconfiguration of knowledge-based organizations and their services. In such a dynamic environment, the significance of what is done and how it is done is continually challenged by questioning why it is done or, in some cases, why it is not done. But with each one of those components being affected by this phenomenon of change, each presents its own challenge to an effective process of change.

PARADIGM SHIFT—MYTH OR REALITY

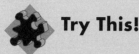 **Try This!**

Mahatma Gandhi once said, "We must become the change we want to see."

Is a paradigm shift in response to changing information service necessary? What external factors are forcing library and information services organizations to do things differently? What are the impediments to change in traditional library organizations?

The most important avenues of change have produced a paradigm shift in the resources, in the services, and in the user orientation within knowledge-based organizations and in knowledge workers' responsibilities for services and systems in those organizations. This continuing paradigm shift now presents the best yet opportunity for comprehensive organizational change.

Change is just as threatening to top managers as it is to other members of the organization. In particular, it threatens autocratic administrators because it can force decision making of a more mundane nature to a lower level in the organization. In addition, the refinement of responsibilities of teams of knowledge workers also diminishes the image of a finger-snapping manager making all the decisions. In such a scenario, there may be a feeling of loss of authority, being unable to control certain outcomes, and that is what occurs if the management style is not one of openness and collaboration. From the top and through every level of the organization, a reorientation requires acceptance of

Figure 3.2—Information Paradigm Shift

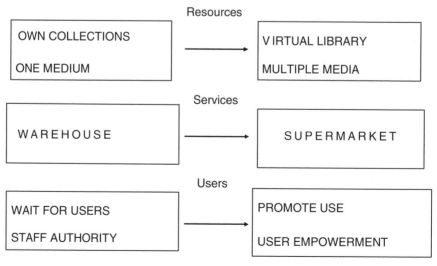

new ideas, learning new techniques and skills, breaking old habits, and adapting to new behavioral patterns. If the process is perceived as threatening, it requires a more delicate, deliberate, calculated approach with much preparation and gentle persuasion. In such a setting, each member of the organization is expected to become somewhat of a risk taker, prepared to abandon approaches that no longer work. Tough questions must be asked: What sort of work is affected as smart technologies are developed and employed? What do knowledge professionals do better than the technologies? How can knowledge workers be organized for optimum impact?

It can be observed that knowledge-based organizations are rapidly moving from individualism, or task orientation, toward more teamwork and process development. Staff participation in the decision-making process; unionization and collective-bargaining efforts; decentralization of information services; flattening of organizational hierarchies; and collaborative employer/employee workplace arrangements, including programs like maternity and parental leave, flextime and flex-place, part-time and job-sharing, and an end of mandatory retirement age—all of which are designed to meet changing needs and interests—are examples of change factors that are having an impact on organizational culture and character and have helped produce a feeling of shared responsibility toward achieving a vision of knowledge-based services.

Empowerment is the key factor and accountability the motto. Because change remains difficult to quantify and somewhat elusive to manage, however, there is no one successful model to follow. The important thing to consider is that change can be accomplished when it is done to improve, innovate, and exploit the knowledge base, and a new organizational profile can emerge. Risk is the primary factor in this equation, but there is no other alternative. A common vision and mission hold the organization together, and team effort provides the vital link to achieving goals, with accountability measurement tracking the success of the mission. Educating, informing, and involving knowledge workers is an important step in planning change because information about needed change helps individuals and organizations adjust to the inevitable and helps motivate so that change can be viewed as an opportunity rather than a threat. Therefore, in the process, an organization cannot abandon recognition of prior achievements of individuals and the organizational whole because that could demoralize people who contributed to those past successes. The corporate memory, that body of data, information, and knowledge residing in files but also primarily in memories of staff, is valuable as a source of knowledge in fulfilling the strategic aims and objectives of an organization. The internally "looking around" aspect of the planning process, the performance evaluation and motivational aspects of the human resources function, the motivational aspects of the leading function, and the feedback options and budgeting applications of the controlling endeavor provide important information about both external and internal forces promoting and facilitating change and offer options for making tough choices, decisions about future directions of the knowledge-based organization. Change also requires constant awareness of each identified organizational role in the goal-oriented, information-intense, knowledge-based organizations in which the previously mentioned teamwork and process are replacing individualism and a task orientation. This involves designing, implementing, and evaluating programs to meet the market's needs and desires and using effective financing of resources, communications of services, and distribution of systems to inform, motivate, and service a market that is also fluid.

Library organizations, as future-focused knowledge-empowering entities, are attempting to anticipate and redefine customer needs on a regular basis and expand and shift services in this fluid environment. In this process they have become more flexible and people centered. This is obvious as many information services organizations have become committed to:

- Reordering priorities.
- Retraining staff.
- Reorganizing space.
- Renewing equipment.
- Restructuring the hierarchy.
- Redirecting financial resources.

 Try This!

It is interesting that there are so many different, sometimes conflicting, ideas about change and what it means for information services organizations. Identify five things that you think need to be changed in the provision of information services and then get a colleague or classmate to make the same list. How many of the characteristics were on both lists? If they were all different, speculate on reasons.

ORGANIZING FOR CHANGE

The past quarter-century has seen enormous change in society and in library and information services. Managers of libraries and other information centers previously spent little time on external matters. Today, a major portion of every manager's time is spent on external matters: with civic organizations, trustees, or corporation members at board meetings and individually; in fund-raising by cultivating relationships with philanthropic-minded individuals and foundations as well as other potential funding authorities; lobbying government officials and other decision makers at many levels; in collective-bargaining sessions, in meetings with friends of libraries groups, and with higher administration and funding agencies or authorities in defense of the budget or support of strategic-planning efforts; and on other public relations matters such as gathering and disseminating information to the press, to decision makers, to customers, and to colleagues.

The primary focus upon customers—gauging their information/knowledge-seeking patterns and assessing their information/knowledge needs in order to develop plans, policies, practices, and procedures that satisfy those needs—presents new challenges and requires changing patterns of service and attitudes. This has precipitated a move away from what might be called an authoritarian hierarchy to smaller work groups in which people manage themselves, with the response time to action being shortened in the process. Workers' roles in adopting a change environment are enhanced as they are allowed, as far as capabilities permit, to grow beyond a traditional hierarchical job to the point of being involved in team problem-solving activities.[6] Work design is becoming more flexible and self-organized, and in many cases human-to-human and human-to-machine networking is replacing the hierarchical organizational form. Information intermediaries working in those no longer institution-bound organizations are challenged to become educators, coordinators, and facilitators. The trend toward the flattening of the organization means that communication and decisions are more immediate and apparent within groups of workers at appropriate levels, and those changes are not easily portrayed in solid lines, or even dotted lines, on organization charts. This flattening of organizations requires greater collaboration as new approaches are developed in management planning, personnel development, systems analysis, and control activities. Seeking a balance between initiative, delegation, and control is a meaningful challenge for those who are ultimately responsible for action, with motivation and trust becoming paramount. Employees are more empowered as they become more sophisticated, articulate, and unwilling to settle for what management theorists call the lower-level needs. "Managing participation is a balancing act: between management control and team opportunity; between getting the work done quickly and giving people a chance to learn; between seeking volunteers and pushing people into it; between too little team spirit and too much."[7] This requires managers to become better teachers and coaches, mentors, and developers of human potential, rather than "whip-wielding autocrats trying to force change."[8] The way change is managed has become as important as the outcome of the change process itself. Managers are learning to acknowledge the transition and to cope with the continuous barrage of new ideas, advanced technologies, sophisticated information access, and the need for interpersonal and intraorganizational relations.

The idea of a virtual organization is no longer unthinkable as the digital or virtual library becomes a reality. To implement new ideas and services requires participation by all who are affected by such change. The thought of restructuring requires consensus and a common vision of and core values for the organization's future. Therefore, understanding what the change process means and then becoming committed to it is a continuing process from the time that an organization first officially recognizes, and therefore encounters, the need to change until the point when change is initiated, internalized, institutionalized, and valued, as illustrated in figure 3.3.

At every point along this continuum of change, the process can be, and sometimes is, aborted for a variety of reasons. For instance, with the "understanding" point in that continuum, a person or group can have a positive perception, in which the process continues, or a negative perception. If it is negative, steps must be taken to bring that person or group along to the point of understanding and having a positive response. This does not mean coercion, but education and gentle persuasion.

Figure 3.3—The Continuum of Change

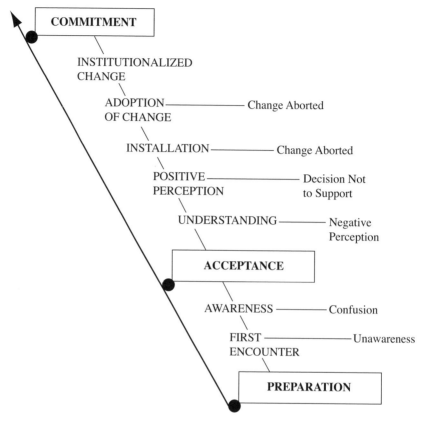

Try This!

Bertolt Brecht once wrote, "Because things are the way they are, things will not stay the way they are." Discuss "things" that are now in place in library and information services organizations that are different than in the "good ole days."

DIAGNOSING CHANGE

Two approaches to change can be identified in organizational structures.

1. Unplanned change is the most prevalent and is likely to be disastrous because it usually presents a situation that forces an organization to react. Such change usually occurs when pressures for change are intense and almost out of control or if the process is being mismanaged. Negative forces, such as poor management and lack of

vision, which can cause organizational decay, are examples of such unplanned change.

2. Planned change, on the other hand, usually encourages all in the organization to buy into the process, thereby bringing about renewal or recommitment on the part of the organization and the people working in it.

Although change is sometimes forced upon an organization from outside, causing it to react, successful change efforts most often come from within as calculated effort on the part of people working in organizations who have recognized the need. An informed approach to managing change enables library and information center personnel to join together in strategic thinking and envisioning a strategic vision for the organization while at the same time deciding upon necessary choices about technological and facility investments, staffing, and service needs. This process involves a deliberate progression toward renewing the organization by creating conditions, encouraging participants, and soliciting resources to accomplish that transition. Change is sometimes costly to implement yet inevitable in the current life cycle of libraries and other knowledge-intensive organizations. It should be obvious that the difference between planned and unplanned change is that of being proactive rather than reactive when the time is right. Proactive change recognizes the need for change, and it is easily revealed in a SWOT analysis that considers the *s*trengths and *w*eaknesses in the organization as well as the *o*pportunities and *t*hreats that exist in the external environment (see chapter on strategic planning). This deliberate approach can guide the identification and establishment of goals for change, can help diagnose relevant variables, and can aid in the selection of a change technique to be employed. It also should set the stage for planning the initiation of change, implementing the process, and then evaluating its impact.

Theorists describe the change process as being either incremental or fundamental, with incremental being based upon preserving successful aspects of what has been created before and building upon that. Fundamental change, on the other hand, is based upon abandoning what has gone before, challenging those old concepts, and doing things in a new, completely different way. There are proponents of both approaches, each stating the strengths and logic of a particular approach. In any case, it is apparent that organizations must be flexible and agile.

Two approaches to bring about positive change in libraries and information centers can be identified. One is that the organization conducts the process in-house with staff assuming responsibilities for developing the plan led by individuals within the organization (self-appointed or management-appointed teams to address various aspects necessary in the process). Guidelines for this method can be found in the professional literature. A second approach is that of employing change agents, brought in from outside the organization, who are responsible for helping adapt the organization's structure to a changing environment, directing the speed and focus of organizational change, and controlling conflict. One effective process using that approach is the Star of Success Model, which provides consultants for change with an objective way of addressing a series of questions and factors to consider in a process of organizational change.[9]

Figure 3.4—Change Is an Evolutionary, Cyclical Process

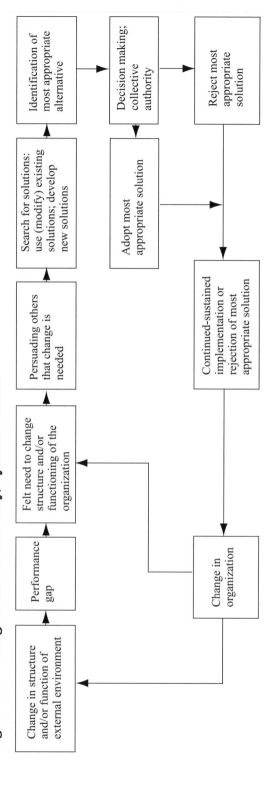

Effective change agents, whether they are brought in from outside or are members of the staff, try to ensure that people are not afraid of what is to come and are able to put the traditions of the organization into some perspective while recognizing that "We've always done it that way" is a strong argument on the side of those satisfied with the status quo. Those doubters must be persuaded that yesterday's success may be tomorrow's failure. Gentle but firm persuasion and inclusiveness all along the way is needed in changing not only the way that people act, but also the way they think. This positive process, then, requires trust and participation by all. An internal environment that fosters change includes the organizational structure itself, the strategic-planning process, the decision-making process, strategies for improving communication and staff morale, team building and conflict management, and the accountability factor that controls what is done and the way it is done, all of which must be encouraged by management and gently directed by leaders in the organization. Modification of attitudes and behavior of individuals, a delicate process and one that cannot be management controlled, is just as important as those other factors in the internal environment. The culture of the organization and the set of beliefs and expectations that are shared by members, those ethical values and social responsibilities, must be identified and preserved.

As with any major process, there must be a plan for change, a road map of getting from where the organization is now to where it wants to be. This process is facilitated by a few simple questions, prevalent in all good planning exercises (who, what, when, where, how, and, most importantly, why). A lack of preparation and imaginative follow-through are ingredients for failure in any change initiative. The change process is evolutionary because tasks, technologies, and even organizational structure are dictated by constantly changing environmental pressures and relationships. Those influence the attitudes, habits, and values of persons working in the organization, in a changing political, economic, social, and technological climate. As an example, change in attitude among elected officials as to the government's role and responsibilities has direct impact on financial support for libraries and information services. Such a shifting focus, as it occurs, should be capitalized upon as elected officials and decision makers begin to recognize the importance of information, converted into knowledge in the social services and economies of countries and local areas. The question of fee-based services versus free services in public libraries, with the concomitant issues of the data-rich and information-poor, is a specific example of a social question that influences individuals working in libraries and information centers and their guiding principles and operations. These are but examples of library and information services reacting internally to external opportunities or pressures. Those various components must be considered as a whole because each one affects and interacts with all of the others.

LIBRARIES AS OPEN SYSTEMS

The library of today can be considered an open system that receives input from the outside, absorbs it, transforms that information, and then transmits it back into the environment. This proactive type of organization includes a number of subsystems that, in turn, respond to this change cycle. This

Figure 3.5—Internal and External Pressures

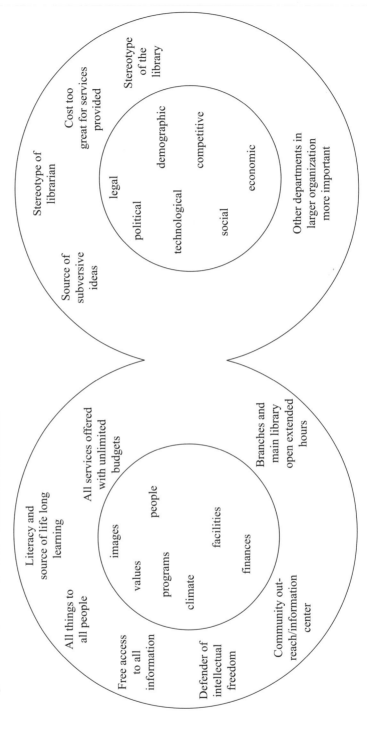

requires that a change in any one component of the organization leads invari-
ably to a change in all components.[10] It also means that goals and objectives
are determined, to a great extent, by that larger environment, and, if the
organization is to be successful, it must depend upon that outside input to be
able to produce usable output against which the success of goals and objectives can be measured. Further, the psychosocial subsystem is formed by
individuals and groups interacting both within the system and with groups
of individuals outside the system. Additionally, the structure of the organization subsystem determines the way assignments are divided and work is
carried out, those being reflected in documents such as organization charts,
performance evaluation processes, policies relating to service and structure,
and procedures manuals. Finally, the technical subsystem is shaped by
the specialized knowledge, skills, and techniques required and the types of
technological equipment involved. These subsystems continually interact in

Figure 3.6—Interrelationships of the Various Subsystems.

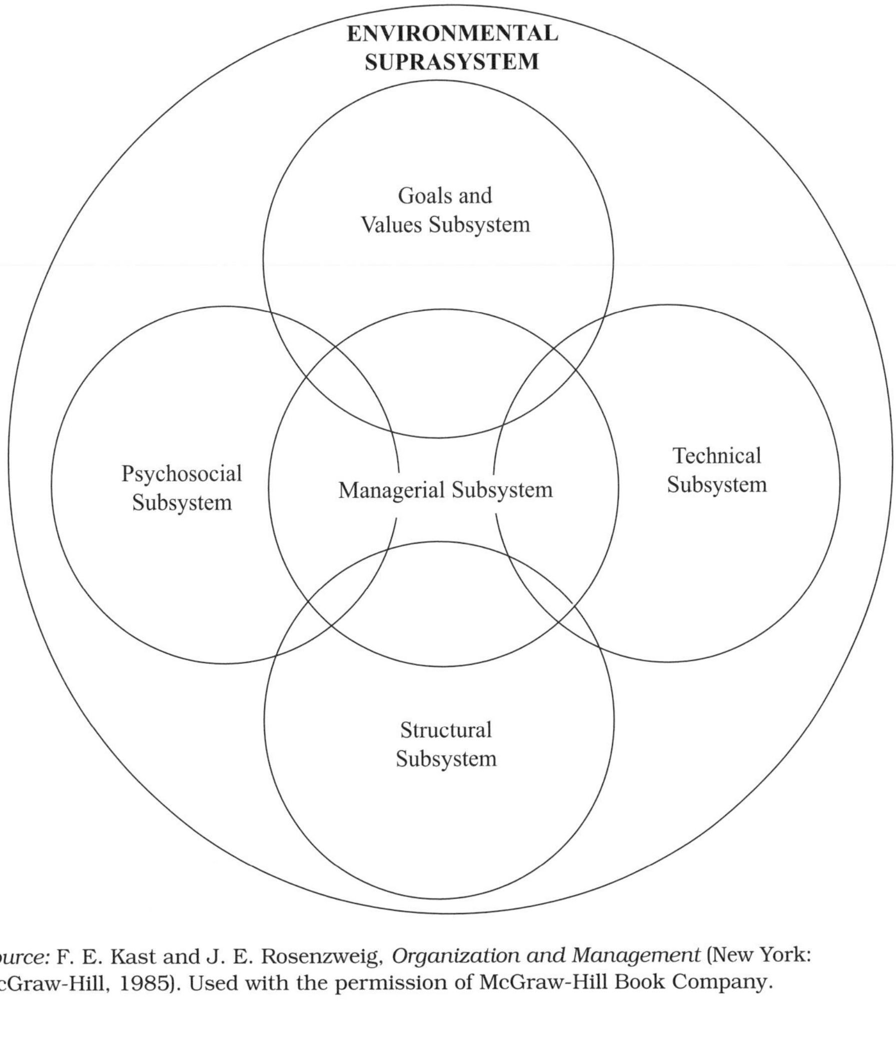

Source: F. E. Kast and J. E. Rosenzweig, *Organization and Management* (New York:
McGraw-Hill, 1985). Used with the permission of McGraw-Hill Book Company.

informal and formal ways within the overall system. Each points to the challenge of developing a multidimensional knowledge-rich, technologically savvy environment and the need to plan for that eventuality. This interaction is reflected in the larger managerial subsystem that encompasses components of the entire organization and is subject to the greatest change.

Change in both placid and turbulent organizations, whether planned or unpredicted, almost always is accompanied by tension, anxiety, resistance, and conflict. Those negative forces can and must be analyzed and minimized to facilitate the success of the change process. Change, affected unilaterally by the hierarchy in which the "definition and solution to the problem at hand tends to be specified by the upper echelons and directed downward through formal and impersonal control mechanisms"[11] is a recipe for disaster because that attitude and approach is one of the major causes of tensions, anxiety, conflict, and resistance to change. Human nature dictates that change initiatives sometimes fail because the primary factor of people working in organizations is not adequately accounted for.

RESISTANCE TO CHANGE

 Try This!

Without changing our patterns of thought, we will not be able to solve the problems that we created with our current patterns of thought.

—*Albert Einstein*

What patterns of thought are prevalent in your view of information services today that are likely to change tomorrow?

Resistance to change, sometimes destructive but oftentimes creative, relates primarily to emotional, philosophical, and procedural conflicts among individuals and groups and within the process. It is in human nature to be tentative about change, particularly if they do not understand why it is being initiated. Resistance, as well as acceptance, can provide important feedback. If it is identified early and managed properly, it can facilitate the change effort with minimum difficulty. Empowerment remains the key factor. Most change initiatives that fail do so because human factors are not taken into account adequately.

Resistance occurs for a variety of reasons:

- People do not understand or do not want to understand the need for change. People have time invested in the status quo. Some truly do not understand, and too often this reaction is interpreted by change advocates as defiance. Other persons may disagree with the need for change, basically denying that it is necessary. Certain categories of people resist change more than others. It has been pointed out that people who have been in an organization longer are more resistant to change because they have more time and money invested in the status quo. People who have less time invested have no strong commitment to the old way and are more adaptable to new situations.

- People are skeptical about the success of the effort. People sometimes have not been fully informed, an indication that effective communication is a key factor that is sometimes lacking. Communication is a two-way street. How a message is transmitted and if it is successfully received are both necessary components. If resistance is viewed as noncompliance with change, it can build the change climate to a higher intensity of resistance. Communication is an important management responsibility to see that everyone is kept fully informed. Sometimes information about change is restricted, thereby causing resistance. Several experts have pointed out that not only will providing opportunities for individuals to have influence over and participate in the change process lessen resistance to change, but also providing continuing involvement after the initial change effort "will produce significant increases in motivation, satisfaction, and performance."[12] A lack of understanding of how and what to change causes confusion.

- People's habits and securities are threatened. They may feel their basic assumptions, their personal values, and their senses of security or friendship are threatened. Change introduces new conditions and requires different skills and knowledge. People may become anxious about their own personal situations and about their future responsibilities or even if they have a future in the organization. Self-preservation becomes paramount in the mind because self-confidence is threatened.

- People may be satisfied with the status quo, with the way things are and with current priorities and working relationships, particularly because groups of individuals may be comfortable working together. Often groups are comfortable together, and the pressure of a group norm influences attitudes. This pressure may influence attitudes toward change, forcing the burden of proof upon those seeking change. In addition, some groups may lack motivation and therefore do little to support its implementation.

- People have vested interest and what they view as a clear perception of what is needed or wanted, and even though they may be somewhat open to change, it is only on their own terms. With increasing complexity in organizations comes a greater disparity of backgrounds, attitudes, and values, thereby allowing greater likelihood of individual or group resistance.

- The speed with which change occurs causes greater strain on the organization. The organization itself may not be able to cope. When overwhelmed by change, people resist. Rapid change makes people nervous, and fear becomes an inhibitor. On the other hand, once the process has begun, some may become impatient with the slowness of progress, which leads directly to the next point.

- Inertia in an organization requires considerable effort in order for it to be redirected. Such strain forces pseudoconsensus on groups and places greater reliance on managers as coordinators, negotiators, and arbitrators, as well as motivators.

- The organization may not be ready for change. Certain preconditions, as previously discussed, are required but may not yet be in place. Speed in instituting those preconditions cannot be forced. Trust must be established at all levels, and leaders must be ready and capable of implementing the proposed change and must exude that confidence.

- Rapidly changing technology and societal conditions render some individuals obsolete. It is impossible to remain in the same job for life, and even if a person did remain in one position, the job itself would change. Obsolescence is one of the most serious problems facing individuals in today's society. Obsolescence means the degree to which a person lacks the up-to-date knowledge or skills necessary to maintain effective performance on the job. In addition, many things, including the information explosion and dynamic change stimulated by the knowledge revolution; personal characteristics, particularly psychological; and work environment and climate, influence obsolescence. The acceleration of change has resulted in a progressive decline in the useful lifetime of previous formal education and training, thereby requiring continual education on the part of individuals and staff development on the part of organizations.

- Change is difficult to implement. Any type of transformation or transition is difficult. It is difficult to let go of a way of doing things, a way of organizing work and working life, to imagine a different future. Change cannot be forced upon the organization by the dictate of managers; no person wishes to have change in the working environment forced upon him or her. Likewise, every effort must be expended to preserve the agreed upon traditions, values, and character that are vital to the organization's life.

In many cases, it can be anticipated that there will be some resistance to change; therefore, resistance must be recognized, valued, and managed. The organization as a whole must explore the core of that resistance, validate its existence, and try to minimize its impact through understanding and problem solving. This kind of negotiation is what experienced change agents are good at, facilitating change in organizations.

A status quo attitude in times of universal change can render stagnation, and stagnation condemns organizations to obsolescence.

CONCLUSION

Change in organizational behavior of libraries and information centers is the result of recognition that today's knowledge-intense climate requires a different structure, attitude, and outcome on the part of those organizations. It requires collaboration and cooperation among all levels of workers, primarily in self-directed teams. Managerial systems and practices in some libraries and information centers were introduced in a more leisurely past without the current rate of change, and some of those systems, created in that more stable, predictable world, may no longer work effectively. For example, bureaucratic control, a holdover from the past, is being replaced by peer control, customer control, and automated control. In many successful library initiatives, teamwork, team building, team sharing of core knowledge and new directions, and team incentives now provide flexibility and total organizational learning modes.

Organization charts now depict new organizations of groups with collective responsibility for service to customers, with a focus on customer requirements. The challenge is to convert resistance into commitment and status quo attitudes into new initiatives as the change concept is implemented. The remaining chapters of this textbook discuss components necessary to be considered as that change is instituted in knowledge-based library and information service organizations.

NOTES

1. Charles Handy, *The Age of Unreason* (Boston: Harvard Business School Press, 1990).

2. Dirk van Gulick, *Encounter with Chaos* (New York: McGraw-Hill, 1992).

3. Daniel Yankelovich, *New Rules: Searching for Self-Fulfillment in a World Turned Upside Down* (New York: Random House, 1981), 79.

4. John Kotter, "Leading Change: Why Transformational Efforts Fail," *Harvard Business Review* 73 (March–April 1995): 59–67.

5. L. Hirschenhorn and T. Gilmore, "The New Boundaries of a Boundaryless Company," *Harvard Business Review* 70 (1992): 104.

6. Victor Turner, *The Ritual Process* (Chicago: Aldine, 1996), 47.

7. Rosabeth Moss Kanter, *The Change Masters: Innovations for Productivity in the American Corporation* (New York: Simon & Schuster, 1983), 275–76.

8. John Naisbitt and Patricia Aburdene, *Re-inventing the Corporation* (New York: Warner Books, 1985), 54.

9. Robert E. Quinn, *Deep Change: Discovering the Leader Within* (San Francisco: Jossey-Bass, 1996).

10. B. Burnes, *Managing Change: A Strategic Approach to Organizational Development and Renewal* (London: Pitman, 1992), 43.

11. L. E. Greiner, "Patterns of Organization Change," *Harvard Business Review* 45 (1967): 120.

12. Alan C. Filley, R. J. House, and S. Kerr, *Managerial Process and Organizational Behavior* (Glenview, IL: Scott, Foresman, 1976), 491.

2

Planning

Planning is the activity that determines where a library and information services organization is going over a period of time, how it plans to arrive there, and how it can determine if it got there or not. The focus is on the entire organization. There is no choice but to anticipate the future and to mold organizational objectives and strategies to accomplish goals. More and more factors determine the success of libraries and other information services organizations. Thinking strategically and taking action to revise and revitalize in order to meet new challenges is the focus of the process. With the future no longer predictable, a recommitment to core values and a vision of the services is embedded in the planning process. Of course, marketing is a vital component in that success. All of these factors must be developed with a keen awareness of outside forces that may facilitate or frustrate the planning process.

An effort to anticipate the future requires choosing from among possible alternatives and with full knowledge and use of techniques and tools available for such action. Thinking and acting strategically enables the organization to continue to move from where it is now to where it wants to be. Planning the services and then marketing the outputs can ensure success in the efforts. Involving stakeholders—users and financial supporters—in the process empowers the organization to move forward in a systematic, more rapid fashion. In order to garner that kind of support for such plans, library and information centers are beholden to the development of marketing strategies for success.

Because planning sustains the viability of an information services organization, discussion of how to facilitate such a process, the trends and techniques, is the focus of this section.

Chapter 4

Planning Information Services and Systems

Overview

Jean Smith is excited to have been the appointed director of libraries in this most prestigious university. In fact, she is the first female appointed to such an august position in this Ivy League institution with a long history and tradition behind it. In the first general information meetings she schedules with her senior staff, the issue of future directions is high on the agenda. Wanting to ease into discussion of planning for the future, she asks each unit chief to describe his or her area of responsibility and to imagine some future directions for the unit. The first old-timer to speak tenaciously presents his unit's responsibilities with a caveat of "Thank you very much; we are doing what we are supposed to do!" By way of gently prodding the discussions, she asks why something is done the way it is. Comes his serious, but defensive, reply, "Because we have always done it that way." Is the response an excuse or a reason?

Planning is one important way of anticipating the future. In the process of futuring, an organization must determine where it is before it can decide where it wants to be and how it will get there. Planning services and systems in libraries and information centers is an all-encompassing concept from recognizing the need to plan and then developing a vision and a mission, through setting goals, motivating individuals, appraising performance of both personnel and systems, evaluating results, developing a financial base to accomplish all of that, and finally adjusting directions to account for the outcome of those activities. Along the way, decisions must be made and policies developed.

This chapter provides an introduction to the organizational planning process. It gives an overview of various planning models and the factors involved in the planning process. Finally it presents some techniques and tools that are useful in the planning process. This is done in preparation for the next chapter on strategic planning.

TECHNIQUES AND TOOLS

A dynamic organization has no choice but to anticipate the future, to attempt to mold future directions, and to balance short-range and long-range goals. Preparing for the future is the core of management activities, with its effectiveness—or in some cases ineffectiveness—being reflected in every segment of an organization's developmental process. As an analytical process, it involves assessing the future, determining a desired direction for the organization in that future, identifying objectives in the context of that future, developing programs of action for such objectives, selecting an appropriate agenda from among those alternatives that are priorities, and pursuing a detailed course of action.

ENVIRONMENT FOR PLANNING

Planning is committing library or information center resources—physical, personnel, and material—based upon the best possible knowledge of the future. It requires systematically organizing the effort needed to use these resources and requires measuring the results of planning decisions through systematic feedback so that needed changes can be effected. In libraries and other information service organizations, the planning process may be resisted by individuals and groups who fear that change—in goals and objectives as well as in responsibilities and organizational structure—will threaten their positions in the organization. In its extreme, this planning climate can create a competitive relationship with other departments in the larger organization—whether they are academic units of an educational institution, departments of a governmental entity, part of a school district, or divisions of a business or foundation—of which the library is a part. This competition places greater responsibility on the librarian to sell programs and exert pressures for their successful execution.

Strategy is the focus of all planning processes, and it usually incorporates purpose, policies, program, action, decision, and resource allocation that serve to define an organization.

 Some Definitions

Planning: An effort to develop decisions and actions in order to guide what an organization does and why it does it.
Policy making: Development of plans, positions, and guidelines that influence decisions and provide direction for the organization.

> **Decision making:** The process of selection of a course of action from among potential alternatives.

PLANNING MODELS

Various change dimensions and predictive management approaches are used in the planning process and are extensively discussed in the literature. Crisis management, contingency planning, and conditional thinking are terms found in the literature to describe the art of predicting and planning. Most new techniques capitalize on opportunities to change, rather than on the threats that unplanned change can bring. They are techniques for minimizing some of the risk and uncertainty in an organization's future, minimizing or replacing uncertainty with some measure of control over the direction and outcome of the future, and placing the organization on a deliberate, successful course through the planning jungle. Planning gives direction, redresses impact of change, minimizes waste and redundancy, and sets standards used in controlling.

A few of those models have some application for library and information services planning. They are presented as a prelude to the strategic planning technique that has most relevance for information services and that is discussed in the next chapter.

Those models include:

- **Issue-based (or goal-based) strategic planning** is a simplified form of strategic planning that is applicable to information services in smaller organizations but has most of the components of the strategic planning exercise.

- **Self-organizing planning** purports to deny the notion that strategic planning is linear or mechanical. Thus, it requires continual attention to common values. It has been likened to the development of an organism; that is, an organic, self-organizing process. This requires an intensive examination of the current organization and clarifying the organization's values and then articulating a vision. It also requires routinely revisiting the process in order to envision what must be done at that point. In that sense, the planning process is never completed; a learning process is continuous, and therefore examination of values is necessary in order to update the process.

- **Alignment modeling and organic modeling** is used to ensure that what the organization does is aligned with its mission. It is useful as a fine-tuning strategy or to explore why strategies, already in existence, are not working. Some of those techniques use computer software in developing the model. The purpose of the model is to ensure strong alignment between the organization's mission and its resources to effectively operate the organization. This model is also undertaken by organizations that are trying to fine-tune strategies or discover why their current strategies are not working. An organization might choose this model if it is experiencing a large number of issues around internal efficiencies. The approach allows not only identifying what is not working well but also what adjustments should be made.

- **Scenario planning** is a particular planning technique that basically requires a group process that promotes creative thinking through a "What if?" attitude. A scenario is formed by developing and describing a desirable future situation and identifying the course of events that enables one to progress from the original situation to that future situation. It encourages participants to discover new ways to solve problems, to develop services, and to institute plans by sharing knowledge and sharing a vision for becoming a more effective and efficient learning organization. Scenario planning has been developed using Peter Senge's five disciplines approach.[1] It maintains that multiple possible futures exist and discusses the process necessary for an organization to create its own future by exploring all possible alternatives to the present structure. This approach is useable in conjunction with other models to aid planners in undertaking strategic thinking. The model is useful, particularly in identifying strategic issues and goals. Often times this technique requires the organization to discuss and develop three different future scenarios: best-case, reasonable-case, and worst-case scenarios that might be foreseen as a result of change. This exercise can encourage motivation for change of the status quo. In addition, each scenario offers potential strategies to cope with change. Of course, the objective is to select the most realistic scenario while identifying the best strategies the information services organization must undertake to respond to change.

The intent of this approach is to develop more than one vision, allowing flexibility in creating views of the future as part of the planning process. The strategies can be addressed in at least three possible scenarios:

1. Probable: Key trends and constraints of current situations are explored and implications for continuation; increase or decline of what is current are explored.

2. Possible: What might change? What would one envision if the organization had better and more? Imagination and speculation are tools for deciding.

3. Preferable: Develop a vision of what is a preferred, idealized condition.

By choosing the most likely to succeed, actions can be converted into an agenda through the planning process. The technique can be potentially useful for libraries and information centers as they try to envision the unknown future.

Each of those mentioned models has certain strengths and weaknesses. Descriptions and application of each can be found in the extensive business and management literature. It is important to note that, although some of the mechanical planning models can be helpful in some situations, the most desirable approach for information services relies upon creativity and innovation.

Despite the obvious need to plan, a systematic planning process remains one of the most elusive and easily avoided activities in information services organizations. This phenomenon continues to exist despite the fact that planning is *the* most basic function—all other functions must reflect it, and the growth or decline of an organization depends in no small measure upon the soundness of its planning process.

Several recently imposed change factors have come together and are now making it imperative to develop planning decisions focused on more detailed, systematic processes than was necessary in a more leisurely past. The multidimensional interrelationship between external and internal forces and between levels of staff in information services organization now demands a systematic approach to developing and marketing the services and their benefits. Changing environments and anticipated future environments—including declining or stabilized budgets, inflation, technological developments, the explosion of information in many formats, staffs' growing sophistication coupled with their own needs and expectations, patterns of use, user interests and satisfaction, and nonuser resistance and reasons thereof—all make planning for information services more vital and more alive today than it has ever been.

 What Would You Do?

The new director is insistent upon approaching management in a new way. Participation is the name and decision is the game You, as the group leader for the upcoming retreat on change, have been asked to come up with an agenda for discussion and action that includes identification of the five most important change factors that are or might soon impact good library and information services. How do you begin to identify those factors that make it more necessary than ever to systematically plan and develop library and information services? In thinking about the assignment, and before even reading articles and treatises on change, what are your initial reactions? Present a persuasive argument to the group as you break out into discussions on this theme.

Such a dynamic environment provides new challenges and opportunities to revitalize and redefine organizations as well as reinvent information sources and services for both growth and survival, with the primarily goal of meeting a growing need in society for access to information. An added benefit is that staff at various levels in information services organizations, as they become more actively engaged in the planning process, are more likely to become committed to an agreed upon vision of the organization and to dedicate their efforts to pursuing the goals and objectives that are the outcomes of that planning. As this happens, all members of the organization are becoming spokespersons and advocates in explaining, enhancing, and enveloping the identified needs and directions not only to other staff members but also to governing agencies and the customer/client/patron/user base.

Although numerous reasons can be given for why many libraries and other information centers have neglected planning, the main reason given is that if it is to be done successfully it is extremely difficult and time-consuming and can be a confusing, sometimes threatening, process. That is further complicated by the macroenvironment, including economic uncertainty, technological innovations that are necessary, shifting demographics, changing societal priorities, and shrinking financial support from primary sources. In addition, changes occur in reporting relationships in organizations of which libraries and information centers are a part—university presidential and corporate officials' tenures are shorter; sometimes another administrative layer is inserted in the chain of command; boards of trustees change, as do school committees; corporate boards and mayors or other chief management officers change. Such changes may force libraries and information centers to make decisions that will affect operations in the foreseeable future and, in some cases, to project needs beyond that immediate future. Added to the complications and resistance is the fact that many managers and other staff members simply avoid proper planning, whereas others naively do not understand how to plan. Some library and information center professionals in decision-making positions tend to emphasize current operations at the expense of planning for the future. Resistance to systematic and comprehensive planning often is couched in such phrases as "Planning is just crystal ball gazing in these days of technological change," or "There is no time to devote to planning because we are too busy with our work." Some managers in libraries and information centers continue to look to past success as a guide for projecting future trends, whereas others rely on intuition as a decision-making device. Former successful operations that were the result of an overabundance of funds are sometimes attributed to the manager's own imagination and intuition. Lack of success, on the other hand, is blamed on "circumstances beyond the library's or the information center's control" instead of on a lack of planning.

Planning styles and approaches, if they can be identified, are sometimes more retrospective in nature, drawing upon past experiences with the hope of projecting those past successes into the future. When the organizational climate, internal and external, was more stable than in current turbulent times, such experience was acceptable as a basis for decision making. This is no longer a realistic approach. Although experience still is one legitimate factor in the overall analysis of a plan, it is no longer the only and certainly not the primary factor. Experience, intuition, and snap judgments made by one person are no longer effective methods with so many new variables now likely to determine eventual outcomes. As libraries and other information centers have matured organizationally, and in order to avoid continual crisis, information professionals have taken it upon themselves or, in some cases, have been mandated by parent institutions to think more strategically and to act more strategically by developing future-oriented plans in an attempt to anticipate the processes, programs, and priorities that will be desirable and sustainable in the future. That future is not what it used to be. The outcome of such planning, then, becomes the basis for financial considerations leading to operational plans covering staff utilization, materials acquisition, technological development, and physical plant maintenance, each of those cost factors being a part of the total service matrix. Many libraries and information centers have introduced a self-evaluation planning process in order to identify strengths and weaknesses that support or hinder priorities identified in the process. Some are surprised that those identified priorities may be completely different from what was previously perceived to be the primary focus of activities.

What Do You Think?

By failing to prepare, you are preparing to fail.

Do you agree with this statement that was made by Benjamin Franklin? Is it really necessary to plan, particularly because there is some indication that the future is already here?

A changing information services environment now demands greater attention to effective planning for information services. This requires an attitude of anticipation, with planning being deliberate, conscious, and consensual. In such an atmosphere, there is greater likelihood of successfully incorporating change as the dynamic force. Because planning is an effort to anticipate future change, it can and should be accomplished by choosing from among several possible alternatives.

Planning in the past was most often accomplished in the performance of managers only, in a direct supervisory relationship. Now many large libraries and information centers have developed cadres of people whose primary function is planning. Those officers in planning staff positions augment and support team-based planning efforts, sometimes acting as information sources, sometimes as catalysts, sometimes as advisers, and sometimes as devil's advocates. Those individuals might, for example, provide factual data and propose new services, but their primary role is to coordinate the entire planning program. Some libraries and information centers have instituted planning committees or groups, whereas others, mainly large public and academic library systems, have created planning offices within the staff structure of the library. Information centers in for-profit organizations are more likely to relate a portion of their activities to a planning division and, with knowledge management becoming such an important component of their responsibilities, are likely to be represented at a high level in the organization because knowledge management plays an important role in those initiatives. These groups are responsible for developing or guiding the development of certain plans, particularly those that are long-range or more strategic in nature. Such groups, with clearly defined responsibilities, are usually able to perform more intensive investigations and to analyze and coordinate plans more thoroughly.

One good example of a centralized planning effort with designated staff is that of the University of California's System Wide Planning Unit within the Office of the President. That group is charged with providing "strategic leadership and support for strategic planning for the long-term sustainable growth of the University of California's library collections and services, consistent with the 'One University, One Library' concept of shared resources, programs, services, and planning."[2]

Now, more than ever before, a new, more formalized approach to planning, based upon forecasting and examination of environmental factors, is the key to success in library and information services. However, this simply stated feat is not easily accomplished. Librarians and information specialists new to the planning process should be cautioned that some formal planning methods and models can be quite complicated and may not apply to current library and information service needs of their own organization. Some of these sophisticated models do not lend themselves to smaller information service operations and, therefore, may not be cost-effective; others are so complex that they may be of no use in a particular library or information center setting. It also must be stated that, because of rapid environmental changes, many plans may become dated or obsolete before they even can be implemented. Therefore, it should be a process that never ends, is continuously revisited and revised as opportunities and circumstances dictate. A balance between efforts expended and outcome is desirable. It should be recognized, however, that there is a downside to an extensive planning process.

THE PLANNING PROCESS

A successful planning approach must build an understanding of the library's or information center's reason for existence and capabilities as an essential first step to identifying future directions. To create a planning attitude, the concept must involve all levels of the organization, beginning at the top and filtering down throughout the various levels to be accepted and implemented through policies, procedures, projects, and programs that are developed as a result. The outcome, a planning document, becomes today's design for tomorrow's action, an outline of the steps to be taken starting now and continuing into the future. The process leading to the development of a written document involves all segments concerned with and affected by the process, both inside the immediate library and information center and outside through customers with programmatic interests and individuals and organizations with vested financial interests. This planning process forces action on the part of the whole of the institution. Although the idea of involving every single person in the process is an idealistic approach, it is so only because it is not feasible for everyone to participate in every single aspect of the stages of a planning process.

Because planning is a delicate, complicated, time-consuming process, it cannot be forced on an organization that is not prepared for self-analysis and the change that will result from the process. A bifurcation exists, in which scientific evidence and rational thinking must be balanced by a planning attitude and the interpersonal skills that facilitate the process. Discretion must be exercised so that overinvolvement in the planning process, by individuals and by groups, does not interfere with fulfillment of the basic mission of the organization, while at the same time they must be assured that they are an important component in the success of the process. Occasionally, services can suffer if resources are diverted to the planning process and staff become so engrossed in planning that current basic library and information services tasks are ignored. On the other hand, the success of the effort requires commitment that must be earned. One cautionary note relates to the fact that when large amounts of energy and resources are committed, expectations are likely to be high, foreseeing miraculous results and significant instant change. Such expectations must be quickly brought into a realistic perspective.

The degree of extensive staff involvement in planning depends on cost, time, the importance of the particular plan, and the perceived knowledge and interest of participants. It is imperative that each person involved knows clearly the purpose of the planning, the expected outcomes, and his or her role as well as that of every other individual throughout the process. Keeping the whole organization informed about the plans that are taking shape is also an important component. If this type of communication and involvement takes place, a greater commitment is likely to be achieved. Even previous to the start of the process, the right organizational climate must be established to encourage the success of the planning process. If the staff, the customers, and the funding authorities are in agreement at this initial stage and buy into the process, then it is realistic to expect that members of the library or other information service organizations will consistently use the written plan as a guide.

After the plan is accepted as a document for future directions, progress toward achieving the intent of the plan should proceed in a timely manner, addressing activities and developing procedures to achieve the objectives identified in the plan. The planning process never should be considered as just an activity that management uses occasionally, when they think there is time for it. Without daily planning as follow-up, decisions revert to becoming ad hoc choices, activities become random, and confusion and chaos can prevail.

 What Do You Think?

Abraham Lincoln once said, "If I had six hours to chop down a tree, I would spend the first four hours sharpening the ax." How does this comment have relevance for planning information services, and what does it entail?

FACTORS IN PLANNING

Impetus for planning is now necessary in all organizations, whether for-profit or nonprofit. This is true because technology is changing, doing business is more expensive, and organizations must be sure of their value and therefore justified in expending the required resources. A plan is basically a blueprint for action, a to-do list for the information services organization. It can be simple, short-term, and basic or more detailed, long-range, and strategic. It helps set priorities or goals and helps establish guidelines for implementing the various tasks identified in the plan. Factors, for purposes of discussion here, are arbitrarily divided into five elements:

Time Frame

There are two basic categories of plans with respect to time: (1) strategic or long-range plans and (2) short-term, annual, or operational plans. This categorization refers primarily to the span of time over which the plan is effective, starting with the time when the plan is initiated and ending with the time when the objectives of the plan are actually measured for achievement.

A variety of terms, including *long-range, normative, strategic,* and *master planning* have been used to describe what is now conceived as the strategic planning process. It is the type of planning that has become most widely used and accepted. There are nuances of differences in each of those approaches, but, for purposes of this text, the focus will be on thinking and planning strategically. Strategic planning has become the most central outcome of many organizations' strategic thinking. Exacerbating, or one should say encouraging, this approach are technological developments and applications combined with circumstances and external forces that are mostly beyond the library or information center's immediate environment and control. Those forces dictate an organized, extended view to planning library and information services operations. The strategic planning concept has more or less absorbed what was previously viewed as the intermediate long-range view. Long-range, strategic, and master planning each necessitate looking at library and information center operations in a critical and comprehensive way in order to develop a planning network and time frame that combines the subplans of departments, divisions, project units, or program coordinators of the library or information center into one master plan that charts the course of the whole organization for a foreseeable future.

On the other hand, short-term, operational, or tactical plans encompass the day-to-day planning that takes place in any organization, a type of planning that is more task oriented. It involves a shorter time frame and the resolution of specific problems, usually of an internal nature. Such plans often coincide with the accounting or bookkeeping year and are deadline driven. Short-term plans provide the guidelines for day-to-day operations and the procedures by which they are accomplished. These plans are much more detail intensive and immediate than strategic plans, and their objectives are much more short term and specific. They encompass more known factors and, therefore, are more quantitative. Short-term plans bring the general guidelines developed in long-range plans to the operational level. One might view the two approaches as complementing each other—strategic plans providing the overview and operational plans providing the specific budgetary factors for a specified period of time. Because short-term plans are specific and immediate, they do not carry the uncertainty that strategic plans do. Both types of plans can be considered action oriented, however, and, therefore, measurable and attainable.

Collecting and Analyzing Data

The more pertinent the information on which a plan is based, the better the planning process will be. Therefore, the second element in planning is collecting and analyzing data. This step includes systematic collection of data concerning the library or information center, its activities, operations, staff, use, and users over a given period of time, as well as the external environment, which affects what the organization wants to do and the way it can do it. In other words, it is an analytical study of the whole organization and its operation. One must resist the urge to allow data collection to dominate or to bog down the planning process, but viewing this step as a means to an end—the collection of data relating to past activities with the view of making decisions about future ones. Needs assessment and data collection cannot be stressed to the exclusion of translating the needs into goals and objectives, developing programs to address those needs, and evaluating the effectiveness of new and ongoing library operations and programs. Evaluation as an element of the planning process, and techniques for collecting data are discussed in later chapters of this textbook.

LEVELS OF PLANNING

All supervisors, coordinators, or team leaders, whatever their level of responsibility within the organizational structure, should be engaged in planning at least on two levels. They should be responsible for planning in their individual units or groups, and they should work with others in the organization to develop the overall plan. In addition, involvement of lower-echelon personnel in planning has the advantage of both incorporating the practical point of view of those closest to the scene of operations while enticing them to recognize the need for planning and to support the direction the plan takes. Traditionally, long-range planning has been carried out primarily by the upper echelons, whereas short-term planning usually is conducted by supervisors or coordinators at the point of impact of services. In libraries and information centers that have planning committees or officers, and in smaller organizations, this hierarchical approach is abandoned in favor of input from all levels and segments of the organization. Strategic planning involves many staff at all levels in the process. Therefore, it is obvious that there are consequences of failing to coordinate long-range and strategic planning with short-term plans because the whole concept of planning is to create a network of mutually dependent components ranging from overall, mission-oriented plans to detailed, technical plans for specific operations.

Flexibility

Flexibility, or adaptability in meeting changing needs, is the essence of good planning. Any planning that is too rigid to accommodate change as it occurs is an exercise in futility. That is why it is important to review plans on a regular basis with the intent of revising priorities that might change over the short term as well as identifying objectives that have been accomplished. In this respect, a planning process is never completed; it is continuously revisited, reviewed, revised, and renewed. At the same time, it is important that the library's or the information center's plans remain compatible with those of the larger organization of which the information unit is a part and that they reflect the changing environment in which the library or information center exists.

Accountability

Accountability is key to future success. Accountability requires commitment to the obligations and taking the initiative to carry out established plans.

For managers, this means delegating authority and assigning responsibility to individuals or teams to achieve the plan's objectives once they have been established. Ultimately, however, the director or manager is accountable for the action—or inaction—in achieving the goals. This incorporates control firmly into the planning process. A plan can be no better than the control mechanisms established to monitor, evaluate, and adjust efficiency and effectiveness toward the ultimate success of the endeavor.[3]

ENVIRONMENTAL ASSESSMENT

Political, economic, social, and technological (PEST) trends all significantly influence success in achieving the mission of a library or information center in today's volatile climate.[4] For instance, commerce and technology are globalizing, international resource needs are increasing, and the world political climate is changing daily as governments and organizations react to changes. Also, economic factors, including publisher price increases, foreign exchange rates, varying tax revenues from funding authorities, increasing costs of electronic resources, inflation, and global intellectual property issues affect buying power. In the social arena, an increasingly urban population, disenfranchised from mainstream society and economically disadvantaged, requires the library and information center to aggressively promote itself to its public, stressing its benefits to society. The technological environment, including the Internet, World Wide Web, and electronic bibliographic and full-text resources that are now ubiquitous, requires customer assistance, both informational and technical, for effective use.

Developing Standards and Guidelines

One concise definition of standards is being able to designate any measure by which one judges a thing as authentic, good, or adequate. Standards are measurable, enforceable, and can be directly related to goals. They should provide guidance for actions in the present climate while being flexible enough to allow for future development. General, industry-wide, or profession-wide standards or guidelines established by various professional groups provide a basis for planning. For example, standards developed by the American Library Association and its various divisions include perspectives on services, resources, access, personnel, evaluation, and ethics.[5] Those serve as guidelines and are based on actual, or known, demands for library services. But these standards are not plans; they are a means of defining acceptable service. Each individual library must develop its own plans based on the demands of its clientele, using those industry standards as guidelines. Both human and technical factors must be considered in developing sound standards.

Forecasting

The term *forecasting* elicits visions of crystal ball gazing but more appropriately designates a process of projection or prediction. Predictions are, basically, opinions about facts. Projections, on the other hand, are based on some type of systematic review, whether that review employs quantitative data analysis or qualitative judgment. Forecasts are predictions based on assumptions about the future. Forecasting helps reduce uncertainty because it anticipates the results of a decision about a course of action described in the forecast. Forecasting is a useful planning technique. It attempts to find the most probable course of events or range of possibilities.

A problem very basic to libraries is estimating future trends, influences, developments, and events that will affect the library but are beyond the control of the library.[6] Forecasts account for some of this uncertainty, offering some foundation upon which to plan. Forecasting requires good information on trends and developments in society and the economy as well as in the profession and its system of user interaction.

Various techniques are being used to predict the future. From opinion polling to informal gathering of information, qualitative approaches are used. Futurology has become particularly popular among managers of business enterprises. Some forecasting techniques used in industry have been adapted for library and information services. These include the survey approach, which is used in technological forecasting. One of the most popular types of technological forecasting is the Delphi technique. Delphi attempts to build a consensus of opinion or view and is most useful when judgment is required, when several responses to an issue might be viable, or when it is politically expedient to have strong support for the alternative that eventually will be chosen. Other forecasting techniques that have been used quite effectively in libraries and other information centers include trend projection and environmental scanning. Through environmental scanning, for instance, the information gathered, including the events, trends, and relationships that are external to an organization, is provided to key managers within the organization and is used to guide management in future plans.[7] In its more formal approach, trend projection graphically plots future trends based on past experience and current hard data. Environmental scanning is carried out to anticipate and to interpret change and sometimes to provide a competitive edge. Many information services organizations are now in the competitive intelligence area of environmental scanning. Seeking basic information about competitors and global scanning are examples of techniques necessary to assimilate the knowledge.

Another technique that has come out of forecasting efforts is that of benchmarking, a process that searches for the best practice, assuming that an organization can be improved by analyzing and copying other successful organizations. Therefore, data are collected and analyzed to determine the performance gaps between that particular organization and others that are more successful. From that analysis, an action plan is developed. These techniques and others will be discussed further in the chapter on coordinating and reporting.

They are mentioned here only as examples of the forecasting techniques that can be used in libraries and information centers. With the availability of computers for modeling and the development of software for that purpose, forecasting techniques are becoming more attractive to and manageable for library and information services planners. The primary attempt is to collect and analyze the most relevant information and introduce that information into a flexible framework to serve as a guide for library and information services development.

Try This!

H. G. Wells, more than a century ago, argued that if the long-term course of events is principally determined by society's collective response to economic and technological circumstances, we can, in fact, make meaningful projections of what the future is likely to bring through the continued use of analytical tools, including forecasting.

Using a forecasting technique project 10 years from now, what information services will entail?

David P. Snyder and Gregg Edwards, *Future Forces* (Washington, DC: Foundation of the American Society of Association Executives, 1984), 1.

THEORY APPLICATIONS

Two examples of techniques that have been used in both for-profit and not-for-profit organizations, including libraries and information centers, are Management by Objectives (MBO) and Total Quality Management (TQM), although neither is as popular as it was a few years ago, perhaps because many of their components have been absorbed into other techniques, some of them into strategic planning.

Management by Objectives (MBO)

One technique that has been used to supplement the planning process relates specifically to merging organizational goals and objectives with the personal ones of individuals working in the organization in order to achieve greater success. MBO has been informally applied in libraries to combine individual and institutional goal setting with the decision-making process. Much has been written on the technique of MBO, a process that has been in and out of favor with industry and commerce for some time. Recently it has lost favor with business enterprises. Some now seem to believe that its time has passed and prefer to focus upon project management, whereas others feel it is now reemerging. It is discussed here because it is a style of thinking that remains widespread and pervasive in both private and public organizations.

Because some of its concepts (relationships between units are closely linked through common technologies, customers, values, goals, and objectives) are so closely aligned with those of strategic management, and its focus for the future is on providing a framework for the management process, some discussion is warranted. A guide, called the SMART method, was introduced to help maintain the validity of objectives. SMART stands for *s*pecific, *m*easurable, *a*chievable, *r*ealistic, and *t*ime-related. The belief is that these parameters are predictors of effective goals. For instance, if the goal is not specific or measurable, it is less likely to guide behavior. It has been used successfully as a long-range planning instrument and has undergone change over the years by integrating individual needs with organizational objectives, and the concept has morphed into other management practices.

One caution about MBO is that although it allows one to direct oneself and one's work, it also can mean domination of one person by another. "Objectives are the basis of 'control' in the first sense; but they must never become the basis of 'control' in the second, for this would defeat their purpose. Indeed, one of the major contributions of Management by Objectives is that it enables us to substitute management by self-control for management by domination."[8] Therefore, it is necessary that supervisor and employee jointly identify the commonly agreed upon objectives, define areas of responsibility in terms of expected outcomes, and use those as guides for assessment of performance. In this process, at the start of appraisal periods, supervisor and subordinates agree upon specific results to be obtained during this period; they establish what is to be done, how long it will take, and who is to do it. This approach makes the person accountable for results. Therefore, objectives are developed and measured as a team, with the two important factors being those of goal setting and performance appraisal. Open communication and follow-up, without fear of retaliation, is the result.

In that regard, MOB remains one of the most evident examples of participative management because it involves supervisors and employees in the management process. It can clarify responsibilities, strengthen planning and control, and establish better relationships between supervisors and other staff members. The process rests upon several premises that are guided by the SMART guidelines and includes:

1. Clearly stated objectives. If they are not clear, they should be clarified.
2. A succession of specific objectives. Benchmarks must be established to measure progress.
3. Delegation of specific objectives. Certain people should be responsible for accomplishing specific objectives.
4. Freedom to act. Subordinates should be given objectives and authority and then be charged with accomplishment of those objectives.
5. Verifiable objectives. To achieve objectives, it is best to quantify them. If they are nonquantifiable objectives, they may relate to quantifiable ones. For example, if one wants to reduce absenteeism by 50 percent, the reasons for absenteeism must be considered. If the reasons relate to morale, then morale must be improved.
6. Clear communication. This exists only when objectives are specific, are agreed upon by all parties, are budgeted, and are known by all individuals who have a reason for knowing.
7. Shared responsibility. Team effort is the key to management by objectives.
8. Personal accountability. Each person must be accountable for the achievement of his or her assigned objectives.
9. Improving management ability. Management is able to plan more objectively when these premises are accepted.

MOB occurs in phases: finding the objectives, setting the objectives, validating the objectives, implementing the objectives, and controlling and reporting the status of the objectives. George Odiorne, a major proponent of MBO back in its formative years, reasoned that it helps solve management problems by:

1. Providing a means of measuring the true contributions of managerial and professional personnel.
2. Defining the common goals of people and organizations and measuring individual contributions to them. It enhances the possibility of obtaining coordinated efforts and teamwork without eliminating personal risk taking.
3. Providing solutions to the key problem of defining the major areas of responsibility for each person in the organization, including joint or shared responsibilities.
4. Gearing processes to achieving the results desired, both for the organization as a whole and for the individual contributors.
5. Eliminating the need for people to change their personalities as well as for appraising people on the basis of their personality traits.
6. Providing a means of determining each manager's span of control.
7. Offering an answer to the key question of salary administration, "How should we allocate pay increases from available funds if we want to pay for results?"
8. Aiding in identifying potential for advancement and in finding promotable people.[9]

Over the years, some libraries and information centers have adapted this technique's potential for their operations. In practicing MBO, one must guard against making the individual's objectives too easy, making them too difficult, setting objectives that conflict with policy, or setting objectives that hold an individual accountable for something beyond his or her control.

Total Quality Management (TQM)

Like MBO, some argue that TQM has proved to be an effective process for improving organizational functioning.[10] Others say that TQM no longer has the success it experienced several years ago. Proponents of TQM argue that setbacks are temporary and that TQM eventually will produce results. Those against TQM say that it does not work, not because its focus on quality is misguided, but because the TQM operations often become so cumbersome that they overshadow the mission of the organization.[11] It is true that TQM can result in the formation of more bureaucracy to implement quality, particularly when it is first being implemented, because it tends to add to the workload of everyone. If TQM is perceived as a quick fix, forgetting that quality is a never-ending journey, or if the managers only pay lip service to the technique, it will not succeed.

TQM has found success in some large library and information services organizations, however, as those organizations have implemented planning processes, by strategic planning, focus groups, or task forces. Some libraries and information centers, like other organizations as they seek to pay more attention to quality, have turned to TQM as a system that allows them to do so. All libraries and information agencies have certain routine processes that can be greatly improved by TQM methods. In addition, the TQM emphasis on improving quality in service can help libraries and other service organizations maintain the support of their customer base in an era of increasing competition. Even though TQM has not been widely accepted by not-for-profit organizations, its emphases on quality and customer service can be examined as a model for managers and staff in these organizations. TQM possesses "two key concepts. The first is the need to focus on the customer in the development of products and the delivery of services. The second is the need to be constantly aware of process both in development and delivery, and vigilant for opportunities for improvement."[12]

It is often easy to dismiss this and some other techniques as just management fads, but those fads often have something valuable to teach us. They provide ways to make libraries and information centers more interested in quality, customers, teamwork, and getting things done right the first time. For instance, reengineering basically calls for complete change. What has happened is that there has been a continuum of planning strategies that has brought libraries from looking first at incremental change to the more dramatic comprehensive change. Some of the best of those techniques have been incorporated in current strategic thinking and planning exercises as libraries and information centers look to the future.

POLICY MAKING

It is important to distinguish between objectives and policy. Objectives emphasize aims and are stated as expectations while policies emphasize rules and are stated as instructions intended to facilitate decision making.

In many discourses, policy making and decision making are used as synonymous terms. In practice, however, policy making is only one part of decision making, in that policies emanate from the original decisions and become general statements or understandings that channel and guide thinking toward future decision making and serve as guidelines for the actions, particularly those of a repetitive nature, in order to create some sense of uniformity in the conduct of an organization. In other words, policies are contingency plans because they are based on decisions that set the action course for the plan. Policies, even though they are sometimes expressed in positive terms, are essentially limiting because they dictate a specific course of action and are aimed at preventing deviations from a set norm. They attempt to guard against and eliminate differences that sometimes result from personality conflicts or irrational forces. Policies become the effective tools for transferring decision making through various levels in the organization. This is true because, within the broad policy outline, individuals at all levels may be charged with making operational decisions. A good working definition of policy making might be "a verbal, written, or implied overall guide setting up boundaries that supply the general limits and direction in which managerial action will take place."[13]

Both policies and objectives are guides to thinking and action, but there are differences between them. Objectives, as already discussed, are developed at one point in the planning process, whereas policies, taken as a higher level, channel decisions along the way toward meeting those established objectives. Another difference is that a policy is usually effective or operational the day it is formulated and continues to be in effect until it is revised or deleted. As mentioned before, policies can give guidance to all levels of the organization. For example, by adopting an equal employment opportunity policy, an institution ensures that all qualified individuals are seriously and equally considered by all hiring units within the organization for any position vacancy. The policy does not dictate the choice of a particular individual but does eliminate the factor of discrimination as an element in a final decision.

Policy making is not just reserved for top management because they include both major policies involving all segments of the organization as well as minor policies applicable only to a small segment of the organization. Many policies in libraries and information centers provide basic direction toward the achievement of stated goals, including policies relating to materials purchasing, personnel employment, equipment use, and monetary allocation. Examples of library and information center policies might be:

1. All new staff will be rotated through all departments during their first year of employment (a staff-development policy).

2. Library materials should present all sides of controversial issues (a materials selection policy).

Policy manuals should enumerate an organization's policies in relation to its goals and objectives. Therefore, a policy manual is an important record and is invaluable as a decision-making guide and as a way of communicating within the organization. It is also a basic tool for indoctrinating new staff members and assuring some degree of uniformity in approaches or responses to issues. Of course, it also serves as a historical record of decisions made.

All libraries have policies, whether they are written or unwritten, sound or unsound, followed or not followed, understood or not understood, complete or incomplete. It is almost impossible to delegate authority and clarify relationships without policies because one has difficulty carrying out decisions without some kind of guideline. It is important to remember that policies can provide freedom as well as restrict it and that there are as many cases of frustration within organizations about the lack of rules, regulations, procedures, and policies as there are about arbitrarily established ones. In the absence of policy, each case is resolved on its own merit and at one particular time, so consistency is lacking.

Lack of policy means that the same question may be considered time after time, by a number of different individuals, in several units of the organization, with the result that energy is wasted, redundancy is established, conflicting decisions are made, and confusion develops. Policies ensure some degree of consistency in the operation. They may be stated in the form of guiding principles (these being broad, comprehensive, and basic) or may be specific or operational and deal with day-to-day activities.

 **Try This!**

Mahatma Gandhi once said, "A policy is a temporary creed liable to be changed, but while it holds good it has got to be pursued with apostolic zeal."

Identify two policies relating to information services that are general, have national appeal, are valid, current, and have stood the test of time.

Sources of Policy

Policies can be categorized according to their source:

1. **Originated policy.** This type of policy is developed to guide the general operations of the library or information center. Originated policies flow mainly from the objectives and are the main source of policy making within the organization. An example of an originated policy is the previously mentioned policy to adhere to the concept of equal employment opportunity.

2. **Appealed policy.** Certain decisions may be needed by managers in their assigned areas of responsibility, and the staff is required to take it through the chain of command, in which a common law is established. This type of policy can cause tension because it forces a decision or policy that, consequently, often does not have the thorough consideration that is required. To draw an extreme example, it may be the appealed policy of the processing department to make no more than two subject headings for each monograph entered into the online system. That policy, derived from practice in the paper-based cataloging process, has a great effect on the information services department's ability to work with patrons. Oftentimes, appealed policies are made by snap decisions.

3. **Implied policy.** This type of policy is developed from actions that people see about them and believe to constitute policy. Usually, this type of policy is unwritten. For instance, repetitive actions, such as promotion from within, may be interpreted as policy. This may or may not be the case. Particularly in areas relating to personnel, staff must be informed so that misunderstandings do not arise. When implied policies are recognized, policies should be developed or other statements used to clarify the issue.

4. **Externally imposed policy.** These policies, which come through several channels, dictate the working of an institution even though they may be beyond its control. For example, local, state, and federal laws have a direct bearing on the policies that libraries may formulate. These laws may be general, such as those relating to destruction of public property (Malicious Damage Act of 1861), or specific, such as those relating to copyright (Copyright Act of 1976, last

amended 2004). When policies are being formulated, they must be checked for compliance with law before they can be finalized.

No matter what policies are set for libraries and information centers, the policies are subject to government regulation, national and sometimes international. In the case of public libraries, objectives must adhere to government policy on the local, state, provincial, and/or national levels. If, for instance, a local authority decides, for local economic reasons, to reduce drastically the library service hours to the point that the library no longer meets that state's standards for allocating funds to that library, such an action could be in conflict with its obligation and thus be illegal. Or, if a library redesignates its service points and closes a branch library, people living nearby may petition their representatives or other local officials, who may decide that such a policy does not secure an improvement and may prevent the library from carrying out its decision on policy.

Laws governing information services often relate to finances. Standards for capital investment, percentage of budget spent on physical and electronic materials, qualifications of staff, and so on are developed by library officials. Because this is an external control upon all public library spending, it necessarily affects the planning and administration of public libraries. The example given is in relation to U.S. regulations, although those same types of laws of principle affect other countries as well.

Effective Policy Development

Policies fall into two basic groups: those that deal with the managerial functions of planning, organizing, staffing, directing, and controlling and those that deal with the functions of the enterprise, such as selection and development of technology, resources, finance, personnel, and public relations. Both types of policies relate to the characteristic behavior of the information services organization to achieve its objectives.

Several basic rules should be considered when policies are being formulated. Some of these may seem simplistic, mundane, and even redundant, but it is surprising how many organizations ignore these basics steps when they are formulating policy. To be most effective, policies should be reflective of the objectives and plans of the organization. These should complement one another and build on that common strength. For this reason, any specific policy being formulated should receive detailed consideration before being proposed and certainly before implementation. Characteristics of good policies would include them being:

1. **Consistent.** This maintains efficiency, and the existence of contradicting policies dissipates the desired effects.

2. **Flexible.** Policies should be reviewed and changed as new needs arise. Unfortunately, many organizations ignore this fact and therefore adhere to out-of-date policies. At the same time, a laissez-faire approach to policy formulation and revision can lead to

disillusionment on the part of those who are charged with carrying out the policies. Some degree of balance and stability must be maintained. Policies should be regularly revisited and controlled through a careful review process and someone should be in charge of that process. Although the application of policies requires judgment, violation of policies, sometimes under the guise of flexibility, should be avoided.

3. **Distinguished from rules and procedures.** Rules and procedures are firm, whereas policies, as already indicated, are guides that allow some discretion and latitude.

4. **Written.** A clear, well-written policy helps facilitate information dissemination. Because many policies affect individuals who have not been involved in their formulation, the policies should be discussed and widely distributed through letters, memoranda, announcements, and policy manuals.

Stated policies have several advantages:

1. They are available to all in the same form.
2. They can be referred to, so that anyone who wishes can check the policy.
3. They prevent misunderstanding through use of a particular set of words.
4. They indicate a basic honesty and integrity of the organization's intentions.
5. They can be readily disseminated to all who are affected by them.
6. They can be taught to new employees easily.
7. They force managers to think more sharply about the policy as it is being written, thus helping achieve further clarity.
8. They generate confidence of all persons in management and in the fact that everyone will be treated substantially the same under given conditions.[14]

Implementing Policy

Policies are carried out or enforced by procedures, rules, and regulations. Procedures are guides to action and therefore are subordinate to policies. They establish a method of handling repetitive tasks or problems and may be thought of as means by which work is performed. Basically, procedures prescribe standardized methods of performing tasks to ensure uniformity, consistency, and adherence to policies. Greater efficiency in routine jobs can be achieved through procedures that identify the best way of getting the job done. Procedures tend to be chronological lists of what is to be done. Examples of procedures include a timetable for budget preparation, a sequence of steps to be followed in searching and ordering library materials, and interlibrary loan procedures. Procedures are helpful in routine decisions because they break down the process into steps.

The relationship between procedures and policies can be best indicated by an example. Library policy may grant employees a month's annual vacation. The procedures specify how vacations are to be scheduled to avoid disruption of service, maintain records to assure each employee is allocated the right length of vacation days, and elucidate procedure for applying for additional entitled time off.

Rules and regulations, constituting the simplest type of a plan, spell out a required course of action or conduct that must be followed. A rule prescribes a specific action for a given situation and creates uniformity of action. Rules may place positive limits (should), negative limits (should not), or value constraints (good or bad) on the behavior of individuals working in the institution or on individuals using the institution as a service. Rules ensure stable, consistent, and uniform behavior by individuals in accomplishing tasks, addressing personnel issues, and relating to both the internal and external environment. Like procedures, rules and regulations guide action, but they specify no time sequence. Similar to decisions, rules are guides, but they allow no discretion or initiative in their application. Examples of rules might be the prohibition of smoking in the library or information center or the fact that materials in the reference collection do not circulate. Regulations also establish a course of action that is authoritative, with failure to adhere to regulations eliciting discipline.

DECISION MAKING

Organizational decision making is an important part of management, one of the very basic planning principles. Selection from among alternatives, that is, the decision making process, is at the core of planning. In simple language, a decision is a judgment and therefore a choice between alternatives. "It is at best a choice between 'almost right' and 'probably wrong'—but much more often a choice between two courses of action neither of which is probably more nearly right than the other."[15] Decision making complements planning because it involves choosing the best alternative for the future, and those decisions with organization-wide implications are related specifically to the planning process. A decision is made with a course of action in mind. Of course, such a choice implies an awareness of alternatives and the important factors that need to be considered. A good decision is by choice, not accident, and is the result of intelligent direction and is the best choice among alternatives.

The organizational decision-making process is a much slower process than some can imagine. The stereotype of finger snapping and button pushing fades with the realization that decisions, affecting important future outcomes, require systematic research and analysis. The decision-making process involves a blend of thinking, deciding, and acting; information is key to the process. Deliberation, evaluation, and thought are all brought into play. Although many decisions are mundane, important organizational ones are of unmeasured consequence and could change the information center's course of action. An example of the latter is the decision to open a new branch library or to purchase a totally integrated online system for the library's or the information center's operation. Such decisions can be made only after long, thoughtful review, analysis, discussion, and deliberation. The manager who has the ultimate responsibility must make a decision that will have a great impact on the operation of the library and on many people, staff, customers, and other stakeholders.

Attention paid to the final act—the decision itself—often obscures the fact that a number of steps and minor decisions are made along the way, and the announcement of the decision is only the final step in the process. Decision making at a formal level involves a series of scientific steps: defining the problem, analyzing it, establishing criteria by which it can be evaluated, identifying alternate solutions, selecting the best one, implementing it, and evaluating the results.

Rational decision making views the process happening in a series of steps in which problems are clearly defined and decision makers are able to know all alternatives, can clearly define the problems, and then can make an optimizing decision.

Steps in Making Decisions

If the organization's goals are clear, the important step in decision making is developing alternatives for solutions to identified problems or issues. This step is possible in almost all situations. Effective planning involves a search for these alternatives. If there is only one solution, management is powerless to devise alternatives, and no decision is required, although some adjustments may be necessary. In most cases, however, several alternatives exist. Final selection of a course of action is a matter of weighing expected results against enterprise objectives.

The first step in the decision-making process, then, is the recognition that a problem exists. Having done that, one can then begin to explore possible causes with the intent of seeking a solution. The environment inside and outside the organization provides information upon which a decision can be made. This requires considering all of the information—where does the issue or problem come from, does it represent several points of view, how accurate has information been gathered, and is it based on fact or opinion? Based upon the evidence gathered, one must consider the alternatives. Weigh the advantages and disadvantages of each alternative. What are the costs, benefits, and consequences? Are there obstacles, and, if so, how can they be overcome? What are the choices available? This process focuses on the articulation of a desired outcome. It builds in a review or assessment phase to measure success of the effort. The process culminates in a selection of the solution that best serves organizational goals and the initiation of action to implement it. Of course, it always requires follow-through on the decision by monitoring the results of implementing the plan. These phases, of course, do not have clear-cut boundaries or strict sequence.

When adopted, the decision is then expressed as policy for the functioning of the organization. The outcome of the selection process involves a great deal of risk taking as well as uncertainty because it is only after the decision has been implemented that one can determine whether it was appropriate. The final step of implementation brings the decision into the control and evaluation aspect of the decision.

Figure 4.1—Steps in the Decision-Making Process

```
┌──────────┐   ┌──────────┐   ┌──────────┐   ┌──────────┐   ┌──────────┐
│ Step 1   │   │ Step 2   │   │ Step 3   │   │ Step 4   │   │ Step 5   │
│ Define   │→  │ Generate │→  │ Select   │→  │Implement │→  │ Evaluate │
│ the      │   │ and      │   │ the      │   │ the      │   │ the      │
│ problem  │   │ evaluate │   │ preferred│   │ planned  │   │ results  │
│          │   │alternative│  │alternative│  │ course of│   │          │
│          │   │ solutions│   │          │   │ action   │   │          │
└──────────┘   └──────────┘   └──────────┘   └──────────┘   └──────────┘
     ↑
     │              ┌──────────────────────┐
     └──────────────┤      FEEDBACK        │
                    │   Repeat steps if    │
                    │      necessary       │
                    └──────────────────────┘
```

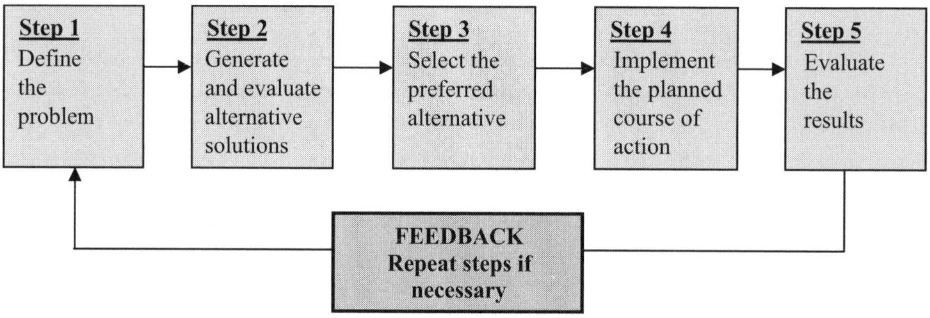

Although this discussion is primarily about the steps in the major decision-making process, it is important to remember that everyone makes decisions every day and that most of these decisions are, to some degree, reached by the same process discussed here. Some organizational decision making, which was once reserved for the executive, is now being delegated to and assumed by others in the organization. The way in which decision making is handled is as important as the decision reached. Decision making can no longer be confined to the very small group at the top. In one way or another, almost every knowledge worker in an organization either will have to become a decision maker himself or herself or will at least have to be able to play an active, an intelligent, and an autonomous part in the decision-making process. What in the past was a highly specialized function, discharged by a small and usually clearly defined unit within the organization, is rapidly becoming a normal if not an everyday task of every single unit in the open system of a large-scale, knowledge-based organization. The ability to make effective decisions increasingly determines the ability of every knowledge worker to be effective. This requires distinguishing between problems for which existing procedures are appropriate and those for which new ground must be broken, because it is inefficient to deal with routine problems as though there are exceptional.

It is also important to remember that decisions involve factual, verifiable elements along with judgment and qualitative evaluation and that the evaluation of the decision should lead to a positive feeling about the results on the part of those affected.

Group Decision Making

The approach to decision making by groups is somewhat different from individual decision making, primarily because of group dynamics. However, group decision making should follow the same process if it is to be constructive. There are, in some cases, several advantages to group decision making, including:

1. **Group judgment.** The old adage "two heads are better than one" applies here. Group deliberation is important in identifying alternative solutions to a problem.

2. **Group authority.** There is a great fear of allowing one person to have too much authority. Group decisions prevent this problem to an extent; however, it must be remembered that one person must ultimately answer for decisions that have been made. Thus, the role of leadership in the organization is not diminished but altered.

3. **Communication.** It is much easier to inform and receive input from all parts of the organization through a group. Also, if various interest groups have been represented during the process of making major decisions, there is less resistance to the decisions. Communication permits a wider participation in decision making and therefore can have some influence on employee motivation.

There are also distinct disadvantages to the group approach. As a cynic once wrote, a committee is a group of "unfits appointed by the incompetent to do the unnecessary." More realistically, disadvantages potentially include:

1. **Cost.** Group decision making requires a great deal of time, energy, and, therefore, money.

2. **Compromise.** Group decisions can be diluted to the least common denominator. Pressures of uniformity force compliance. There are two ways to view this. The major drawback may be that majority rules. The desirability of a consensus should not take precedence over critical evaluation in such a situation. On the other hand, a group can prevent an individual from going off the track by forcing him or her into line with the thinking of the rest of the group.

3. **Indecision.** There are delays in reaching a final decision because of the lengthy deliberations required. Groups often are accused of engaging in too much irrelevant talk and not enough concrete action.

4. **Power.** One individual usually emerges as a leader. This person should be in a position of influence in the organization. The authoritarian personality of an administrator can be used as a tactical weapon so that the group process simply becomes one of minimizing opposition to an action that already has been decided on by the administrator. The cohesiveness of the group and the attitudes of one person toward another are important factors in the group process.

5. **Authority.** Groups are frequently used to make decisions that are beyond their authority. This can cause great delay and only enhances a feeling of frustration on the part of members, particularly if the group decision is rejected by management. The responsibility and authority of the group should be clearly set out at the beginning.

The democratic approach of group decision making improves morale, stresses the team approach, keeps individuals aware, and provides a forum for free discussion of ideas and thoughts. Traditionally, librarians and information managers have not demanded a greater voice in decision-making affairs because they have had an employee rather than a professional orientation. In the past, the higher a person was on the administrative scale, the less aware he or she was of the inadequate opportunities available for staff participation. This is an area of great discussion and disagreement in all types of organizations and one that is rapidly changing as team-based organizations proliferate.

Try This!

The truth is that many people set rules to keep from making decisions.

—*Mike Krzyzewski*

Discuss the realities behind this statement and actions that must be in place to refute that attitude. In the process, consider if there any significant differences in the effectiveness of group versus individual decision making.

Factors in Making Decisions

Several factors influence decision making for libraries and other information centers. The PEST analysis, to be detailed later, suggests a community analysis should be conducted before certain major decisions can be made on services to be offered by the library. Selection from among alternatives is made on the basis of:

1. **Experience.** In relying on one's experience, mistakes as well as accomplishments should act as guides. If experience is carefully analyzed and not blindly followed, it can be useful and appropriate.
2. **Experimentation.** This approach toward making major decisions from among alternatives, although legitimate in many situations, is expensive where capital expenditures and personnel are concerned.
3. **Research and analysis.** Although this is the most general and effective technique used, it also may be somewhat expensive. The approach is probably more beneficial and cheaper in the long run, however, particularly for large academic, public, school system, and special libraries. This topic is discussed in the chapter on controlling.

Another important factor, mentioned previously, in the decision-making process is the perceived level of importance of a particular decision. There are two basic types of decisions: major ones affecting the total organization and lesser and routine ones, which have less effect on the overall organization but are nonetheless important. Those routine decisions constitute as much as 90 percent of decisions made in an organization. Most decisions of lesser importance do not require the thorough analysis described.

There are frequently two dimensions to the potential effectiveness of a decision. The first is the objective or impersonal quality of the decision, and the other is the actual acceptance of the decision, the way people react to it. Politics is paramount in decision making, as is consideration of the human factor. Acceptance of change is essential to the success of a decision. Therefore, it is desirable that those who will be affected also be involved in the decision from the beginning. Traditionally, emphasis has been placed on the quality of a decision, that is, on getting the facts, weighing them, considering them, and then deciding. Although this position is technically sound, it may not involve other people. The optimal decision should include high acceptance as well as high quality.

The following suggestions may facilitate involvement in the decision-making process:

1. Distinguish big from little problems to avoid getting caught in a situation that is rapid-fire and not effective.
2. Rely on policy to settle routine problems, and subject the big problems to thorough analysis.
3. Delegate as many decisions as possible to the level of authority most qualified and most interested in handling the problem.
4. Avoid crisis decisions by planning ahead.
5. Do not expect to be right all the time; no one ever is.

Decision making is at the heart of any organization. The approach that the librarian and the information specialist take to decision making and to the involvement of others will determine the direction the library or information center will take in the future.

CONCLUSION

Preparing for the planning process is an important aspect of sustaining an organization's viability. It requires examining the factors in the process, setting a proper environment within the organization, and making decisions based upon sound guidelines. Once the process is in place, an organization can view the big picture and begin to address the questions of "Why are we here?" and "Where do we want to be?" organizationally. There are several techniques to help an organization do that. Perhaps the most widely used one is strategic planning, which is discussed in the next chapter.

NOTES

1. Peter Senge, *The Fifth Dimension* (New York: Doubleday, 1990).
2. University of California, Office of the President, "Systemwide Library Planning" (2006), http://www.slp.ucop.edu/.
3. See, for example, the National Library of Australia's "Public Accountability" annual report, 2002, http://www.nla.gov.au/policy/annrep02/pages/corpoverview6.html.
4. See, for instance, Brown University Library's "Environmental Assessment," http://www.brown.edu/Facilities/University_Library/MODEL/SPSC/EnvAssT.html
5. Association of College and Research Libraries, "Standards & Guidelines" (2005), http://www.ala.org/ala/acrl/acrlstandards/standardsguidelines.htm.
6. See, for instance, Norman Oder, "The New Wariness," *Library Journal.com* (January 15, 2002), http://www.libraryjournal.com/article/CA188739.html.

7. Kendra S. Albright, "Environmental Scanning: Radar for Success," *Information Management Journal* 38, no. 3 (May/June 2004): 38.

8. Robert Rodgers and John E. Hunter, "A Foundation of Good Management Practices in Government: Management by Objectives," *Public Administration Review* 52 (January–February 1992): 27–39.

9. George S. Odiorne, *Management by Objectives* (New York: Fearon-Pitman, 1965), 555.

10. Thomas Packard, "TQM and Organizational Change and Development" (1996), http://www.improve.org/tqm.html.

11. Oren Harari, "Ten Reasons TQM Doesn't Work," *Management Review* 38 (January 1997): 38–44.

12. Susan Jurow, "Tools for Measuring and Improving Performance," in *Integrating Total Quality Management in a Library Setting*, ed. Susan Jurow and Susan B. Barnard (Binghamton, NY: Haworth Press, 1993), 125.

13. M. Valliant Higginson, "Putting Policies in Context," in *Business Policy*, ed. Alfred Gross and Walter Gross (New York: Ronald Press, 1967), 230.

14. Dalton E. McFarland, "Policy Administration," in *Business Policy*, ed. Alfred Gross and Walter Gross (New York: Ronald Press, 1967), 230.

15. Peter F. Drucker, *The Effective Executive* (New York: Harper & Row, 1967), 143.

Chapter 5

Strategic Planning—Thinking and Doing

 Overview

The university library director has just met with the new president of his institution. During the conversation, the president asked about the development of information services at the university and wondered, aloud, why there did not appear to be a strategic plan developed as a guide for the library and as a public document to enlighten the academic community about systems and services. The director, somewhat chagrined, acknowledged that most large academic libraries and several smaller ones, as well as other types of libraries, have developed proactive plans. However, he secretly feels that it is a fad that does not carry substance. He does recognize, from that discussion, that a plan is expected and quite necessary for the future of information services on the campus. He searches out several Web sites of libraries in other universities and colleges, in addition to conducting a literature search through library literature, with particular attention to some of the projects and programs that have been instigated and implemented by the Association of Research Libraries and the American Library Association's Library Administration and Management Association (LAMA) and like institutions in other countries.

This is but one example of the important role that accountability planning plays in offering information services in all types of information services institutions, whether they are public libraries funded by local or state governments, school learning resource centers supported by local tax dollars, university or college libraries supported by governments and tuition, or specialized information centers in both for-profit and private organizations. A manager or management group must determine the most appropriate way of demonstrating accountability while developing needed services. This chapter will present an introduction to the topic of strategic planning for information services.

Thinking strategically means focusing upon a vision for the organization as it attempts to create distinctive value for those whom its services exist. Strategic planning can be useful only if it supports such strategic thinking as a step in the organization's strategic management; those three steps are the basis for an effective organization. Strategic thinking means asking not only if the organization is doing things right but also, more importantly, "Are we doing the right thing?" More precisely, it means making a strategic thinking assessment by keeping in mind an awareness of the greater environment in which the organization operates. Those outside factors are likely to affect the fulfillment of the organization's purpose. This awareness allows the information services organization to be more creative in developing effective responses to those forces. Strategic thinking facilitates the conversion of a vision and mission into goals and action plans. Therefore, a strategic planning process is only as good as the strategic thinking that leads to its development and actions. In order to be most successful in the planning effort, this thinking precedes planning and planning precedes actions. The whole process requires some degree of looking around or so-called futuring, by considering the many important factors, inside and outside, that have potential effect on the organization's future. Strategic thinking most oftentimes involves brainstorming, including such actions as what-if scenario planning. Successful thinking requires looking backward and identifying successful accomplishments that need to be capitalized upon as well as looking forward by letting go of some things that have been maintained "because we have always done them that way." In other words, it means challenging assumptions so that new directions and initiatives can be created. Without strategic thinking, a strategic planning process is likely to be no more that an exercise in futility.

Strategic thinking, then, is a process of creating a better tomorrow for the information services organization, and it requires insight through synthesis as well as analysis, nonlinear as well as linear thinking, visual as well as verbal conceptualizing, implicit as well as explicit thinking, and the need to engages the heart as well as the head.[1]

 Some Definitions

Strategic visioning: A proactive view, leading to a plan to anticipate the future of the library organization.

Strategic acting: A process of strategically analyzing the organization's efforts.

Strategic planning: A systematic method used by organizations to adapt to expected changes.

Core values: A set of common beliefs held by the organization.

PLANNING STRATEGICALLY

Many systems, methods, models, and options for strategic planning are being developed in many not-for-profit organizations in preparation for an unpredictable future. This is why strategic thinking as a basis for the development of information services is not just desirable but mandatory. To be truly strategic in actions, however, some ambiguity must be tolerated, meaning that some uncertainty becomes acceptable. Faced with that unknown future, library and information services organizations are challenged to maintain the process of converting information to knowledge, through staff initiatives, for the benefit of customers. Such strategic planning involves a continuous process of making entrepreneurial, even risk-taking, decisions systematically, with the greatest possible knowledge of future consequences.

The process of strategic thinking and then planning is a proactive one and as such provides the underlay for initiative, by developing and employing a mindset that guides organizational thinking and acting. It calls upon members of an information services organization to discern what is truly important and to position it within a relatively long-term context by imagining and exploring the identified innovative possibilities. In a sense, the process can be described as a way of taking control of the future by developing the vision of the results that the organization wants to achieve. This requires revisiting and reenvisioning the organization and the service mission that is most desirable. It involves reexamining the organization's strengths and weaknesses and identifying threats as well as opportunities that exist and ones that can hinder or encourage that future state of information services. Management and staff colleagues, working together, are required to participate in the exploration of future options and directions in a systematic way. Three primary questions guide this future strategic thinking exercise:

1. What seems to be happening? Answering that question requires addressing, meaning perceiving, how one builds the relevant knowledge base.
2. What possibilities are presented? This requires addressing, meaning understanding, how one determines the significance or use of the knowledge base.
3. What is the organization going to do about it? This requires reasoning, how to determine the significance or use of the knowledge base.[2]

Resolving this questioning mix involves identifying the *political, economic, sociological,* and *technological* (PEST) forces external to the organization. The outcome of this PEST analysis, an acronym for the process, has an influence on what eventually can be accomplished. A knowledge base developed from identifying and describing those forces, plus input from customers, allows the information services organization to develop scenarios of what information services appear reasonable and desirable. If those are then compared to the identification of an organization's own *strengths* and *weaknesses,* as well as *opportunities* and *threats* (SWOT), possibilities for the future begin to emerge. Intangible inputs also are identified in this strategic thinking process, including the organizational culture and values, that play a role in developing a vision and mission. There should be an attempt to convert those intangibles into outputs of trust identified through honesty, openness, and reliability; satisfaction; team spirit; and commitment of pride, loyalty, and ownership of the process. Strategic planning can assist libraries and information centers in developing this kind of thinking mode that facilitates projecting the organization into a desired future.

PLANNING—THE OUTCOME

Strategic planning, then, is the systematic outcome of a thinking process that enables libraries and information centers to organize efforts necessary to carry out major decisions and to measure the results of these decisions against the expectations through organized, systematic feedback and adjustments. Libraries and information centers as customer-focused organizations develop services to meet their needs and also market to nonusers who are potential customers. Therefore, strategic planning must start with the customer. That focus is primary in all types of libraries and information centers today. Just as with strategic thinking, several questions must be addressed in the process:

- Who are we? Requires reaffirming or creating the organizations vision and mission.
- Where are we now? Requires a SWOT analysis, which includes both an internal examination and an external view of trends and threats.
- Where do we want to be? Requires the visioning aspect and then preliminary goal and objective setting.
- How do we get there? Requires the development of specific action, financial and communications plans.
- How are we doing? Requires periodic review of the plan, noting successes and shortcomings, and preparation of a revitalized plan.

Figure 5.1 illustrates this strategic planning process common to library and information centers that have initiated strategic plans.

Strategic planning was introduced in the business world more than half a century ago to address market shifts. However, it now has much wider, almost universal, application in not-for-profit organizations as well. Despite its usefulness, the concept has not been universally applied in libraries, whether in higher education planning, city or regional or state planning, school system planning, or corporate planning. However, most large library and information centers and many smaller ones are now involved in some form of strategic planning.

Many organizations automatically associate strategic planning with growth and new resources management. In today's world of "doing more with less," however, it is equally important for successful retrenchment and maintenance of efforts and particularly with the development of technological systems that enable services, developed and maintained by libraries, to be available

Figure 5.1—Strategic Planning Is a Continuous Process

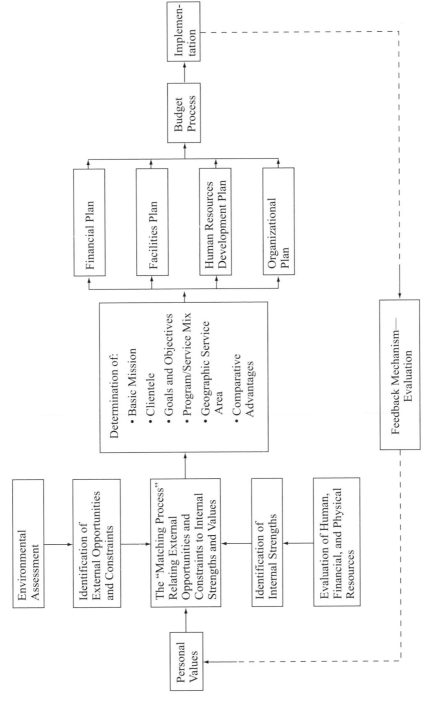

beyond the walls of a physical building. Strategic planning requires developing a vision for the organization's information services, identifying a mission within that context, setting realistic goals, establishing attainable objectives, and developing activities that can be carried out as policies and procedures that accomplish those goals and objectives. In its simplest definition, it is a process of translating decisions into policies and policies into actions so that a successful transition can take place in moving from the current scenario to one envisioning the future.

Systematic, planned change is the most effective way to implement new services and preserve important existing ones, while eliminating those programs and services whose usefulness has passed. This scenario requires an organizational arrangement that makes systematic, orderly change possible and attainable within a realistic time frame. Flexibility in development, implementation, and time constraints presents the greatest challenges to a strategic planning effort. "Change at the Speed of Thought" is the metaphor of the day, and this requires a flexible process, perhaps even "preferred futuring."[3]

In order to implement a successful strategic planning process, two criteria are necessary:

1. The entire organization should be informed of the process and buy into its success, with all participants being kept informed of it progresses.

2. The administration of the larger organization—academic institution, town officials, school district, or company CEOs—should be aware of decisions, commitments, and efforts as a result of the planning activities.

Within such an acknowledged scenario, the library or information center can proceed with a systematic planning process that has a chance of maximum success with a minimum amount of resistance. Most experts agree that a strategic plan should attempt to project at least five years into the future, while recognizing that there should be an ongoing, periodic planning process in place, not a one-time affair resulting in a document that is never again consulted. In fact, with today's changing climate, many libraries and information centers are revisiting their strategic planning efforts on a more retracted basis.

The question of time frame addresses one of the most difficult aspects of strategic planning, which is that of projecting and making assumptions about external forces and the likelihood of change—demographics, technology, and so forth. It must be recognized that the farther ahead one plans and projects, the greater the uncertainty and, therefore, the greater the challenge. Such uncertainty makes it imperative that strategic plans receive continuous review and assessment so that certain aspects can be updated, deleted, or rethought as the library's goals are achieved and as priorities shift. Such a review also can indicate how realistic and achievable the goal-setting process has been.

One weakness in many strategic plans is that seldom, if ever, is there a contingency plan for failure or shortcomings. With shortened timelines, however, more effective and realistic monitoring is achieved.

ENVIRONMENT—THE ASSESSMENT

 What Do You Think?

"Would you tell me, please, which way I ought to go from here?" asked Alice. "That depends a good deal on where you want to get to," said the Cat.

—*Alice in Wonderland*

How can an organization get from where it is now to where it would like to be? What steps must be taken to accomplish that goal?

One primary benefit of strategic planning is that it serves as a necessary self-analysis or self-study that allows the organization to identify its strengths and weaknesses and then develop priorities within the framework of those physical and financial capabilities. The need for such an assessment has been heightened by the increasing pace of change in library and information services—what is done and the way it is done. The library or information center as an open, social system with specific goals of service interacts with the larger environment through the underlying values that it exists to support. Strategic planning assumes that an organization is responsive to a dynamic, changing environment. Being strategic, then, means having a clear understanding of the organization's objectives, while at the same time being aware of the organization's resources, and incorporating both into being consciously responsive to a dynamic external environment. The process is disciplined in that it calls for a certain order and pattern to keep it focused and productive. This self-examination begins with identifying the beliefs, values, and ethos that guide the library's or information center's service goals. Commitment of individuals working in the organization to develop organizational strategies is vital and is evident in common values and shared beliefs or ideologies that are deemed good and desirable and that can act as guidelines for actions and the implementation of decisions.

Self-examination allows the library or information center to formulate actions that address threats and weaknesses while taking advantage of opportunities that promote the vision of what it would like to be, envisioned in a mission statement, with what it can afford to be, regulated by the organization's physical and financial capabilities. If great disparity exists, a resolution must be sought by reducing expectations and/or increasing resources. Most organizations focus their planning strategies on concerns relating to new directions, services and systems, marketing and public relations, growth and finances, and performance and personnel development. This process of mining information that is vital to the organization's survival, the self-analysis and environmental scanning process, produces several obvious benefits. Perhaps the most important one is that of viewing itself in relation to the greater environment.

Strategic issues often arise as a part of the planning process and may produce conflicts among both internal and external sources. They are critical challenges that particularly affect the organization's mission and values. They may involve philosophy (why), means (how), ends (what), persons advantaged or disadvantaged by outcome (who), location (where), and timing (when). An open system is prepared to deal with those conflicts and to resolve them. From an analysis emerges a concise understanding of what the organization is and whom it serves—those primary stakeholders whose satisfaction guides ultimate services—and how it intends to achieve a plan by identifying priorities of service and directing decision making.

The planning process analyzes capabilities, assesses environmental pressures and opportunities, sets objectives, examines alternate courses of action, and implements a preferred course. However, the distinguishing mark of strategic planning from other forms of planning is through the deliberate attempt to concentrate resources in areas that can make a substantial difference in future performance and capability. Thus, strategic planning is as much a frame of reference and a way of thinking as it is a set of procedures identified in the planning tool. The process does not concentrate upon projecting past experiences into future practices. Rather, it concentrates upon understanding the ever-changing environment in which the library or information center plays a vital role. It encourages creativity, has the potential of improving communications within the organization, markets the initiative to its users, and allows libraries and other information organizations and their staffs to identify and adopt options that may be unique to their individual settings and at a particular time in the organization's life.

The plan itself encourages managers to experiment with various alternatives before committing resources by promoting a systems approach in:

- Providing a mechanism to avoid overemphasizing organizational parts at the expense of the whole.
- Guiding managers to make decisions that are in line with the aims and strategies of the whole organization.
- Providing a basis for measuring the performance of the organization as a whole, of an operating unit, and of an individual.
- Forwarding to higher levels of management those issues of strategic importance with which they should be concerned.
- Serving as a training device by requiring participants to ask and answer the very questions that managers must address.
- Improving managerial motivation and morale through a sense of creative participation in the development of known expectations.[4]

Before beginning a strategic planning process, an organization must seriously address and adequately answer several basic questions: Why it is necessary to plan strategically, and why at this particular point in the organization's life? Who should be involved and how involved should they be? How does strategic thinking lead to strategic planning for this organization and what needs to be known beforehand? Is there understanding among all the primary players of

Figure 5.2—Development of a Strategic Plan

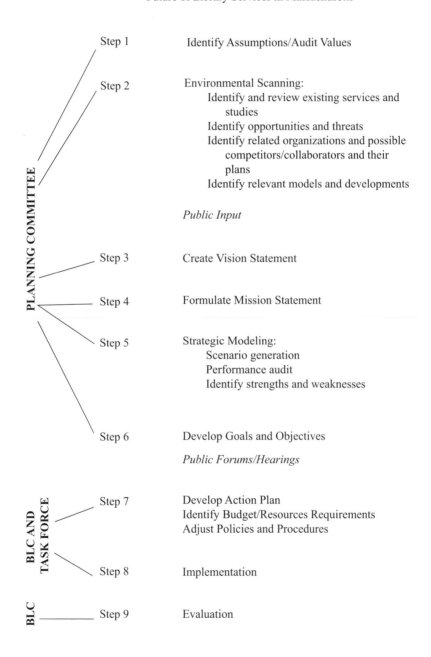

MASSACHUSETTS BOARD OF LIBRARY COMMISSIONERS

Proposed Process for Development of a Strategic Plan
for the
Future of Library Services in Massachusetts

PLANNING COMMITTEE

Step 1   Identify Assumptions/Audit Values

Step 2   Environmental Scanning:
         Identify and review existing services and
            studies
         Identify opportunities and threats
         Identify related organizations and possible
            competitors/collaborators and their
            plans
         Identify relevant models and developments

Public Input

Step 3   Create Vision Statement

Step 4   Formulate Mission Statement

Step 5   Strategic Modeling:
         Scenario generation
         Performance audit
         Identify strengths and weaknesses

Step 6   Develop Goals and Objectives

Public Forums/Hearings

BLC AND TASK FORCE

Step 7   Develop Action Plan
         Identify Budget/Resources Requirements
         Adjust Policies and Procedures

Step 8   Implementation

BLC

Step 9   Evaluation

the factors to be considered and how they interrelate? What additional resources are needed and how will they be made available? Is a strategic planning consultant necessary? How long will the process take? Is the larger organization of which the library or information center is a part committed to supporting the strategic planning effort and what type of support is committed to the outcome and to facilitate success? How will the process be implemented and how will it be evaluated? After those initial questions have been answered to the satisfaction of members of the organization, the important first step in a strategic plan process is the identification of a coordinating team or task force with the responsibility for the major planning phases. In addition, other work teams and task forces are likely to be involved, as appropriate, at various times and levels in the process.

To facilitate the activities, some organizational planning teams work with strategic planning consultants. The primary role of that consultant is to help the team or task force decide what data are to be collected, how they will be collected and by whom, and how they will be analyzed and used. A consultant acts as both a catalyst and facilitator in identifying organizational goals and objectives. He or she does not force opinions on the group because no two organizations are alike and a cookie-cutter approach cannot be imposed upon an organization's missions and goals. A realistic time frame must be set for the strategic planning process.

One vital issue is to consider factors that are in place or have the potential of being developed in the larger context in which information services plays an important role, including the global environment, and that have the potential of affecting the end result of a plan. This issue is answered using a formal environmental scanning process of "looking around."

A part of that looking around can be accomplished by the SWOT analysis, basically an environmental scan, which involves a formalized examination of the *s*trengths and *w*eaknesses that are internal to the organization as well as the *o*pportunities and *t*hreats that are factors not specifically under the control of the organization but important to the future of information and knowledge services.

The process examines the microenvironment, that is who the customers are and what their needs are, as well as the internal environment, meaning facilities, structure of the organization, personnel resources, finances available, and organizational structure. Positive and negative events inside and outside of the library or information services organization can influence changes in any or all of these categories. The microenvironment might be considered a simple dichotomy: the external opportunities and constraints.

A second segment of the macroenvironment process sometimes includes the PEST analysis, which helps identify the opportunities and threats by viewing overlapping layers in the greater environment: economic trends, governmental regulations, inflation, demographics, and technological factors among them. PEST analysis includes examining *P*olitical issues, including governmental institutions' attitude toward information services and information policies and external stakeholders that affect resources, and *E*conomic forces, including looking at systems and general economic conditions and trends within and outside the country, can be observed and documented. *S*ocial forces,

Figure 5.3—Looking-Around Aspect of the Planning Process

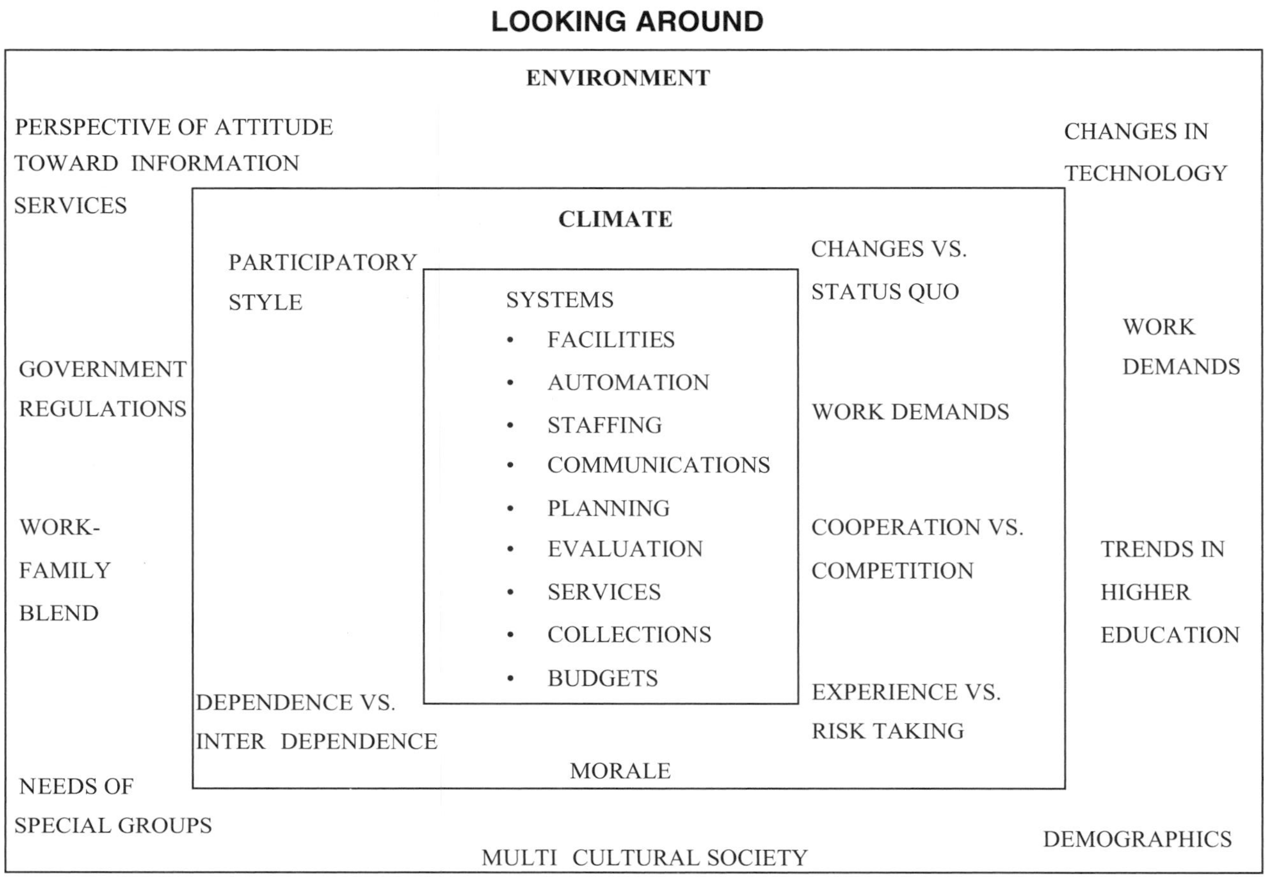

LOOKING AROUND

ENVIRONMENT

CHANGES IN
TECHNOLOGY

WORK
DEMANDS

TRENDS IN
HIGHER
EDUCATION

DEMOGRAPHICS

PERSPECTIVE OF ATTITUDE
TOWARD INFORMATION
SERVICES

CLIMATE

CHANGES VS.
STATUS QUO

WORK DEMANDS

COOPERATION VS.
COMPETITION

EXPERIENCE VS.
RISK TAKING

PARTICIPATORY
STYLE

SYSTEMS

- FACILITIES
- AUTOMATION
- STAFFING
- COMMUNICATIONS
- PLANNING
- EVALUATION
- SERVICES
- COLLECTIONS
- BUDGETS

MORALE

GOVERNMENT
REGULATIONS

WORK-
FAMILY
BLEND

DEPENDENCE VS.
INTER DEPENDENCE

NEEDS OF
SPECIAL GROUPS

MULTI CULTURAL SOCIETY

Figure 5.4—Strengths, Weaknesses, Opportunities, and Threats (SWOT)

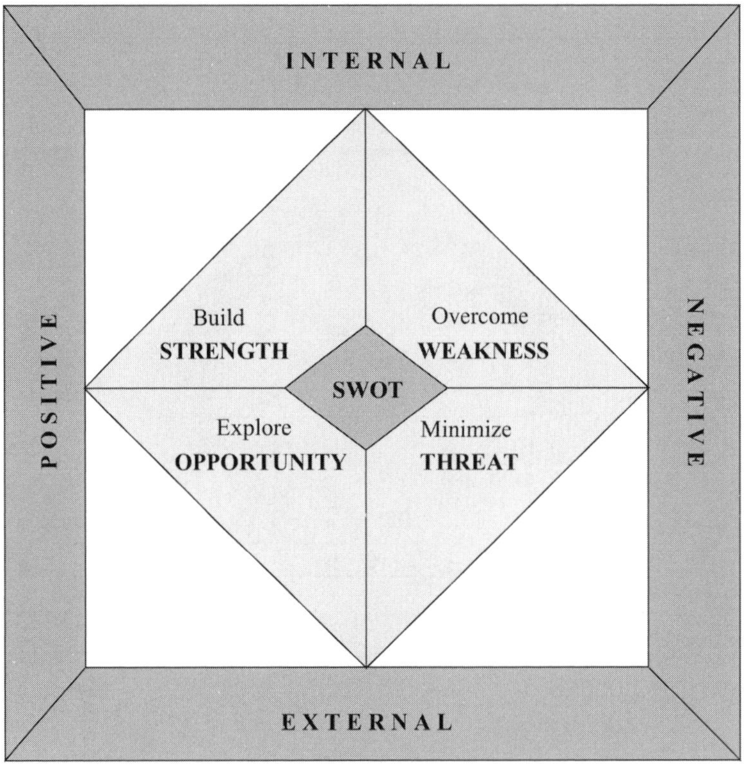

INTERNAL

POSITIVE

NEGATIVE

Build
STRENGTH

Overcome
WEAKNESS

SWOT

Explore
OPPORTUNITY

Minimize
THREAT

EXTERNAL

SWOT Analysis

including the norms and values that characterize the local culture, and Technological forces, developing software and hardware systems that are likely to have impact, change what is occurring or may occur in the near future.

Both the SWOT analysis and the PEST analysis help focus planning on the mission and vision of the organization and help develop strategies to monitor external and internal forces. The external environmental scan and the internal self-analysis merge in the process to provide the focus for developing strategies and converting them into plans, policies, processes, and procedures.

The steps in the strategic planning process, after the planning team has been identified and the environmental scan and strengths/weaknesses exercise have been carried out, are to:

- Identify the organizational culture and the values or assumptions that are the organization's guiding principles. This leads to creation of a vision statement that focuses on a better future by communicating enthusiasm and excitement.

- Formulate the vision and mission statements that identify a distinctiveness.

- Develop the goals and objectives.

Figure 5.5—Political, Economic, Social, and Technological (PEST) Factors Impact Planning

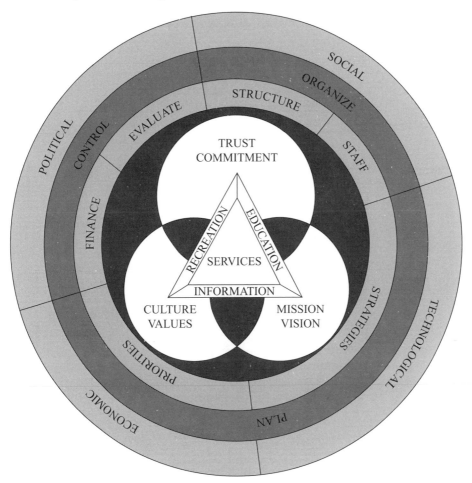

- Develop strategies and action plans. This requires identifying resource funds and developing policies and procedures to accomplish the objectives.
- Implement the strategic plan.
- Monitor, evaluate, and adjust the plan as objectives are accomplished and as priorities shift.

 Try This!

Develop a vision statement for a large public library in a diverse population setting. What are the criteria to be considered and how have they been identified?

Figure 5.6—Several Factors Must Be Considered in Initial Strategic Planning Steps

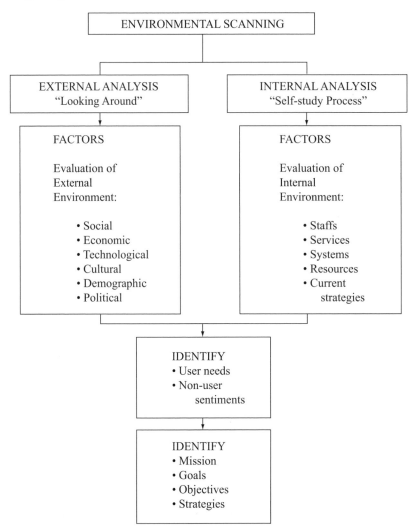

An initial strategic planning exercise, just as with planning of any magnitude, should be viewed as only that—the initial step in a continuous process. No plan, no matter how well formulated, can or will implement itself. Success in the process requires direction and commitment to succeed. Therefore, the final step in the cycle is one of monitoring, the evaluating and adjusting that is essential to the process. Following through with clearly developed implementation steps, measuring progress toward the goals, and incorporating feedback are a continuation of the process of planning. The greatest cause for failure of the process lies in poor execution of the plan, a lack of follow-through accompanied by a lack of commitment to see that it is accomplished or that adjustments are made so that it can be accomplished.

In order for the process to proceed smoothly at the operational level, there should be a common understanding of the meanings of terms used in the strategic planning process.

Vision

Vision drives the planning process. A vision statement, as an act of foresight, outlines what the organization wants to be. It is inspirational; set within a context of the future, it is timeless, and it provides clear decision-making criteria. It envisions changes that will affect systems and services. It is as simple or as complex as necessary to stretch the organization's capabilities and image of itself. It gives shape and direction to the organization's future. An example of a simple, yet comprehensive, statement is one from the Calgary Public Library, which states the vision is "A world of information and ideas within reach of every Calgarian."[5]

Developing a vision statement requires drawing upon the imagination of good information services. Sometimes the sophisticated technique of visioning is used by organizations to help develop vision statements as part of their strategic planning by examining and understanding all of the possibilities available for them to envision a scenario for the future. Vision focuses on the ultimate end result of an effort, not how to get there. As a guiding statement, it should answer the question "What is the preferred future for this organization?" The procedure of visioning seeks to create a compelling picture of a desirable future that represents quantum changes from the past. It has many critics who maintain that it can generate impractical and ungrounded concepts. When visioning focuses on generating a thoughtful vision statement, a process engaging people in the exploration of possibilities, it can be energizing and enlightening for an organization. It can help distance a library from a constrained view of the future and is a particularly powerful way of tying values to action.

Simply stated, it should be an inspiring statement of the future, which can become the guide for actions and behaviors toward the accomplishment of a mission.

Values and Culture

Values are the organization's essential and enduring tenets—a small set of general guiding principles that are proved, enduring guidelines for human conduct. Values are usually stated in terms of respect for other people, their honesty and integrity, a commitment to the social responsibilities and diversity in the organization's work force; engagement in activities with commitment to innovation, collaboration and excellence in services, and social responsibility.

Following from the identified values and a vision for the future, other components necessary to accomplish the strategic plan can be stated. One of the difficulties in stating components in the strategic thinking and planning process is the confusion that exists in the terminology used. In the literature,

Figure 5.7—University of California–Berkeley Library's Value Statement

> **The University of California Berkley Libraries**
> **Value Statement endorses:**
>
> 1. Collegiality and cooperation by working together to build a civil environment, cooperation, and supporting each other and appreciate diversity;
> 2. Effective communication through regular and ongoing open communication throughout the system;
> 3. Excellence and creativity through quality services within the organization's stated needs and priorities;
> 4. Fairness, by recognizing the importance of everyone and every part of the organization's function;
> 5. Participatory decision making that affects daily work;
> 6. Professional growth and development given through opportunities and challenges;
> 7. Recognition through clear and fair rewards policy and competitive pay structure and recognition of individuals successes; and
> 8. Provide a safe, comfortable, and healthy environment for staff and users.

Source: Library Staff, University of California–Berkeley Library (2002), http://www.lib. berkeley.edu/AboutLibrary/values.html.

objective is often used as a generic term variously referring to philosophy, vision, mission, purposes, goals, guiding principles, strategies, targets, quotas, policies, activities, and even deadlines. Because of the lack of consistency in the use of the terms, confusion often arises.

A hierarchical process, with integral relationships, can then be developed among components after the vision has been articulated, with the mission preceding goals, which precede objectives, which precede activities and strategies from which policies and procedures emanate and then evaluation is possible. Each of these components builds on the previous one.

With that understanding, activities and policies can be developed and directed toward the achievement of the goals and objectives based upon mission, vision, and value formulation. Clear commitment to and formulation of all components at the different levels encourage consistent planning and decision making over the long term and at various levels of the organization. Unfortunately, in some organizations parts of that whole exist only in the unilateral thinking of management and are not made explicit by verbalizing and sharing them. Such a casual approach must be avoided, because it can lead to confusion, discouragement, and resistance. A great deal of energy can be expended on such faulty and secretive assumptions. It should be recognized by all in the organization that it is difficult, if not impossible, to be accountable for achieving portions of a plan if they have not been clearly articulated and communicated to all involved in implementing them.

Mission

Identification of this broad service aspiration is one primary step in the planning process. The mission statement is a short, succinct statement focusing on the purpose of the organization, its reason for existence, and what it hopes to accomplish. This overarching, comprehensive concept or principle is intended to guide the organization in establishing goals and developing strategies to achieve those goals. Defining its mission is the most important strategic step an organization can take. The effort is based upon the values and beliefs previously identified in the organization's vision. The mission statement should answer three primary questions: "Who (customers)?" "What (services)?" and "How (activities)?" all focused by the previously answered question of "Why (the vision)?" It demonstrates the value the organization can make in the lives, personal and professional, of those it serves.

Only by closely examining external forces and perceived constraints can an effective mission statement be formulated. A clearly formulated, broadly discussed, and mutually accepted statement enables all parts of an organization to work toward common goals. Taken together, these should provide the focus for policy making and for management decisions of all types and at all levels. Only after this analysis has been completed, and the mission has been embedded in the strategic thinking and culture of the organization can quantitative and qualitative goals and objectives, to achieve the mission, be considered. This requires that the concise mission statement be shared with all members of the organization, funding authorities, and supporters so that everyone understands and is committed to its basic principles. This sharing action reduces the possibilities of fragmentation and dissension and enables the statement to be used as an important marketing tool.

Of course, all types of libraries and information centers are typically created with a mission of service. For public libraries, this mission has traditionally included education, information, and recreation or entertainment, and the

Figure 5.8—Components of a Mission Statement

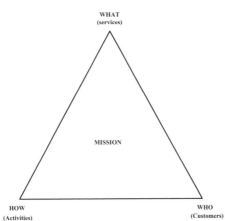

library's services have emerged as a vehicle to accomplish a broader mission. A concise mission statement, for example, from the Boston Public Library states, "The mission of the Boston Public Library is to preserve and provide access to the historical record of our society and to serve the cultural, educational and informational needs of the people of the City and the Commonwealth."[6]

Some form of an organization's mission statement is often set forth in a charter, the constitution and bylaws, annual reports, or other authoritative pronouncements of the organization. Although one might assume that the mission will not change, it does, sometimes subtly, sometimes dramatically. Therefore, the statement process is not set in stone; it may be constant and fluid, with the flexibility to accommodate change in internal and external forces. Consider, for example, the Baltimore County, Maryland, system. Thirty years ago, its mission was "to make readily available to the greatest possible number of county residents the most wanted library materials of all kinds, and to serve as a point of access for any needed information." A later system's mission statement was "to make readily available to Baltimore County residents library materials and information services in a cost-effective manner, proportionate to levels of demand and use, and to provide access to resources outside the library system," and in the current statement it is to " provide innovative, quality services responding to the needs of our diverse community as we: Promote the love of reading; Excel at providing resources to customers of all ages; and Create welcoming spaces for our community."[7]

To ensure that a library or information center continues to respond appropriately to the changing environment, it should be obvious from this example that its mission should be revisited and reviewed periodically.

Goals, Themes, and Directions

In formulating goals, planners are required to delve one step deeper by resolving the overlap between the needs of the users and a desire to provide appropriate services with the physical and financial capabilities of the library or information center. This intersection provides the foundation for identifying and describing the library's goals. Failure to identify concisely and correctly this common ground leads to the selection of goals—and later objectives and activities—that may be unrelated, unrealistic, unattainable, and subject to false starts that could lead to ultimate failure. Likewise, goals and objectives are likely to change over time and, therefore, must be viewed as flexible, timely, and changeable.

Goals are the organization's broad aspirations defined in operational terms, leading to measurable objectives with strategies and activities emanating from them. Goals provide direction and are intended to produce effectiveness. They also provide a framework for future planning and help motivate individuals and groups in the work environment. Goals must be flexible and are subject to constant modification to reflect changing expectations and focus. Because goals are not specific enough to be termed operational, however, lower-level objectives and activities are required to quantify goals, but goals are the basis for development and measures against which the success or failure of the plan can be determined. Goals are action oriented with that action following through in the form of objectives that specify means of achieving the goals. It must be recognized that sometimes there are two types of goals functioning in an organization: stated goals and perceived goals. Although stated goals and real goals may be identical, sometimes they are different. If they are real goals, they will have an impact on the organization's policies, structure, operations, and, in general, on the behavior of people. The differences between stated goals and real goals are subtle and often financially driven. For instance, a library may want to offer bookmobile service (stated goal), but if it does not adequately finance the operation, it cannot offer high-quality bookmobile service (real goal). One beneficial way of developing a goal statement is to place it within the larger environmental context. For example, the Purdue University Libraries identifies one trend as "The Libraries' virtual presence will be enhanced by integration into the University learning and discovery environment."[8] This leads to the identification of how best to serve the needs of library users.

Objectives, Initiatives, Pathways, and Strategies

Several action terms are used to describe the next level of specific activities. *Objectives* is the most generic term used to set a pattern for the structure of the activities. Those activity-oriented objectives provide direction as well as incentive toward achievement. Objectives can be conservative or expansive but always should be stated in terms and conditions that stretch the enterprise. They are specific objectives to achieve goals that specify activities to be accomplished in order to achieve the vision. There is a real danger of setting objectives that are really hopes and not attainable ends or, on the other hand, so easily attainable that they are not challenging. In setting objectives, many things must be taken into account: the strengths of the library, the limitations of the organization and how much can be accomplished with the financial and material resources available, and the mission of the larger institution of which the library or information center is a part. Questions that must be addressed in the objective-setting exercise are:

- Is the objective suitable for this library/information center at this time?
- Does the objective help achieve the goal to which it is related?
- Does it take the organization in the direction it wants to go?
- Does it support the overall mission of the library/information center?
- Is it compatible and complementary with other objectives?
- Is it acceptable and understandable to the majority who will be charged with implementing it?
- Is it affordable for the organization?
- Is it measurable and achievable?
- Is it ambitious enough to be challenging?

The library or information center must be able to prove to both itself and to the funding authority that the objectives are suitable, sustainable, and measurable.

An example goal of the Evanston (Illinois) Public Library at the beginning of its strategic plan in 2000–2010 was to "annually establish 25,000 child book links." (A child book link is defined as each time an individual child hears a story read to them in a library-sponsored program.) The library began this planning cycle with the target of 8,000 child book links annually, and two years later the actual number increased to 24,126.[9]

Primary elements involved in objectives formulation include:

- **Clients.** Who they are and who they are not (with the potential of converting those who are not).
- **Services.** What new services are needed, which existing ones should be retained, and which should be deleted.
- **Personnel resources.** What professional and support skills are needed to provide identified services.
- **Technological resources.** What can be accessed when and where (many organizations are now instituting a separate strategic plan for technological development).
- **Financial resources.** What and where they are and how to maintain them.
- **Community responsibilities.** The library's obligations as a social institution.

A maximum degree of compatibility should exist between the identified goals and specific objectives to achieve them if the organization is to be successful in its mission. It is also important to remember that many forces influence the process of planning and achieving goals; therefore, the process must be viewed from a number of perspectives. The three primary perspectives are:

1. **Environmental.** Considering constraints imposed on the organization by society in general.
2. **Organizational.** Considering the organization as an open system.
3. **Individual.** Considering the personal goals of the individuals working in the organization.

A balance must be achieved between what is realistic and what is obtainable, what is challenging and what is idealistic but not necessarily completely attainable. As was mentioned under the goals discussion, the greatest problem in planning is bridging the gap between what is desirable (the stated objectives) and what is possible (the real objectives).

Unlike for-profit organizations, in which the first objective is often to create the greatest profit base, most libraries and other information centers have among their primary objectives to provide a useful and needed service and to attract a competent staff. Libraries and information centers, however, are responsible to higher authorities that may restrict some other more social objectives. Still other objectives may be forced upon libraries and information centers by the community, through social obligations, or by the employees, through collective bargaining or other means. Therefore, just as profit objectives in business organizations and their sometimes conflicting social objectives can dictate opposing courses that force compromise, so in information services organizations an individual's personal objectives and those of the organization as a whole can create conflict and sometimes force compromise.

Additionally, specific organizational subobjectives can be departmental, unit, or team-based objectives or even short-range objectives of the whole organization. Most objectives are tangible and measurable, but others are not. For example, one objective may be to improve morale, but how can one measure morale? Nonetheless, objectives should be stated in terms of activities that are in some way quantifiable and measurable.

 What Do You Think?

Challenges sometimes result from multiple service goals and related objectives, with attempts being sought to avoid conflict in those activities.

Example: What should a primary service goal of a university library be: to provide needed curricular materials and information, in whatever format, for students at the undergraduate leave, or to provide more sophisticated, scholarly materials that will enhance the research efforts of faculty and graduate students and advance the state of knowledge?

How can such issues be resolved? Are the goals mutually exclusive? Can one be chosen over the other? How does this relate to the mission of the organization?

Activities, Tasks, and Initiatives

These elemental tasks are directly related to the objectives and are a way of achieving the objectives. They are usually short term, repetitive, measurable, and numerous at the operational level. They require effective policies and procedures to facilitate their achievement. Activities guide the everyday functioning of the organization and in that sense are pragmatic and narrow.

EVALUATION—ACCOUNTABILITY IN ACTION

Just developing a strategic plan on paper is not enough, and therefore evaluation is vital to any strategic effort. At the end of the established time periods, reports are made to appropriate individuals and groups as to the progress and success. Operational plans that support the goals and benchmarks of the overall strategic plan should be established on a regular yearly basis. Performance measures are required to indicate the progress and anticipated success of the planning effort. Those benchmarks indicate adjustments that may need to be made along the way and should be a part of the process.

Once the body of a strategic plan has been developed, guidelines should be established for monitoring progress in terms of operational adjustments as well as guidelines for overarching decisions for policy making and measurement of success. The measurement and evaluation plan helps ensure that the expected outcomes are reasonable and measurable. In addition, such evaluation tends to sharpen the organization's thinking about the process. They relate to four basic actions:

- Applying the strategies in operational form by identifying specific performance measures and developing implementation strategies with a view toward ensuring that all understand the goals and objectives that guide performance measures.
- Ensuring that all the various work units within the organization are linked, both tactically and philosophically to achieving the goals and objectives, thus instilling a synergy for the work to be accomplished.
- Communication is important to ensure total understanding of the strategies and how they impact the organization's mission.
- Link the plan to the budgeting process, thereby ensuring a continuing initiative.

The end of the cycle and the beginning of a new stage is the final formal evaluation process, which is based upon data collected since the initiation of the plan. This evaluation component requires a focused design that provides for measuring program success and recommending program improvement, when necessary. Factors such as success, efficiency, effectiveness, benefits, and costs all play a role in this effort.

The kinds of information and how it is collected are decided as the final component of the initial planning process and are key to the success of the library or information center's plan. They must be built in as a systematic part of the plan. The results are useful for both internal purposes—guiding the future of the organization—and external—as communication with the greater community. Involvement of staff, users, and other stakeholders in this process is valuable in improving programs and activities. Stakeholder participation in the evaluation sometimes proves extremely useful in helping the organization verify its effectiveness, or lack thereof. A systematic collection of data and other information about the program of information services also enables stakeholders to better understand the organization, recommend improvements its effectiveness, and thereby buy into future programming.

Someone should be designated as responsible for monitoring progress toward each objective that has been established. A person or team can be identified in relation to the success of each goal, and that person or team becomes responsible for developing a timeline for accomplishing the objective, identifying measures to evaluate progress, and establishing processes and procedures at the functional level. Individual strategies can be assigned to one or more units or teams within the organization for execution, and these units in turn assign activities to individuals or specific sections of the unit. If this process is followed, the strategic plan can automatically be used at the functional level for decision making. This, of course, entails designating responsibilities for implementing the various steps in the planning process. A mechanism is required for coordination, evaluation, and monitoring the various activities and tasks that are necessary for the implementation of a plan. Such an implementation plans provide an opportunity to specify recommendations for resource allocation strategies, assignments of responsibility, coordinating mechanisms, and priority-setting criteria.

Performance indicators will have been built into the plan, and ideally each unit can execute several subplans simultaneously, making consistent progress toward various objectives in keeping with the established priorities. In practice, this may not always work effectively because, by nature, some people tend to invest more time in fulfilling objectives related to their own particular interests, thus slighting the priorities established for the unit. In addition, unforeseen circumstances, such as the loss of a key person, can jeopardize the achievement of objectives or can, at least, force major revisions or delays.

It is obvious that organizations with clear goals and objectives tend to have higher staff morale. Understanding those goals and objectives and their environment and actively participating in understanding them and carrying them out is the best assurance of loyalty to the plan of service. Unfortunately, some people carry out tasks; they do not achieve objectives. Some employees do not even know the objectives of an organization. Ask that person what justifies their position, and some will answer by listing the work they do, the tasks they perform, or the machines they control or supervise. These individuals are concerned with means and methods and may be unable to describe the goals and objectives.

Perhaps a simplistic, yet primary, benefit of setting goals and objectives is to provide a new way to look at those jobs; it concentrates thought and gives a sense of purpose and commitment. By developing a plan and establishing written goals and objectives and communicating them to the staff and the organization's customers, the organization encourages individuals to think through logical courses of action and provides a yardstick for decision making and ongoing activities. Such a planning exercise is the most effective way of measuring output for the organization.

Therefore, reviewing strategies, revising priorities, reassessing the plan, and reassuring the primary constituency is a vital element, a prelude, to the next round of strategic planning, a continuing process, a circle from initiating, developing, instituting, and reviewing. In that process, attention is paid to what has worked (successful strategies) and what has not worked (failed attempts, with a review of why), what efforts have been successful and should be retained, as well as a review of which have not been totally successful and should be adjusted, phased out, or immediately discarded. No library or information center can afford to put forth the same goals and programs on a continuous basis. Customer needs, financial outlays, larger organizational priorities, operating methods, and market needs are in continuous flux. This requires revisiting objectives and strategies on a periodic basis, probably no longer than a five-year period. Change is required as circumstances dictate.

PLANNING HIERARCHY—AN EXAMPLE

An example of the hierarchy of mission to goals to objectives to activities is illustrated in figure 5.9 from the strategic plan of Highland Park Public Library. Only one example is selected from each of the elements in goals and objectives of the strategic plan.

Figure 5.9—Highland Park Public Library Strategic Plan

HIGHLAND PARK PUBLIC LIBRARY

STRATEGIC PLAN

2006–2010

MISSION

The Highland Park Public Library's mission is to provide the highest quality Library services to community members for life long learning, cultural enrichment, and enjoyment.

VALUES

The Highland Park Public Library firmly believes in and supports each of the following:

• *Free access and services.*

All residents of Highland Park have a right to free, equitable, and convenient access to Library resources in an inviting, comfortable, and safe environment.

• *Intellectual freedom.*

The Library supports freedom of speech and the right of residents to receive uncensored information. It provides a forum for debate and exchange of ideas in the community.

• *Fostering education for all age levels.*

The Library supports early reading readiness, formal and alternative education, and lifelong learning.

• *A climate of respect and trust.*

Mutual respect and trust are honored both internally and externally. Patrons and staff are valued, supported, and respected.

• *Privacy.*

The Library preserves the discreet use of its services and materials.

• *Patron-centered service.*

The Library strives for excellent, personalized service. It creates and makes available information, materials, and programs that anticipate and respond to patron needs.

• *Diversity.*

The Library reflects and encourages diversity in its services, collections, and staff.

• *Strong partnerships within and beyond the community.*

The Library's resources, involvement, and leadership in the community are extended through partnerships with community members and organizations.

VISION

The Highland Park Public Library strives to be an essential center for community learning and discovery.

Programming Goal

Continue to expand services and resources, which reflect diversity and stimulate learning. **Objectives**

A. Provide resources, services, and programs to help children under five develop a foundation for language development and literacy.

Objectives - Programming

Provide resources, services, and programs to help children under five develop a foundation for language development and literacy.

Potential Activities

• Expand storytime offerings for children under three and their caregiver.

• Create a preschool activity center.

CONCLUSION

Strategic planning is the most popular approach in management of today's knowledge-based organizations. It helps define the organization's reason for being and mission. Because the planning process can be a costly proposition, improper selection or faulty specification of objectives wastes planning time and money, resulting in frustrations and disenchantment, rendering the entire planning activity futile. Every information services organization needs to spell out its own goals and objectives, instead of relying on those of other organizations, because those components determine the policies, procedures, and organizational structure of the library or information center. Planning represents the beginning of a process upon which other principles are based.

NOTES

1. Richard L. Hughes and Katherine Colarelli Beatty, *Becoming a Strategic Leader* (San Francisco: Jossey-Bass, 2005), 45.

2. Stuart Wells, "To Plan, Perchance, to Think; Aye, There's the Rub," *Information Outlook* 5 (September 2001): 10–11.

3. Ronald Lippitt, "Futuring before You Plan," in *The NTL Managers' Handbook*, ed. R. A. Ritvo and A. G. Sargent (Arlington, VA: NTL Institute, 1983).

4. Benjamin B. Tregue and John W. Zimmerman, "Strategic Thinking," *Management Review* 68 (February 1979): 10–11.

5. Calgary Public Library, Alberta, Canada, "Vision" (n.d.), http://www.calgarypubliclibrary.com/library/vision.htm.

6. Boston Public Library Board of Trustees, "Mission Statement" (n.d.), http://www.bpl.org/general/trustees/mission.htm.

7. Baltimore County Public Library, "Mission Statement" (n.d.), http://www.bcplonline.org/libpg/lib_facts.html#mission%20statement.

8. Purdue University Libraries, "Strategic Plan 2006–2011" (2006), http://www.lib.purdue.edu/admin/stratplans/.

9. Evanston Public Library, "Strategic Plan 2000–2010: A Decade of Outreach" (2003), http://www.epl.org/library/strategic-plan-00.html.

Chapter 6

Marketing Information Services

 Overview

The Riverview Public Library, in a medium-size New England town, has been notified by the town manager that it will sustain another serious budget cut, the second in less than 10 years. Staff are frustrated and demoralized, and administrators are perplexed and angry. "Why isn't the library *really* appreciated by the community, how can they do that to us?" After all, everyone in the community should know the value of good library and information services that enrich both their work lives and their personal lives.

Faced with what seems to be inevitable layoffs and curtailment of services, the director of thirty years finally decides, for the first time, to bring a few of the staff together with a group of townspeople to discuss issues and plan strategies. After an uneasy start, the dialogue turns to "What can be done?" short of closing the two small branches. It does not take long, in the tense dialogue, to come to an uneasy conclusion that some community members do not know or understand about many of the information services the library offers and others do not have a clue as to what the library is capable of providing. Why? Over the years, the librarians have assumed the purpose and services were being acknowledged by the community. After all, at any one time there are people in the library reading the newspapers, checking out new best sellers, and such things.

A relatively healthy collection-development policy, supported by the town's budgetary allocations, had allowed the library to become one of the best-stocked medium-size public libraries in the state. Likewise, some automated services had just been introduced through the initiative of a couple of recently graduated professionals who had written a grant to the state library

agency and had received initial funding to put in place some electronic services, including subscription to one well-known database that could provide some good, basic information on social services—health, housing, and
educational opportunities—that can be beneficial to the community.

It is obvious that this library is long overdue in addressing questions
that are being faced by numerous library and information services organizations in school, academic, public, and special information services
organizations. "Why are not our services recognized and appreciated.
What do we need to do to address the issue?"

Effective marketing of library and information services is a vital segment in every type of library and information services organization today.
Customer-centered marketing is at the core of successful service, and
understanding the marketing mix and creating value is vital.

This chapter will present an introduction to the topic of marketing,
what it entails, and why it is necessary.

MARKETING—A STRATEGIC COMPONENT

One of the most important yet seemingly elusive concepts of a strategic
plan is the development of a marketing strategy, an outcome of the planning
process. Basically, the two activities are inextricably tied together. For purposes of discussing this component of information services, marketing can be
simplistically described as the process of identifying the wants and needs of
the population of library and information center customers and identifying the
capabilities of the organization to address those needs and then developing or
adjusting services and products to satisfy various targeted segments of that
market. This requires knowing the organization's own capabilities, establishing commitments, and identifying customer needs. The marketing analysis
process can facilitate making strategic decisions about product design, promotion, and distribution to satisfy those needs.

This marketing strategy requires primary understanding of the mission
and vision of the information services organization. That vision and mission,
developed as the primary guiding principle of the strategic plan itself, serves as
a basis for initiating and developing the process of communication and marketing within the library's community. Therefore, the most important guiding
principles already have been identified for the library organization. The outcome
of a more focused marketing strategy can now fulfill one important aspect of the
overall plan: good information services. The rigor necessary for implementing
such a plan focuses upon the value of information and knowledge as well as the
promotion of information services as a primary factor in customer satisfaction.

Initiative for developing or enhancing this particular segment will have
been built into the overall strategic plan, which began by involving the whole
community—administration, staff, and users—in the planning process and,
thereby, encouraging every segment of the information organization to buy
into the outcome of a strategic plan. That basic planning process will have not
only identified goals and objectives but also initiated the discussion of means
by which the library and/or information center would accomplish them. Just

as with the strategic plan, this marketing component requires a separate, analytical approach in its own right to ensure a successful marketing effort, and this process starts with a specific mission statement for marketing.

The most likely focus of such a statement, which leads to eventual action, is one of assuring or reassuring an identified customer base that their needs, identified in the process, will be met through organized commitment to the library mission, values, and philosophy of service identified in the strategic plan. That fact ultimately will be translated into actionable terms that can be understood by everyone involved in this marketing-driven process. Specific focus is on implementation of a communication plan promoting the basic priorities of information services.

A comprehensive marketing program encompasses not just the strategic plan's primary concern of "what are we here for?" It also requires a follow-through to market many of the goals and objectives of that plan. The marketing plan has several subgoals, including validating or changing perceptions in terms of developing products and services, delivering those products and services in an efficient and effective manner, and analyzing use and satisfaction with those identified products and services to confirm success or as a signal to adjust systems and processes to ensure success. Such a plan becomes the showpiece of a wide range of activities that are involved in meeting the needs of customers and giving value to those efforts. In that sense, the marketing component is obvious in every aspect of the strategic plan. Otherwise, once a strategic service goal is identified and implementation is begun, how do customers know it exists and how can its success or failure be validated? Viewing strategic planning and marketing in the same context strengthens both the major plan and recognizes marketing as a necessary process for the plan's success.

 Try This!

1. Think of a library you are familiar with that has a good marketing strategy.
2. List two outstanding examples of outreach services that impress you.
3. Think of a library that is failing to live up to its expectations and potential, then identify two public relations activities they are lacking.
4. How do these two libraries differ?

A clear strategy determines what resources are available or will be available, and how all the resources and energies of the library organization will be applied to achieve the goals set out by the marketing initiative. It provides the checks and balances approach in offering the services and products. This is necessary because it is of little value to have a strategy if either the resources or the expertise to implement the program are not available. Clearly, this strategy determines how all the resources and the energies of the library will be applied to achieve the goals. Several components can be identified as necessary in the development of such a marketing strategy. In this process, an old reliable method, commonly identified as the "marketing mix," can be considered.

Some call it a cliché of describing the process around the *Cs* (customer, convenience, and communication) and *Ps* (product, price, place, process, participants, and promotion) of the mix. Those critics maintain that working through this approach is passé. However, it does provide a legitimate structure for developing a marketing strategy. Basically, the overall marketing plan, inherent in those catchwords, focuses upon structuring a strategy to achieve a desired primary marketing outcome.

How does one begin to address those basic philosophical questions of service? In the strategic plan, and this integral marketing component, a process of marketing research is required to identify the demands for services or products. Effective marketing commences with understanding users, their expectations, the patterns of access by seekers and their preferences, and the barriers that exist in attracting potential customers. It also requires establishing an ongoing relationship that links information services with that primary user population and, just as vital, a larger public, including donors and potential donors, governments, the media, taxpayers and others who might have a financial interest, or public/organizational opinion about the library's success. The beginning of this identification process is an integral part of the environmental scan conducted as part of the strategic plan that identified the strengths and weaknesses, opportunities, and threats (SWOT) set in the political, economic, social, and technological (PEST) climate. Parts of that initial phase, most often identified as the marketing audit, should have been introduced in the community analysis and user needs components of the strategic plan. Therefore, revisiting the initial analysis of the market situation identified in that process can now help develop specific marketing objectives and provide a solid base for a marketing plan. If that has not been done, however, it must be accomplished at the beginning of a marketing strategy.

 What Do You Think?

John D. Rockefeller once said, "Next to doing the right thing, the most important thing is to let people know you are doing the right thing."

Do you agree that is most important? If so, how should it be accomplished?

There are two important components in the total marketing strategy, starting with the one of internal marketing, which includes good internal communications and a unified concept of customer consciousness among all staff. In other words, staff must be aware of and embrace the value of customer satisfaction. Only when this happens can an effective strategy be developed to address the second component, one of customizing services to meet community needs. In today's information-intense electronic environment, with access to databases, including journals and other information resources, and even customized portals, such customization becomes much more important with the virtual library partly existing outside the physical library.

MARKETING—THE AUDIT

A follow-up focused marketing audit, emanating from that strategic planning process, identifies the needs and activities necessary to promote those systems and services. From the marketing perspective, answering "Who?" "What?" "When?" "Where?" and "How?" provides guidelines for developing the necessary marketing strategy. Each of those basic questions must be answered through the analytical process of identifying the market and its various segments, ensuring that the organization can provide the necessary services, developing a responsive schedule of when the service can be provided, and then developing an infrastructure for success. All of this activity is related to the primary goal of developing a strategy to enhance an ongoing relationship between the users and the providers of information services.

The strategic planning process, leading into this specific segment of a plan, will have identified the more philosophical question of "Why?"—that being the essence of the library's existence. From that base, the library and/or information center will have identified the mission of information services for that particular organization and in that process will have addressed the philosophical question of why there is a need for marketing.

For marketing purposes, the most important reasons can be enumerated:

1. Competition for customers and resources; recognition that the library may no longer be the primary, and certainly not the only, information source available and that this fact brings new meaning to the need to promote the library's value in a crowded arena.

Figure 6.1—Ten Reasons for Marketing Library and Information Services

Ten Reasons For Marketing Library and Information Services

1. **Competition for customers**
2. **Competition for resources**
3. **Maintaining your relevance**
4. **Stop being taken for granted**
5. **Promote an undated image**
6. **Visibility**
7. **Valuable community resource**
8. **Rising expectations**
9. **Survival**
10. **Beneficial to library image**

Source: "Library and Information Services Marketing" (September 2003), compiled and annotated by Marianne Steadley at the University of Illinois Graduate School of Library and Information Science and the University of Illinois Libraries, *UI Current LIS Clips,*

2. On a benign level, libraries, "like motherhood and God," are good. Therefore, by certain segments of the population, they have been taken for granted. However, neither library staffs nor the users of their services can any longer assume that complacent attitude. An aggressive strategy is required.

3. At a different level, many libraries remain virtually irrelevant to funding authorities because those who hold the purse strings do not perceive the value. There appears to be a misplaced perception of "stuffing loads of money into a rat hole, and for what?" This attitude requires better public understanding of why libraries are vital.

4. With changing social trends and technological development, the needs and expectations of seekers of information are constantly changing. This changing scenario requires libraries to create an infrastructure, both physical and personal, that is responsive and conducive to customer satisfaction. It also requires educating the public, with information entering cyberspace, of the importance of accurate and authentic information—or misinformation—in society.

It must be understood that marketing is not just publicity or promotion, product creation, public relations, or even pricing and distribution. Rather, each of those is but one component of the overall marketing process to be developed through this detailed internal marketing audit and assessment. The ultimate success of this comprehensive process is customer satisfaction, the primary goal of every information services organization. With the library's mission statement addressing information delivery as a primary objective, the institution already should be prepared to develop an effective and efficient marketing plan. Marketing collects and uses demographic, geographic, behavioral, and psychological information to fulfill the organization's mission and inspires public awareness and educates.[1]

A primary step is to revisit the assessment of the organization's capabilities, the strengths and weaknesses as well as the opportunities and threats that would have been originally identified as the components of the SWOT analysis of the overall strategic planning process. This specific exercise, as already mentioned, for marketing purposes is commonly called the marketing audit. By examining the organization's profile, one is able to assess its capabilities to develop a marketing program. What systems and services are already in place, how might they be adjusted if desirable, and what new ones might need to be developed? Can the organization afford the development of a new or greater program with current resources? If not, what is the likelihood of additional resources being allocated or sought through donations or redirection of existing resources? What technological capabilities are in place to ensure success of expanded efforts? What other organizations compete with or, more desirably, complement those services? What expertise is present among the staff to effectively, efficiently, aggressively develop such a program? Recognizing the importance of this complex yet valuable process, many large libraries and information centers now have dedicated management staffs—with various titles, including director of marketing and publishing, development officer, or public relations coordinator—to coordinate activities relating to marketing and fund-raising.

MARKETING—THE VALUE FACTOR

In some ways, marketing presents a relatively new challenge as well as an opportunity for many librarians who have traditionally recognized the public good of information services and have assumed an automatically agreeable, willing, and eager public. Now, greater political, economic, social, and technological pressures, those PEST components of every librarian's life, mandate a concerted effort to demonstrate the organization's value. This can be accomplished through several ways. It requires:

1. Determining what customers and potential users want and how they perceive the library as the most appropriate instrument for meeting those needs. This process is usually accomplished through a variety of means: for example, surveys, interviews, and focus groups.

2. Segmenting the population so that specific services can be identified and tailored to the needs of those specific groups. The market segmentation process categorizes customers by identifying unique characteristics and common needs, such as location, technical competence, profession, age, and so forth. The common thread is access to information.

3. Recognizing and enumerating what it will take to provide these services in terms of staff, expertise, physical layout, access, collections, technology, and so forth.

4. Developing affordable strategies to satisfy information-delivery goals and objectives based on the results of that audit and research. Price and value are both components in this mix, with a balance between the two being required. In this reasoning, one can paraphrase Oscar Wilde's comment, "In these days people know the price of everything and the value of nothing."

5. Detailing the place(s) that is the most convenient location of services from the perspective of the customer. This also includes directions for use, including displays and signage directing potential users to the services—in-house, through media, or at locations that are remote from the primary facility.

6. Promoting the results of that effort through identified channels so that users and potential users know what products and services are available. Those include, among others, personal skills, print on paper, and electronic; that is, a description of "what we do and how we do it." Promotional approaches to users include advertising, public presentations, working with media outlets and other public relations efforts, direct marketing, publications (including such things

as flyers and newsletters), book sales, friends' groups and other lobbying groups, Web pages, and so forth.

7. Periodically and routinely evaluating the process.

COMMUNICATION—PROMOTION AS A BASIC ELEMENT

 What Would You Do?

Marla Mann sits, drumming her fingers on her desk, in the office of Allentown University's main library. As vice president for information, she has to make a tough decision that will have significant impact on information services at the university. Her administrative responsibilities include not only the university libraries but also the bookstore, the computer center services, and the university press. But it is to the libraries that her thoughts now turn.

She mulls over comments made at a recent faculty meeting and later repeated in the monthly university management team's meeting regarding the cost of marketing initiatives to enlighten the university community of the benefits and services offered by the information services units of the university libraries. Marla's attempt has been to create a greater awareness of those services in order to preserve them at an acceptable level and ensure they remain politically viable. She knows that the information services are "the best kept secret in the university." What can she do to get the secret out; to enlighten the doubters?

Ongoing public relations is the best tool for explaining to the public the values that all libraries and information centers uphold.[2] Previously, marketing communication was a one-way, no-response approach. However, today's interactive media, including Web sites, online services, blogs, and so on, enable librarians to develop and maintain a more interactive, responsive dialogue with their public. Successful marketing requires identifying reasons that customers use and potential customers might use the information services of a particular type of library, in a particular location, at a particular time, in a particular format, for a particular reason. The process of identifying some of those intangible values is difficult, because it requires developing profiles of various user groups, mentioned previously, that are intended to be the recipient base for services. It requires recognizing different needs in different groups that might use information services in different ways. Then it requires developing different products and services to meet those varying needs.

With this analysis in place, various methods can be employed in the process of getting the message across to likely users so that the services will justify the means. Internal motivation of the staff is a primary factor that affects the bottom line. That promotional commitment builds staff morale, enhances productivity, and creates team spirit. The marketing goals and objectives identified in the strategic plan present an opportunity to move from the so-called push mentality of persuasion to a pull mentality of identifying what is needed, a process that has been carried out in the strategic planning process. This helps organizations manage change in order to stay competitive and efficient. Therefore, success in this effort begins with an informed, positive, dedicated staff committed to information services.

Each of the following concepts forms one important segment of a comprehensive marketing package:

1. **Public relations:** Public relations help an organization and its publics adapt mutually to each other. Libraries must acknowledge various attitudes and values of potential users and the notion that because they reflect the external environment, they also will guide the development of services. Libraries cannot develop a product or service in a vacuum without knowing what is needed and wanted. This requires analyzing and interpreting needs as well as understanding attitudes. It requires interaction between providers and potential seekers of information services. Public relations is an ongoing process, not a one-time activity. It is an attempt to develop an understanding, among users and potential users of information services, about the value of information to people—in their professional life and in the development of the organization of which they are a part—as well as in their personal life, whether seeking pleasure or factual knowledge. Developing an image of the library by inducing those potential users requires some proof of successful "information fulfillment," some indication of past success or potential success in the product or services of the library. The American Library Associations "@ Your Library" has many public relations suggestions, materials, and so on.

2. **Publicity:** Publicity is a way of creating awareness of the systems and services in place to address various segments of the population's information and knowledge needs. It is a tool of public relations meant to persuade. Several obvious ways of communicating with those identified primary audiences are through the traditional print-on-paper and broadcasting modes, as well as, more recently, electronically. A positive message is the library's and the librarian's most important role as information provider and intermediary, eager to connect seekers with the information and knowledge they seek. Much of the time, this type of marketing is through public sources, not directed by the library. Examples are interviews with staff or externally produced articles in newspapers or online. In-house productions of publicity items include displays, posters, bookmarks, and so forth. Recently, blogging has become an effective publicity tool with the library's blog Web page, including short, frequently updated postings of what is new. Libraries are using blogs to keep patrons up to date on library events, staff picks, and news.

3. **Advertising:** Marketing is not just advertising, as is so often assumed because it is one of the most obvious aspects. By focusing

on advertising, other aspects of the program are often overlooked. The advertising subset should fit with all the other components of a marketing program. Because it is an important part of the program, it is a key to reaching the target population. This is a less common way of promoting library services, because it often requires substantial financial resources to support. The core purpose of such advertising is to communicate information about service(s), sometimes new services or to keep the library in the public's eye or to announce the opening of a new facility. With the dot-com revolution, though, few libraries are forced to budget advertising in their profile promotions. If advertising is used in any format, however, care must be taken to ensure that this subset of the program flows logically from, and is consistent with, other parts of the overall marketing strategy.

4. **Ambiance:** The environment should support the message. Physical layout and design offer libraries one of their greatest marketing opportunities. Attractive and inviting design and layout provide a vision through inspirational spaces that embody the values and qualities of the service, attract and retain the public, and can be responsive to their changing needs. Workplace routine cannot outweigh user convenience, including hours of opening. Other factors, such as availability of public transportation or parking, handicap-friendly entrances, and so forth, are vital.

5. **Fund-raising:** Although this is a primary activity within itself and many libraries consider it too important to be conducted as a subset of marketing, it is mentioned here to support the proposition that it is a process that supports marketing efforts. An alternative term, preferred by many, is *library development*. This involves securing funds, through an organized effort, to augment traditional monies in order to provide additional or special services, programs, or other resources identified as desirable in order to achieve the stated goals and objectives of the library. A number of avenues are available, including foundation and corporate funding, gifts from bequeaths or in kind, endowments, and capital campaigns. Much of fund-raising relates to marketing the library and information services, and common avenues, such as exhibits, newsletters, programming, and so on, tie the two closer together.

EVALUATING—CHECKS AND BALANCES

In this complex and changing world, there is little time for action without a carefully reasoned rationale. In addition, accountability demands evaluative data to document the status and quality of library services.[3] Even well-thought-out services, if not appropriately marketed, may fail. How does one measure success? As with all planning processes, a follow-up activity must be integral to a successful initiation, implementation, and evaluation of a marketing program. One can anticipate or even expect certain outcomes of the process. The most obvious one is increased customer satisfaction that might result in willingness to financially support certain services offered or willingness on the part of the larger organization—local, regional, or national government; university or college; school district; private or public company or foundation—to increase funding based upon demonstrated goal achievements through proactive measures that both create and prove value for the larger community.

One problem with trying to evaluate the success of a library's marketing program is that product—satisfaction of users—is often intangible and difficult to measure. Customers' wants and needs remain somewhat elusive and changeable. Shifting demographics in public library communities, shifting academic programs in higher-education institutions, and shifting company foci in special library customer bases are threats to inflexible programs. In addition, commitment of time, effort, and financial resources in order to address the perceived needs of newly formed user profiles is viewed by some as potentially risky. Change brought about by shifting priorities with a marketing focus, is also threatening. A status quo attitude toward products and services on the part of both customers and staff argues against innovation. Managers cannot afford to let that happen.

CONCLUSION

Marketing information services have moved from being a nice innovation to being a required component in every library organization's program of services. A well-thought-out, well-constructed marketing strategy supports the organization's goals of information services. Marketing is a valuable tool available to libraries in demonstrating their organizational effectiveness; the evaluation of a marketing strategy addresses the question of "How are we doing?" In a way, it is an accountability check. It is one way of ensuring that libraries are responding effectively to what their public wants and needs. It is also a way of establishing a desirable relationship not only with users but also with other segments that have the potential of providing support—governments, media outlets, donors, corporations, and publishers. That is why marketing is so important to the life of the library organization and why it must be valued by both library staffs and seekers and users of information and knowledge.

NOTES

1. Paul Argenti, *The Portable MBA Desk Reference: An Essential Business Companion* (New York: Wiley, 1993), 87.

2. Lisa Wolfe, *Library Public Relations, Promotions, and Communications,* 2nd ed. (New York: Neal-Schuman, 2004), 5.

3. Darlene E. Weingand, *Future-Driven Library Marketing* (Chicago: American Library Association, 1998), 2.

Organizing

The planning and organizing functions are closely linked. The planning process described in the previous section helps an organization define its goals and objectives. After these are established, the next function of management is to design an organizational structure that will facilitate the achievement of those goals and objectives. Organizing involves determining what tasks are to be done, who is to do them, how the tasks are to be grouped, and how all the tasks are to be coordinated. So organizing divides an organization into smaller, more manageable units and makes the work done in each unit compatible with that done in the others. As a result of organizing, the structure of the organization is formed.

In this section, the component pieces of the organizing process are examined. Ways in which the organization is broken apart (specialization) as well as the ways in which the organization is brought back together (coordination) will be discussed. Various aspects of organizing, covering the why, how, and when—why organizing is important, how to choose the most appropriate structure, and when reorganization should be considered—are examined. The classic theories of organization are covered in addition to more contemporary views on the topic. Finally, the different types of organizational structures that libraries and other information agencies have adopted are examined.

Chapter 7

Organizations and Organizational Culture

 Overview

The academic library at Madison College has a collection of 400,000 volumes and serves 150 faculty and 3,000 students. The library has a director and two assistant directors and is divided into six departments, each with a department head. The atmosphere at the Madison College library is fairly formal; the director is always addressed as Dr. Gossman, and all of the other administrators are addressed using their titles. Most of the librarians wear business attire to work. The academic library at nearby Monroe College has a collection of about the same size and serves approximately the same number of students and faculty. However, that library is very different. There are no formal departments. Instead, the library director closely interacts with the other employees in a team-based organizational structure. There is a much more casual feel to the library. All employees are on a first-name basis, and all of them dress very casually—often in jeans. Although the two libraries are similar in size and purpose, they have very different organizational structures and cultures.

All libraries are organizations, but, like other organizations, they can differ in many aspects. They often differ in structure; this difference can be easily seen on an organizational chart that shows all of the positions and their relationship to others within the organization. Libraries have been experimenting with their structures in an attempt to create cost-effective organizations in which both employees and patrons can achieve satisfaction. Much of the reorganization in libraries has resulted in flatter organizations that reflect the growing importance of the use of teams.

> Libraries also vary in their organizational culture, which is the shared as-
> sumptions, beliefs, and behaviors of the people within the organization.
>   This chapter will provide an introduction to organizations and their
> importance in the modern world. It includes a discussion of organizational
> charts and how they reflect (and sometimes do not reflect) the reality of
> the organizational structure. The chapter concludes with a discussion of
> organizational culture and its influence.

There is a close link between the planning and the organizing functions of management. First, managers plan in order to establish the organization's goals and objectives. Then, managers organize to provide a structure that will allow the organization to achieve its strategic objectives. Today, managers in both for-profit and not-for-profit organizations are very attentive to the organizing function because the structure of the organization is seen as a key element in making an organization successful. It is essential for both managers and nonmanagers to understand the function of organizing. Although most of the decisions about organizing are made by upper-level managers (often with the input of midlevel managers), all employees work within an organizational structure, and it is important to know why the organization is shaped as it is. In addition, most organizations today face rapidly changing environments, and it is often necessary for organizations to change their structures. An understanding of organizing as a managerial function will help employees to understand both the organization they are working in now and the structure of the one they may be employed in tomorrow.

ORGANIZING

As the word implies, *organizing* provides shape and structure to an organization. Organizing involves looking at all the tasks that have to be done and deciding how they will be done and by whom. Organizing has long been central to the study of management. The classical management writers such as Henri Fayol provided more guidelines and principles about organizing than about any other managerial function. These classical writers viewed an organizational structure as a lasting entity. Their overall perception was that organizations were stable structures, almost always arranged in hierarchical fashion, with the power flowing in an orderly manner from the individuals at the top of the hierarchy to those below.

As Henry Mintzberg has written:

> It probably would not be an exaggeration to claim that the vast majority
> of everything that has been written about management and organization
> over the course of this century ... has had as its model, usually implicitly,
> [this] form of organization. With its dominant vertical hierarchy, sharp
> divisions of labor, concentration on standardization, obsession with con-
> trol, and of course, appreciation of staff functions in general and plan-
> ning in particular [this] type has always constituted the "one best way" of
> management literature.[1]

One of the most striking changes in management in the past decades has been a rethinking of organizational structure. Much of this rethinking has been forced on managers by rapid changes in the environment, especially increasing competition and the growing importance of computerized information in all types of organizations. The old conventions about organizational stability have been challenged and discarded in many types of organizations, including libraries and information centers.

In an attempt to become more efficient and effective, organizations have begun to change their structures. Hierarchies have been flattened by the removal of layers of middle managers. The new model of organization being touted by management experts is flexible and adaptable to change, has relatively few levels of formal hierarchy, and has loose boundaries among functions and units.[2] Many of these new organizational structures employ teams of workers who work together on a specific task on a semipermanent or permanent basis.

Libraries, like other organizations, are restructuring in response to changes in their external environments. Unlike many other organizations, however, libraries have an additional compelling reason to reorganize. Over the past few decades, libraries have evolved from organizations in which traditional print resources predominate into ones in which these traditional resources coexist with digital electronic resources. Today's libraries are hybrids, containing both print-based and electronic materials, with the proportion of electronic resources in most libraries increasing year by year. Users who once expected to have to come to the library to gain access to resources now expect access to much material to be available through electronic gateways both inside and outside the library. Libraries now are as much about access to materials as the materials themselves. It is not surprising then that libraries, which have always been structured to provide on-site access to print resources, need to change their organizational patterns.

What organizational structure is best suited for the new hybrid library? As will be seen in this section, there is no one answer to that question. At the present time, there is a growing interest in organizational structure, and many librarians are actively engaged in looking for a way to restructure their organizations to answer the challenge presented by the change from print-based to digital materials. What is required for this transformation? What organization best suits the new reality of libraries? In this section, various approaches that libraries have taken and are taking to organizing will be discussed.

But, before discussing organizing, it is important to understand what organizations are.

WHAT AN ORGANIZATION IS

What are organizations? One definition is that organizations are goal-directed, boundary-maintaining, and socially constructed systems of human activity.[3] Let us examine that definition a bit more closely. Organizations are socially constructed; that is, they are deliberately formed by humans. They are goal directed, which means that they are purposive systems in which members attempt to achieve a certain set of goals. They are boundary maintaining; that is, there is a distinction between members of that organization and nonmembers, which sets organizations off from their environments. Those boundaries are almost always permeable because organizations are affected by their environments.

Organizations are the basic building blocks of modern society. The development of organizations is inevitable in any complex culture because of the limitations of individuals. When a single person cannot do all the work that needs to be done, there is no choice but to organize and to use more people to accomplish the task. There are many types of organizations, and they vary greatly in size and in purpose. Although they differ in many ways, the local Rotary Club, the Little League baseball team, and Microsoft are all organizations.

An organization is a human group, composed of specialists working together on a common task. Unlike society, community, or family—the traditional social aggregates—an organization is purposefully designed and grounded neither in the psychological nature of human beings nor in biological necessity. Yet, although a human creation, it is meant to endure—not perhaps forever, but for a considerable period of time.[4]

Throughout most of human history, organizations have played a less important role in people's lives than they do now. For instance, over the past 200 years, the United States has changed from a country in which almost all workers were self-employed, either as farmers or independent craftspeople, into one in which almost all workers are employed by organizations. Even as recently as the beginning of the twentieth century, farmers constituted more than one-third of the total U.S. workforce.[5] Today, most people spend their work life as one employee among many others working in an organization.

Organizations are, therefore, groups of individuals joined together to accomplish some objective. But organizations are more than simply an aggregation of individuals. Organizations have characteristics of their own, over and above the characteristics of the people who make them up. For example, organizations have a distinct structure; they have rules and norms that have developed over time; they have a life cycle that goes beyond the lives of individuals; and they usually have goals, policies, procedures, and practices. They exist in an environment that affects many of these characteristics. They are likely engaged in processing some kind of input and turning it into an output. They interact with other organizations, and they have to change internally to keep up with external pressures.[6]

Although there are many organizations in existence in the modern world, most are quite small. In the United States, the Small Business Administration has estimated that about 90 percent of the approximately 5 million businesses employ fewer than twenty workers. A similar size distribution is seen in the European Union.[7] Libraries display the same type of size distributions: There are many small libraries and a few very large ones. According to the latest American Library Association statistics, there are more than 117,000 libraries in the United States, and almost 94,000 of these are school libraries. These libraries employ approximately 400,000 people, about one-third of whom are classified as librarians.[8]

Organizations, like people, have life cycles: They come into existence, they grow, and they become mature. They may flourish for a while, but they then usually begin to decline and, unless they are revitalized, they often die.

Although some organizations, such as the Roman Catholic Church, the Icelandic Parliament, and a few universities, have been in existence for a long time, most organizations are short lived, coming and going in a much shorter time period than the humans who formed them.[9] If they wish to continue to exist, organizations have to adapt to meet changing conditions. As can be seen in Figure 7.1, organizations that are not able to revitalize themselves will cease to exist.

The environment in which organizations function has become more competitive and complex, so, as mentioned earlier, many of these entities have begun to experiment with changing their organizational structure. Not surprisingly, most of this restructuring has occurred in the corporate world, the sector that usually leads the way in organizational transformation. Publicly supported organizations, including libraries, have been slower to change and move away from the traditional organizational structures. Although libraries and other information centers as a whole have not been as radically altered as many organizations in the private sector, they have still begun to reshape and restructure. Few libraries have completely revamped their organizational structure; instead, the reorganization in most libraries has been "incremental rather than dramatic."[10]

The need to examine and perhaps reshape the organizational structure is as imperative in libraries as in other organizations. As was discussed in chapter 3, fast-paced change is certainly a part of the environment of all types of libraries. These changes have led managers in libraries, like managers in other types of organizations, to consider possible restructuring. Many of the same forces that have resulted in the reshaping of other types of organizations also have affected libraries and information centers: increased automation, reduction in budgets, changing information needs and expectations of users, and the need for staff to have more autonomy and control over their work.[11] The boundaries of many libraries, like other organizations, have become more permeable or fuzzy as they have collaborated with other libraries in joint ventures, such as statewide licensing consortia, and as they have used outsourcing as a means to attain from outside sources goods and services that they once produced in-house. As librarians have had to reconsider their systems and the roles their libraries play, they also have had to reexamine the organizational structure of the library itself.

The critical task for management in each revolutionary period is to find a new set of organizing practices that will become the basis for managing the next period of evolutionary growth. Interestingly enough, these new practices eventually sow the seeds of their own decay and lead to another period of

Figure 7.1—The Life Cycle of Organizations

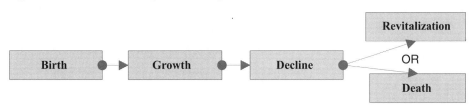

revolution. Managers therefore experience the irony of seeing a major solution in one period becoming a major problem in a later period.[12]

There are no pat answers about the way libraries or any other organization should be structured. But wise managers are exploring the options. Clinging to the organizational structure that worked well yesterday may mean that an organization cannot meet the challenges of either today or tomorrow.

ORGANIZATIONAL STRUCTURE

The terms *organization* and *organizational structure* often are used interchangeably, but more precise definitions are available. The organization is the group of individuals joined together to achieve an objective. An organizational structure (sometimes called an organizational design) results from the organizing process and is the system of relations, both formally prescribed and informally developed, that governs the activities of people who are dependent on each other for the accomplishment of common objectives.

Organizational structure is one of the interrelated components that define any organization. Structure refers to the definition of individual jobs and their relationship to each other as depicted on organization charts and job descriptions. An organization's structure is the source of how responsibility is distributed, how individual positions are coordinated, and how information is officially disseminated. When an organization's structure is changed, the process is referred to as *restructuring* or *reorganization.*

Because the structure of an organization is created by people, it should in no way be considered permanent, fixed, or sacred. Traditionally, many managers have been reluctant to alter an organizational structure once it has been established. This may be due to fear of change or failure to recognize that new activities necessitate new or modified organizational structures. It has been said that most of the organizations existing today were created to meet goals and objectives that no longer exist for those organizations. When managers continue to use an old organizational structure to achieve new goals and objectives, the result is inefficiency, duplication of endeavor, and confusion. In a period when there is little competition or when changes in the outside environment are occurring slowly, it is possible to get by with an outdated organizational structure, but when competition becomes more intense and the environment more turbulent, an outdated structure will lead to problems.

It is not easy to develop an organizational structure that provides for the efficient achievement of planned goals and objectives. And as organizational structures get larger and involve more people, more complex problems are encountered. The organizational structure must provide for the identification and grouping of similar or related activities necessary for achieving the organization's goals and objectives; it must permit the assignment of these activities to appropriate units. It must provide for the coordination of activities under a manager and the delegation of authority and responsibility necessary for the manager to carry out the assigned activities.

Even in the corporate world there is much indecision about reorganization and the best type of structure. As Robert Johansen and Rob Swigart write: "We have outlived the usefulness of models from the industrial era but don't yet have robust organizational models for the information era."[13]

In the 1990s, many organizations tried to restructure following the principles of business process reengineering (BPR). BPR was the latest of a long line of managerial reforms adopted by businesses in an effort to make organizations more effective and efficient. Two books published in the early 1990s, *Process Innovation: Reengineering Work through Information Technology*[14] and *Reengineering the Corporation: A Manifesto for Business*,[15] triggered the explosive interest in BPR, and organizations all over the world started to reengineer.

As the name implies, business process reengineering consists of rethinking and transforming organizational processes through the use of information technologies in order to achieve major improvements in quality, performance, and productivity. BPR is not for the timid; it is radical and difficult to implement. It does not involve gradual change; instead, it calls for the total overhaul of an organization. According to Michael Hammer and James Champy, BPR is "the fundamental rethinking and radical redesign of business processes to achieve dramatic improvements in critical, contemporary measures of performance such as quality, service, and speed."[16] One of the results of this reengineering was a change in organizational structure as a result of the rethinking of processes.

Although BPR was heavily used in the 1990s, in the past few years even some of the strongest early advocates of BPR have backed away and begun to point out some of its problems. Many of these difficulties resulted from a misunderstanding of the purpose of BPR. Undoubtedly, one of the reasons BPR was so popular when introduced was because of the generally adverse economic conditions of the early 1990s. Management literature was full of dire predictions of what would happen to companies that did not become more cost efficient in the face of global competition. Many of the organizations that adopted BPR did so primarily as a cost-saving measure, and in numerous cases BPR was used as an excuse to reduce the number of employees. Managers thus were able to avoid taking direct responsibility for making staff redundant; they could argue that these cuts were required by the reengineering effort.[17] Many organizations claimed to be reengineering when their primary purpose was reducing headcount, so, in the eyes of many, BPR became inextricably linked with downsizing and layoffs.

 ## What Do You Think?

Business organizations are changing, whether they want to or not. The changes are chaotic—the experience from inside or close to a large corporation, as well as the feeling inside your stomach. The pyramids of corporate strength have flattened into a web of organizational ambiguity. Individual employees no longer have a sturdy structure to climb. Instead, planning a career is more like crawling out on a webbing of rope, grasping for stability that comes and goes quickly.

> Johansen and Swigart describe the chaotic feeling that results from working inside an organization that is in the midst of restructuring. What can managers do to help make the experience less chaotic? Does organizational change always have to be threatening?
>
> Robert Johansen and Rob Swigart, *Upsizing the Individual in the Downsized Organization: Managing in the Wake of Reengineering, Globalization, and Overwhelming Technological Change* (Reading, MA: Addison-Wesley, 1994), x.

BPR also fell from favor because it seemed to devalue people. Reengineering often resulted in a demoralization of the organization's staff, especially when the employees did not understand or had little input into the organizational changes. From the employee's point of view, it seemed that the organization's structure was far more important than the people who worked there. Even Thomas Davenport, one of the creators of BPR, called it a failed process: "The rock that re-engineering foundered on is simple: people. Re-engineering treated the people inside companies as though they were just so many bits and bytes, interchangeable parts to be re-engineered."[18] As more and more business organizations reported problems with the process, BPR began to fade from use, at least in the U.S. corporate sector.

However, it would be foolish to ignore the real benefits associated with BPR. BPR, as originally designed and sold to organizations, had flaws, but many of its underlying concepts were sound. Properly designed processes (e.g., how work is carried out) are vitally important to the success of any organization. Periodically, all organizations need to examine both the need for and the design of their processes. Any organization that ignores the need to change and improve its processes is risking its future. The pace of change in all organizations, including libraries, is accelerating, and most are experiencing increased competition. Information technology has been widely adopted and should be permitting people to do their jobs in different and better ways. Organizations cannot continue to use yesterday's processes or organizational structures if they want to be in business tomorrow.

Although a number of libraries used some of the principles of BPR in redesigning their internal processes,[19] none followed all of its principles. Instead, most libraries that have reorganized have done so by keeping at least some of the previous structure intact while making incremental changes in departments and subunits. Libraries and information centers currently are organized in a variety of ways, ranging from very flat to traditional hierarchical organizations. Although libraries and information centers may have many different structures, each of them may be appropriate; having different structures does not necessarily mean that some are right and some are not. As this section will show, there is no optimum way to organize and no consistent prescription for the best type of organizational structure. Although the trend now is toward flatter structures, it is not true that they are always superior to more hierarchical ones. Traditional hierarchies do work best in some situations, whereas flatter structures are more suitable in others. As in so many other areas of management, the best organizational structure depends on the circumstances in a specific case.

Organizational theorists have moved away from a prescriptive approach and now agree that there is no one best answer. They urge the organization to think about what it hopes to accomplish and to adopt the type of organizational structure that allows it to best achieve its goals. The question then becomes, "Which organization design performs better in a particular market and location, and which design best enhances the company's core competencies.... The executive's operating focus becomes how to create congruency—the fit among all organizational components consistent to the chosen organization design—so that the organization is the most efficient."[20]

But restructuring is a difficult task. Often, organizations have restructured to solve one problem, but the new structure inadvertently created many more. There are no easy answers to how organizations should be designed, but managers of all types should be addressing the question of the most appropriate structure for their organization.

GETTING STARTED WITH ORGANIZING

One of the most important aspects of organization is choosing the design of the enterprise, both its structure and the allocation of its jobs. As long as the work to be accomplished in an enterprise can be done by one person, there is little need to organize. But as soon as an enterprise grows so that more than one worker is necessary, decisions must be made about its organization.

As managers move up the hierarchy, and/or as the size of their organization grows, they become more concerned with issues of organizational design. Managers are concerned with three related goals when they make design decisions: (1) to create an organizational design that provides a permanent setting in which managers can influence individuals to do their particular jobs; (2) to achieve a pattern of collaborative effort among individual employees, which is necessary for successful operations; and (3) to create an organization that is cost effective.[21]

Most organizations need little structure when they are first started because they are still very small. There are advantages to small organizations: They are flexible, fairly inexpensive to maintain, and have clear accountability. When OCLC (then the Ohio College Library Center) was founded in 1967, the organization consisted of Frederick G. Kilgour and one secretary. The people at OCLC in its earliest days probably gave little thought to formal organizational structure. When organizations are small, there is less need for organizational structure because decisions can be made by just a few people, and communication can be very informal. If an organization is successful and grows larger, however, the need for a formal structure becomes more critical. There is a need to have written policies and guidelines and to divide the responsibilities and the authority for decision making. OCLC now employs a large number of people and has operations worldwide. As OCLC expanded and grew into a global organization, its managers needed to think about how to organize the corporation so it could achieve its objectives. Today, OCLC's organizational structure reflects the larger, more complex corporation it has become.

What Would You Do?

The first Apple computers were built in 1976 in the Cupertino, California, garage of Steve Jobs's parents. He and fellow computer buff Steve Wozniak built 50 computer boards that they sold through a local dealer. The Apple II computer was introduced two years later. Sales began to skyrocket. When Apple went public in 1980, sales hit the billion-dollar mark. The two Steves became instant multimillionaires. Apple was founded to be a new type of company in which the old corporate rules were scrapped. No dress codes, no formal meetings—nothing to get in the way of what really mattered: creating computers that, Apple promised, would change the world. As the company grew, however, more employees were hired, and seasoned managers were needed to handle the rapid growth of the organization. Soon friction developed between the two cofounders and the new management, and by 1985 both Jobs and Wozniak were no longer associated with Apple Computing.

New start-up organizations often flourish with creative and charismatic leaders who have both an understanding and a passion for the technology underlying their success. But as organizations grow, they need chief executives with a different set of skills, including the ability to delegate and to operate in a highly structured setting. If you were hired as a consultant to a fast-growing new organization and asked to provide advice on how to manage the organization, what would you advise? Is it possible to keep the same type of organizational structure and culture in a larger organization as was present in a smaller one? Do organizational cultures marked by creativity and informality have to give way to a more formal and structured way of operating?

Based on information taken from Steven Levy, *Insanely Great: The Life and Times of Macintosh, the Computer that Changed Everything* (New York: Viking, 1994).

Some organizations remain small and never get to the point at which they have to think seriously about organizational structure. For instance, a small public library with a handful of employees will be able to remain relatively informal in its organizational structure. But every organization that grows reaches the point at which a formal organizational structure becomes essential, and those that do not implement such a structure will not be able to make a successful transition from a small to a large organization.

Few successful start-ups become great companies, in large part because they respond to growth and success in the wrong way. Entrepreneurial success is fueled by creativity, imagination, bold moves into uncharted waters, and visionary zeal. As a company grows and becomes more complex, it begins to trip over its own success—too many new people, too many new customers, too many new orders, too many new products. What was once great fun becomes an unwieldy ball of disorganized stuff.[22]

Library and information agencies reflect the same increasing complexity of organizational structure as they grow larger. For example, consider the case of a small special library in a fast-growing corporation. When the library is first established, one librarian may be sufficient to perform all the tasks associated with operating the library, including acquisitions, cataloging, reference, interlibrary loan, and online searching. But as the parent corporation grows larger and the demand for information supplied by the library increases, more employees are needed. Now decisions must be made about the organization of that library. The expanded library and its new employees could be structured in many ways. The task of the manager is to try to establish the most effective and efficient structure. It is possible that each employee could do a portion of all the tasks that need to be done, with each one spending some time doing acquisition, reference, cataloging, and so forth. More likely, however, the work will be divided in such a way that each employee will specialize, at least to some extent, in one or more of these tasks.

Since the publication of Adam Smith's *The Wealth of Nations* more than 200 years ago, it has been recognized that division of labor leads to greater efficiency. Smith believed that a nation's wealth could be increased if organizations used a high degree of worker specialization. Instead of having one individual complete an entire job, the job is broken up into its component parts, and each discrete part of the job is completed by a different individual. Smith described one factory in which pins were produced. In this factory, 10 workers produced as many as 48,000 pins a day. The task of making a pin was subdivided into a series of smaller tasks, such as straightening the wire and cutting it. If each worker had been working alone to make the whole pin alone, he or she could produce only about twenty pins a day.[23] Division of labor leads to role differentiation and specialization of function and thus is an efficient way to structure tasks.

So, specialization usually leads to more efficiency in jobs, but as will be discussed in sections 4 and 5 of this book, too much specialization often results in jobs that are too narrow in scope and thus are boring and dissatisfying to the employee. Specialization is more often found in larger organizations; in smaller ones, employees often have to perform many types of functions, and there is much less differentiation of roles. Contrast the difference between a school library media specialist working as the only librarian in a media center and a librarian working in a large academic research library that employs 300 professionals. Obviously, the school library media specialist will, of necessity, perform a wider range of tasks than the librarian in a specialized position in the large academic library. Persons working in what have been termed *one-person libraries*[24] have to be generalists who are able to perform many functions well. In the case of the corporate library described previously, it is likely that the library organizer would decide that each employee should specialize to some extent. In that case, the manager would divide the tasks to be performed, and the tasks would be allocated so that one employee would be in charge of acquisitions, two would focus on cataloging, two would work in reference services, one would perform online searches, and so on. Probably, there also would be one employee accountable for the operation of the entire library. One of that person's responsibilities would be to coordinate all the tasks that have to be done so as to be sure that all processes work together and all objectives are accomplished. That person would be the library director, the manager who makes the ultimate decisions about the structuring of the organization.

The restructuring of this library illustrates two key concepts in organization: specialization and coordination. When more than one person is working toward an objective, each worker must know what part to do, in order to avoid confusion and duplication of effort. No matter how precisely the work is divided, the workers' efforts will not mesh exactly unless some means of coordination is provided.

Every organization must decide how it wants to divide its tasks or specialize; this specialization involves breaking the whole organization into parts. Then the organization must decide how to integrate all the specialized parts to create a whole product or service. The latter goal is achieved by coordinating. All large organizations must both specialize and coordinate. The methods that libraries use to specialize and coordinate will be discussed in chapter 8.

FORMAL AND INFORMAL ORGANIZATIONS

Organizations may be classified as formal or informal. A formal organization is legally constituted by those in authority. This is the organization as it is supposed to function, based on the deliberate assignment of tasks, functions, and authority relationships. The formal organization is the set of official, standardized work relationships. An informal organization, on the other hand, is more loosely organized and flexible. It is often created spontaneously. Informal organizations can exist independently of formal organizations; for instance, four people who gather to play bridge constitute an informal organization.

However, many informal organizations are found within the confines of a formal organization. After the formal organization has been established, informal organizations arise naturally within its framework. The unofficial relationships within a work group constitute the informal organization. These informal groups often have leaders whose positions never show up on the organizational chart. Unlike the formally appointed leader who has a defined position from which to influence others, the informal leader does not have officially sanctioned authority. Instead, the leader of an informal group is typically the person that the other members feel is critical to the satisfaction of their specific needs at a specific time. Leadership in informal groups often changes rapidly, and different individuals revolve in and out of leadership.

Informal organizations are never found on the organization chart, but they often have a profound impact on the formal organization. Their influence can either contribute to or subvert the organization's effectiveness. Classical management principles usually ignored the existence of informal organizations, and many managers still underestimate the importance of these informal ties. For the individual who is employed by an organization, both the formal and informal relationships affect his or her organizational role.

LIBRARIES AS ORGANIZATIONS

This chapter focuses on formal organizations. Libraries are one type of formal organization; most libraries are not-for-profit, service organizations with special organizational characteristics. As Lowell Martin has pointed out, libraries:

- are service agencies, not profit-making firms;
- purvey information, not more tangible services or products;
- perform functions both of supply and guidance, a combination that in the medical field is shared among the doctor's office, the hospital, and the pharmacy;
- provide professional service without, in most cases, having a personal and continuous client relationship;
- are, for all their general acceptance, currently marked by ambiguous goals rather than clear-cut objectives;
- have, during their long history, accumulated set conceptions of function and method that make for rigid structure and resistance to change;
- respond both to resources and to clientele in a dual and sometimes conflicting orientation, with some staff characterized as resource-minded and others as people-minded;
- function as auxiliaries to larger enterprises, such as universities, schools, and municipalities, and not as independent entities;
- are, because of their auxiliary role, subject to external pressures from political bodies, faculties, and users;
- are staffed in the higher echelons by personnel with graduate training, making for a highly educated core staff;
- are administered by professionals who are promoted from the service ranks, not by career managers;
- seek identity and domain within a host of communication and information sources in the community at large and in their parent organization.[25]

Although libraries are one distinct type of organization, they share many characteristics with other kinds of organizations. Throughout this section, libraries will be the focus of attention, but the theories and principles of organizing discussed are the same used in all organizations.

ORGANIZATION CHARTS

A useful aid for visualizing the horizontal and vertical differentiation within an organization is the organization chart. An organization chart is a graphic representation of the organizational structure. These charts are so prevalent that, when "they hear the word *structure,* most people think of boxes on charts."[26] Although an organizational chart includes staff units, its primary function is to show how lines of authority link departments. Such a chart provides valuable information about the organizational structure of the organization, but it must be remembered that the "orderly little boxes stacked atop one another ... show you the names and titles of managers but little else about the company—not its products, processes, or customers—perhaps not even its line of business."[27]

Lines of authority are usually represented on organization charts by solid lines. Lines that show staff organizational units are often represented by broken lines. Formal communication follows the lines of organizational units and authority. Informal lines of communication are not shown on the traditional organization chart.

On an organization chart, authority flows down and out; it does not return to the point of origin. For example, in figure 7.2, the main line of authority flows from the director down to the assistant director and from that position down and out to the three functional departments. The business office is supervised by the director only. Authority flows from the director down to the assistant director and down and out to the business office, where it stops. In other words, in this library, the assistant director reports to the director, as does the head of the business department. The heads of the circulation, reference, and technical services departments report to the assistant director. Understanding that authority flows out and stops is very important in interpreting organization charts. The business office has no authority over the assistant director or the other organizational units shown in the figure.

In the library represented in figure 7.3, the director has authority over the human resources office. Because the human resources office performs a staff function, this authority is depicted with a broken line. The human resources office serves in an advisory capacity to the director and to all other units of the organization, without authority over any unit. However, the human resources office, in its internal operation, has line authority in that it supervises the payroll functions.

Some of the blocks in figures 7.2 and 7.3 seem to represent individuals (e.g., director and assistant director), whereas others represent functions (e.g., circulation, reference, and technical services). The blocks that represent functions include all assigned activities, including those performed by the manager. The blocks that seem to represent individuals actually represent all

Figure 7.2—Organization Chart Showing Authority Lines

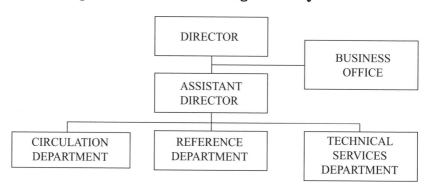

the activities assigned to that position. For the director, activities include the direct supervision of the business office in figure 7.2 and the human resources office in figure 7.3. In addition, both charts assume that the director will perform activities such as planning; working with outside groups, organizations, and individuals (such as the public library board or, in a university library, the vice president for academic affairs); and evaluating library services. In both charts, the assistant director is responsible for day-to-day supervision of the three operating units, but other activities also are assigned to this position. Although it may appear that a unit of the organization structure is designated by an individual's title, one must recognize that the organizational block includes all the activities of that position.

Not many organizations are as simple as those represented by figures 7.2 or 7.3. Some are very complex. Various means have been developed to show the authority relationship of one unit to another. Some organizational charts are very complex and, because of their size, sometimes confusing. It is commonly believed that the higher on the chart the unit appears, the greater is its status and authority, and, occasionally, the organizational status of a unit is misunderstood because of its location on the organization chart. The importance of an organizational unit is determined not by its position on the organizational chart but by the line of authority and the number of managers that authority passes through before reaching the final authority.

The organizational charts in figures 7.2 and 7.3 are traditional. They are based on the hierarchical concept and are designed to show the relationship of one organizational unit to another through lines of authority. A few organizations, although structured traditionally, depict their structure in a nontraditional organization chart. Figure 7.4 is an example of this type of chart. This chart model consists of a series of concentric circles, each of which shows a different level of operation. Top administrators are shown in the center, and successive circles represent the various levels of the organization.

Figure 7.3—Line and Staff Organizational Units

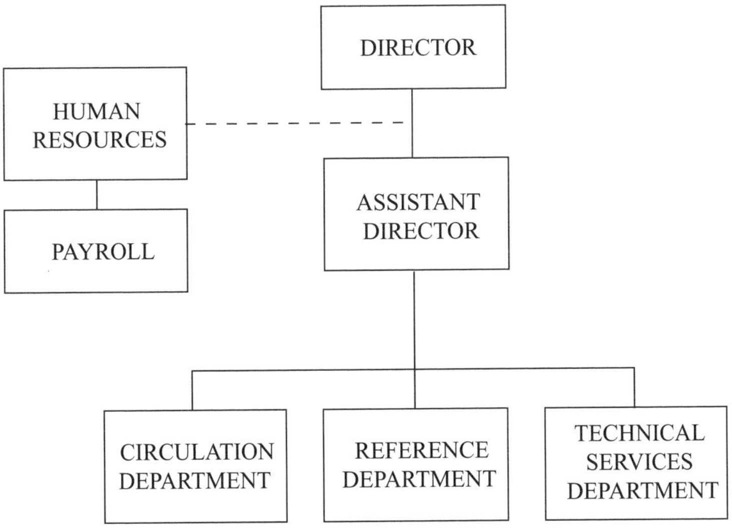

Other organization charts have configurations even further removed from the traditional one.

Figure 7.5 shows the organization as spokes around a wheel. All of these charts simply represent different ways of illustrating the same traditional, hierarchical structure.

Organization charts can be used to define and describe channels of authority, communication, and information flow. They can be used to show the status or rank of members of the organization, and the span of control of each supervisor can be readily detected on them. Developing an organization chart helps the manager identify problems or inconsistencies in the organization, such as the assignment of unrelated or dissimilar activities to a unit.

Every library, regardless of size, should have an up-to-date organization chart. It should be available to all staff to help them understand relationships within the library. But it also must be understood that an organization chart, a static model of a dynamic process, is limited in what it can do. It shows division of work into components, who is (supposed to be) whose boss, the nature of the work performed by each component, and the grouping of components on the levels of management in terms of successive layers of superiors and subordinates. It does not show the importance or status of the organizational units, the degree of responsibility and authority exercised by positions on the same management level, clear distinctions between line and staff, all channels of communication and contact (only the formal ones are shown), all key links

Figure 7.4—Organization Chart Presented as a Circle

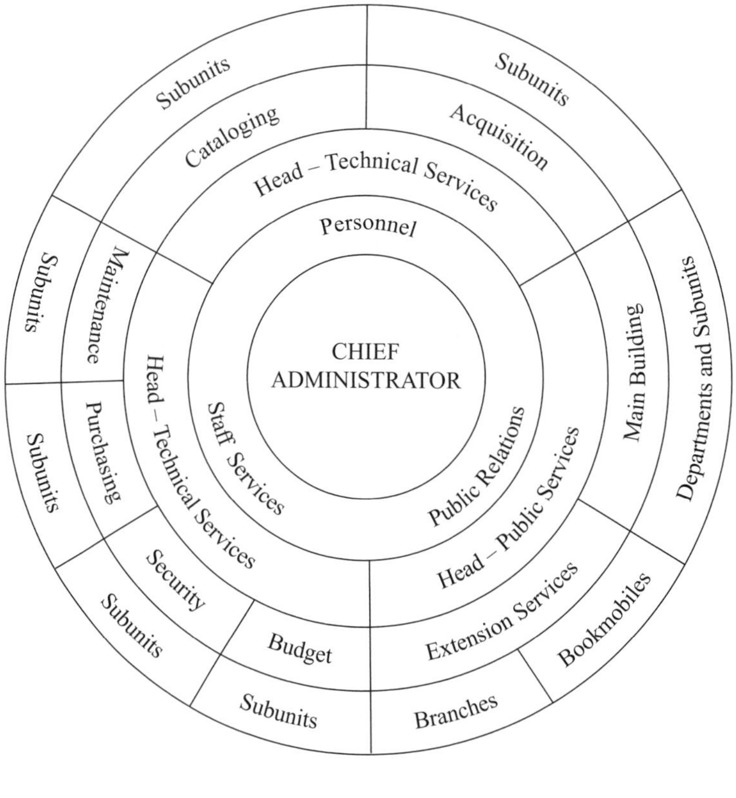

Figure 7.5—Organization Chart Presented as Spokes around a Wheel

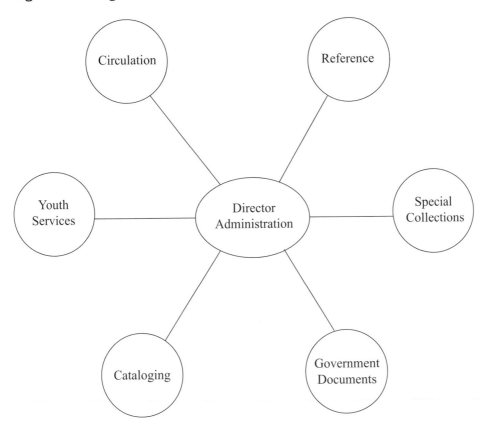

or relationships in the total organizational network, or the informal organization that is a logical and necessary extension of the formal structure.[28]

This book's Web site (http://www.lu.com/management) contains a number of organization charts from libraries and links to the charts of others. Analysis of the charts indicates that the principles of organizing are sometimes violated. On some of the charts, some positions have two or three supervisors. The span of control of some supervisors is larger on some of the charts than is usually recommended. An organization chart often reflects local situations that may be historical or may represent the intent of the top administrator, regardless of the general principles of organizational design.

ORGANIZATIONAL CULTURE

Each organization tends to develop its own organizational, or corporate, culture as norms of the organization arise and become manifest in employee behavior. In the corporate world, many organizations have very strong cultures. Wal-Mart, for example, has developed a culture based on the belief that its founder's, Sam Walton's, thriftiness, hard work, and dedication to customers is the source of the company's success. IBM has a strong corporate culture that is very different from that at Dell Computer. Organizations with a strong culture are viewed by outsiders as having a certain style or way of doing things.[29]

Most libraries have their own culture. For instance, in some, the employees dress in a businesslike manner; the men wear coats and ties, and the women wear tailored suits and dresses. In others, the employees dress in a much more casual manner. In some libraries, the workers tend to socialize a great deal off the job, whereas in others there is little interaction outside of work hours. In some libraries, the director is always addressed formally using a title, such as Dr. Brown or Ms. Smith. In other libraries, everyone is on a first-name basis. The ways in which workers dress, socialize, and interact with one another are just a few examples of organizational culture.

Organizational culture is defined as the "assumptions that a group discovers it has as it learns to cope with problems of external adaption and internal integration." *External adaption* refers to how the organization finds a niche in and copes with the external environment. *Internal integration* is concerned with establishing and maintaining effective working relations among members of the organization. In both of these categories, the assumptions that have worked well are taught to new members of the group as the correct way to perceive, think, and feel in relation to those issues.[30] In other words, the culture reflects the values of the organization. Organizational culture comes from three main sources: (1) the beliefs, assumptions, and values of the organization's founder; (2) the learning experiences of group members as the organization evolves; and (3) new beliefs, values, and assumptions brought in by new members and leaders.[31] The major influence on an organization's culture is usually the organization's top management, which "not only creates the rational and tangible aspects of organizations, such as structure and technology, but also is the creator of symbols, ideologies, language, beliefs, rituals, and myths."[32]

 Try This!

According to Kilmann, organizations themselves have "an invisible quality—a certain style, a character, a way of doing things—that may be more powerful than the dictates of any one person or any formal system. To understand the soul of the organization requires that we travel below the charts, rule books, machines, and buildings into the underground world of corporate cultures."

Think about an organization you know well, either a library or another type of organization, and try to tease out the various elements of its organizational culture. Can you identify its symbols, special language, heroes, slogans, myths, or ceremonies? Would you say that this organization has a weak or a strong organizational culture?

R. H. Kilmann, "Corporate Culture," *Psychology Today* 28 (April 1995): 63.

Organizational culture is composed of many elements. Among the most common are:

- Symbols are objects or acts that convey meaning to others. Some symbols that are found in libraries are whether employees work in traditional offices or in cubicles, the type of decorations on the wall, and whether supervisors keep their office doors open or closed.

- Language is the shared terminology that helps cement an organization's identity. In libraries, there is much use of various acronyms, such as LC or AACR2, that are understood by most librarians but by few outsiders.

- Group norms are the implicit standards or ways of acting that evolve within an organization. In some libraries, all staff meetings start exactly on time; in others, they tend to start five to ten minutes late.

- Slogans are phrases or sentences that express an organization's values. Sometimes these slogans are found in the organization's mission statement.

- Heroes are the men and women who exemplify the attributes of the culture. The experienced reference librarian who always finds the right answer or the library director who is able to defend the library against proposed budget cuts might be held up as heroes within their organization.

- Myths or stories are the retellings of real (or sometimes imagined) things that happened to figures associated with the organization, typically in the past. These stories are retold to new employees because they reinforce the organization's values. Stories about the founder or an early leader of an organization are common.

- Ceremonies are the rituals that mark a special event. Many libraries have ceremonies each year—for example, an employee appreciation dinner or a reading of banned books during National Library Week.

Global Differences in Organizational Culture

Geert Hofstede, a Dutch scholar, studied national differences in organizational behavior. He identified five characteristics that are affected by national and regional differences. These characteristics are:

- **Power distance.** The degree to which a society expects there to be differences in the levels of power.
- **Uncertainty avoidance.** The extent to which a society accepts uncertainty and risk.
- **Individualism versus collectivism,** Whether people are expected to act primarily as individuals or as members of a group.

- **Masculinity versus femininity.** —The worth placed on traditionally male or female values.
- **Long- versus short-term orientation.** The importance attached to the future versus the past and present.

To find out more about Hofstede's cultural differences and to see the scores for your own country, go to http://www.geert-hofstede.com/.

All of these elements and often many more go into defining an organization's culture.

Organizational culture has various levels. Some of it is visible, and some of it is less easy to see. Edgar Schein describes three levels of culture: artifacts, espoused values, and shared basic assumptions:

- Artifacts are visible manifestations of underlying cultural assumptions, such as behavior patterns, rituals, physical environment, stories, and myths. Artifacts are easily discerned and relatively easy to understand. For example, the dress codes that some organizations have are artifacts. Schein warns that it is dangerous to try to infer the deeper levels of organization culture from the artifacts alone because individuals inevitably project their own feelings and reactions onto a given situation. For example, if an individual sees a very informal organization, he or she may interpret that as a sign of inefficiency if that individual's own perceptions have been colored by the assumption that informality means playing around and not working.

- Espoused values are the shared values of the organization. For example, many libraries have mission statements that inform both employees and patrons about what the library strives to accomplish. Codes such as the American Library Association's Code of Ethics could, if they are adopted, be considered to be part of the espoused values of a particular library. These values are statements of why things should be as they are. The set of values that becomes embodied in an organization serves as a guide to dealing with uncertain or difficult events.

- Basic assumptions are the invisible but identifiable reasons why group members perceive, think, and feel the way they do about certain issues. These basic assumptions can be so deeply held in a group that members will find behavior based on any other premise inconceivable. Basic assumptions are so deeply embedded that they are likely to be neither confronted nor debated, and thus they are extremely difficult to change. These assumptions often deal with "fundamental aspects of life—the nature of time and space; human nature and human activities; the nature of truth and how one discovers it; the correct way for the individual and the group to relate to each other; the relative importance of work, family, and self-development; the proper role of men and women; and the nature of the family."[33]

Schein argues that the pattern of basic underlying assumptions can function as a cognitive defense mechanism for individuals and the group; as a result, culture change is difficult, time consuming, and anxiety provoking. "The bottom line for leaders is that if they do not become conscious of the cultures in which they are embedded, those cultures will manage them. Cultural understanding is desirable for all of us, but it is essential to leaders if they are to lead."[34] Schein stresses the need for senior management to focus upon the third level of culture. Artifacts can be changed and new values articulated. But unless the basic assumptions are addressed, the organization's culture is likely to stay the same.

GETTING TO KNOW THE CULTURE

One of the first things that newly hired employees learn is "the way things are done here," including information about the organization's history, its cast of characters, and expectations about employee behavior. Often when employees are unhappy in a job, it is because there is not a good fit between the organization's culture and what the employee had expected. In many cases, when this mismatch occurs, employees resign from their jobs or are asked to leave because they cannot conform to the culture. So it is important for prospective employees to find out as much about the organizational culture as possible before they accept a job.

Just as employees are always happier when they can accept the culture of the organization in which they work, organizations look for a good organizational fit when filling positions. They do this because an organization's culture is largely maintained through recruiting employees who fit into that culture. In addition to hiring individuals they think will fit into it, managers reinforce the organizational culture by (1) what they pay attention to; (2) the way they react to critical incidents and crises; (3) how they allocate rewards; (4) the way they

Figure 7.6—The Three Levels of Corporate Culture

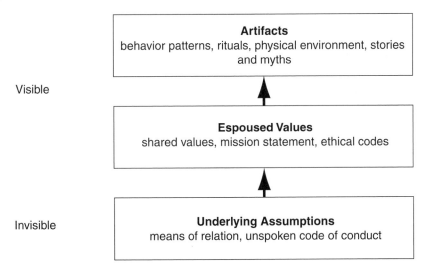

carry out role modeling and coaching; (5) what methods they use for selection, promotion, and removal; and (6) their various organizational rites, ceremonies, and stories.[35] If an organization wishes to change its organizational culture, it has to restructure all of the factors listed previously.

As can be seen, each organization has its own individual culture. Although the culture of two organizations of the same type may be similar, each one will have its own distinctive features. In the corporate world, in which there have been so many mergers in the past few years, one of the most difficult things to accomplish has been the bringing together of the corporate cultures of two different firms. Although mergers are less common in the not-for-profit sector, libraries, too, sometimes face the need to merge. In academic libraries that have merged with university computing centers, the clash of cultures between these two types of institutions often has been a challenge. Public libraries that have merged with academic libraries, as in San Jose, California, or Cologne, Germany,[36] face a similar challenge in making the two institutions one. Autonomous libraries that are integrated into a unified system also often find it hard to merge the preexisting individual organization cultures into a unified whole.[37]

Obviously, it is not easy to change the culture in an organization, because it is usually deeply ingrained in the employees and managers who work there. Organizational culture is thus often the cause of inflexibility in organizations. Employees are resistant to change because they have "always done it that way." However, some organizations, such as Toyota, have consciously shaped a corporate culture that welcomes change.[38] Research has shown that the most successful organizations not only have strong cultures, but they also have adaptive ones.[39] The so-called learning organization described in chapter 2 is distinguished by its adaptive culture. Employees in learning organizations are rewarded for questioning the status quo and the current way of doing things. This type of organization values risk taking and change. Most experts feel that an adaptable organizational culture will be critical for the success of tomorrow's organizations.

Organizational culture needs to be able to change, because cultural values that have worked in the past may become outdated, and an organization needs to adapt its culture to new conditions Ironically, it is sometimes the most successful organizations that are the most resistant to change; their past success has convinced them that their ways are the right ones. They think that they have the answers, and so they are not as responsive to their constituencies. They are not willing to take risks. They become resistant to change, which allows new organizations to gain ground on them and to begin to take away their market share.

Libraries have an organization and a structure that have worked well in the past, but now they are faced with increasing competition as they make the transition from paper-based to digitally based collections. It is easier to cling to the tried and true than to make changes, especially when there is no new model that has been shown to be a reliable replacement. But if libraries wish to continue to exist in the future, they have to continue to experiment with changes in their organization and their culture. As Philip Evans and Thomas Wurster state: "The paralysis of the leading incumbent is the greatest competitive advantage enjoyed by new competitors. It is an advantage they often do not deserve, since if the incumbent would only fight all-out by the new rules, the incumbent would often win."[40] But it is hard to make radical changes in the way things are done, and it is very difficult to walk away from the things that organizations have done well over the years—from those "core competencies that were built over decades, the object of personal and collective pride and identity."[41]

What will happen if libraries refuse to change? Unlike commercial enterprises that fail to keep up with changing customer expectations or that make a product that no longer sells, libraries will not go out of existence, at least in the near future. But it is likely that they will be gradually supplanted by competing information providers. Individuals who can go elsewhere for what they need, and who can get it more quickly and with less hassle, are unlikely to keep coming to libraries if they continue to depend on old models—for example, providing assistance only at desks physically located within library buildings.

Libraries of all sorts have a rich tradition of access to information and preservation of knowledge. But if libraries are to continue to flourish, they must do more than rest on their laurels. They must make changes. Library managers face an enormous challenge in trying to organize libraries to meet the demands of tomorrow. They must develop a different mindset, one that welcomes change, and welcoming change is far easier to accept intellectually than in actual practice. Librarians will need to persist in experimenting with different types of organizational structures and with modifications in the organizational culture. If librarians are not willing to make these changes, not willing to deconstruct their own organizations, someone else will do it to them.[42]

CONCLUSION

This chapter has provided an overview of organizations and their cultures. Chapter 8 will cover the methods that organizations use to specialize and coordinate. Chapter 9 will look at the prevailing organizational designs of libraries and the ways that some libraries are beginning to redesign their organizational structures.

NOTES

1. Henry Mintzberg, *The Rise and Fall of Strategic Planning: Reconceiving Roles for Planning, Plans and Planners* (New York: Free Press, 1994), 399.

2. Rosabeth Moss Kanter, Barry A. Stein, and Todd D. Jick, *The Challenge of Organizational Change: How Companies Experience It and Leaders Guide It* (New York: Free Press, 1992), 3.

3. Howard E. Aldrich, *Organizations Evolving* (London: Sage, 1999), 2–3.

4. Peter Drucker, *Post-Capitalist Society* (New York: HarperBusiness, 1993), 48.

5. John Naisbitt, *Megatrends: Ten New Directions Transforming Our Lives* (New York: Warner Books, 1982), 14.

6. John H. Jackson and Cyril P. Morgan, *Organization Theory: A Macro Perspective for Management* (Englewood Cliffs, NJ: Prentice-Hall, 1978), 3.

7. Ibid., 10.

8. See American Library Association, "ALA Fact Sheets" (n.d.), http://www.ala.org/ala/alalibrary/libraryfactsheet/Default1446.htm.

9. Aldrich, *Organizations Evolving*, 8.

10. Joanne D. Eustis and Donald J. Kenney, *Library Reorganization and Restructuring* (SPEC Kit 215) (Washington, DC: Association of Research Libraries, 1996).

11. Joe A. Hewitt, "What's Wrong with Library Organization? Factors Leading to Restructuring in Research Libraries," *North Carolina Libraries* 55 (Spring 1997): 3.

12. Larry E. Greiner, "Revolution as Organizations Grow," *Harvard Business Review* 76 (May–June 1998): 58.

13. Robert Johansen and Rob Swigart, *Upsizing the Individual in the Downsized Organization: Managing in the Wake of Reengineering, Globalization, and Overwhelming Technological Change* (Reading, MA: Addison-Wesley, 1994), 13.

14. Thomas N. Davenport, *Process Innovation: Reengineering Work through Information Technology* (Boston: Harvard Business School Press, 1993).

15. Michael Hammer and James Champy, *Reengineering the Corporation: A Manifesto for Business Revolution* (New York: HarperBusiness, 1993).

16. Ibid., 46.

17. E. Munford and R. Hendricks, "Business Re-engineering RIP," *People Management* 2 (1996): 22–26.

18. Thomas Davenport, "The Fad that Forgot People," *Fast Company,* no. 1 (October 1995), http://www.fastcompany.com/magazine/01/reengin.html.

19. For example, see B. J. Shapiro and K. L. Long, "Just Say Yes: Reengineering Library User Services for the 21st Century," *Journal of Academic Librarianship* 20 (1994): 285–90; T. W. Shaughnessy, "Lessons from Restructuring the Library," *Journal of Academic Librarianship* 22 (1996): 251–56; N. R. Smith, "Turning the Library Inside Out: Radical Restructuring to Meet the Challenge of Sudden Change," in *Computers in Libraries International 96* (Oxford: Learned Information Europe, 1996), 71–82; Nurit Roitberg, "Library Leadership and Re-engineering—An Israeli Experience," *IATUL Proceedings, New Series* 8 (1999); Sandra Yee, Rita Bullard, and Morell Boone, "We Built It and They Came: Client Centered Services in a New Building," *Proceedings of the ACRL Tenth National Conference* (Chicago: American Library Association, 2001), 261–64.

20. Miles H. Overholt, "Flexible Organizations: Using Organizational Design as a Competitive Advantage," *Human Resources Planning* 20 (1997): 23.

21. Jay Lorsch, "Organizational Design," in *Managing People and Organizations,* ed. John J. Gabarro (Boston: Harvard Business School Publications, 1992), 313–14.

22. Jim Collins, *Good to Great: Why Some Companies Make the Leap and Others Don't* (New York: HarperBusiness, 2001), 121.

23. Jay R. Galbraith, *Organization Design* (Reading, MA: Addison-Wesley, 1977), 13.

24. For more information about one-person libraries, see Guy St. Clair, *Managing the New One-Person Library* (New York: Bowker Saur, 1992).

25. Lowell A. Martin, *Organizational Structure of Libraries* (Lanham, MD: Scarecrow Press, 1996), 12–13.

26. Robert Fritz, *Corporate Tides: The Inescapable Laws of Organizational Structure* (San Francisco: Berrett-Koehler, 1996), 14.

27. Harold Steiglitz, "What's Not on the Organization Chart," *The Conference Board RECORD* 1 (November 1964): 7–10.

28. Ibid.

29. John P. Kotter and James L. Heskett, *Corporate Culture and Performance* (New York: Free Press, 1992), 15–18.

30. Edgar H. Schein, "Organizational Culture," *American Psychologist* 45 (February 1990): 111.

31. Edgar Schein, *Organizational Culture and Leadership* (San Francisco: Jossey-Bass, 1992), 211.

32. Andrew Pettigrew, "The Creation of Organizational Cultures" (paper presented to the Joint EIASM-Dansk Management Center Research Seminar, Copenhagen, Denmark, May 18, 1976), 11; quoted in Thomas J. Peters and Robert H. Waterman Jr., *In Search of Excellence: Lessons from America's Best-Run Companies* (New York: Harper & Row, 1982), 104.

33. Schein, *Organizational Culture and Leadership,* 25–26.

34. Ibid., 377.

35. Ibid., 228–53.

36. Ilene Rockman, "Joint Use Facilities: The View from San Jose," *Library Administration and Management* 13 (1999): 64–67.

37. Barbara B. Moran, "Continuity and Change: The Integration of Oxford University's Libraries," *Library Quarterly* 75, no. 3 (2005): 262–94.

38. A. Taylor, "Why Toyota Keeps Getting Better and Better and Better," *Fortune* 122 (November 19, 1990): 66–79.

39. John P. Kotter and James L. Heskett, *Corporate Culture and Performance* (New York: Free Press, 1992).

40. Philip Evans and Thomas S. Wurster, *Blown to Bits: How the New Economics of Information Transforms Strategy* (Boston: Harvard Business School Press, 2000), 65.

41. Ibid., 66.

42. Ibid.

Chapter 8

Structuring the Organization— Specialization and Coordination

Overview

All organizations have to be structured or organized. The tasks that are performed must be divided among the workers, and the work being done must be coordinated so that various tasks are performed at the right times. As organizations grow in size and complexity, the need to structure becomes more critical. An increased emphasis on structure is reflected in the history of all organizations that grew in size as they became successful. Take, for example, the U.S. Library of Congress, the largest library in the world, which was established in 1800 with an appropriation of $5,000. The library's first collection consisted of 740 books and three maps, and its first librarian also served as clerk of the House of Representatives.[1] A library of that size with a part-time librarian did not need to pay much attention to structure and organization. Today's Library of Congress is a much different organization. It has a collection of more than 130 million items on 530 miles of bookshelves. The library has more than 4,000 employees and adds more than 10,000 items to its collection each day.[2] The Library of Congress now has a very elaborate organizational structure.[3] Obviously, it is essential that an organization of this size and complexity have a structure that not only allows its workers to specialize in the type of work each does but also permits its managers to coordinate this work.

This chapter will cover some key concepts in the managerial function of organization, including the ways in which an organization is subdivided (specialization), as well as the ways in which it is brought back together (coordination). Other key elements of organization, such as span of control, delegation, power and authority, unity of command, and line and staff, also will be discussed. The chapter also will cover the advantages and disadvantages of centralized organizational structures.

The larger the organization, the more complex its structure will be. As was discussed in chapter 7, small organizations can have very simple organizational structures. When there are only one or two or three people working in a library or any other type of organization, there is not a great need for either specialization—that is, breaking down the tasks to be done into discrete parts for various individuals to accomplish—or coordination—that is, being sure that all the tasks are being accomplished in the appropriate sequence. As organizations grow larger, however, attention has to be paid to both specialization and coordination if the goals of the organizations are to be accomplished. Structuring involves these two fundamental requirements: the division of labor into distinct tasks and the achievement of coordination among these tasks.

SPECIALIZATION

An organization divides all the tasks to be done (or specializes) in two ways. The first is by establishing horizontal specializations, which results in the creation of various departments, each performing specific tasks. The second is by establishing vertical differentiation, or a hierarchy of positions. Vertical differentiation involves structuring authority, power, accountability, and responsibility in an organization.

An organization is structured horizontally by identifying and grouping similar or related activities or tasks into subunits or departments. Grouping tasks creates blocks of activity-oriented tasks and people-oriented tasks. Blocks of activity-oriented tasks, such as cataloging books or acquiring materials, put primary emphasis on process, procedure, or technique. These tasks can vary from the most routine, requiring little skill, to the very complex, requiring extensive ability and knowledge as well as conformity with a process, procedure, or technique. Examples of routine activity-oriented tasks in a library are shelving books or copy cataloging; complex activity-oriented tasks might include the selection of books in accordance with a book-selection policy, creating metadata or the development of an Internet user instruction module. People-oriented tasks, which place primary emphasis on human relationships, require the ability to communicate, to guide or direct, and to motivate other individuals. People-oriented tasks include the relationship of the reference librarian to the library user, the attitude of the supervisor to subordinates, or the ability of a public library director to work with higher officials in government.

Once a manager has identified blocks of tasks that need to be accomplished, then those tasks must be grouped in a logical order. The manager must answer the questions, "What blocks should be put together or kept apart?" and "What is the proper relationship of these blocks?" Some of the blocks will be of primary importance; others will be secondary.

According to Peter Drucker, it is more important to identify the key tasks within the organization than to identify all the tasks. He proposes that someone designing an organization start with the following questions: In what areas is excellence required to obtain the organization's objectives? In what areas would lack of performance endanger the results, if not the survival, of the enterprise? He recommends, in short, that organizers ask why the organization exists and build on that basis.[4] These are questions that all library managers need to ask and have answered before structuring the organization.

What Do You Think?

Like powerful elephants, many companies are bound by earlier conditioned constraints. "We've always done it this way" is as limiting to any organization's progress as the unattached chain around the elephant's foot. Success ties you to the past. The very factors that produced today's success often create tomorrow's failures.

James Belasco compares organizations to elephants that are constrained by chains. Do you agree that the factors that produce success today may creature failure tomorrow? Can you think of any examples from libraries that illustrate his point? What can organizations do to avoid this?

James A. Belasco, *Teaching the Elephant to Dance: Empowering Change in Your Organization* (New York: Crown, 1990), 2.

In a similar vein, other management experts urge organizations to ask, "What business are you in?" They point to the plight of the U.S. railroad companies, which almost became extinct because they thought they were in the business of trains, not realizing that they were actually in the transportation business.[5] Pitney Bowes provides an example of a corporation that was able to reenvision itself. After Pitney Bowes lost its monopoly on postage meters, it went through a troubled financial period until it was able to move beyond viewing itself as a postage meter company and realize that it could be highly successful if it thought in a broader fashion and concentrated on providing so-called messaging to organizations.[6] In a similar fashion, libraries and information centers have had to reexamine their purpose during the past few decades. Libraries have refocused and now consider themselves to be in the information business (and not just in the book or printed material business). They also realize that they have competitors in the private sector that did not exist before. Modern libraries have had to redefine themselves, and this redefinition has necessitated a change in their structure to reflect their new mission.

PARTS OF AN ORGANIZATION

Organizational design can be seen as the putting together of a fairly standardized set of building blocks; it is a process similar to building a house. Although houses may have many types of design, ranging from traditional colonial to modern contemporary, and although their sizes may range from small cottages to large mansions, almost all houses share common characteristics. They will all have a foundation, a roof, certain essential rooms, and ways to provide such services as electricity and water. Organizations are designed in a similar fashion. Although the variety and number of blocks will vary with the size and the type of institution, with pieces that can be put together in different ways, all organizational structures have a great deal in common. Managers who are attempting to organize (or reorganize) are, metaphorically speaking, the architects of the structure—they are shaping the space to meet the needs and aspirations of the organization.[7] So, most organizations contain the same basic parts. Henry Mintzberg has categorized the five basic elements of organizations as:

- A strategic apex, which consists of the organization's top management and is responsible for the overall functioning of the organization.
- The middle line, which is composed of the midlevel managers who coordinate the activities of the various units. They serve to link the operating core to the strategic apex. One of the major activities of the midlevel managers is to transmit information about the operating core to the top-level managers.
- The operating core, which is made up of the workers who carry out the mission of the organization.
- The technostructure, which consists of those units that provide the organization with technical expertise.
- The support staff, which is composed of the workers who provide the organization with expertise in areas such as labor relations or personnel.[8]

These components are illustrated in figure 8.1.

In a large library, the director and the assistant and associate directors form the strategic apex. The heads of the various departments make up the middle line. Employees in units such as library systems and original cataloging make up the technostructure, whereas employees in units such as personnel and public relations constitute the support staff. The largest group, the operating core, consists of the employees who work in areas such as circulation and reference. They are the ones carrying out the organization's mission of linking people to information. Although some small organizations do not contain all of Mintzberg's categories, most larger ones do, although the size of each component in relation to the others varies according to factors such as type and complexity of endeavor, age of the organization, and its size.

METHODS OF DEPARTMENTALIZATION

In the past, organizations have traditionally used five methods to establish departments: function, territory, product, customer, and process. In addition, libraries have developed two other methods to establish departments: subject and form of resources. In both businesses and libraries, these methods are

Figure 8.1—Mintzberg's Model of the Organization

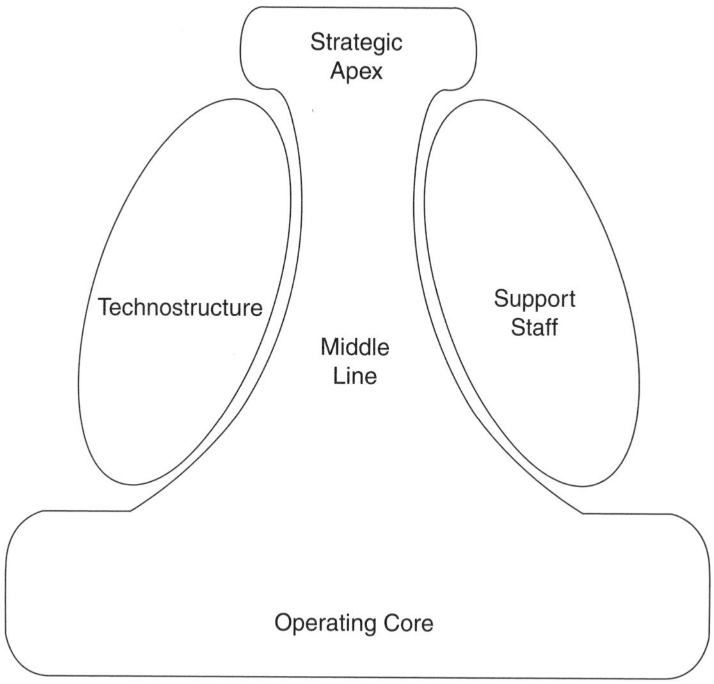

Source: From Henry Mintzberg, *Structure in Fives: Designing Effective Organizations* (Englewood Cliffs, NJ: Prentice-Hall, 1983). Reprinted by permission of Prentice-Hall, Inc., Englewood Cliffs, NJ.

used in varying combinations to produce a hybrid structure. Although these methods of departmentalization are being affected in many organizations by new approaches to organizational structure, they still serve as the primary approach for establishing subdivisions within an organization. Each method of departmentalization is discussed in the following sections.

Function

In business, the most common organizational design is the functional structure. For instance, a company that makes furniture would have departments dealing with production, marketing, sales, and accounting. In libraries, too, this method of departmentalization is extensively used. Functions such as circulation, reference, acquisition, cataloging, and management historically have been the bases of library organization.

Functional design has a number of advantages. It groups together specialists with similar backgrounds and interests, and it allows specialization within that function. For instance, a library might have both a Slavic and an East Asian cataloger. Functional design also ensures that higher organizational levels will be aware of the contributions and the needs of the various subunits of the organization. There are, however, three major disadvantages of functional division. First, it may lead to competition among various departments—for example, competition for resources or disagreements over the most appropriate procedures. In some libraries, the reference and cataloging departments may disagree about the best classification or subject headings for a particular book. Second, workers in functional settings may lose sight of the end product of the whole organization, especially when they are distanced from the ultimate users of the product. Finally, this organizational design is not as effective if the organization has units in different locations. The functional design appears to work best in organizations that do not need close collaboration among the functional departments.

Territory

In industries that operate over a wide geographic area, all activities in a designated geographic territory are commonly grouped together and placed under the direction of a manager. For instance, multinational organizations have divisions to deal with specific parts of the world, such as North America, South America, or Europe. This structure permits the organization to adapt to local situations, as far as the local labor market, local needs and problems, and local production issues are concerned. Libraries also use this principle of territory or area in their organizational structure. For instance, public libraries always have been very concerned about the location of their central facility and the areas to be served by their branch libraries, bookmobiles, and storefront libraries. Academic libraries that have branches, such as a science library, an architecture library, or an education library, are concerned that these facilities be in the area where the appropriate clientele will be located. School systems usually have individual schools and their media centers located throughout their service area, and students typically will go to the school geographically nearest to their homes.

The primary advantage of this type of organization for libraries is that the individual units can be located close to their users, can get to know these users' needs better, and, it is hoped, can thus serve them better. Territorial organization also provides a training ground for managers because it gives a manager a chance to work relatively autonomously in managing a smaller unit that is geographically separated from the central organization. It is not uncommon for a librarian who has directed a branch library to be promoted to head of the library system.

The biggest disadvantage of territorial organization is that it increases the difficulty of coordination and communication within the organization. In addition, rivalries often crop up between the different locations. Many large public libraries hard hit by funding cuts have had to make difficult decisions about whether it is better to maintain the quality of the central collection or to maintain service to various neighborhoods through the branches. Finally, territorial organization often leads to duplication, for example, in resources like standard reference books.

In librarianship, there always has been disagreement about the degree of geographic centralization that should prevail. Typically, library administrators have favored a more centralized organization because of the tight control and budgetary advantages associated with that design. On the other hand, users typically prefer a more decentralized system because of its convenience and more personalized service (in spite of the special problems of users working in interdisciplinary areas).

The degree of decentralization varies according to country and type of library. For example, academic libraries in the United States traditionally have been more centralized than those in Europe, especially those within the older European universities where individual units such as institutes or colleges often provided library service before it was provided centrally. Some of the arguments against decentralization have been weakened by the increasing importance of information technology and the advent of new methods of document storage and retrieval that lessen some of the costs involved in the duplication of material in decentralized locations.[9] The advent of online catalogs and online access to reference and bibliographic material and full-text journals and books has made decentralization less expensive.

Product

Organization by product is particularly useful in diversified industries in which the production of one product is sufficiently large to employ fully specialized facilities. In such cases, departmentalization by product allows a product manager complete control over all functions related to that product, including profit responsibility. For instance, Time Warner is organized into divisions that are based on product lines: AOL; Time, Inc.; Turner Broadcasting; Warner Brothers; and so forth.[10] Product organization is used infrequently in libraries. Although the product of a print shop (a bibliography or a brochure) or a product of the systems office (such as the library's Web site) might be considered a product, in almost every case this product is a minor part of the total operation of the library.

Customer

Businesses, especially retail stores, use this structure to appeal to the needs and desires of clearly defined customer groups. Department stores have children's, preteen, men's, misses, and petite departments to cater to specific customer groups. Libraries often use the same structure. Since the late 1800s, special children's sections have been one of the most used sections in public libraries. Public libraries also have aimed their services at other customer groups, such as young adults or business users. Academic libraries have used this structure when establishing undergraduate libraries.

The advantage of this type of departmentalization is that it allows libraries to meet the special and widely varying needs of users. The disadvantages are similar to those involved in territorial departmentalization. Coordination among departments is difficult, and competition among various departments, especially for resources, may arise. In addition, when budgets get tight, services to some groups may have to be eliminated. For example, some public libraries have eliminated their young-adult departments. In some universities, previously existing undergraduate libraries have been closed because it was felt that undergraduates could be better served by the main library.

Process

In the process method of departmentalization, workers are grouped together based on process or activity. A process is "a set or collection of activities that take more than one kind of input and that, taken together, produce a result of value to the customer."[11] So a process approach to departmentalization focuses upon how work is done within an organization. Processes usually have two characteristics. The first is that the process has customers, either internal or external. Second, processes usually cross organizational boundaries; they occur across organizational subdivisions. Consider the common library process of getting a specific book on the shelf. That process could involve several departments, including collection development, acquisitions, cataloging, and so forth.

So a process is not a function or a department but a series of activities that result in an output that is a value to a customer. An organizational output that is of value only to the organization itself is one that likely should be either improved or eliminated.[12] Looking at functions instead of processes often leads to fragmentation and low customer satisfaction because no single department owns the entire process. Because customers are not interested in the steps in the process but in the output, designing libraries around process should lead to greater customer satisfaction.[13]

Focusing on improving processes usually provides a competitive advantage for an organization. Michael Porter and Victor Millar suggest the use of the so-called value chain as a means of analyzing processes.[14] The value chain is a representation of the activities carried out in an organization. An organization may gain competitive advantage by managing its value chain more efficiently or effectively than its competitors. Each step in the value chain has both a physical and an information processing element. Competitive advantage is often gained by increasing the information content of parts of the value chain.

Maxine Brodie and Neil McLean have described the components involved in restructuring the provision of information resources within a library and also have provided an outline of the organizational impact of adopting a process framework. These can be seen in table 8.1.

Business process reengineering, discussed in chapter 7, is built around the restructuring of process. Total quality management also focuses upon processes. For organizations that have departmentalized using functional or other traditional approaches, changing and focusing upon process is difficult. Although a few libraries have reorganized using the process approach,[15] to date process is not a widely used method of departmentalization in libraries. However, team and matrix organization, discussed in chapter 9, usually do provide more attention to process than more traditional structures.

In addition to these five conventional ways of establishing departments, libraries have used two additional methods: subject and form of resources departments.

TABLE 8.1 The Results of Adopting a Process Framework in Restructuring a Library

Steps in the process will be performed in natural order.
Work will be done where it makes most sense.
Work units will change from functional departments to process teams.
Jobs will change from simple to multidimensional.
Processes will not be standardized but will have different versions for different clients.
Staff will become empowered to make decisions.
Performance appraisal measures will shift from activities to results.
Values will cease to be protective and become productive.
Managers will become coaches, not supervisors.
Organizational structure will become flatter.
Top managers will become leaders, not scorekeepers.
A hybrid centralized/decentralized structure may be used based on shared information systems.
A "one-stop shopping" case manager with easy access to all information systems will serve as a single point of contact for users.
Checks and controls will be introduced.

Source: Maxine Brodie and Neil McLean, "Process Reengineering in Academic Libraries: Shifting to Client-Centered Resource Provision," *CAUSE/EFFECT* 18 (Summer 1995): 45.

Subject

Large public and academic libraries use this method extensively. It provides for more in-depth reference service and reader guidance, and it requires a high degree of subject knowledge on the part of the staff. There is no one pattern of subjects included in a subject department and no set number of subject departments. In academic libraries, subject departments are usually broad in scope and include all related subjects in areas like humanities, social sciences, or science. In large public libraries, subject departments such as business, fine arts, and local history are common.

There are definite advantages of subject departments. All materials dealing with one topic are gathered together, which is convenient for users. The librarians working with this material usually have special training in the subject matter. The disadvantages include the increased cost of the necessary duplication of material and the hiring of specialized personnel. Each department must be staffed, even when usage is low. One reference librarian might be sufficient to handle all reference inquiries at a central desk when demand is low, but if there are four subject-area reference desks, four librarians are required, even if there are few inquiries. In addition, although subject divisions are convenient for users working strictly within a subject field, users pursuing interdisciplinary topics must go to many departments to find the materials they need.

Form of Resources

Many libraries have used format, or the form in which resources are issued, as a basis for organization, especially as the quantity of nonbook and nonprint material has increased. It is not unusual to find separate map, microform, audiovisual, periodicals, online services, electronic resources, or documents departments in a library. Many of these specialized forms present special problems in acquisition, storage, handling, or organization. Often, librarians working in format-based departments handle all functions relating to that department's resources, including functions that are normally performed centrally. For instance, a government documents department may order, process, provide reference service for, and circulate all government documents. Format-based departments are most useful for patrons seeking one type of resource, such as audiovisual materials. More commonly, however, users seek information on specific topics, and they may easily miss relevant materials that are housed in various format-based departments. As digital material replaces printed material in libraries, departments based on form of resources will need to be restructured.

Summary

As can be seen in figure 8.2, libraries use a number of ways to establish their departments. Only in the most specialized library would a single organizational method be used. A large public library, for example, generally has a circulation department (function), subject department (combining several functions), branch libraries (territory), children's services (customer), business services (customer), government documents collections (form), and several others.

There is no one right way to establish departments in an organization. There are advantages and disadvantages associated with each method, and a manager interested in organization should be aware of both of them. Also, as stated previously, no organizational structure, no matter how good, is intended to last forever. Institutions change, and organizational structures must change to reflect new situations. Managers need to look first at the tasks that need to be accomplished, the people involved in accomplishing them, the users being served, and the pertinent external and environmental factors, and then they need to design a suitable departmental organization. Often, employees feel threatened by any change in organizational structure; managers should communicate the reasons for changes and provide reassurance to employees who need it.

THE HIERARCHY

Within the structure of an organization, specialization exists in two dimensions. We have just discussed the specialization found on the horizontal

Figure 8.2—Types of Departments Found in Libraries

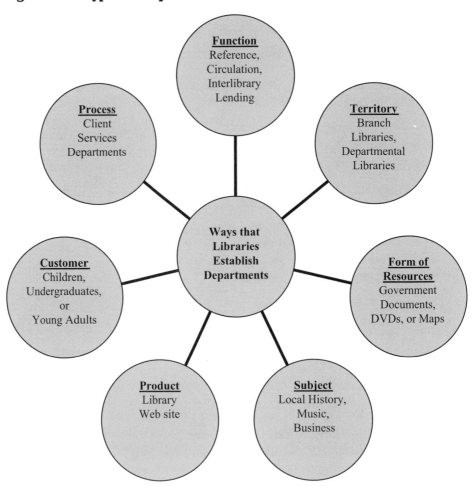

axis—the grouping of tasks into departments and subunits. The vertical axis contains a different type of specialization—the structuring of authority. In organizations, authority is the degree of discretion conferred on subordinates that makes it possible for them to use their judgment in making decisions and issuing instructions. A manager is assigned to each department or subunit within an organization. Each manager has a measure of responsibility and authority, delegated by his or her superior. The need for such delegation is obvious; if managers are responsible for the accomplishment of designated tasks and the supervision of employees, they must have the authority to guarantee efficient performance. The vertical hierarchy provides a channel through which authority flows from top management down to the managers of subunits. It also provides a means to coordinate the efforts of many individuals performing a variety of tasks. The concept of a vertical hierarchy is central to the classic theories of organizing. Now that so many organizations are using teams, encouraging horizontal communication, and instituting multiple reporting patterns, the vertical hierarchy may be less critical than it used to be.

Figure 8.3—Vertical and Horizontal Specialization within Libraries

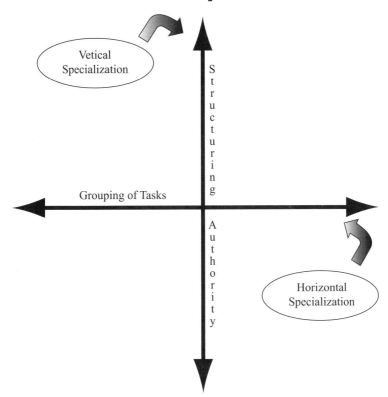

Nonetheless, it is important to understand this concept, even if many organizations are deemphasizing its importance.

THE SCALAR PRINCIPLE

As departments and subdepartments are assigned various tasks, primary and secondary units of the organization emerge. Primary organizational departments have numerous tasks and broad responsibilities; secondary or subdepartments have specific tasks and limited responsibility. For example, a copy catalog unit would be a subdepartment of a cataloging department. A subdepartment's tasks contribute to the fulfillment of the responsibilities of the primary department. The manager of the primary department supervises the manager of the subdepartment to assure compliance with the needs of the primary department. Authority flows from the primary to the secondary manager.

The scalar principle requires that there be final, ultimate authority and that lines of authority descend to every subordinate position. The clearer the line of authority, the more effective the organizational performance and communication. Henri Fayol described the scalar principle as "the chain of supervisors ranging from the ultimate authority to the lowest ranks. The line of authority is the route followed—via every link in the chain—by all communications which start from or go to the ultimate authority."[16]

A clear understanding of the scalar principle by each subordinate is necessary for an organization to function effectively. Subordinates must know to whom and for what they are responsible, and the parameters of each manager's authority should be clear.

This vertical hierarchy develops as a result of the ranking of organizational units. A scalar hierarchy may be illustrated as a pyramid, with the ultimate authority at the apex and authority fanning out as it flows downward. The positions at the top of the pyramid deal with broader tasks and responsibilities, those at the bottom with more specific tasks and responsibilities. Even though the vertical hierarchy may remain stable over a period of time, tasks and responsibilities may shift as managers and supervisors delegate.

POWER AND AUTHORITY

The words *power* and *authority* are sometimes used interchangeably, but these terms are not synonymous. A person may possess power but still not necessarily possess authority. Authority is the legitimate right of a supervisor to direct subordinates to take action within the scope of the supervisor's position. Authority flows down the vertical chain of command within the organization. The authority is vested in the organizational position, not in the person holding that position, and it is accepted by subordinates. Power is the potential ability to influence the behavior of others. John French and Bertram Raven have identified five types of power:

- **Legitimate power** is the power that comes from a formal management position and is based upon authority recognized in accordance with position in an organizational structure.
- **Reward power** stems from the power to provide rewards for people.

Figure 8.4—The Flow of Authority within a Traditional Organization

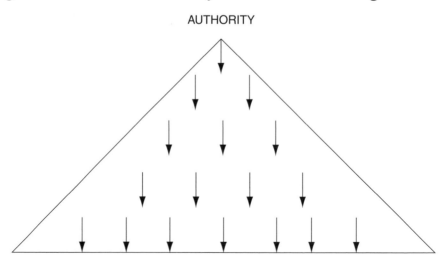

AUTHORITY

- **Coercive power** is power that derives from the potential to inflict punishment.
- **Expert power** is the power derived from expertise or knowledge. Often people whose positions are not high in the chain of command have a great deal of power because of their knowledge.
- **Referent power** refers to power that derives from the respect and esteem accorded to an individual by virtue of personal attributes that command respect and admiration.[17]

Authority is the ability to influence that is associated with a person's position within the organization. Power can be derived from sources other than a formal position. In many organizations there are people who have more power than might be expected as a result of their position.

 Try This!

The Kingsbury Group is a medium-size information consulting company with about fifty employees. Bob Smith has just been appointed the new chief executive officer of the group. He will be in charge of all operations of the company. Also working at Kingsbury is Mark Simonds, who is in charge of all the firm's information technology (IT) and computers. He has a keen sense of what is needed to keep the company's complicated IT system running well. Whenever there is an IT problem, the employees always turn to Mark for a solution. Mary Malone is Bob Smith's administrative assistant. She has worked at Kingbury for more than twenty years and makes the decisions about how vacation days are allocated and how travel expenses are reimbursed. Name the type of power that each of these individuals possesses and give one example of how he/she might demonstrate that power for the benefit of the organization.

DELEGATION

A supervisor with authority may delegate some of that authority downward. Delegation is the transfer of authority within prescribed limits. In an effective organization, the person in the position holding ultimate authority delegates authority to subordinate managers. The delegation of authority to subordinates does not relieve the manager from ultimate responsibility; a manager is responsible for the actions of subordinates, even if authority has been delegated. A manager can delegate to subordinates almost anything for which that manager has responsibility. Of course, managers cannot delegate all authority without abdicating their managerial role. This is rarely a problem, however. Most managers delegate too little; some clutch tenaciously to authority and dislike delegating anything.

Many managers find it difficult to delegate adequate authority because they fear that a subordinate might make a mistake or perform poorly. In addition, some managers feel that they are not doing their jobs unless they make all of the decisions, even the smaller ones that subordinates could easily make. These managers spend a disproportionate amount of time on minor decisions, not realizing that, by doing so, they are taking time and attention away from the more important decisions that only they can make.

Effective managers have learned to delegate. They are willing to let go of some of their authority and to trust their subordinates. They know that these subordinates sometimes make mistakes, and they are still willing to take the risk because they realize that delegation is necessary in any organization. In addition, effective managers always remember that responsibility cannot be delegated without authority. A subordinate given responsibility without authority probably will be unable to function effectively.

 ## What Do You Think?

Delegation without authority is empty. Before delegating think carefully whether you are willing to permit work to be done without your direct oversight or review. Too much review, especially of professionals, breeds apathy, dependency, and passive resistance, and destroys motivation.

Do you like to be micromanaged? Why do you think that so many supervisors find it hard to delegate? What can be done to encourage managers to feel more confident in delegating work to their subordinates?

Allen B. Veaner, *Academic Librarianship in a Transformational Age* (Boston: Hall, 1990), 129.

CENTRALIZATION AND DECENTRALIZATION

In describing the departmentalization process in organizations, the issues of centralization and decentralization were discussed. These same issues, although in a different form, are also relevant to a discussion of hierarchy. In the context of the vertical hierarchy of an organization, centralization and decentralization do not refer to geographic dispersal but to the dispersal of authority for decision making. In highly centralized organizations, authority is concentrated in the highest echelons of the hierarchy; almost all decisions are made by those at the top. For example, in the traditional organization, authority was highly centralized in the hands of top managers. These types of organizations have been termed *command and control* organizations because they were structured to centralize both the command and control of the organization in the ranks of top management. It was assumed that whoever was in command also would tightly control the organization.

In contrast, in decentralized organizations the authority to make decisions is pushed down the organizational structure. As institutions become larger and more complex, there is a tendency toward decentralization. Centralization and decentralization can best be envisioned as two ends of a continuum.

Organizations marked by a high degree of retention of power, duties, and authority by top management are centralized; those marked by a high degree of delegation of duties, power, and authority at lower levels of the organization are decentralized. Decentralized organizations are often described as "participative" because they allow for greater employee participation in decision making. As mentioned earlier, many of today's organizations are moving away from a command and control configuration toward a more decentralized structure. The advantages of decentralization are several. First, the decisions to be made in many organizations are so numerous that if they are centralized, the manager may be overwhelmed by the amount of decision making that needs to be done. The organization may therefore become paralyzed by the inaction of these managers. Today, more libraries allow decisions to be made at the levels in the organization at which the most information about these decisions exists.

This greater access to inclusion in the decision-making process is contrary to practice in the typical bureaucracy, in which decisions and the information needed to make them are pushed up the hierarchy to a top manager. Most modern organizations attempt to bring together people who have the necessary information and let them make the decisions that will affect them. The effect is to create groups that can focus on problems, projects, or products better than the traditional hierarchy can. These overlays allow the organization to cut across departmental lines and to decentralize decision making. They make the organization more flexible.

A second advantage of decentralization is that it permits organizations to be more responsive to local conditions. Because the transmission of information for decision making takes time, a decentralized organization is able to make more timely decisions. A final advantage of decentralization is that it serves as a stimulus to motivation. An organization that wishes to attract and retain creative and intelligent people is better able to do so when it permits them considerable power to make decisions.

 What Do You Think?

James Neal, the vice president for Information Services and university librarian at Columbia University was quoted recently as saying:

> We invest enormously in the people who work in a library organization both in terms of the responsibilities we assign them and in their growth and development; yet we don't always provide them with the authority to make decisions and carry out their assignments effectively.

Has there ever been a time when you have felt as though you lacked the authority to carry out something you had been assigned to accomplish? What is the result of failing to provide appropriate authority to accomplish a task?

Gregg Sapp, "James Neal on the Challenges of Leadership: An LA&M Exclusive Interview," *Library Administration and Management* 19, no. 2 (Spring 2005): 64.

Both centralization and decentralization offer advantages.[18] The major advantage of centralization is that it offers the tightest means of coordinating decision making in the organization. Managers have a great deal of control over the decisions that are made because only a small number of managers are permitted to make them.

As mentioned previously, most large organizations have cut back the number of middle managers, resulting in a flatter, more decentralized structure. Much of this flattening has been permitted by the introduction of information technology. Technology has the potential to increase top-down control and to demotivate and deskill jobs, but, if it is used to provide employees with information needed for decisions, it can empower them. Information technology makes more reliable information available much more quickly than it ever was before to both top managers and those who work at lower layers in an organization.[19] Midlevel managers have been replaced with information technology.

Now top managers can receive up-to-the-minute information on operations via their computers—information that once was collected and interpreted by middle managers. Information technology also permits the easy sharing of information both up and down the organizational ladder. In organizations such as libraries and information centers, where there are a number of highly educated and skilled workers, it is likely that technology will play a key role in permitting further decentralization of decision making.

UNITY OF COMMAND

A classic management principle that provides clarity in the vertical hierarchy is that of unity of command. This principle states that organizational structure should guarantee that each employee has one supervisor who makes assignments and assesses the success of the employee in completing those assignments. In many organizations, however, employees have several supervisors. In libraries, this is often true; for example, in many large libraries, subject bibliographers are responsible to both the head of collection development and the head of technical services. An employee with more than one supervisor is placed in the awkward position of determining whose work to do first, how to do the work, and which instructions to follow. Unity of command protects the employee from such undesirable situations. As modern organizations have become more complex, theorists have realized that employees are often subject to multiple influences. When faced with these conflicting pressures, the employee should have a single supervisor who can resolve the conflict. In addition, job descriptions should clearly spell out the worker's duties and the amount of time to be spent on each.

SPAN OF CONTROL

Just as employees should not be accountable to too many supervisors, managers should not be responsible for too many employees. Span of control (sometimes called span of management) refers to the number of people or activities a manager can effectively manage. When a manager supervises a large number of employees, that manager is said to have a wide span of control, whereas one who supervises a small number is said to have a narrow span of control. When the number of subordinates exceeds the span of control of a single manager, something must be done to reduce their number. Managers usually solve the problem by grouping some of the jobs and by placing an individual in charge of each of the groups. The manager then deals primarily with the individuals in charge of the groups rather than with all of the subordinates. Obviously, span of control is closely related to how many levels exist in an organization's hierarchy. When there is a broad span of control, there are fewer managers, and the organization tends to be flatter.

 ## What Do You Think?

The Manning University Library is growing at a rapid rate. A few years ago, the library employed only 20 people. Now, it has 150 employees. The heads of more than twenty diverse departments report directly to Wilma Smith, the library director. Lately, Ms. Smith has felt that that all she does is supervise and respond to problems. There is never time to concentrate on her other managerial responsibilities, and she feels as though she is getting further and further behind in planning and budgeting. Using management terminology, what problem does she face and what do you recommend that she might do to improve the organizational effectiveness of the library?

There is no set number of subordinates that constitutes the ideal span of control. Recent research shows that the size of an effective span of control varies widely, depending on the type of organization and the type of activity being supervised. Managers have moved away from trying to specify the so-called ideal span of control to considering which is most appropriate to a specific situation.

One of the criteria used to determine the number of people a manager can adequately manage is the number and variety of tasks being managed. If the activities of the units assigned to one manager are similar, the span of control can be increased. If the activities vary extensively and require thorough knowledge, the span of control should be decreased. One must consider what knowledge the manager must have to do an adequate job; the broader and more detailed the required knowledge, the fewer units that should be assigned to him or her.

Another criterion used to determine span of control is the amount of time available to be spent on communication. Time is a critical element in many enterprises. A manager who has many subordinates must reduce the time spent supervising each. Thus, it will be necessary for a manager with a large number of subordinates to spend more time on the initial training of each new supervisor, to give assignments in broad terms of goals or objectives to be achieved, and to delegate authority so that the supervisors may manage their personnel. If the span of control is wide and the manager fails to function as described, time will be consumed by frequent conferences, daily meetings, and repetitive instruction.

When many organizational units report to one manager, a flat or horizontal organization is created, and a wide span of control prevails. There are few levels of operation in a flat organization. Figure 8.5 shows only two levels of operation: the director and the manager of each unit to which specific activities have been assigned. But the scope of knowledge required of the director is extensive indeed. When a manager has many subordinates, supervision of each unit is likely to be minimal. In organizations with narrow spans of management, a tall, vertical organization is created. Figure 8.6 shows a vertical organization with four levels of operation. Each supervisor's span of control is narrow—in this organization, the director has direct supervision over only two people—a great reduction from the 12 positions shown in figure 8.5.

LINE AND STAFF POSITIONS

An important but sometimes confusing authority relationship in any organization is that of line and staff positions. The concept of line and staff has been used for many years, but it still causes friction and difficulty. Line positions are those that are responsible and accountable for the organization's primary objectives. Staff positions are those that provide advice, support, and service to the line positions. Line and staff also are distinguished by their decision-making authority. Because line positions are responsible for accomplishing the organization's primary objectives, they have the final authority to make decisions. Staff positions, on the other hand, provide suggestions and advice for the line positions but cannot, theoretically, make decisions for them. As the old saying goes, "Line tells; staff sells." In other words, people in line positions have the authority to give orders, whereas those in staff positions must convince the line managers to adopt their suggestions. By maintaining final decision-making authority in the line positions, an organization seeks to keep it in those positions accountable for results and to preserve a clear chain of command from the top to the bottom of the organization.

As libraries have grown in size and complexity, they have relied more heavily on staff positions to provide support, advice, and information. Many li-

Figure 8.5—A Flat Organization Chart

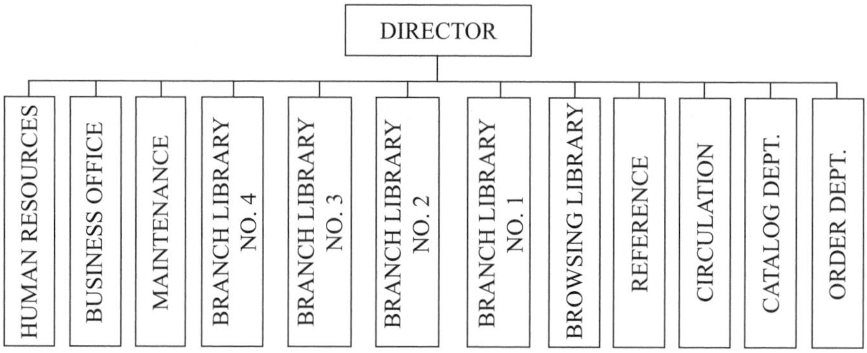

Figure 8.6—A Vertical Organization Chart (figures in parentheses indicate level according to authority lines)

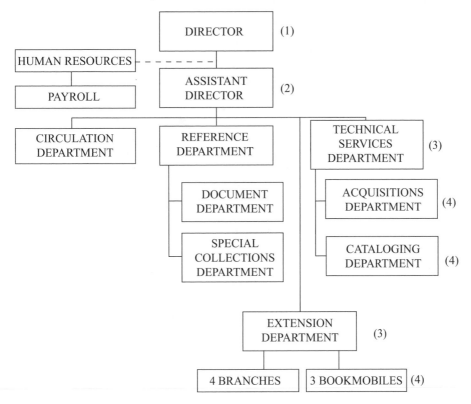

braries now have a number of staff positions dealing with public relations, systems, personnel, planning, fund-raising, and budgeting. These staff positions are held by individuals skilled in specific functions who provide the facts and information needed by the decision makers. A library human resources office, for example, may be responsible for receiving applications, interviewing applicants, maintaining personnel files, and recommending promotion or transfer. But, generally, the human resources director does not have the authority to make human resources decisions. For instance, the human resources department facilitates the search for a new department head, but the actual decision about whom to hire is made by someone else—most likely by the library director, often with input from a search committee. Only individuals in a line position—the authority position—make these kinds of decisions. Although the head of the human resources department serves in a staff position for the entire library, he or she would, at the same time, have a line position within the human resources department and make decisions relating to its operation.

Conflicts often develop between line and staff personnel, usually when there are unclear notions of duties and authority. If staff employees do not understand their role in the organization, they will be frustrated and confused. On the other hand, if line managers continually disregard the advice of the staff, fearing that staff members may undermine their position and authority, the staff will be underutilized and its expertise wasted. Managers should be sure that authority relationships are understood and should encourage line personnel to listen to staff and keep them fully informed so that staff positions can play their intended role of offering support and advice.

 What Would You Do?

Samuel Shea has been employed by the Sullivan State University Library for the past 45 years. He came to SSU (when it was still Sullivan State College) as a new graduate from library school. He rose through the ranks and has been library director for 36 years. When he was first hired there were only three professionals on the staff. Since then, the library has grown and now employs 12 professionals, 25 clerical workers, and a number of student assistants. Nonetheless, Mr. Shea still runs the library like a one-man show. He tightly controls everything that goes on. He originates every procedure and service. He even draws up the schedules for the student assistants because he is sure he knows better than anyone else when and where they are needed. After 45 years, Mr. Shea is retiring next month, and you have just been hired as the new director. You are excited but a bit concerned about what you learned when you were interviewed.

- There is no organizational chart, but the library seems to be organized as it was 45 years ago. Although there are the usual departments, the department heads are ignored. Everyone goes to Mr. Shea for answers because he makes all of the decisions.
- There have never been any regularly scheduled staff meetings.
- Orders for supplies are only placed once a year, because Mr. Shea handles them.
- There is no user instruction provided, because Mr. Shea thinks college students should arrive knowing how to use the library.
- Mr. Shea refuses to have either telephone or online reference, because he feels that people should come to the library for service.

What difficulties do you see in making changes in a library like this one? Where will you start? What changes will you try to implement first?

COORDINATION

Division of work, or specialization, is one important task in setting up an organization, but it is equally important to make provisions for coordination. As mentioned earlier, every organization must specialize by dividing the tasks to be done. It also must coordinate or integrate these activities, bringing together all the individual job efforts to achieve a particular objective.

It is sometimes hard for a manager to strike the right balance between too much and too little coordination between departments. If there is too little, each department will focus inward on its own responsibilities. There will be too little attention given to the organization's overall objectives, and likely there will be both duplications and omissions in what is done because of the lack of the overall big-picture view. At the same time, too much coordinating can lead to departments getting in one another's way and little getting accomplished. Sometimes in libraries, one hears the complaint that librarians spend all their time in committee meetings and hence do not have time to do their "real" work. Although this is almost always an exaggeration, it is true that in all types of organizations a great deal of time is consumed by committees and meetings. These are good means of achieving coordination and integration among units, but if allowed to proliferate uncontrolled, they can take far too much time away from the real work of the organization. Therefore, managers need to strive to maintain a balance between specialization and coordination.

COORDINATING MECHANISMS

There are a number of ways that coordination can be achieved. The vertical hierarchy is the primary means of providing coordination and integration, because the power and accountability associated with the hierarchy help ensure that all parts of the organization work compatibly with one another. The planning techniques discussed in chapters 4 and 5 provide another means of coordinating. Policies, procedures, and rules provide guidance for members of the organization. When organizational members follow agreed-upon guidelines, they are more likely to perform in a manner that is consistent with the organization's overall goals. In a similar fashion, the organizational manual serves as a coordinating mechanism by specifying the activities that are to be conducted in each unit. The functional statements in the manual are designed to ensure that all work is covered and that the separation of the overall duties and functions provides the mix necessary to achieve organizational objectives. Committees provide another means of coordination among specialized units, because they often draw members from various parts of the organization and because they encourage communication and participation in decision making. Staff positions, because they provide assistance and advice to managers throughout an organization, also promote coordination.

Many management experts recommend that organizations maintain a basic simplicity of form. Thomas Peters and Robert Waterman, in their study of successful organizations, found that the most successful organizations had a simple form that was easily understood by their employees. In their words, "making an organization work has everything to do with keeping things understandable for the tens or hundreds of thousands who must make things happen. And that means keeping things simple."[20] Any good organization structure has to have a clear delineation of boundaries and accountabilities. Thus, simplicity in form aids in coordination.

Henry Mintzberg provides another viewpoint on coordination. He identifies five mechanisms that explain the fundamental ways organizations coordinate their work. These five mechanisms—mutual adjustment; direct supervision; and the standardization of work processes, outputs, and skills—provide the means to hold the organization together.

- Mutual adjustment means informal communication. Because it is such a simple mechanism, mutual adjustment is the coordinating mechanism used in the simplest of organizations, such as in a small library with a limited number of employees. Where there are just a few workers, there is no need for an elaborate hierarchy, and direct communication among all workers is unimpeded. Hence, informal communication permits the coordination of activities without the use of a more complicated mechanism. And as will be discussed later, mutual adjustment also is used by the most complex of organizations, in which sophisticated problem solvers facing extremely complicated situations must communicate informally to accomplish their work.

- In direct supervision, one individual takes responsibility for the work of others, issuing instructions to them and monitoring their actions. In a library that has individual departments, mutual adjustment does not suffice to coordinate work. A hierarchy in which, as Mintzberg says, "one brain coordinates several hands,"[21] needs to be established.

Mintzberg's remaining methods of coordination all involve standardization. With standardization, coordination is achieved before the work is undertaken. In a sense, standardization incorporates coordination into the design of the work; this reduces the need for external coordinating mechanisms.

- Standardization of work processes occurs when the content of specific jobs is specified and programmed; that is, the processes are standardized to a high degree. Supervisors overseeing such workers have little need to coordinate because a high degree of specificity is built into the jobs that are to be performed. The classic case of this type of standardization is found on assembly lines where workers perform highly specified tasks.

- Standardization of outputs occurs when the results of the work—for example, the dimensions of the product or the performance—are specified. Certain outputs are standardized in libraries and information centers; for instance, the records in an online catalog are usually standardized by means of a tool like AACR2.

When neither the work nor its outputs can be standardized, some coordination is attained by standardizing the worker.

- Standardization of skills occurs when the training required to perform the work is specified. In most libraries and information centers, an ALA-accredited master's degree is required for entry-level professional positions. Although curricula differ among LIS schools, it is assumed that a person who has earned an accredited MLIS degree possesses the initial skills and knowledge needed.

Mintzberg sees the five coordinating mechanisms as a continuum; as organizational work becomes more complicated, the means of coordination shifts from mutual adjustment to direct supervision and then to standardization of

TABLE 8.2 Examples of Mintzberg's Coordinating Mechanisms in Libraries

Mutual Adjustment	Direct communication among workers in a small library
Direct Supervision	Paraprofessional and clerical workers supervised by professionals
Standardization of Work Processes	Processing of material for mailing for interlibrary loan
Standardization of Outputs	Using tools such as AACR2 to produce uniform records
Standardization of Skills	Requiring an MLIS degree for all professionals

work processes, to standardization of outputs, and, finally, to standardization of skills. As mentioned previously, the most complex organizations revert to the beginning of the continuum and use the coordinating device of mutual adjustment.[22]

Although organizations may favor one coordinating mechanism, no organization relies on a single one, and most mix all five. At the least, a certain amount of mutual adjustment and direct supervision is always required, regardless of the extent to which the organization relies on standards. Libraries use all five of the coordinating mechanisms.

Managers should remember the importance of coordination. It serves as the glue that permits the various units of the organization to move together toward the achievement of organizational objectives. The larger and more complex an organization becomes, the more those coordinating mechanisms are needed.

CONCLUSION

This chapter has covered the methods that organizations use to decide how to subdivide into smaller subunits to permit specialization, as well as the approaches they use to integrate the organization to permit coordination among the functions. The next chapter will look at the various overall organizational structures that are found in libraries and other organizations today and also will discuss how those structures may be different in the organizations of tomorrow.

NOTES

1. John Cole, "Jefferson's Legacy: A Brief History of the Library of Congress," Library of Congress (2006), http://www.loc.gov/loc/legacy/librs.html.

2. For these and other interesting facts about the Library of Congress, see "Fascinating Facts" (2005), http://www.loc.gov/about/facts.html.

3. An organizational chart (2004) for the Library of Congress may be seen at http://www.loc.gov/about/LC_org_Sep04.pdf.

4. Peter Drucker, *Management: Tasks, Responsibilities, Practices* (New York: Harper & Row, 1974), 530.

5. Theodore Leavitt, "What Business Are You In?" *Harvard Business Review* 84, no. 10 (October 2006): 128.

6. Jim Collins, *Good to Great: Why Some Companies Make the Leap and Others Don't* (New York: HarperBusiness, 2001), 133–34.

7. Robert Howard, "The CEO as Organizational Architect: An Interview with Xerox's Paul Allaire," *Harvard Business Review* 70 (September/October 1992): 120–21.

8. Henry Mintzberg, "Organization Design: Fashion or Fit?" *Harvard Business Review* 59 (January–February 1981): 103.

9. Vesa Kautto and Joma Niemitalo, "Organization and Efficiency of Finnish Academic Libraries," *Libri* 9 (December 1996): 201–8.

10. See TimeWarner, "About Us: Our Company" (2007), http://www.timewarner.com/corp/aboutus/our_company.html.

11. Michael J. Hammer and James Champy, *Reengineering the Corporation: A Manifesto for Business Revolution* (New York: HarperBusiness, 1993), 3.

12. Maxine Brodie and Neil McLean, "Process Reengineering in Academic Libraries: Shifting to Client-Centered Resource Provision," *CAUSE/EFFECT* 18 (Summer 1995): 42.

13. Ibid.

14. Michael E. Porter and Victor E. Millar, "How Information Gives You Competitive Advantage." *Harvard Business Review* 63, no. 4 (July–August 1985): 149–174.

15. See, for example, Sandra Yee, Rita Bullard, and Morell Boone, "We Built It and They Came: Client Centered Services in a New Building," *Proceedings of the ACRL 10th National Conference* (Chicago: American Library Association, 2001), 261–64.

16. Henri Fayol, *General and Industrial Administration* (New York: Pitman, 1949), 14.

17. John R. P. French Jr. and Bertram Raven, "The Bases of Social Power," in *Group Dynamics: Research and Theory,* ed. Dorwin Cartwright and Alvin Zander (Evanston, IL: Row, Peterson, 1960), 607–23.

18. Edward E. Lawler III, *From the Ground Up: Six Principles for Building the New Logic Corporation* (San Francisco: Jossey-Bass, 1996), 90.

19. Kenneth Chilton, "American Manufacturers Respond to the Global Marketplace," in *The Dynamic American Firm,* ed. Kenneth Chilton, Murray L. Weidenbaum, and Robert Batterson (Boston: Kluwer Academic, 1996), 166.

20. Thomas J. Peters and Robert H. Waterman Jr., *In Search of Excellence: Lessons from America's Best Run Companies* (New York: Harper & Row, 1982), 306.

21. Henry Mintzberg. *The Structuring of Organizations* (Englewood Cliffs, NJ: Prentice-Hall, 1979), 4.

22. Ibid.

Chapter 9

The Structure of Organizations—
Today and in the Future

 Overview

Sydney Smith has just been appointed director of the Piedmont University Library and, as is often the case, has arrived with ideas about how to make the library function better. The staff expects that there will be changes made in many aspects of the organization as a result. The Library has had the same organizational structure since 1982, and both the director and the staff feel it is outdated. Although the provision of digital resources and services has become a primary focus of the library, its organizational structure does not reflect this. In addition, Smith came from an institution that successfully used teams in the library and thinks that a team-based structure might work in this library also. The staff knows that changes need to be made, but, at the same time, they are a bit apprehensive about losing their old, comfortable ways of doing things. The director has appointed a committee to recommend what modifications should be made in the library's organization and to propose a timetable for restructuring.

This scenario has become common in all types of libraries. As a result of changing technologies and missions, many libraries are experimenting with restructuring to allow them to serve their patrons better. Restructuring is never easy, and there is no one best method to accomplish it, for each institution has its own particular needs that must be satisfied. Even when change is needed, the transition between the old and the new is difficult because reorganization cannot occur without abandoning long-established practices that may be obsolete but are also familiar. Change, especially if it is on a large scale, can be very threatening to employees used to the old way of doing things.

This chapter will first examine the characteristics of bureaucratic organizations, because most libraries are still organized as bureaucracies. Some of the criticisms of bureaucracies as a form of structure also will be discussed and alternatives to the bureaucratic structure introduced. Next, factors that need to be kept in mind by an organization considering restructuring are covered. The chapter concludes with a brief discussion of the types of organizational structures likely to be used in the future.

Organizations can be of many types and structures. It is widely recognized that no one structure is suitable to all organizations, and factors such as growth, competition, technology, and environmental uncertainty have to be considered when choosing a structure.

This is a world in which there are now many more choices about organizational alternatives than there have been in the past. It is also a world in which technological alternatives are many and the variations proliferating. We have gone from a world in which there were only a few tried-and-true organizational designs to one in which there are many. It requires a great deal of organization design skill to achieve a good fit between the organizational and technical alternatives available.[1] Nonetheless, some types of organizations are very common. Today, throughout the world, most large organizations, including libraries, are still structured as bureaucracies.

BUREAUCRACIES

The term *bureaucracy* is used often in a derogatory fashion, with a connotation of cumbersome structure, red tape, and overorganization. However, bureaucracies were initially viewed in a very positive manner, because they were considered to be much more effective and rational types of organizations than their predecessors. Bureaucracies (as discussed in chapter 2) were first described in the early part of the twentieth century by Max Weber, a German sociologist trained in law, economics, history, and philosophy. His perceptive and incisive theoretical analysis of the principles of bureaucracies is undoubtedly one of the most important statements on formal organizations; it has had a profound influence on almost all subsequent thinking and research in the field.[2] Weber created the concept of bureaucracy as a model for use in his analysis of organized industrial society. He attempted to construct a model of a perfectly rational organization, one that would perform its job with maximum efficiency. Weber based his model on reasoning rather than on empirical evidence; the characteristics of this model can be seen in table 9.1.

Weber's concept of bureaucracy has been the basis for much influential thought and investigation into organizations. His work brings together a large number of the concepts already discussed in this section: division of labor, horizontal specialization, hierarchy of authority, and standardization of work

TABLE 9.1 Characteristics of a Bureaucracy

Characteristic	Reason
Impersonal and formal conduct.	Because personality and emotional-based relationships interfere with rationality; nepotism and favoritism not related to performance should be eliminated.
Employment and promotion on the basis of technical competence and performance.	Using these criteria ensures that the best-qualified people will pursue a career in the organization and remain loyal to it.
Systematic specialization of labor and specification of responsibilities.	All of the work necessary to accomplish the tasks of the organization should be divided into specific areas of competence, with each employee and supervisor having authority over his or her functions and not interfering with the conduct of others' jobs.
A well-ordered system of rules and procedures that regulates the conduct of work.	These rules serve (a) to standardize operations and decisions, (b) as receptacles of past learning, and (c) to protect incumbents and ensure equality of treatment. The learning of rules represents much of the technical competence of incumbents because the rules tell them what decisions to make and when to make them.
Hierarchy of positions such that each position is controlled by a higher one.	The hierarchy of authority is impersonal, based on rules, and the superior position is held by the individual having greater expertise. In this way, compliance with rules and coordination is systematically ensured.
Complete separation of the property and affairs of the organization from the personal property and affairs of the incumbents.	This serves to prevent the demands and interests of personal affairs from interfering with the rational, impersonal conduct of the business of the organization.

Source: Max Weber, *The Theory of Social and Economic Organizations,* ed. and trans. A. M. Henderson and T. Parsons (Oxford: Oxford University Press, 1947).

processes. The organization of a typical library includes many characteristics of bureaucracy. Almost all libraries are marked by a hierarchical structure, a large number of rules (ranging from cataloging to circulation rules), the demands of technical competence, and the systematic specialization of labor.

Since the time of Weber, many critics have written about the dysfunctional aspects of bureaucracies. A great deal of this criticism of bureaucracy focuses on the internal workings of the organization, especially the unintended consequences of control through rules.[3] Other criticism centers on the relationship of the bureaucratic organization to its environment and the tendency of the traditional bureaucracy to ignore the outside world. The bureaucratic organizational model is seen as flawed because it treats the organization as if it were a closed system unaffected by the uncertainties of environment.[4] Other criticism faults the bureaucratic model for being overly mechanical and ignoring individual and group behaviors in organizations.[5]

 What Do You Think?

Although the bureaucratic form of organizational structure has been criticized in recent years, it still has many proponents. Elliot Jaques, in an article entitled "In Praise of Hierarchy," wrote: "The hierarchical kind of organization we call bureaucracy did not emerge accidentally. It is the only form of organization that can enable a company to employ a large number of people and yet preserve unambiguous accountability for the work they do. And that is why, despite all its problems, it has so doggedly persisted."

What aspects of the bureaucratic structure allow it to preserve accountability for a large number of employees? Why have libraries always favored this form of organization?

Elliot Jaques, "In Praise of Hierarchy," *Harvard Business Review* 68 (January–February 1990): 127.

In stable environments, changes occur slowly. For organizations, stable environments mean that customer needs change slowly, and, thus, organizations are under little pressure to change their established methods. In a stable environment, organizations handle information that is largely predictable. Carefully developed plans can be made in advance, and exceptions are so few that there is time for upper-level decision makers to decide what to do. The rules and procedures that are a characteristic of bureaucracies function best in this type of environment. In large organizations in stable environments, bureaucracies are likely to be the most efficient types of organizational structure.

Today, however, the environment is not stable but turbulent. The rapid changes now taking place in the external environment cause many to question the suitability of the bureaucratic method of organization. Organizations that exist in unstable environments encounter change frequently. They must be adaptable and flexible. Long lists of policies and rules cannot be relied upon; circumstances change too quickly for decisions to be adequately covered by rules. As technology evolves rapidly, frequent product and service changes result from both the changing needs of customers and the pressure of competitors. Bureaucracies are less efficient because they lack the ability to adapt easily to change; instead, they "are geared to stable environments; they are performance structures designed to perfect programs for contingencies that can be predicted, not problem solving ones designed to create new programs for needs that have never been encountered."[6]

MECHANISTIC ORGANIZATIONS

Although the bureaucracy is the most common form of organizational structure, there are other forms. Tom Burns and G. M. Stalker were among the first to distinguish between two types of organizations: One they called the mechanistic, and the other the organic.[7]

Mechanistic organizational structures are shaped in the traditional, pyramidal pattern of organization. This type of organization is designed to be like a machine, hence the name. "People are conceived of as parts performing specific tasks. As employees leave, other parts can be slipped into their places. Someone at the top is the designer, defining what the parts will be and how they will fit together."[8] Burns and Stalker found that a mechanistic, or bureaucratic, structure worked best for organizations that perform many routine tasks and operate in a stable environment but was not successful in organizations that were required to adjust to environmental changes. Instead, another form, the organic, functioned best in these environments.

ORGANIC SYSTEMS

The organic organization's structure is completely different from the mechanistic organization. This structure is based on a biological metaphor, and the objective in designing such a system is to leave it open to the environment so it can respond to new opportunities. The organic form is appropriate to changing conditions that constantly give rise to fresh problems and unforeseen requirements for action. Organic structures are often more appropriate than bureaucracies for today's better-educated workers who seek greater freedom in their work. An organic structure is characterized by:

- an emphasis on lateral and horizontal flows of communication within the organization;

- organizational influence based largely on the authority of knowledge, rather than an individual's position in the structure;

- members of the organization tending to have a systemwide orientation rather than narrow, departmental views;

- job definitions that are less precise and more flexible and duties that change as new problems and challenges are confronted;

- a commitment by many members to professional standards developed by groups outside the formal organization. For instance, many librarians identify as much with their profession as with the institutions that employ them.[9]

In almost every respect, the organic institution is the opposite of the classical bureaucracy, which emphasizes standardization and formal relations;

Figure 9.1—The Mechanistic and Organic Organizational Structure

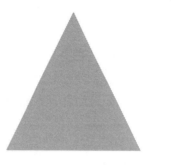   

A Mechanistic Structure   An Organic Structure

organic structures are marked by loose, informal working relations and problems worked out as needs arise.

Burns and Stalker are careful to emphasize that, whereas organic systems are "not hierarchic in the same sense as are mechanistic systems, they remain stratified." Positions are differentiated according to seniority or greater expertise. The lead in joint decisions is frequently taken by senior staff members, but it is an essential presumption of the organic system that the lead, or the authority, is taken by those who show themselves most informed and capable. The location of authority is settled by consensus.[10]

Because of the departure from the familiar clear and fixed hierarchical structure, many managers feel uncomfortable in organic organizations. Much more ambiguity is associated with the organic pattern of organizing, and managers must be able to tolerate that ambiguity. It takes a different style of management to succeed in organic structures. And, as we will see, it is not easy for a manager to switch from managing one type of structure to managing the other.

Mechanistic and organic systems are on the extreme ends of a continuum. A small group of scientists working in a laboratory represents an organic structure; a highly structured factory producing a standard product for a stable market represents a mechanistic one. Most institutions fall somewhere between these two extremes, and an organization can contain both organic and mechanistic units.[11]

Few libraries are structured as pure organic systems. This type of organizational structure is possible only when the number of people working in an organization is relatively small. Some small public and school libraries are organic in structure. Smaller special libraries often use this model, as do small academic libraries that have adopted a collegial system of organization similar to that used in academic departments.[12]

 ## What Do You Think?

The librarians in one small library who decided to change from a hierarchical to a collegial structure explained their reasoning as follows:

[W]e previously had a vestigial hierarchy, laid out in a pyramid shaped chart, that mimicked standard library organizations: we had a director, heads of technical and public services, and the remaining librarians in a third tier. But having three layers of hierarchy among six librarians makes about as much sense as having a captain and a first mate in a rowboat.... In fast-changing times, we couldn't work within a system, however vestigial, in which some of us stood around waiting for orders—or in which people best positioned to make informed decisions felt compelled to go through layers of command for approval. And in practice, we usually ignored those vestiges of traditional hierarchy. It made sense to us that the best decisions are made by a group of people working together with a shared knowledge base and a shared sense of responsibility for the entire operation.

What would be gained by eliminating the hierarchy in this library? What might be lost?

David Lesniaki, Kris (Huber) MacPherson, Barbara Fister, and Steve McKinzie, "Collegial Leadership in Academic Libraries," *Proceedings of the ACRL Tenth National Conference* (Chicago: American Library Association, 2001), 234.

In the collegial system, instead of a single final authority position, a group of individuals participates in making decisions that affect the whole organization. The collegial organization has been successful in some small libraries, but the large number of employees in most libraries makes this form of organization impossible. But, even in large libraries, subunits of the library are becoming more organic in structure. For example, using teams is one way to make a mechanistic organization more organic.

MODIFYING LIBRARY BUREAUCRACY

Although many organizations are moving away from the bureaucratic model, most libraries, because of their size, the technology they use, and the services they perform, are still organized in this fashion. But, as libraries "have been criticized for their inability to keep up with social and individual expectations and their failure to change quickly enough to meet competitive challenges,"[13] they have begun to search for new forms of organizational structure. There is a growing acceptance of the fact that the traditional hierarchical system needs to be modified.

There has been a widespread belief that the adoption of new technologies will inevitably lead to radical changes in the organizational structures of libraries. To date, those radical changes have not occurred, but there is still a vast amount of restructuring going on in libraries. One of the best places to see this restructuring is in large libraries, because the number of employees in these libraries has always resulted in their having more complex organizational structures.

Since 1973, the Association of Research Libraries (ARL) has published a series of volumes containing the organizational charts of the large research

libraries that are members of ARL.[14] In addition, the association has monitored organizational restructuring in other publications, which reveal that,
although the hierarchical structure still prevails in large academic libraries, there is still a great deal of organizational restructuring occurring. Many
libraries have either completed a library-wide reorganization or have reorganized specific units. There has been great interest in reshaping former
circulation departments into broader access services departments.[15] Many
libraries also have combined parts of the reference department and computer
lab services and resources and formed a so-called information commons or
similarly named department in the library.[16] The growth of electronic resources has prompted a number of libraries to form new electronic resources
departments.[17] Other libraries have reorganized their systems office[18] or their
preservation activities.[19] Services such as chat reference or user instruction sometimes are located in reference departments or sometimes in newly
formed units. Without a doubt, these libraries are undergoing a number of
organizational structure changes, but most seem to have reorganized around
the edges instead of completely discarding their old structure and beginning
anew.

Instead of radically restructuring, many libraries have changed in a way
that is not reflected on their organizational charts. Libraries and information
centers are becoming more hybrid in structure, by organizing some departments more organically than others or by employing so-called overlays, or
modifications imposed on the basic bureaucratic organizational structure. The
pyramid remains largely intact, but modifications are in place in many libraries that are flattening the pyramid and allowing more employee input into
decision making.

 What Do You Think?

Carl Guarino, a top executive of SEI, a large successful financial services organization recently stated, "We reject the idea that because
people sit at the top of the organization, power resides with them
and control comes down the line.... Power is much more diffused
and dispersed in this organization. Power doesn't come from position
but from influence and the ability to engineer consensus—not in the
Japanese sense of unanimity but in terms of the participation and
support required to get things done.

The approach at SEI violates many of the tenets of bureaucracy. What
do you see as the major advantages and disadvantages of this type of organization?

William C. Taylor and Polly LaBarre, *Mavericks at Work: Why the
Most Original Minds in Business Win* (New York: HarperCollins, 2006):
238.

SOME COMMONLY USED MODIFICATIONS

Libraries rely heavily on various types of coordinating positions and temporary groups to deal with increasing complexity, but, in most cases, these modifications are superimposed upon the traditional bureaucratic structure. Modifications may be traditional, such as committees, or innovative, such a teams; they may be permanent, such as matrix organizations, or more transitory, such as temporary task forces. A discussion of some of these modifications to the traditional hierarchical structure follows.

Committees

One of the most common modifications to libraries' hierarchical structure is the formation of committees. Committees are especially useful when a process does not fall within the domain of any one chain of command, and so a committee consisting of representatives from the units involved needs to be established. Standing committees often deal with ongoing issues, such as staff development, automation, and personnel. Ad hoc, or temporary, committees are formed as required. For instance, many libraries use search committees in the hiring process. The power held by committees varies from library to library. In some libraries, committees have the authority to establish policy; in others, they play only an advisory role.

Committees provide a means to bring a wide variety of knowledge and experience to bear on a topic. Because they permit the participation of staff members, they also are useful in obtaining commitment to policies and decisions. Committees are often slow to act, however, and they are costly because of the time required of participants. All of the advantages and disadvantages of group decision making discussed in chapter 4 pertain to decision making by committees.

Task Force

Task forces are similar to committees, except that their assignment is often full time rather than part time; employees generally leave their primary jobs to devote all their time to the task force. A task force has a specific, temporary task to perform, and when the task is completed, the members of the group return to their primary jobs. Task forces are particularly valuable when the undertaking is a one-time task that has a broad scope and specific, definable results; is unfamiliar or lacks precedent; calls for a high degree of interdependence among the tasks; and is of high importance. In libraries and information centers, task forces are often called upon to deal with new, unfamiliar, or involved projects, such as the installation of a new online catalog or the building of a new facility.

Matrix Organizational Structure

One of the more recent innovations in organizational design is the matrix structure. In task forces or project management, group members are withdrawn from their departments and temporarily assigned to the project manager. For the duration of the project, group members have a reporting responsibility to both the project manager and their department supervisor. In matrix management, dual assignments become part of the permanent organizational pattern. Matrix management represents an attempt to retain the advantages of functional specialization, while adding project management's advantage of improved coordination. Aerospace firms were the first to use the matrix structure by experimenting with organizational structures that combined project management with departments organized by function. Functional departments continued to exist in the traditional vertical hierarchy, but project management was superimposed over those departments as a horizontal overlay, hence the name *matrix*.

The matrix is a fairly complex structure that violates many management principles, especially the principle of unity of command. Although many businesses, including banks and insurance and chemical companies, have implemented a matrix organizational pattern, it is still not common. One reason that this type of structure has not been more widely adopted is that it is often confusing: The simple chain of command is replaced by multiple authority relationships, and managers need to function as team leaders rather than as traditional managers.[20] People working in such an environment need to be able to tolerate a great deal of ambiguity. As two library managers wrote, matrix management is "difficult to implement. It runs against our cultural bias, and it is sufficiently complex and ambiguous that it requires virtually constant monitoring to keep it running well. Most of us have lived in hierarchical organizations all of our lives, and it is difficult for us to even visualize, much less adapt to, another form of organization."[21]

Few libraries have adopted a pure matrix organization. One that did was the library at San Francisco State University (SFSU), which was looking for a way to increase organizational effectiveness, particularly in reference services and collection development. After considering the options, the library decided to adopt a matrix management organization. Program coordinators were chosen for the various services provided by the readers' services division: user education, online, reference, and collection development. Librarians working in the readers' services division had a dual-reporting responsibility to the assistant director for public services and to the program coordinator of their specific service unit.[22] The organizational structure of that library after the reorganization is illustrated in figure 9.2.

The library at SFSU has now moved away from the matrix model and gone with a more traditional style of organization. Even in the for-profit sector, a number of corporations experimented with and then eliminated the matrix management organizational pattern because of its complexity and lack of clear-cut authority lines. Although few libraries have adopted the pure form of matrix organization, matrixlike structures exist in many libraries today, either as part of their overall organizational structure or in specific units of the library. Libraries that are using teams or task forces as organizing devices are good examples of the incorporation of matrixlike structures into the organization.[23]

Figure 9.2—A Matrix Organizational Structure

A Schematic of Matrix Organization
for the Readers Services Division of the
San Francisco State University

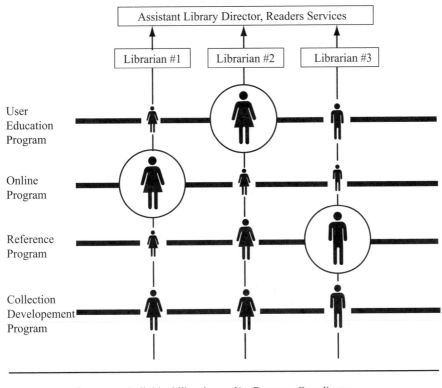

Individual librarian and/or Program Coordinator
interaction with the Division Head

Relationship of individual librarian participation to
various divisional programs

Individual librarian and/or Program Coordinator
interaction with peers and/or other Program Coordinators

Circled figure represents Program Coordinator

Size of figure represents librarian time commitment
to specific program

Source: From Joanne Euster and Peter Haikalis, "A Matrix Model of Organization," in *Academic Libraries: Myths and Realities, Proceedings of the Third Annual ACRL Conference* (Chicago: American Library Association, 1984). Reprinted with permission of the American Library Association.

Teams

There has been an increased interest in the use of teams in all types of libraries. The team approach provides a basic redesign of how work is accomplished: Instead of groups being managed, there is a shift to groups that manage themselves. When a number of employees work as a group to perform related tasks, it is possible to redesign the overall work, not as a set of individual jobs but as a shared group task. Self-managing or autonomous teams take over many of the functions traditionally reserved for managers, including determining their own work schedules and job assignments. Self-managing teams sometimes have other names (self-directed, self-maintaining, self-leading, and self-regulating work teams, to name a few) depending on the organization, but their duties are similar. They are groups of employees who are responsible for a complete, self-contained package of responsibilities that relate either to a final product or to an ongoing process. Team members possess a variety of technical skills and are encouraged to develop new ones to increase their versatility, flexibility, and value to the work team. The team is responsible for monitoring and reviewing the overall process or product (through performance scheduling and by inspecting the team's own work) as well as for assigning problem-solving tasks to group members. Teams create a climate that fosters creativity and risk taking, a climate in which members listen to each other and feel free to put forth ideas without being criticized.[24]

Self-managed teams began to be used in libraries in the late 1980s, and their use grew in the 1990s. Since the turn of the twenty-first century, self-managing work teams are the most common overlay to the bureaucratic structure of large libraries. Whereas some of these libraries, such as the ones at California State University at San Marcos or the University of Arizona, have used the team approach for the entire library, others use teams only in a few departments.[25] Many libraries have reorganized their technical services department into a team structure. University libraries that recently have instituted this type of organization in their technical services department include Tufts, University of Nevada at Las Vegas, and McMaster University in Canada.[26]

One suburban Chicago public library that recently reorganized its reference department into a team-based structure used the reasons listed in Table 9.2 in deciding to make the change.

The use of team structure in this library allowed for more differentiated work between professional and nonprofessionals and permitted the library to focus on some previously neglected services and collections.

The role of a manager changes when teams or work groups are used. In an organization that uses teams, the core behaviors of a manager are developing the talents and skills of the team members, getting them excited about the mission of the team, and fostering effective working relations.

Work teams are gaining increasing popularity in library settings, and they provide yet another way to provide greater decentralization within the hierarchical structure. As all of the accounts of organizations that have switched to the team approach note, it is not an easy or a fast process. The hierarchical approach, with all of its deficiencies, is the one that both managers and employees are most familiar with, and sometimes the old certainties look very alluring. It is important for any library considering teams to understand that

TABLE 9.2 Reasons for Adopting a Team Approach in One Public Library

Current Situation	Under the Team Approach
MLS and associate staff do the same work	Clear distinctions—MLS will be team leaders; job descriptions will incorporate that responsibility
Too many staff for one manager	Clearer organization with current staff
Everyone trains the public (information literacy)	Information literacy team will train
Staff training is sporadic	Each team has staff training component
Print reference collection is underutilized	General reference team assigned to highlight print reference sources
Department manager provides goals, objectives, tasks	Department manager develops department goals based on library's long-range plan, teams determine tasks to meet the goals
Evaluation of services neglected	Teams assigned evaluation piece for each of their focus areas
Reference Web site bloated	Web content management team will focus on making the site lean and integrated with Illinois Clicks
MLS staff have limited team experience	All reference staff gain formalized team experience, MLS staff as team leaders

Source: Barbara Brattin, "Reorganizing Reference," *Public Libraries* 44, no. 6 (November/December 2005): 343.

becoming a team-based organization means undergoing a radical change in organizational culture. Chapter 17 contains more information on managing teams and team building.

RESHAPING THE LIBRARY'S ORGANIZATIONAL STRUCTURE

Although there are as yet few signs of a radical reorganization of libraries, librarians in all types of libraries and information centers are thinking about the future and trying to devise organizational structures that will allow them to reach their goals most successfully. Most libraries are considering ways to flatten their structures and make their organizations more flexible and responsive. These changes are being considered while the library is "getting on with essential daily tasks." Any reorganization is of course complicated because "current services must be maintained while the infrastructure is being built to support the information needs of the [twenty-first] century."[27] But libraries do seem to be following the recent advice of Lowell Bryan and Claudia Joyce, who state that if organizations want to raise the productivity of their professionals, they, "must change their organizational structures dramatically, retaining the best of the traditional hierarchy while acknowledging the heightened value of the people."[28]

If a library decides to proceed with reorganization, the first step is to decide what type of structure is needed. Peter Drucker, who has written much about organizational structure, provides three ways to determine the type of structure necessary for a specific organization: (1) activities analysis, (2) decision analysis, and (3) relations analysis.[29] The activities analysis requires the manager to perform a detailed and thorough analysis of activities so that it can be determined what work has to be performed, what activities belong together, and where these activities should be placed in the organizational structure. The decision analysis identifies the kinds of decisions that are needed, where in the structure of the organization they should be made, and the degree of involvement of each manager in the decision-making process. The relations analysis emphasizes the relationships among the units of the organizational structure and the responsibilities of each manager to the various units as well as the responsibilities of the various units to each manager. After performing these three analyses, a manager would have the information needed to begin determining the structure needed for the organization.

 Try This!

When Warren Newport Public Library, a medium-size library outside of Chicago, decided to reorganize, it went about it in this way:

> Whereas the standard corporate reorganization often involves merging departments, this exercise began at the task level with a zero-based approach to what we were doing and who would most logically get it done. The exercise began with a comprehensive listing of current library activities at all levels of service, both in contact with our customers and behind the scenes. Every activity was evaluated for relevance in relation to the library's current long-range planning goals, and we culled unnecessary activities from the final list. Each of the remaining activities were then grouped together functionally, and logical patterns of oversight emerged.

Think about a library with which you are familiar. Assume that the library has decided to reorganize and to adopt the approach described in the preceding excerpt. Identify the list of activities that are currently done, evaluate each for current relevance, and then group them together in a logical fashion that could be the basis of a restructuring.

Barbara Brattin, "Reorganizing Reference" *Public Libraries* 44, no. 6 (Nov./Dec. 2005): 340.

Analyses such as the ones Drucker proposes would be helpful in gathering information about the type of structure to be implemented. Often other data, especially on library use and satisfaction, are gathered. Techniques, such as those used in business processing reengineering, that focus upon reexamining the critical processes within an organization also can be useful.

Managers interested in implementing changes in an organization's structure should learn as much as possible from reading on the topic and talking to others who have implemented change, but the structure chosen for a particular organization should be based on that organization's specific needs and not chosen because it is being implemented elsewhere. Some libraries have used consultants in this planning process, others have done it with planning committees drawn from library employees, whereas others have used both of these approaches.

The second step in any structural change is a consideration of whether the employees will be able to work well in the proposed new structure. One part of this consideration concerns the personal style of the organization's managers. Not all managers adjust well to a flatter, less bureaucratic style of organization. They learned to manage in the command-and-control mode and feel more comfortable using that style. If a library is considering drastic changes to its structure, it needs to consider whether this new structure will be congruent with the present managers' styles. If not, it will likely fail, unless the structural changes are adopted in tandem with other changes, such as replacing managers or providing them with in-depth training on how to manage in the new environment.

It is not just top-level managers, however, who likely will need help in adjusting to a new structure. Many lower-level staff and middle managers also may find the adjustment difficult. Staff development needs to be provided to all employees to ready them for the new structure. The human side of the organization will be critical in the success or failure of a new type of organizational structure.

It cannot be stressed too much that different types of structures will demand different types of management expertise and different types of employee skills and that training will be important. As the director of one library that has reorganized wrote:

> The key to making the reorganization work is staff education and training. This point cannot be overemphasized. Moreover, educational efforts must target all staff, including management. The staff needs to learn how to participate in the new organization.... Not only do staff members need to acquire new knowledge and skills, but, also their attitudes and philosophies must be reexamined and refined.[30]

The staff development and training required to bring about organizational transformation successfully, both in the planning and implementation phases, require a large amount of investment of time and money.

The third step is to develop the strategy for moving from the current configuration of the organization to the new configuration. This is the implementation stage of the process. Recently published accounts of how certain libraries have approached restructuring can provide some insights into some of the strategies being employed. The accounts of successful restructuring have all included a great deal of employee input. Unless employees understand the reasons for the change and buy into the change proposed, it is unlikely to be effective. Staff members must understand the concepts underlying the new structure to ensure their full participation.

Role-Play a Situation

The Brickton Public Library, a large municipal library in a major U.S. city, has just restructured its organization and has implemented team-based management throughout the system. You are the director. It has been brought to your attention that Ms. Kasey, the former head of the cataloging department, is not doing well under the new system. She is now a member of the cataloging team but appears to be very unhappy. She is disruptive at team meetings, speaks out publicly against the new type of organization, and is even suspected of trying to sabotage the work of the cataloging team. You have scheduled a meeting to speak with Ms. Kasey. What is going on here and what approach would you take to try to solve this problem? What would you say during your meeting?

There is a critical need throughout the entire process, beginning from its inception, for effective communication. This communication needs to be both external—for the library is usually a part of a larger organization that must be informed about the proposed changes—and internal. Organizational communication will be discussed in chapter 16, but it should be noted here that, if employees are not kept well informed of proposed changes, rumors will be rampant. Changes in organizational structures can be very threatening; good communication keeps everyone informed about proposed changes and helps alleviate employee anxiety.

Almost all the descriptions of organization transformation in libraries and other settings have stressed the time and effort involved in the process, with most commenting that it took longer to implement than they had anticipated. It is also not an inexpensive undertaking. As the librarians at one institution described:

> The process has been expensive. It has taken an enormous amount of time, in total length and in staff weeks. It has required consistency and constancy of vision over a span of several years. Sometimes it also has required, uncomfortably, that we remain flexible and adaptable and that we recognize that ambiguity is an ongoing part of our organization life, not an occasional problem to be eradicated. Would we do it again? Most emphatically *yes*.[31]

The last step is to realize that, once the reorganization is accomplished, the process is likely not finished. A method of assessment needs to be built into the process so it can be determined if the new structure is successfully carrying out the organization's goals and objectives. This assessment should attempt to pinpoint the things that are working well and the things that still need to be changed. In most settings, the reorganization is viewed as an iterative process. Typically, everything does not work well with the first reorganization attempt; some things need to be fine-tuned, and mistakes need to be corrected. Once greater flexibility is built into the system, it will be easier to face future changes and to view any restructuring process as an evolutionary one.

In summary, any structural reorganization requires effort and cannot be implemented quickly. Mistakes will be made in the process, and there will be many times when almost everyone will wonder why they ever wanted to consider reorganization. It is important to reward small successes along the way and to keep employees focused on the expected results of the reorganization. It should be encouraging to any organization that feels itself mired in structural change to look to the published reports of libraries that have finished the initial stages of reorganization. Almost all report greater productivity, increased flexibility, better communication, and improved decision making.

THE LIBRARY ORGANIZATION OF THE FUTURE

Libraries and information centers, like all other institutions, are moving toward new organizational structures. They are changing, slowly, away from rigid hierarchies to more organic forms of organization. The move is appropriate because there often has been tension in libraries between the professional status of many of their employees and the traditional bureaucratic form.

Libraries have been struggling to identify the most appropriate organizational structure for many decades now. During that time, writers have speculated about the type of libraries that will exist in the future. Most of these writers have expected increased decentralization. These early advocates of decentralization were thinking in terms of the decentralization of the library as a physical entity. Today, we have moved away from thinking of libraries just as places because the growing electronic information component of libraries is making place less important.

A great deal has been written about the virtual library and the library without walls. In the strictest sense, this type of library would not be a physical entity at all, and the storage function traditionally performed by libraries would be eliminated, because all information would be available via computer technology. The libraries in some corporations have gone the farthest in assuming this type of structure. In some large multinational corporations, much of the information provision is done by professionals in widely separated locations using electronic resources. Typically, these types of libraries have very small collections. The professionals employed in these libraries function as parts of virtual teams and work together, although they rarely see one another face-to-face.[32]

It is in these types of libraries that we see the closest approximation to a new model of organization structure being implemented in some for-profit organizations. These new organizations, often called boundaryless, virtual, or networked organizations, give us a preview of what the organizational structure of a completely new type of library might be. The terms *virtual, boundaryless,* and *networked* are used slightly differently by different people, but in general they all describe a new type of organizational structure that is geographically dispersed and supported by information and communication technology. These types of organizations are not defined or limited by horizontal, vertical, or external boundaries imposed by a predetermined structure. Rather than being housed under one roof, these organizations are widely dispersed and grow and shrink as needed. Usually, they have a small hub that coordinates the organization's functions, but most of the rest of the organization is subcontracted.[33] Firms such as Dell Computers, which buy all of their products ready-made or handle only the final assembly, are examples of networked organizations.

These types of organizations provide a high level of flexibility. They can grow or contract as circumstances demand. They are able to change directions swiftly. There is little administrative overhead. At the same time, these organizations have disadvantages. They are hard to coordinate because the parts are so scattered. There is very low employee loyalty because there is a very weak link between employees and the organization.[34] A networked organization is shown in figure 9.3.

As libraries become less dependent on place, more of them may begin to assume a networked or virtual structure. Perhaps the first true virtual library might be part of one of the universities that has been established to serve only distance students. These universities are not places but are so-called knowledge servers linked into a vast network that provides classes to students situated in geographically diverse locations across the country and the world.[35]

Figure 9.3—A Networked Organization

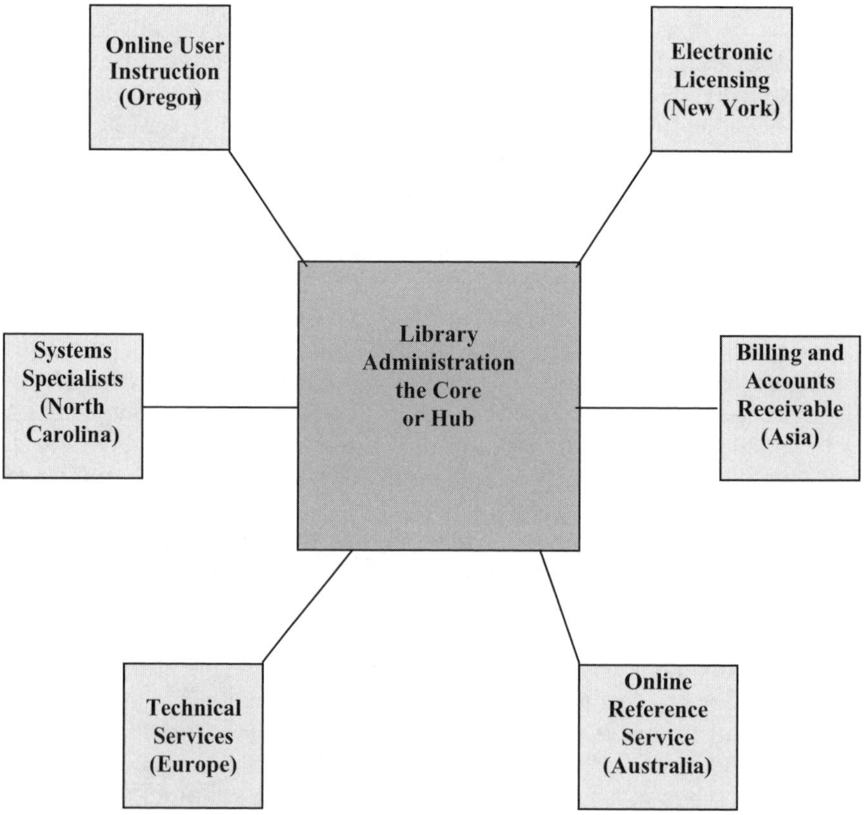

These emerging universities provide one model of higher education in the future, and it is possible to imagine a library with a network type of organizational structure associated with them. In such a networked organization, there is a central core or hub that coordinates the organization, and all of the other functions are subcontracted or outsourced to other groups that are linked electronically to that core. Rather than being housed under one roof, the functions of the library would be geographically dispersed. The individuals in the core of the library might still be housed near the central offices of the university, but the other units could be almost anywhere in the world, with all of them electronically linked to the core. The individuals in the core would outsource the acquisition and licensing of electronic materials, user assistance, and perhaps user instruction to help students wherever they might be. If users were billed for the use of material, the accounting department could be located off-site. Systems specialists also could be located at a distance. The people in the center would be the nexus. They would administer and coordinate this networked library, but all of its functions would be supplied from elsewhere. The only interaction between librarians and users would be electronic. This type of library would be truly virtual.

At least in the foreseeable future, however, few libraries will take this route. Instead, libraries will be hybrids—combining both paper and electronic resources. But many of these hybrid libraries are displaying at least some components of virtual organizations. For instance, the libraries that are member of the Global Reference Network provide professional reference service to their users wherever they are located through an international, digital network of libraries.[36] Almost all libraries now have access to collections of electronic resources that are not owned or managed by the library itself but by some sort of a library aggregator.

Despite these moves toward the virtual organization, libraries as physical places will continue to exist in the near future, but they likely will become more and more boundaryless each year. For instance, universities could have small satellite libraries scattered throughout the campus containing just a few books and journals; these libraries would provide most access to information electronically. Students and faculty also would have access to electronic resources from their dormitory rooms, offices, or homes. Public libraries also could be much more decentralized, with small branches or kiosks in government offices, businesses, shopping malls, or other locations. The branches would not have to own a large number of materials, but the librarian could have needed material available electronically and respond to users' needs upon request. Public library patrons who own computers would have access to materials from their homes. Most special libraries will continue to have small collections, and more and more of their information will be provided electronically.

New technologies will doubtless continue to have a major impact on the departmental patterns of all types of libraries, but, at this point, one only can speculate about what the ultimate effects will be. It can be conjectured that technological advances will permit libraries of the future to be more decentralized and thus provide their users with the geographically dispersed, individualized service that they have always preferred. It also seems likely that efforts to introduce more flexibility into libraries and information centers, including the use of cross-functional teams, will lead to libraries and information centers where the barriers between departments are much less fixed. There likely will be more changes in library structure, and workers will become accustomed to working in organizations that are periodically reshaped to fit new needs.[37] In the libraries of the future, it will be even more important for managers to observe closely the organizational structure of the library to see whether it is still adequate to achieve its objectives.

We are still moving toward those new organizational structures. Today's libraries are not like the ones of twenty years ago, but we must also realize that the libraries of 2025 also will be different from those of today. To date, the biggest changes in the organizational structure of libraries is the flattening of the hierarchy, the use of teams, and the greater inclusion of employees in decision making that has resulted from decentralization.

But the perfect organizational design for today's libraries has not been found, and many failures can be expected as part of the process. There will not be just one successful model but a number of different models. The design of an organization should be contingent upon the environment in which it operates, the tasks the employees must perform in this environment to achieve the organization's objectives, and the characteristics of these employees.[38] Each library will need to discover what works best for it, which organizational structure is most effective and efficient in allowing the organization to achieve its purposes and reach its objectives. And, as one expert wrote, there is no need for just one type of structure for an entire organization:

> For example, would anyone seriously contend that you want the management of your accounts receivable "organized" in the same way with the same amount of control as a team working on developing software for an artificial intelligence (AI) system? I certainly hope not. In one case, there is a clear need for tight control and adherence to procedures, whereas the other situation begs for unbridled creativity.[39]

Although organizations must be ready to change their forms to meet changing conditions and needs, it can be disastrous if they engage in too much or too frequent reorganization. There must be a core of stability built into the structure, because no organization or its employees can function effectively if there is frequent complete restructuring. In the early 1980s, Thomas Peters and Robert Waterman wrote that the most effective organizations "appear to be reorganizing all of the time. They are; but most of the reorganization takes place around the edges. The fundamental form rarely changes that much."[40] In their view, the most effective organizations have found a way to build stability into their structure but, at the same time, have incorporated organizational features that allow innovation and responsiveness to the external environment.

Robert Kaplan and David Norton reiterated this same notion in a recent article in which they stated that following the latest trends about restructuring can sometimes lead to "nightmares as companies start engaging in expensive and distracting restructurings." They argue that it is far more effective to choose a design that works reasonably well then to develop a system to keep the structure in tune with the organization's strategy.[41] As they point out, reorganization is extremely expensive, and new structures often create new organizational problems that replace the ones that they were designed to over-come. Restructuring an organization is not to be undertaken lightly; the fact that most libraries have not abandoned their traditional structures but merely redesigned around the edges is likely to have been a wise decision. Fine-tuning an existing structure is far easier than implementing a completely new one.

Like everything else, management trends change over time. Right now, the flat organizational structure is in fashion. Although some experts predict that the age of hierarchical structures is over, others take a different viewpoint and think that today's flatter structures are merely trends and that the bureau-cratic structures will return to popularity soon.[42]

What we should learn from the pendulum swing of management trends of all types is that there is not just one answer to any problem and that it is a mistake to adopt any prevailing model, dealing with organizing or anything else, without seeing whether that answer suits the circumstances of a particu-lar organization. The rush to flatten structures has taught us a great deal, and in certain types of organizations, flatter structures will provide more efficiency and effectiveness. However, flattening is not the only or necessarily the best approach to use in fashioning every organization's structure. Library manag-ers need to try to avoid the pendulum swings by systematically addressing the entire range of organizational issues, including organizational structure and culture. Each organization must consider its own needs and design a struc-ture to allow it to achieve its objectives. And, as much as possible, managers should involve the library's employees in the design of the new organization. Broad employee participation will create a better structure because the em-ployees' detailed knowledge of the way that specific parts of the organization work will ensure that the rationale behind the new structure is understood. This participation also will make implementing the new structure easier be-cause participation builds people's commitment to change.

CONCLUSION

Each organization must be structured to achieve its goals and objectives. The organizational structure must allow workers to specialize while coordinat-ing and integrating the activities of those workers at the same time. Although organizing is one of the most important managerial functions, it must be re-membered that it is not an end in itself but merely a means to allow the orga-nization to reach its objectives. The design principles discussed in this section are tools, which are neither good nor bad in themselves. They can be used properly or improperly, and that is all. To obtain the greatest possible simplic-ity and the greatest fit, organization design has to start out with a clear focus on key activities needed to produce key results. They have to be structured and positioned in the simplest possible design. Above all, the architect of the organization needs to keep in mind the purpose of the organization he or she is designing.

Organizational structures fail if they do not encourage workers to perform at their highest levels. As many experts have noted, too much reengineering and reorganization can result in a demoralized workforce, especially when the employees do not understand or have little input into the organizational changes. From the employees' point of view, it can appear that the organizational structure is far more important than the people who work there. In many of the reengineered structures, reorganization and downsizing have resulted in many workers losing their jobs and in feelings of instability and overwork among those who remain. At the same time, the managers in these restructured organizations are stressing the importance of their employees and touting the importance of "the performance of people." An organization's structure is important, but it is never more important than its employees. So, while libraries and other types of organizations search for better, more efficient structures, they must keep in mind that the effectiveness of the structure depends primarily on the performance of the people working there. Today, the most successful organizations are those in which top executives recognize the need to manage the new environmental and competitive demands by focusing less on the quest for an ideal structure and more on developing the abilities, behavior, and performance of individual managers.[43]

The next two sections of this book will focus on the organization's employees and will discuss the managerial functions dealing with human resources and leading. They will deal with the important and challenging issues associated with the people who work within an organization.

NOTES

1. Harvey F. Kolodny, "Some Characteristics of Organizational Designs in New/ High Technology Firms," in *Organizational Issues in High Technology Management,* ed. Luis R. Gomez-Mejia and Michael W. Lawless (Greenwich, CT: JAI Press, 1990), 174.

2. John H. Jackson and Cyril P. Morgan, *Organization Theory: A Macro Perspective for Management* (Englewood Cliffs, NJ: Prentice-Hall, 1978), 77.

3. See, for example, Robert K. Merton, "Bureaucratic Structure and Personality," *Social Forces* 18 (May 1940): 560–68; Philip Selznick, *TVA and the Grass Roots* (Berkeley and Los Angeles: University of California Press, 1969); Alvin W. Gouldner, *Patterns of Industrial Bureaucracy* (New York: Free Press, 1954).

4. See, for instance, James D. Thompson, *Organizations in Action: Social Science Bases of Administrative Theory* (New York: McGraw-Hill, 1967).

5. Warren G. Bennis, *Changing Organizations: Essays on the Development of Human Organization* (New York: McGraw-Hill, 1966); Rensis Likert, *The Human Organization: Its Management and Value* (New York: McGraw-Hill, 1967).

6. Henry Mintzberg, *The Structuring of Organizations: A Synthesis of the Research* (Englewood Cliffs, NJ: Prentice-Hall, 1979), 375.

7. Tom Burns and G. M. Stalker, *The Management of Innovation* (London: Tavistock, 1966), 119–20.

8. Michael B. McCaskey, "An Introduction to Organizational Design," *California Management Review* 17 (Winter 1974): 14.

9. Burns and Stalker, *The Management of Innovation,* 122.

10. Ibid.

11. Paul R. Lawrence and Jay W. Lorsch, *Organization and Environment: Managing Differentiation and Integration* (Boston: Graduate School of Business Administration, Harvard University, 1967).

12. David Lesniaki, Kris (Huber) MacPherson, Barbara Fister, and Steve McKinzie, "Collegial Leadership in Academic Libraries," *Proceedings of the ACRL Tenth National Conference* (Chicago: American Library Association, 2001), 233–39.

13. Susan Jacobson, "Reorganization: Premises, Processes and Pitfalls," *Bulletin of the Medical Library Association* 82 (October 1994): 370.

14. The latest of these ARL volumes devoted specifically to restructuring was published in 1996. See Association of Research Libraries, *Library Reorganization and Restructuring* (SPEC Kit 215) (Washington, DC: Association of Research Libraries, May 1996).

15. Association of Research Libraries, *Access Services* (SPEC Kit 290) (Washington, DC: Association of Research Libraries, November 2005).

16. Association of Research Libraries, *The Information Commons* (SPEC Kit 281) (Washington, DC: Association of Research Libraries, July 2004).

17. Association of Research Libraries, *Electronic Resources* (SPEC Kit 282) (Washington, DC: Association of Research Libraries, August 2004).

18. Association of Research Libraries, *Library Systems Office Organization* (SPEC Kit 271) (Washington, DC: Association of Research Libraries, November 2002).

19. Association of Research Libraries, *Integrating Preservation Activities* (SPEC Kit 269) (Washington, DC: Association of Research Libraries, October 2002).

20. Alex Bloss and Don Lanier, "The Library Department Head in the Context of Matrix Management and Reengineering," *College and Research Libraries* 58 (November 1997): 499–508.

21. Joanne R. Euster and Peter D. Haikalis, "A Matrix Model of Organization for a University Public Services Division," in *Academic Libraries: Myths and Realities* (Chicago: American Library Association, 1984), 359–60.

22. Ibid.

23. For example, see Bloss and Lanier, "The Library Department Head," 499–508.

24. Moshen Attaran and Tai T. Nguyen, "Self-Managed Work Team," *Industrial Management* 41 (July/August 1999): 24.

25. See, for example, Joseph F. Boykin Jr. and Deborah Babel, "Reorganizing the Clemson University Library," *Journal of Academic Librarianship* 19 (May 1993): 94–96; Joanne R. Euster, Judith Paquette, and Judy Kaufman, "Reorganizing for a Changing Information World," *Library Administration and Management* 11 (Spring 1997): 103–14; Joan Giesecke, "Reorganizations: An Interview with the Staff from the University of Arizona Libraries," *Library Administration and Management* 8 (Fall 1994): 196–99; Jacobson, "Reorganization," 369–74; John Lubans, "I Ain't No Cowboy, I Just Found This Hat: Confessions of an Administrator in an Organization of Self-Managing Teams," *Library Administration and Management* 10 (Winter 1996): 28–40; Nancy Markle Stanley and Lynne Branche-Brown, "Reorganizing Acquisitions at the Pennsylvania State University Libraries: From Work Units to Teams," *Library Acquisitions: Practice and Theory* 19 (1995): 417–25.

26. Bradford Lee Eden, ed., *Innovative Redesign and Reorganization of Library Technical Services* (Westport, CT: Libraries Unlimited, 2004). This book contains a great deal of information about the restructuring of technical services departments and a number of case studies that describe the reorganization process.

27. Joanne D. Eustis and Donald J. Kenney, *Library Reorganization and Restructuring* (SPEC Kit 215) (Washington, DC: Association of Research Libraries, 1996), 2.

28. Lowell Bryan and Claudia Joyce, "The 21st-Century Organization," *McKinsey Quarterly* no. 3 (2005). http://www.mckinseyquarterly.com/home.aspx

29. Peter F. Drucker, *The Practice of Management* (New York: Harper & Row, 1954), 195–201.

30. Jacobson, "Reorganization," 373.

31. Euster et al., "Reorganizing for a Changing Information World," 105.

32. Mike Knecht, "Virtual Teams in Libraries," *Library Administration and Management* 18, no. 1 (Winter 2004): 24–29.

33. Sirkka L. Jarvenpaa and Blake Ives, "The Global Network Organization of the Future: Information Management, Opportunities, and Challenges," *Journal of Management Information Systems* 10 (Spring 1994): 25–57.

34. Janet Fulk and Gerardine DeSanctis, "Electronic Communication and Changing Organizational Form," *Organization Science: A Journal of the Institute of Management Sciences* 95 (July/August 1995): 337–39.

35. James Duderstat, "A Choice of Transformations for the 21st Century University," *Chronicle of Higher Education,* 4 February 2000, B6.

36. See Library of Congress Global Reference Network Page, http://www.loc. gov/rr/digiref/ for more information.

37. Charles B. Lowry, "Continuous Organizational Development—Teamwork, Learning Leadership, and Measurement," *Portal* 5, no. 1 (January 2005): 1–6.

38. Jay Lorsch, "Organizational Design," in *Managing People and Organizations,* ed. John J. Gabarro (Boston: Harvard Business School Publications, 1992), 315.

39. Clifford Haka, "Organizational Design: Is There an Answer?" *Library Administration and Management* 10 (Spring 1996): 75.

40. Thomas J. Peters and Robert H. Waterman Jr., *In Search of Excellence: Lessons from America's Best-Run Companies* (New York: Harper & Row, 1982), 311.

41. Robert S. Kaplan and David P. Norton, "How to Implement a New Strategy without Disrupting Your Organization," *Harvard Business Review* 84, no. 3 (March 2006): 100.

42. David Fagiano, "Pendulum Swings Back," *Management Review* 86 (September 1997): 5.

43. Christopher A. Bartlett and Sumantra Ghoshal, "Matrix Management: Not a Structure, a Frame of Mind," *Harvard Business Review* 68 (July–August 1990): 138.

Human Resources

First a library plans and establishes its goals and objectives. As a result, an organizational structure is put into place to allow the organization to reach its goals. Establishing the structure would be meaningless unless there were qualified people to fill the positions in the structure. The human resources functions encompass all the tasks associated with obtaining and retaining the human resources of an organization. These tasks include recruitment, selection, training, evaluation, compensation, and development of employees.

Until recently, all of these functions dealing with human resources were termed *personnel management*, but in recent years that term has been displaced by another: *human resources management*. Although the two terms are still sometimes used synonymously, human resources management has been the favored term since 1989, when the American Society for Personnel Administration (ASPA) voted to change its name to the Society for Human Resources Management (SHRM). The name change was symbolic of the expanding role that human resources, another term for the organization's employees, play in the modern workplace. Employees are no longer looked upon just as costs to the organization; instead they are resources, just as the budget and the physical plant are resources. All resources are important, but good human resources are the greatest asset an organization can have.

The "Human Resources" section of this textbook provides an overview of the major activities associated with the employees who work in libraries and information centers. Chapter 10 describes the different types of staff found in a typical library, discusses the organizational framework of various types of positions that must be established before an organization can hire a staff, and provides an overview of the process of recruiting and hiring staff to fill those positions. Chapter 11 focuses on the functions that relate directly to individuals holding jobs within an organization. These employee functions include training, developing, evaluating, compensating, and disciplining. Finally, chapter 12 looks at some of the general issues that have had a major impact on human resources in libraries. That chapter will cover topics such as personnel procedures and policies, career development, mentoring, health and safety, external regulations, and unionization.

Chapter 10

Staffing the Library

Overview

Terry is just about to graduate with an MLIS degree and is looking for a first position in a library. Terry is entering the profession at a propitious time. Today's libraries are stimulating organizations in which new graduates usually assume positions that provide a good measure of responsibility, autonomy, and creativity. New librarians also are entering a profession in which there is a looming shortage of LIS graduates and a pressing need to recruit new librarians and develop new leaders in order to replace those about to retire. Terry begins to read the professional job advertisements in print and online and applies for a number of openings that appear promising. The libraries that have these open positions have done preparatory work before advertising. Each has had to look at its vacant position and decide whether it should be restructured or left the same. The position description has been updated or rewritten in preparation for the new hire, and the library has designed a recruitment plan to attract good applicants. If all goes well, there will be a good match between Terry's aspirations and the needs of one of those libraries, and Terry will be offered a position as a professional librarian.

One of the most important functions that managers do is structuring the human resources aspect of the organization. There are many elements in this human resources function, but one of the most basic is that of structuring the positions within an organization and then finding capable individuals to fill those jobs.

This chapter will provide an introduction to the human resources function of management. It will give an overview of the type of workers employed by libraries and how their positions are structured. Finally, it will look at the process of recruiting and hiring employees to fill positions in libraries.

Although, in the past, employees often were considered to be interchangeable, easily replaced components of their organizations, a different view predominates today. Employees are now seen as resources, just as the funding to operate the organization and the building in which it is housed are resources. All resources are important, but good human resources are the greatest assets an organization can have.

The human resources function of management has been transformed by this new attitude toward employees. Now that human resources (usually abbreviated as HR) are recognized as one of the most valuable assets of organizations, individuals who hold positions as HR specialists are considered to be a strategic part of the management team, instead of merely paper-pushing, clerical workers. Today's HR specialists spend a large part of their time matching organizational problems to human resources solutions and, by doing so, demonstrating the impact that HR has on the bottom line of the organization.[1]

Large libraries usually have specially trained individuals who work exclusively on the HR aspects of management. These individuals, usually called human resources or personnel directors, are responsible for overseeing the HR function. In libraries, human resources/personnel directors are often individuals who have MLIS degrees with additional course work and experience in HR management. Many libraries and information agencies, however, are too small to have one person serve as a full-time HR or personnel specialist. Instead, the director usually performs those top-level HR functions that relate to the entire organization, or many of the HR functions are done by the library's parent organization (for instance, the appropriate county or city government office for a public library).

But, in every library, even in those large enough to have an HR department, all managers, from directors down to first-line supervisors, are involved in HR functions. Because the largest allocation of the budget goes toward personnel costs, library managers must be able to handle people if they want their organization to be effective and efficient. Although the degree of responsibility for HR increases as a manager moves up the hierarchy, the principles of good HR management should be widely understood throughout the organization.

Often, one of the most challenging and sometimes frustrating aspects of every manager's job is dealing with people-related problems. Because no organization is static, the people in it and the problems associated with them change. There are times when no sooner is one personnel problem solved than another develops. It is much more difficult to deal with people than with inanimate objects, because each person is different. Some managers proceed on the mistaken notion that everyone can be treated identically, but techniques that have worked well with one employee frequently will not be effective when dealing with another. So, although it is relatively easy to learn the basic principles of HR management, dealing with employees is a never-ending challenge.

THE INCREASING COMPLEXITY OF HUMAN RESOURCES MANAGEMENT

Managing HR has become more complex in the last few decades for a number of reasons. One of these reasons is the increasing diversity of the workforce. As the workforce becomes less homogenous, a manager has to learn to deal with people from many different backgrounds. *Diversity* is a broad term encompassing not only race, ethnicity, and gender, but also characteristics such as age and physical ability. This diversity enriches the organization, but it also can present problems unless managers understand the needs of these new workers and accept the challenge of managing a heterogeneous workforce.

Another reason for the increasing complexity of HR management centers around the expectations of most contemporary workers, especially well-educated employees who expect to have jobs that are meaningful and that provide opportunities for promotion and career advancement. No longer are most employees content to remain in dead-end jobs in which they have no input in the decisions that affect them and their jobs. The library profession is thus seeking ways to empower library employees by decentralizing decision making and increasing employees' control over their work environment.

Yet another factor that is changing the nature of managing people in libraries and information centers is technology. In the past two decades, technology has restructured many library jobs, created others, and eliminated still others. Technology brings many benefits for library employees and users; at the same time, it complicates the jobs of managers and employees. Some employees find it difficult to adapt to an environment in which technology is constantly changing. Also, in some organizations, technology is used to monitor the amount of work that employees perform, which produces stress for many employees. In addition to psychic stress, technology also can produce physical problems, often caused by the repetitive motions involved in using keyboards for long periods of time. Managers have had to become more knowledgeable about the potential and pitfalls of technology and its impact on employees.[2]

Jobs not only are being restructured because of technology, but, as discussed in the previous section, many of the hierarchical organizational patterns also are being modified. Instead of a group of workers reporting to one supervisor, in many types of organizations the workforce is now structured into teams, which, to some extent, manage themselves. Team organization brings benefits to workers, but it also presents new challenges to managers.

In addition, many organizations have downsized, and in many cases, fewer employees are employed doing more work than had been done previously. Other organizations are relying more heavily on part-time or temporary workers or have outsourced processes that used to be performed internally. Both organizations that are in the process of downsizing and those that have a large number of temporary employees provide additional complexities to HR managers.

Finally, the job of the manager has become more complicated because of the growing number of external regulations, especially those from state and federal governments. The purpose of these regulations is to make organizations safer and more equitable. External regulations are not new; laws relating to pay, safety, and labor relations have been in place for decades. However, the number of regulations with which organizations must comply has increased, and managers dealing with people need to be knowledgeable about the various, often complex, regulations that pertain to their employees.

All of these factors will be discussed in greater depth in the three chapters of this section, which provide an overview of the HR functions in libraries and information centers. This chapter provides a description of the different types of staff found in a typical library, presents information about the organizational framework that must be established before an organization can hire a staff, and then discusses recruiting and hiring. Chapter 11 focuses on the HR functions that relate directly to individuals holding jobs within an organization. These functions include training, evaluating, compensating, and disciplining employees. Finally, chapter 12 examines some of the external issues, especially legal issues and unionization, that have had a major impact on HR in libraries.

TYPES OF STAFF

Like other types of organizations, libraries employ a diverse group of employees with various levels of education and responsibility. As libraries have incorporated more technology into their processes, the staff employed by them necessarily has become more varied. Professional librarians almost always constitute the smallest group of library employees. Usually, to be considered a professional librarian, an individual must have earned a master's degree in library or information science (MLIS). Sometimes these professionals also hold a second master's degree in a subject field or a doctorate. The professional staff works at those tasks that are predominantly intellectual and nonroutine, those requiring "a special background and education on the basis of which library needs are identified, problems are analyzed, goals are set, and original and creative solutions are formulated for them, integrating theory into practice, and planning, organizing, communicating, and administering successful programs of service to users of the library's materials and services."[3] Professional librarians serve in leadership roles, directing the total organization and the various departments and subunits. They also provide the expertise needed to fulfill the information needs of the library's patrons.

The support staff consists of workers with a varied set of skills, from paraprofessional to clerical. The support staff is usually the largest group of full-time employees in a library, and their activities cover a wide range of essential duties, including the tasks of entering, coding, and verifying bibliographic data; maintaining book funds; ordering; circulating materials; claiming serials; filing; and copy cataloging. This support staff handles the routine operations in most departments. The educational background of these workers varies widely. Some may have only a high school diploma, but many have a bachelor's degree, and some have graduate degrees of various kinds. And, in the past few decades especially, libraries have needed both librarians and support staff with a strong technology background. Many libraries and information centers now employ specialists to work specifically with technology—for instance, to manage the library's local area network or to maintain Web pages. These technology specialists also have a variety of types of degrees and training.

In addition, libraries usually employ a large number of part-time employees. Part-time employees, such as pages in public libraries and student assistants in academic libraries, work at easily learned, repetitive tasks, such as retrieving items from the stacks or shelving returned books. Because these workers typically remain at their jobs for only a limited period of time, they require a great deal of training and supervision in proportion to the number of hours they work.

As mentioned previously, libraries are labor-intensive organizations, and, traditionally, the largest part of their budgets has been devoted to staff. In the past, the traditional rule of thumb for dividing library budgets was 60 percent for personnel, 30 percent for materials, and 10 percent for other expenses. This budget ratio is rapidly being discarded. Many libraries are now confronted with no-growth or shrinking budgets, whereas costs for library technology and library materials are climbing rapidly. A number of libraries have tried to reduce the size of their staff in order to cut their HR costs. Like private corporations, libraries have become "leaner and meaner" organizations. Some feel that, for libraries to remain viable, still larger changes must be made. For instance, one library director has advocated that research libraries "reverse the current standard in budget ratios. The new look should be 33 percent for staff, 50 percent for materials/access, and 17 percent for 'other.'"[4] A change of this magnitude will be difficult to implement without an accompanying reduction in service and a loss of employee morale.

Nonetheless, libraries and information centers, like other organizations, must strive to improve their productivity. Many of them are turning to part-time and contract workers in an attempt to achieve more flexibility and to save money. A recent survey showed that about 17 percent of 2005 MLIS graduates are working in part-time professional positions.[5] Other libraries and information centers are using part-time and contract workers to perform such services as janitorial and groundskeeping functions.

A number of libraries have decided to outsource certain functions, including such core tasks as cataloging, to outside agencies. The term *outsourcing* refers to purchasing from an outside source certain services or goods that an organization previously provided or produced for itself. A recent study found no evidence that outsourcing has a negative impact on library services or management.[6]

All of these new methods of getting work done with different types of workers have the possibility of presenting problems to a manager. There is often a potential clash of attitudes about values and service between the permanent staff and these more temporary workers.[7] Long-term contract workers, hired as a cost-cutting measure to do basically the same job as regular employees but without receiving benefits, often resent the dual standard of compensation. A library has less control over employees who are doing outsourced work than it does over employees who work within the organization itself. Libraries, like other organizations, must become more productive, but managers need to realize that these economizing measures can make both the manager's work and the employees' lives more difficult.

Despite all of these attempts to reduce the number of employees,[8] there has not been a significant reduction in the percentage of library budgets devoted to staff. According to the National Center for Education Statistics, in 2004 public libraries still devoted more than 65 percent of their budgets to staff.[9] Academic libraries reported that a lower percentage of their budget, 50.1 percent, was spent on salaries and wages.[10] When information technology was first introduced into libraries, it was predicted that the number of employees would decline as a result. This has not proved to be true. Like other types of organizations, libraries have invested large amounts of funding in information technology but have still not seen an increase in productivity.[11] To date, this new technology has done more to change the nature of the jobs in libraries than it has to cut the number of people needed to provide effective library service. Ironically, in many cases, technology actually has increased the demands for library services and has therefore resulted in the need to add staff to meet these demands.

What Do You Think?

Bill Gates has stated that "Job categories change constantly in an evolving economy. Once all telephone calls were made through an operator.... Today there are comparatively few telephone operators, even though the volume of calls is greater than ever. Automation has taken over."

What are some jobs in libraries that have been affected by technology and automation?

How have the HR policies and procedures of libraries been changed by the increasing importance of technology in libraries of all types?

Bill Gates, *The Road Ahead,* with Nathan Myhrvold and Peter Rinearson (New York: Viking, 1995), 253.

One of the most difficult issues that library administrators continue to face is matching the appropriate level of work to the appropriate type of employee. For many years, professional librarians spent at least part of their working day engaged in tasks that did not require a professional background. This was especially true in small libraries, because, in many, the only employee was a professional librarian. During the 1930s and early 1940s, it was not uncommon to find libraries in which 50 percent or more of the total staff was classified as professional librarians. In the past few decades, the tasks that professional librarians perform have become more clearly demarcated from those done by other staff members, and, in many cases, tasks that previously had been done by professionals have been transferred to the support staff. These transfers have been made possible by the increase in the number of staff members in most libraries, as well as by the introduction of new technologies. Allen Veaner has described this shift in task-oriented work from the professional staff to the support staff as a "technological imperative." Once a technology is applied to carry out a routine job, that work is driven downward in the work hierarchy, away from professionals whose work then expands to include new and more challenging responsibilities. This change has provided professional enrichment opportunities for librarians and similarly has enriched the jobs of support staff.[12]

Although some small libraries still have only one professional librarian and perhaps a clerical worker, in most larger libraries today the ratio is usually one professional librarian to three support staff members. In some libraries, the proportion of professional to support staff is even smaller. As library technology advances, it may be feasible to turn over still more functions to support staff, and the ratio of professional to nonprofessional workers may decrease even further.

THE LIS EDUCATION AND HUMAN RESOURCE UTILIZATION POLICY

The most comprehensive attempt to clarify desirable staffing patterns in libraries is the American Library Association's revised Library and Information Studies Education and Human Resource Utilization policy.[13] This document demonstrates: (1) that skills other than those of librarianship are needed in libraries and (2) that nonlibrarians must have equal recognition in both the professional and the support ranks of libraries.

Skills other than those of librarianship have an important contribution to make to the achievement of superior library service. There should be equal recognition in the library for those individuals whose expertise contributes to its effective performance. To accomplish this goal, the document recommends that libraries establish a dual career lattice that allows both librarians and nonlibrary specialists to advance in their chosen careers.

In addition to recognizing the importance of specialists, the LIS Education and HR Utilization policy recommends that librarians be permitted to advance within an organization without becoming administrators. In many libraries, promotion and advancement are possible only when an employee assumes greater supervisory responsibility. However, there is a great need for administrators to recognize and to reward financially the important role that nonadministrative librarians play. The LIS Education and HR Utilization policy states:

> [There are] many areas of special knowledge within librarianship which are equally important [as administration] and to which equal recognition in prestige and salary should be given. Highly qualified persons with specialist responsibilities in some aspects of librarianship—archives, bibliography, reference, for example—should be eligible for advanced status and financial rewards without being forced to abandon for administrative responsibilities their areas of major competence.[14]

Although the original version of the LIS Education and HR Utilization policy was produced more than thirty-five years ago, most libraries and information centers have yet to deal successfully with some of its recommendations. Many libraries, despite the influx of nonlibrarian specialists, have not yet adopted dual career lattices to allow nonlibrarians to advance, nor do they have procedures for allowing employees to advance in salary and rank without becoming administrators.

The strict demarcation that was once observed in most libraries between support staff and professional librarians has been eroded as virtually all

Figure 10.1—Dual Career Lattices

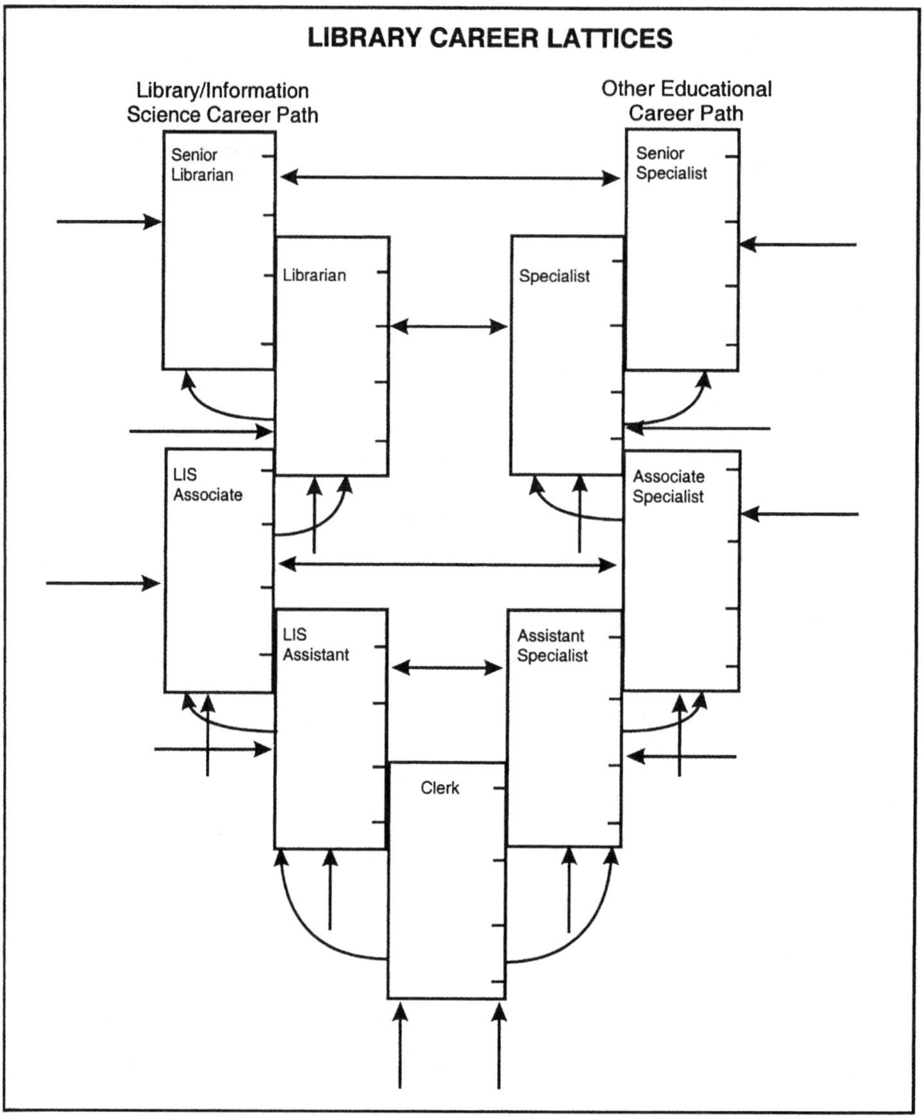

Source: From "Library and Information Studies Education and Human Resource Utilization" (Chicago: American Library Association, 2002), 5. Reprinted by permission of the American Library Association.

employees of libraries have become knowledge workers.[15] Support staff members are being increasingly used in "new and reconfigured roles, in many cases performing tasks previously considered to be the exclusive province of librarians."[16] This overlap sometimes causes tension, and even resentment, among support staff as they, "see themselves performing the tasks they have watched librarians perform for years, as well as the challenging new tasks created by automation, but for less money and lower status."[17]

Both professional librarians and support staff have new names that reflect this increasing diversity. For instance, librarians are not just called librarians anymore. Increasingly, their titles provide a framework for the technological role that they play within the library. Professional journals and electronic mailing lists reflect these new roles; they are filled with openings for technology consultant, technology training coordinator, head of the Digital Information Literacy Office, information systems librarian, head of computer services, Web master, cybrarian, and Internet services librarian.[18]

In a similar way, the old clerical functions of library support staff have been transformed. The types of support workers employed in libraries and information agencies have increased in number, reflecting the changing and varied responsibilities of the support staff in today's libraries.[19] Some of the many job classifications of support personnel can be seen in table 10.1.

The library profession has not yet come up with a uniform model that addresses these types of staffing patterns. Libraries and librarians need to look at the necessary qualifications for all levels of library work and then hire a workforce that has qualifications matching those needs. It seems inevitable that the staffing patterns of libraries will continue to shift in the twenty-first century and that the realities of budgeting will force libraries to look for economical ways to provide the staffing they need.

Charles Handy has suggested that the organizations of the future will be "shamrock" organizations, made up of three different groups of workers, "groups with different expectations, managed differently, paid differently, organized differently."[20] The first leaf of the shamrock is composed of the core workers, those employees who are essential and permanent. This core group

TABLE 10.1 Types of Support Staff

Delivery Worker	Applications Systems Analyst	Human Resources Specialist
Development Associate	Systems Specialist	LA Specialist/ Coordinator
TV Repair Supervisor	Public Information Officer	Photographer
Curatorial Assistant	Business Coordinator	Fiscal Officer
Learning Disabilities Specialist	Graphic Design Specialist	Adult Literacy Specialist
Bookmobile Driver	Marketing Specialist	Volunteer Resources
Gallery Manager	Electronic Technician	Network Specialist

is becoming smaller in all types of organizations. Work increasingly is being done by workers in the two other leaves: the contract workers and the part-time and temporary workers. Although these other groups of workers always have existed, what is different today is the relative size of the three groups. Although the core workers are decreasing in number, the other two groups are increasing in size because their use allows greater flexibility if budget cuts need to be made.[21] Like other types of organizations, many libraries are relying on a smaller core group and are therefore using more part-time workers or are outsourcing tasks that used to be performed by core workers.

THE ORGANIZATIONAL FRAMEWORK FOR STAFFING

As described in the previous section, organizations are formed and jobs are created when the overall task of the organization is too large for any one individual. Libraries, like all organizations, are networks of interacting components. Jobs are the individual building blocks upon which the organization is built.

Although the terms *job, position,* and *occupation* are often used interchangeably, each actually has a distinct definition in human resources terminology. A position is a collection of tasks and responsibilities that constitute the total work assignment of one person. Thus, there are as many different positions in an organization as there are people employed there. The Slavic language cataloger in a large academic library holds a position, as does the bookmobile driver in a public library. A job, on the other hand, is a group of positions that generally involve the same responsibilities, knowledge, duties, and skills. Many employees, all performing slightly different work, may be classified under the same job title. A library may employ many catalogers, all of whom have different responsibilities but whose duties are similar enough to be classified in the same job group. An occupation is defined as a general class of job found in a number of different organizations; for example, librarianship is considered to be an occupation.

A job always should be a planned entity consisting of assigned tasks that require similar or related skills, knowledge, or ability. Ideally, jobs should never be created haphazardly at the whim of an employee or to suit the special knowledge or ability of a particular individual. Instead, jobs should be designed carefully to ensure maximum organizational effectiveness. It is the responsibility of the library administration to identify the tasks that are to be included in a job. The tasks should be similar or related. All the tasks to be accomplished by a specific job should require approximately the same level of education. One task should not be so excessively complex that extensive education is required, whereas another be so simple that it could be performed by an individual with much less education. Further, the tasks assigned to any one job should require comparable experience. Some tasks can be performed only after extensive experience, whereas others can be executed by novices. And finally, tasks assigned to a job should require comparable responsibility. Some tasks have end responsibility, which means that there is no review of the task after it has been completed. The action of the individual in a job having end responsibility is final. Such end responsibility is frequently found in reference services, book selection, and top administration. Other jobs require little or no end responsibility. Revisers in a catalog department may have end responsibility, whereas the catalogers whose work is revised have no end responsibility. To summarize, a well-defined job has assigned to it tasks that are (1) comparable in the amount of education required, (2) comparable in the amount of experience required, and (3) comparable in the degree of responsibility required.

It was long a principle of job design that all the tasks that constituted a job should, if possible, be related to the accomplishment of a single function, process, or program or should be related to the same subject field or type of material. In large institutions, this was easily accomplished; in small institutions, however, workers often had to work in multiple areas. Although the assignment of a single function, process, or program to a job makes sense in terms of efficiency, it still can be carried too far. There is now a much greater interest in jobs that allow workers to practice multiple skills. This new interest reflects a growing belief that to make a job too narrow may, in many cases, be detrimental to both workers and managers. To increase the flexibility within organizations, jobs are now being designed to take advantage of multiple skills. More organizations are encouraging cross-training; that is, having employees learn the techniques associated with jobs that are not their own. This is so that, if the need arose, there would be additional employees who would know how to get a specific job done. Workers are being encouraged to work both with and across multiple functions and units.

This flexibility and broadening of job responsibilities is a change in the way that jobs traditionally have been structured. The allotment of narrow, specialized portions of a large task to specific workers is known as division of labor. Adam Smith, in *The Wealth of Nations* (1776), first wrote about the benefits of division of labor.[22] When each job consists primarily of a few simple, repetitive tasks, the skill level and training required for performing that job are low.

In the United States, during most of the twentieth century, both the scientific management principles popularized by Frederick W. Taylor and the Detroit style of mass production introduced by Henry Ford heavily influenced the thinking of individuals who designed jobs. There was widespread acceptance of the principle of dividing tasks into small component units and then having each worker responsible for just a small portion of the overall task. This type of job design promoted efficiency and ease of training. More recently, however, there has been a realization that this approach to job design often leads to worker dissatisfaction and alienation. Workers who perform one small task over and over begin to feel like cogs in a machine. Now, many industries are trying to provide job enrichment by redesigning jobs so that they comprise a wider variety of tasks and more responsibility. In addition, all organizations, including libraries, are rethinking the design of their jobs in an attempt to find better ways of accomplishing the objectives of the organization.

Although few library jobs were ever as narrow and confining as those on an assembly line, the principle of job enrichment is especially important in organizations like libraries and information centers. The educational level of most of the employees in a library is typically quite high, and well-educated workers usually seek jobs that are intellectually challenging. A job should not be so restrictive that assigned tasks are quickly mastered and soon become monotonous and boring. Instead, the scope of a job should be large enough to challenge and encourage employees to increase their skills, knowledge, and abilities. Some jobs in libraries must be performed according to prescribed procedures to maintain uniformity or because of standardized methodologies. These jobs are generally low in the hierarchy. Nevertheless, even at this level, the employee should be given every opportunity to be creative, to exercise initiative, and to vary the routines of the job, as long as the established standards are maintained.

Technology has had the greatest impact on lower-level jobs, in which work is routine, and it has had less on higher-level jobs, in which decision making is concentrated. Still, just adding technology to a job function does not in itself make the job more interesting. Instead, sometimes information technology can lead to deskilling when the computer takes decision making away from an employee. One study of paraprofessional technical services positions found that the introduction of technology had changed the positions over time primarily by changing the tools with which the work was done. It had done little to add autonomy, authority, and decision making to the positions.[23]

Although the buzzword now in all types of organizations is "empowerment," it must be remembered that there are some workers who do not want to be empowered. A basic rule of HR management is to match the individual to the job. Following that principle, workers who do not want autonomy and empowerment should not be placed in positions in which they will need to work without supervision and direction. Nonetheless, the talents of a great number of workers are underutilized at the present time, and it benefits both the worker and the organization to create jobs that allow these employees to work to their full potential. If libraries want their employees to be innovative and responsible, they must provide jobs that give the employees an opportunity to develop these attributes.

J. R. Hackman and G. R. Oldham have proposed a model of job enrichment that identifies five core job dimensions that are essential to job enrichment. These dimensions are:

- Skill variety—the extent to which a job requires a number of different activities using a number of skills and talents.
- Task identity: the extent to which a job requires completing a whole piece of work from beginning to end.
- Task significance: the worker's view of the importance of the job.
- Autonomy: the extent to which employees have the freedom to plan, schedule, and carry out their jobs as desired.
- Feedback: the extent to which a job allows the employee to have information about the effectiveness of their performance.

As figure 10.2 illustrates, these core job characteristics lead to critical psychological states that allow the worker to experience the meaningfulness of the work, responsibility for the outcome of the work, and knowledge of the actual results of the work. These psychological states affect an employee's feeling of motivation, quality of work performed, and satisfaction with work and lead to low absenteeism and turnover.[24]

Just as organizations are changing, so are the jobs within organizations. Managers need to look at the jobs in their organization and see if they are

Figure 10.2—Hackman and Oldham's Core Job Characteristics

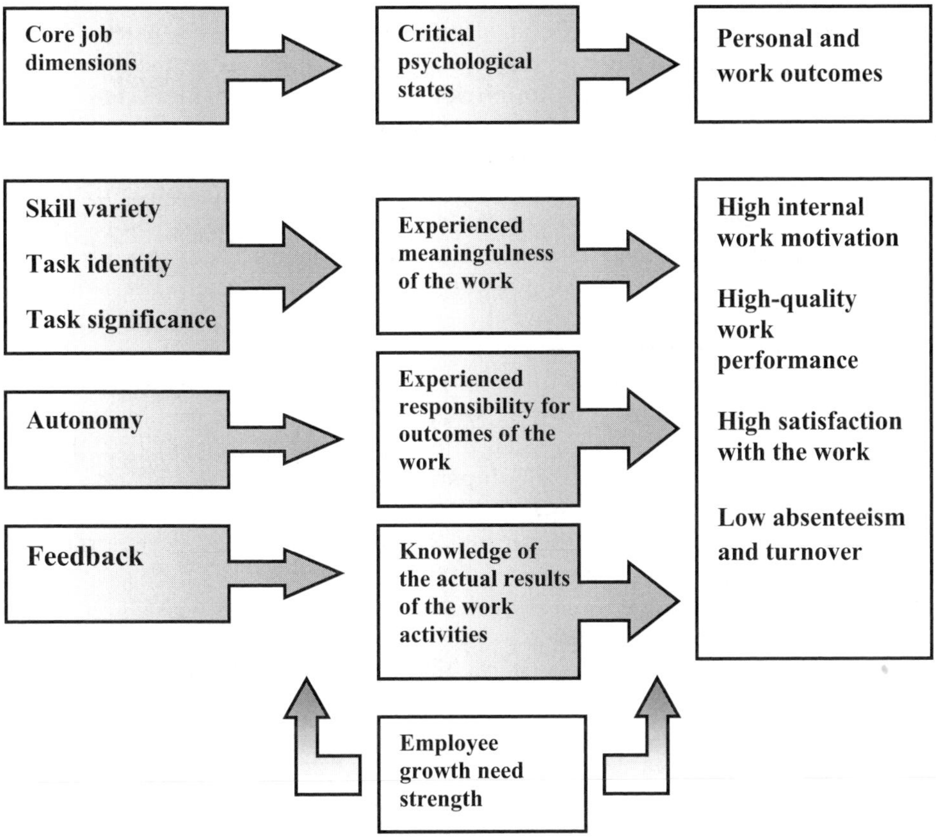

Core job dimensions	→	Critical psychological states	→	Personal and work outcomes

Skill variety / Task identity / Task significance	→	Experienced meaningfulness of the work	→	High internal work motivation
Autonomy	→	Experienced responsibility for outcomes of the work	→	High-quality work performance / High satisfaction with the work
Feedback	→	Knowledge of the actual results of the work activities	→	Low absenteeism and turnover

Employee growth need strength

Source: Adapted from J. R. Hackman and G. R. Oldman, *Work Redesign* (Reading, MA: Addison-Wesley, 1980).

designed in a way that balances the need for efficiency with the need for a more enriched job to ensure employee motivation.

Job Descriptions

After a job has been established, the next step is to write a job description that specifies the duties associated with that job; the relationship of the job to other units of the institution; and the personal characteristics, such as education, skill, and experience, required to perform the job. Today, most government agencies and private companies require job descriptions for all employees. Job descriptions vary from organization to organization but generally contain the following elements:

1. Job identification. This section of the description typically includes the job title, line number, and department.
2. Job summary. This section of the job description provides details of the job's major responsibilities and provides a justification for its existence.

3. Job activities and procedures. This section includes a description of the tasks performed by the incumbent of the job, sometimes including the percentage of the job that is devoted to each of its tasks. There should be a clear delineation of what the duties and responsibilities of the job are, although some flexibility is often inserted by the use of a phrase such as, "and other duties on occasion as assigned." The enumeration of the job's activities and procedures is the most important part of the job description. This enumeration identifies for the employee the exact tasks for which he or she will be responsible. It also indicates to the supervisor those tasks that require training, supervision, or task evaluation. Without this section of the job description, neither the employee nor the supervisor knows what the employee is expected to do.

4. Relationship of the job to the total institution. This section states the title of the person to whom the incumbent reports, the number of employees or the organizational unit supervised by this job, and the internal and external relationships required by the job.

5. Job requirements. Job requirements are established by each organization and identify the minimum acceptable qualifications required for an employee to perform the job. Requirements often include amount of education; amount of experience; and special skills, knowledge, or abilities. All job requirements should be necessary for the successful performance of the job. For some jobs, requirements are set unrealistically high, which artificially restricts the pool of possible applicants. Sometimes, job specifications reflect the characteristics the organization would like the employee to have and not what is actually necessary to perform the job effectively. Job specifications (e.g., an educational requirement such as a college degree) that are not essential for successful job performance are invalid and may violate Title VII of the Civil Rights Act of 1964.

Job descriptions fulfill several important administrative and HR needs. A job description may be used in recruiting new employees. Not only does the recruiter know exactly the capabilities for which to search, but the candidate also knows exactly what would be expected if the job were accepted. For this reason, the job description always should be made available to applicants for their study and review. After an individual has been hired, the job description becomes the basis for determining training needs and for identifying tasks that require special effort before the employee can perform them well. Later, the job description becomes the basis for the employee's formal performance appraisal. Job descriptions also are used to evaluate a job's worth, in order to aid in developing a compensation structure. Figure 10.3 shows a job description from an academic library. Other job descriptions can be seen on this book's Web site (http://www.lu.com/management).

Job Analysis

In principle, a job should be stable over time. Once it has been defined and the characteristics necessary to perform it have been specified, the job should

Figure 10.3—Job Description from an Academic Library

Collection Development Librarian, Rare Book, Manuscript, and Special Collections Library

The Collection Development Librarian, along with other staff, contributes to the growth, organization, interpretation, and conservation of RBMSCL collections in a broad range of subject areas.

<u>**Responsibilities**</u>
• Identifies, selects, solicits, and acquires by purchase and gift a broad range of materials, including books, newspapers, maps, manuscripts, ephemera, broadsides, photographs, and electronic media; works in close consultation with faculty, subject librarians, library staff, donors, and dealers.
• Develops, maintains, and implements collecting policies in areas of responsibility. In consultation with faculty, subject librarians, and other library staff, determines priorities for collecting activities and coordinates development of special collections with other Duke Libraries' collections.
• Manages and expends funds, including restricted and endowed acquisition funds in areas of responsibility.
• Provides specialized reference assistance to students, faculty, and visiting scholars, both on-site and remotely; participates in weekend RBMSCL reference rotation.
• Working with RBMSCL research services staff and with the Perkins Library System instruction and outreach programs, provides library instruction and other outreach services related to RBMSCL resources.
• Plans and prepares exhibits, publications, online guides, public programs, and other activities or products that promote the Library's collections.
• Serves as appropriate on Perkins Library System groups relating to collecting and on other Perkins and RBMSCL committees and task forces.
• Performs other relevant duties as needed.

Qualifications: Required: Master's degree from an ALA-accredited program or an advanced degree in a relevant discipline. At least one year of rare book and manuscript collecting and librarianship experience; strong reading knowledge in one or more modern European languages; excellent interpersonal, oral and written communication skills; creativity, flexibility, initiative, and interest in non-traditional as well as traditional collecting areas; ability to work independently and as a member of a team; working knowledge of MS Office applications; demonstrated commitment to providing outstanding customer service. **Preferred:** Advanced degree in a subject relevant to RBMSCL collections. Ideal candidate will have 1-3 years professional librarian experience, equivalent to an Assistant Librarian rank. Diverse experience in successfully acquiring rare books and manuscripts for an academic library; reading knowledge of two or more European languages, especially German, French and/or Italian; knowledge of archival practices, book history and bibliography; experience in the antiquarian book and manuscript trade; experience producing exhibits, publications, guides, and web sites; familiarity with the ExLibris integrated library system.

not be appreciably changed by the incumbents holding the job or by different situations. In reality, though, jobs are dynamic and often change considerably over time. New machinery or equipment may be introduced. Departments or even entire libraries may be reorganized. Changing technology may alter the skill requirements of a job. In libraries, for instance, the job of cataloger has changed greatly since the introduction of bibliographic utilities. Thus, it is important to remember that job descriptions and specifications must be kept up-to-date to ensure that they still describe the activities and characteristics of that job.

Because all jobs change over time and because employees, by emphasizing or deemphasizing certain portions of their jobs, can produce drastic changes in their jobs, all organizations should occasionally perform a job analysis. This analysis allows the institution to gather information about what is actually being done by employees holding specific jobs. A variety of methods may be employed for a job analysis. Some of the most common include direct observation of the job, interviews, written questionnaires, and requesting employees to record what they do on a job in a daily log or diary. Each of these methods has its advantages and disadvantages. It is beneficial to acquire data using more than one of these methods in order to make sure that sufficient information is gathered. The results of a job analysis can be useful in writing new job descriptions, in specifying the skills and abilities needed by workers holding the job, and in determining the appropriate compensation for that job. A job analysis also can indicate when a job needs to be redesigned. Although employees sometimes feel threatened by a job analysis, in most cases, the data provided by the analysis allow an organization to manage its HR effectively and to provide better training, performance evaluation, and promotion and compensation opportunities.

Because a complete job analysis of all positions is not only time-consuming but also demands extensive expertise, complete analyses are not performed regularly in libraries. When they are, library administrators often call in special HR or management consultants to help accomplish the analysis. Another approach found in some libraries is to use the HR department of the parent institution to perform the analysis. For example, the HR department of a municipal or county government or of a college or university might assist in designing and carrying out the job analysis program.

To keep jobs up-to-date between complete analyses, supervisors should report any significant changes in the makeup of tasks in their units. Also, some institutions conduct periodic audits of the jobs in every department. The audit involves checking the tasks that actually are being performed against the ones specified in the job description. When discrepancies are found, either changes are made in the work habits of the employee, if certain essential tasks are not being carried out, or changes are made in the job description, so that it reflects the changes that have occurred in the job for legitimate reasons (e.g., the introduction of new equipment or technology).

Job Evaluation

After jobs have been designed and accurate job descriptions written, all the jobs within the organization are arranged in a hierarchical order. An attempt is made to enumerate the requirements of each job and its contribution to the organization and then to classify it according to importance. Skill, education, experience, and the amount of end responsibility are common criteria used in making this evaluation. A number of methods can be used to assign jobs to ranked categories.

Some organizations use the point method. These organizations develop a quantitative point scale that identifies the factors involved in a job, and they then assign weights to these factors. The higher the number of points, the higher the job is in the hierarchy. Other organizations use a factor system, in which job rank is calculated by comparing jobs with one another and also by subdividing them into factors that have dollar values attached to them. The factor method is similar to the point method but with a monetary scale in place of a point scale.

Two nonquantitative systems are widely used for evaluating jobs. Simple ranking systems compare actual positions to one another to create a ranked hierarchy. Similarly, a job classification system defines classes of jobs on the basis of duties, skills, abilities, responsibilities, and other job-related qualities. The jobs are grouped into classes arranged in a hierarchy. Regardless of the system used, it is always the job that is classified, not the employee holding the job.

The hierarchically arranged jobs are divided into groups, which vary from library to library. Usually, all professional librarian positions fall into one group; library associates or paraprofessionals into another; and library technicians, clerks, and custodians into still others. Within each group, there will be hierarchical levels based upon the experience, education, and responsibility associated with each job. A job title is assigned to each level, usually modified by the use of a numeral. Jobs requiring the same level of education, experience, and responsibility are given the same title, although the tasks associated with each may be different. Both an experienced reference librarian and an experienced cataloger could be classified as Librarian III. Figure 10.4 shows a hierarchy of professional library positions.

Figure 10.4—A Hierarchy of Professional Positions

Job Title	Education	Experience	End Responsibility
Librarian IV	MLIS from an accredited LIS school plus an Advanced Certificate	10 years with 3 years in supervisory position	Final responsibility for the operation of the institution
Librarian III	MLIS from an accredited LIS school plus subject specialization	5 years of professional experience	Under general supervision and according to policies, end responsibility for a department
Librarian II	MLIS from an accredited LIS school	2 years of professional experience	Under general supervision and according to policies, responsible for a unit of a department
Librarian I	MLIS from an accredited LIS school	0 years of professional experience	Under general supervision and according to policies, performs assigned task

The same procedure is used for all other job groups. A hierarchy of clerical-level jobs is shown in figure 10.5. There is no standard for the number of levels in each group. In larger institutions there may be many, in smaller ones only a few.

Figure 10.5—A Hierarchy of Support-Level Positions

Job Title	Education	Experience	End Responsibility
Clerk III	High school plus business school graduate	3 years of experience	Under general supervision, end responsibility for payroll
Clerk II	High school plus some business school	2 years of experience	Under general supervision, end responsibility for verifying invoices
Clerk I	High school diploma	0 years of experience	Under close supervision, perform assigned tasks

RECRUITMENT AND HIRING

Once a library has its positions established, they need to be filled. Filling these jobs is a multistep process, which is illustrated in figure 10.6. The first step is recruiting applicants to apply for the jobs. Recruitment involves seeking and attracting a pool of applicants from which qualified candidates for a vacant position can be chosen.

Recruiting has become an especially important consideration because some libraries are finding it difficult to attract enough qualified applicants to fill vacant librarian positions. This need to attract new professionals is especially critical for libraries because of the demographics of the library workforce. Research has shown that, overall, librarians are significantly older than most other professionals. For instance, a study that examined the age of librarians in the large Association of Research Libraries (ARL) institutions showed that, relative to comparable professions, librarianship contains one-third the number of individuals aged 35 and younger and almost 75 percent more individuals aged 45 and older.[25] Another recent study that looked at age distribution of librarians showed that a very large percentage of librarians will reach the age of 65, the traditional age of retirement, between 2005 and 2014.[26] The numbers can be seen in figure 10.7.

Figure 10.6—The Stages in Recruiting and Hiring

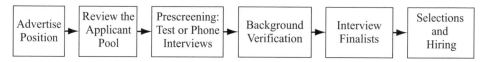

Figure 10.7—U.S. Librarians Reaching Age 65, 1990–2034

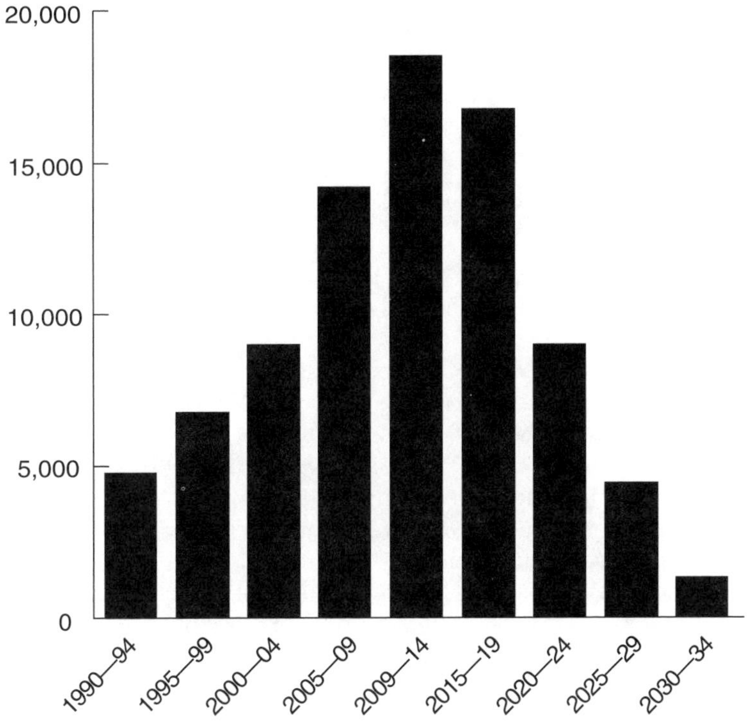

Source: Reprinted by permission of the American Library Association.

Filling Vacant Positions

When librarians begin to design a search to fill a vacant position, they first need to consider the labor market from which candidates will be drawn. In most libraries, support staff positions are filled from the local labor market. Openings are advertised only in local publications, and almost all of these positions are filled by individuals already living in the area. On the other hand, in many libraries, professional vacancies are filled from the national labor market. Almost all libraries and information centers recruit top administrators nationally. In these cases, libraries and information centers advertise in national periodicals, such as *American Libraries, Library Journal,* or *The Chronicle of Higher Education,* in the hope of attracting a large number of well-qualified applicants.

The Internet is changing the way that open positions are being advertised. The classified sections of many newspapers and specialized publications are available on their Web sites. For instance, *The Chronicle of Higher Education*'s position openings can be seen at http://chronicle.com/jobs/, and the ALA's *American Libraries* position openings can be seen online at http://joblist.ala.org/. There are also sites specifically devoted to employment advertisements (such as Monster.com at http://www.monster.com/), where job seekers can search job openings by category and find useful tips to aid in their job search. Many individual libraries publicize open positions on their own Web sites. Others post positions to be filled on specific Listservs that are apt to be read by people with the appropriate background and interest for the job vacancy. Advertising using the Internet is advantageous to both the organization with the open position and the job seeker, because it usually permits access to information about positions to be distributed to individuals who might not see the printed ad, especially if it were in a regional newspaper that the job seeker did not usually read.[27] The cost is generally lower as well.

Attracting a Diverse Workforce

Diversity among staff is becoming increasingly more valued in all types of institutions. Because libraries serve a multicultural clientele, most libraries try to hire a culturally diverse staff. Despite attempts to increase the number of minorities in the profession, however, they are still underrepresented. Recent statistics show that in academic and public libraries fewer than 15 percent of the librarians belong to racial or ethnic minorities, and the percentages are far below the representations of these groups in society.[28] In an attempt to increase the number of minorities in libraries, both libraries and LIS schools have tried a number of approaches. Some libraries have introduced undergraduate internship programs designed to bring more minorities into the profession. Others have established minority residency programs to attract new MLS graduates. In addition, many libraries have instituted diversity plans to coordinate their efforts to produce a more diverse workforce. LIS schools have attempted to diversify their enrollment by more active minority recruitment efforts and by offering special scholarships. The American Library Association has instituted a new Spectrum Initiative to provide scholarships to African American, Latino/Hispanic, Asian/Pacific Islander, and Native American/ Alaskan Native students for graduate programs in library and information studies.

 What Do You Think?

In the twenty-first century, "nearly one out of two Americans will be a member of what today is considered a minority group. America will be many faces and many races with no one majority group in the workforce. The question is not whether there will be change but how we manage that change so that all may benefit."

What advantages does a diverse workforce bring to an organization? What are some of the challenges of managing such a workforce?

U.S. Department of Labor, *Futurework: Trends and Challenges for Work in the 21st Century* (Washington, DC: Department of Labor, 1999), 10;

excerpt also available in U.S. Department of Labor, "Futurework: Trends and Challenges for Work in the 21st Century," *Occupational Outlook Quarterly* (Summer 2000): 31–37, http://www.bls.gov/opub/ooq/2000/Summer/art04.pdf.

Librarianship must compete with more lucrative professions in hiring a diverse workforce, and it has not succeeded in attracting as diverse a workforce as would be desirable. Nonetheless, at each hiring opportunity, managers should make an effort to attract qualified minority applicants in an attempt to increase diversity.

Internal and External Applicants

Applicants for a job often include both internal candidates—individuals already employed by the organization who are seeking job transfers or promotions—and external candidates—individuals from outside the organization. There are advantages and disadvantages associated with both the external and internal recruiting of personnel. The first advantage of recruiting external candidates is the larger pool of talent that can be tapped. The second advantage is that new employees bring fresh insights and perspectives to the organization. The major disadvantage of external recruiting is that filling a position with an external candidate generally takes longer and is more expensive than filling it with an internal candidate. It also takes longer for an employee hired from the outside to become oriented to the new organization.

The biggest advantage of filling positions with internal candidates is that it usually fosters high morale. Employees in organizations that have a policy of promotion from within have an additional incentive for good performance because of the possibility of a promotion when openings occur. Another advantage of recruiting from within is that management can more accurately appraise the suitability of the candidate. The internal candidate is a known factor, whereas the external candidate is less well known; therefore, there is less risk in the selection and placement of an internal candidate. However, if the position is an attractive one and there are many internal candidates, the ones not chosen may react very negatively. For that reason, it is extremely important to build procedural fairness into this, as well as every other, search, so that the unsuccessful candidates will feel that the process was a fair and objective one.[29]

There are, however, inherent problems and limitations in always relying on internal promotion. Probably the most dangerous is organizational inbreeding. When internal candidates are promoted, they tend to perpetuate what they have seen done in the past, and the organization therefore may not be exposed to new ideas and innovation. In general, the best policy is probably filling the majority of vacancies from within when there are fully qualified individuals to assume these positions. But it is also wise to fill at least some high-level positions by outsiders to inject new ideas into the organization.

What Would You Do?

On the whole, Ethel Shea reflected, the first week had gone quite well. Just last Friday afternoon she had been one of four assistant librarians in the technical services department of the Calhoun Public Library. Now she sat at the corner desk as head of the department, and her three former coassistants and the six clerks reported to her. Soon she would be interviewing applicants for her old job.

Shea recalled her fear and apprehension when the chief librarian (now her immediate supervisor) had offered her the promotion. Certainly she wanted the job, but would the other three assistants accept her? Would there be resentments? Could she assume the managerial role and still maintain the congenial but guarded camaraderie that passes for friendship among professional rivals? In particular, would she be able to handle Steve Cannon?

(See http://www.lu.com/management for the rest of this case study.)

Internal promotions often present some problems both to the person who received the promotion and to their former peers. What steps can be taken to minimize such problems?

Matching the Applicant to the Position

Selection refers to the process of actually choosing the individual who will be most likely to perform the job successfully. The fundamental goal of selection is to achieve a good fit between the qualifications of the applicant and the requirements of the position. The successful matching of an applicant to a position is very important, because failures are costly not only to the persons hired but also to the organization. If the match is bad, corrective measures, such as training, transfer, demotion, or termination of employment, often are required.

The time spent selecting the right person for a position is time well spent. Oftentimes, organizations do not realize the large investment of scarce resources that may be committed to each new employee. One study that looked at the investment a library would make in a new entry-level librarian who would stay in the job for 25 years estimated that the investment would be in excess of $1 million, not including the costs of office furnishings, training, travel expenses, moving costs, or even the cost of recruitment itself.[30] Offering the position to the wrong applicant can be an expensive mistake, both in time and in money. An interesting calculator on the Internet allows an employer to calculate the cost of a bad hire (see http://www.adphire.com/badHireCalculator.html). Selecting the right candidate always has been important but is even more so now when there is often little staff turnover in many libraries. If the right candidate cannot be found the first time, it is better to readvertise the position and try again than to hire someone just to fill the position.

The Selection Process

Each organization should have a well-designed selection system. Typically, the selection process includes application forms, applicant testing, personal interviews, verification of past performance and background, and hiring.

Application Forms. Libraries often use standard application forms for vacant positions. In some cases, a cover letter and a résumé are substituted for the application form. A typical application form contains questions that identify the applicant, such as name, address, and telephone number; questions about an individual's education and work experience; and questions related to the specific requirements of the job or the organization. The employer receiving an application form must ensure that the applicant has the experience and the education needed for the job. The employer looks for steady progress in experience and for unexplained gaps in work history. Information on the application form allows tentative judgments to be made about an applicant's suitability for a position; it also screens out obviously unqualified candidates.

Applicant Testing. Some libraries use tests to see if an applicant possesses the skills needed for a specific job. These tests are most useful when the job requires certain skills that can be easily tested. For instance, an applicant for a clerical position might be given a keyboarding test to check that his or her speed and accuracy are satisfactory. The most useful tests are a sample of the work itself or a task that closely resembles the work and requires the same skills and aptitudes. If a test is used for selection, the U.S. Equal Employment Opportunity Commission (EEOC) requires that the employer establish the validity and reliability of the test.

INTERVIEWING THE CANDIDATE

When the pool of candidates has been narrowed down, the most promising applicants are invited for an interview. Sometimes, libraries initially interview candidates by telephone to narrow the pool of candidates and then choose those who will be invited for a personal interview. The job interview is the single most important tool in the candidate selection process. Although few libraries use tests in selecting employees, almost all interview the candidate. In many libraries, multiple interviews are held, thus allowing wider participation in the selection process.

The purpose of the interview is to supplement information obtained through other sources. The interviewer uses this opportunity to find out more about the applicant's technical and professional knowledge, experience, and personal characteristics. The applicant finds the interview a useful way to learn more about the job itself, to clear up any uncertainties about the position or the organization, and to be introduced to the staff that he or she would work with if hired.

The sole focus of the interview should be job requirements, and questions should be designed to provide information about an individual's suitability for the job that is being filled. All questions asked during an interview should be job related. The EEOC has forbidden the use of interview questions that are not related to job requirements. Candidates may not be asked questions about race, religion, gender, national origin, age, or handicaps. Specific questions that are prohibited are listed in table 10.2.

Interviewing is a skill that can be improved with practice. To start, interviewers should prepare for the interview. They should be familiar with the information provided by the candidate on the application form. An interviewer also should plan an outline of questions to be asked and specify the information that needs to be obtained. The same basic questions should be asked of all individuals being interviewed for a specific position. In addition, the interviewer should arrange a place for the interview that will be private and free of interruptions.

TABLE 10.2 Permitted and Prohibited Questions in Employment Interviews

Topic	Permitted Questions	Prohibited Questions
Marital Status	None	Are you married? Are you planning to get married? Do you have children? Do you plan to have children? What does your spouse do?
Sexual Orientation	None	Do you live alone?
National Origin	What is your name?	Where were you born?
Citizenship	Are you a citizen of the United States? If hired, can you prove eligibility to work in the United States?	Of what country are you a citizen? Are you a naturalized U.S. citizen?
Religion	None. If you wish to know if an applicant is available to work on Saturday or Sunday, ask about working on those days and ask the questions to each applicant.	Do you go to church? Synagogue?
Race	None	What is your race?
Criminal History	Have you ever been convicted of a crime?	Have you ever been arrested?
Age	If hired, will you be able to prove you are at least 18 years old?	How old are you?
Disability	Are you capable of performing the essential functions of this position with or without reasonable accommodation?	Are you disabled? Do you have any health problems?

During the actual interview, an interviewer should try to put the applicant at ease. A relaxed applicant will display a more normal behavior pattern than a tense applicant. The candidate should be encouraged to talk, but the interviewer must maintain control of the interview and remember that its objective is to gather information that will aid in the selection process. Too often, interviewers spend an excessive amount of time discussing the organization and the position and thus never obtain from the applicant the information needed to make a good hiring decision. The best interview is one in which the applicant does most of the talking.

 Try This!

It is well known that first impressions are the most important aspect of an interview. Imagine that you are interviewing for a position that you wish to obtain. Develop a one-minute opening statement to be used in the interview with recruiters or at a job fair. The statement should provide a succinct overview of your strengths and your fit with the position available. Practice presenting this overview to a friend, and ask him or her to assess how effective it is in marketing you for the position.

The interviewer must listen carefully and note pertinent facts. He or she should refrain from excessive note taking, however, because it will inhibit the applicant. Questions should be phrased correctly. Open-ended questions elicit the best answers because they force a candidate to think through a situation. The interviewer should avoid leading questions; that is, questions that signal the desired answer. Instead of asking, "You wouldn't object to weekend work, would you?" say, "Tell me how you feel about working weekends." The interviewer should never be judgmental. By refraining from expressing disbelief or shock at a candidate's response, the interviewer encourages the person to reveal failures as well as successes. As soon as the interview is over, the interviewer should record his or her impressions about the applicant. If this is delayed, valuable information and impressions about the applicant will be forgotten.

Background Verification

At some point, either before or after the interview, the employer will want to verify the information provided by the candidate by contacting references and previous employers. Most jobs require that the applicant list references, which can be either personal, academic, or professional. Personal references are unreliable, because few applicants would list a person who would not give a highly favorable reference. If the applicant has a work history, previous employers are the most valuable source of information. An applicant should give written permission to have his or her references checked before the individuals listed are contacted.

Reference checking is frequently conducted by telephone. It is felt that individuals provide more frank and specific information on the telephone than in writing. Some organizations, however, divulge information about past employees only in writing, and the amount and type of information provided varies from organization to organization. Fear of lawsuits has made reference checking harder than in the past, as former employers have become hesitant about giving references for fear of possible lawsuits from their ex-employees. A few organizations are now willing to confirm only that an individual had been employed there. Usually, however, a prospective employer is able to verify the accuracy of the information that the applicant has provided, such as position held, last salary, supervisory responsibilities, and reasons for leaving. The prospective employer may also ask whether the previous employer would be willing to rehire the employee and why. Although previous or present supervisors usually provide accurate assessments, sometimes they may give a better recommendation than the applicant deserves, either because they would like to see that applicant leave his or her present place of employment or because they do not feel comfortable giving negative information about individuals. The reference checkers should probe and follow up if they feel that the person giving the reference is hesitant or not responding to the questions being asked.

The same set of basic questions should be asked of all references about all candidates. Only questions relating to an applicant's job performance should be asked. Even if references are checked on the telephone, the prospective employer also should ask to have a written reference, so that there will be written documentation if there are ever any questions about the hiring decision.

If an applicant does not list supervisors from recent jobs as references, a prospective employer might want to contact them anyway. Very few applicants falsify their credentials, but it is always wise to verify the information given. If a particular educational background is required, the applicant's school record should be confirmed. A few recruiters and employers are now using social networking sites such as Facebook or MySpace and search engines such as Google to check to see if there is publicly available information on the Internet about an applicant that might affect a hiring decision. The investigation into an applicant's background is sometimes overlooked by prospective employers. However, it costs little in either time or money and is worth the effort because it cuts the risks that an organization will make an unwise hire.

Making the Hiring Decision

The last step in the selection process is choosing the individual who will be hired to fill the vacant position. In some libraries, many people contribute to the final decision, especially for professional positions. Search committees, which are commonly used in academic and other types of libraries, are one way of allowing peer involvement in the selection process. The search committee usually recommends a ranked list of finalists for the position, and then an administrator usually makes the final choice.[31] In some libraries and information centers, the director always makes the final decision; in others, the immediate supervisor is allowed to choose, subject to the approval of higher management. If the appropriate information has been gathered and if the steps in the selection process have been performed effectively, the likelihood of making a good decision is quite good; the applicant's qualifications will match the job requirements, and the fit should be successful.

If good hiring practices are not followed, an organization may be plagued by a high level of turnover in its staff. Even though a certain amount of turnover is healthy and allows an organization to bring in employees with new ideas and experiences, excessive turnover can be costly because an employee has to be replaced and a new one trained. A great deal of turnover can also threaten morale in an organization because the remaining employees feel that the organization is in a constant state of change. An excessive amount of turnover should be a warning to a library to examine carefully its hiring and recruitment practices.

CONCLUSION

After the steps that are delineated in this chapter are finished, a library's positions will be established, and there will be individuals hired for each of those spots. Hiring the staff is just the first step in working with HR in a library. Chapter 11 will look at some of the processes involved in training, evaluating, and compensating those employees.

NOTES

1. Sharon Lobel, "In Praise of the 'Soft' Stuff: A Vision for Human Resource Leadership," *Human Resources Management* 36 (Spring 1997): 135–39.

2. For a thoughtful discussion of the impact of technology on work, see Shoshana Zuboff, *In the Age of the Smart Machine* (New York: Basic Books, 1988).

3. American Library Association, *Library and Information Studies and Human Resource Utilization* (Chicago: American Library Association, 2002), 4.

4. Jerry D. Campbell, "Academic Library Budgets: Changing 'The Sixty-Forty' Split," *Library Administration and Management* 3 (Spring 1989): 78.

5. Stephanie Maatta, "Starting Pay Breaks $40K—Placement and Salaries 2005," *Library Journal.com* (October 15, 2006), http://www.libraryjournal.com/article/CA6379540.html.

6. Robert S. Martin, *The Impact of Outsourcing and Privatization on Library Services and Management* (Chicago: American Library Association, 2000), http://www.ala.org/ala/oif/iftoolkits/outsourcing/outsourcing_doc.pdf.

7. Ann Lawes, "Managing People for Whom One Is Not Directly Responsible," *The Law Librarian* 26 (September 1995): 421–23.

8. For a description of how to downsize in a more humane fashion, see "Changing the Way We Downsize," *Library and Personnel News* 8 (January–February 1994): 3.

9. U.S. Department of Education, National Center for Educational Statistics, *Public Libraries in the United States: Fiscal Year 2004* (August 2006), 82, http://nces.ed.gov/pubs2006/2006349.pdf.

10. U.S. Department of Education, National Center for Educational Statistics, *Academic Libraries: 2000* (November 2003), 37, http://nces.ed.gov/pubs2004/2004317.pdf.

11. Chris Hare and Gary Geer, "The Productivity Paradox: Implications for Libraries" (paper presented at the ACRL 9th National Conference, 1997 in Nashville), http://www.ala.org/ala/acrlbucket/nashville1997pap/haregeer.htm

12. Allen B. Veaner, "Librarians: The Next Generation," *Library Journal* 109 (April 1984): 623–24.

13. American Library Association, *Library and Information Studies and Human Resource Utilization: A Statement of Policy* (Chicago: American Library Association, 2002); see the complete statement at http://www.ala.org/ala/hrdr/educprofdev/lepu.pdf.

14. Ibid., 2.

15. Allen B. Veaner, "Paradigm Lost, Paradigm Regained? A Persistent Personnel Issue in Academic Librarianship, II," *College and Research Libraries* 55 (September 1994): 390.

16. Larry R. Oberg, "Library Support Staff in an Age of Change: Utilization, Role Definition, and Status," *ERIC Digest,* EDO-IR-95-4 (May 1995), http://www.ericdigests.org/1996-1/support.htm

17. Ibid.

18. Linda W. Braun, "New Roles: A Librarian by Any Name," *Library Journal* 127 (February 1, 2002): 46.

19. Ed Martinez and Raymond Roney, "1996 Library Support Staff Salary Survey," *Library Mosaics* (March/April 1997): 6–10.

20. Charles Handy, *The Age of Unreason* (Boston: Harvard Business School Press, 1989), 90.

21. Ibid., 94.

22. Adam Smith, *An Inquiry into the Nature and Causes of the Wealth of Nations* (New York: Modern Library, 1937).

23. Carol P. Johnson, "The Changing Nature of Jobs: A Paraprofessional Time Series," *College and Research Libraries* 57 (January 1996): 59–67.

24. J. R. Hackman and G. R. Oldman, *Work Redesign* (Reading, MA: Addison-Wesley, 1980).

25. Stanley J. Wilder, *The Age Demographics of Academic Librarians: A Profession Apart* (Binghamton, NY: Haworth Information Press, 1999).

26. Mary Jo Lynch, "Reaching 65: Lots of Librarians Will Be There Soon," *American Libraries* 33 (March 2002): 55–56.

27. Marydee Ojala, "Recruiting on the Internet," *Online* 21 (March/April 1997): 78–81.

28. Mary Jo Lynch, " Librarian Salaries: Annual Increase Drops Below Average" (Chicago: ALA, 2002). (available online at http://www.ala.org/hrdr/salaries.html; also available as "Racial and Ethnic Diversity Among Librarians: A Status Report," at http://www.ala.org/Template.cfm?Section=diversitytools&template=/ContentManagement/ContentDisplay.cfm&ContentID=8582

29. Ken Jordan, "Play Fair and Square when Hiring from Within," *HR Magazine* 42 (January 1997): 49–52.

30. Constance H. Corey, "Those Precious Human Resources: Investments that Show You Care Enough to Keep the Very Best," *Library Administration and Management* 2 (June 1988): 128.

31. Hiring done by search committees, especially in academic libraries, often moves at a very slow pace. For tips about how the process can be improved for the job seeker, see Todd Gilman, "Endlesse Searche," *Chronicle of Higher Education,* 27 July 2006, xx.

The Human Resources Functions in the Library

Overview

Terry had great luck in her job search. She applied for 20 positions and had 4 on-site interviews. Just before graduation, she was offered a position in her top-choice institution, and two weeks after receiving her MLIS degree, she began work as an adult services librarian in a growing public library system in the Southwest. Terry went through a day-long orientation her first day on the job and then was trained in the procedures and activities of her specific position. Over the first few months, she was given a chance to learn more about the library and was socialized into its norms and expectations. Recently, after six months on the job, her probationary period came to an end, and she had her first performance appraisal. She was told that she was performing up to expectations and, as a result, was given a small increase in her salary. As part of the appraisal, her supervisor helped her develop a list of objectives to be met during the next year. Together, Terry and her supervisor outlined the additional training and experience that would be needed to allow Terry to be successful in meeting these goals. Terry is now planning to attend a day-long workshop in readers' advisory at an upcoming conference, and she is scheduled to be trained on a new computer system that will be installed soon. She is also receiving cross-training from Bill, a colleague who is an expert in business reference, so that she can fill in for him on his days off. After less than a year in the position, Terry feels as though she is contributing a great deal to the organization, and she looks forward to continuing her professional growth and development, with the hope of being promoted within the library system in a few years.

235

The previous chapter discussed staffing, one of the key responsibilities in human resources (HR) management, but staffing the organization is just the beginning. All employees need to be oriented, trained, evaluated, and compensated. Occasionally there is a need to discipline or even terminate a problem employee. This chapter will discuss these HR functions and give examples of how they are implemented in libraries.

Hiring an employee is just the first step. The new employee arrives at the library for the first day of work, and immediately there is a need for the orientation and training of this new worker. There has to be a compensation and benefits package already in place. And, for as long as the employee remains on the job, there is a need for various other HR functions to be performed. In this era of rapid change, there are always demands for training and staff development. At least once a year, an employee's performance needs to be evaluated and possibly considered for a salary increase. Sometimes an employee has to be disciplined or wishes to file a grievance, and occasionally an employee needs to be terminated. All of these activities are an integral part of the HR responsibilities of managers. This chapter will provide an overview of the major HR functions from an employee's initial day on the job until he or she leaves the organization.

TRAINING AND STAFF DEVELOPMENT

Training is a never-ending process. There are always new employees that need training or new systems that need to be taught. In a library, there are many levels of training, some of which are received by everyone and some of which are more individualized. Although training can be expensive, it is false economy to try to minimize these expenses. Over a period of time, the cost to the institution is returned in quality performance.

Orientation

The first type of training typically received is an orientation. After an employee has been hired, he or she needs a general orientation to the organization. Usually, if a number of new employees come in at about the same time, a general orientation session is held to provide information that all new employees need, regardless of level or area of employment. Even if some of the information was transmitted during the selection process, it is wise to reinforce that knowledge.

An orientation usually includes both general information and information about the goals, objectives, and philosophies of the organization. The general information part of the orientation covers rules and policies applicable to all employees, including information concerning pay periods, how vacation and sick leave are accumulated and used, requirements for reporting illness, and the use of time sheets. Units, such as the HR office, the public information office, and various subject or functional departments, are described, so that employees see their role within the total organization. Using visual presentations and permitting extensive discussion and questions makes such sessions more productive. Many libraries have specific ways of doing things, and the reasons for these procedures are explained.

The second purpose of orientation is to help the new employee become familiar with the culture of their new organization. All new employees, regardless of level or place in the organization, need to be socialized into the institution's culture and understand its history, traditions, and norms.[1] To begin this socialization, orientation meetings often include presentations by the director or another top manager, which allow new employees to get a feel for the organization's culture and what will be expected of them.

Although some libraries still treat orientation sessions in a casual manner, most now give careful thought to what should be included. For instance, figure 11.1 illustrates the checklist used by Kent State University in its orientation for new employees. This form asks for the signatures of all the individuals involved to ensure accountability.[2] More orientation forms and links can be found on this book's Web page (http://www.lu.com/management).

Initial Job Training

As soon as a new employee reports for work, the immediate supervisor begins training him or her in the specific tasks of the job. Occasionally, this training is given by the person leaving the job, but this is a risky practice. Having the departing employee train a new one perpetuates the work habits and patterns of the former employee and frequently establishes attitudes and opinions toward the supervisor, the department, and the organization. For these reasons, it is recommended that the immediate supervisor be in charge of training new employees.

There are many ways of training. The worst way is to describe briefly the tasks to be performed and then let the employee figure out the rest. The new employee, already uneasy from being in a new environment with new responsibilities, will absorb little of the supervisor's remarks. Some employees are able to observe co-workers, figure out the job from the job description, or learn the job on their own, in spite of the supervisor. Others fail, and their failure is the fault of the supervisor for not providing appropriate training.

Training must be carefully planned. Table 11.1 contains principles to guide a trainer.

A library's responsibility for training and education does not end when a new employee is properly trained for his or her position. It takes a long time for a new employee to become socialized into the organization's culture, with its norms for acceptable and unacceptable behavior. Experienced staff play a vital role in helping new employees make an effective transition to a new setting.[3] New employees will look to more senior staff members to serve as role models. When they are faced with a gap in knowledge, they usually will turn to these more senior employees to act as their teachers or coaches.

Figure 11.1—Orientation Checklist for New Employees

What Every New Libraries/Media Services Employee Should Know
CHECKLIST

✓ DIRECTOR OF STAFF SERVICES discusses:

I. Introduction to Kent State University and Libraries/Media Services

DATE

- University ID card
- Parking permit
- Map of campus; tour of especially relevant offices, such as Personnel
- Tours: department, main library, branch libraries, regional libraries as appropriate
- Introductions to staff
- Promotional materials about University services and organizations (e.g., Wellness Center, physical fitness facilities, Audio Visual Services, Professional Women of Kent State University)
- Copies of undergraduate and/or graduate catalogs

DATE

- Community information: what does Kent offer ... Portage and Summit Counties ... greater Akron/ Cleveland metropolitan areas ... Ohio
- Library circulation policies
- When the library operates
- List of University paid holidays
- Keys and getting into the building outside of normal work schedule
- Completion of *Confidential Vital Information Record*
- Safety manual
- University/corporate perks (e.g., Sea World, Sam's Club, American Express card)

II. Personnel Policies and Procedures

DATE

- Breaks: length, frequency, where allowed physically, coordination with co-workers, etc.
- Lunch/dinner, including bringing food into the library
- Flextime availability
- Calling supervisor, forms to fill out for sick leave, vacation, leave of absence
- Court leave
- Use of radios and radio/headphones on the job
- Making/receiving personal telephone calls
- Dress codes
- Attending classes, completing class assignments

DATE

- Changing one's regular schedule
- Attendance at University and library functions and meetings, such as May 4 Remembrance, Women's Day events, etc.
- Timecards
- Professional development: meetings, conferences, seminars; travel reimbursement
- Pay raises
- Promotions
- Exiting the University
- Faculty issues: reappointment, tenure, sabbatical, faculty committees, mentors, library liaison program, use of research leave, exit interviews

III. Information About the Job and the Organization

DATE

- Information about the relationship with the supervisor, including: chain of command; administering discipline/ rewards; performance evaluations; communicating with supervisor, including what supervisor needs to know and what is confidential
- Information about relationships with co-workers: when and how to discuss mutual interests and concerns; what to tell the supervisor
- Information about relationships with supervisees: policies as for supervisors above

DATE

- L/MS personnel structure: organizational charts, personnel rosters, descriptions of committees, how to become involved
- L/MS communication methods: memo writing protocol, telephone protocol, availability of committee reports, *Local Data Record, Inside, Matrix, Connect,* other publications and reports, communicating with others
- List of L/MS telephone numbers
- List of radio stations to tune in if snow might close down University operations

---

Director of Staff Services sign-off:

New Employee sign-off:

---

continued

Figure 11.1a—Orientation Checklist for New Employees

✓ SUPERVISOR discusses:

	DATE		DATE
• Training information: how long is training period, when reviewed, who reviews performance, when is a decision about employment binding, implications with respect to layoffs	————	• Getting into the department outside of regular working hours	————
• Job description/outline of job responsibilities	————	• Relationship with supervisor: the chain of command, expectations of the supervisor, departmental meetings, how to request other meetings, when and how to discuss issues and concerns	————
• Procedures manuals: personal copy or knowledge of ready availability	————	• If new employee supervises others, the supervisor may make recommendations on how the new employee should relate with supervisees	————
• When the department operates	————		
• Work schedules of co-workers and supervisor	————	• Word processing: availability of computers and software for on and off the job	————
• Personal schedule: regular working hours, timeliness	————	• Supplies and equipment: when and how to request	————

Supervisor sign-off:

_____

New Employee sign-off:

_____

✓ PERSONNEL – STAFF BENEFITS OFFICE discusses:

	DATE		DATE
• Benefits: tuition waiver, insurance (life, medical, dental), retirement, travel reimbursement	————	• Explanation of Benefits Fest	————

Personnel Office sign-off:

_____

New Employee sign-off:

_____

Source: From Shelley L. Rogers, "Orientation for New Library Employees: A Checklist," *Library Administration and Management* 8 (Fall 1994): 213–17. Use by permission of the American Library Association.

TABLE 11.1 Training Principles

• Teach the simple tasks first.
• Break down the task into its basic components.
• Teach only the correct procedures.
• Keep teaching cycles short and reinforce them with practice.
• Develop skills through repetition.
• Do not train too far in advance to avoid the employee forgetting what was learned.
• Motivate the trainee by emphasizing the relationship between the training and good job performance.

Training and Staff Development for Established Employees

It is not only new employees who need training. Any staff member who works in a library needs continuous updating to stay current. The rapid changes taking place in all types of libraries compel library managers to attach new importance to training and staff development. Although the terms *training* and *staff development* often are used synonymously, a distinction is sometimes made. Training frequently refers to learning skills or knowledge that are to be used on the present job, whereas staff development involves learning of a larger scope that goes beyond the present job and looks toward the future. But because it is often difficult to make a distinction between these two types of continuing learning, this book will treat them together. Another related function, career development, will be covered in chapter 12.

Training and staff development can be offered in various ways. On a recurring basis as specific training needs are identified, selected groups of employees might receive training in specific topics, such as how to conduct good performance evaluation interviews, how to prepare performance evaluation reports, how to prepare departmental budget recommendations, or how to do task analysis for job description revisions. These training sessions, which concern all units of the organization, may be conducted by a specialist within the institution or by an expert brought into the institution for this purpose.

The training programs described so far are developed and presented by the institution. In addition, many training and educational programs exist outside the institution; these also should be available to employees. Attendance at local, regional, and national conferences and workshops provides opportunities for employee development and growth. In addition, more and more training is being offered by means of online courses or teleconferences. The need to take courses beyond the first professional degree increases as library operations become more complex. Many institutions provide tuition funding for employees who take formal courses that are job related.

Some libraries are attempting to transform themselves into so-called learning organizations. These are organizations in which "people continually expand their capacity to create the results they truly desire, where new and expansive patterns of things are nurtured, where collective aspiration is set free, and where people are continually learning how to learn together."[4] More information about learning organizations is available in chapter 2, but, in general, the learning organization is marked by a team-based culture, open flows of information, empowered employees, and decentralized decision making.[5] As a result, the learning organization is able to grow and change in response to environmental changes. These learning organizations attempt to formalize exchanges of information. Managers in learning organizations must be open to suggestions, be able to admit mistakes without fear of reprisal, and be willing to make changes. Learning organizations have become adept at translating new knowledge into new ways of behaving.[6] The move toward learning organizations brings with it an emphasis on continuous growth and training.

Another change in attitude toward training comes from the newly adopted practice in many libraries to view managers and supervisors as coaches for the employees that they supervise. Like a good coach, a supervisor should act as a role model, help the employee set realistic goals, give feedback on performance, supply suggestions on how to improve that performance, and provide reinforcement and encouragement. The supervisor and the employee should not view themselves as adversaries. Instead, they are on the same team, each trying to improve the overall performance of the organization. A commitment to coaching "sends the message that continuous learning is the accepted practice. By coaching, we model how we must interact with each other if we are to achieve our best individual and organizational performance."[7] More information about coaching is contained in chapter 17.

No library is exempt from change, and at times it seems that the pace of change becomes more rapid each year. If librarians are to remain up-to-date, they have no choice but to continue to learn. Every library, regardless of size or type, needs a planned staff development program. Such activities are not haphazardly scheduled but are organized on a structured continuum. Such programs provide the means by which employees can grow on the job and prepare to advance as opportunities become available. Good staff development programs contribute to employees' career development. Also, through such programs, employers can identify potential supervisors and prepare them for that responsibility. Human resources are too valuable for any institution to fail to invest in the training programs needed to develop employees to their full potential.[8]

PERFORMANCE APPRAISALS

A performance appraisal is the systematic evaluation of an individual employee's job-related strengths and weaknesses. In all types of organizations, employees have to be evaluated. Some workers are better than others at specific jobs. Some workers take the initiative and carry through an assignment with little supervision, while others may be unreliable or must be closely supervised to ensure the successful completion of a project. When decisions have to be made about pay increases or promotions, the supervisor must have a way to distinguish the excellent performers from the mediocre ones. Before systematic performance appraisals were developed, such decisions often were made on the basis of subjective, spur-of-the-moment impressions. A systematic, written appraisal system provides a sounder method of distinguishing among the performances of employees.

There has been a shift, in some organizations, in the focus of evaluations as a result of other changes in the organization. Especially in team-based organizations, there has been, as we have seen, a move to see the supervisor as more of a coach than a boss. If the supervisor is functioning as a coach, the feedback to the employee is continuous, even though formal performance assessments may still be done only once a year.

Learning theory suggests that immediate feedback helps learners increase their performance. Regardless of the type of organization, all employees need feedback more than once a year, and good supervisors provide it. Usually, the frequent feedback is done in a more informal, spontaneous fashion, whereas the annual evaluation is done in a more formal, structured manner.

Judging another's performance is difficult, and often both supervisors and subordinates feel ambivalent about performance appraisals. Some writers have likened appraisals to paying taxes. They are something that managers are obligated to do but would prefer to avoid. And, although most employees want feedback on how they are doing, they would prefer feedback that is consistent with their image of themselves as good performers needing no improvement.[9]

 What Do You Think?

Personnel Appraisal (pers'-n-el a-pra'zel) noun: given by someone who does *not want to give it to someone who does not want to get it.*

This definition is an accurate description of what happens in many organizations. What makes personnel appraisals so difficult for both the supervisors doing them and the employees being appraised? How can organizations improve this process?

From James S. Bowman, "Performance Appraisal: Verisimilitude Trumps Veracity," *Public Personnel Management* 28 (Winter 1999): 557.

Why Appraisals Are Done

Formal performance assessments have two main objectives. The first is to determine how well an employee performs on the job. The second objective is to help an employee understand how well he or she is doing. This way, if improvement needs to be made, the employee knows where his or her deficiencies lie. To achieve this second objective, the findings of the evaluation must be communicated to the employee. Without this transfer of information and the subsequent development of a remedial process or plan, the employee cannot be expected to achieve improvement or redirection in performance.

The results of performance appraisals are used as the basis for making important HR decisions relating to promotion, demotion, and termination of employees. A good performance appraisal system facilitates the promotion of outstanding workers and the weeding out or transfer of poor performers. Systematic, written assessment of a worker by a number of raters over a period of time helps make these decisions reasonable and sound. Performance appraisal also can serve as the basis for setting wages or salaries. Many organizations relate at least some decisions about pay increases to an employee's performance appraisal rating. The appraisal process also can facilitate understanding between supervisors and employees. Performance appraisal provides concrete feedback to employees that allows them to improve their performance. The performance appraisal process should help employees establish personal goals that will enable them to grow and develop and that, in turn, will further the goals of the institution. Finally, performance appraisals can serve as information-gathering tools that provide data to be used in determining both organizational and individual training needs.

Good performance appraisal systems are careful to make a distinction between the variations of employee performance caused by shortcomings on the part of the employee and those caused by the inadequacies of the organization. For instance, the best employee cannot be productive if there is a problem with getting materials—a cataloger cannot catalog if there is a backlog in acquisitions that prevents the books getting to the cataloging department. An appraiser must be careful never to blame the deficiencies of the organization on the individual employee, because such improperly done appraisals "can jeopardize morale, adversely affect teamwork, and leave an individual feeling unfairly criticized."[10]

When to Do Appraisals

Each organization has to decide when performance appraisals will be administered, although often the schedule is mandated by external authorities such as a state government. But there always should be a definite schedule, and this schedule should be public knowledge. Performance appraisals are most commonly done on a yearly basis. Ideally, though, performance appraisals should be done frequently enough to let employees know if their performance is satisfactory and, if not, the steps that need to be taken for improvement. For some employees, an annual performance appraisal is not frequent enough. As mentioned previously, it is recommended that informal performance appraisals be done several times a year to supplement the formal annual appraisal.

New employees need more frequent appraisals than do long-established workers. In most organizations, new staff members serve a probationary period before permanent appointment is made. A performance rating should be administered at the end of the probationary period, but a good supervisor will review the job description and the quality of job performance with the new employee several times during the probationary period.

After the probationary period, performance appraisals are administered on a recurring basis. Some institutions schedule all of these evaluations at the same time. This practice permits the supervisor to compare the performance of all subordinates. But grouping all the appraisals also presents drawbacks. Supervisors with a large number of appraisals to complete can be overwhelmed, resulting in poorly prepared performance evaluations. To avoid overload, some institutions do performance evaluations on each anniversary of an employee's appointment to permanent status. This timetable distributes the workload over the entire year and thus permits careful judgments to be made.

Who Does the Appraisals?

By far, the most common practice in libraries, as in other institutions, is to have the immediate supervisors evaluate the performance of their subordinates. This is because supervisors have the greatest opportunity to observe the work performance of these employees. Because supervisors are accountable for the successful operation of their units, it is appropriate that they have authority over HR functions affecting that unit.

Although the custom of having the immediate supervisor evaluate subordinates is most common, other types of evaluations replace or supplement this practice in some institutions.

Peer Appraisals. Peer ratings are used to evaluate some professional librarians, primarily academic ones. Because many academic librarians have faculty status, they have adopted the same type of peer review of performance that is used for most faculty members in institutions of higher education. Professional librarians interact with one another and are usually familiar with one another's work. In addition, many elements of the librarian's work, particularly at the departmental level, require cooperative work. Thus, they should be good judges of one another's performance.[11]

Appraising Superiors. In some organizations, subordinates are allowed to appraise the performance of their immediate supervisor. Considerable trust and openness are necessary to make this type of appraisal successful, and, in most cases, subordinates do not assess their bosses without guaranteed anonymity. When subordinates do evaluate their superiors, the appraisals are not seen by anyone but the managers, and they serve primarily as tools for the guided self-development of the supervisor and as a way of giving employees a chance to express their opinions. Upward evaluations provide supervisors with information that can be very useful. But, because inaccurate and inadequate information gathered about a supervisor could lead to a distorted view of the supervisor's performance and thus potentially could lead to legal challenges, it is important that a formal process be developed and a valid and reliable instrument used.[12]

Three-Hundred-Sixty-Degree Appraisals. A growing number of organizations are using what is termed *360-degree* or *multirater* feedback, a process in which an employee's performance is assessed through confidential feedback from a variety of sources, including direct reports, managers, peers, internal and external customers, and the individual employee. The reviews from each of these sources are anonymous, and usually the HR department collects and compiles the reviews into a report to be given to the employee. This 360-degree feedback allows an employee to get feedback on facets of his or her performance that often are overlooked in a traditional top-down performance assessment. Another reason for its growing use is the number of organizations that have eliminated layers of middle managers, leaving managers with wider spans of control. Thus, it has become more difficult for managers to provide accurate assessments of the larger number of employees under their supervision. The increasing number of organizations using self-directed teams is another impetus for the adoption of 360-degree feedback. In this situation, the members of the team are in the best position to know the performance of other team members.

This type of evaluation yields valuable data, but it can be very threatening to individual managers.[13] It also can be very time consuming. If a library had 30 employees and decided to institute this type of performance appraisal, and on average each employee was to be evaluated by six other employees using an appraisal instrument that took 45 minutes to complete, it is easy to see how this appraisal would become expensive in terms of time and effort expended.

If a library decides to institute 360-degree appraisals, the process it uses to develop them should be planned carefully. It will take time to implement a well-designed system. As with all other appraisal systems, there needs to be support from top management, and because employees know their jobs best, they should be involved in the development of the appraisal criteria. Training in both giving and receiving 360-degree feedback should be given to everyone participating in the process. If employees are given feedback without being told what to do with the results, they do not know what actions to take. As one expert states, "There is often too much focus on getting the feedback and mining the data and too little focus on using the feedback for job-related or behavior change."[14] As with any new system, the procedure probably should be pilot tested in one area before being adopted library-wide, and managers should monitor the system to be sure it is performing as designed and be ready to modify it if it is not.

Self-Appraisals. Some organizations permit employee self-evaluation. If an employee is accurate in identifying strengths and weaknesses, the supervisor only has to confirm this information and then help the employees set goals to improve the weaknesses. Individuals are much less defensive if they themselves have pointed out their shortcomings, instead of having those shortcomings pointed out by their manager. Unfortunately, however, not all employees are able to evaluate themselves accurately, and there is often little agreement between the employee's evaluation and that of the supervisor.[15] If self-appraisal is used as part of evaluation, it is almost always used in conjunction with another type of appraisal.

Whatever type of performance appraisal program is instituted, it must be supported by senior managers, and these managers must orient and train supervisors. Unless the upper echelons of management indicate support, the program likely will be ineffective. Management also must give supervisors sufficient time to carry out the appraisals. Most supervisors dislike the process of evaluating their employees and, in particular, try to avoid discussing deficiencies with them. One of the major challenges of performance appraisal is establishing the standards of performance against which an employee's work is judged. Standards that need to be established usually fall clearly into three categories:

1. **Quality-Quantity Standards.** How well does the employee perform the various tasks in the job description, and how much of each task is actually accomplished?

2. **Desired Effect Standards.** Is work complete, accurate, and performed on time, benefiting the goals and objectives of the institution and users? Are sound data gathered as a basis for judgment and decisions?

3. **Manner of Performance Standards.** Is the work accomplished in cooperation with others, without friction? Can the employee adapt to new programs or processes?

Because no two supervisors interpret these standards in exactly the same way, top management must define the standards. If supervisors interpret standards differently or give greater weight to one standard over the others, inequity in evaluation from department to department will result. To avoid this, many organization provide supervisors with a performance evaluation manual to help in defining standards.

Problems in Rating

Because appraisals are carried out by humans, they are subject to a number of weaknesses and errors. The most common errors found in performance appraisal can be seen in table 11.2

A number of techniques can reduce errors in performance appraisal. As mentioned previously, training can reduce errors. Some errors can be lessened by keeping good records of employee performance. Errors also can be reduced if supervisors have input into the type of appraisal system that is used. If raters have participated in developing the system, they will use it more effectively. Finally, errors can be minimized if the organization's top management makes it clearly understood that all supervisors are to take performance appraisal very seriously. Not only should good appraisals be expected, they should be rewarded. When the organization not only expects good appraisals but also systematically rewards supervisors who carefully and conscientiously perform those appraisals, it lays the foundation for an effective system of performance evaluation.

Methods of Performance Appraisal

There are no standard methods of performance appraisal and no method that works best in all settings. Instead, there are a number of effective methods that can be used. Although institutions do not have to select a single method, one method or combination of methods is still generally agreed upon for the entire institution. The method used may be that used by the parent institution, as in the case of a library that is part of a larger municipal or academic

TABLE 11.2 Errors Made in Performance Appraisals

1. The *halo effect*. Letting the rating assigned to one characteristic unduly influence rating on all factors. For example, if a supervisor thinks an employee is outstanding in one area, he or she gives that individual high ratings on all the factors being evaluated.
2. *Prejudice and partiality*. Letting personal feelings about a subordinate affect the rating given to that subordinate. It is a serious error for a supervisor to let personal likes and dislikes affect performance appraisals. In addition, it is illegal to consider race, creed, color, religion, politics, nationality, or gender in evaluating work performance.
3. *Leniency or strictness*. Supervisors using different standards for evaluation, thus resulting in employees receiving vastly different ratings. Some supervisors give all their subordinates high ratings because they do not want to face the resentment or disappointment resulting from low ones. Equally damaging is giving low ratings to all employees because supervisors have set artificially high standards that few subordinates can ever achieve.
4. *Central tendency*. Reluctance to use either the high or low extremes of the rating scale, resulting in all ratings clustering about the center. On a normal distribution curve, more people will be rated closer to the mean than to any other point. However, when all ratings are clustered at the center, most of the value of the performance appraisal is lost.
5. *Contrast*. Not measuring the work the employee has actually done but the work the supervisor thinks the employee has the potential to achieve.
6. *Association*. Supervisors with a large number of evaluations to complete rating factors at the same level merely because they follow each other on the page. Often occurs when the supervisor is tired and tries to make hurried judgments without all the facts.
7. *Recency*. A supervisor appraising only the work the employee has done in the recent past, rather than the work done over the entire period of time covered by the appraisal.

system. Some examples of performance appraisal forms are available on this book's Web site (http://www.lu.com/management).

If the library is free to select its own method, staff committees may have input into this decision. In larger libraries, the HR office often plays a key role in the selection and development of the method used. The performance appraisal methods most commonly used are essays, ranking, forced distribution, graphic ratings scales, and the behaviorally anchored rating scale. Management by objectives also provides a means of performance appraisal (for more information, see chapter 4). Regardless of the type of instrument used, all factors being assessed should be job related.

In the essay method, the rater describes an individual's performance in a written narrative. The essay can be unstructured, but usually the rater is asked to respond to general questions relating to the employee's job knowledge, strengths and weaknesses, and promotion potential. The major drawback of essays is that their length and content may vary, and consistency is therefore hard to achieve. The rater's writing ability also may affect the appraisal. An employee might receive a comparatively poor rating because the rater does not write well. Essays are most effective when they are combined with some other appraisal technique.

Several ranking systems are used in employee appraisal. Using the simple ranking method, the supervisor ranks the employees from highest to lowest— from best employee to worst. In alternative ranking, the supervisor first chooses the best and the poorest performers. Then the next-best and the next-poorest performers are chosen, alternating from top to bottom, until all employees have been ranked. The paired comparison method is an organized way of comparing each employee with every other employee, one at a time. The advantage of the ranking systems is their simplicity. The major disadvantages are that they do not reveal the degree of difference between persons in adjacent ranks, and individuals with the same performance rating must be given separate ranks. In addition, it is difficult to compare various groups of employees, because the ones ranked highest in one unit may not be as good as those ranked highest in another unit.

A common problem with rating scales is that too many people are rated on the high end of the scale. The forced distribution rating system is designed to prevent this clustering. Forced distribution requires the rater to place a certain percentage of employees at various performance intervals. Usually, a supervisor must allocate 10 percent to the highest category and 10 percent to the lowest, with the other employees proportionately assigned. This process results in a distribution identical to that found in the normal bell-shaped curve (figure 11.2).

The forced distribution method assumes that performance in a group of employees is distributed according to a normal curve. In many units, this assumption may be untrue. This method is most difficult to use when evaluating a small number of people.

The graphic rating scale is the most commonly used method of performance appraisal in libraries and information centers. The rater evaluates the employee on such factors as quantity of work, dependability, initiative, job knowledge, and accuracy. Some organizations use a very simple form, with the factor being evaluated listed and defined, followed by a multiple-choice format for the rating. The supervisor indicates the rating of the employee for each factor by placing a mark on the horizontal line.

Accuracy Is the Correctness of Work Performed

Poor   Fair   Average   Good   Excellent

One problem with the graphic rating scale has been that it is very difficult for supervisors to agree on the meaning of terms such as *average* or *good*. No matter how much training supervisors receive, individuals will interpret these terms differently. In recent years, most institutions have improved the graphic rating scale by eliminating these terms. In their place, a short phrase is used to describe the different levels of performance. The most difficult part of developing these new scales is to provide a short phrase that cannot be misinterpreted, thus assuring comparable interpretations by different supervisors. In this type of form, accuracy might be evaluated as follows:

Figure 11.2—Performance Rankings in a Forced Distribution Rating System

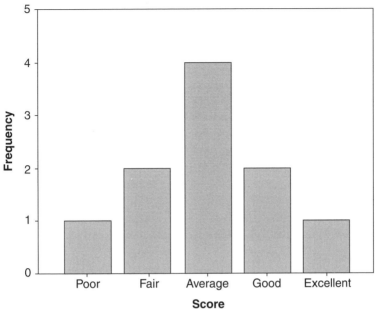

Accuracy Is the Correctness of Work Performed

| Makes frequent errors | Careless, often makes errors | Usually accurate; only makes average number of errors | Requires little supervision; is exact and precise most of the time | Requires absolute minimum of supervision; is almost always accurate |

The fact that graphic rating scales require relatively little time to construct and administer doubtlessly contributes to their popularity. They also force an evaluator to consider several dimensions of performance, and they are standardized and comparable across individuals. Their biggest drawback is that they are susceptible to errors such as halo, central tendency, or leniency. In addition, all rating scales tend to look backward, judging an employee's performance over the period of time being assessed, instead of helping the employee set goals for improvement. An example of a graphic rating scale may be seen in figure 11.3.

Behaviorally anchored rating scales (BARS) were created to correct some of the deficiencies of the graphic rating scale. In developing BARS, the active participation of jobholders and supervisors helps to identify key job dimensions and areas of responsibility. Each job is likely to have several job dimensions and separate scales for each. The anchors are specific, written descriptions of actual job behaviors that supervisors agree represent specific levels of performance. To carry out a performance appraisal using BARS requires the rater to read through the list of anchors on each scale (i.e., for each job behavior) until the anchor that best describes the employee's job behavior is identified.

Figure 11.3—A Graphic Rating Scale

Parkville Public Library

Employee Performance Evaluation

Employee's Name _____   Classification_____

Evaluation Period: From _____ To_____   Department _____

PLACE CHECK MARK IN BOX THAT MOST APPROPRIATELY INDICATES YOUR JUDGMENT ON EACH FACTOR BEING APPRAISED. COMPLETE ALL ITEMS FOR ALL EMPLOYEES.				
Job Knowledge				
1 Serious gaps in knowledge of essentials of job	2 Satisfactory knowledge of essentials of job	3 Adequately informed on most phases of job	4 Good knowledge of all phases of job	5 Excellent understanding of job
Attitude				
1 Uncooperative, resents suggestions, no enthusiasm	2 Often cooperates and accepts suggestions	3 Satisfactory cooperation; accepts new ideas	4 Responsive, cooperates well; helpful to others	5 Excellent in cooperation and enthusiasm; welcomes new ideas; very helpful
Judgment				
1 Decisions often wrong or ineffective	2 Judgment usually sound but makes some errors	3 Good decision resulting from sound analysis of factors	4 Sound, logical thinker	5 Consistently makes sound judgments
Quantity of Work				
1 Falls below minimum requirements	2 Usually meets minimum requirements	3 Satisfactory quantity	4 Usually well exceeds minimum	5 Consistently produces high quantity
Quality of Work				
1 Poor quality, many errors	2 Quality usually all right, some errors	3 Satisfactory quality	4 Quality exceeds standards	5 Consistently high quality

The scale value corresponding to this anchor is checked. The evaluation is a combination of the rankings on the scale values for each job dimension. BARS take more time to develop than graphic rating scales, and a separate form must be developed for each job. The use of BARS can help reduce errors if good behavioral statements are provided as anchors. Also, because BARS are developed with the participation of managers and jobholders, the likelihood is higher that this appraisal method will be accepted. Figure 11.4 shows a scale that might be used to evaluate the job dimensions of program promotion and public relations. A BARS such as this could be used to evaluate librarians who have responsibility for program promotion in a public library.

BARS are often impractical because each job requires its own scale, and often in smaller organizations there are not enough employees in each specific job to use them.[16] Because of the difficulties of implementing this system, it is not widely used in libraries.[17]

Figure 11.4—A Behaviorally Anchored Rating Scale

| *Job Dimension: Program Promotion and Public Relations* |
| *This section includes standards for evaluating behaviors in promoting programs and using the mass media* |

Scale Values	Anchors
7 Excellent	Conducts one of the best PR progr ams in the state. Always gets extensive media coverage for library programs.
6 Very Good	Constantly works on developing good public relations. Is willing to work with all groups and organizations for promotion of programs. Communicates effectively with the mass media.
5 Good	Has developed a city wide mailing list of interested individuals. Makes some original use of mass media. Has adapted some of the promotional material supplied by the American Library Association for local use. Makes reports to advisory groups and public officials on request or as opportunities arise.
4 Average	Maintains communication with some local leaders, organizations, and groups.
3 Below Average	Assists with planning and implementing public relations programs even though efforts may lack consistency. Does not make sufficient use of one or more of the mass media.
2 Poor	Makes no effort to speak to community clubs or organizations. Continually mentions media that should be contacted to increase potential audiences, but does nothing about it. Is not interested in certain parts of the library's program and does not publicize them.
1 Unacceptable	Shows disrespect for local values and customs. Fails to communicate events and activities to those interested.

The Performance Appraisal Review Process

Institutions structure their performance appraisal process in various ways, but some elements are common to almost all of them. First, someone from the office responsible for appraisals (probably either HR or the library director's office) distributes the appropriate forms. Information is provided about the individual whose performance is to be evaluated, the name of the person responsible for completing the form, and the date the form is due back in the initiating office. In an increasing number of organizations, computer software is used in performance appraisals as a means of making the process more efficient and standardized.

The person who receives the form then needs to evaluate the employee's performance. It is the rater's responsibility to complete the form thoughtfully and carefully. Usually, it is wise for the rater to base judgments on notes or a diary kept over a period of time. The rater must have proof of the evaluations given, particularly negative evaluations. The rater must consider the employee's work from the last period of rating to the current time; evaluation should not be based solely on what happened recently.

The rater must not be afraid to give a negative rating. With today's emphasis on accountability, it is the rater's responsibility to be accurate and truthful in the evaluation of an employee's performance. If the performance is bad, the evaluation should reflect it, but there also should be evidence to show why such an evaluation was justified.

In order to make sure that no prejudice or bias influences an evaluation, the rating should be reviewed by the supervisor's supervisor. Together, the rater and his or her supervisor should review the proposed performance evaluation and come to a consensus on its accuracy.

The Performance Appraisal Interview

After the evaluation form is complete, the rater must share the results with the employee. This information is usually provided in a performance appraisal interview. Conducting the performance appraisal interview is probably the most difficult part of the process—at least, it is the part most dreaded by employees and supervisors. Both the employee and the supervisor need to prepare for the interview. The supervisor should make an appointment with the employee and make the purpose of the appointment clear. Before the meeting is held, the supervisor should give the employee the completed performance appraisal form. The employee should have at least twenty-four hours to review the evaluation and to consider its fairness and appropriateness. In addition, the supervisor must prepare for the meeting. The supervisor might examine previous performance appraisals to review the employee's progress. Certainly, the supervisor will plan the meeting's structure. Most employees are apprehensive about these performance appraisal interviews. Once an interview time has been established, the supervisor should make every effort to hold to the schedule because postponements or other schedule changes increase the employee's worry and concern. Because of the sensitivity of this interview, the supervisor must establish as informal an atmosphere as possible. Frequently, supervisors move away from their desks to an area with more informal furniture because the supervisor's desk, a symbol of authority, functions as a barrier and a psychological obstacle to many workers. Supervisors should ensure that there will be no telephone calls or other interruptions during the interview.

What Would You Do?

At 9:05 A.M., Jeanne Leforte was walking briskly toward the entrance of the Deuxville Public Library, one of the nation's largest urban libraries. Despite the heaviness of the air, she felt happy, almost light-headed. Why? Last evening, her doctor had given her the news she had been eagerly hoping for: She was going to have a baby. She and her husband, John, had wanted a baby for a long time, and this exciting development helped offset the unfortunate reality of John's predicament: He had been seriously injured several months ago in a car accident and would be unable to work for some time. But there was also another reason why she felt happy. This feeling of happiness was based on the belief that her salary shortly would be increased by 15 percent. Every year at this time, the library requires performance evaluations for all employees. In the years she had worked at the Deuxville Public Library, her annual evaluations had been superior in each of the categories on the library personnel office's evaluation form; the comments sections also contained warm words of praise for her and her work. Consequently, she always had received the city's maximum possible raise. So, although her husband could not resume work for a while, they would be able to get by on her salary—that is, as long as she got the raise she expected. She was to have her appraisal interview with her supervisor, Marshall Edmonds, at 9:30. She looked at her watch and mounted the long flight of stairs leading to the offices on the first floor.

Her first hint that all was not well was the sudden appearance of Consuelo Feng. As Feng swept by with an almost inaudible "Good morning, Jeanne" escaping from her lips, Leforte thought she detected the telltale indications of crying on her face: the red, swollen eyes, the puffiness.

Performance appraisal interviews can be threatening to both employer and employee. What steps can be taken to ensure that these interviews proceed as smoothly as possible?

(For the rest of this case study, see http://lu.com/management.)

The supervisor should not lecture the employee but should ask questions or make comments that encourage the employee to talk. If the employee is encouraged to talk, the discussion naturally will center on the performance appraisal. The employee has the opportunity to express concerns about, or approval of, the appraisal, and the supervisor can explain why certain elements were rated as they were.

In this interview, the supervisor's objectives are to identify problems that the employee has in performing any assigned tasks; to plan methods or procedures by which these problems might be resolved; to determine the employee's general level of satisfaction with the job, the institution, and the working environment; and to help the employee plan personal programs and activities that will improve job effectiveness or help in preparation for advancement. The last objective is particularly important. Together, the employee and the supervisor establish current and long-range goals for the employee. After mutual agreement, the goals are recorded on the performance evaluation form; at the next evaluation interview, progress toward the goals is measured. By signing the form, the employee indicates acceptance of the evaluation and proposed goals.

Of course, not all interviews go smoothly. Sometimes supervisors have to tell employees they are not working up to the library's standards. In some cases, the supervisor may have to demote or terminate an employee. The supervisor should be able to anticipate when such action might be necessary and be prepared. Previous and current performance appraisals, as well as the known attitude and behavior of the employee, provide indications that difficulty might be encountered. The wise supervisor is seldom caught unprepared for any direction the interview takes.

Performance appraisal is a necessary though difficult part of HR administration. Good performance appraisal systems help employees understand how well they are doing and provide an opportunity for employee growth and development.

DISCIPLINE AND GRIEVANCES

At one time or another, almost every manager has to deal with an employee who fails to comply with the requirements of the job or the organization. That employee's supervisor may need to invoke some sort of disciplinary procedure to resolve the issue. Conversely, sometimes an employee has a complaint about the organization or its management. In that case, the employee may need to use the organization's grievance procedure to resolve the problem.

Discipline is the action taken by an organization against an employee when that employee's performance has deteriorated to the point where action is necessary or when that employee has violated an institutional rule. Discipline is a method of communicating to employees that they need to change their behavior to meet established standards. Discipline may need to be administered for reasons ranging from excessive absenteeism to theft. Supervisors must be aware of the dual objectives of discipline: preserving the interests of the organization and protecting the rights of the individual.

Most organizations have formal policies and procedures for handling discipline. It has been estimated that only about 5 percent of employees ever need discipline; the vast majority are good workers who want to do the right thing.[18] But policies and procedures relating to discipline must be in place to deal with the few who need them. Before establishing disciplinary procedures, each institution must develop rules and regulations governing employee performance and must take measures to ensure that these rules and regulations are clearly understood by each employee. If an employee violates a rule or work standard, disciplinary action is taken. Before this is done, however, it should be established that the poor performance is not caused by external factors, such as poor training, insufficient supervision, or inadequate equipment.

Role-Play a Situation

You are head of reference in an academic library. One of the student workers who is scheduled to work 20 hours per week is late again. The student has been showing up for work at least 20 minutes late since the new semester began three weeks ago. This is causing a great deal of inconvenience to all the other staff and has resulted in gaps in coverage at the desk. You have scheduled an appointment to speak with the student tomorrow. How will you structure the interview? What points will you want to make? What do you hope the outcome of the interview will be?

Ask a friend or fellow student to play the role of the student worker in this scenario.

Disciplinary actions take various forms, depending on the nature and frequency of the offending behavior. Most organizations employ what is known as progressive discipline, which provides for a series of steps before dismissal so that an employee will have the opportunity to correct the undesirable behavior. The mildest disciplinary action is the simple oral warning. After this, the penalties escalate to an oral warning noted in the employee's personnel record, then to a written warning, then to suspension without pay for varying lengths of time, and, finally, to the harshest penalty, discharge from the job. However, in the case of gross misconduct, such as assault on a supervisor or theft, an employee can be dismissed without going through all these steps. To prevent litigation, documentation should be kept at each step of the process.

To administer discipline effectively, the penalties must be imposed in the right manner. Many HR experts refer to the so-called red-hot-stove method of administering discipline. When someone touches a red-hot stove, the punishment is immediate, given with warning, consistent, and impersonal. The best disciplinary systems have these characteristics. Discipline should be carried out impersonally, without a feeling that there is any animosity on the part of the supervisor. A supervisor should never hesitate to use discipline when necessary but should always remember that discipline is not intended to humiliate an employee but to correct a problem or to modify job behavior. Discipline should be administered privately and in a calm manner. The supervisor should encourage two-way communication and allow the employee to speak. A follow-up plan for improving behavior should be agreed upon. If possible, the interview should end on a positive note, leaving the employee with the belief that both the supervisor and organization want him or her to succeed.[19]

No one likes to administer discipline, but, if handled properly, a disciplinary system can be an effective tool in handling job-related employee problems. In addition to the individual being disciplined, discipline may prevent others from acting in a similar fashion, assure others that inappropriate behavior will not be tolerated, and communicate the manager's commitment to a high standard of conduct.[20]

Firing or Termination

When none of these disciplinary procedures are effective, a manager may have to discharge an employee. *Firing* is the term that is usually used for a for-cause dismissal. An employee who has committed a major transgression, such as stealing, gross insubordination, or the like, would be fired. Termination results from an employee's failure to meet job expectations after a reasonable amount of time. Discharging an employee is never easy, but the process must be handled correctly because the mishandling of terminations is a major cause of employee lawsuits. Documentation is important in all HR decisions, but it is especially important in the case of terminations. All evidence supporting the need for termination should be available in case of litigation.[21] Managers should treat the employee with respect and understand how traumatic it is to lose a job for whatever reason. At the same time, however, it is the duty of a manager to remove poorly performing employees before they affect the morale of other workers and impede the work being done in the unit.

Grievance Systems

Discipline is concerned with the problems organizations have with employees. A grievance system, on the other hand, provides a method for employees to deal with the problems they have with supervisors or with the organization. A grievance is any dissatisfaction relating to one's employment that is brought to the attention of an organization's management. Grievance procedures are found in both unionized and nonunionized organizations, but the procedure is apt to be more formal and well defined in unionized situations.

In many nonunionized institutions, the open-door policy is used to solve employee grievances in an informal manner. This policy is based on the assumption that, when supervisors encourage employees to come to their office voluntarily at any time to discuss problems and complaints, they will feel free to do so. The open-door policy works only when the supervisor has been able to instill in employees a feeling of trust. Employees must feel that any problem or complaint will be objectively heard and fairly resolved and that the supervisor will not hold it against them or consider them troublemakers. The open-door policy is successful when the supervisor is skilled in human relations and is sensitive to employee needs and feelings. The open-door policy gives the supervisor an opportunity to explain why a certain action was taken and to resolve the complaint or grievance through direct communication. Factual problems are probably the easiest to resolve, because they involve easily verified situations such as working conditions, hours of work, or changes in the procedures of a job. Problems involving feelings or emotions are often much more difficult to handle.

In a unionized institution, the collective-bargaining agreement establishes the procedures to be used for handling grievances. These procedures proceed through certain steps outlined in the union contract. In general, the first step is for the aggrieved employee to meet with the union steward, who is the union representative for that employee's unit. The employee and the union steward discuss the grievance and together bring the grievance to the grievant's supervisor. If a mutually satisfactory solution cannot be reached, the grievance is put in writing, and the process is continued with the next level of management. If the problem is still unresolved, higher management and the HR department usually become involved. If a solution to the grievance cannot be arrived at within the organization, the grievant can request arbitration, a process by which both the employer and the union representing the employee agree to settle the dispute through an outside, neutral third party. The decision made by the arbitrator is binding for all parties involved.

It is best for all organizations to have formal grievance procedures. In a unionized organization, this procedure is part of the union contract. In a nonunionized organization, management must see that such procedures are established. A grievance procedure defines the manner in which grievances are filed (written or oral), to whom the grievance is submitted, how the grievance proceeds through the organization's hierarchy, where decisions about the grievance can be made, and the final point of decision. Usually, the procedures identify actions that aggrieved employees can take if they are not satisfied with the final decision.

Grievance procedures are ways of removing the employee from the direct and complete control of his or her immediate supervisor. Grievance procedures may discipline supervisors and act as guarantees to employees. They exist to assure employees that justice is available when they have a legitimate complaint against the organization.

EMPLOYEE COMPENSATION

The ultimate aim of salary administration is to arrive at an equitable system of compensating employees for the work they perform. Most libraries offer employees only salaries and benefits, unlike for-profit corporations, which often provide annual bonuses, stock options, or other special incentives to reward employees. HR specialists differentiate between wages and salaries. Wages refers to the compensation of employees whose pay is calculated according to the number of hours worked each week, and salary refers to compensation that is uniform from one pay period to the next. Wages are usually reported by the hour; salaries by the year.

Two other terms are used to differentiate between these types of employees. Wage-earning employees are often referred to as *nonexempt* personnel. Generally, nonexempt employees work in nonsupervisory positions and are covered by the Fair Labor Standards Act. Nonexempt employees must be paid time-and-one-half (the hourly wage multiplied by 1.5) for overtime work. Salaried workers are often referred to as *exempt* personnel. Exempt employees are usually managerial or professional employees who are exempt from the Fair Labor Standards Act. Employers are not required to pay such employees overtime, regardless of the number of hours worked.

Most libraries receive the bulk of their salary funding from their parent institution. In addition, a few libraries receive a smaller amount of personnel funds from endowments, federal or foundation grants, or, occasionally, from earned income. Funds received from federal or foundation grants are allocated to specific projects or programs on a temporary basis; such funding is often called *soft* money.

Private businesses and institutions are not required to make public the wages or salaries of any individual employee or group of employees. Indeed, in many industries, salary information is a closely kept secret. The justification for salary secrecy is that it prevents discontent among employees. Most public institutions, on the other hand, are required to make salary information available. In many states, the salaries of state employees are considered a public record and are available in personnel offices and/or in newspapers.

Some employees dislike having salaries disclosed because they feel that the disclosure violates their privacy. Sometimes, public disclosure of salaries may lead to envy and a loss of morale. On the other hand, open disclosure of salaries is thought to curb favoritism and to lessen pay discrimination among employees. Many HR specialists feel that, if possible, a compromise between the two positions is best. An organization should disclose the pay ranges for various jobs within the organization but not reveal what any particular individual is earning.

In libraries as in other organizations, a salary administration program consists of three parts: the determination of what salary to pay, the development of a salary scale, and the process of awarding salary increases.

Determination of Salary

All institutions that pay personnel for services rendered must determine what is fair and equitable compensation for the education, experience, and responsibility required for the job. The determination of the salary associated with any job should be directly related to the requirements for that job; the higher the job requirements, the higher the salary.

Institutions must provide competitive salaries in order to attract and retain good employees. Individuals who have specialized education, a demonstrated capability resulting from successful work experience, and a willingness to accept responsibility are always in demand. Thus, the compensation must be adequate to attract them. Although money may not be the most important motivator for some people, it is still very important to most. Institutions that strive to obtain and retain the best people usually will offer salaries higher than institutions that will accept lower performance and higher turnover.

In the private sector, more and more companies are paying employees on the basis of some sort of performance measure.[22] This pay for performance can range from the piece-rate method of paying factory workers to the lump-sum bonuses given to employees who are considered to have contributed to a company's productivity or profits. These programs differ from the usual compensation systems because they link pay directly to productivity or performance, not just to the time spent at a job. This type of compensation system is rarely found in publicly funded libraries.

The question of fair pay generally involves two general issues: (1) internal equity, or what the employee is paid compared to what other employees in the same organization are paid, and (2) external equity, or what the employee is paid compared to what employees in other organizations are paid for performing similar jobs. Pay dissatisfaction can have a negative influence on the employee's work. If organizations are to avoid this dissatisfaction, employees must be convinced that both internal and external equity exist.

In general, the salaries of professional librarians are competitive nationally, although there are sometimes regional and local conditions that affect them. In large metropolitan centers, such as New York City or San Francisco, the cost of living is greater than in smaller communities. Factors of this nature affect the level of salary offered. The annual report of professional salaries received by current graduates of accredited schools of library and information science, usually published in an October issue of *Library Journal*,[23] shows the regional variation of beginning salaries as well as the national average and median salaries.

In addition to the *Library Journal* survey, there are several ways to gather information on entry-level salaries as well as on the salaries of other professional levels. Periodically, the Special Libraries Association conducts an in-depth survey of its members.[24] The American Library Association periodically reports information about salaries in *American Libraries*.[25] The Association of Research Libraries publishes an annual salary survey.[26] Some state libraries issue salary data for all libraries in that state. An institution may wish to gather these data by conducting a salary survey or by simply evaluating salaries offered in advertisements in professional periodicals. Regardless of the method used, great care must be taken to assure that all the data gathered apply to positions that have the same job requirements.

Salaries for library positions other than those held by professional librarians usually are determined by the going rate of pay in the community in which the library is located. The Allied Professional Association and Office for Research and Statistics of the American Library Association now provide a national overview of salaries for library support staff.[27] Information concerning local salaries can be obtained from institutions such as the school system, local government, employment agencies, or Chamber of Commerce. Some Internet sites, such as http://www.salary.com, provide information about salaries for specific jobs in various geographic locations.

Information technology has altered the jobs of most librarians, and often the job classifications and the pay scales have lagged in recognizing these changes. In many organizations, the tasks that librarians perform are similar to those performed by computer or systems workers, but, because they are classified differently, they are paid less.

If libraries and information centers wish to attract the most talented employees, efforts must be made to be sure that the salary offered to their employees is as attractive as that offered to employees performing similar functions working elsewhere. The disparity in salaries of technologically proficient workers in libraries and in the corporate world is one of the reasons that libraries today are having problems in recruiting new employees.

Development of a Salary Scale

A salary scale establishes the amount of money that will be paid for the accomplishment of the duties designated in the job description. The scale has a minimum and a maximum amount that will be paid for that job. The minimum represents the beginning or entry-level salary, and the maximum amount should indicate the value of the job to the institution when it is performed with maximum efficiency and thoroughness. The difference between the minimum and the maximum are steps on the salary scale that designate salary increases awarded to the employee as proficiency increases or as experience is gained. After an employee has reached the top step of a grade, the only way he or she can receive a pay increase is by moving to a higher range.

Each library has to develop its own salary scale, but such scales are influenced by many external factors. For instance, there are numerous constraints on how these scales can be developed. Federal and state laws concerning the minimum wage put a floor under the compensation of the lowest-paid employees. In early 2007, the federal minimum wage remained at $5.15 per hour although bills have been introduced into the U.S. Congress that will likely increase the federal minimum wage in the near future. Already some states and cities require a higher minimum wage.[28] The existence of a union contract may affect how employees are paid. The salaries paid in competing institutions also influence the salary scale. Finally, the law of supply and demand plays a part; employees in high-demand specialties may have to be paid more than other employees with more commonly available expertise.

The establishment of the salary scale is closely linked to the process of job evaluation. Regardless of which method of job evaluation has been used (e.g., the factor method or the classification method), the ultimate objective is to ascertain the correct rate of pay for all jobs in the organization and the relationship in terms of salary between them. Although some institutions have salary scales that do not overlap, it is much more common for the ranges of adjacent pay grades to do so. The use of an overlapping pay scale allows an outstanding performer in a lower grade to make a higher salary than a below-average worker in a higher grade. In a like fashion, an experienced worker in a lower grade would make a higher salary than a beginning worker in a higher grade.

In administering a salary scale, some commonsense principles should be kept in mind. First, there should be equal pay for equal work. If two jobs have equal requirements in terms of education, experience, and responsibility, the pay should be the same. Of course, this does not prevent having a salary range with individuals at different steps within the range. Second, employees are not required to enter a salary scale at the first step. Most institutions recognize previous related work experience and allow a new employee to enter higher on the scale. Third, if an employee is promoted from one rank to another, for instance, from Librarian I to Librarian II, the employee should not be forced to take a pay cut if the beginning salary of Librarian II is lower than the salary the employee earned as Librarian I. Instead, the employee should be given a somewhat higher salary to compensate him or her for assuming more responsibility.

Salary Increases

Three common methods of determining salary increases in libraries and information centers are length of service, merit, or some combination of these two factors. Length of service equates increased pay with seniority. The underlying assumption is that an organization should recognize the fact that an experienced worker is more valuable than an inexperienced one. Librarians working in public schools usually have pay schedules with predetermined steps; with each year of experience, the librarians advance a step on the salary scale. Sometimes, government employees receive a uniform salary increase (e.g., a 5% increase), and all employees receive the same percentage increase to reward increasing seniority. The automatic increase, though easy to administer, does not allow the organization to reward exceptional performers.

The merit system is based on the concept that salary increases should be awarded only for quality performance. In any organization, some workers contribute more than others. Merit pay allows the organization to reward the employees who work the hardest and who are the most valuable. It is assumed that a merit-based system will encourage all employees to work better in the hopes of receiving a larger pay increase. It is almost impossible to construct a plan of merit increases that will please all employees. Supervisors are often accused of using merit systems to reward their favorite employees. The merit system also presents problems when employees receive no pay increase at all. During periods of high inflation, employees who are given no salary increase are seriously affected by a loss of spending power and thus will not be able to maintain the same standard of living from year to year. If a merit system is used, it should be carefully designed, well publicized, and closely related to the employees' performance appraisals.

Most libraries use some combination of merit and seniority to award pay increases. All employees may be awarded an increase of a certain monetary amount or percentage if their job performance is meritorious. This approach allows all employees to receive some pay increase when raises are awarded.

The use of teams has complicated the awarding of salary increases. Traditionally, employees have been compensated based on their individual performance, but in team-based organizations, many employees are being evaluated and paid according to the performance of their teams. Obviously, if an organization wants to reinforce the value and importance of teams, it is important to reinforce team behavior. Rewarding team performance, not individual performance, achieves that goal. But the team-based reward only works well when all team members contribute equitably. Team-based pay has the potential of giving free riders as great a pay increase as those who have worked much harder. Determining equitable pay for team members is difficult, but libraries need to continue to find a way to provide equitable ways of administering team-based rewards.[29] Whatever compensation system is used, it should be one that can be communicated easily and that is felt to be fair by the employees.

Recognition and Rewards

Individuals working in libraries rarely receive the monetary rewards, such as stock options or bonuses, that are available to employees in the private sector. Nonetheless, many libraries have tried to structure some no-cost or low-cost way to reward and express appreciation for employees. Employee recognition programs usually are successful because employees are motivated by recognition. People who feel appreciated identify with the organization and are more productive. Managers of reward systems must be sure that rewards are tied to the organization's needs, that the reward system is flexible and fair, and that rewards are publicized and, if appropriate, presented in a public forum. It is best to schedule frequent reward presentations so employees receive the reward soon after the achievement is recognized.[30] Celebrations and awards can be effective morale boosters and can increase productivity and quality. They also contribute to building a strong organizational culture.

 Try This!

Work with a group of other people. Try to think of as many ways as you can that a library could provide nonmonetary rewards or recognition to employees. What are the advantages and disadvantages or these types of rewards?

Employee Benefits

A major portion of employees' compensation packages consists of benefits. The number and variety of benefits provided by libraries and information centers has grown over the years to the point where benefits constitute a major factor in total compensation. The package of benefits offered to employees is determined by the individual library or by the library's parent institution. Some benefits are required by federal or state law, and, in unionized institutions, some are mandated as part of a collective-bargaining agreement. Federal and state regulations apply to almost all workers in the United States. Among the benefits required by these laws are Social Security, unemployment insurance, and workers' compensation. Unemployment insurance and workers' compensation are financed solely by employer contributions. Social Security is financed by equal contributions from employer and employee. The amount of Social Security tax has increased rapidly over the years. In 1937, the combined employer-employee tax rate was 2 percent on a maximum of $3,000 in earnings. In 2006, the combined rate was 12.4 percent on a maximum of $94,200.[31] For many low-paid employees, contributions to Social Security are larger than their federal income tax.

In addition to benefits mandated by federal or state law, organizations provide other types of benefits. For some, the employer pays the full cost, and for others, the employee pays a portion of the cost. In private industry, a recent trend is the use of flexible, or cafeteria, plans, which allow employees some discretion in choosing the specific elements of their benefit program from a range of options. This approach allows employees to tailor a program to fit their needs. For example, an employee who is covered by a spouse's health insurance plan might forgo the health insurance option and instead select a larger amount of life insurance. To date, however, few public institutions provide such cafeteria plans.

Most libraries offer several types of group insurance plans. Medical insurance, often including major medical coverage of catastrophic illness, is commonly provided. The cost of medical insurance has escalated in the past few years, and, as a result, many organizations have shifted more of the cost of this insurance onto the employee and have increased his or her deductibles. In addition to health insurance, many organizations provide both group life insurance and disability insurance; the latter tides employees over during periods of disability caused by sickness or accident. Dental insurance is provided by some libraries. The payment for these types of insurance varies; some institutions pay the full cost, but more commonly, the employee pays a portion, especially for the coverage of dependents.

Paid time off includes holidays, vacations, and various types of leave. It is also standard practice in many organizations to pay employees for rest periods and lunch breaks.

Employee retirement plans are pension or retirement plans that offer an addition to the retirement coverage offered by Social Security. Commonly, both the employer and employee make contributions to these plans.

Many employees are offered access to Employee Assistance Programs (EAPs), which provide assessment and referral for employees who have problems with depression, family dissension, substance abuse, and financial or legal matters. At one time, employees with personal problems were fired if these problems got in the way of work performance. EAPs help employees work through these problems and stay on the job.

Librarians may be offered a wide variety of other benefits, depending on where they work. Some of these monetary benefits include travel and moving expenses, tuition refunds, and access to subsidized day care.

Some of the benefits offered by libraries are related to the rise in the number of two-career families. Especially when couples in a two-career marriage have children, benefits that allow them flexibility in order to meet family responsibilities are among the most valuable that an organization can provide.

A nonmonetary benefit found more and more in libraries and information centers is the alternative work schedule. Instead of requiring all employees to work the same hours, alternative work schedules, such as flextime or the compressed workweek, allow employees some freedom in choosing the hours and days they work. This flexibility, of course, can be granted only if appropriate provision is made to cover service to users and supervisory and training responsibilities. Before instituting any type of alternative work schedule, administrators should develop clear plans of action, with targeted jobs tested in advance to determine the likely effects of the new schedule.

 ## What Do You Think?

For the vast majority of working families, Ozzie and Harriet are demographic dinosaurs. For others, they were always a myth. Today, Harriet usually does not stay home. Nearly three out of four women with children are in the workforce. Often, neither Ozzie nor Harriet gets home by 5:00 P.M. The time that married women with children spend working outside the home nearly doubled in 30 years—translating into 22 fewer hours per week families can spend with their children.

> Most employees in libraries are women, and many of them have children and other family responsibilities. What can employers do to help women (and men) balance the responsibilities of work and family? Do you think that employees with children should get any special benefits or consideration?
>
> U.S. Department of Labor, *Futurework: Trends and Challenges for Work in the 21st Century* (Washington, DC: Department of Labor, 1999): 10; excerpt also available in U.S. Department of Labor, "Futurework: Trends and Challenges for Work in the 21st Century," *Occupational Outlook Quarterly* (Summer 2000): 31–37, http://www.bls.gov/opub/ooq/2000/Summer/art04.pdf.

Telecommuting refers to working away from the office, on a full-time or part-time basis, often at home, usually using an Internet connection, telephone, and/or fax machine as a way to keep in touch with the office. Telecommuting has advantages for both employer and employee. The employer does not have to provide a place for the employee to work. The employee benefits from a more flexible job schedule, lack of interruptions, lack of a commute, and the maximum amount of freedom in terms of structuring the work environment. Although telecommuting is becoming increasingly popular in the for-profit sector, it is not used as frequently in libraries. Where it is used, it is usually on a temporary or part-time basis. However, some librarians are allowed to work out of their homes at least part-time for such tasks as Web site design, online reference, and writing projects. To be a successful telecommuter, it is important "to be self-motivated, focused, and organized, and to have a family life that won't create frequent work interruptions."[32] Telecommuting provides ultimate flexibility for people holding the type of job that lends itself to being done off-site.

A few libraries have instituted the practice of job sharing. Job sharing splits one job between two individuals. Usually, the salary is shared; benefits, such as medical insurance, are sometimes prorated, but, in the best cases, both employees receive benefits. Flextime, telecommuting, and job sharing are attractive to employees with small children because these alternative approaches to work enable them to spend more time with their children. Other employees also find these options beneficial; their existence sometimes allows organizations to keep valuable employees they otherwise would lose.

Many employees take their benefits for granted, not realizing that benefits are a sizable part of the total labor cost of any organization. Benefits add significantly to the salary of an employee because of the contributions made by the employer. On a percentage basis, the cost of benefits has increased substantially in recent years. The Bureau of Labor Statistics reports that, for all domestic industries in 2006, the total cost of all benefits was almost 30 percent of total annual wages.[33]

Both employers and employees gain from a well-designed and well-administered benefits program, despite its cost. In considering a benefits program, a manager must carefully study each element of the program to determine its future financial impact on the institution. After determining that the program is needed and desired by the employees, the manager must carefully define the program and establish the policies and procedures necessary to assure its fair and equitable implementation. Finally, the manager should communicate information about the benefits package to all employees to inform them what is available, when they are eligible, and what procedures are involved in obtaining the benefits. Supervisors should be able to speak knowledgeably about the entire benefits package because many employees turn to their immediate supervisors for information of this type.

CONCLUSION

This chapter has covered the primary functions related to maintaining the HR of a library. The next chapter looks at some of the general issues affecting HR management. That chapter will cover topics such as personnel procedures and policies, career development, mentoring, external regulations, and unionization.

NOTES

1. Janice Simmons-Welburn and William C. Welburn, "Organizational Entry, Sense Making, and New Professional Employees in Academic Libraries" (paper presented at the ACRL 11th National Conference, April 2003, Charlotte, North Carolina), http://www.ala.org/ala/acrl/acrlevents/simmons-welburn.PDF.

2. Shelley L. Rogers, "Orientation for New Library Employees: A Checklist," *Library Administration and Management* 8 (Fall 1994): 213–17.

3. Mary M. Nofsinger and Angela S. W. Lee, "Beyond Orientation: The Roles of Senior Librarians in Training Entry-Level Reference Colleagues," *College and Research Libraries* 55 (March 1994): 161–70.

4. Peter M. Senge, *The Fifth Discipline: The Art and Practice of the Learning Organization* (New York: Doubleday, 1990): 3.

5. Ibid, 6–16.

6. David A. Garvey, *Learning in Action: A Guide to Putting the Learning Organization to Work* (Boston: Harvard Business School Press, 2000).

7. Ruth F. Metz, *Coaching in the Library: A Management Strategy for Achieving Excellence* (Chicago: American Library Association, 2001), 2.

8. For a more in-depth look at staff development, see Luisa Paster, "Current Issues in Staff Development," in *Human Resource Management in Today's Academic Library,* ed. Janice Simmons-Welburn and Beth McNeil (Westport, CT: Libraries Unlimited, 2004), 37–44.

9. Michael Beer, "Making Performance Appraisal Work," in *Managing People and Organizations,* ed. John J. Gabarro (Boston: Harvard Business School Publications, 1992), 196.

10. Brendan McDonagh, "Appraising Appraisals," *The Law Librarian* 26 (September 1995): 425.

11. Necia Parker-Gibson and Lutishoor Salisbury, "The Process of Peer Review," *Arkansas Libraries* 53 (February 1996): 3–7.

12. Richard Rubin, "The Development of a Performance Evaluation Instrument for Upward Evaluation of Supervisors by Subordinates," *Library and Information Science Research* 16 (Fall 1994): 315–28. This article provides considerable detail about the development of a valid and reliable instrument used in one public library.

13. Bodil Jones, "How'm I Doin'?" *Management Review* 86 (May 1997): 9–18.

14. Susan J. Wells. "A New Road—Traveling beyond 360-Degree Evaluation," *HR Magazine* 44 (September 1999): 84.

15. George C. Thornton, "The Relationship between Supervisory and Self-Appraisals of Executive Performance," *Personnel Psychology* 21 (Winter 1968): 441–55.

16. James S. Bowman, "Performance Appraisal: Verisimilitude Trumps Veracity," *Public Personnel Management* 28 (Winter 1999): 561.

17. Joyce P. Vincelette and Fred C. Pfister, "Improving Performance Appraisal in Libraries," *Library and Information Science Research* 6 (April–June 1984): 191–203.

18. "Breaking with Tradition: Changing Employee Relations through a Positive Employee Philosophy," *Library Personnel News* 8 (January–February 1994): 4.

19. D. Day, "Training 101: Help for Discipline Dodgers," *Training and Development* 47 (May 1993): 19–22.

20. Richard E. Rubin, *Human Resource Management in Libraries: Theory and Practice* (New York: Neal-Schuman, 1991), 157–58.

21. Karen L. Vinton, "Documentation that Gets Results," *Personnel* 67 (February 1990): 43.

22. Fred Luthans and Alexander Stajkovic, "Reinforcing for Performance: The Need to Go Beyond Pay and Even Rewards," *Academy of Management Executive* 13 (May 1999): 49–56.

23. The last survey available, published in 2006, reported the 2005 results. The average beginning salary for a 2005 MLS graduate was $40,118, up 2.58 percent from the previous year's average. Stephanie Maatta, "Starting Pay Breaks $40K," *Library Journal* 131 (October 15, 2006): 28–36.

24. Information about the latest survey can be seen at Special Libraries Association, "2005 SLA Salary Survey and Workplace Study" (2006), http://www.sla.org/content/resources/research/salarysurveys/salsur2005/index.cfm.

25. For the latest, see Denise M. Davis and Jennifer Grady, "Librarian Salaries: Revised Survey Yields Broader Results," *American Libraries* 36 (December 2005): 73.

26. For the latest ARL salary survey, see Association of Research Libraries, *The ARL Annual Salary Survey 2006-2007.* http://www.arl.org/stats/annualsurveys/salary/.

27. American Library Association, *ALA-APA Salary Survey 2006: Non-MLS—Public and Academic* (Chicago: American Library Association, 2006).

28. An interactive map of the minimum wage laws in the states is available from the U.S. Department of Labor, "Minimum Wage Laws in the States—January 1, 2007" (2006), http://www.dol.gov/esa/minwage/america.htm.

29. Michael Ray, "Making Systems Visible," *ARL Bimonthly Report* no. 208/209 (February/April 2000), http://www.arl.org/newsltr/208_209/index.html.

30. Philip C. Grant, "How to Make a Program Work," *Personnel Journal* 71 (January 1992): 103.

31. U.S. Social Security Administration, "Electronic Fact Sheet, Update 2007" (January 2007), http://www.socialsecurity.gov/pubs/10003.html.

32. Karen Schneider, "The Untethered Librarian," *American Libraries* 31 (August 2000): 72.

33. United States Department of Labor, Bureau of Labor Statistics, "Employer Costs for Employee Compensation Summary" (September 2006), http://stats.bls.gov/news.release/ecec.nr0.htm.Figure 11.2—Performance Rankings in a Forced Distribution Rating System

Chapter 12

Other Issues in Human Resource Management

 Overview

It has been 10 years since Terry began her career as an adult services librarian in a large public library system. She is still in the same library system but not in the same position. Five years ago, she was promoted to head of the Reference Department and discovered that she was not only a good manager but also enjoyed managing. Now, Terry has just been appointed associate director for Human Resources in her library system. She is excited about the new possibilities of this position. She had become accustomed to such HR functions as training, staff development, and employee performance appraisals in her previous department head position, but her new role gives her the opportunity to work full time in human resource (HR) administration, and she is looking forward to it. She already has plans for reviewing and updating the system's personnel policies and procedures and for getting them online so that they will be more easily accessible. She intends to implement a new career progression structure in response to the requests of many long-term employees who have asked for the system to help them advance in their careers. Terry soon will be working with the city's Disaster Preparation Office to come up with a plan to be implemented in the event of injuries or medical emergencies in the main library or any of its branches. The director also has asked her to serve as the library system's representative in the upcoming collective bargaining between the union that represents the clerical employees and the city. Terry knows that she will be busy, but she thinks that her new position will allow her to contribute not only to making the library a better place to work but also to it being a more effective organization overall.

In addition to the human resource management that is the responsibility of every manager, there are some larger HR responsibilities that usually are assumed either by designated HR managers in the library or by the library director. This chapter will discuss these more specialized HR functions and give examples of how they are implemented in libraries.

Many HR functions such as the ones discussed in the previous chapter are related to day-to-day activities and are carried out by managers throughout the organization. There are, however, some things that lie at the periphery of the HR functions that, nonetheless, are very important to the management of the human resources in any organization. This chapter will look at some of those topics, ranging from policies and procedures to health and safety issues in the workplace. In addition, there are a number of external forces that affect HR management. Two of the most important of these, legal protections for workers and unionization, will be discussed as well.

HUMAN RESOURCES POLICIES AND PROCEDURES

Throughout this section of the book, much has been written about HR policies and procedures. The development of policies and procedures is an integral part of the HR function of libraries and information centers. Clearly defined policies are essential to an effective HR program in every library. A policy is a statement of action that commits management to a definite plan or course of action. Policies—concerning hiring and promotion, for example—play an important role in every organization. They are used as guidelines for decision making. By reducing ad hoc decision making, HR policies lead to greater consistency and continuity in an organization. All employees need to understand, through written policy statements, topics such as why salaries are administered in a particular way, how and when performance appraisals will take place, and what benefits are available.

Even in larger libraries with specialized HR departments, the formulation of policy is ultimately the responsibility of the director. In most libraries, however, the director establishes policy with input from others. For instance, a group of supervisors or staff members might recommend the establishment or modification of a particular policy. Discussing, evaluating, and writing the policy statement can encourage the participation of the groups that will be affected by it.

An effective set of HR policies serves a number of functions. First, the formulation of such policies requires library management to think through the needs of both employees and the organization. Second, such policies provide consistent treatment for all employees. Because each supervisor follows the same policies, the equal treatment of each employee is assured. Clearly stated policies minimize both favoritism and discrimination. Third, such policies assure continuity of action, even during periods when managers or supervisors change. New managers have a written standard to follow, and policy remains stable. Employees need not endure vacillations in policies when supervisors resign or retire.

A human resources policy may be broad. For instance, "The X Library does not discriminate against any employee on the basis of age, gender, race, religion, or national origin." Policies also may be narrow. For instance, "All employees are entitled to four weeks of paid vacation each year." It must be remembered that a policy is a general statement of intent and does not spell out the exact methods by which it will be implemented. That function is accomplished by the procedure, which provides methods for carrying out a policy. It sets forth the steps that are needed to accomplish a particular result. A library will have procedures as to how vacation times will be allotted or how equal opportunity will be assured. For instance, if choice of vacation time is governed by length of service to the organization, this process would be described in the procedure manual.

In addition to policies and procedures, organizations also have rules. A rule is defined as a regulation or prescribed guide for conduct or behavior. Rules are the minimum standards of conduct that apply to a group of people and should apply uniformly to everyone in that group. Examples of rules are ones concerning the number of work hours required per day or the number of allowable absences. Rules serve to ensure predictability of behavior so that the organization can achieve its goals and function without undue disruption.

Obviously, the policies, procedures, and rules of an organization should be written and available to all. If they exist only in the mind of the director, they fail to serve the purposes for which they are developed. However, they must be more than written; they must be communicated to and understood by all employees. Policies locked in the director's desk are just as ineffective as those that are unwritten.

How are policies, procedures, and rules communicated through an organization? First, special care must be taken to communicate these documents to supervisors so that they can administer them equitably and uniformly. Often, organizations have special training sessions to acquaint supervisors with policies or to review them periodically. Nonsupervisory employees commonly learn about policies, procedures, and rules through the employee handbook or manual, which usually is given to each new employee during orientation. In many libraries, employees can access such information through the library intranet. When any changes in policies, procedures, or rules are implemented, they should be communicated and explained by the employee's immediate supervisor. Manuals should be updated, as should any material maintained online.

CAREER DEVELOPMENT

The topics of training and staff development were covered in chapter 11. However, career development differs from both training and staff development. A career is usually defined as a series of positions occupied by an individual during the course of a lifetime, and career development is a long-term attempt to help employees shape careers that are satisfying to them. Ultimately, of course, career development is the responsibility of the individual employee; nonetheless, the best organizations pay attention to this topic. Helping employees, especially high-performing employees, achieve a satisfying career reduces turnover and enables an organization to retain valuable human resources. At the very least, an organization should recognize the complex issues that employees face as they attempt to manage careers in the changing workplaces of the twenty-first century.

Typically, careers are thought to go through certain stages. These stages are illustrated in figure 12.1.

Figure 12.1—The Stages of a Career

Each of the stages is marked by different needs and perceptions. The first stage is precareer, when a person is beginning to think about what type of profession or job he or she would like to pursue as a career. The early career stage takes place at the time of organizational entry, when an individual enters the job market and begins to establish a career. A newly minted MLIS graduate taking a first professional job in a library would be at this entry stage. The challenges of this stage are getting a first position and becoming established in the organization. After a few years in a career, the individual enters the midcareer stage. He or she is familiar with the field now and perhaps has been promoted into some sort of managerial position. Plateauing, discussed later in this chapter, is one of the common problems associated with the midcareer stage. The late career stage is when individuals are firmly established in an organization and are typically of great value to it because of their expertise and organizational knowledge. These are the people who likely will serve as mentors to younger professionals. Individuals toward the end of that stage are likely to be looking ahead to retirement. The last stage in a career is retirement. Once, most people retired at age 65, but with the end of mandatory retirement, employees are retiring at different ages. Even some of those who have retired return to the workplace as part-time or temporary workers, either at their previous organization or at another one. These career stages are not always as clear-cut as figure 12.1 might imply. People move through the stages at varying rates of speed, and, in an era when many people switch careers, some may not go through all the steps outlined, whereas others might go through them several times. Some of the arrows in the figure point both forward and backward to reflect the reality that many people change careers and often retirees go back into the workforce.

In the past, employees often expected to go to work for one company and stay there until they retired. That expectation has been destroyed by the increased number of companies that have downsized, merged, or turned to temporary or contract workers. No longer can an employee, especially in the for-profit sector, expect a career working in a single company. Instead, the new pattern is one in which individuals are active agents in their own career development. In the not-for-profit sector, the organizational upheavals have been fewer, but employees still are affected by the new organizational rules that are in effect. The career ladders in most libraries are flatter than they used to be. An entry-level librarian who wants to move up the ladder to become a library director encounters many obstacles. The flattened organizations discussed in chapter 9 do not have as many levels of hierarchy as the ones they replaced, and new team-based organizations found in many libraries also have eliminated the need for many midlevel managers. The career progression pattern that used to exist in most large libraries, of becoming a department head and then an assistant or associate director and finally a director, is thus not as commonly available as before.

What Do You Think?

An article in *Fortune Magazine* contained the following quotation:

> Close your eyes and picture an object that embodies the word "career." If you joined the workforce say 15 or 20 or 25 years ago you're probably hard-wired, as the techies say, to visualize your working life as a predictable series of narrow and distinctly separate rungs that lead straight up (or down)—in other words a ladder. Ha! Ha! Ha! My friend, the ladder has been chopped up into little pieces and dumped in the garbage pile. A crew of sanitation engineers disposed of it at dawn while you were dreaming.

The traditional system of career progression has been affected by the downsizing of organizations and the resulting loss of job security, the erosion of employee loyalty to the employer, and an environment in which new technology is always demanding fresh skills.

Do you think that the traditional ladder exists in the workplaces you know? If not, what is taking its place? How can organizations keep employees motivated without it?

Anne Fisher, "Six Ways to Supercharge Your Career," *Fortune* 135 (January 13, 1997): 46.

In fact, careers are being viewed differently. There is a realization that not everyone wants to be a library director or a manager of any type. Different people have different aspirations. That is why the dual career ladders found in the LIS Education and Human Resources Utilization policy statement discussed in chapter 10 are helpful in allowing individuals who do not aspire to management to progress within a library. Also, there is some evidence that there are differences between age cohorts and that the wants of Generations X and Y may be different from those of the baby boom generation.[1] These younger employees do not identify job stability as an objective, and most expect to move and work at different institutions.[2]

Furthermore, it appears that today there are fewer people of all ages who want to move into jobs with more responsibility. The Families and Work Institute, a nonprofit research organization, conducted a national study to determine differences in the way generations view issues related to employment. Among college-educated men of Gen Y, Gen X, and the baby boom, only 52 percent wanted to move into jobs with more responsibility in 2002 compared to 68 percent in 1992. Among college-educated women, the decrease was even greater. Only 36 percent aspired to jobs with more responsibility in 2002 versus 57 percent in 1992.[3]

But, assuming an individual does want to progress up the administrative ladder, there are still roadblocks for many. Most libraries have been in a nongrowth stage for a number of years. Well-qualified employees may find their career advancement blocked because there are no openings in the positions directly above them, and, even worse, many of these positions are held by individuals who are only slightly older than the employee who is seeking advancement. Until the large number of baby boomers employed in libraries begins retiring, this situation likely will prevail.

Plateauing

When employees wish to progress but are unable to do so, they are said to be *plateaued.* Plateauing usually occurs during midcareer and can occur in two ways. Structural plateauing occurs when an individual is no longer promoted within the organization; content plateauing means that a job has become routine, and no challenging tasks are added to it.[4] A special type of plateauing is sometimes referred to as the *glass ceiling.* The glass ceiling is an invisible barrier that prevents women and minorities from ascending the institutional hierarchy. Although, in the past two decades, women and minorities have made significant progress into lower and middle management levels, neither is represented in upper management in proportion to their numbers in the general population.

All types of plateauing can result in employees who are stuck and are no longer stimulated by the promise of promotions or of new job content. Often, plateaued workers are frustrated, depressed, and nonproductive. More than half of the workforce are midcareer employees between the ages of 35 and 54. A recent survey of this group of employees found that they work longer hours than their older and younger counterparts, yet "only 43 percent are passionate about their jobs, just 33 percent feel energized by their work, 36 percent say they feel that they are in dead-end jobs, and more than 40 percent report feelings of burnout."[5]

Although some employees accept plateauing as an inevitable part of a career, others do not. Supervisors often find that personnel problems such as irritation with fellow employees and intolerance of bureaucracy develop more frequently with plateaued employees than with others. In addition, valuable workers often seek employment elsewhere when they feel that they are stuck in a no-promotion situation.[6]

Managers can use a number of strategies, including those listed in table 12.1, to help employees overcome the stress of plateauing. These strategies include job enrichment, lateral transfers, cross-training, restructuring organizations to make them more horizontal so that decision-making power increases in the lower ranks, and educating employees about plateauing so that they will be prepared for periods of stagnation in their career development.[7] Employees can be encouraged to take advantage of mentoring and networking opportunities that offer career support and possibilities for change. Managers of libraries, as well as other organizations, should attempt to find ways to make jobs interesting and to keep workers' enthusiasm alive if they want to maintain the effectiveness of employees whose careers have become plateaued. To crack the glass ceiling, managers should encourage women and minorities to apply for promotions as openings occur.

TABLE 12.1 Human Resources Practices that Help Overcome the Problems of Plateauing

Performance Management
1. Fight negative stereotyping with accurate appraisals
2. Ask around to appreciate fully how employees contribute
Training
1. Train for the future, not for advancement
2. Train everyone to contribute, not just the fast-trackers
Career Development and Staffing
1. Broaden opportunities to grow on the job
2. Remove roadblocks to lateral and downward moves
3. Help employees identify new challenges
Compensation
1. Pay employees for performance, knowledge, or teamwork
2. Look beyond financial compensation
3. Check to see if your perks send the right messages
Human Resources Planning
1. Determine how many employees are plateaued
2. Determine what proportion of plateaued employees are successful

Source: Adapted from Deborah E. Ettington, "How Human Resource Managers Can Help Plateaued Managers Succeed," *Human Resource Management* 36, no. 2 (Summer 1997): 228.

It must be remembered, however, that some employees welcome plateauing, at least at certain times in their careers. It is not unusual for employees to feel overwhelmed by their jobs, especially because the growth of technology is breaking down the barrier between work and personal lives. Although some employees still derive their primary sense of who they are from their jobs, many others seek fulfillment in different ways. These employees would prefer to focus their energy not on their jobs but on their families, volunteer work, hobbies, or other activities. It also must be recognized that employees place a different amount of emphasis on success in the workplace at different times in their lives. This is especially evident when employees are attempting to balance family responsibilities with those of the job. Someone who is caring for small children or an elderly parent may need reduced pressures at work for awhile, but that individual may wish to become more job focused and advance in his or her profession a bit later. Once again, employers need to realize that there is no one right approach. There must be flexibility to meet the needs of different employees. One expert has suggested that the corporate ladder be replaced by a corporate lattice—a more adaptive kind of framework, which allows an individual to move in many different directions, not just up and down.[8]

Mentoring

Mentoring is a specialized form of career development. The term *mentor* is used to describe an influential person who significantly helps another, usually younger, person reach his or her major goals. Although mentoring always has existed in organizations of all types, only in the last few decades has the importance of this process been fully recognized. There has been a growing interest in mentoring in all fields. The reason for this is the clear link between career success and having a mentor. Many studies provide evidence of this link; their findings are fairly consistent in stating that very few individuals advance to the top administrative ranks in an organization without the help of a mentor or several mentors.[9]

There are four functions that can be a part of mentoring: teaching, psychological counseling and emotional support, organizational intervention, and sponsoring. The context and meaning of the term is adjusted slightly by each mentor and protégé. No two mentoring experiences are exactly alike, because no two people or set of organizational circumstances are exactly alike.[10]

The need for the mentor varies at different points in the protégé's career, and the things a mentor does for a protégé also differ. New employees need a mentor to help them learn more about the details of the job and the organization. As the protégés become more technically competent and begin to ascend the organizational ladder, the need for teaching might be less important than the need for emotional support. When the appropriate times for promotion and advancement occur, the mentor can be most helpful by providing organizational intervention and sponsoring the protégé to individuals in the higher echelons of the organization.

The advantages to the protégé are clear. But, because mentoring involves a considerable investment on the part of the mentor, it may be harder to understand what causes individuals to serve in such a capacity. Most mentors do not enter into such a relationship from altruism alone. The benefits are almost always mutual, and the mentoring role is almost always professionally rewarding. Sometimes, the mentor receives job assistance from the protégé and secures a valuable ally within the organization. In addition, the mentoring procedure causes the mentor to reexamine the day-to-day workings of the organization, which usually causes the mentor to learn more about it. A protégé who succeeds can make a mentor look very good. One of the responsibilities of present-day management is developing talent. The protégé therefore validates the mentor's worth to the organization. Having protégés who can help perform the mentor's job shows that the mentor is a manager who knows how to delegate well. And as a protégé advances, the mentor not only shares in the glory but also builds up a strong network of past and present protégés. Finally, many mentors derive great personal pleasure out of the process. They enjoy teaching and feel a sense of personal gratification as the protégé's career advances. They are pleased to see the continuity of their own work carried on by the protégé.

Try This!

If you are at a stage in your career at which you could use a mentor, try to find one. First, clarify your mentoring needs. Think about individuals who might be able to serve as your mentor. Are there possible mentors you have served with on committees or someone whose ideas you respect? If so, you might approach the individual and indicate that you are interested in learning more about the organization and ask if he or she would be willing to meet with you periodically on an informal basis to offer advice and insight into the organization. If you do not personally know someone who might serve as a mentor, try networking with your friends and colleagues to see if they might have suggestions.

There are more individuals who would like to have mentors than those who actually have them. Some organizations have established formal mentoring programs in which new employees are provided a mentor. These programs sometimes succeed, but mentoring relationships that arise spontaneously usually are more successful because both the mentor and the protégé see the value of each other without being forced into a relationship. Some mentors are now off-site and advise through e-mail.[11]

Mentoring relationships, both formal and informal, should be encouraged by organizations as a means of career development and growth. But mentoring sometimes can have a darker side. Roma Harris has pointed out that because mentoring is by definition designed just for a few individuals, it may pose barriers that impede the progress of many librarians who are interested in career advancement but are not chosen as protégés.[12] Another problem with mentoring is that mentors usually are drawn toward mentoring those who are like themselves, and this unconscious bias often leads to an uneven availability of mentoring opportunities. And because mentoring requires the development of a personal relationship between the mentor and the protégé, it occasionally results in claims of sexual harassment or discrimination.[13] There may be a need for formal guidelines to accompany a mentoring program. Overall, however, the benefits of a well-designed program to provide mentoring seem to outweigh the disadvantages.

HEALTH AND SAFETY ISSUES IN THE LIBRARY

Employers have a responsibility to ensure the health and safety of their employees. Today's workers are demanding a more healthful environment in which to work, and most managers are trying to provide such a workplace. Most libraries today are smoke free so that nonsmokers are not exposed to secondhand smoke. Many libraries have security and disaster procedures in place to attempt to prepare for unexpected emergencies.

Physical Stress

Overall, libraries provide fairly safe workplaces. However, one type of physical problem found more commonly in libraries today is injury caused as a result of the use of computers. Now that computers are used as a tool by almost every category of worker in a library, more and more employees are suffering from a condition known as repetitive stress injury (RSI), most frequently carpal tunnel syndrome. RSI has been common for a long time in employees working in factories who perform the same motion repetitively throughout the day. Now, the same condition is appearing in libraries and information centers where staff spend a large part of the day working on computer keyboards. According to the U.S. Occupational Safety and Health Administration (OSHA), over the past 25 years ergonomic injuries have gained recognition as a major factor in workplace health. One survey found that 3.1 percent of staff members in Association of Research Libraries libraries are affected by carpal tunnel syndrome.[14] As more employees spend more time in front of computers, the number of these repetitive stress injuries is likely to increase.

Libraries and information centers have begun to take steps to prevent RSI and to provide relief to those already exhibiting symptoms. Many libraries have invested in ergonomic chairs, workstations, and keyboards. Other libraries have instituted more frequent breaks, increased the types of activities within a job, started exercise sessions, or provided training in attempts to alleviate and prevent RSI. Many libraries have established ergonomic standards and policies to govern the use of computers.[15] Because the use of computers will continue to be an essential part of the work life of most library employees, managers of all types need to be mindful of this physical stress to prevent the development of more cases of carpal tunnel syndrome.

RSI appears to be the most harmful result of using computers. Although a few years ago there was concern about radiation resulting from video display terminals (VDTs), studies have shown that the radiation produced by computer terminals of all types is slight. More common complaints are of eyestrain, back and neck aches, and body fatigue, which probably result from sitting in one position for too long. Again, good ergonomic practices, such as proper positioning of monitors, supportive chairs, good lighting, adequate ventilation, and more frequent breaks from working on the computer can alleviate many of these complaints.

Job-Related Mental Stress

Employees in all types of organizations are susceptible to stress, which is defined as the body's response to any demand placed upon it. Although libraries sometimes are considered to be stress-free environments, they are not, and library employees can be subjected to various sources of stress.

What Do You Think?

A recent article in the *Journal of Academic Librarianship* began:

> Our subject, a college librarian, is near the end of an exhausting workday which included teaching three hour-long library instruction sessions to first year students enrolled in a required, multiple section English Composition course. He ate lunch while attending still another campus committee meeting. He has spent the last month at work in a similar fashion and has been feeling quite stressed, perhaps even "burned out." While at the reference desk, he interrupts his collection development activities (for which he is facing a deadline) to help a student get background information on a future profession she is considering. As she leaves with the information she needed, he thumbs through one of the reference books he had shared with her, the 2000 edition of the Jobs Rated Almanac, curious to see how it has rated his profession in terms of stress. Imagine our subject's feelings on learning that, of the 250 occupations considered, librarianship is ranked ninth-lowest in terms of job stress, about the same as for book-keeper. Bookbinder and barber are ranked higher in terms of stress.

> Is librarianship a stressful profession? If you think so, what produces the stress? What can libraries do to promote less stressful workplaces?

Deborah F. Sheesley, "Burnout and the Academic Teaching Librarian: An Examination of the Problem and Suggested Solutions," *Journal of Academic Librarianship* 27, no. 6 (November 2001): 447.

Today, more employees in all types of organizations, including libraries, are reporting feeling stress or tension as a result of their jobs. Without a doubt, among librarians, part of the cause of this stress is the increasing rate of change within the profession. Librarians, now more than ever, are being asked to master new methods and technologies for doing their jobs. Technology has speeded up the way things are run; e-mail, faxes, and instant messaging have cut the time needed for communication but also have added pressure to get things done faster. Organizational change of all types, if too rapid and frequent, may result in stress. In addition, because of the budget cutbacks in many libraries, librarians often are asked to assume more responsibilities.

Stress arises from many sources. Role ambiguity arises when positions are poorly defined and employees do not know what is expected of them. Some librarians feel the stress of what is known as role conflict when different groups of people hold different views about how that employee should behave. Oftentimes in libraries and information centers, there is tension between the professional and support staff when roles are blurred and changing.[16] In some organizations, interpersonal demands cause stress when an employee must constantly deal with unpleasant or abrasive co-workers or supervisors. In addition, in many libraries, the effect of downsizing has resulted in a smaller number of employees doing the same amount of work.

Of course, not all stress-related disorders are caused by workplace stress; many employees have stresses caused by off-the-job factors, such as family or financial problems. Sometimes, stress can be produced by the conflict between job and home responsibilities, especially in two-career families with children. Table 12.2 shows some of the common causes of stress.

Stress is not always bad, and different employees are able to tolerate different levels of stress. Without some stress in organizations, there likely would be much less energy and productivity. Many people work more effectively under conditions of mild stress. When there are deadlines looming, many people work faster and better. However, the same deadline often can cause other employees to experience extreme stress. It is when stress is severe and unending that it becomes destructive.

Although it has been commonly thought that managers feel more stress than lower-level employees, recent research has shown that this is not true. For example, a study of 270,000 male employees at a large corporation found that the rate of coronary disease increased at successively lower levels of the organization. It is thought that top-level executives feel less stress because they have greater control over their work than employees at lower levels.[17] The more control employees have over their own work and the more information they have about possible changes that will occur, the less likely they are to feel job-related stress.

Stress may be evidenced in a number of ways, including absenteeism, irritability, tardiness, and inability to perform well. One of the jobs of the manager is to help identify the cause of the stress and try to help eliminate it, if possible. All managers need to be aware of the individual differences in their employees and help them cope with the stresses in their lives. If the effects of the stress are more than the manager can handle, the employee should be referred to a health professional for diagnosis and treatment.

TABLE 12.2 Common Causes of Stress

Personal causes	Financial problems Family problems Illness	Personality traits[1]
Organizational causes	Interpersonal demands Role conflict or ambiguity Technology	Downsizing Leadership Constant change

[1] An interesting study that investigates the relationship between personality traits and various aspects of job satisfaction, including stress, is Jeanine M. Williamson, Anne E. Pemberton, and John W. Lounsbury, "An Investigation of Career and Job Satisfaction in Relation to Personality Traits of Information Professionals," *Library Quarterly* 75, no. 2 (2005): 122–41.

Burnout

Burnout is a specific type of stress-induced condition that affects individuals engaged in so-called people work. Burnout results from emotional strain and the stress of interpersonal contact, especially from dealing with people who are having problems. Individuals suffering from burnout typically experience exhaustion, both physical and emotional; a negative shift in the way they respond to other people; and a loss of self-esteem. Remedies for burnout can be found at two levels. At the personal level, employees should structure their lives outside of work to give them a sense of comfort and control. Employees should pursue an active life outside of the work environment. The managerial responsibilities for aiding workers with burnout include knowing the symptoms of burnout and making workers familiar with them, holding staff meetings that can be used for staff support, and fostering a sense of teamwork among the staff. If staffing patterns permit, managers also may restructure jobs so that librarians do not spend as much time with patrons or revise schedules to shorten periods of time spent at public services desks. Workshops in stress management or time management also can be useful.

 Try This!

Are you feeling burned out or overstressed because of your job? Try these tips suggested in *Library Mosaics* to reduce those feelings.

1. **Find time to play.** You need to get away from the workplace and spend time with family and friends.
2. **Get physical.** Try to work physical activities into your day and focus on something else besides work when you are exercising.
3. **Set realistic objectives.** Most stress arises when you feel overwhelmed at work. Try to prioritize your projects. Do not strive for perfection; good enough will do.
4. **Use your support network.** Turn to people who will support, encourage, and give you candid feedback.
5. **Keep your options open within your present organization.** Individuals who burn out usually feel that they have no way out. Look for other areas of the organization in which you might be happier. Update your résumé and be prepared to show what you can contribute to the organization in other areas.
6. **Leave if you have to.** If there is no sign that the situation will change, prepare to look for another job. Check out job advertisements, network, and begin to look for another position.

"Snuffing Out Burnout," *Library Mosaics* 11, no. 2 (March/April, 2000): 22.

Managers should pay special heed to recent research that has demonstrated the importance of the organizational context on burnout. Burnout can be caused by managers who do not respect the work done by employees. When employees do not feel that the organization values and respects them, they often experience burnout. Managers who belittle or patronize employees can be a cause of burnout and rapid staff turnover.[18]

It is important to try to prevent burnout because it is rarely confined to one worker. Employees with burnout who display a negative attitude toward their jobs, customers, or colleagues are sure to have a negative effect on their fellow employees. To keep burnout from spreading, managers need to recognize the symptoms and prevent it whenever possible.

Violence and Crime in the Workplace

Violence and crime are increasingly serious problems in almost all workplaces. Although libraries are not places where violence often occurs, violence is still not unknown in them. There have been several recent cases of librarians being murdered while on the job, and assault and robbery (of both staff and patrons) and vandalism are unfortunately relatively common in libraries. Libraries have tried hard to make themselves seen as accessible places, and this accessibility has sometimes left them vulnerable. There is a perception among most people that libraries are safe places, and often users are not as vigilant as they should be. Many libraries, especially in urban areas, have been affected by the increasing numbers of homeless and mentally ill individuals who come to the library to get off the street. Library buildings, with their often relatively deserted stack areas and isolated work spaces, provide secluded spots for individuals who are attempting to prey either upon property or upon other individuals. There is also a perception that violators will not be prosecuted in libraries as readily as they would be in other types of organizations.

Library managers are now more aware than they once were of the possibility of workplace violence, and many are now taking measures to attempt to lessen it. Many libraries have installed surveillance cameras to increase patron and employee safety and to decrease vandalism. Other libraries have hired additional security people.[19]

There is no way to make any environment completely safe for workers and customers, but libraries should consider implementing the following measures to increase their safety:

1. Have policies in place that ban all weapons, including weapons in vehicles in the parking lot.
2. If conditions warrant, require employees to submit to searches for weapons or to determine their fitness for work.
3. Have an organizational policy that states that no violence or threat of violence will be tolerated.
4. Have an organizational policy that requires employees to report acts or threats of violence to management.

5. Develop relationships with mental health experts who may be contacted for assistance and recommendations in dealing with safety and emergency issues.

6. Train managers and all who work with the public to recognize the warning signs of violence and train them in techniques to diffuse potentially violent situations.

7. Equip desks in public areas with panic buttons to alert security officers immediately if help is needed.[20]

Most libraries have preparedness programs for natural disasters such as floods or hurricanes, but fewer have instituted such programs for violence in the workplace. All libraries need manuals relating to emergencies, and librarians should be trained in what to do in the event an emergency arises. There also should be clearly stated security policies to protect librarians and patrons. A partial example of a security policy may be seen in figure 12.2. All managers hope that they never need to use such a policy, but they always should be prepared in the event something does occur.

Overall, most libraries are focusing more than ever before on the health and safety of their employees. Many encourage employees to participate in exercise, weight loss, or other wellness programs. Employee assistance programs have been instituted at a number of organizations to provide help to employees

Figure 12.2—A Part of the Security Policy of the Decatur Public Library

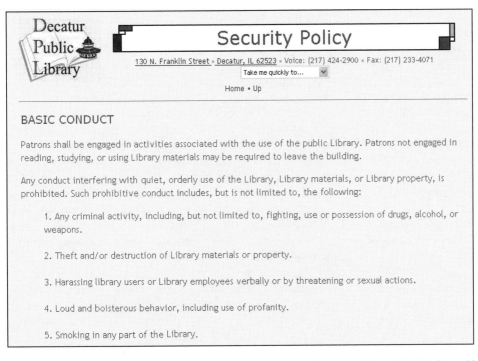

Decatur Public Library

Security Policy

130 N. Franklin Street • Decatur, IL 62523 • Voice: (217) 424-2900 • Fax: (217) 233-4071

Take me quickly to...

Home • Up

BASIC CONDUCT

Patrons shall be engaged in activities associated with the use of the public Library. Patrons not engaged in reading, studying, or using Library materials may be required to leave the building.

Any conduct interfering with quiet, orderly use of the Library, Library materials, or Library property, is prohibited. Such prohibitive conduct includes, but is not limited to, the following:

1. Any criminal activity, including, but not limited to, fighting, use or possession of drugs, alcohol, or weapons.

2. Theft and/or destruction of Library materials or property.

3. Harassing library users or Library employees verbally or by threatening or sexual actions.

4. Loud and boisterous behavior, including use of profanity.

5. Smoking in any part of the Library.

Source: See the complete policy at Decatur Public Library, "Security Policy" (2000), http://www.decatur.lib.il.us/policies/security.html.

with various types of personal problems, such as alcoholism or drug use. Many library managers are becoming better at helping prevent both physical and mental stress. Managers realize that it is cost-effective to invest in the health of employees, because healthier employees are more productive than those who are suffering from physical or mental conditions. Making the library workplace environment a safe and healthy one is a win-win situation for employees and employers.

EXTERNAL IMPACTS ON HUMAN RESOURCES— LEGAL PROTECTIONS

All of the subjects discussed so far relate to specific internal HR functions found in libraries of all types. There are, however, two broader external forces that have had a profound impact on human resources work in many libraries. These issues are (1) legal protections for employees and (2) unionization.

The number of federal and state regulations relating to the HR function of management has increased over past decades, and, today, virtually every HR function from hiring to firing is affected by them. These regulations have provided workers with more legal protections, especially in the area of equal employment opportunity. Nonetheless, there are still some areas in which employees have very few rights. Almost every employee not covered by a collective-bargaining contract or civil or state service rules is at risk for dismissal because of the employment-at-will principle that permits either party in an employment contract to cancel it at will. Although legislation protects workers from being fired for such reasons as age, gender, national origin, or disability, workers not covered by either collective bargaining or civil service regulations have few legal remedies to combat being fired or discharged.

There are other areas in which workers have limited protection. Although the right to free speech is guaranteed by the First Amendment to the U.S. Constitution, managers in the private sector can legally discipline workers who say something damaging about the corporation or its practices.

The right to privacy is another area in which employees, especially those in the private sector, do not have clear protections. Privacy issues have become a growing concern for workers with the growth of electronic technologies of all types. For instance, although the Electronic Communications Privacy Act of 1986 prohibits outside interception of electronic mail by a third party, the act does not affect inside interception. This means that, unless an individual organization has a policy prohibiting it, employers can read their staff's e-mail, listen in on telephone conversations, install small video cameras anywhere, and search employees' lockers and desks. The use of electronic surveillance is growing as more and more organizations monitor people using personal computers by counting keystrokes and mistakes.[21] On the whole, these new monitoring technologies are considered to be extensions of managerial prerogatives, and employees currently have few legal tools to combat them.[22] Obviously, this electronic monitoring can be beneficial if it can prevent or disclose misconduct or if supervisors use it in training to give constructive feedback to help individuals improve. But studies also have shown that employees who know that they are monitored are more likely to be highly dissatisfied and to suffer from such conditions as fatigue and hostility.

Suggestions for reform of electronic monitoring have come from many sources, and the proposed reforms almost all agree in advocating that employers do the following: monitor in the open, monitor only relevant activities, monitor only periodically, and encourage employee participation in setting up the monitoring standards and practices.[23] Employers have the right to monitor employees' communications and activities but still should take care that they do so only when necessary. Employees should be familiar with and understand the policies relating to surveillance and monitoring.

Another challenging legal issue in the workplace is that of random testing for the use of drugs. Many employees feel that drug testing is a violation of their privacy, but, in most states, employers of all types have the right to screen employees for drug and alcohol use. These types of tests are often mandatory for certain positions, such as airline pilot.

Although the rights of employees are better protected now than they were in the past, there are still areas in which few protections exist. Because the employment-at-will rule allows employers the right to discharge workers for any cause, employees who wish to maintain a job sometimes are subjected to practices in the workplace that they feel violate their privacy. Many of these privacy violations are extremely resented by workers and cause mistrust and ill feelings on the job. The rights of both employers and employees need to be balanced. Supervisors should strive, as much as possible, to show respect for employees' privacy and dignity, even when they are not legally obliged to do so.

Equal Employment Opportunities

Many of the legal protections enjoyed by workers are found in the area of equal employment opportunity (EEO). Equal employment opportunity refers to the right of all people to be hired and to advance in a job on the basis of merit or ability. Discrimination against protected classes of people in any aspect of employment is now prohibited by law in the United States.

Before the passage of EEO laws, employers were able to hire, promote, or fire whomever they wished. It is sometimes forgotten how much various civil rights rulings have changed the entire field of HR management. For just one example of this change, see the job advertisements listed in table 12.3. These advertisements were printed in *Library Journal* in 1959, before the advent of civil rights protections for job applicants. Advertisers were free to look for applicants of a specific gender or age.

Today, women, racial minorities, older workers, and people with disabilities have acquired substantial employment rights under the law. The equal employment opportunity laws have exerted a profound influence on the U.S. labor scene. HR functions, such as hiring, interviewing, testing, training, promoting, appraising, disciplining, and compensating, have been affected by equal employment opportunity laws.

TABLE 12.3 Position Descriptions from the Classified Advertising Sections in the January 15 and July 1959 Issues of *Library Journal*

Stymied in your present job? Want to broaden your experience? Like to work in a brand-new building under ideal conditions? Insist on liberal fringe benefits? Want faculty status? If so, and if you are a male, you may be interested in the position of Assistant Cataloger ...
Director, Male, Challenging opportunity in fast-growing Long Island suburb of 40,000. New air-conditioned building ...
Assistant Director. Male. Newly enlarged public library in historic ...
Position in small college for young woman interested in cataloging and general reference.
Cataloger (Assistant Librarian) needed for small, Midwestern liberal arts college. MA, MS in librarianship, or M.Lbn. desired. Either young female or male (preferred) ...
Cataloger (half time or less) Reference, rank of assistant librarian, faculty status, needed by small Midwestern university. Woman under 40 ...
Assistant librarian, Responsibility for main library service in a city-county. Man or woman under forty.
Circulation-Reference Librarian needed immediately for active modern library in progressive community with 20,000 residents. Real opportunity for young woman with initiative ...

The Civil Rights Act of 1964 and Other Important Federal Legislation

Although federal laws prohibiting discrimination against certain groups of employees go back more than one hundred years to the Civil Rights Acts of 1866 and 1871, the most powerful impetus to equal employment opportunity came with the passage of the Civil Rights Act of 1964. Title VII of that act prohibits discrimination based on race, color, religion, sex, or national origin in all employment practices, including hiring, firing, promotion, compensation, and other conditions or privileges of employment. The primary aim of this legislation was to make overt discrimination actionable in all phases of employment. Title VII has been interpreted in the courts many times since its passage. These court decisions have established that an employer's practices are discriminatory if they affect any one of the groups protected by Title VII in an adverse manner, even if the employer had no intention to discriminate.

It is against the law for any organization to have policies and practices that have an adverse impact on any protected groups, unless that organization can demonstrate that those policies and practices are justified by business necessity. Business necessity has been narrowly interpreted to mean that the employer must show overriding evidence that a discriminatory practice is essential to the safe and efficient operation of the firm. Once a plaintiff shows a prima facie case of discrimination by demonstrating adverse impact upon any protected group, the burden of proof falls on the organization to justify its employment policy or practice.

Title VII as amended by the Equal Opportunity Employment Act of 1972 covers all private employers of 15 or more people, all private and public educational institutions, state and local government, employment agencies, labor unions, and apprenticeship and training programs. Thus, most libraries in the United States are covered by Title VII. It is enforced by the Equal Employment Opportunity Commission (EEOC), a five-member independent agency appointed for a five-year term by the president of the United States with the advice and consent of Congress. The EEOC investigates discrimination complaints and develops guidelines to enforce Title VII.

The federal laws relating to EEO are too numerous to discuss comprehensively in this section. Highlights of the legal framework are presented in a table 12.4. Most states also have antidiscrimination laws that are sometimes more comprehensive than the federal laws. For instance, at the present time the federal antidiscrimination laws do not extend to cover sexual orientation, but discrimination on the basis of sexual orientation is part of the antidiscrimination laws of many states.

Affirmative Action and Comparable Worth

Today's workplaces are much more diversified than those in the past because of the passage of legislation requiring equal opportunities in hiring, promotion, and other personnel practices. Although it has been more than forty years since the passage of the Civil Rights Act of 1964, there are still many unsettled areas in EEO. Two of these are affirmative action and comparable worth.

Affirmative action refers to a set of specific procedures designed to ensure an equitable distribution of women and minorities within an institution. Affirmative action was created in 1965 by Executive Order 11246, which required government contractors to have a written plan to remedy the effects of past discrimination. Any organization that holds a government contract of a certain size is required to have a written affirmative action plan. Many other institutions have voluntarily produced such plans.[24] The Office of Federal Contract Compliance Programs (OFCCP) of the Department of Labor administers the order.

Despite the belief of some, affirmative action does not require fixed quotas, preferential hiring, or the employment of unqualified people. Affirmative action does, however, require an organization to determine whether there are fewer minorities and women working in particular jobs in the organization than reasonably would be expected by their availability in the workforce. It also requires organizations to establish goals and timetables for remedying any underutilization that might be identified.

Despite the impact of affirmative action legislation over the past three decades, both the federal and state commitment to affirmative action seems to be weakening, and the future of affirmative action is unclear. Opponents of affirmative action have two major objections to it. They argue either that it has worked so well

TABLE 12.4 Major U.S. Federal Legislation Relating to Equal Opportunity in the Workplace

Federal Law	Date	Provisions of Legislation
The Equal Pay Act	1963	This act requires all employers to provide equal pay to men and women who perform work that is similar in skill, effort, and responsibility and that is performed under similar working conditions. The only disparity permitted in payment of wages is disparity resulting from a seniority system, a merit system, a system that measures earning by quantity or quality of production, or a differential based on any factor other than sex.
The Civil Rights Act	1964	Title VII of this act prohibits discrimination based on race, color, religion, sex, or national origin in all employment practices, including hiring, firing, promotion, compensation, and other conditions or privileges of employment.
The Age Discrimination Act	1967	Prohibits age discrimination against persons who have reached the age of forty in hiring, discharge, retirement, pay, and conditions and privileges of employment decisions. The act also restricts mandatory retirement.
Occupational Health and Safety Act (OSHA)	1970	Establishes mandatory health and safety measures in organizations.
Vocational Rehabilitation Act	1973	Prohibits discrimination based on physical or mental disability. Its provisions were strengthened in the ADA described below.
Consolidated Omnibus Budget Reconciliation Act (COBRA)	1985	Requires employers to offer health insurance coverage on a temporary basis to employees who have been terminated or laid off. The insurance is to be paid for by the employee and ordinarily is available for up to 18 months after the change in employment status.

Americans with Disabilities Act (ADA)	1990	Bars discrimination against individuals who have disabilities. A person is considered disabled if he or she has a physical or mental impairment that substantially limits one or more of life's major activities, has a record of such an impairment, or is regarded as having such an impairment. An employer must not deny a job to a disabled person if the person is qualified and able to perform the essential functions of the job, with or without reasonable accommodation. If a disabled person is otherwise qualified but unable to perform an essential function without accommodation, the employer must make the accommodation, unless that would cause undue hardship.
Civil Rights Act	1991	Creates rights to compensatory and punitive damages, including the right to jury trial, for individuals who are the victims of intentional discrimination as defined by Title VII of the Civil Rights Act of 1964 and the Americans with Disabilities Act. There are caps on both the compensatory and punitive damages, except for racial discrimination; these caps are based not on the seriousness of the discrimination but on the size of the employer's work force.
The Family and Medical Leave Act (FMLA)	1993	FMLA requires covered employers to provide up to 12 weeks unpaid, job-protected leave to employees for causes including childbirth, adoption, their own serious health problems, or those health problems of a close family member.
Health Insurance Portability and Accountability Act	1996	Allows employees who change jobs to switch health insurance plans and get new coverage despite preexisting health conditions.

that it is no longer needed or that it is a means of reverse discrimination against individuals who are not in the preferred classes and thus favors women and minorities at the expense of more qualified white males.[25] Recent court decisions have narrowed the scope of affirmative action while still upholding its value. As the workforce becomes more diversified and as former minority groups become the majority in parts of the United States, affirmative action programs are coming under increasing scrutiny, and their future is uncertain.

Comparable worth, an issue that is closely related to equal pay, began to be discussed in the 1980s. At the heart of this issue is the fact that many occupations in our society are segregated by gender; men are heavily concentrated in certain types of occupations, and women are concentrated in others. At the same time, women who work are, on average, paid less than men who work. In 2003, the median earnings of women who worked full time were 80 percent of the earnings of men who worked full time.[26] Part of this disparity can be attributed to the fact that the occupations in which women are concentrated pay less than the occupations in which men are concentrated. Because librarianship is a profession that is approximately 80 percent female, salaries of both male and female librarians are adversely affected. The Equal Pay Act, passed in 1963, made it illegal to pay one gender less than the other for doing substantially the same work on jobs under similar working conditions requiring equivalent skills, effort, and responsibilities.

Advocates of comparable worth say the concept of equal pay for equal work should be broadened to include equal pay for comparable work. For example, a job in a profession dominated by women, such as librarianship, which requires a certain level of education and experience, should pay the same salary as a job in a profession dominated by men, such as engineering, if that job requires comparable (but not identical) education and work experience. Comparable worth is based not on jobs being the same, but on them being comparable, based on an evaluation of the intrinsic worth or difficulty of that job in relation to other jobs in that organization or community.

 What Do You Think?

The Equal Pay Act of 1963 requires equal pay when men and women are doing substantially the same work. Comparable worth would extend this principle to work requiring comparable skills, training, effort, and responsibility. People hold widely varying views on comparable worth. What do you think? Should librarians continue to work for this principle? What might be the results of this?

There are two main problems with instituting comparable worth: the difficulty of establishing the mechanism to measure the worth of jobs and the sizable increase in labor costs to employers. There is still a great deal of controversy concerning comparable worth, and perspectives on the topic differ widely, even among librarians. Recent court decisions indicate that courts will not require employers to implement comparable worth policies nor find them liable of discrimination for using market values in setting salaries. But nothing prohibits an employer from adopting comparable worth standards. There is no doubt that employees in many fields, especially those employed by state or local governments, will continue to press to have comparable worth issues addressed. Professional organizations also are continuing to advance this concept. One of the primary focuses of the recently established American Library Association's Allied Professional Association (ALA-APA) is comparable worth.[27]

Sexual Harassment

Sexual harassment is a relatively new area of federal regulation and, according to the Equal Employment Opportunity Commission, it is now the fastest growing employee complaint. In 2005, the EEOC received 12,679 charges of sexual harassment: 14.3 percent of those charges were filed by males. In 2004, the EEOC resolved 12,859 sexual harassment charges and recovered $47.9 million in monetary benefits for the charging parties and other aggrieved individuals.[28] This increase is attributed to an increased willingness on the part of women to file formal complaints and to a Supreme Court ruling, *Harris v. Forklift Systems, Inc.,* that made it easier for plaintiffs to win their cases.[29]

Sexual harassment violates Title VII of the Civil Rights Act of 1964. According to the EEOC, sexual harassment includes, but is not limited to:

- The victim as well as the harasser may be a woman or a man.
- The victim does not have to be of the opposite sex.
- The harasser can be the victim's supervisor, an agent of the employer, a supervisor in another area, a co-worker, or a nonemployee.
- The victim does not have to be the person harassed but could be anyone affected by the offensive conduct.
- Unlawful sexual harassment may occur without economic injury to or discharge of the victim.
- The harasser's conduct must be unwelcome.[30]

There are two types of sexual harassment. One, the quid pro quo type, occurs when a supervisor or someone in authority demands a sexual favor in exchange for some type of employee benefit, such as a pay raise or promotion. The other type of sexual harassment, the hostile work environment, occurs when an employee is forced to work in an environment in which behaviors considered offensive to the employee, such as sexual jokes or teasing, occur.

Sexual harassment is a violation of federal law, and, in most cases, employers are considered liable for the actions of supervisors. In addition, employers can be held liable for the harassment of employees by nonemployees or third parties such as customers and/or clients. If, for example, a public services librarian were continually harassed by a library patron and the employer knew of the harassment but took no corrective measures, the employer could be held liable.[31] Although most victims of sexual harassment are female, the regulations also apply to female-on-male harassment and homosexual harassment.[32]

What Would You Do?

As Robert walked into the library for the evening shift, he had a feeling that this was going to be another one of those evenings. Robert worked as a paraprofessional at the Information Desk at Fairmead Public Library. Recently, his manager had resigned and had been replaced by Ms. Price. Ever since, Robert had worried that his job was in danger.

Robert did not think that he was the best library employee Fairmead had ever seen. After all, this was his second job, and he often came in tired after spending all day working in the accounting office at the hospital. Despite this, he enjoyed his library job, especially getting to interact with people after a long day shut up in his office alone. He even had suggested some changes to the way the library handled their cash transactions, giving the library the benefit of his long years of accounting experience and volunteering to train staff in the new methods.

But even that had caused the latest in a string of conflicts with Ms. Price. On a fairly slow Saturday, Robert had attempted to teach one of the newer staff members the new cash procedure, and Ms. Price had sent word—through another employee—that he was to stop immediately, that he was distracting patrons. This had made Robert's blood boil: How dare she interfere with training that had to be done? And to humiliate him by sending an order through another employee?

She had been practicing this guerrilla warfare nearly since she had started her job three months prior. She would sit nearby while he worked at the desk but never talk to him the way she did with the other employees. She would send e-mail messages reminding him to do routine tasks that he had never failed to do but did not send them to the other employees she supervised; he had checked.

At first, the idea that Ms. Price might have a problem with his gender had been the furthest from his mind. Robert had gotten used to the idea that he was one of the only men working at the library and so had gotten out of the habit of thinking of himself as different. However, Robert had noticed that Ms. Price acted very differently to male patrons at the Reference Desk than to females.

Sexual harassment can be a real problem in many workplaces. Is Robert the victim of sexual harassment? What can be done to lessen the possibility of such conduct?

(For the rest of this case study, see http://www.lu.com/management.)

The field of equal employment opportunity is rapidly changing. The interpretations of the laws pertaining to EEO are changing as new regulatory agency rulings and court decisions are issued. Library managers dealing with any of the HR functions should attempt to remain abreast of changes in these regulations and apply them to their organizations. Although federal and state EEO laws have constrained employers in their human resources actions, the laws have worked to make U.S. workplaces more diversified and equitable. The ultimate aim of all EEO regulation is to ensure that every individual, regardless of age, race, gender, religion, or national origin, has an equal right to any job for which he or she is qualified.

Unionization

From the 1970s onward, there was an accelerated movement toward unionization in various white-collar and professional jobs. A substantial number of public school teachers are unionized, as are a large number of nurses and college professors. Like their colleagues in other professions, a significant number of librarians belong to labor unions. Although there are no exact figures available, the most recent estimate is that approximately 30 percent of librarians work in unionized situations.[33]

The history of U.S. workers' attempts to get fair and equitable treatment and to have a voice in the decisions that affect their lives goes back to the earliest days of the colonies, but the real foundation of the U.S. labor movement was laid in 1935, when the National Labor Relations Act, popularly known as the Wagner Act, was passed. This act gave employees the right to organize unions and to bargain collectively with employers. The purpose of the act was to encourage the growth of unions and to restrain management from interfering with this growth. To investigate violations and unfair labor practices, the act established the National Labor Relations Board (NLRB). This board has the authority to establish the rules, regulations, and procedures necessary to carry out the provisions of the Wagner Act.

After passage of the Wagner Act, unions began to grow rapidly and continued to grow until the mid-1950s. However, the proportion of the total labor force that is unionized has shown a decline since then. This decline is attributed primarily to the decreasing number of jobs in manufacturing industries, in which the greatest numbers of unionized workers traditionally were found. But the downsizing and cost-cutting efforts of many organizations also have led to a new interest in unionization in many organizations in which the workers who remain feel overworked and underpaid.

To compensate for this loss of membership in the blue-collar industries, many unions initiated extensive organizing campaigns in the white-collar sector, particularly of public-sector employees such as government workers and public school teachers. Until the mid-1950s, white-collar workers constituted a minority of the nation's workforce. Since that time, they have come to outnumber blue-collar workers, and the gap continues to widen as automation and foreign competition reduce the demand for factory workers.

In 2005, union members totaled 12.5 percent of all workers.[34] This is a decline even from 1983, when slightly more than 20 percent of all workers were unionized. The decline in unionization has been concentrated in the private sector. Although 36.5 percent of workers in the public sector are members of unions, the percentage in the private sector has dropped from 16.5 percent in 1983 to 7.8 percent in 2005.[35] The percentage of workers in labor unions varies from state to state. In 2005, New York, Hawaii, Alaska, New

Jersey, and Michigan had union membership rates higher than 20 percent, whereas North Carolina and South Carolina had membership rates lower than 3 percent.[36]

Some white-collar workers, particularly professionals, have been ambivalent about joining unions. Many professionals have felt that membership in a professional organization is the best way to advance their interests and the profession. Some professionals have believed themselves to be more allied with management than with production workers. Other professionals felt that, although unions might be desirable for hourly workers, professionals, with their higher status, did not need them. Nonetheless, as unionization has become more common in the public sector, increasing numbers of librarians, like other professionals, have joined unions. Often, librarians are given little choice when the library is part of a larger bargaining unit, such as municipal or university employees. The two factors influencing employees' interest in unions are dissatisfaction with their working conditions and a perception that they cannot change these conditions.[37] One of the major attractions of unions for most workers is the hope that collective bargaining will improve their salaries and benefits. Because many librarians are joining unions or wondering whether such a move might be in their best interest, an understanding of the unionization process is very important to human resources managers regardless of whether their own library is presently unionized.

To date, unionization in libraries has brought mixed results. On the plus side, unions have contributed to the formalization of human resources policies and procedures, improved communications, increased fringe benefits, and improved working conditions. According to the Bureau of National Affairs, in 2004 union librarians made an average of 39 percent more than nonunion librarians. The difference is even more dramatic among support staff as statistics show that staff covered by a union contract make 42 percent more than those without a union.[38] According to one study, university librarians in California who are represented by unions feel great loyalty to them. They feel greater loyalty to their membership in the union than to their membership in professional organizations.[39]

On the negative side, unions have caused substantially more paperwork, contributed to the establishment of more rigid work rules, and created an adversarial relationship between librarians and library managers. A recent study showed that unionized professional librarians in academic research libraries were less satisfied with their jobs than nonunionized librarians, although the relationship between job satisfaction and unionization also was affected by the variables of salary and part-time status of the respondents.[40]

Not enough research has been done yet about the effects of unionization on libraries. Unionization is a complex issue, and, because of its importance and possible impact on the library profession, more facts are needed to document and implement future planning.[41] In libraries, as in all other types of organizations, harmonious working relations are necessary between management and workers. The adversarial relationship that often has resulted from unionization needs to be overcome so that organizations can function more effectively—for the good of both the managers and the workers.

CONCLUSION

The human resources function is becoming increasingly important in all types of libraries and information agencies. As these organizations become larger and more complex, HR becomes an even more vital part of library management. In the present era of downsizing and tight budgets, managers need to pay even more attention to HR processes than ever before. As this section has shown, the tasks involved in HR are many and diverse. For an organization to function efficiently, the HR function must be a high priority for every manager. All of the component parts of this function must be integrated into a smoothly functioning system that enables employees to fill their work roles in such a way that the organization can operate effectively.

Providing the best human resources to meet the needs of today presents problems and challenges, but these problems and challenges must be met. Effective organizations are those that are constantly trying to provide the best HR so that the organization can fulfill its mission, both now and in the future.

NOTES

1. Marisa Urgo, *Developing Information Leaders: Harnessing the Talents of Generation X* (New Providence, NJ: Bowker-Saur, 2000).

2. Pixey Anne Mosley, "Mentoring Gen X Managers: Tomorrow's Library Leadership Is Already Here," *Library Administration and Management* 19, no. 4 (Fall 2005): 185–92.

3. Families and Work Institute, *Generation and Gender in the Workplace* (New York: American Business Collaboration, 2004), http://familiesandwork.org/eproducts/genandgender.pdf.

4. Judith M. Bardwick, "Plateauing and Productivity," *Sloan Management Review* 24 (Spring 1983): 67.

5. Robert Morrison, Tamara Erickson, and Ken Dychtwald, "Managing Middlescence," *Harvard Business Review* 84, no. 3 (March 2006): 80.

6. Barbara Conway, "The Plateaued Career," *Library Administration and Management* 9 (Winter 1995): 14.

7. Bardwick, "Plateauing and Productivity," 69–72.

8. "Plateauing: Redefining Success at Work," *Knowledge@Wharton* (October 4, 2006), http://knowledge.wharton.upenn.edu/article.cfm?articleid=1564&CFID=2595079&CFTOKEN=2604561.

9. Suzanne C. de Janasz, S. Sullivan, and V. Whiting, "Mentor Networks and Career Success: Lessons for Turbulent Times," *Academy of Management Executive* 17, no. 4 (2003): 78–91; David Marshall Hunt and Carol Mitchell, "Mentorship: A Career Training and Development Tool," *Academy of Management Review* 8 (July 1983): 475–85.

10. Michael Zey, *The Mentor Connection: Strategic Alliances in Corporate Life* (New Brunswick, NJ: Transaction, 1990).

11. Tinker Massey, "Mentoring: A Means to Learning," *Journal of Education for Library and Information Science* 36 (Winter 1995): 52–54.

12. Roma Harris, "The Mentoring Trap," *Library Journal*, 15 October 1993. 37–39.

13. Jonathan A. Segal, "Mirror-Image Mentoring," *HR Magazine* 45 (March 2000): 157–66.

14. Joyce K. Thornton, "Carpal Tunnel Syndrome in ARL Libraries, *College and Research Libraries* 58, no. 1 (January, 1997): 9–18.

15. Many libraries have ergonomic information available online. See, for instance, the University of Texas at Austin policy, "Library Ergonomics" (2001), http://www.lib.utexas.edu/ergonomics/.

16. Julita Nawe, "Work-Related Stress among the Library and Information Workforce," *Library Review* 44 (1995): 30–37.

17. Stanley J. Modic, "Surviving Burnout: The Malady of Our Age," *Industry Week* 238 (February 20, 1989): 28–34.

18. Lakshmi Ramarajan and Sigal Barsade, "What Makes a Job Tough? The Influence of Organizational Respect on Burnout in the Human Services," *Knowledge@Wharton* (November 2006), http://knowledge.wharton.upenn.edu/papers/1327.pdf.

19. Robert L. Willits, "When Violence Threatens the Workplace: Personnel Issues," *Library Administration and Management* 11, no. 2 (Summer 1997): 166–71.

20. Patrick Mirza, "Tips Offered on Minimizing Workplace Violence," *HR News* 16 (July 1997): 15.

21. Janine Kostecki, "Privacy Issues in the Workplace Increasing," *Library Personnel News* 8, no. 2 (March-April 1994): 1–2.

22. Michael Levy, "The Electronic Monitoring of Workers: Privacy in the Age of the Electronic Sweatshop," *Legal References Quarterly* 14 (1995): 12–14.

23. Edward D. Bewayo, "Electronic Management and Equity Issues," *Journal of Information Ethics* 4 (Spring 1995): 70.

24. See, for example, the Association of Research Libraries, Systems and Procedures Exchange Center, *Affirmative Action in ARL Libraries* (Washington, DC: Association of Research Libraries, 1998).

25. *Congressional Quarterly Almanac, 104th Congress, 2nd Session, 1996*, vol. 52 (Washington, DC: Congressional Quarterly, 1996), 5–37.

26. U.S. Department of Labor, Bureau of Labor Statistics, *Highlights of Women's Earnings in 2003* (Washington, DC: U.S. Department of Labor, 2004), http://www.bls.gov/cps/cpswom2003.pdf.

27. The ALA-APA has produced a very helpful booklet on the topic of comparable worth and other compensation issues. See Campaign for America's Librarians, *Advocating for Better Salaries and Pay Equity Toolkit*, 3rd ed. (Chicago: American Library Association, 2003), http://www.ala-apa.org/toolkit.pdf.

28. U.S. Equal Employment Opportunity Commission, "Sexual Harassment" (2007), http://www.eeoc.gov/types/sexual_harassment.html.

29. Larry Reynolds, "Sex Harassment Claims Surge," *Human Resources Forum*, May 1997, 1.

30. U.S. Equal Employment Opportunity Commission, "Sexual Harassment."

31. Teresa Brady, "Added Liability: Third-Party Sexual Harassment," *Management Review* 86, no. 4 (April 1997): 45–47.

32. Laura N. Gasaway, "Sexual Harassment in the Library: The Law," *North Carolina Libraries* 49 (Spring 1991): 14–17.

33. U.S. Department of Labor, Bureau of Labor Statistics, "Occupational Outlook Handbook: Earnings" (2006), http://stats.bls.gov/oco/ocos068.htm#earnings.

34. U.S. Department of Labor, Bureau of Labor Statistics, "Union Members Summary" (2007), http://www.bls.gov/news.release/union2.nr0.htm.

35. Ibid.

36. Ibid.

37. J. M. Brett, "Why Employees Want Unions?" *Organizational Dynamics* 8, no. 4 (1980): 47–57.

38. Bureau of National Affairs, *Union Membership and Earnings Data Book 2005 Edition* (Washington, DC: BNA Books, 2005).

39. Renee N. Anderson, John D'Amicantonio, and Henry DuBois, "Labor Unions or Professional Organizations: Which Have Our First Loyalty?" *College and Research Libraries* 53 (July 1992): 331–40.

40. Tina Maragou Hovekamp, "Unionization and Job Satisfaction among Professional Library Employees in Academic Research Institutions," *College and Research Libraries* 56 (July 1995): 341–50.

41. An overview of the advantages and disadvantages of unions in public libraries is covered in an overview section edited by Skip Auld, "The Benefits and Deficiencies of Unions in Public Libraries," *Public Libraries* 41, no. 3 (May/June 2002): 135–42.

Leading

One common definition of management is "getting things done through people." Leading (sometimes also referred to as directing or commanding) is the managerial function that enables managers to get things done through people—individually and in groups. Leading is related to the human resources function because both of these are concerned with the organization's employees, but the two functions are quite different. They each focus on distinct aspects of working with people. Human resources is concerned with providing and maintaining the individuals working in an organization. The function of leading, as the name implies, involves directing and motivating these human resources. Leading builds upon the human resources function; it takes the human resources of an organization and guides and coordinates them toward achieving the organization's goals. So, although both functions are concerned with the human side of the organization, they are distinct and different.

Leading is complex because it requires that managers understand the human element in the organization. Thus, it draws heavily on the behavioral sciences such as psychology and sociology for the insights they provide in understanding individuals and their behaviors in the workplace. To be effective at leading, managers must be familiar with what type of rewards are most effective in motivating individuals, and they must know what styles of leadership are most likely to work best in any given situation. They also must understand the importance of communication within the organization. Because each individual is different, leading can be a complicated and time-consuming part of a manager's work. Indeed if a manager is not careful, the interpersonal aspects of leading can consume inordinate energy and time.

This section presents an overview of the leading function. First, the major research relating to human behavior in the work environment is examined. The three major aspects of leading—motivating, leadership, and communication—are discussed. This section also contains chapters on leading in a team-based environment and on ethics and concludes with a discussion of the contingency approach to management that integrates the many theories of leading into a method that managers can use to match their styles to the needs of specific groups of employees in specific work settings.

13

Motivation

 Overview

You have just accepted a position as the head of the Library Media Center (LMC) at Hillside Elementary School. Hillside is a fairly large school, with an enrollment of 800 students in kindergarten through sixth grade. The only employees in the LMC are you and Mrs. Smith, a clerical aide who has worked in the library for almost ten years. You have been told that the library relies heavily on parent volunteers to provide service to the students, and you realize that managing these volunteers will be an important part of your job. From a discussion with the previous head of the LMC, you learn that many of the volunteers seem to be very dispirited and burned out and that fewer of them are actually showing up for their assigned work. Also, there are 20 percent fewer volunteers signed up to help than there were last year. You are worried about this situation. How do you motivate volunteers who receive no monetary reward for the work they do? How do you get busy people interested in providing needed services for their children's school? You know you need to attract good volunteers and keep them satisfied, but you are puzzled about what to do next. You are facing a problem common to all managers: How can you structure the work environment to get individuals to work up to their fullest potential? What is the best way to motivate workers?

Although the function of leading has many aspects, the three major ones are motivation, leadership, and communication. This chapter will begin with a brief overview of human behavior in the work environment. Then the first major aspect of leading, motivation, will be discussed. Some of the early motivation theories will be described, followed by a discussion of current ideas about motivation. The section on leading will continue on to cover the topics of leadership and communication. In addition, two important aspects of leading, creating an ethical climate and promoting teamwork within an organization, will be covered in separate chapters in this section.

THE HUMAN ELEMENT OF THE ORGANIZATION

This chapter begins a new section of this textbook, one that discusses the managerial functions that are grouped under the classification of "leading" (also sometimes called directing or commanding). Among the most important of these functions are motivation, communication, and leadership. All of the functions encompassed under this classification share a common focus upon the human element of the organization. Sometimes this aspect of management is downplayed or ignored, but this is always a mistake. Although many of the facets of this human element are not apparent at first glance, they play an important role in any organization. Employees' attitudes, personality attributes, and perceptions affect the way they work. As Abraham Zaleznik has written, each employee brings to his or her job "all the frailties and imperfections associated with the human condition," and the "complexity in human nature ... leads managers to spend their time, smoothing over conflict, greasing the wheels of human interactions, and unconsciously avoiding aggression."[1] Zaleznik urges managers to maintain a balance between what are often two competing organizational functions: functions he terms the *interpersonal* and the *real work,* such as marketing and production. Obviously, managers do a disservice to the organization if they spend a disproportionate amount of time on the interpersonal aspects of management. However, the interpersonal functions of management cannot be neglected, because the human element is essential to the performance of the real work of the organization.

The managerial function of leading draws heavily upon the field of study known as organizational behavior (OB). As the name implies, organizational behavior is the study of how people, both individually and within groups, behave in organizational settings. For the last century, managers have looked to the behavioral and social sciences (such as psychology, sociology, anthropology, and political science) for useful insights to help in dealing with the people working in an organization, and they have applied many of their findings to the workplace. This borrowing has been useful because it has provided managers with many theories to explain human behavior. However, because there has been so much research and because the results of this research often seem contradictory, a manager seeking information on the best way to lead often becomes confused and frustrated. It must be remembered that the research was never intended to provide a single, simple prescription for all managers. Indeed, it has become clear that there is no one best way to lead and no universal theory that is appropriate in all cases.[2] What this scientific research does provide, however, is a framework for managers to use in assessing their methods for dealing with people in organizations as well as a mechanism to suggest possible avenues of improvement. The more managers know about the research relating to motivation, leadership, and communication, the more they are able to draw from this research the elements that will be most useful to them.

What Do You Think?

Joan Giesecke, the dean of libraries at the University of Nebraska–Lincoln, posed the following questions:

> Managing professionals can present a true dilemma for today's managers. How do you manage, in the traditional sense, professionals or other managers who expect to have the authority and freedom to do their jobs? They are trained as experts in their fields. Why would they want you to manage them? Why would you think you could or should manage them?

What are the problems with managing professionals in today's libraries? How can managers rise to the challenge posed by Giesecke?

Joan Giesecke, *Practical Strategies for Library Managers* (Chicago: American Library Association, 2001), 41.

Like other managerial functions, leading is done by managers at different levels of the organization. As was discussed in chapter 1, in most typical organizations, including libraries, management can be divided into three levels. Top management, which in libraries usually means the director and the assistant and associate directors, is responsible for the overall functioning of the entire organization. In most organizations, managers on the highest levels have the power to establish organization-wide policy and are influential in setting the style of leading throughout the organization. Middle management is in charge of specific subunits or functions of the organization. In libraries and information centers, department heads are middle managers. Their management functions are concentrated on the successful functioning of individual areas of the library. Middle managers, in addition to leading their specific subunits or functions, also serve as liaisons between top management and supervisors. These supervisors, sometimes also called first-line managers, are the managers in the lowest position of the management hierarchy. They lead the activities of individual workers in accomplishing the desired organizational objectives. Because supervisors lead the work of all nonmanagement employees, they play a major role in influencing the performance, job satisfaction, and morale of the individuals in a work unit. Because they are usually the managers in direct contact with most employees, much of the leading function in an organization is done by these lower-level managers; they, like upper-level managers, must be skilled in leadership and human relations functions.

Although this tripartite division of management is being affected by the organizational changes discussed in section 3 and although the layers of management may be much less distinct in team-based structures, even the flattest organizations still will have managers who need to practice the components of leading each day.

Managers at all levels should be familiar with the techniques of good leading so that they can create a climate in which people can work together to fulfill the organization's goals. Leading is a difficult undertaking because its focus is on human behavior. This behavior is always unpredictable because it arises from people's deep-seated needs and value systems. As Keith Davis and John Newstrom state, "There are no simple formulas for working with people. There is no perfect solution to organizational problems. All that can be done is to increase our understanding and skills so that human relations at work can be upgraded."[3]

STRUCTURING THE HUMAN ELEMENT IN ORGANIZATIONS

Research concerning people in organizations provides managers with some insight into how to structure the human element of their organizations. As Davis and Newstrom point out, there are four basic assumptions about people that every manager should keep in mind:

1. **Individual differences.** People have much in common, but each person is an individual. Each person is born unique, and subsequent individual experiences make one even more different. Because of these individual differences, no single, standard, across-the-board way of dealing with employees should be adopted.

2. **A whole person.** Although some organizations wish they could employ only a person's skill or brain, they must employ the whole person. Various human traits may be separately studied, but, in the final analysis, they are only parts of the system that make up an entire person. People function as total beings. Good management practice dictates trying to develop a better employee, but it also should be concerned with developing a better person overall in terms of growth and fulfillment.

3. **Motivated behavior.** Psychology has shown that normal behavior has certain causes. These may relate to an individual's needs or to the consequences that result from a person's acts. In the former case, people are motivated not by what we think they ought to have but by what they want themselves. To an outside observer, an individual's needs may be illusory or unrealistic, but they still control that person.

4. **Value of the person.** This is more of an ethical philosophy than a scientific conclusion. It confirms that people are to be treated differently from other factors of production, because they are of a higher order of the universe. It recognizes that, because people are of a higher order, they want and deserve to be treated with respect and dignity. A person working any job, regardless of how simple it may be, is entitled to proper respect and to recognition of his or her unique aspirations and abilities. This concept of human dignity rejects the old idea of using employees only as economic tools.[4]

What Do You Think?

Henry Ford, the automotive pioneer, once complained that his employees asked too many questions. He is reported to have said, "Why, when I only want to hire a pair of hands, do I get a whole person?"

Why cannot managers employ just a pair of hands? How do good managers handle the human element in the organization?

To a large extent, the human factor of any organization is shaped by managerial actions. Managers have a tremendous impact on the growth and development of individual employees. J. Sterling Livingston used the George Bernard Shaw play *Pygmalion* (the basis of the later musical *My Fair Lady*) as an analogy for the role he thinks managers play in developing able subordinates and in stimulating their success.[5] Just as in *Pygmalion*, in which Henry Higgins transformed the flower girl into the society lady by treating her as if she were a lady, managers have the potential to transform their employees into something greater. According to Livingston, a manager's expectations are the key to the subordinate's performance and development. If a manager thinks the employee is going to succeed, that employee usually will succeed, because he or she will want to live up to the manager's high expectations.

When a new worker comes into an organization, he or she may be treated in one of two ways. Typically, if the manager has high expectations of that new worker, the manager will be friendly and give the employee opportunities to assume responsibility. If that new worker then fails at some task, the manager will be likely to view the failure as the result of a lack of proper training and will then see that training is provided. On the other hand, if a manager has low expectations, he likely will oversee the worker closely; will not trust the worker to do much independent work; and, if mistakes are made, will blame the worker. The manager with the low expectations is setting the worker up to fail.[6]

First impressions are very important. The first information received about a person may evoke reactions that lead to a self-fulfilling prophecy. For instance, a poorly dressed new worker may evoke a reaction from a manager that ultimately leads to that new worker failing in his or her job. Whatever assumption is adopted may serve as a self-fulfilling prophecy, because if managers believe that something is true, they will behave in a way that helps that belief turn into reality. If a manager believes that employees are irresponsible, immature, and lazy, he or she will treat them as if they were. The employees will respond by being frustrated, aggressive, and apathetic, and thus the manager's beliefs will be fulfilled. On the other hand, if employees are treated as responsible, capable, and interested in the organization's goals, they usually will respond in like fashion and thus fulfill that prophecy.

MOTIVATION

Managers are interested in motivation because it affects both employee performance and organizational effectiveness. Managers motivate by providing an environment that induces workers to contribute to the furthering of the goals of the organization. Many questions about employees' behavior can be best understood by understanding motivation. In every organization, there are some employees who work very hard and others who do as little as possible, some employees who show up on time for work every day and work after hours when necessary, and others who are frequently late and sometimes fail to come to work at all. It is often said that the first group of employees is motivated and the second is not. But what causes some workers and not others to be motivated? This is a question that has puzzled managers for a long time.

Motivation is the willingness to expend energy to achieve a goal or a reward. Thus, motivation is a process governing choices made by individuals between alternative voluntary activities. Motivation at work has been defined as the sum of the processes that influence the arousal, direction, and maintenance of behaviors relevant to work settings.[7]

Evidence has shown that most people do not work to the fullest extent of their capabilities and that most jobs do not require that they do so. In some of the earliest research on motivation, William James of Harvard University discovered that hourly workers working at 20 percent to 30 percent of their ability were performing well enough not to lose their jobs.[8] He also found that highly motivated workers performed at 80 percent to 90 percent of their ability. That gap between 20 percent to 30 percent and 80 percent to 90 percent is the area that can be affected by motivation. Many, if not most, people do not work up to their full potential. Because the success of any organization depends on how well its employees perform, it is not surprising that motivating workers is a major concern of managers. The motivation process can be seen as a sequence, with the efforts of an employee resulting in the achievement of the goals of the organization, which then leads to the employee's needs being satisfied.

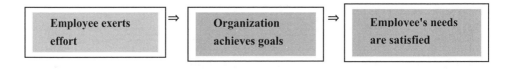

What motivates people varies from individual to individual and even within the same person over time. Motivation is influenced by a number of internal and external forces. Because each human being has a complex psychological makeup, motivation is a complicated, multifaceted quality that is related to various drives, needs, and wishes. A human need is a "personal unfilled vacancy that determines and organizes mental processes and physical behavior so that fulfillment can occur."[9] Individuals may recognize some of their needs and take care of them, but other needs are not as well recognized and may be working subconsciously.

Many theories and models have been developed to explain human motivation. These theories and models fall into two major groups: the content models and the process theories. The content models try to explain what workers want and need. They attempt to explain the nature of individual needs, because, according to these theories, workers' needs are tools that managers can use to motivate them. The second group of theories is categorized as the process theories, which focus on how managers can use their knowledge of workers' needs and desires to motivate behavior.

THE CONTENT MODELS

Because workers are so individualistic in what appears to motivate them, a number of motivational theories and models attempt to specify the exact needs and desires that motivate each person. All of these theories assume that individuals possess preexisting needs and that, although these needs are complex, organizations can motivate employees by addressing them. The relationship between the individual and the organization is a synergistic one; the individual has his or her needs fulfilled, and the organization obtains productivity. Psychologist Abraham Maslow proposed one of the earliest and best known of these theories of motivation in the 1940s.

Maslow's Hierarchy of Needs

Maslow postulated that all individuals have needs and that these needs can be ranked on one predetermined hierarchy. One level of need must be satisfied before an individual pursues the satisfaction of a higher-level need. As needs are satisfied, they lose their motivational properties until they are again aroused. Only unsatisfied needs serve as motivators. Maslow identified five levels of needs:

1. **Physiological.** The basic needs of a human are food, water, shelter, sleep, and other bodily needs. All are essential to human survival, and until they are satisfied to the degree necessary to sustain life, the other needs will provide little motivation.

2. **Safety and security.** These are the needs to be free of the fear of physical danger and of the fear of the deprivation of basic physiological needs.

3. **Social or affiliation.** After the first two needs are met, an individual develops a need to belong, to love and be loved, and to participate in activities that create a feeling of togetherness.

4. **Esteem.** After the social needs are met, people need to be more than just a member of a group. Individuals want to be held in esteem, both by themselves and by others. The satisfaction of these needs produces feelings of power, self-confidence, and prestige.

5. **Self-actualization.** At the highest level, the individual achieves self-actualization, which means maximizing one's potential to become everything that one is capable of becoming.[10] Figure 13.1 is a graphic presentation of Maslow's hierarchy of needs:

Figure 13.1—Maslow's Hierarchy of Human Needs

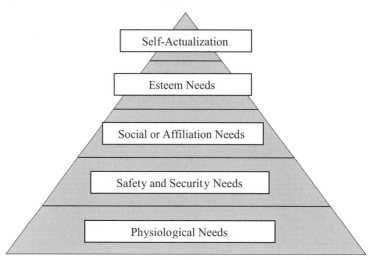

The implications of this hierarchy of needs can be useful in understanding what motivates workers. If a person's basic physiological needs are not met—if he or she does not have sufficient food, water, clothing, and shelter—then none of the higher-level needs will be of sufficient strength to be a motivator. In most cases, physiological needs can be satisfied as long as an individual has enough money. Thus, money, not in itself but because of what it will purchase, is a powerful motivator. In an affluent society like ours, the physiological needs of most individuals are fulfilled and, thus, do not serve as effective motivators.[11]

After a worker's physiological needs are met, fulfilling the security or safety needs becomes paramount. Some security needs are clear: for example, the need to avoid physical harm, accidents, or attacks. Most organizations provide physically safe places to work. However, the need for security extends beyond the present and into the future. Organizations are able to allay some concerns about the future by providing benefits, such as life and accident insurance and pensions. Job security is very important to most workers; the desire for job security is thus often a strong motivator, especially when jobs are scarce and unemployment is high.

After the physiological and safety needs have been fulfilled, the worker's social needs become predominant. Humans are social animals; they want to interact with others and be affiliated with a group. For example, the informal organization described by Elton Mayo in the Hawthorne studies discussed in chapter 2 arises to fulfill workers' needs to socialize and belong to a group.

The esteem needs include both self-esteem and the esteem of others. Workers desire to have their work valued not only by their superiors and their peers but also by themselves; they need to derive self-satisfaction from their work. Some employees stay on a job that does not pay well because of the self-satisfaction they get from it. The desire for prestige and power is also a part of the esteem needs, as is the competitive desire to outdo others. These esteem needs are rarely completely fulfilled. The desire for recognition is never ending for most, and esteem needs can be a potent and reliable source of motivation.

The final level of need described by Maslow is self-actualization, or the need to maximize one's potential. This is the most complex of Maslow's levels. Self-actualization goes beyond the boundaries of everyday life and requires individuals to have an almost religious fervor to fulfill their human potential.[12] This need is rarely completely satisfied.

Maslow's hierarchy has been criticized for being simplistic and artificial. Because every individual is different, many individuals do not pursue needs in the order postulated by Maslow, especially at the higher levels. In addition, it appears that the needs frequently overlap and combine.

Because Maslow's theory was based upon U.S. culture, it is also limited in its applicability to other cultures. Although other Western countries might have cultures that are similar, countries with different value systems might have different hierarchies. For example, E. C. Nevis studied individuals in China and found that the hierarchy of needs there was very different from those that Maslow had proposed. Maslow's hierarchy was based upon workers fulfilling their own individual needs, whereas Chinese culture stressed the importance of needs related to society. According to Nevis, the order of needs in the proposed Chinese hierarchy are:

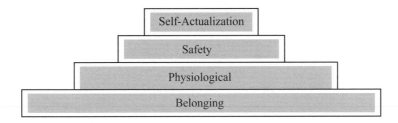

The need for belonging is the most basic need in Chinese culture, and there is no category for self-esteem. Even self-actualization is defined by the contributions made to society.[13] Most of the models of motivation discussed in this chapter are, like Maslow's, based upon U.S. culture, and although they may be applicable in other Western cultures, they are not meant to be universal.

Although Maslow's theory does have flaws and limitations, it has been popular with managers because it provides a conceptual means of understanding the motivation of employees. By identifying an employee's current position in the hierarchy, the manager has an indication of what motivator would be most effective when guiding, counseling, and advising the employee to achieve better performance. The hierarchy tells managers that unfulfilled needs are more motivating than fulfilled needs, and it points out that all needs never can be satisfied, because an individual who satisfies one need immediately begins to try to satisfy another. Managers must realize that need satisfaction will be a continuous problem for any organization.

Herzberg's Two-Factor Theory of Motivation

In the late 1950s, Frederick Herzberg and his research associates built upon and modified Maslow's ideas. Herzberg formulated a theory of motivation that focused specifically upon the motivation of employees in a work environment.[14] Figure 13.2 compares the two theories.

To gather information about what leads to high morale in employees, Herzberg and his associates looked at the factors that made employees feel happy and satisfied and at what kinds of things made employees feel dissatisfied. After the data were analyzed, the researchers discovered that one group of factors contributed to employees feeling good about their jobs. Herzberg called these factors *motivators.* These motivators, which are closely related to the actual content of the job itself, include such things as achievement; recognition by supervisors, peers, customers, or subordinates of the work accomplished; the work itself—the aspects of the job that give the worker personal satisfaction; responsibility—being able to work without supervision and being responsible for one's own efforts; and advancement. These factors lead to job satisfaction and are effective in motivating individuals to superior performance.

Another group of factors, which Herzberg labeled *hygiene* or *maintenance factors,* pertains not to the content of the job itself but primarily to the conditions under which a job is performed. These hygiene or maintenance factors

Figure 13.2—Comparison of Maslow's and Herzberg's Motivation Theories

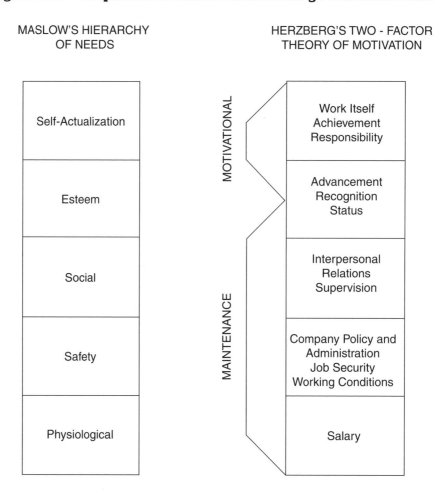

include salary, job security, status, working conditions, quality of supervision, company policy and administration, and interpersonal relationships. These factors do not lead to satisfaction on the job, nor do they serve as motivators. If these factors are inadequate, however, they do lead to dissatisfaction.

These two sets of factors are relatively independent of each other, and each set affects behavior in different ways. When people are satisfied with their jobs, the satisfaction is connected to the work itself. When they are dissatisfied with their jobs, they are usually unhappy with the environment in which they work. The factors that motivate workers are intrinsic to the job itself; the factors that cause dissatisfaction are extrinsic to it.

Later research has both supported and rejected Herzberg's model. Nevertheless, the two-factor motivational theory still has relevance to managers. It implies that the hygiene or maintenance factors must be satisfactory, because they provide a base on which to build. If employees are unhappy about their salary, status, or working conditions, they will be dissatisfied in their jobs. But merely providing these maintenance factors is not enough. If managers want employees to be motivated, they must provide what Herzberg called the motivators; that is, managers must ensure that jobs are interesting and challenging to employees. They must emphasize achievement, recognition, the work itself, and growth, all of which are factors that workers find intrinsically motivating.

Herzberg argued that job enrichment is one of the most effective methods of motivating employees.[15] However, he cautioned against horizontal job loading, merely adding more meaningless tasks to be performed by the worker. In a library, allowing a shelver to shelve both books and periodicals is not likely to improve motivation. True job enrichment involves vertical job loading, which consists of both making jobs more challenging and allowing the worker more responsibility. An enriched job uses more of the employee's talents and provides more freedom in decision making. (More information about job redesign may be found in chapter 8.)

Herzberg's research shows that job enrichment leads to better motivated and more productive employees. Although today Herzberg's theory does not have the wide popularity it once had, it still has had a strong influence on how jobs are designed and on how managers view the relationship between a worker's job and job satisfaction.

As a result of interest in job enrichment and its motivational force for workers, many organizations have established Quality of Working Life (QWL) programs. QWL is a broad approach to job enrichment that attempts to satisfy the personal needs of employees through their work experience. The QWL focus on individual needs contrasts sharply with traditional personnel programs, with their emphasis on the productive capability of the worker. Proponents of QWL claim that work can be redesigned to meet workers' psychological needs, such as feelings of competency and self-esteem, while at the same time improving productivity. The six major characteristics usually included in QWL programs are autonomy, challenge, expression of creativity, opportunity for learning, participation in decision making, and use of a variety of valued skills and abilities.[16] There is evidence that links exist not only between QWL programs and employee satisfaction but also between QWL programs and an institution's financial success.[17] Even in libraries that do not have formal

QWL programs, attempts are being made to improve working conditions and make jobs more satisfying, both for professional librarians and for the support staff. Many individuals who work in libraries are motivated by such workforce innovations as flextime and the ability to telecommute to work at least part of the time.

McClelland's Need Theory

David McClelland's work offers us a different perspective on what motivates workers. McClelland proposed that there are three major categories of needs among workers:

1. **The need for achievement** (nAch), which is the drive to excel in relation to a set of standards. It is the drive to succeed.
2. **The need for power** (nPow) is the desire to have an impact on an organization and to be influential.
3. **The need for affiliation** (nAff) is the desire for close interpersonal relationships.

Workers with a high need for achievement wish to succeed and advance. They seek situations in which they can assume responsibility. Accomplishment is important for its own sake. Those workers with a high need for power want to influence people and make an impact on their organizations. They want to be in charge. If workers have a high need for affiliation, they have a drive to relate to people on a social basis and to have close interpersonal relationships. They prefer cooperative rather than competitive situations.

McClelland used a projective test, the Thematic Apperception Test (TAT), in this research. Each subject was shown a picture and asked to write a story about it. For instance, a picture might depict a boy at a desk with a book. A subject identified as low in nAch might write a story about the boy daydreaming, whereas someone high in nAch would write that the boy was studying hard to do well and was worried about a test that he had to take. In addition to the TAT, McClelland and his associates also used questionnaires asking about such things as career preferences, the role of luck in outcomes, and similar subjects.[18]

McClelland's theory differed from earlier ones in that he thought that the three needs were learned.[19] "Motivation is inculcated in children through the stories and role models presented to them as things admired in their society. As adults, they seek to emulate the heroes and values of their childhood lessons."[20] But McClelland also believed that adults are changeable, and some of his later work deals with the idea of developing greater nAch, especially in workers of other societies. He attempted to train managers in organizations in less developed countries to increase their nAch, thereby increasing the success of these organizations. He claimed that this attempt was successful. For instance, 50 businesspeople he had trained in India invested more money in local ventures, participated in more community development activities, and created more jobs than a control group that had not been trained.[21]

What Would You Do?

The Serials Department at the library at Heaton University is facing a severe personnel shortage. As the department head, Muriel O'Brien, explains to the library director:

"Sarah, Inez, Zoë, and I have been working two extra hours a day for several weeks to try to keep up. And even with that we're way behind. Now, Sarah has gotten ill, and I don't know what we're going to do. I can't ask Inez and Zoë to work any more hours. They've been good sports. I've also been working every Saturday, as well as the two extra hours a day."

"I'm sorry about that," the library director said, "and I greatly appreciate what you have been doing. Since we can't pay you overtime the way we do with the clerks, Ill try to arrange some compensatory time when things get to normal—if they ever do."

Heaton University has a freeze on new hiring, and student assistants cannot handle the work that needs to be done in the serials department.

If you were Muriel O'Brien what would you do next?
(For the rest of this case study, see http://www.lu.com/management.)

A manager using McClelland's theory of motivation would try to match various aspects of the work with the employee's need. Like many of the other theories, McClelland suggests that the worker has to be matched with a job that fulfills his or her needs if that worker is to be as successful as possible. For instance, a worker with a high nAch should be given a job that challenges him or her and that allows personal responsibility.

THE PROCESS MODELS

In contrast to the content models of motivation, which try to identify the specific needs or values that contribute to motivation, the process models of motivation focus on the psychological and behavioral processes involved in motivation. The basic assumption underlying the process models is that "internal cognitive states and situational variables interact in the motivational process. The individual is an active factor, selecting behaviors based on his or her needs and based on expectations about what kind of behavior will lead to a desired reward."[22] Four of the best-known process models of motivation are the equity, the expectancy, the behavioral modification, and the goal-setting theories.

Adams's Equity Theory

John Stacey Adams, a behavioral psychologist, developed the equity theory of job motivation. This theory relates to the balance that exists between the inputs and the outputs of a particular employee's job in comparison to the inputs and outputs of other employees' positions. The other positions that employees use as reference points for comparison can be either within the same organization or in another one. The equity model states that an employee compares the perceived inputs and outputs and then tries to achieve equity between the positions. The inputs are thing such as hours worked, how much effort is expended on the job, the requirements of the job, and the ability or educational level required for the job. The outputs are things such as amount of pay, vacation time, job security, recognition, and praise. Employees compare the inputs and outputs of their particular position to those of similar positions, and if they do not think that there is equity between the two, they are motivated to reduce the perceived inequity. For example, if employee A compares himself to employee B and thinks that the ratios of the inputs and outputs are not equitable, employee A may begin to expend less effort on his work. Employee A also might ask for a raise to try to increase his rewards, or he might try to get employee B to work harder. If equity cannot be achieved, employee A might try to get a different job. Employees who feel underpaid will usually make efforts to readjust the equity by working less, whereas those who feel overpaid usually will try to do the same by working harder. The equity theory emphasizes the importance of a reward system that is perceived as fair by employees. Good managers will try to maintain an equitable reward system and be sure that employees understand how highly visible rewards, such as pay or promotions, are apportioned.[23]

 What Would You Do?

You are the supervisor of a 12-person copy cataloging department in a very large public library. Sydney Brown, one of your employees, has just had his position reclassified, which will result in a higher pay level. Sydney has long been working at a higher level than his present job classification, and you are delighted that this reclassification, which you have been trying to achieve for months, has finally been approved. When word about the reclassification becomes public, you are surprised that a number of Sydney's co-workers do not share your feelings about it. Several complain to you that they have the same level of responsibility in their work that Sydney does, but they have not been promoted. They think you have treated them unfairly by pushing for a reclassification of Sydney's position.

What would you do in a case like this?

Vroom's Expectancy Theory

A number of individuals have developed expectancy theories of motivation.[24] Expectancy theories are based upon the belief that individuals act in such a way as to maximize desirable results and minimize undesirable ones.

Among the best known of these theories is one put forth by Victor Vroom.[25] This theory is more complex than the content theories. It emphasizes how motivation takes place, given an individual's needs and objectives. The theory focuses on an individual's decision making and on the process that he or she goes through in deciding whether to exert the effort to attempt to achieve a particular goal.

Vroom's theory states that people will be motivated to perform to reach a goal if they believe in the worth of the goal and if they perceive that what they do will contribute to the achievement of that goal. The expectancy model is composed of four elements. Force is the motivational drive to achieve a goal. Valence is the extent to which an individual desires a certain outcome or goal. Expectancy is the perceived probability that a particular outcome will lead to a desired result, a result that is called the first-level outcome. Instrumentality is the degree to which an individual believes that a first-level outcome is related to a second-level outcome, which is defined as some human need, such as companionship, esteem, or accomplishment. Vroom's model can be stated in the following formula:

Force = Valence × Expectancy × Instrumentality

To illustrate this theory, consider a worker who wants to be promoted. This individual thinks that the best way to achieve the promotion would be to increase job performance. The motivation (force) to improve job performance would be a product of the intensity of the desire for promotion (valence) multiplied by the worker's perception of how likely it is that working harder can improve job performance (expectancy) multiplied by the worker's perception of how likely it is that improved job performance will lead to a promotion (instrumentality). In this example, improved job performance is the first-level outcome and promotion is the second-level outcome.

Vroom's formula is a multiplicative one; as soon as the value of any element drops to zero, so does the motivational force. In the previous example, if the worker felt that, despite improved job performance, there was no chance for promotion, the motivation to improve job performance would be zero. Likewise, if the worker felt that, despite any effort, there was no way to improve job performance, again the motivation would be nonexistent.

Vroom's theory is important because it highlights how people's goals influence their efforts; the behavior of an individual is a function of (1) his or her belief in the efficacy of that behavior in achieving a goal and (2) his or her desire to achieve a goal. Because the theory recognizes the importance of various individual needs and motivations, it demonstrates to managers that motivation is highly individualized. A manager must try to learn the special concerns of each employee and what each individual values. The manager also must make clear to employees the connections between performance and reward. This theory also points out some situations that should be avoided in organizations. If an organization says it has a merit system for awarding pay raises, and if more employees get high evaluations than there is money available for pay raises, there obviously will be less motivation in the future to try to work well enough to get a high evaluation because the reward that was promised was not forthcoming.

What Do You Think?

Jeanne works in the cataloging department of a large academic library. She has been told by her manager several times in the last few years that good performance will result in a promotion. Although Jeanne's evaluations have been consistently good, she has not been promoted. Now her manager has asked her to take responsibility for a special project and has promised her a promotion if this project is successful. If you were Jeanne how likely would you be to take on this new responsibility?

Vroom's theory, because it emphasizes the individual, is more difficult to apply than those of Maslow and Herzberg, which are general theories of motivation. But Vroom's theory avoids some of the more simplistic features of the content theories, and it also seems to more adequately account for the diversity in motivational needs seen in employees. There has been extensive research done on this model, and the research bears out the premise that people tend to work hard when they think that working hard either will lead to desirable outcomes or will avoid undesirable ones.

Behavior Modification

B. F. Skinner, one of the leading proponents of the behavioristic school of psychology, provides managers with yet another process model of motivation. Behavior modification, unlike the other motivational theories discussed, is based on observed behavior, not on individual attitudes, desires, and emotions. Skinner's emphasis is on operant behavior, behavior that has been shaped and modified—that is, controlled—by its consequences. Individuals act as they do because of reinforcements received in the past for similar behavior. Reinforcement is defined as a consequence that follows a response and that makes a similar response more likely in the future. Reinforcements can be tangible (e.g., money or food) or intangible (e.g., praise or attention). According to Skinner, there are four methods for modifying behavior: positive reinforcement, negative reinforcement, no reinforcement, and punishment.[26] Positive reinforcement, according to Skinner, is the most effective long-range strategy for motivating individuals. Positive reinforcement is a reward given after a behavior that the motivator wishes to see continued. Positive reinforcement tends to strengthen this behavior and to make it more likely to occur again. Managers can offer a wide range of positive reinforcements, including pay increases, promotions, and praise. When a behavior or act is followed by the termination or withdrawal of something unpleasant, it is called negative reinforcement. For instance, if a supervisor criticizes a worker for coming to work late, the worker's desire to eliminate this criticism may cause the worker to come to work on time. No reinforcement leads to the extinction of a behavior. Because the behavior is not reinforced in one way or another, it decreases in frequency and then stops. If the manager neither praises nor criticizes the worker who talks loudly to attract the manager's attention, the unwanted behavior is not being reinforced, and it should stop eventually. Punishment is an unpleasant event that follows unwanted behavior; punishment is intended to decrease the frequency of that behavior. Punishments that managers can inflict include demotion and firing.

Skinner's work has been criticized by those who say it treats humans as passive objects and denies the existence of individual free will. In practical terms, it is more difficult to apply behavior modification principles in the workplace than in the controlled setting of a laboratory. Scientists working with rats are able to deprive the animals of food so that they are hungry and then provide food immediately after the desired behavior occurs. They can do this and be certain that no uncontrolled variable has influenced the rats' behavior. Although the workplace provides managers many opportunities to practice behavior modification on employees, managers who try this must do it in an environment in which uncontrolled variables are always intruding. Nevertheless, some organizations have used Skinner's principles of behavior modification to motivate employees. One of the most frequently cited success stories of the use of behavior modification in business occurred at Emery Air Freight, where, over a three-year period, $2 million was saved by identifying performance-related behaviors and strengthening them with behavior modification.[27]

Behavior modification, although difficult to institute systematically and thoroughly, provides managers with several principles that can be applied in any type of organization. Be sure that employees who are performing as desired receive positive reinforcement, and remember that positive reinforcement is more effective in modifying behavior than either negative reinforcement or punishment. Although negative reinforcement and punishment traditionally have been popular means of control among managers, they have serious drawbacks and side effects. Among these drawbacks are temporary suspension of behavior rather than permanent change, dysfunctional emotional behavior, behavioral inflexibility, permanent damage to desirable behavior, and conditioned fear of the punishing agent.[28] For example, employees who are punished for talking on the job learn not to talk when supervisors are around but likely still talk in their absence. Also, they are likely to feel resentful about being punished and will find unproductive ways of acting out such feelings by thwarting the supervisors' goals.

Behavior modification works best when a job has specific variables that can be identified and reinforced. Some of the clerical jobs performed by library support staff fall into this category. For instance, error rate is subject to behavior modification techniques. Employees who complete tasks error free could be rewarded in some fashion. However, when jobs are more complex, it is more difficult to use behavior modification. Much of the work done by librarians is largely intellectual, and it would be difficult to identify, measure, and reinforce many of the behaviors that constitute such work.

Goal-Setting Theory

The last of the process theories that will be discussed is the goal-setting theory. This theory, first propounded by Edwin Locke, states that specific goals increase performance and that difficult goals, when accepted by employees, lead to higher performance than do easier goals.[29] There have been more than 500 studies on goal setting in organizations in at least eight countries; about 90 percent of these studies have shown positive results.[30] This theory has a number of propositions:

- The more difficult the goal, the higher the performance achievement.
- The more specific the goal, the more explicitly performance is regulated.
- The best way to get high performance is to make goals both specific and difficult.
- Goal setting is most effective when there is feedback.
- In order to maximize performance, one must have both goals and feedback.
- To get people committed to a goal, they must be convinced that the goal is important and that it is reachable or partially reachable.
- The higher an individual's self-confidence, the higher the goals the person will be willing to set, the more committed the person will be to difficult goals, the more resilient and persistent the person will be in the face of failure, the better task strategies the individual likely will be to develop, and the better the person will perform.
- Participation is more valuable as an information exchange device for developing task strategies than as a method of gaining commitment to goals.
- The more successful the performance in relation to the goals, the greater the degree of satisfaction experienced.[31]

Goal setting helps point employees toward what is important in the organization. Setting difficult yet achievable goals (sometimes called stretch goals) helps employees know what they should be attempting to achieve. Imagine that you are an original cataloger in a large library. Would it be more motivating to be told that you should do the best you can or to be told that you are expected to do original cataloging for 12 English-language books a day? Having a goal to meet allows an employee to know the expectations of the employer and gives that employee an objective to try to meet. Finally, achieving a goal that has been set is very satisfying and fulfills both the need for self-esteem and the need for achievement. It often stimulates an employee to try to do even more the next time.

Goal setting that incorporates only a few of these elements will not be successful. To implement goal setting successfully, the elements illustrated in figure 13.3 must be included.

HOW SHOULD MANAGERS MOTIVATE?

Motivation is a complex factor, and managers face a wide array of approaches for promoting commitment to jobs within an organization. As one expert states:

Figure 13.3—Elements of Effective Goal Setting

Specificity of Goals	Challenging, yet Reachable, Goals
Effective Goal Setting	
Acceptance of Goals	Feedback

Source: Adapted from Edwin A. Locke, "Motivation by Goal Setting," in *Handbook of Organizational Behavior,* 2nd ed., ed. Robert T. Golembiewski (New York: Marcel Dekker, 2001).

The issue of how to understand and influence human motivation has proven to be one of the most recalcitrant problems in human psychology. The fundamental reasons for this are that motivation at root comes from within the individual and is most directly controlled by the individual. Since motivation is "inside" the person, it cannot be observed directly, and since individuals possess freedom of choice ... people cannot be controlled directly from the outside.[32]

 Try This!

Although employees usually appreciate monetary rewards, cash incentives are definitely not the only way to motivate employees. Elisha F. Topper, director of the Dundee Township Public Library, offers these suggestions:

Don't forget to say "thank you" when staff put in extra effort on the job, and be sure to carry this practice over into staff meetings by adding to the agenda time to issue thanks and compliments.

Create an employee motivation program with departmental awards for exceptional work, perhaps with an emphasis on customer service.

Make a "thanks for your help" box and ask staff to drop in the names of fellow employees who go beyond the call of duty; then hold a monthly drawing for a small gift.

> Celebrate the completion of major projects with a special coffee break with treats.
>
> Be sure to acknowledge the anniversary date for each employee either with a paper or electronic card.
>
> Try thinking of some other nonmonetary ways to thank employees.
>
> ---
>
> Elisha P. Topper, "Working Knowledge: Knowing How to Say 'Thank You,'" *American Libraries* 35, no. 1 (January 2004): 96.

Raymond Katzell and Donna Thompson have endeavored to summarize the vast body of research on motivation into a series of seven imperatives:

1. Ensure that workers' motives and values are appropriate for the jobs in which they are placed.
2. Make jobs attractive to and consistent with workers' motives and values.
3. Define work goals that are clear, challenging, attractive, and attainable.
4. Provide workers with the personal and material resources that facilitate their effectiveness.
5. Create supportive social environments.
6. Reinforce performance.
7. Harmonize all of these elements into a consistent sociotechnical system.[33]

To carry out all of the seven imperatives is a daunting task, but one that managers need to attempt. A manager must adopt a managerial style that motivates workers to perform tasks efficiently, but, unfortunately, no one prescribed style assures success. Rather, managers must develop individual approaches based on their personality, managerial philosophy, and knowledge of their workers. The effective manager takes advantage of the worker's reasons for working and offers inducements related to those reasons. Thus, a system of inducements, rather than a single inducement for all workers, emerges. Some inducements may have to be negative, but the majority should be positive. A system of inducements is not designed for across-the-board application but is designed to provide workers with those inducements that best motivate them.

A sound motivational system is based on principles derived from motivation research, on the policies of the organization, and on the manager's philosophy of human needs. Essential to any motivational system is the organization's ability to satisfy employee needs. This is difficult to accomplish because the needs of humans vary greatly and are subject to change. Maslow's hierarchy of needs gives the manager a guide to the range of needs, from basic life requirements to social, ego, and creative needs. Herzberg's studies provide information about the need for recognition, achievement, advancement, and responsibility. McClelland's work shows that different individuals have different learned needs that affect the way they approach a work situation.

Vroom's research demonstrates the importance of considering each individual's aspirations and of coupling performance to reward. Skinner's work makes evident the importance of positive reinforcement in ensuring continued desirable behavior. Locke's goal-setting theory shows the significance of goals as a means of helping employees achieve a higher level of performance.

The policies of the organization should be structured so that the capacity to do good work is encouraged. Good productivity reflects the quality of employee motivation. Ideally, an organization's goals and objectives motivate an employee who wants to be part of and contribute to their achievement. Certainly this is so in the library profession. A high degree of success in achieving the goals and objectives creates a positive image of the organization; the worker is proud to be part of the organization and is motivated to promote its success through efficient work.

CONCLUSION

Any system of motivation depends on managers. The manner in which they apply their knowledge of employee needs and desires, the organizational environment that releases the capacity for work, the quality of training received by capable employees, and the pride these employees have in the organization establish the basic climate of the motivational system. It is the manager's responsibility to exercise sound judgment to make the system work.

NOTES

1. Abraham Zaleznik, "Real Work," *Harvard Business Review* 75 (November–December 1997): 56.

2. John J. Morse and Jay W. Lorsch, "Beyond Theory Y," *Harvard Business Review* 48, no. 3 (May–June 1970): 61–68.

3. Keith Davis and John W. Newstrom, *Human Behavior at Work: Organizational Behavior*, 8th ed. (New York: McGraw-Hill, 1989), 4.

4. Ibid., 9–12.

5. J. Sterling Livingston, "Pygmalion in Management," *Harvard Business Review* 47, no. 4 (July–August 1969): 81–89.

6. Jean-Francois Manzoni and Jean-Louis Barsoux, "The Set-Up-to-Fail Syndrome," *Harvard Business Review* 76 (March–April 1998): 101–13.

7. Meshack M. Sagini, *Organizational Behavior: The Challenges of the New Millennium* (Lanham, MD: University Press of America, 2001), 449.

8. Cited in Paul Hersey and Kenneth H. Blanchard, *Management of Organizational Behavior: Utilizing Human Resources* (Englewood Cliffs, NJ: Prentice-Hall, 1982), 4.

9. O. Jeff Harris and Sandra J. Hartman, *Organizational Behavior* (Binghamton, NY: Haworth Press, 2002), 200.

10. Abraham H. Maslow, *Motivation and Personality*, 2nd ed. (New York: Harper & Row, 1970), 35ff.

11. It is important to remember that workers' basic needs are not fulfilled in all cultures. See, for example, Kalu U. Harrison and P. Havard-Williams, "Motivation in a Third World Library System," *International Library Review* 19 (July 1987): 249–60.

12. Dennis M. Daley, *Strategic Human Resource Management: People and Performance Management in the Public Sector* (Upper Saddle River, NJ: Prentice Hall, 2002) 56.

13. E. C. Nevis, "Using an American Perspective in Understanding Another Culture," *Journal of Applied Social Behavior* 19 (1983): 249–64.

14. Frederick Herzberg, Bernard Mausner, and Barbara Bloch Snyderman, *The Motivation to Work,* 2nd ed. (New York: Wiley, 1959).

15. Frederick Herzberg, "One More Time: How Do You Motivate Employees?" *Harvard Business Review* 46 (January–February 1968): 53–62.

16. Charles Martell, "Achieving High Performance in Library Work," *Library Trends* 38, no. 1 (Summer 1989): 82.

17. R.S.M. Lau and B. E. May, "A Win-Win Paradigm for Quality of Work Life and Business Performance," *Human Resource Development Quarterly* 9 (October 1998): 211.

18. Hal G. Rainey, "Work Motivation," in *Handbook of Organizational Behavior,* 2nd ed., ed. Robert T. Golembiewski (New York: Marcel Dekker, 2001), 27.

19. David C. McClelland, *The Achieving Society* (New York: Free Press, 1961); David C. McClelland, *Power, the Inner Experience* (New York: Irvington, 1975).

20. Daley, *Strategic Human Resource Management,* 58.

21. David McClelland and D. G. Winter, *Motivating Economic Achievement* (New York: Free Press, 1969).

22. Sagini, *Organizational Behavior,* 462.

23. J. Stacy Adams, "Towards an Understanding of Inequity," *Journal of Abnormal and Social Psychology* 67 (1963): 422–36.

24. See, for example, Edward E. Lawler, *Motivation in Work Organizations* (Pacific Grove, CA: Brooks/Cole, 1994); and Victor H. Vroom, *Work and Motivation* (New York: Wiley, 1964).

25. Vroom, *Work and Motivation.*

26. B. F. Skinner, *Science and Human Behavior* (New York: Macmillan, 1953).

27. E. J. Feeney, "At Emery Air Freight: Positive Reinforcement Boosts Performance," *Organizational Dynamics* 1 (Winter 1973): 41–50.

28. F. Luthans and R. Kreitner, *Organization Behavior Modification* (New York: Scott, Foresman, 1975), 118.

29. Edwin A. Locke, "The Ubiquity of the Technique of Goal Setting in Theories and Approaches to Employee Motivation," *Academy of Management Review* 3 (1978): 594–601.

30. Edwin A. Locke, "Motivation by Goal Setting," in *Handbook of Organizational Behavior,* 2nd ed., ed. Robert T. Golembiewski (New York: Marcel Dekker, 2001), 48.

31. Ibid., 44–48.

32. Ibid., 43.

33. Raymond A. Katzell and Donna E. Thompson, "Work Motivation: Theory and Practice," *American Psychologist* 45 (February 1990): 151.

Chapter 14

Leadership

 Overview

For the third time in five years, the library at Longleaf College is searching for a new director. Edward Ravenal served as director of the library for 27 years until his retirement five years ago. Since then, there has been no consistency in leadership at the Longleaf College library. Each search process brought in a promising replacement, but once the new director began work, library employees began to complain about the changes being made and the new director's leadership style. The first new director lasted two years and then accepted another position out of state. His replacement was forced to retire after 18 months due to ill health brought on by stress, and an interim director is now in charge of the library. As the search committee begins the search for yet another library director, it is trying to understand what has gone wrong with the previous searches. What has caused these failures after promising new leaders were hired? Is the fault in the organization or in the individuals being selected? Why is it so hard to find a good leader these days?

This search committee is grappling with the same questions that are being faced by numerous organizations in all segments of today's society. Throughout history, people have struggled with the question, "What makes a good leader?" but there are still many aspects of leadership that are not fully understood. Can leadership be taught? Are the skills of leadership the same in all organizations? What is the difference between a manager and a leader? What do good leaders do? How do they invest their time? How can a good match between an individual leader and the organization he or she is leading be assured?

This chapter will present an introduction to the topic of leadership, examining what leadership is, what leaders do, and how the topic of leadership has been studied in the past and at present. The chapter will end with suggestions for preparing future leaders.

WHAT IS LEADERSHIP?

Because having a good leader is so important to organizations of all types, leadership has long been a topic of interest, but there is far more interest in leadership than there is agreement upon it. Leadership is an often perplexing topic with numerous debates about what leadership is and even what leaders actually do. Our failure to understand leadership is not the result of any lack of literature on the topic. Writers in a number of fields have churned out hundreds of books and thousands of articles. A recent review listed more than 7,000 books, articles, or presentations on the topic of leadership.[1] In 1999 alone, there were more than 2,000 books on leadership published, exhibiting many varying viewpoints on the topic, with "some of them repacking Moses and Shakespeare as leadership gurus."[2] There is so much advice available about how to be a successful leader that it is almost overwhelming.

The definitions of the term *leadership* are not much clearer. James MacGregor Burns, one of the most respected experts on leadership, once wrote, "Leadership is one of the most observed and least understood phenomena on earth."[3] Leadership is a difficult subject to understand because it defies easy analysis. Indeed, it is even a difficult term to define. There are many books and articles that define leadership, but often these definitions do not agree with one another. The most common definition of leadership is that it is an ability to inspire confidence and support among followers that permits a group to reach its goals. Regardless of how we define leadership, there are certain elements that are usually included. The words *influence, vision, mission,* and *goals* are almost always a part of the definition. It is commonly accepted that an effective leader has the ability to influence others in a desired direction and thus is able to determine the extent to which both individuals and the organization as a whole reach their goals. Leadership transforms organizational potential into reality.

MANAGERS AND LEADERS

Because leaders often function in an organizational or institutional setting, the terms *manager* and *leader* are closely related, but they are not the same. Managers are often associated with qualities of the mind, such as rationality, analytics, and authority, and leaders more with the qualities of the soul, such as vision, creativity, passion, and inspiration.[4] As one expert said, a manager takes care of where you are, but a leader takes you to a new place.[5] In general, leaders are viewed as being able to take control of situations, whereas managers learn to live with them. Other distinctions include: Leaders create vision and strategy, whereas managers implement the outcome; leaders cope with change, whereas managers cope with complexity; and leaders focus upon interpersonal aspects of the jobs, whereas managers deal with administrative duties.[6]

But because individuals in both managerial and leadership roles are often at the top of an organizational structure, there is often overlap in the roles. Perhaps the most helpful distinction that can be made between the two is an examination of where the power to lead comes from: With managers, it comes from their positions, whereas with leaders, it may come from more personal attributes. But individuals often play both roles in libraries, and without a doubt, managers can be leaders, and it is beneficial when they can be because one of the things that is known about leadership is that the successful organization is almost always set apart from less successful ones by the fact that it is headed by a dynamic and effective leader. For this reason, both managers and organization theorists long been have interested in how leadership can be encouraged and developed.

 What Do You Think?

Warren Bennis and Burt Nanus, two leading scholars of leadership, once wrote, "Managers are people who do things right and leaders are people who do the right thing."

What is the difference between doing things right and doing the right thing? Do you agree that managers do things right and leaders do the right thing?

Warren G. Bennis and Burt Nanus, *Leaders: The Strategies for Taking Charge* (New York: Harper & Row, 1985), 21.

However, individuals can be good managers without being leaders. Our organizations also need good managers. Effective managers are highly valued by those who work for them because good managers facilitate employees getting their jobs done. Of course, some managers also may be leaders, but it is a mistake to denigrate what managers do by assuming that they are failures if they are not also leaders.[7] Leadership may not be as important to an organization that is enjoying a favorable, nonturbulent environment. But when an organization needs innovation more than standardization, it needs a leader rather than a manager as the top administrator. An organization may be managed well but led poorly.[8]

LEADERSHIP QUALITIES

If managers and leaders are not synonymous, are there qualities that every leader possesses? It always must be remembered that there is no one model of a successful leader, and leaders differ in different cultures and historical periods. Despite this variability, according to most experts, each leader must fulfill two major roles. First, a leader must exercise power, and second, each leader must through actions, appearance, and articulated values present a vision that others will want to emulate.[9] Let us look at these two roles a little more closely.

Exercising Power

The first role, that of exercising power, obviously has close connections to what a good manager does. Good leaders exercise power wisely and efficiently;

they must be temperate and fair, must set objectives and see that they are carried out, and must make good decisions. The characteristics that we usually associate with a good manager are also found in a good leader.

Unfortunately, not all leaders are good. A few people become leaders not to advance the good of an organization but to gain personal power or achieve their own objectives. A recent book has characterized these individuals as toxic leaders—those who are destructive to their employees, their organizations, and even to their nations.[10] Leaders such as Adolf Hitler or Jeffrey Skilling from Enron were destructive leaders, although in very different ways. Barbara Kellerman, in another recent book, provides a typology for measuring bad leadership.[11] This typology ranks bad leadership from bad to worst (see "Try This!" for more about the typology). Both of these books emphasize that bad or toxic leaders have followers who tolerate and remain loyal to them and who enable them to remain in leadership positions. As Kellerman points out, managerial literature often tries to accentuate the positive by discussing only good leadership and ignoring the so-called elephant in the room—bad leadership. She argues that ignoring bad leadership is analogous to a medical school that claimed to teach health while ignoring disease.[12] So, although it is true that most leadership literature focuses on the good leader, it is important to acknowledge that there is a dark side of leadership and that all leaders are not good. Many of the traits that allow a person to become a leader can be used for either good or for evil.

 Try This!

Kellerman has developed a classification scheme that can be used to categorize bad leaders. The characteristic of the leaders in each group are summarized in the following list with the typology ranging from bad leaders who are merely incompetent to those who are evil. Can you think of examples of leaders in each of these categories?

- **Incompetent:** lack of skill or will to sustain leadership.
- **Rigid:** stiff, unyielding, and unwilling to adapt to new ideas, new information, or changing times.
- **Intemperate:** lacks self-control.
- **Callous:** uncaring or unkind; ignores or discounts the needs of the rest of the organization, especially subordinates.
- **Corrupt:** lies, cheats, or steals; puts self-interest above the public interest.
- **Insular:** disregards or at least minimizes the health and welfare of those outside their own inner group.
- **Evil:** commits atrocities inflicting severe physical or psychological pain on others.

Barbara Kellerman, *Bad Leadership: What It Is, How It Happens, Why It Matters* (Boston, Harvard Business School Press, 2004).

Presenting a Vision

The second role, that of presenting an image that others will want to emulate, is the aspect of leadership that is called vision. A leader must provide a vision, a difficult undertaking in itself, and a lack of vision is one of the major problems of leaders today. Although a leader must present a vision so that an organization will not drift aimlessly, presenting a vision is not enough. A leader must have his or her vision accepted by the followers; the followers must buy into the vision and adopt that vision as their own. They must be energized so that the vision can be accomplished.[13] With an effective leader at the helm, the goals of the leader and the followers are meshed and congruent.

When leaders fail, it is often because they have not been able to create a vision that is shared. Sometimes, people are hired in an organization, and they bring with them a predetermined vision that they want to see fulfilled. They begin to move too quickly, before their vision is accepted by the individuals who are going to have to carry it out. These individuals inevitably fail because they did not sell the vision to those who had to implement it.

In discussing leadership, sometimes the importance of followers is forgotten. A leader is not a leader without followers. Garry Wills has stated that three elements—leaders, followers, and a shared goal—are necessary for effective leadership. He defines a leader as "one who mobilizes others towards a goal shared by leaders and followers."[14]

Figure 14.1—Three Elements of Effective Leadership

Leader

Effective Leadership

Followers

Shared goals

The Elements of Effective Leadership

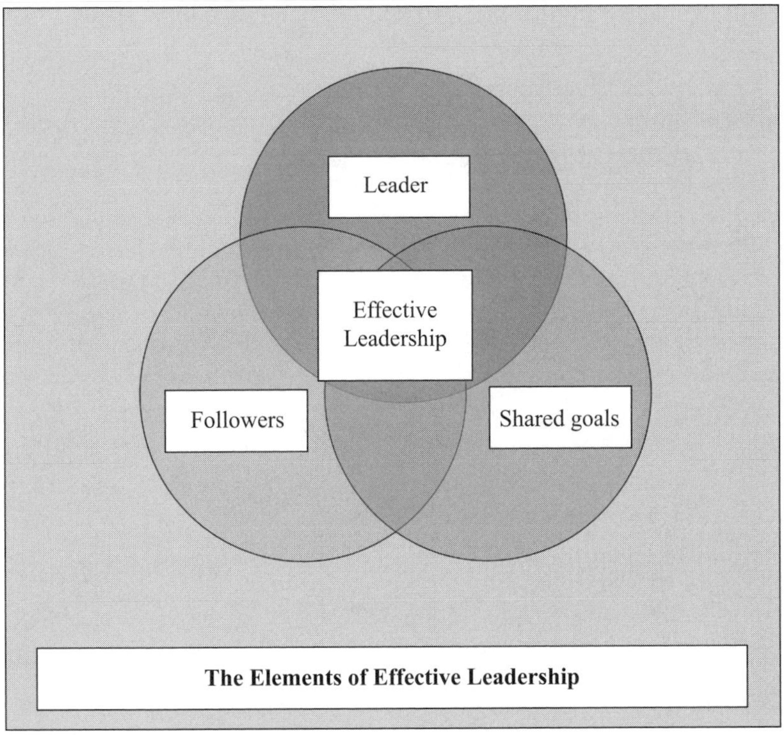

Getting individuals to buy into a vision is perhaps the hardest task confronted by a leader. As the great Chinese philosopher Lao-tzu said long ago, a leader is best when people barely know he exists. When his work is done, his aim fulfilled, they will say, we did this ourselves. The leader's vision has been so thoroughly ingrained in the followers that they think it was their idea to start.

An effective leader has the ability to influence others in a desired direction and thus is able to determine the extent to which both individual employees and the organization reach their goals. Leadership too often has seemed to be in short supply. For these reasons, both managers and organization theorists long have been interested in how leadership can be encouraged and developed. There have been a number of approaches to studying leadership. Because managers and leaders share many responsibilities and attributes, a number of the studies cited actually studied high-level managers as a method of investigating leadership. Some of the most important studies are discussed in the following sections.

THE TRAIT APPROACH TO THE STUDY OF LEADERSHIP

Early studies on the subject of leadership were concerned with identifying the traits or personal characteristics associated with leadership. The studies were based on the premise that leaders were born, not made, and only those who were born with these traits could be leaders. The assumption was that once the traits were identified, leadership selection could be reduced to finding people with the appropriate physical, intellectual, and personality traits. Leadership training would then consist of developing those traits in potential leaders.

Lessons in Leadership

Ron Yeo was a former chief librarian of the Regina Public Library in Saskatchewan, "whose extraordinary vision and leadership led to a new order in Canadian public libraries." A recent article in *Public Libraries* distilled his leadership wisdom into 21 lessons that are helpful to leaders in any type of library.

Lesson 1: Want to Succeed
Lesson 2: Have a Central Vision
Lesson 3: Share the Power
Lesson 4: Be Strategic
Lesson 5: Keep a Wide-Open Mind
Lesson 6: Don't Back Off from Conflict
Lesson 7: Make Some Key Commitments
Lesson 8: Act with Conviction
Lesson 9: Exceed Expectations
Lesson 10: Harness Respect

Lesson 11: Favor the Best
Lesson 12: Make More Leaders
Lesson 13: Don't Confuse Scholarship with Leadership
Lesson 14: Be an Intrapreneur
Lesson 15: Make Your Cause Their Cause
Lesson 16: Bet on the Future
Lesson 17: Take Responsibility
Lesson 18: Be Undeterred
Lesson 19: Raise the Bar
Lesson 20: Go to the Community
Lesson 21: Lead from the Outside

To read more about each of these lessons, see Gary Deane, "Lasting Lessons in Leadership: How a Former Book Trade Rep Took a Library from Good to Truly Great," *Public Libraries* 44, no. 3 (May/June 2005): 163–68, http://www.ala.org/ala/pla/plapubs/publiclibraries/mayjune2005.pdf.

Many trait studies were conducted, and traits that were said to be associated with leadership, such as energy, aggressiveness, persistence, initiative, appearance, and height, were identified.[15] However, summaries of this research demonstrate its shortcomings: Each study tended to identify a different set of traits. In one summary of more than one hundred studies, only 5 percent of the traits were found in four or more studies.[16] Eugene Jennings concluded, "Fifty years of study have failed to produce one personality trait or set of qualities that can be used to discriminate between leaders and non-leaders."[17] Although some traits have been found to be weakly associated with leadership, these studies show that there is no such thing as a single leader type. Instead, there is much variation in the skills, abilities, and personalities of successful leaders.

 Try This!

It is interesting that many individuals have different ideas about the characteristics associated with leadership. List five different characteristics that you think most leaders possess and then get a colleague or classmate to make the same list. How many of the characteristics were on both lists?

BEHAVIORAL APPROACHES TO THE STUDY OF LEADERSHIP

After the trait studies fell out of favor, interest grew in the actual behavior of leaders. Researchers turned from looking for a single configuration of leadership characteristics to investigating leadership style. This research examined the behavior of leaders: what they did, what they emphasized, and how they related to subordinates. Three of the most important of these studies are discussed. All of these studies looked at managers as leaders within organizations.

The University of Iowa Studies

One of the first of these studies was done at the University of Iowa by Kurt Lewin and his associates. These researchers primarily used controlled experiments with groups of children to examine three types of leadership styles: autocratic (a leader who centralizes decisions and makes decisions autonomously), democratic (a leader who allows subordinates to participate in decision making and delegates authority), and laissez-faire (a leader who gives the group complete freedom in decision making).[18] The results of this experiment demonstrated that there was more originality, friendliness, and group cohesion in democratic groups and more hostility, aggression, and discontent in laissez-faire and autocratic groups.[19]

Ohio State Studies

Other early studies were conducted at Ohio State University in the late 1940s and early 1950s. These studies identified two relatively independent dimensions on which leaders differ. One of these dimensions—consideration—refers to the extent to which a leader establishes mutual trust, friendship, respect, and warmth in his or her relationship with subordinates. Initiating structure refers to the leader's behavior in organizing, defining goals, emphasizing deadlines, and setting direction. Consideration and initiating structure are independent of each other; they are not separate ends of a continuum. A high score on one does not necessitate a low score on the other. A leader could be high in both consideration and initiating structure.[20]

University of Michigan Studies

A group of researchers at the University of Michigan's Institute for Social Research conducted similar studies at about the same time as the researchers at Ohio State.[21] These studies tried to identify managers' supervisory styles and their effects on employee productivity. The researchers identified three types of managers: predominantly production-centered managers, predominantly employee-centered managers, and those with mixed patterns. Because no person is always the same, the word *predominantly* is important. A production-centered manager was one who felt full responsibility for getting the work done; departmental employees were to do only what the manager told them to do. An employee-centered manager recognized that the subordinates did the work and therefore should have a major voice in determining how it was done. Employee-centered managers thought that coordinating and maintaining a harmonious environment was the supervisor's main responsibility.

The research results were surprising. Contrary to traditional management thinking, which emphasized that permissive management led to employee laxity and carelessness, the departments that had employee-centered managers produced more than those with production-centered managers. The Michigan researchers had to make an assumption that was radical at the time; that assumption was that many workers like their jobs, want to be productive, and would be productive if given a share of control over their jobs.

STYLES OF LEADERSHIP

The next trend in the study of leadership was the development of ways to assess the style of a leader. The proponents of these typologies used the findings of the leadership behavioral studies to categorize the ways in which leaders lead. The style theorists thought that although many different leadership behaviors were possible, some styles were better than others. Three of the best known of these style theories are Likert's Systems of Management, the Leadership Grid developed by Robert Blake and Jane Mouton, and the transactional/transformational model of leadership.

Likert's Systems of Management

Rensis Likert, in *New Patterns of Management,* built on the research done at the University of Michigan Institute for Social Research.[22] Likert describes four prevailing ways that managers lead within organizations. These styles can be depicted on a continuum ranging from System 1, exploitative-authoritative, to System 4, participative.

- System 1 management is exploitative-authoritative. In this system, management has no trust or confidence in subordinates. Managers are autocratic, and almost all decisions are made at the top of the organization. Subordinates are motivated by fear and punishment and are subservient to management. Almost all communication in the organization comes from the top of the hierarchy.

- System 2 management is benevolent-authoritative. Management is condescending to employees, who are expected to be loyal, compliant, and subservient. In return, management treats the employees in a paternalistic manner. This system permits more upward communication than System 1, but top management still tightly maintains control.

- System 3 is consultative. In this system, management has substantial but not total trust in subordinates. Top management still makes most of the major decisions but often solicits ideas from subordinates. Control is still primarily retained by top management, but aspects of the control process are delegated downward. Communication flows both up and down in the hierarchy.

- System 4 is participative. Managers have complete trust in subordinates, and much of the decision making is accomplished by group participation. Decision making is found on all levels of the organization. Communication flows up, down, and horizontally among peers. Because of their participation in decision making, employees are strongly motivated to achieve the organization's goals and objectives.[23]

In short, System 1 is a highly structured and authoritarian system of management. The assumptions made about employees under this system closely approximate Douglas McGregor's Theory X. System 4 is a participative system based on trust and teamwork. Here, the assumptions made about employees are similar to McGregor's Theory Y. Systems 2 and 3 fall between the two extremes.

Likert concludes that the most effective organizations use the System 4 style of management. Although System 1 may yield favorable results in terms of productivity in the short run, over a period of time, production in System 1 organizations will taper off. In addition, the negative effects of System 1 upon people more than offset any short-term gains in productivity. Today's organizations can be found at all points on the continuum. Those that have adopted innovations such as self-directed work teams are moving toward System 4. Undoubtedly, there are more organizations using System 4 now than in the past, but the true System 4 organization is still rare. Most libraries and information centers are still at the System 2 or System 3 level.

The Leadership Grid

The Leadership Grid (first termed the Management Grid) was developed by Robert R. Blake and Jane S. Mouton.[24] The Leadership Grid involves two primary concerns of the organization: concern for production and concern for people. The term *production,* as used here, "covers whatever it is that organizations engage people to accomplish."[25]

Managers who are most concerned about productivity focus almost exclusively on the tasks that have to be accomplished; managers who are concerned about people are more interested in the human relations part of the organization. These two concerns and the range of interactions between them are illustrated in figure 14.3. Concern for production is represented on the horizontal axis, and concern for people is represented on the vertical axis. Each rating is expressed in terms of a nine-point scale of concern, with one in each case indicating minimum concern and nine indicating maximum concern. A manager with a rating of nine on the horizontal axis has maximum concern

Figure 14.2—Likert's Four Systems of Leadership

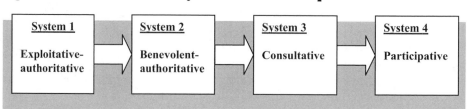

| System 1

Exploitative-authoritative | System 2

Benevolent-authoritative | System 3

Consultative | System 4

Participative |

for production; a manager with a rating of nine on the vertical axis has a maximum concern for people.

Based on the grid, Blake and Mouton describe five leadership styles. A rating of 1,1 is considered impoverished leadership. Minimum effort is exerted to get the required work done, and minimum concern is paid to employees. A leader with this rating is essentially doing nothing at all for either people or production; he or she has abdicated leadership responsibility. A rating of 1,9 is called country club leadership. Thoughtful attention to people's need for satisfying relationships leads to a comfortable, friendly atmosphere and work tempo. There is no concern for production. A rating of 9,1 is considered task leadership. Here, operational efficiency results from arranging work conditions in such a way that human elements interfere to a minimum degree. Leaders with this rating are autocratic taskmasters. A rating of 5,5 is middle-of-the-road leadership. Adequate organization performance is achieved by balancing production

Figure 14.3—The Leadership Grid

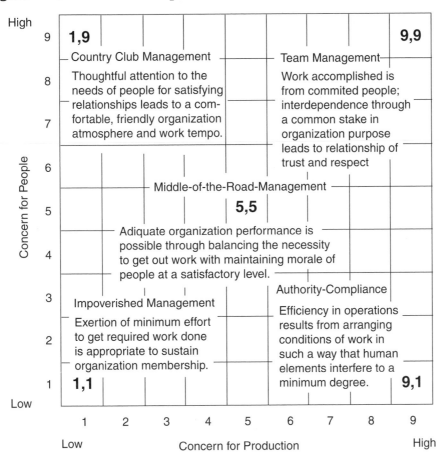

Source: From Robert R. Blake and Anne Adams McCanse, *Leadership Dilemmas—Grid Solutions* (Houston, TX: Gulf, 1991), 29; formerly the Management Grid figure by Robert R. Blake and Jane S. Mouton. Reproduced by permission of the owners.

with maintaining a satisfactory level of morale. Leaders with this rating are adequate in dealing with both people and production but are not outstanding in either capacity. Finally, a rating of 9,9 is team leadership. Work is accomplished by committed people; interdependence, resulting from a common stake in the organization's purpose, leads to relationships of trust and respect. According to this theory, leaders with a 9,9 rating are outstanding in their concern for both people and production.[26]

The Leadership Grid is most helpful for identifying and classifying leadership styles. It is useful as a theoretical framework for understanding human behavior in organizations. Using this grid, managers at any level should be able to identify their level of concern for people and for productivity.

Transformational/Transactional Leadership

James MacGregor Burns was the first person to popularize the terms *transactional* and *transformational* to describe leadership styles.[27] Transactional leaders see job performance as a series of transactions with subordinates. The transactions consist of exchanging rewards for services rendered or punishments for inadequate performance. On the other hand, transformational leaders are skilled at getting subordinates to transform their own self-interest into the interest of the larger group. Transformational leaders bring out the best in their subordinates. The described differences between these two types of leaders are reminiscent of the differences that often are said to exist between managers and leaders. The transactional leaders are more like managers, being sure that the job is done, whereas the transformational leader is more like a leader because he or she inspires subordinates. Transformational leaders usually allow more participation on the part of subordinates. Another researcher described transformational leaders as working "to make their interactions with subordinates positive for everyone involved. More specifically, [they] encourage participation, share power and information, enhance other people's self-worth, and get others excited about their work."[28] Later research has shown that these two types of leadership are not in opposition to each other.[29] Instead, transformational leadership often builds upon transactional leadership. But of the two types of leadership, transformational leadership usually has a greater positive effect on an organization than does transactional leadership.[30] However, transformational leadership, like so many other models of leadership, is not the answer in every situation. It has been found that transformational leadership alone does not always produce better results. Other factors such as organizational culture, structure, and employee receptiveness influence the effectiveness of transformational leadership.[31]

SITUATIONAL OR CONTINGENCY MODELS OF LEADERSHIP

Likert's Systems of Management, the Leadership Grid, and the transformation/transactional model imply that there is a preferred leadership style. More recent theorists have turned away from the idea that there is one best way to provide leadership. They assert that earlier theorists had little success in identifying consistent relationships between patterns of leadership behavior and group performance. Instead, these contingency, or situational, theorists argue that there is no single ideal type of leader but, instead, a number of leadership styles that may be appropriate, depending on the situation. Employee-centered leadership may be best under some circumstances, and production-centered leadership may be best under others. According to advocates of contingency theories, the task of a leader is to use the style that is most appropriate in any given situation.

Fiedler's Leadership Contingency Model

Fred Fiedler developed one of the best-known contingency theories. According to Fiedler's model, three situational variables determine how favorable any particular situation is for the leader. These three situational variables are:

- **Leader-member relations:** the degree to which group members like and trust a leader and are willing to follow him or her.
- **Task structure:** the clarity and structure of the elements of the tasks to be accomplished.
- **Power position:** the power and authority that are associated with the leader's position.

Fiedler produced and studied eight combinations of these three variables. The combinations range from the situation that is most favorable to a leader (good relations with followers, highly structured task, and strong power position) to the situation that is most unfavorable to a leader (poor relations with followers, unstructured tasks, and weak power position). Figure 14.4 lists each of the combinations. Fiedler then attempted to assess what would be the most effective leadership style in any of these situations. His theory predicts that the task-oriented leader is most effective in situations at either end of the continuum. When situations are most favorable or least favorable for a leader, the production-oriented style is most effective. The human relations, or employee-oriented, style works best when conditions are either moderately favorable or moderately unfavorable for the leader.

Fiedler's research is helpful to managers because it improves their understanding of the relationship of the various situational variables involved in leadership. Leadership effectiveness depends as much on the organizational variables as it does on the leader's own attributes.

Path-Goal Theory of Leadership

Another contingency theory of leadership is called the path-goal theory. This theory, first developed by Robert House, differs from Fiedler's contingency theory because its central focus is on the situation and leader's behavior instead of the personality traits of the leader.[32] Unlike Fiedler's view that leaders could not change their behavior, the path-goal model assumes that leaders can adopt different leadership goals depending on the situation.

Figure 14.4—Fiedler's Contingency Model Relating Style of Leadership to Situational Variables

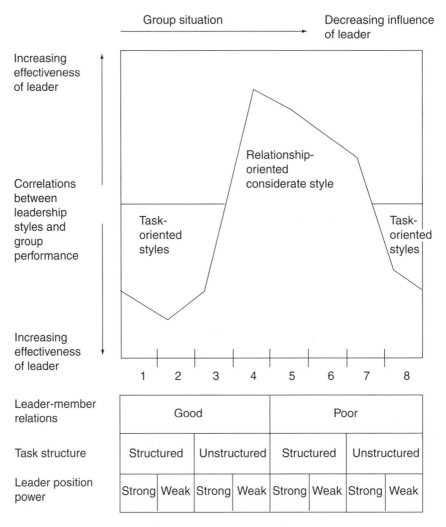

Source: From Fred Fiedler, "Correlations between Leadership Styles and Group Performance," *Psychology Today,* March 1969, 42. Copyright American Psychological Association.

The path-goal theory arises from a belief that effective leaders clarify the path to help followers achieve work goals, and they make the journey along the path easier by reducing any pitfalls or roadblocks. House thought that the role of a leader is to increase "personal pay-offs to subordinates for work-goal attainment and make the path to these pay-offs easier to travel by clarifying it, reducing road blocks and pitfalls, and increasing the opportunities for personal satisfaction en route."[33] This theory suggests that managers have three ways to motivate: first, by offering rewards for reaching performance goals; second, by making the paths toward these goals clear; and third, by removing obstacles to performance.

House identified four types of leadership behaviors:

1. **Directive leadership** occurs when specific advice is given to the group and clear rules and structure are established.
2. **Supportive leadership** occurs when the needs and well-being of subordinates are considered.
3. **Participative leadership** occurs when information, power, and influence are shared. Subordinates are allowed to share in the decision making.
4. **Achievement-oriented leadership** occurs when challenging goals are set and high performance is encouraged. Achievement-oriented leaders show high confidence in subordinates and help them in learning how to achieve high goals.

A leader may use any of the four types of leadership behaviors, depending on the situation. The two most important situational contingencies in the path-goal theory are:

1. The personal characteristics of the workers, such as their experience, ability, motivation, needs, and locus of control.
2. The environmental factors, including the nature of the work to be done, the formal authority system, and the work group itself.

So, the leader has to take into account both the environment and the characteristics of the followers. For instance, a new employee in an uncertain environment might need directive leadership, whereas an established employee performing a familiar task would be better off with supportive leadership. As is seen in figure 15.5, different situations require different types of leadership behavior.

The path-goal theory is complex, but it is one of the most respected theories of leadership today. Research to validate its conclusions generally has been encouraging, with most studies supporting the logic underlying path-goal theory.[34] It makes sense that both an employee's performance and satisfaction are likely to be positively influenced when a leader is able to adapt different leadership behaviors to compensate for differences in either the employee or the work setting.

 ## What Would You Do?

Chris Adams has just been hired as the new library director at Plainville State University (PSU). The new director is replacing Dr. Zachary Longstreet, who was the founding director of the PSU library. PSU is a medium-size state institution founded in 1964, which today enrolls approximately 14,000 students and offers undergraduate degrees in a number of fields and master's degrees in education and business. Chris received an MSLIS degree 10 years ago and had worked in several academic libraries, most

Figure 14.5—Situations and Preferred Leader Behaviors According to the Path-Goal Theory

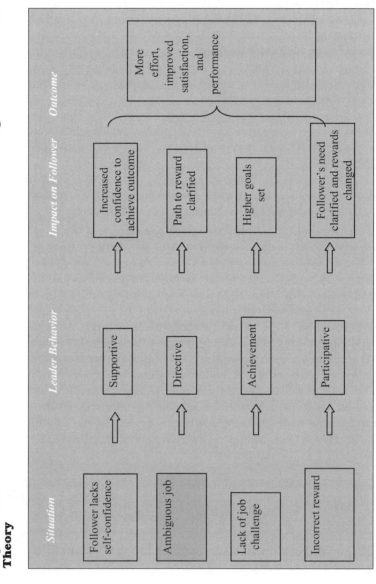

Source: Adapted from Gary A. Yukl, *Leadership in Organizations* (Englewood Cliffs, NJ: Prentice-Hall, 1981), 146–52.

recently as head of reference. The new director is eager to move into a leadership position at PSU but is a bit worried about the best way to proceed. It seems to Chris that the library at PSU is at least twenty years behind most libraries. There is an early-generation online catalog and access to a few databases but little else in terms of information technology. The library has never engaged in strategic planning, and there have been no staff meetings at the library for years. The PSU library is still using the same organizational structure it used when it opened more than forty years ago. It seems that Dr. Longstreet ran the PSU library in an autocratic fashion, and its employees are used to being told how to do everything and are certainly not used to changes. Chris would like to implement a number of innovations but is unsure of what to do first and how to do it. If you were Chris, how would you proceed? What things would you do first? What actions might you delay.

LEADERSHIP IN THE TWENTY-FIRST CENTURY

The pressure is building to walk the talk. Call it whatever you like: post-heroic leadership, servant leadership, distributed leadership, or, to suggest a tag, virtual leadership. But don't dismiss it as just another touchy-feely flavor of the month. It's real, it's radical, and it's challenging the very definition of corporate leadership for the 21st century.[35]

What is the best leadership style for the twenty-first century? Some experts have postulated that we are entering a postheroic period of leadership. In the past, leaders often have been viewed as heroes. James MacGregor Burns wrote a great deal about heroic leadership, which he described as a relationship between leaders and follows in which followers put great faith in the leaders' ability to overcome crises and problems.[36] The leader has all the answers, and the followers follow his or her directives. Peter Senge described the heroic leader as follows: "Especially in the West, leaders are heroes—great men (and occasionally women) who rise to the fore in times of crises.... At its heart, the traditional view of leadership is based on assumptions of people's powerlessness, their lack of personal vision and inability to master the forces of change, deficits which can be remedied only by a few great leaders."[37] The heroic style of leadership consists of powerful leaders and fairly powerless followers. Making leaders play the role of hero is detrimental both to a leader and to those who are being led. Extraordinary pressures are placed on heroic leaders; many feel that they have to be perfect and cannot acknowledge mistakes or the negative impacts of their actions. Heroic leadership is also harmful to followers who become overly dependent and disempowered. The heroic leadership style does not match the needs of today's flatter, more participative organizations. In response, a new concept of leadership—postheroic leadership—has been emerging, which stresses the importance of shared power.[38]

One of the most important proponents of this new style of leadership is James Collins, who has introduced the notion of Level Five leadership. Collins and his research associates formulated the concept after research done on 11 companies that made the leap from "good" to "great."[39] The researchers found all of these highly successful companies had one characteristic in common: At the time they made the transition from good to great, they were led by a Level Five leader. Collins defines a Level Five leader as one with a paradoxical blend of personal humility and professional will. Level Five leaders are very ambitious, but they focus their ego needs not on themselves but on their organizations. They are not weak or vacillating but combine a respect toward people with a powerful commitment to achieve results. Their lack of ego is combined with a strong will to do the right thing for the organization at all costs. This type of leader, according to Collins, brings out the best in subordinates.

All of the levels of Collins's hierarchy of leadership styles are illustrated in figure 14.6. Workers at the lower level can be successful and contributing members of an organization, but the most successful leaders have reached the top level.

This postheroic way of envisioning leadership is a change from what has been thought in the past, but it fits well with the pattern of distributed leadership found in many of today's organizations. It requires "many of the attributes that have always distinguished the best leaders—intelligence, commitment, energy, courage of conviction, integrity. But here's the big difference: It expects those qualities of just about everyone in the organization."[40] At present, there is a great deal of interest in postheroic leadership. As the twenty-first century progresses, there doubtlessly will be other new theories about leadership, because leadership is a topic that continues to be of interest to managers both in libraries and in all other types of organizations.

THE LEADERSHIP CHALLENGE

So, as can be seen, there are many theories to suggest what makes a leader successful. None of the theories completely explains leadership; however, they do help explain many of the variables that contribute to being a successful leader. But as was discussed at the beginning of the chapter, leadership is a complex topic and one that has no easy answers.

 What Do You Think?

Herb White, a former dean at the LIS school at Indiana University, once wrote, "We believe in leaders and leadership, but ... on a personal basis few of us want to be led."

Do you agree with this and if so, why?

Herbert S. White, "Oh, Where Have All the Leaders Gone?" *Library Journal* 112 (October 1987): 68–69.

Figure 14.6—Collins's Five Levels of Leadership

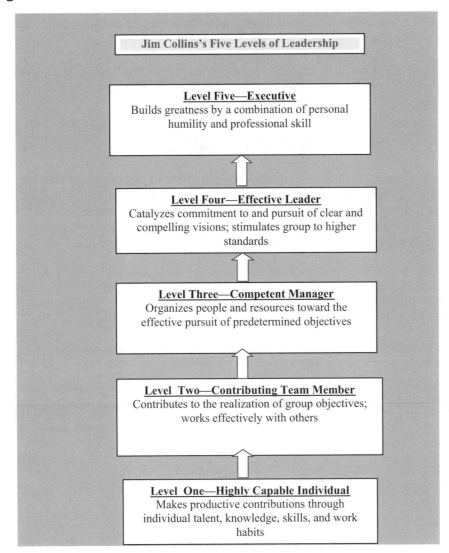

It is more difficult for individuals to succeed in leadership roles now. In the past, people were far less likely to question the authority of a leader. Today's leader must try to inspire confidence and trust in followers who are likely to be at least partially distrustful of authority of all types.

Managers who are concerned with leadership should keep in mind that, despite all the theories about leadership style, research still has not shown whether one style of leadership is superior to the others. The analysis of leadership style is a complex topic, and much of the research that has been done to date has been short-term and scattered. The situational theories, such as Fiedler's contingency model and the House's path-goal theory, seem to be the most helpful in dealing with real-life situations. However, such theories, with their emphasis on matching a leadership style to a particular environment or work situation, complicate the manager's task. Many managers would like to be told how to lead; the situational theories say there is no one right way. Instead, effective leaders adapt their style of leadership behavior to the needs of the followers and the situation. Because these factors are not constant, discerning the appropriate style is always a challenge. And if the postheroic theorists are correct about the type of leadership that will be most effective in twenty-first-century organizations, we need to find a way to encourage and develop leadership in all parts of our organizations.

DEVELOPING LEADERSHIP

One of the most important lessons that successful leaders must learn is that no one can lead alone. By definition, leaders do not operate in isolation. Nor do they command in the literal sense of the word, issuing a one-way stream of unilateral directives. Instead, leadership almost always involves cooperation and collaboration.[41] As Peter Senge wrote:

> In the knowledge era, we will finally have to surrender the myth of leaders as isolated heroes commanding their organizations from on high. Leadership in the future will be distributed among diverse individuals and teams who share responsibility for creating the organization's future.[42]

It is impossible for any one individual to succeed as a leader if they are working without help. It is no longer possible for any one person to run an organization successfully. For contemporary organization to function effectively, "interdependent teams at different levels need leaders."[43] Leadership has to be found throughout the organization, and leadership skills must be nurtured and developed in many individuals. Some individuals, such as the library director, might have an ongoing leadership role, while others might assume leadership responsibility based on specific activities or projects. If leadership is to be exercised on all levels, libraries need to develop leadership capacity throughout the organization and nurture the leadership proclivities of individuals working in all levels of the organization.

Today, it is commonly accepted that leadership is a quality that can be developed. Leadership is an acquired competency that is the result of many circumstances, including chance. As the old saying goes, being in the right place at the right time often provides an opportunity for a person to discover that he or she can exert leadership.

 Try This!

1. Think of someone you consider a great leader.
2. List three traits this person possesses that contribute to his or her leadership ability.
3. Think of someone you consider to be an ineffective leader.
4. How do the two people differ?

There always will be some people more successful at becoming leaders than others. And obviously, everyone cannot be a leader at all times—an organization cannot have only leaders and no followers. But people can exercise leadership in different ways and at different times. As society and institutions become more complex, it will be even more important to expose more individuals to the opportunity to learn leadership skills. Leaders are not born, although leadership may come more naturally to some than to others. As a society, we cannot afford to waste the leadership skills that can be developed in the majority of people. In most modern organizations, leaders may be found at all levels of the organizational hierarchy, and to envision the person at the top as the only leader is to accept an artificially constrained view of leadership. More and more employees at all levels are participating in management and thus also are providing leadership within the organization.

How can leaders be developed? What can be done to ensure that new librarians entering the field this year or next can play appropriate leadership roles? And what can be done to enable individuals already working in libraries who perhaps aspire to more responsibility to move into leadership positions?

Leadership development consists of two intertwined components. First, there are the skills that need to be learned. Although many of the skills of leadership can be taught, they will be learned with varying rates of success by different people. Then there is the personal component of leadership. Knowing the behaviors associated with leadership is important, but an individual also needs to have a basic aptitude and will to lead. Most people can develop these aptitudes, but there always will be some who will not or who cannot.

Assuming that the aptitude and will are there, however, the skills associated with leadership not only need to be learned but also need to be practiced. First, a prospective leader needs to master skills associated with leadership, and then he or she needs to practice these skills. So, like so much else, leadership development is a mix of theory and practice. The best preparation for leadership allows individuals to learn a skill and then to practice it. All of this is to say that it is not easy to transmit leadership skills. True leadership cannot be taught in a course or learned in a leadership institution. These provide a start, but they alone will not make a person a leader.

A number of the leadership development attempts in librarianship are designed to help a person attain leadership skills. Many of the LIS schools are beginning to teach courses in leadership. These courses can be helpful in imparting to new practitioners what research tells us about leadership and the skills of leaders, but they provide few opportunities for the participants to practice leadership within a real organization. Luckily, however, many students get a chance to actually practice and demonstrate leadership within the various student organizations, community service projects, and internship programs that are part of LIS programs today.

The chance to develop leadership begins for most in the work setting. Here, many libraries have instituted programs to help new practitioners. Many of these programs are designed to provide additional management training, but leadership training is often a by-product because there is such a close connection between management and leadership in libraries. Libraries function as laboratories for beginning leaders, who all learn from doing. Often, mistakes are made when a person is learning to manage or to lead, but making mistakes is one way of learning. People learn a great deal from failure, and perhaps the most important lesson is that no one is ever always right. Everyone makes mistakes, and it is all right to make some mistakes. A manager or a leader who has never made a mistake has never taken a risk or made significant changes in an organization.

One of the best ways to learn about leadership is to observe other leaders. People who aspire to leadership positions can learn a great deal from more experienced leaders who already have acquired many of the skills and the characteristics associated with leadership. Even better than observing is actually being mentored by a leader. Many libraries have mentoring programs in place, and a quality that has been identified with many of the best leaders is their desire to mentor and pass along their leadership experience. Leadership has many stages, from beginning leaders to those about to retire. As leaders progress through the stages, mentoring is always helpful, and it is very common for a leader to be both a mentor and a protégé at the same time.

 What Do You Think?

Nigel Nicolson writes:

> Leaders come to power through both internal and external selection. The internal is self-selection, the force that induces some to seek and others to avoid leadership. Even when one is handed a leadership position on a plate, one's inner self has to acquiesce, especially around three attributes. Are you ready to take on the risks and responsibility (drive)? Do you believe you have the skills to take on the challenge and succeed (ability)? Can you withstand the demands on your energies (constitution)? Many people have succumbed to the lure of the rewards or the encouragement of others and have become bad leaders, when they would have done better to heed their inner doubts.

> What attributes allow a person to become a good leader? Do you agree with Nicolson that people should forego leadership roles if they have inner doubts?

Nigel Nicholson, *Managing the Human Animal* (London: Texere, 2000), 115–16.

As will be discussed in chapter 17, many libraries are using teams to accomplish their missions. Often, being a part of a team is one of the first places that an entry-level librarian is able to act as a leader. Success in leadership within a team often encourages a new leader to want to achieve more. Chairing committees can be another way to provide some leadership experience. Work within professional organizations is another. Often, individuals who never had considered themselves leaders find that they have a knack for it and want to go on to practice leadership at a higher level. Because high-level leaders need to get a feel for the entire organization, some libraries have used cross-training and job rotation as another form of leadership development. Other libraries have used interim department head or associate director positions to let individuals get experience working in a leadership position. Those who have an inclination for leadership often use these positions as springboards into permanent leadership positions.

In addition to leadership development that happens on the job, there are a number of leadership institutions that are designed to help individuals who have been identified as prospective leaders acquire the skills that are needed in leadership. These institutes are not all alike, but they have some common characteristics. Usually, the participants have had several years in the profession and have been identified as individuals with leadership potential. The institutes are often week-long events in a residential setting and usually mix an academic introduction to leadership topics with a number of exercises designed to help the individual participants learn about themselves and their potential for leadership. This type of leadership institution has been very popular not only in librarianship but also in many other fields. Similar to free-standing leadership institutions are the numerous courses on leadership taught in schools of business or public administration, which many librarians take for continuing education.

All of these opportunities help individuals learn about the skills associated with leadership, but perhaps more important, they help individuals discover whether they really want to lead. Wanting to lead is crucial. Warren Bennis says that potential leaders always should ask themselves two questions: Do I really want to lead, and am I willing to make the sacrifices leaders must make? The self-awareness must go further, and potential leaders must understand and be able to articulate their values. The best leaders are the principled ones who know and follow their own convictions. They also must examine their fortitude. Are they willing to act on their principles despite resistance and questioning? Individuals considering leadership should consider carefully whether their skills and personal characteristics will allow them to be successful leaders in their institutions.

Leadership skills should be taught to all who are willing to learn, and librarians at all levels should be encouraged to engage in the self-reflection that is necessary to determine whether leadership is a role that they want to play. Transitioning from an entry-level library employee to a managerial position to a leader is a journey that not all will want to take, but as our libraries become flatter and more decentralized, more and more people will need to take this journey. The recognition of a diversity of leadership styles means that the routes to leadership will be different, because individuals must lead in ways that will draw upon their individual strengths. Libraries, like all organizations, must be willing to support and help those who are willing to take the steps toward providing the leadership that will be necessary in the libraries of the future.

NOTES

1. Bernard M. Bass, *Bass and Stogdill's Handbook of Leadership*, 3rd ed. (New York: Free Press, 1990).

2. Robert Goffee and Gareth Jones, "Why Should Anyone Be Led by You?" *Harvard Business Review* 78 (September–October, 2000): 63.

3. James MacGregor Burns, *Leadership* (New York: Harper & Row, 1978), 2.

4. Genevieve Capowski, "Anatomy of a Leader: Where Are the Leaders of Tomorrow?" *Management Review* 83 (March 1994): 12.

5. James E. Colvard, "Managers vs. Leaders," *Government Executive* 35, no. 9 (July 2003): 82–84.

6. Robert G. Isaac, Wilfred J. Zerbe, and Douglas C. Pitt, "Leadership and Motivation: The Effective Application of Expectancy Theory," *Journal of Managerial Issues* 13 (Summer 2001): 213.

7. For an illuminating discussion of the differences between management and leadership, see Joseph C. Rost, *Leadership for the Twenty-First Century* (Westport, CT: Praeger, 1991), 140–52.

8. Warren Bennis, *Why Leaders Can't Lead* (San Francisco: Jossey-Bass, 1989), 17.

9. Michael Maccoby, *The Leader* (New York: Simon & Schuster, 1981), 14.

10. Jean Lipman-Blumen, *The Allure of Toxic Leadership* (New York: Oxford University Press, 2004).

11. Barbara Kellerman, *Bad Leadership: What It Is, How It Happens, Why It Matters* (Boston, Harvard Business School Press, 2004).

12. Ibid, 11.

13. Fred A. Manske Jr., *Secrets of Effective Leadership*, 2nd ed. (Columbia, TN: Leadership Education and Development, 1990), 5.

14. Garry Wills, "What Makes a Good Leader?" *Atlantic Monthly* 273 (April 1994): 70.

15. Ralph M. Stodgill, *Handbook of Leadership* (New York: Free Press, 1974).

16. Howard M. Carlisle, *Situational Management: A Contingency Approach to Leadership* (New York: AMACOM, 1973), 124.

17. Eugene E. Jennings, "The Anatomy of Leadership," *Management of Personnel Quarterly* 1 (Autumn 1961): 2.

18. Kurt Lewin and Ronald Lippitt, "An Experimental Approach to the Study of Autocracy and Democracy: A Preliminary Note," *Sociometry* 1 (1938): 292–300.

19. Kenneth E. Reid, *From Character Building to Social Treatment: The History of the Use of Groups in Social Work* (Westport, CT: Greenwood, 1981), 115.

20. Ralph M. Stodgill and Alvin E. Coons, eds., *Leader Behavior: Its Description and Measurement* (Research Monograph no. 887) (Columbus, OH: Bureau of Business Research, 1957).

21. Saul Gellerman, *The Management of Human Relations* (New York: Holt, Rinehart &Winston, 1966), 32.

22. Rensis Likert, *New Patterns of Management* (New York: McGraw-Hill, 1961).

23. Rensis Likert, *The Human Organization* (New York: McGraw-Hill, 1967), 4–10.

24. Robert R. Blake and Jane S. Mouton, *The Managerial Grid* (Houston, TX: Gulf, 1964).

25. Ibid., 9.

26. Ibid., 9–11.

27. Burns, *Leadership*.

28. J. B. Rosener, "Ways Women Lead," *Harvard Business Review* 68 (1990): 120.

29. Joseph Seltzer and Bernard M. Bass, "Transformational Leadership: Beyond Initiation and Consideration," *Journal of Management* 16 (December 1990): 693–703.

30. See, for instance, A. L. Geyer and J. M. Steyrer, "Transformational Leadership and Objective Performance in Banks," *Applied Psychology: An International Review* 47 (July 1998): 397–420.

31. Badrinarayan S. Pawar and Kenneth K. Eastman, "The Nature and Implication of Contextual Influences on Transformational Leadership: A Conceptual Examination," *Academy of Management Review* 22 (January 1997): 80–109.

32. Robert J. House, "A Path-Goal Theory of Leader Effectiveness," *Administrative Science Quarterly* 16 (September 1971): 321–38.

33. Ibid., 324.

34. See, for example, J. C. Wofford and L. Z. Liska, "Path-Goal Theories of Leadership: A Meta-Analysis," *Journal of Management* (Winter 1993): 857–76; and A. Sagie and M. Koslowsky, "Organizational Attitudes and Behaviors as a Function of Participation in Strategic and Tactical Change Decisions: An Application of Path-Goal Theory," *Journal of Organizational Behavior* 15 (January 1994): 37–47.

35. John Huey and Ricardo Sookdeo, "The New Post-Heroic Leadership," *Fortune*, 21 February 1994, 42.

36. Burns, *Leadership*.

37. Peter Senge, *The Fifth Discipline: The Art and Practice of the Learning Organization* (New York: Doubleday/Currency, 1990), 340.

38. Huey and Sookdeo, 42–50.

39. Jim Collins, *From Good to Great: Why Some Companies Make the Leap and Others Don't* (New York: HarperCollins, 2001).

40. Huey and Sookdeo, 50.

41. William G. Pagonis, "The Work of the Leader," *Harvard Business Review* 70 (November–December 1992): 123.

42. Peter M. Senge, "Communities of Leaders and Learners," *Harvard Business Review* 75 (September–October 1997): 32.

43. Maccoby, *The Leader*, 21.

15

Chapter

Ethics

 Overview

A public library director has been instructed to provide information to government officials about the material borrowed by a patron. The director knows that providing library patron records violates the Code of Ethics of the American Library Association and is confused about what she should do.

A recent MLIS graduate has been offered a job in an information center in a bank that has been accused of discrimination in approving mortgages and other financial services to residents living in low-income neighborhoods. This practice conflicts with her personal values, and she wonders if she could be happy working in that organization.

The director of a small academic library has been invited for an all-expenses-paid visit to a vendor's corporate headquarters. He knows he would gain valuable information about the vendor's products but fears that the trip might influence his future purchasing decisions.

An employee in a special library is concerned that the software on his computer is illegal. His supervisor did not purchase enough site licenses for the department in an attempt to keep costs under control.

All of these examples are descriptions of incidences in which individuals in a workplace setting have to determine the right or ethical way to handle a problematic situation. In the past, many organizations just assumed that managers and employees would behave ethically. Since the early 2000s and the scandals that occurred in organizations such as Enron, World-Com, and Arthur Andersen, however, much more emphasis has been put on ethics in the workplace. Managers now realize that encouraging ethical behavior is an important part of managing in every organization.

This chapter will present an introduction to the topic of ethics and provide information about how to foster ethical working environments in libraries.

ETHICS IN MODERN ORGANIZATIONS

Every day individuals must make decisions and then act according to their beliefs about what they consider to be right or wrong. Ethics helps answer the question, "What should I do?" Ethics is usually defined as a set of principles and values that govern the behaviors of an individual or a group with respect to what is right and what is wrong. Whenever decisions need to be made, it is important to reflect on the ethical aspects of the choice as part of the process. Individuals face ethical issues both in and outside of the workplace. In this book, the discussion of ethics will be focused primarily on managerial and professional ethics, that is, the ethics that are found in the workplace.

Ethical problems are inevitable in any type of organization; library managers need to know about ethics and how to apply ethical principles to the decisions that confront them in the organizations they are managing. A chapter on ethics logically follows the preceding chapter on leadership because research has shown that the leaders in any type of organization set the ethical tone of that organization.[1] One study of more than a hundred corporate managers found that 90 percent of them agreed that employee attitudes toward ethical issues directly mirrored executive beliefs.[2] Other researchers have found that the best single predictor of how employees handle ethical dilemmas is the perceived values of top management.[3] A recent British study found that when employees were asked to rate 20 qualities they would want a manager to have, honesty was the top-rated attribute.[4] If the top managers in an organization routinely engage in questionable ethical principles, such as inflating expense accounts, taking supplies home for personal use, or revealing material that should be kept confidential, then others in the organization will consider those acceptable ways of behaving. It is important for any organization to be clear about its ethical expectations, and the individuals who most commonly act as role models in establishing those expectations are the organization's leaders. They provide guidance for the rest of the organization's employees in what is expected ethically.

ETHICS—A DEFINITION

The whole idea of ethics can be a bit confusing, and many people find if difficult to precisely define what they mean when the use the term *ethics*. Ethics is often confused with morals or even law, but these three terms refer to different concepts. Although the terms *ethics* and *morals* are often used interchangeably, they are not identical. Morals typically refer to the practices of individuals, whereas ethics refers to the overarching rationales behind such practices. Some people feel that it is immoral to drink alcoholic beverages, but that is an individual moral belief or value that does not mean that drinking itself is unethical.

There is also often confusion in many people's minds about the differences between ethical standards and the law. Usually what is considered ethical is also legal, but that is not always so. Ethics is a branch of philosophy, and its principles are derived from theories of what is right and wrong. Law is more concerned with rules that stabilize societies than promoting social ideals. It is incorrect to assume that if something is legal, it is also ethical. Ethics often requires a higher standard than laws, and although what is ethical is usually legal, in some cases, ethics conflicts with law. Capital punishment is legal in many states in the United States, but many citizens think that the death penalty is unethical even where it is legal. Some physicians have broken the law by prescribing marijuana to dying patients to ease pain. For them, the ethical requirement of lessening suffering is a more important concern than laws regarding use of illegal drugs.

Another factor that leads to confusion about ethics is that ideas about ethical behavior can change over time. At one time, slaveholding was considered ethical by most people in society, and now it is been abolished as an abhorrent practice in almost all societies. In addition, ethics are affected by societal and cultural norms. Practices that are considered ethical in some countries would not be consider ethical in others. For instance, polygamy is recognized as ethical in a few places but not in most. Child labor is still common in many developing countries, but it would be considered unethical (as well as illegal) to employ children in factories in most of the world.

 Some Definitions

Ethics: The rules or standards governing the conduct of a person or the members of a profession.
Morals: Rules or habits of conduct, especially of sexual conduct, with reference to standards of right and wrong.
Laws: The body of rules and principles governing the affairs of a community and enforced by a political authority; a legal system.

The American Heritage Dictionary of the English Language, 4th ed. (New York: Houghton Mifflin, 2000).

Because ethical standards are not codified like laws and are not uniform across time and place, it is often difficult to decide what action should be taken when an ethical decision needs to be made. Often individuals must make decisions based on their judgments rather than on indisputable facts. Many times there seems to be no one right ethical solution, instead there are alternative choices, none of which is perfect. These situations are referred to as ethical dilemmas. One common example often used to illustrate an ethical dilemma concerns stealing. Stealing is usually considered to be unethical, but would stealing would be justified if stealing food were the only way to feed a family? Which is of higher value, personal property or feeding one's family?

In organizations, employees are faced with similar ethical dilemmas. For example, you supervise a single mother who is often absent from work. You have given her warnings, but she continues to be absent about one day a week—often because one or more of her children are ill. You know she is the only source of support for her family. Are you justified in dismissing her for excessive absenteeism? Managers often experience situations in which their professional responsibilities come into conflict with their personal values. Many times there is no clear-cut right or wrong decision. Knowing about ethics helps in solving these situations.

What Do You Think?

Albert Einstein once said, "Relativity applies to physics, not ethics."
Do you agree with this statement? Are ethical principles always the same, or do they change with the situation?

THE IMPORTANCE OF ETHICS

Although some individuals consider ethics in the workplace to be a frill or an add-on, ethics is an integral part of good business. Organizations that exploit the labor force, take advantage of customers, or deny product defects incur huge costs that ultimately hurt the organization. Consider the difference in ethical approach between the large tobacco companies, which attempted to deny the ill effects of nicotine, and Johnson & Johnson, which voluntarily recalled all of its Tylenol products in an early product-tampering case. The tobacco companies were severely punished by penalty costs imposed by the courts, whereas Johnson & Johnson won widespread praise and customer loyalty by its ethical stand. Organizations that are well respected and profitable are almost always marked by good ethical practices.

Of course, individual employees sometimes act in opposition to the organizational norms. Each employee brings his or her individual ethical values to an organization. These values have been shaped in an individual's early years by parents, relatives, teachers, and culture, and they represent an individual's basic convictions about what is right and what is wrong. Because these individual values usually differ from person to person, any one organization can have individuals working in it with widely varying ethical values. Each employee, with his or her own values, is then exposed to the norms of the organization. Ideally, these norms would conform to the individual's values, but sometimes they do not. Finally, the behavior of individuals in the workplace is affected by external factors such as the norms of society or laws and regulations. These three sets of factors influencing ethical behavior can be seen in figure 15.1.

Even though the ethical behavior of individuals is influenced by many factors, research has shown that an organization's ethical norms have a strong

Figure 15.1—Factors Influencing Ethical Behavior

Factors Influencing Ethical Behavior in the Workplace

The Individual
- Family values
- Religion
- Values of peers outside of work

The Workplace
- Behavior of managers and colleagues
- Policies and codes

External Environment
- Norms of society
- Laws and regulations
- Professional codes of ethics

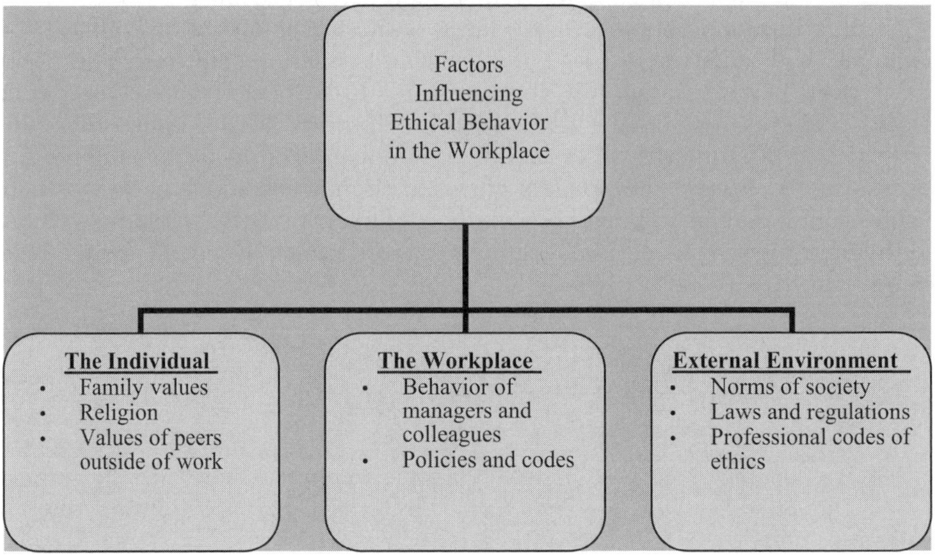

influence on how employees act and their ideas of right and wrong within that organization. James Weber and Janet Gillespie found that corporate culture is recognized as a key contextual influence in establishing and maintaining ethical norms.[5] Linda Trevino and Michael Brown state that much unethical conduct is the result of "neglectful leadership and organizational cultures that send mixed messages about what if important and what is expected."[6] So employees' organizational values are influenced by the organization's ethical climate. Unethical actions within an organization "involve the tacit, if not explicit, cooperation of others and reflect the values, attitudes, beliefs, language, and behavioral patterns that define an organization's operating culture. Ethics, then, is as much an organizational as a personal issue."[7] Thus it is the responsibility of mangers to provide leadership in ethics because those "who fail to provide proper leadership and to institute systems that facilitate ethical conduct share responsibility with those who conceive, execute, and knowingly benefit from corporate misdeeds."[8]

Some companies such as Johnson & Johnson have been known for decades as institutions that pride themselves on integrity and ethical behavior. Robert Wood Johnson, one of the early presidents of Johnson & Johnson, developed a credo for the organization in the 1940s, and this simple one-page document has guided the actions of the employees of Johnson & Johnson from that date. The credo clearly states the organization's responsibilities to four separate sets of stakeholders in the company—customers, employees, communities, and stockholders—and emphasizes that the organization puts its responsibility to customers before profits.[9]

In the past few years, ethics has become an increasingly important concern to all organizations. The corporate scandals that occurred in organizations such as Enron and WorldCom not only brought adverse publicity to the organizations but they also caused great damage to the people who worked in these organizations or who had relied upon them for service. These cases have resulted in a new wave of corporate reform efforts, primarily the Sarbanes-Oxley Act passed by the U.S. Congress in 2002, which was designed to make accounting practices more transparent and to protect investors. Some of the most egregious corporate misdeeds took place at the Enron Corporation. It has been suggested that one could teach an entire ethics course by using Enron as an example of what not to do. Although Enron was considered to be a "company of the future," it "sought to circumvent or avoid systems that were designed to protect the company and its shareholders and to bolster the credibility of its dealings."[10] Although no library has had an ethical scandal as immense as that at Enron, given the frequent occurrence of unethical and illegal behavior in highly respected organizations, it is critical to understand and to promote ethical conduct in all types of organizations, including libraries.

THE ETHICAL INFORMATION PROFESSIONAL

Ethics are especially important to practicing professionals such as doctors, lawyers, and librarians because there are specific ethical issues that need to be confronted in all these professions. Subfields of ethics such as biomedical and legal ethics have developed that are particularly relevant to certain professions. One subfield of ethics that relates directly to librarians and information specialists is the field of information ethics. Information ethics is the "branch of ethics that focuses on the relationship between the creation, organization, dissemination, and use of information and the ethical and moral codes governing human conduct in society."[11] Information ethics has become more important since the burgeoning of technologies, such as the Internet, which have posed new problems relating to our ethical understanding of such issues as privacy, censorship, and intellectual property. This subfield of ethics is concerned about issues such as relationship between information and the good of society and the relationship between information providers and the consumers of information. Information ethics also covers other areas such as access to information, intellectual freedom, plagiarism, copyright, and digital divide issues.

Although many of the problems relating to ethics that are confronted in libraries are similar to those in other organizational settings, each type of organization encounters some problems that are unique to that type of setting, and the context must be considered. Martha Smith has provided a model of the conflicting loyalties that are often experienced by information professionals.[12] This model can be seen in figure 15.2. The multiple loyalties of information professionals include loyalties to:

Self; includes personal integrity, job security, and personal responsibilities.

Clients or patrons; includes privacy of information, freedom of access, serving patron needs.

Figure 15.2—Multiple Loyalties of Information Professionals

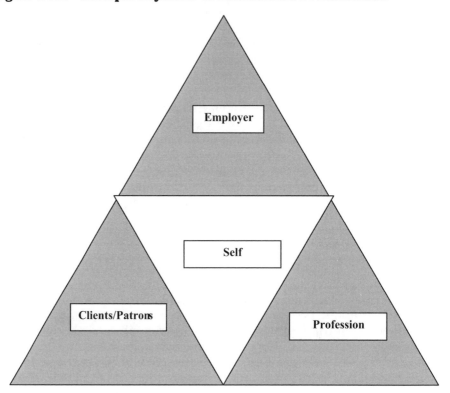

Profession; includes professional standards of service and the responsibility to raise the public knowledge of issues identified by the profession.

Employing institution; includes loyalty to employer, upholding the goals and priorities of the institution, and working for its good.[13]

Ideally, these four loyalties would function together, but sometimes there is conflict among the loyalties, and then a professional has to negotiate among conflicting claims. Smith provides the following example. Imagine a situation in which a library director is asked by city officials to monitor circulation records to aid in the investigation of the illegal manufacturing of drugs. Which loyalty will have priority? Loyalty to the patron and to the profession would likely cause her to refuse. However, loyalty to the employing institution or to self might cause her to comply.[14]

This model demonstrates the complexity that is involved in making ethical professional decisions and can be a useful tool when managers in libraries need to reason through a multifaceted situation that causes conflict between personal, professional, and institutional loyalties. When managers confront difficult decisions, they should first think of the alternative solutions or actions that might be taken and then review them in light of the four loyalties discussed previously to see if their decision is being unduly influenced in any way.

PROBLEMATIC ETHICAL SITUATIONS

Managers confront many different types of ethical problems on the job. Problematic ethical situations or ethical dilemmas often consist of a conflict between the needs of a part and the needs of the whole. These may be the conflicts between the needs of an individual employee and the organization as a whole or between the needs of an organization and society as a whole. Pharmaceutical companies have come under increasing criticism because of their decision to make profits for the stockholder and charge high prices for AIDS drugs instead of making them available at low costs, especially to impoverished individuals or nations.

In the for-profit world, a great deal of the unethical behavior that has occurred has been a result of trying to maximize profits at any cost, including engaging in unethical or illegal activities. Because most libraries are not-for-profit organizations, they do not usually face the problem of trying to balance ethical behavior with increasing profits to stockholders or owners.

Libraries, like other organizations, often face ethical issues in the area of human resource management. Need for confidentiality and conflict between the rights of the individual and the rights of the institution were the top two ethical issues identified in one survey of library administrators. The other top ethical issues mentioned were fair treatment of employees, affirmative action/equal opportunity, discipline and firing, and performance appraisals.[15] Some of the ethical issues relating to human resources and staffing were discussed in previous chapters in this book.

Another type of ethical dilemma often found in a professional situation is that of individual conflict of interest. A conflict of interest exists when an individual who has to make a job-related decision has an outside interest in the outcome that may influence the objectivity of the decision making. Usually these interests are financial, but sometimes they may be personal, for instance, when an individual hires as a summer intern the daughter of a friend instead of doing an objective job search to fill that position.

Kenneth Kernaghan and John Langford list seven types of conflicts of interest. All of them might be confronted by librarians in the course of their official duties.

1. **Self-dealing.** This means using a management position for personal advantage. For example, self-dealing would be a librarian who uses his or her position to secure a contract for a private consulting firm partially owned by that librarian's spouse.

2. **Accepting benefits.** These are any benefits that might be thought to affect independent judgment. For instance, some libraries have policies against allowing collection development librarians to be entertained by vendors to avoid having any suggestion that a vendor selection decision might be influenced by accepting a certain vendor's hospitality.

3. **Influence peddling.** This consists of an individual soliciting benefits in exchange for unfairly advancing the interests of another party. For example, a librarian who is instrumental in the selection of a new

automated system might be accused of influence peddling if that individual agreed to advocate for a particular system in return for the vendor offering him or her a part-time position.

4. **Using an employer's property for private advantage.** This could involve taking office supplies for home use or using software licensed to an employer for personal use.

5. **Using confidential information** involves using information that you become privy to as part of your position to your own advantage. For example, a reference librarian who becomes aware of confidential information about a person by means of a reference interview and reveals that information in a way that advantages the librarian.

6. **Outside employment or moonlighting.** For example, a conflict of interest would arise if an employee spent so much time on an outside consulting job that the regular job was neglected.

7. **Postemployment** conflict of interest occurs when an employee uses knowledge or information gained in a position to benefit after leaving that position. Perhaps an employee in the library of a private corporation resigns and uses knowledge from the previous employment to compete directly with his or her former employer.[16]

 ## What Would You Do?

You are the reference librarian on duty at a large public library. Two teenagers come in and ask for instructions on how to build a car bomb. Would you:

- Help them all you could?
- Call the police?
- Ask your supervisor for advice?
- Ask them why they want the information?

You are the director of a small academic library. An automation vendor offers to take you to dinner at a national meeting. Would you:

- Accept with thanks?
- Go ahead but pay your own way?
- Decline the invitation?
- Ask if another director friend could come too?

Patrons in your small inner-city public library have complained about homeless people taking baths in the library rest room and sleeping on the furniture. Would you:

- Lock the restrooms and have people get a key from the staff so that restroom use could be monitored?
- Put signs up discouraging inappropriate use of the library?

- Have the police remove persons who are sleeping or using the library to bathe?
- Suggest that patrons start a shelter for the homeless?

Adapted from Martha M. Smith, "The Ethics Quiz," *North Carolina Libraries* (Spring 1993), 28–30, and used by permission. (To continue to test your knowledge of ethics, see more questions on this quiz at http://www.lu.com/management.)

The Ethics Quiz allows you to try to decide what you would do in response to a few examples of ethical dilemmas that might arise in a library setting. As you can see, deciding what is the ethical thing do is not always clear-cut or easy.

TOOLS FOR ETHICAL DECISION MAKING

When managers or employees are confronted with an ethical dilemma, what should they do? How should they think through the issue, and what factors should they consider?

Obviously, an important first step in analyzing any ethical issue is to gather all the information that is available. Sometimes individuals make wrong decisions because they are not aware of all of the facts concerning the case. But getting the facts is not enough. Facts give us information about a decision, but they do not tell us what should be done. There are a number of different approaches that people can use to deal with ethical issues.

Normative Ethical Frameworks

Philosophers have developed a number of different approaches to dealing with ethical issues, including the development of a variety of normative ethical frameworks that can be used for evaluating behavior. The frameworks can be seen in figure 15.3. In brief, the most common frameworks are:

- **Utilitarianism.** Using this framework, an individual would behave in a way that produces the greatest good for the greatest number of people. For instance, a manager might decide to ban all smoking in the workplace because more employees will benefit from this policy than will be hurt by it.

- **Individual rights.** This is the framework that states that all individuals have inalienable rights, such as rights to privacy, freedom of speech, and due process, and that these rights should not be abridged. An employer might make the decision not to look at e-mail logs because he or she considers that a violation of employees' privacy rights.

- **Social justice.** This approach holds that decisions must be based on standards that involve the fair treatment of all, fair application of rules, and fair compensation. This framework would ensure that there would be no discrimination among employees on such factors and race, religion, or gender. An employer would compensate all workers doing the same job equally.

Figure 15.3—Normative Frameworks

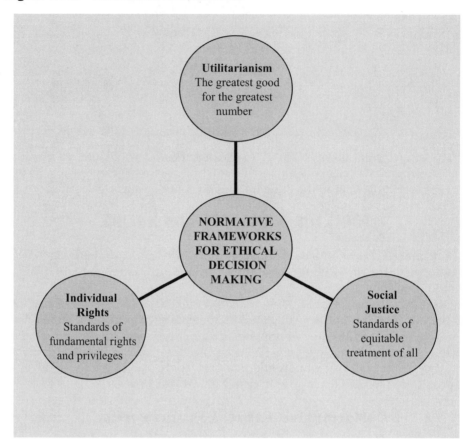

These ethical frameworks give a manager a context to use in considering ethical problems and a means of identifying the most important ethical considerations, but they often do not provide clear-cut solutions. Instead, sometimes they provide different, often contradictory, answers to the problem. For instance, in 2000 the North Carolina Museum of Art had to make a difficult choice about a painting that the museum had bought to be part of its permanent collection. After its purchase, this painting was found to have been stolen by the Nazis during World War II. The descendents of its original owner asked the museum for restitution of the painting.[17] It could be argued using the utilitarian framework that the greatest good would be produced by leaving it in the museum where many visitors could see it on display. However, other arguments could be mounted using the other two frameworks, which would support the rights of the descendents of the owner from whom the painting was stolen. In this particular instance, a compromise was reached. The museum paid compensation to the owner's descendents for the painting, and it remained in the museum. Unfortunately, there are often no real right and wrong answers in ethical situations, and compromises have to be made. The frameworks give managers a way of viewing ethical dilemmas and putting them in a broader perspective.

Codes of Ethics

Many organizations have codes of ethics designed to guide individuals within the organization in acting ethically. In addition to individual codes in specific organizations, many professional organizations have developed codes of ethics designed to guide individual conduct within a profession. Most large corporations in the United States and many in other countries around the world have developed their own codes of ethics.[18] Many of these companies' codes of ethics are available on their Web sites. For instance, BellSouth[19] and Lockheed Martin[20] have their codes of ethics posted on their Web sites. Fewer libraries have developed their own individual codes of ethics. Although there have been suggestions that libraries develop codes of ethics for library administrators, such codes have never been developed.[21] Instead, most libraries have subscribed to a professional code of ethics. For example, the American Library Association has a code of ethics that can be seen in figure 15.4. The Medical Library Association also has developed its own code of ethics for health sciences librarians.[22] National libraries or librarians' associations around the world have developed professional codes of ethics. A large number of such professional codes can be seen at the International Federation of Library Associations and Institutions (http://www.ifla.org/faife/ethics/codes.htm). It is interesting to compare and contrast the elements found in each of these professional codes and to see how each group's code varies in some aspects from the others.

The value of both institutional and professional codes of ethics depends on how they are used. If the importance of a particular code is taught to all employees, if top managers affirm such codes, and if individuals who go against the code are punished, codes can be important in shaping behavior. If such a code is used only as window dressing, it will be ineffective in providing a guide to ethical behavior. Enron had a 64-page code of ethics that was distributed to all employees, but obviously the code was ignored by many of the managers in the company.[23]

 What Do You Think?

It often has been said that reputation is how others perceive you and character is how you act when no one is watching. Is it inevitable for people to behave differently when they are being observed by others, or does the truly ethical person always behave the same?

Other Frameworks for Ethical Decision Making

Experts provide other frameworks, including a list of questions that individuals can use to assess whether they are confronting any problematic situation in an ethical way. For instance, questions such as the ones in table 15.1 provide guidance to an individual trying to reach an ethical decision. Other managers use such guidelines by asking such questions as: "Would you be proud to tell

Figure 15.4—The Code of Ethics of the American Library Association

> ## Code of Ethics of the American Library Association
>
> As members of the American Library Association, we recognize the importance of codifying and making known to the profession and to the general public the ethical principles that guide the work of librarians, other professionals providing information services, library trustees, and library staffs.
>
> Ethical dilemmas occur when values are in conflict. The American Library Association Code of Ethics states the values to which we are committed and embodies the ethical responsibilities of the profession in this changing information environment.
>
> We significantly influence or control the selection, organization, preservation, and dissemination of information. In a political system grounded in an informed citizenry, we are members of a profession explicitly committed to intellectual freedom and the freedom of access to information. We have a special obligation to ensure the free flow of information and ideas to present and future generations.
>
> The principles of this Code are expressed in broad statements to guide ethical decision making. These statements provide a framework; they cannot and do not dictate conduct to cover particular situations.
>
> *1. We provide the highest level of service to all library users through appropriate and usefully organized resources; equitable service policies; equitable access; and accurate, unbiased, and courteous responses to all requests.*
>
> *2. We uphold the principles of intellectual freedom and resist all efforts to censor library resources.*
>
> *3. We protect each library user's right to privacy and confidentiality with respect to information sought or received and resources consulted, borrowed, acquired, or transmitted.*
>
> *4. We recognize and respect intellectual property rights.*
>
> *5. We treat co-workers and other colleagues with respect, fairness, and good faith and advocate conditions of employment that safeguard the rights and welfare of all employees of our institutions.*
>
> *6. We do not advance private interests at the expense of library users, colleagues, or our employing institutions.*
>
> *7. We distinguish between our personal convictions and professional duties and do not allow our personal beliefs to interfere with fair representation of the aims of our institutions or the provision of access to their information resources.*
>
> *8. We strive for excellence in the profession by maintaining and enhancing our own knowledge and skills, by encouraging the professional development of co-workers, and by fostering the aspirations of potential members of the profession.*
>
> Adopted June 28, 1995, by the ALA Council

Source: Reprinted with permission.

your parents or grandparents about the decision you have made?" "Are you able to sleep well at night?" "How would you feel if interviewers from your local television station showed up with cameras to ask about your actions?" Questions like these may help focus an individual's response to a perplexing problem. But

TABLE 15.1 Questions for Examining the Ethics of a Business Decision

1. Has the problem been defined accurately?
2. Would you define the problem differently if you stood on the other side of the issue?
3. How did the situation occur in the first place?
4. To whom and to what do you give your loyalty as a person and as a member of the organization?
5. What is your intention in making this decision?
6. How does this intention compare with the likely results?
7. Whom might your decision or action injure?
8. Can you discuss the problem with the person or persons likely to be affected before you make the decision?
9. Are you confident that your decision will be just as valid over time as it seems now?
10. Could you disclose without qualm this decision to your boss, your board of directors, your family, or to society as a whole?
11. What is the symbolic potential of your action if understood? If misunderstood?
12. Under what conditions would you allow exceptions to this decision?

Source: L. L. Nash, "Ethics without the Sermon," *Harvard Business Review* 58, no. 6 (November–December 1981): 81.

ethical dilemmas are not easy; sometimes there are no readily apparent correct answers, or there is more than one approach that might be taken.

ETHICS TRAINING

Managers must realize that all of the ethical frameworks, codes, and question-asking approaches described previously are useless unless they are communicated to employees and employees are taught to use them. As was mentioned earlier, individuals have their own set of ethical guidelines, and these guidelines can differ a great deal even among employees who are largely homogeneous. As organizations employ a greater diversity of employees, it is important to remember that different cultures often have different beliefs about what is acceptable ethical behavior, and it can never be assumed that an employee understands the ethical expectations of an organization without training. A number of institutions in the private sector have instituted ethics training programs to train employees about the ethical standards expected within the organization on topics varying from sexual harassment to insider stock trading. In addition, some have set up hotlines to allow employees to seek guidance or to report wrongdoings.[24] Although trying to teach people to behave ethically is not an easy thing to do, ethics training can be useful because it reinforces the organization's standards and reminds the employee that these standards are important to the organization.

What Would You Do?

Drew Pope put down his pencil, pushed back in his chair, stretched his arms over his head, and looked out the window. It was a warm Indian-summer day. The maple trees that lined the Allenby Public Library parking lot reached toward the sun like a hedge of orange fire. The smell of their dry, aromatic leaves spiced the gentle breeze. "What a day to be inside!" he said, meditatively addressing the emptiness of the room. With considerable reluctance, he spun his chair around and was about to return to his papers when Preston Huish put his head into the room.

"Have a minute, Drew?" the selectman asked, perkily.

"Sure," smiled the library director, "Glad to see you. Won't you sit down, Preston?" He didn't know the selectman well, but they were on a first-name basis.

Pope studied him with questioning eyes, his hand reaching for the remainder of his coffee.

Huish spoke, "My daughter, Lisa, applied for a page's job at the beginning of September, and yesterday she stopped by to see the circulation head to find out when she would be starting. Ms. Wren told her that she was number 18 on the waiting list and that it would be quite some time before she would be called."

The dim thought at the back of the director's mind, "You're about to ask a favor of me. I can tell." But he kept his own counsel.

The selectman continued, "Would you personally look into this and see if she can't be moved up on the list? She's in her final year of high school, and she's saving to go away to college next year. She's bright and a really reliable kid. I'd appreciate it if you'd move her to the top of the list."

For the rest of this case study, see http://www.lu.com/management.

GUIDELINES FOR MANAGERS TO PROMOTE ETHICAL BEHAVIOR

Ethics are crucial to every organization, but as a recent article by Trevino and Brown stated, "Ethics isn't easy." Unethical conduct has been with us throughout history, but today there are more gray areas and more opportunities for people to engage in unethical behavior. These authors provide a set of guidelines for improving ethics management in any type of organization. These guidelines are:

1. Understand the existing ethical culture. To manage effectively, a manager must understand the ethical culture. Tools such as anonymous surveys and focus groups can help a manager find out what employees really think the ethical climate of the organization to be. Do employees feel that people who act ethically are rewarded and those who do not are punished? What do employees think you need to do to succeed in the organization?

2. Communicate the importance of ethics. Managers need to be sure that they send clear and consistent messages that ethics is essential. It is not enough to tell people to do the right thing. Employees need to be educated about the types of ethical issues that may arise in the organization and discuss ethics and values when decisions are being made.

3. Focus on the reward system. Managers should be certain that ethical behavior is rewarded, not punished. Be sure that employees realize that getting ahead, no matter how you do it, is not tolerated.

4. Promote ethical leadership. The top managers in a firm must demonstrate ethical behavior themselves if they want to encourage it in those who are below them in the organization. Managers must send out explicit messages about ethics because ethical cultures go hand in hand with ethical leaders. Ethical leadership also must be stressed by middle managers and supervisors. In for-profit organizations, it is important to stress that ethical behavior is more important than short-term, bottom-line profits.[25]

CONCLUSION

Ethics is an important topic, and it is often complex because there are so many gray areas. Obviously, there are some elements, such as restrictions on physically harming another person, that would be agreed upon by almost everyone. But there are many other areas in which ambiguity exists, and even people with the best of intentions often will disagree about the right thing to do. All managers should demonstrate the importance of ethics by their own behavior, should be certain that appropriate codes of behavior are in place and that employees are informed of them, and should monitor the behavior of employees to be sure that they are complying. Managing ethically is not easy, but it is a responsibility of all managers to uphold high ethical standards within their organizations.

NOTES

1. See, for instance, Robert Jackyll, "Moral Mazes: Bureaucracy and Managerial Work," *Harvard Business Review* 61 (September–October 1983): 118–30.

2. Marshall B. Clinard, *Corporate Ethics and Crime* (London: Sage, 1983).

3. Shelby D. Hunt, Lawrence B. Chonko, and James B. Wilcox, "Ethical Problems of Marketing Researchers," *Journal of Marketing Research* 21 (1984): 304–24.

4. Adrian Furnham, "Rating a Boss, a Colleague, and a Subordinate," *Journal of Managerial Psychology* 17 (December 2002): 668.

5. James Weber and Janet Gillespie, "Differences in Ethical Beliefs, Intentions, and Behaviors," *Business and Society* 37 (December 1998): 447–68.

6. Linda Klebe Trevino and Michael E. Brown, "Managing to Be Ethical: Debunking Five Business Ethics Myths," *Academy of Management Executive* 18 (May 2004): 80.

7. Lynn Sharp Paine, "Managing for Organizational Integrity," *Harvard Business Review* 72 (March–April 1994): 106.

8. Ibid.

9. The Johnson & Johnson credo (2005) can be seen at http://www.jnj.com/our_company/our_credo/index.htm.

10. Ronald Berenbeim, , "Enron's Syllabus of Errors: A Primer on Ethics," *Directorship* 22 (March 2002): 8

11. Joan M. Reitz, *Dictionary for Information and Library Science* (Westport, CT: Libraries Unlimited, 2004).

12. Martha Montague Smith, "Infoethics for Leaders: Models of Moral Agency in the Information Environment," *Library Trends* 40, no. 3 (Winter 1992): 553–70.

13. Ibid., 558–60.

14. Ibid., 562.

15. "Ethics and Personnel," *Library Personnel News* 2, no. 2 (1988): 21–22.

16. Kenneth Kernaghan and John W. Langford, *The Responsible Public Servant* (Halifax, NS: Institute for Research in Public Policy, 1990).

17. Emily Yellen, "North Carolina Art Museum Says It Will Return Painting Tied to Nazi Theft," *The New York Times,* 6 February 2000, 22.

18. Gary R. Weaver, Linda K. Trevino, and P. L. Cochran, "Corporate Ethics Practices in the Mid-1990s," *Journal of Business Ethics* 18 (1999): 283–94.

19. See Office of Ethics and Compliance, BellSouth Corp., "About Us" (n.d.), http://www.ethics.bellsouth.com/.

20. See Lockheed Martin, "Code of Ethics: Code of Ethics and Business Conduct" (2006), http://www.lockheedmartin.com/wms/findPage.do?dsp=fec&ci=13120&rsbci=12911&fti=0&ti=0&sc=400.

21. Sharon L. Baker, "Needed: An Ethical Code for Library Administrators," *Journal of Library Administration* 16, no. 4 (1992): 1–17.

22. See Medical Library Association, "Goals and Principles for Ethical Conduct," MLANET (1994), https://www.mlanet.org/about/ethics.html.

23. If you would like to read the code, see the *Enron Code of Ethics* (2000) at The Smoking Gun, http://www.thesmokinggun.com/graphics/packageart/enron/enron.pdf.

24. M. J. McCarthy, "How One Firm Tracks Ethics Electronically," *The Wall Street Journal,* 21 October 1999, 81.

25. Trevino and Brown, "Managing to Be Ethical," 78–80.

Chapter 16

Communication

Overview

The head of the cataloging department has scheduled a performance review for a beginning cataloger later today. The new cataloger has an unacceptably high error rate, and the department head is contemplating how she can convey the need to improve to the new employee without discouraging him. In the same library, the librarians in the instruction department are discussing the best way to alert faculty and students about a comprehensive new user instruction program that is being implemented next semester. They are especially concerned about the large number of distance-education students and wonder how they can most effectively inform these off-campus users. In the library's administrative suite, the director has just received news from the university president that the library's budget will be cut next year by another 5 percent as a result of a legislative budget reduction. She is concerned about the best way to convey this message to the library's employees, especially to those who have been worried that they might be laid off their jobs if there were another budget cut.

Each of these librarians is confronting a need to communicate information in the most effective manner possible. Although some managerial functions such as budgeting and planning are done only periodically, every manager (and every employee) engages in communication on a daily basis. If there are problems in communication, inevitably there are problems within the organization.

This chapter will provide an overview of organizational communication, looking first at communication as a function within an organization. Types of communication and ways to promote effective communication will then be discussed. The chapter will close with an overview of conflict and how it can be managed.

Communication is a key ingredient in effective leadership. Since 1938, when Chester Barnard identified the main task of an executive as that of communication, it has been commonly accepted that communication is a critical skill for any manager. Barnard viewed communication as the means by which people in an organization are linked together in order to achieve a central purpose.[1] Most managers spend a large part of their time communicating with other people; some estimates of the percentage of time a manager spends in communication range as high as 95 percent. In his study of managerial behavior, Henry Mintzberg found that most managerial time was spent in verbal communication, on the telephone, and in meetings.[2]

THE IMPORTANCE OF COMMUNICATION

Communication in organizations is more varied today than ever before because so many new communication options are available. Electronic mail, voice mail, cell phones, PDAs, instant messaging, and teleconferencing provide new channels of communication for organizations to use both internally and externally. New forms of communication such as blogging are becoming more and more popular.[3] These methods have helped minimize the effects of time and distance, which slow down the communication process. In knowledge organizations, such as libraries and information centers, communication is the lifeblood of the organization. Employees in such organizations are constantly involved in the absorption and dissemination of information and ideas. In fact, sometimes people working in information agencies feel that there is so much communication available through so many channels that it leads to information overload and confusion. Many employees receive more information than they can assimilate and are unable to filter the less important so they can concentrate on what really matters. In addition, with the growing popularity of cell phones and PDAs, some employees are rarely out of range of organizational communication, and there is no longer a clear dividing line between professional and personal communication.

A MODEL OF COMMUNICATION

At first glance, it appears that communication should be simple. We all communicate every day, and we all have been doing it since we learned to talk (actually before we learned to talk). But what at first glance seems simple is actually quite complex. It is a process composed of many factors. A number of models of the communication process have been developed to help explicate it. Although these models vary, they typically include the following components:

- **A source.** This is the sender of the message. The source has some thought, need, or information to communicate.

- **A message.** The source has to encode the message in some form that can be understood by both sender and receiver.

- **The channel.** The channel is the link between the source and the receiver. The message is transmitted over the channel. A channel can take many forms. For instance, a telephone is an example of a channel that can be used to link the source and the receiver.

- **The receiver.** The receiver is the recipient of the message. The receiver has to decode the message for it to be understood.

- **Noise.** Noise is anything that hinders communication. Noise may occur in the source, the message, the channel, or the receiver. For instance, if the receiver cannot understand the message, noise has occurred. This could be because the message contained ambiguous phrases, because there was static on the channel, or because the message was in a language not understood by the receiver. Even the simplest communication is filled with opportunities for noise to occur.

- **Feedback.** After the receiver receives and decodes the message, the receiver can become a source and provide feedback by encoding and sending a message through some channel back to the original source. Feedback is a response to the original message. Feedback is always useful because it allows the original source to know if the message was properly encoded, transmitted, decoded, and understood. It is this feedback loop that is the difference between one-way and two-way communication. One-way communication is almost never as effective as two-way communication because the sender has no way of knowing if the message was received and understood.

 Try This!

Remember the telephone game you used to play when you were a child? One person begins with a message and whispers it to the next person until the message has gone around the entire room. Usually, the message that is heard by the last person bears little resemblance to what the first person said. Besides being fun, this activity demonstrates how easily information can become garbled by indirect communication and noise. Try the traditional telephone game with a group, and then try it with a variation. Each person who receives the message is allowed to check with the person transmitting it to be sure they understood correctly. How much more accurate was the second message than the first?

To illustrate this model, imagine a library director wanting to let a department head know about an important meeting. The library director would be the source of the communication. When the library director provided information about the meeting in the form of an e-mail announcement, the e-mail would be the message. The channel employed for the communication would be the library's e-mail system. The receiver is the department head who receives the message and reads it. If the e-mail system crashes or if the e-mail message goes into the department head's spam filter, that would be noise. The feedback would be the response the department head sends the library director about the meeting. The elements in this simple communication model are illustrated in figure 16.1.

Communication exists in many forms and in many settings. Often, we think of communication primarily in terms of personal communication. However, every organization must have some way to bind its disparate parts if it is to achieve its goals and purposes. Communication provides cohesiveness and direction. As Alex Bavels and Dermot Barrett state, "It is entirely possible to view an organization as an elaborate system for gathering, evaluating, recombining, and disseminating information.... Communication is not a secondary or derived aspect of an organization—a 'helper' of the other and presumably more basic functions. Rather, it is the essence of organized activity and the basic process out of which all other functions derive."[4] Communication is so important that Peter Drucker has argued that organizations should not be built around hierarchies but around communication.[5] Communication is the process that makes it possible to unify organizational activity.

ORGANIZATIONAL COMMUNICATION

Organizational communication has been defined by Gerald Goldhaber as "the process of creating and exchanging messages within a network of interdependent relationships to cope with environmental uncertainty."[6] All organizational communication shares certain characteristics. It occurs within a complex, open system that is influenced by and influences its environment; it involves messages and their flow, purpose, direction, and media; and it involves people and their attitudes, feelings, relationships, and skills.[7]

Figure 16.1—A Model of the Communication Process

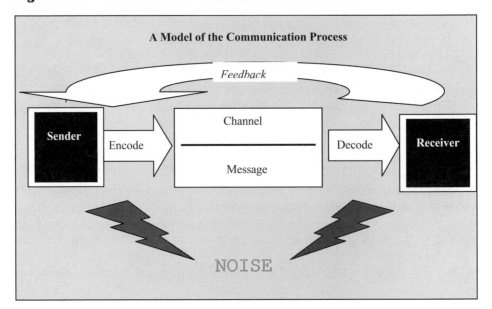

What Do You Think?

Communication problems are very common in all organizations. It is sometimes said that if we could only communicate better within organizations all our problems would disappear. Do you agree with this statement?

Managers never should assume that all workers will understand the messages communicated. This is especially important to remember as the workforce becomes more diversified. Studies have shown that various ethnic groups and that men and women have different styles of communication. Deborah Tannen studied gender differences in communication and found that men's and women's styles vary greatly. She attributes this to different values assimilated by young girls and boys. Males are taught to prize status, independence, and individual power, but females are taught to value connection, interdependence, and the power of community. These differing values lead men and women to communicate in different ways. The resulting differences in the communication styles of men and women can cause misunderstanding in the workplace.[8]

Different ethnic groups also have different styles of communication. For example, in some cultures, it is considered rude to maintain eye contact with someone while they are speaking. Some cultures encourage interruption. Every communication practice is based on certain cultural rules, and as our workplaces become more diversified, managers need to understand the cultural differences that may affect communication flows. Just because two people share a common language does not mean that they can communicate easily. These differences are often more than linguistic and instead are frequently sociopolitical-attitudinal in nature. Everyone should try to be aware of the cultural biases that may impede his or her communication and interactions with others.[9]

Another barrier that sometimes gets in the way of communication is the use of jargon. Jargon is the specialized language that is developed by individuals in groups, and each profession tends to have its own jargon. That is certainly true of librarianship. Think of all the acronyms and technical terms that are associated with the LIS profession. AACR2, ACRL, ARL, ALA, AASL, ASIS&T, ASCII, ALCS, abstracts, acquisitions, accessions, and authority control are just a few of the ones that begin with the letter *a*. Even within the profession, not every individual understands all of these terms, and when librarians begin to communicate with nonlibrarians, it is not surprising that the nonlibrarians are often completely befuddled. Using the language of the communication model presented earlier, it is easy for anyone who understands the jargon to encode it in a message, but it is much more difficult for receivers to decode if they are not familiar with the jargon. Because jargon has the potential of creating noise, it should be avoided unless it is absolutely certain that the receiver will understand it.

TYPES OF COMMUNICATION

Communication can be classified in three general categories: written, oral, and nonverbal. Each of these types of communication plays a specific role in organizational communication, and each has certain associated advantages and disadvantages.

Written Communication

Formal channels of command often require written communication. Managers write memos, e-mail messages, letters, reports, directives, and policies. Written communication provides a lasting record and ensures uniformity in matters like policy, but this type of communication often is flawed. Some of these communications may be poorly written, may not fully explain the action desired, or may not completely define the scope of the problem. Employees may be left with ambiguous instructions. Words used in this type of communication are frequently unclear and ill defined, and written communication allows no opportunity for immediate feedback and clarification. Hence, it may take a long time to know if the message has been received and understood.

Many organizations have tried to improve their written communication, especially their communication with customers. Organizations are urged to scrutinize their written communication to "see if they have value-added components and eliminated fillers and gobbledygook that dilute our purpose and waste the recipient's time."[10] Electronic mail is a new type of written communication that has become "as common as the sticky note in organizations around the world."[11] Trillions of e-mail messages are sent each year (with recent statistics showing that more than two-thirds of them are spam messages).[12] Organizations of every sort are connecting people to networks that permit the sending of e-mail both internally and externally. E-mail in organizations presents a special set of opportunities and problems. Although e-mail is considered written communication, it is generally not viewed as being as formal as a paper copy of a letter or a memorandum. It is very convenient for the sender, it speeds the delivery of information, and it can be relatively inexpensive in providing wide distribution of messages for little cost.

E-mail presents its own set of communication difficulties, however. It has grown as a method of communication faster than have rules governing its use. There are well-established codes of manners concerning face-to-face or telephone communication. No such niceties exist in the e-mail world where it is "frighteningly easy to get into conflicts and misunderstandings with people" because of the "generally hasty, ill-considered, and uncrafted nature of electronic communication."[13] There have been many attempts of codify appropriate Web etiquette (or netiquette, as it is often called). A good source for information on how to avoid offending others with e-mail can be found at the Netiquette Home Page (http://www.albion.com/netiquette/).

 What Would You Do?

You are a first-line supervisor and it is time for your annual performance appraisal. One issue you would like to address with your boss is your need for timely information. Twice in the last month you failed to appear at crucial meetings because your boss did not communicate the date and time with you. Then just two weeks ago, your boss neglected to give you a copy of the new vacation/sick leave policy that you were to discuss with your staff in the weekly meeting. You are finding it increasingly difficult to act as a supervisor when you are kept in the dark about the basic policies you are expected to implement.

When you receive your written evaluation, you are astounded to see that your boss has awarded you "Superior" ratings in every category except one. You have been rated as only average in "Effectiveness with Others"—a matter that concerns you because you pride yourself on your ability to get along with others. When you ask your boss for more clarification on this rating, you receive the reply that recently many of the people you supervise have been complaining to your boss saying that you failed to pass on crucial information. Several of your subordinates were especially upset last week when they found out they had filled out their vacation leave requests incorrectly. They stated that you had failed to fulfill your supervisory duty by communicating the new policy to them.

How would you handle this situation?

Users are often surprised to learn that e-mail is not necessarily private or completely destroyed when they press the delete key. Just as organizations usually have policies relating to the use of telephones, fax machines, and mail, there should be policies in place concerning the appropriate use of e-mail and corporate practices toward its retention and preservation.[14] And as with all such policies, these should be shared with employees.

Oral Communication

Oral communication, conducted through individuals or groups, usually is considered to be the richest communication medium, but it also has problems. Not all oral messages are clearly stated. There remains the problem of the ambiguous or misunderstood word. But in oral communication there is opportunity for feedback through which clarification can be accomplished. Face-to-face oral communication also provides an opportunity for nonverbal communication to help amplify a message. Oral communication often is the best way to resolve conflict situations. On the other hand, oral communication can be time consuming, especially when many people need to be told individually about something. And unlike written communication, oral statements are not preserved.

Nonverbal Communication

Nonverbal communication is any type of communication that is not spoken or written. Nonverbal communication often consists of various types of body language, such as facial cues, hand or arm gestures, or posture. Nonverbal cues also are provided by things such as dress and the positioning of furniture in an office. Nonverbal communication can provide many clues to an observer; as the old saying goes, actions speak louder than words. Some examples of nonverbal communication include:

- Avoiding eye contact.
- A steady stare.
- Crossing your arms in front of your chest.
- Sighing.
- Biting your lips.
- Rubbing the back of your head or neck.[15]

Nonverbal communication can contradict, supplement, substitute for, or complement verbal communication. A manager must be especially careful that nonverbal signals do not contradict verbal ones. For instance, consider a supervisor who claims to have an open-door policy and who encourages employees to come to him to discuss any problems that they may encounter. Imagine the nonverbal message that is sent if when an employee enters the supervisor's office to discuss a problem, he or she finds that the supervisor continues to work, does not look up, and fails to establish any type of eye contact with that employee. The supervisor's verbal invitation to feel free to come in to discuss problems is contradicted by the powerful nonverbal message encountered when the employee accepts the invitation. Nonverbal behavior, although sometimes overlooked, is vital to the process of communication. Anytime people communicate using non-face-to-face methods such as fax or e-mail, they do not have the benefit of nonverbal communication, and hence misunderstandings sometime occur.

Different types of communication have different advantages and disadvantages. The truly good communicator knows to pick the right communication channel or medium with which to communicate. Different media vary in degree of richness; information richness is defined as the information-carrying capacity of an item of data. A rich medium is one that conveys a great deal of information, whereas a lean medium is one that conveys the bare minimum.[16] Figure 16.2 shows a classification of different types of communication media according to their richness. Face-to-face communication is the richest in terms of information conveyed because it relies on multiple channels (e.g., words, body language, facial gestures) to reinforce the message. In addition, face-to-face communication provides an opportunity for immediate feedback.

According to Robert Lengel and Richard Daft, the most important thing for managers to remember in terms of matching media richness to communication needs is to use richer media for nonroutine messages and to use leaner media for routine, simple messages.[17] Complex, highly important messages should be communicated by information-rich media to be sure that the issues are clearly understood, but it is a waste of time to use information-rich media to convey routine messages. For instance, a supervisor would never want to tell an individual through an e-mail message that he or she was being disciplined, but an e-mail would be perfectly appropriate method to tell a subordinate the dates of a trip out of town.

Figure 16.2—A Classification of Types of Media According to Their Communication Richness

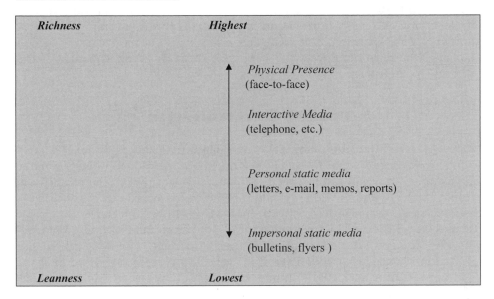

COMMUNICATION FLOWS

Within an organization, communication flows in three directions: down, up, and horizontally. Each of these types of communication will be discussed in the following sections.

Downward Communication

Downward communication, or communication that flows from superiors to subordinates, is the most common type of communication within the organization. The five most common types of downward communication are specific job directives or job instruction; information designed to produce understanding of the task and the relationship to other organizational tasks, or job rationale; information about organizational procedures and practices; feedback to the subordinate about performance; and information of an ideological character to inculcate a sense of mission, or indoctrination of goals.[18]

Although employees expect to receive communication from managers, problems often are associated with downward communication in an organization. The first is that organizations rely too heavily on written methods, such as manuals, booklets, e-mail messages, and newsletters to diffuse downward communication, even when personal contact and face-to-face communication might be more effective. Second, many organizations suffer from message overload. Because of the ease of sending messages via e-mail and by photocopied documents, some employees are overburdened with memos, bulletins, letters, announcements, and policy statements. Many employees who are inundated with too many messages respond by not reading any of the communications at all. Communication also can be hampered by poor timing.

Managers should consider the timing of any communication to be sure it is advantageous for both management and employees. Finally, there is always the problem of filtering of information. Because downward communication usually goes through several layers in an organization, messages may be changed, shortened, or lengthened, and some employees may not receive a message at all. For these reasons, downward communication in many organizations is relatively inefficient.[19]

Upward Communication

Upward communication consists of messages that flow from subordinates to superiors. Most of these messages ask questions, provide feedback, or make suggestions. An organization that is inhospitable to upward communication inhibits such communication, despite the fact that upward communication is essential to an organization's effectiveness. Even in organizations that pride themselves on their open-door policy, it is not uncommon to find employees who are afraid to take information to their superiors, especially when that information concerns problems or bad news. Employees are more likely to send upward messages that enhance their own status or credibility and are much less likely to send up messages that make them look bad.

 What Do You Think?

In many organizations, employees are hesitant to be completely truthful in their communications with their supervisors. Often they do not want to pass along bad news or point out shortcomings. It is the rare organization that is so attuned to its employees and so trusted by them that employees feel comfortable in openly communicating both good and bad news. How can organizations create the type of environment that allows them to get the kind of unfiltered and complete information that is essential for their operations?

Davis points out that it takes a certain amount of courage for workers, especially lower-level workers, to approach their supervisors. "A manager often does not realize how great the upward communication barrier can be especially for blue-collar workers."[20] A manager has status and prestige, often talks and dresses differently from lower-status workers, and has more practice in communication skills. The worker is further impeded because he or she is usually not familiar with the work or the responsibilities of the manager. For that reason, there is often little upward communication in an organization unless the manager encourages it.[21] Managers who want to benefit from the flow of upward communication should be sensitive to the barriers that can be placed in the way of such communications. If managers want to remove some of the barriers, they must be sympathetic listeners and make a practice of encouraging informal contacts with workers. Some methods commonly used to achieve upward communication include grievance procedures, suggestion systems, focus groups, hotlines, group meetings, opinion surveys, and informal meetings between the manager and workers. In addition, managers should remember that the same sort of filtering and misinterpreting that is found in downward communication is also prevalent in upward communication.

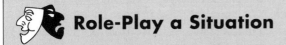

Role-Play a Situation

You are the director of communication at a large public library. You return from your break to find a note on your desk from the library director stating that you should come to the director's office as soon as possible to discuss this year's rewrite of the brochure describing the employee benefits available from the library.

You dread this discussion. The last time you undertook this task, your painstaking arrangements with the printer were countermanded by your boss, who decided at the last minute on doing a revision of your carefully researched and creatively presented brochure. The resulting brochure was a disaster—late, inaccurate, and ugly. To top it all off, your name was on it as editor.

Find a partner. One of you role-play the disgruntled director of communications and the other the library director. Then reverse the roles.

Horizontal Communication

Horizontal communication is the lateral or diagonal exchange of information within an organization; it typically fulfills the following purposes: task coordination, problem solving, information sharing, and conflict resolution. In today's flatter, team-based organizations, horizontal communication is more important than it ever was in the past. This type of communication may occur within or across departments.

Several factors tend to limit horizontal communication within organizations. Information is not always shared in competitive organizations because the employee who possesses the information wants to retain a competitive advantage over others. Specialization also impedes horizontal communication. Most organizations are subdivided into specialized subunits, and members of these subunits may want to further their own subunit's goals rather than communicate with other managers on the same level in order to advance company goals. In addition, excessive specialization may make it difficult for members of one subunit to speak the language of another; even if they were willing to exchange information, they might find it difficult to bridge the horizontal communications gap. Finally, horizontal communication often does not take place because managers have not encouraged frequent horizontal communication nor have they rewarded those who engage in such practices.

Because horizontal communication does not follow the chain of command, precautions must be taken to prevent potential problems. This type of communication should rest on the understanding that these relationships will be encouraged when they are appropriate, subordinates will refrain from making commitments beyond their authority, and subordinates will keep superiors informed of important interdepartmental activities. Although horizontal communication may create some difficulties, it is essential in most organizations to respond to the needs of a complex and dynamic environment. As organizations grow more dependent on a team approach to work, the importance of lateral communication increases.

Much horizontal flow of information takes place in meetings. Some employees spend a great deal of their time in meetings; often these meetings are frustrating and ineffective because they are poorly planned and conceived. Managers at all levels should try to develop the skills and understanding about how to make meetings successful.[22]

CHANGING FLOWS OF COMMUNICATION

There is some indication that new channels of communication, such as e-mail, may be changing the flow of communication within the organization. As John Seely Brown stated, "Email plays quite a different role than it did five years ago. Email has started to erode hierarchical differences. It keeps you more aware of the edge of what's happening in your company. You can sense the heartbeat of the organization when you skim the messages. It's like reading body language."[23]

Because it is more informal than a letter and less threatening than face-to-face conversation, some workers send electronic mail not only to workers on their own level but upward in the organization, to immediate supervisors and to managers even higher up in the organizational structure. Some employees are using e-mail messages or Web sites to raise complaints publicly against organizations and their practices.[24] As Robert Zmud has stated, "Traditionally, an organization member's zone of influence has been limited by a number of constraints, most of which reflect task design, authority relationships, and physical, geographic, and temporal boundaries. New information technologies are relaxing many, if not most, of these constraints."[25] Just as the telephone revolutionized organizational communication, the new communication media will bring vast changes to how employees within organizations communicate with each other and the outside world. There is evidence that effective communication through computer-mediated channels may be a unique skill that needs to be developed and that "even experienced email users will not necessarily be able to communicate richly with a new partner, or about a new topic, or within a new organizational context, without first developing these unique knowledge bases."[26] More research needs to be done to discover how new communication media such as e-mail, instant messaging, voice mail, cell phones, and teleconferencing are affecting organizational communication.

Virtual Communication

In today's modern organization, many managers have to communicate with individuals who are not physically present. This type of communication has become more prevalent in the past few years as the number of telecommuting employees has increased and as more workers are working as parts of virtual teams. A recent report found that 25 percent of U.S. workers work outside of the office at least eight hours a week.[27] Communicating with remote workers is a difficult task. Workers who are not on-site are not able to take advantage of communication transmitted through informal chats and body language. Communication with these workers is essential if they are to succeed. Managers need to pay special attention to communication with this type of employees, giving them clear guidance about the expectations for their work and how they will be assessed. It is important for managers to find ways to be accessible to these off-site workers and to communicate with them according to their preferred preferences. Remote work is still uncharted territory for most managers and organizations, but as the number of virtual workers increase, managers will need to become more knowledgeable about how best to communicate with workers who are not physically present on the work site.[28]

INFORMAL ORGANIZATIONAL COMMUNICATION

Most of what has been discussed so far concerns the formal communication channels within an organization. These are the message channels that follow the official path directed by the organizational hierarchy. But every organization also has an informal communication system. Two of the most common of these are the grapevine and the activity often referred to as "managing by walking around." Although informal channels are neither as predictable nor as neatly designed as those of the formal communication structure, they are remarkably efficient at moving information.

The Grapevine

Every organization has an informal communication network commonly termed the *grapevine*. The grapevine "moves upward, downward, and diagonally, within and without chains of command, between workers and managers, and even within and without a company."[29] Studies of the grapevine have shown that this means of communication is fairly accurate, with more than 75 percent of the messages being transmitted correctly.[30] In addition, the grapevine is usually much faster at moving information than are formal channels. However, nearly all of the information within the grapevine is undocumented and thus is open to change and interpretation as it moves through the network.

Although the grapevine sometimes can cause trouble, this informal communication channel is endemic in all organizations. Managers are not able to destroy it because it serves an essential human need for information. Given the existence of the grapevine, a manager's task is to make it contribute to the accomplishment of the organization's objectives. Managers can do this by using it, either personally or through trusted staff members. It can be very useful in supplementing formal channels. A manager who wants to relay information can feed the grapevine accurate information, which will be transmitted quickly throughout the organization. In addition, managers should be aware of the messages that circulate on it in order to be able to intercept and correct misleading rumors that could damage morale.

The grapevine can be curtailed somewhat by clear, concise, timely, and complete communication through formal communication channels. Rumors often arise because workers are anxious about some situation about which they have received little or no information. Fewer rumors would circulate on the grapevine if managers would provide sufficient information about issues of interest and concern to workers.

 ## What Would You Do?

"What do we do now?" wondered Ann, Lee, and Thomas. It had been two months since the meeting with their supervisor, Phyllis, and nothing had changed: Communication was poor, morale was low, and defenses were up. Even the student assistants were beginning to notice the tension between their supervisors and Phyllis. Although Ann, Thomas, and Lee each had noticed the lack of communication from Phyllis because they worked in different departments, they did not have the opportunity to compare notes. And then David, the circulation supervisor, was fired, suddenly and abruptly. When Ann reported to work that afternoon, David's desk was cleared and he was gone. Ann sought out Phyllis for confirmation. Phyllis acknowledged David's being fired, gave no additional information, but told Ann that because there was a job freeze, David's position could not be filled until and unless the freeze was lifted, and that until that happened, it would be up to Ann to "work things out." Ann, Thomas, and Lee began to share observations, and what they realized was that David's firing was merely an extreme example of what had been taking place since Phyllis had arrived. There had been no memos, no staff meetings, and no briefings in spite of the fact that plans for a library expansion were underway, the job freeze had affected library hours and staff, and that personnel were generally confused and becoming frustrated.

What is the problem here? If you were an employee in this library, what would you do? (For the rest of this case study, see http://www.lu.com/management.)

Managing by Walking Around

Another good way for managers to supplement information received from formal channels of communication is for the managers to get out of their offices, walk around the organization, and spend some time with employees. This means of ensuring informal communication is usually referred to as *managing by walking around*, or MBWA. Just as managers should be aware of what is being circulated on the grapevine, they also should be aware of what is going on in parts of the organization away from their offices.

Managers need to make themselves visible and to spend time getting a general feel for what is going on throughout the organization. The best managers spend a part of their time visiting employees in their work locations. Whether it is walking through the catalog department, visiting the mail room, or talking to shelvers as they do their job, a manager finds out things about the library that he or she would never know without emerging from the office on a periodic basis. Most workers are flattered when top administrators come to their work area and speak with them. It makes them feel significant. As Robert Goffee and Gareth Jones have written, "Followers will give their hearts and souls to authority figures who say, 'You really matter,' no matter how small the followers' contributions may be."[31] The most highly regarded managers are those who are able to communicate to their employees that they are interested in them and in what they are doing. MBWA is a proven way to allow managers and workers to communicate on an informal basis, and because it is done on the employee's turf instead of in the manager's office, it provides a different dimension to organizational communication.

In summary, both formal and informal communication is critical to organizations. Managers should pay close attention to the communication within an organization in an attempt to make it as open and free from distortion as possible. Managers always should be trying to improve their communication skills. Twenty tips for good communication can be seen in table 16.1.

CONFLICT

One of the common results of poor communication is conflict. Conflict situations often arise from problems in communication. One person may misunderstand another. Someone may have said something that he or she really did not mean to say. Or someone may have missed a message that was supposed to be sent. Communication or miscommunication often leads to conflict. Then once conflict exists, people cease to talk to one another, which exacerbates the conflict. Good communication skills are an important part of preventing and resolving conflicts.

Some managers will do almost anything to try to avoid conflicts within the units they manage. Some even feel that the mere existence of conflict is a reflection of their ability to manage. This is not so. Conflict is not bad in itself, and it may result in either positive or negative outcomes. Although uncontrolled conflict can be detrimental to an organization and its employees, properly managed conflict often can be helpful.

Managers who feel that they spend a great deal of time trying to resolve conflict situations are probably correct. One study showed that managers reported spending up to 20 percent of their time dealing with conflict and its impact.[32] Another study showed that 42 percent of a manager's time is spent on reaching agreement with others after conflicts occur.[33]

Conflict usually is characterized as being interpersonal or intergroup. Interpersonal conflict, conflict between two people, is often the result of

TABLE 16.1 Twenty Ways to Communicate with Your Employees

1. Include affected employees in goal setting.
2. Give frequent and meaningful recognition for a job well done.
3. Interact with employees on an informal basis.
4. Go to employees' work areas. Meet them on their own turf.
5. Ask for workers' opinions and listen with an open mind. Try to understand their points of view.
6. Share nonconfidential information with employees and ask for their input.
7. Offset demoralizing actions and events by emphasizing what went well, and use the experience as a learning opportunity.
8. Listen 80% of the time and talk 20%.
9. Ask employees what rumors they have heard, and address them.
10. Get into the trenches with employees. Look for opportunities to understand employees' jobs better.
11. Give information to employees after management meetings.
12. Ask employees, "Have I made our vision, mission, and goals clear and understandable?"
13. Ask employees, "What can I do to help you with your job, and what am I doing that gets in your way?"
14. Ask employees, "What is making our clients/customers the most and/or the least satisfied?"
15. Praise in public and give feedback in private.
16. Find something to like about each staff member with whom you work.
17. Actively make a point of speaking to all employees whom you see in a day.
18. Build bridges with people with whom you are uncomfortable.
19. Set goals each month on ways to accomplish "Managing by Walking Around."
20. Occasionally have lunch with staff members. Use this as an opportunity to build trust.

Source: Adapted from Robin Reid, "A Checklist for Managers" (1999), http://www.improve.org/mbwa.html.

incompatible personalities or different values or points of view. Intergroup conflict, conflict between groups of employees, can be caused by a number of factors within organizations and often arises as a result of competition over scarce resources. Both interpersonal and intergroup conflicts often are heightened by poor communication.

People react to conflict situations in different ways. Research has identified five primary styles of handling conflict: avoiding, compromising, competing, accommodating, and collaborating. Avoiders try to prevent conflict; usually they suppress their feelings and withdraw from conflict situations. Compromisers try to seek a solution that satisfies both parties; they are willing to split differences down the middle. Competitors seek to dominate and impose their viewpoints. Accommodators almost always give in to opposition and acquiesce to the demands of others. Collaborators try to work to find a mutually satisfactory outcome for all parties.[34] These approaches are affected by how assertive and how cooperative individuals are. These different styles are illustrated in figure 16.3; although the figure shows five discrete positions, it is possible for an individual's orientation on conflict to fall anywhere on the diagram.

Of the five styles, the collaborative one is generally considered best because it leads to a result that is usually described as a win-win outcome. This type of outcome occurs when all parties perceive that they have emerged from the conflict in a better position than before. For instance, if two employees were in conflict about the scheduling of weekend and evening hours, it is possible that you might end up with a win-win situation if you discovered that one really did not mind working weekend hours, and the other really did not mind working

Figure 16.3—Five Styles of Handling Conflict

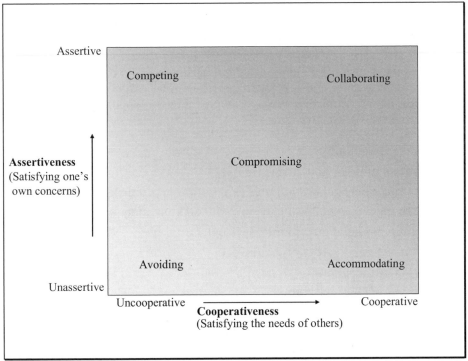

Source: Kenneth W. Thomas, "Conflict and Conflict Management," in *Handbook of Industrial and Organizational Psychology,* ed. Marvin D. Dunnette (Chicago: Rand McNally, 1976), 889–936.

evenings, and thus you were able to arrange their schedules to conform with their preferences. Although win-win solutions are not possible in all cases, managers who are skilled as negotiators often are able to deal effectively with conflict by arriving at solutions that make all parties feel that they have come out ahead.

Results of Conflict

Organizational conflict can have both negative and positive effects. The more negative effects are usually thought of first. Working in an environment with a great deal of conflict can lead to stress and divert employees' attention from the work that has to be done. The morale of employees often suffers, as well as their motivation to perform well. In cases of extreme conflict, workers have been known to disparage or even sabotage the work of others. Conflict between departments can cause groups to close ranks and hamper cooperation. Unmanaged and unresolved conflict is a destructive force. It can destroy relationships, decrease productivity and quality of work, break down communication, and make people feel at odds with others in the group or organization.

On the other hand, sometimes conflict plays a useful role. Conflict can bring previously hidden problems to light so that solutions may be sought. Conflict is considered essential to innovation. If everyone thinks the same thing, changes will not occur. Innovation "takes place when different ideas, perceptions, and ways of processing and judging information collide."[35] At Microsoft, one of the most innovative U.S. corporations, the former chief executive officer, Bill Gates, advocated a management style called "armed truce" because employees were encouraged to challenge everyone, including Gates. Conflict was at the heart of every decision in a company "constantly at war with not only outsiders but also with itself."[36] Properly managed conflict can be energizing. When individuals debate opposing ideas and positions in a calm and reasonable fashion, this type of conflict may:

- prevent stagnation;
- stimulate interest and curiosity;
- encourage the examination and exploration of problems;
- lead to the solving of problems and the making of decisions;
- facilitate personal growth and development;
- promote group identity and cohesion;
- help relieve tensions;
- provide the basis for change;
- encourage interpersonal communication, better understanding, and critical self-reflection;
- strengthen personal relationships;
- promote the exploration and awareness of feelings, needs, and opinions of other people.[37]

In summary, conflict is an inevitable part of working in organizations. Whenever people are put together in an organization, they become interdependent, and thus grounds for competition and conflict arise. The ability to discuss topics openly is a strength in any organization. It is far healthier for individuals to be able to debate, to present opposing viewpoints, and to invite freewheeling conversation on any topic than to keep opinions bottled up inside. Conflicts that are suppressed typically reemerge.

However, there some people think that we have become too contentious and have begun to argue for the sake of argument.[38] In our culture, people have been conditioned to compete and to achieve, and the cultures that develop within organizations tend to exaggerate this trait. Deborah Tannen has termed this an *argument culture*, which she describes as one that urges us to approach the world—and the people in it—in an adversarial frame of mind. It rests on the assumption that opposition is the best way to get anything done. The best way to discuss an idea is to set up a debate; the best way to cover news is to find spokespeople who express the most extreme, polarized views and present them as "both sides"; the best way to settle disputes is litigation that pits one party against another; the best way to begin an essay is to attack someone; the best way to show you are really thinking is to criticize.[39] Unfortunately this type of opposition does not lead to truth because usually an issue is not composed of two opposing views but is multifaceted.[40]

 ## What Would You Do?

You are steaming. Your supervisor, Mrs. Romley, has just asked you to be in charge of the circulation desk this Saturday night. AGAIN. You were on duty last Saturday night and the one three weeks ago. The library policy is that each worker is responsible for one Saturday night a month, but as far as you are concerned, that policy is just a myth. You are assigned to work at least two and often three Saturday nights each month. Other workers always seem to have things that conflict with working on Saturday—spouses who will be out of town, elderly parents who need help with something, or a child's piano recital or football game. You know that Mrs. Romley is trying to make the department "family friendly," but you feel as though you are being asked to do more than your fair share because you are the only full-time employee who is not married with young children. Should you go ahead and accept this week's schedule or try to set up a time to talk with Mrs. Romley? If so, what would you say?

Managers need to find a way to strike the right balance between too much conflict and not enough. In other words, they have to find a way to manage conflict so that the organization will reap its benefits and avoid its negative aspects.

Managing Conflict

How can conflict be managed? The first step is for managers to realize that a certain amount of conflict is inevitable within any organization. The worst thing managers at any level can do is to try to suppress conflict. It is much better to bring it out, to open the lines of communication, and to try to come to a mutually beneficial solution. Even if a win-win solution cannot be achieved, employees will be better satisfied if conflicts are recognized and solutions are sought in a supportive manner.

The second step is to try to deal with the conflict before it escalates. Conflicts typically escalate in three ways:

1. **Expansion of interests.** The conflict goes from a relatively simple one focused on a few issues to one with a larger number of areas of disagreements. Such escalation can be very destructive and makes the conflict far harder to resolve.

2. **Involvement of self-esteem or self-image.** Suddenly the conflict switches from one that is issue oriented to one that is personal. People become defensive and try to save face.

3. **Creation of a new reality.** The final form of escalation occurs when the conflict itself begins to create its own reality. Participants base their choices on only the immediate conflict situation. Winning the conflict takes on a symbolic importance that transcends everything else. Individuals begin to focus wholly on their incentives to compete rather than on their incentives to cooperate.[41]

The third step is to try to resolve a conflict in a way that allows the participants to feel positive about the outcome. The best result will be if the manager can help the parties to the conflict emerge with a win-win solution.

Conflict management is a necessary managerial skill. Inevitably, managers will be called in to act as the third party in management of a great number of conflict situations. Managers get better at handling conflict with experience. Understanding conflict and its impact on others increases a manager's ability to make interventions. Managers learn from smaller conflict situations how to deal with larger ones, and they learn from their successes as well as their failures. Managers may fear conflict but always should be ready to manage the conflicts rather than having the conflict control them or the situation. Some practical tips for managing conflicts may be seen in table 16.2.

CONCLUSION

Communication has been described as the glue that holds an organization together.

Managers spend the majority of their time engaging in communication of various types. Unless managers learn to communicate successfully, they will not be successful in carrying out the other managerial functions of planning, organizing, staffing, leading, and controlling. Communication skills are essential, and the improvement of these skills in both managers and other employees should be made a priority because without communication no organization can function effectively.

TABLE 16.2 Some Practical Tips for Managing Conflicts

• Don't let conflict situations go on. Take care of conflict as soon as possible.
• Avoid power struggles in which someone has to win and someone has to lose.
• Show concern for both the problem and the individuals involved.
• Beware of projecting your own beliefs and standards onto others because this often leads to misperceptions about the motivations for others' actions.
• Listen more than you talk; don't be dogmatic or argumentative.
• Avoid exaggerating the problem
• Restrain your emotions; becoming angry or upset usually adds to the problem.
• Realize that learning to manage conflict is an investment in a better organization.

Source: Adapted from Lucile Wilson, *People Skills for Library Managers: A Common Sense Guide for Beginners* (Englewood, CO: Libraries Unlimited, 1996), 72–73.

NOTES

1. Chester I. Barnard, *The Functions of the Executive* (Cambridge, MA: Harvard University Press, 1938).

2. Henry Mintzberg, "The Manager's Job: Folklore and Fact," *Harvard Business Review* 53 (July–August 1975): 52.

3. A July 2006 Pew Internet Survey showed that 8 percent of U.S. Internet users are bloggers and 39 percent read blogs. See Amanda Lenhart and Susannah Fox, *Bloggers: A Portrait of the Internet's New Storytellers* (Washington, DC: Pew Internet and American Life Project, 2006), http://www.pewinternet.org/pdfs/PIP %20Bloggers%20Report%20July%2019%202006.pdf.

4. Alex Bavels and Dermot Barrett, "An Experimental Approach to Organization Communication," *Personnel* 28 (March 1951): 368.

5. Peter F. Drucker, *Managing the Non-profit Organization* (New York: HarperBusiness, 1990), 115.

6. Gerald M. Goldhaber, *Organizational Communication,* 6th ed. (New York: McGraw-Hill, 1993), 14–15.

7. Ibid.

8. Deborah Tannen, *You Just Don't Understand: Women and Men in Conversation* (New York: William Morrow, 1990).

9. Patrick A. Hall, "Peanuts: A Note on Intercultural Communication," *Journal of Academic Librarianship* 18 (September 1992): 211–13.

10. Kathleen Huddleston, *Back on the Quality Track: How Organizations Derailed and Recovered* (New York: American Management Association, 1995), 113.

11. Marco Adria, "Making the Most of E-Mail," *Academy of Management Review* 14 (February 2000): 153.

12. John E. Dunn. "Has Spam Growth Stabilized?" *PC World,* 12 January 2005, http://www.pcworld.com/news/article/0,aid,119285,00.asp.

13. Nigel Nicholson, *Managing the Human Animal* (London: Texere, 2000), 205.

14. Jenny C. McCune, "Get the Message," *Management Review* 38 (January 1997): 10–11.

15. These and other examples of nonverbal communication can be found in Jack Griffin, *How to Say It at Work* (Englewood Cliffs, NJ: Prentice-Hall, 1998), 26–28.

16. Robert H. Lengel and Richard L. Daft, "The Selection of Communication Media as an Executive Skill," *Academy of Management Executive* 2 (1988): 225–32.

17. Ibid.

18. Daniel Katz and Robert L. Kahn, *The Social Psychology of Organizations* (New York: Wiley, 1966), 239.

19. Goldhaber, *Organizational Communication,* 141–42.

20. Keith Davis, cited in ibid., 138–39.

21. Ibid.

22. A helpful guide to effective meetings is Barbara I. Dewey and Sheila D. Creth, *Team Power: Making Library Meetings Work* (Chicago: American Library Association, 1993).

23. Karen Southwick, "Back in Touch," *Forbes* 169 (March 25, 2002): 46.

24. Bill Leonard, "Cyberventing," *HR Magazine* 44 (November 1999): 35–39.

25. Robert W. Zmud, "Opportunities for Strategic Information Manipulation through New Information Technology," in *Organizations and Communication Technology,* ed. Janet Fulk and Charles Steinfield (Newbury Park, CA: Sage, 1990), 115.

26. John R. Carlson and Robert W. Zmud, "Channel Expansion Theory and the Experiential Nature of Media Richness Perceptions," *Academy of Management Journal* 42 (April 1999): 163.

27. Caroline Jones, *Teleworking: The Quiet Revolution* (Stamford, CT: Gartner Research, 2005), http://www.gartner.com/resources/122200/122284/teleworking_the_quiet_revolu_122284.pdf.

28. Jenifer Robison, "Getting the Most out of Remote Workers," *Gallup Management Journal Online,* 8 June 2006, 1, http://gmj.gallup.com/content/default.aspx?ci=23209&pg=1.

29. Keith Davis, "Grapevine Communication among Lower and Middle Managers," *Personnel Journal* 48 (April 1969): 272.

30. Keith Davis and John W. Newstrom, *Human Behavior at Work: Organizational Behavior,* 8th ed. (New York: McGraw-Hill, 1989), 371.

31. Robert Goffee and Gareth Jones, "Followership," *Harvard Business Review* 79 (December 2001): 148.

32. Kenneth W. Thomas and Warren H. Schmidt, "A Survey of Managerial Interests with Respect to Conflict," *Academy of Management Journal* 10 (June 1976): 315–18.

33. Carol Watson and Richard Hoffman, "Managers as Negotiators," *Leadership Quarterly* 7, no. 1 (1996): 63–85.

34. Ibid.

35. Dorothy Leonard and Susana Straus, "Putting Your Company's Whole Brain to Work," *Harvard Business Review* 75 (July/August 1997): 111.

36. Herbert S. White, "Never Mind Being Innovative and Effective—Just Be Nice," *Library Journal* 120 (September 15, 1995): 47.

37. Gregory Tillett, *Resolving Conflict: A Practical Approach* (South Melbourne, Australia: Sydney University Press, 1991), 6.

38. Charles Conrad and Marshall Scott Poole, *Strategic Organizational Communication: Into the Twenty-First Century,* 4th ed. (New York: Harcourt, Brace, 1998), 340.

39. Deborah Tannen, *The Argument Culture: Stopping America's War of Words* (New York: Ballantine, 1999), 3–4.

40. Ibid., 10.

41. Conrad and Poole, *Strategic Organizational Communication,* 338–40

Chapter 17

Participative Management and the Use of Teams in Libraries

 Overview

The year is 1937. Mary Jones is a recent library school graduate whose first job is in a large academic library. Mary works in the cataloging department, where her orders are given to her by the department head, who receives his own orders from the library director. Each day, Mary does the work she is assigned. She has little contact with other employees outside her own department and little input into decisions that are made concerning her job. Libraries of that time are like other organizations of the same era: managed from the top down with the director making almost all decisions.[1]

Flash forward to the present ...

Mary's grandson, Ben, received an MSLIS degree last year and also has gone to work in an academic library. The environment he works in as a beginning librarian is vastly different from that his grandmother encountered. He frequently works on committees and teams with people outside of his department. He expects to have some input into decision making. He spends time in meetings in which he learns about overall library issues and contributes his knowledge and efforts to many activities outside of his department.

There have been vast changes in the library workplace in the past few decades. Once top managers were expected to have all the answers; now it is widely assumed that lower-level employees are able to solve many problems effectively, and problem solving usually is pushed down to the level where there is the most expertise related to the problem. Often problems are solved by groups of employees working together.

> This chapter discusses participative management and its advantages. Because management by teams is becoming increasingly popular, the chapter also provides an overview of management in a team environment. The preceding chapter on communication is very relevant because good communication is essential, but other skills are also important. The use of teams affects most aspects of management, and additional information on topics such as group decision making and the impact of teams on organizational structure can be found in previous chapters.

PARTICIPATIVE MANAGEMENT

One decision every manager must make is how much employee participation to allow in management. As has been discussed previously, in the past most libraries and information centers were organized in a traditional hierarchical structure, and the normal management style was authoritarian. Authoritarian organizations are controlled from the top down, with upper-level managers making all essential decisions. In these types of organizations, orders are passed down from above using the chain of command, and employees are expected to carry out the tasks demanded of them. Today's directors find authoritarian leadership styles to be less effective as librarians demand increased input into decision making.

This demand for increased input has resulted in many organizations changing the way they are managed to permit employees to participate in management and decision making. Participative management has been defined as:

> Both a philosophy and a method for managing human resources in an environment in which employees are respected and their contributions valued and utilized. From a philosophical standpoint, participative management centers on the belief that people at all levels of an organization can develop a genuine interest in its success and can do more than merely perform their assigned duties.[2]

Participative management involves employees in sharing information, making decisions, solving problems, planning projects, and evaluating results.[3] Those who favor greater participation base their view on their beliefs that the rank-and-file library staff benefit from having a chance to participate in governance, that better decisions are made with staff involvement, and that such a management style leads to increased job satisfaction that results in better library service. Writers who favor less participation usually support their stand by concentrating on the inexperience of most librarians in management, the amount of time that is consumed by participation, and the inappropriateness of the participative model as a means of operating a complex service organization.

Participative management has the virtue of forcing decision making down to the level where the most relevant information can be found and where the effect of the decision will have the greatest impact. Although few libraries could be considered to operate on Rensis Likert's System 4 level (described in chapter 14), most libraries permit some employee input into decision making, and there is almost always some consultation before decisions are made.

Participative management does not mean that the management relinquishes its responsibility for the final decisions that are made; participative management should not be confused with management by consensus. As one expert wrote, "Librarians will have to accept that participatory management is no substitute for individual responsibility and leadership. There will likely always be library directors and just as likely they will be paid considerably more than the rest of the non-administrative staff ... because they are accountable for the operation of the library."[4] Nor does participative management mean that managers involve all their employees in every decision every time, nor do all employees have the same amount of involvement in decision making. The involvement is usually based on familiarity with the decision that needs to be made.[5]

Although management theory advocates the use of participation by employees, it is sometimes difficult to implement with employees who have not had experience with it before. And, on the other hand, it is not easy for some managers to give up control and to let others contribute to decision making and problem solving. Switching to a more participative system of management requires changes on the part of both managers and employees.

 ## Some Definitions

Participative management: A type of management characterized by the delegation of authority and power to lower level employees.
Empowerment: The process of sharing power with employees.

Today, there is a great deal of talk in organizations of all types about empowering employees. Participative management empowers employees to make decisions relating to their work. Employees who report feeling empowered make statements such as:

- My supervisor supported my idea without question.
- Financial data were shared with me.
- I was able to make a financial decision on my own.

Employees that are not empowered make statements such as:

- I had no input into a hiring decision of someone who was to report directly to me.
- I worked extremely hard on a project and my manager took full credit for it.
- The project was reassigned without my knowledge or input.
- My suggestions were never solicited; or if they were, they were ignored.
- I am treated like a mushroom and always kept in the dark.[6]

Empowered employees are given information about the decisions that need to be made as well as the power to make the decisions that give them control over their own work. Empowering employees does not mean that they are left to work with no supervision; instead, they are given instructions about what needs to be accomplished but are given flexibility and the opportunity for some risk taking in how the goal is to be achieved.

Southwest Airlines is a well-known corporate example of a company that empowers its employees. This Dallas-based airline has had unprecedented success and a continued tradition of excellent customer service. Southwest employees work in teams without outside supervision. The employees have the authority to make decisions and do whatever it takes to ensure that the customer is satisfied. Southwest has created an organizational culture than treats both its employees and passengers with respect.[7] Many libraries could take lessons from Southwest in how to create an organizational culture that becomes a competitive advantage.

In an attempt to empower employees, some organizations have begun a practice called open-book management. Organizations that use the open-book management provide employees with all relevant financial information about the company, including information about cost of goods, cash flow, revenue, expenses, and profit. These companies treat employees as partners because they think that if workers are given all relevant financial information they will be able to make better decisions and will take responsibility for the numbers under their control.[8] Employees who are entrusted with financial data and the ability to understand are being empowered by their managers.

WHY EMPOWER EMPLOYEES?

Why would organizations want to involve workers in decisions that are being made? As has been mentioned previously, modern organizations face many challenges, and the traditional hierarchy often no longer performs well. Many times decisions have to be made quickly if the organization is to remain competitive. Because of the information technology revolution, libraries face a demand for greater productivity as well as increased pressure to change structures and services. Greater staff participation can help libraries meet these challenges. Empowering employees can lead to better customer service. More participative management also allows libraries to be successful in developing staff flexibility and creativity and in satisfying the increased expectations of staff members for self-realization.

 ## What Would You Do?

Brickham University Library, the academic library at the largest public university in a midwestern state, had been long regarded as a classical bureaucratic organization. For years, the library has been structured with many layers of management, with power and information carefully controlled by the top echelons of the organization. A new director has just been hired who wants to make changes. This director believes that employees at all levels of the company need to know what is going on and need to have some participation in decision making.

Imagine that you are this new director. What changes would you make and how would you implement the changes? What type of program would you design to allow employee participation? What difficulties, if any, would you anticipate in making this change? Could you take any lessons from Southwest Airlines?

As was discussed in chapter 9, one of the reasons that modern organizations have been made flatter is so that decisions can be made by people close to the action. And modern workers, especially professionals, expect to play a part in making the decisions about matters that concern them and their work. Studies that have looked at the effect of organizational culture on performance have found that in for-profit organizations a higher degree of employee participation produces higher returns on investments and improved financial results.[9] Similar studies carried out in libraries have shown that participation in decision making is a factor that positively affects job satisfaction. The relationship between participative management and job satisfaction in libraries has been found in studies done in the libraries of many countries, including the United States, Canada, South Africa, and Greece.[10]

Participative management is another manifestation of the move from the tightly structured bureaucratic organizations of the past to more modern ones that are becoming increasingly more people centered. Edward Lawler summarized the new principles of management in his book ... *From the Ground Up: Six Principles for Building the New Logic Corporation.* These principles can be seen in table 17.1.[11]

Lawler states that the "logic" of organizations (i.e., how everything is ordered, defined, and operated) needs to move beyond those principles that are based

TABLE 17.1 New Principles of Management (adapted from Lawler's ... *From the Ground Up: Six Principles for Building the New Logic Corporation*)

Old Principles	New Principles
Organization is a secondary source of competitive advantage	Organization can be the ultimate competitive advantage
Bureaucracy is the most effective source of control	Involvement is the most effective source of control
Top management and technical experts should add most of the value	All employees must add significant value
Hierarchical processes are the key to organizational effectiveness	Lateral processes are the key to organizational effectiveness
Organizations should be designed around functions	Organizations should be designed around products and customers
Effective managers are the key to organizational effectiveness	Effective leadership is the key to organizational effectiveness

Source: John J. Morse and Jay W. Lorsch, "Beyond Theory Y," *Harvard Business Review* 48 (May–June 1970): 68.

upon the traditional hierarchical paradigm because those principles no longer work in today's dynamic organizations. "Unfortunately for many of those who use it, the hierarchical command-and-control approach works best only as long as work is simple and stable. As work becomes more complicated and more knowledge based, it runs into problems."[12] Lawler's argument for a more people-centered organization is based on earlier contributions by management theorists such as Douglas McGregor (see chapter 2), who said that if employees are truly involved in their work, they will figure out what should be done and do it without needing bureaucratic controls. Although bureaucracies can be efficient in stable environments because they allow lower-level employees to act quickly with a high degree of precision and conformity by the use of already programmed decisions, this type of organization prevents employees from acting on their own to meet a demand or to respond to a unique problem. Thus they often result in slow or poor decisions because the individuals who know the most about a particular area are not involved in the decision making. Lawler advocates that organizations need to adopt new principles that will distribute knowledge, information, power, and rewards more widely throughout the organization.[13]

LEVELS OF PARTICIPATION

Participative management can be viewed as a continuum with top managers varying in how much they allow employees to participate in management decisions. The use of participative management ranges from those organizations in which the employees are informed about decisions that have to be made to those in which the employees actually make the decisions. One expert has proposed a hierarchical model with eight levels, ranging from least participation to most:

1. Employees need not be informed about decisions made by management unless they directly affect their work.
2. Employees are informed after decisions have been made.
3. Employees are given an opportunity to express views but management makes the decisions.
4. Employees are consulted informally before a decision is made.
5. Employees must be consulted before a decision is made.
6. Employees participate informally with management in decision making and under some collective-bargaining agreements have the right of veto over some issues.
7. Management and employees jointly make decisions.
8. Employees have the final say in all decision making.[14]

Examples of employee participation on each of these levels exist in libraries, with relatively fewer libraries at the extreme ends of the hierarchical model and most libraries providing employee participation in the middle range. At the lowest levels, employees are informed of decisions, perhaps before they are implemented, and are sometimes told some of the reasoning behind them. In the middle levels, librarians are involved to some extent in making decisions.

For instance, many libraries use committees or task forces to gather information and then those groups recommend what decision should be made. As was discussed in chapter 10, libraries commonly use search committees to screen candidates and to make recommendations about which individual should be hired. In these cases, the decision is not solely the committee's but the committee members play an important role in the decision-making process. In the most participative organizations, those at levels 7 and 8, employees actually make the decisions. In some libraries, teams are given such responsibilities. Organizations that use teams, especially self-managed teams, are representative of the most participative organizations. The rest of this chapter will focus on teams and their use in libraries.

TEAMS IN ORGANIZATIONS

A managerial innovation that is becoming more common in many types of organizations, including libraries, is the use of teams. These organizations are employing teams to do work that previously had been done by individuals. To use teams successfully, managers need to call upon all of the skills of leading that have been discussed thus far. Effective team management requires managers who are skilled at motivating, leading, and communicating.

 What Do You Think?

> Michael Jordan, the basketball legend, wrote, "One thing that I believe to the fullest is that if you think and achieve as a team, the individual accolades will take care of themselves. Talent wins games, but teamwork and intelligence wins championships."
>
> This statement is obviously true about basketball, but does it also apply in the workplace? How can teams make individuals successful?
>
> Michael Jordan, Mark Vancil, and Sandro Miller, *I Can't Accept Not Trying: Michael Jordan on the Pursuit of Excellence* (San Francisco: Harper San Francisco, 1994): 24.

Although many multinational organizations are employing virtual teams—that is, teams whose members are geographically dispersed and who work together using computer technology and groupware—this chapter will focus primarily on teams working in the same physical location, because that is the type of team that is most prevalent in libraries. However, librarians who work with off-site colleagues, who are active on committees in professional associations, or who work with consortia have to function, at least part of the time, as members of virtual teams. As more libraries permit at least some workers to telecommute, that type of team likely will become more common in the future.[15]

The Use of Teams in Libraries

It is hard to get any exact numbers about how many libraries are actually using teams. Teams are fairly common in large academic libraries. The Association of Research Libraries (ARL) surveyed its members in 1998 and found that teams are at least being experimented with in most ARL libraries. Five respondents to the survey described their organization as "team-based"; these libraries had completely restructured and moved from the traditional departmental organization of academic libraries to an organization that used teams instead. Sixty-four percent of the respondents reported having at least one permanent team in their organization, whereas 73 percent reported having at least one project team. Of the respondents, 72 percent had used teams for less than five years, which provides some indication of the growth in the use of teams in large academic libraries. The teams in the ARL libraries were used to accomplish many functions, including bibliographic services, library services assessment, project coordination, outreach, Web development, document delivery, and digital collections management.[16] A more recent study of academic medical libraries also found a growing number that use teams.[17] Some academic libraries, for instance those at the University of Arizona and the University of Maryland, have been completely restructured into team-based organizations.[18]

Teams are common in many other types and parts of libraries. They frequently are found in technical services departments where they perform functions such as acquisitions, cataloging, and database and Web site maintenance.[19] Teams also are used in many reference departments. For instance, the Ohio State University Health Sciences Library has a Reference and Information Services Team (RIST) that manages the library's reference services and oversees access, outreach, and education services. RIST has a team coordinator position that rotates among members on a semiannual basis. The team coordinator is responsible for preparing team agendas and facilitating team meetings. Some libraries are using virtual teams consisting of librarians, library technicians, and information system specialists from different library departments or institutions to span temporal and geographic barriers by communicating by e-mail and other electronic media in order to accomplish specific projects.[20] Even though most of the libraries that have adopted the team approach have been large academic libraries, teams are now being implemented in smaller libraries. The Teton County Library, a public library in Wyoming with a collection size of about 100,000 and 34 full-time employees, has reorganized itself into a team-based organization.[21] All indications show that the number of libraries using the team-based approach is growing steadily.

There are also libraries that have not adopted team management but use working groups or committees as an integral part of their structure. Although, as discussed in a following section, there is a difference between true teams and other types of work groups, many of the principles related to team building and developing are applicable to committees and other types of groups used in library management.

Some Definitions

Team management: The use of teams in organizations in lieu of a traditional hierarchical management structure.

Self-directed or self-managed teams: Teams that have been given a charge by senior management relating to a specific project or ongoing process and that have almost complete discretion in deciding how to accomplish their objectives.

Project teams: Teams that are constituted for a set amount of time to work on a specific project or task. Sometimes called a task force.

Cross-functional teams: Teams that include participants from a number of departments or specializations.

Virtual teams: Teams that have members who are located in different geographic locations and rarely meet face-to-face. Team members communicate and work through electronic technologies such as the Internet and teleconferencing.

Although teams are becoming more common, library managers need to think carefully about the implications of changing to a team approach before they begin to implement the process. A manager cannot just create teams and expect them to work effectively. Instead, successful teams are built and developed. Individuals act differently when they are part of a group than when they are alone, so any manager contemplating establishing teams should become familiar with the literature concerning group behavior. Using teams often complicates the pay structure of organizations as managers have to decide whether all team members are paid the same or given the same percentage of pay increase.[22] It is also sometimes difficult for managers to switch from managing in a hierarchical organization to a team-based one because it takes different skills to manage teams.

Even the use of the word *team* can produce confusion. Obviously there are many types of teams, ranging from sports teams to debating teams. Although all teams share a number of similarities, the focus in this chapter will be on work teams. A work team is a group of people who interact and coordinate their work in order to accomplish specific work goals. Teams differ from groups in many aspects. The most important of these are listed in table 17.2.

As can be seen in table 17.2, teams differ from groups in that there is greater unity of purpose and loyalty in a team. There is also a greater tendency in teams to hold one another (rather than a supervisor) mutually accountable for achieving the team's goals. Work teams typically are led in one of two ways. Some of them are self-managed or self-directed; that is, they provide their own leadership. Other teams have a leader who coordinates the team's activities. That position sometimes rotates among the members of the team. A team almost always is able to perform at a higher level than a group because its members are committed to a team goal that they are willing to put ahead of

TABLE 17.2 Differences between Teams and Groups

Teams	Groups
Share or rotate leadership roles	Have a designated leader
Share authority and responsibility	Have little sharing of authority or responsibility
Have individual and group accountability	Have individual accountability
Have members who work together to produce results	Have results that are produced by individual effort
Have collective work products	Have individual work products
Share results and rewards	Have little sharing of results and rewards
Discuss, decide, and share work	Discuss, decide, and delegate work to individuals.

Source: David I. Cleland, *Strategic Management of Teams* (New York: Wiley, 1996), 38.

their own self-interests. "Teamwork is purposeful interdependency, which has the synergistic effect of accomplishing more than the sum of the parts."[23]

Because the use of teams is becoming increasingly popular, it is likely that although some managers say that they use team management in their libraries, they merely are giving lip service to the concept of true team management. Just because you call a group a team, it does not make it one. Renaming an existing department a team without changing how the work is done will not make a department a true team. As Ruth Metz writes:

> A group of people does not make a team. Naming a group a team does not make it one. A group saying that it is a team does not make it one either. For instance, a group of managers is not a team just because they call themselves a management team and meet together regularly. A work unit may call itself a team when it is actually more like an armed camp. Effective, high-performance teams have structure and operate under conditions that enable the team to perform effectively.[24]

Implementing teams in the truest sense is a profound change for most organizations and their staffs. There is often apprehension that use of teams might result in a loss of productivity because more time would need to be spent in meetings. Some people fear that the use of teams will produce mediocre decisions or a decline in productivity. In addition, there is often a fear of loss of control. As the ARL report mentioned earlier states: "The command and control cultures that team-based cultures replace are quite persistent, and the transition to teams can be especially difficult for middle managers, who may perceive it as a loss of power and influence."[25]

There is evidence that the use of teams in organizations can be effective, especially if the work to be done is complex. Advocates of team management say that teams are beneficial because they increase productivity, lead to better decisions, enhance employee commitment to work, foster creativity and innovation, increase organizational flexibility, and lead to greater customer satisfaction.

However, the use of teams has some disadvantages. It sometimes takes a group longer to achieve a goal than it would take an individual because group decision making is almost always slower than individual decision making. If teams are not carefully selected, they may have members who lack interest or motivation and do not assume their fair share of the responsibility. Social loafing is the tendency of some group members to reduce their work effort in groups and let the other team members take up the slack. This social loafing can cause tension and resentment within a group. Also, sometimes group decisions are not as good as individual decisions because team members begin to think alike and do not consider alternative solutions (sometimes called groupthink). Finally, teams sometimes make riskier decisions than an individual would because the members feel that no one individual is responsible for the decision. The group dynamics that are inevitable in any team situation can complicate the workings of the team.

Nonetheless, organizations that have moved to a team-based approach are growing in number, and it is likely that even more libraries increasingly will use teams in part or all of their organizations in the future. Teams can be effective if the organization that employs them understands the complex nature of teams and group dynamics. The next sections of this chapter will look at ways to build effective teams.

Characteristics of Effective Teams

No team that will be expected to work well together should be put together haphazardly. Instead, managers need to choose team members carefully, ensuring that the mix is right for the task that has to be accomplished. Research on teams has shown that certain characteristics are associated with successful teams. The most successful teams demonstrate:

- **Relevant skills.** The members of a team have to have both the technical and the interpersonal skills needed to allow the team to be effective.
- **Mutual trust.** The participants in effective teams trust the other members of the team.
- **An appropriate size.** Although teams will vary in number of members, the most effective team size usually is considered to be from 5 to 12 members. These numbers produce a team large enough to have varying points of view but still small enough to remain workable.
- **Good communication.** The most effective teams have learned to communicate well. They convey messages that are understood, and they have learned to incorporate feedback from other team members and from management.
- **Appropriate leadership.** Effective teams have leaders to help them achieve their goals. These leaders are not necessarily managers; they can be members of the team itself, as is common in self-managed teams. The role of the manager in a team is not so much to provide direction as to serve as a coach and a facilitator.

- **Clear goals.** The most effective teams know what their goals are and how to measure progress toward those goals. This clarity of goals helps ensure the team members' commitment to the achievement of the goals.

- **Loyalty.** Effective team members display loyalty to their group. They identify with the team and are willing to work hard to help the team accomplish its goals.[26]

Stages of Team Development

No team, no matter how carefully its members are chosen, functions at a high level of efficiency when it is first formed. People who are asked to work together for the first time have to get to know each other and learn how to work together. There is a sequence of development that most teams go through. The best-known model of how teams evolve over time is called the five-stage model.[27] These stages—forming, storming, norming, performing, and adjourning—are illustrated in figure 17.1.

Figure 17.1—Five Stages of Team Development

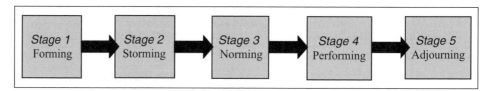

Source: Adapted from. Brucc W. Tuckman and Mary Ann C. Jensen. "Stages of Small Group Development Revisited," *Group and Organizational Studies* 2 (1977): 419–27.

When individuals are first placed in a team, the team begins to take shape. In organizations, people are usually placed in a team because of a work assignment. The first stage, that of forming, occurs when the team is first organized and when the definitions of its purpose, structure, and leadership begin to be decided. The second stage, usually called storming, takes place in the early stages of a team's development. The new members of the team are questioning many things, including who has control of the team and what is the team's direction. After the storming stage is finished, the norming stage begins. This is a relatively tranquil period. There is now a sense of the team's identity and purpose. The team has assimilated a common set of expectations, the norms, concerning what is expected of each team member.

One Library Team's Behavioral and Procedural Norms

The Reference Department at the University of Albany, State University of New York, is organized as a team known as RefTeam. Among other tools developed by that library team was an agreed-upon set of written behavioral and procedural norms. The behavioral norms, which relate to acting within the group, include:

RefTeam members communicate developments relative to other team members' areas or responsibilities.

RefTeam members agree to participate and voice opinions at meetings.

RefTeam meetings are a high priority. Members unable to attend will submit information to the RefTeam leader.

RefTeam members advocate for RefTeam and RefTeam initiatives, perspectives, and projects.

RefTeam members use supportive language about RefTeam.

The procedural norms are the methods by which the team agrees to function. Among the agreed-upon procedural norms are:

Keep RefTeam meeting time restricted. Meetings should last no longer than one hour.

Focus on the agenda during RefTeam meetings.

Revisit RefTeam goals and projects on a quarterly basis.

Annually visit role of each member.

Share RefTeam decisions; inform others outside of RefTeam when appropriate.

Seek feedback from non-RefTeam members who work at the reference desk: What do you need from us?

William F. Young, "Reference Team Self-Management at the University of Albany," *Library Administration and Management* 18, no. 4 (Fall 2004): 185–91.

The performing stage exists when the team is fully functional. Team energy has gone from getting to know one another and setting the norms to accomplishing the tasks.

The last stage, adjourning, takes place in teams that have a limited time span, such as a task force. The team has completed its task and is preparing to disband. The team turns away from task performance and directs its attention to disbanding. If the team's work has gone well, there is a feeling of accomplishment. Many in the team may feel sadness and loss because of the breakup of the team and the loss of camaraderie.

 What Would You Do?

The Avondale Public Library has decided to begin to use teams in most parts of its organization, and a number of new teams have just established. You have been put on one of these teams and have been working as a team member for two weeks now. You are beginning to think that working in teams is not very effective. The workplace is full of conflict. People seem to be constantly testing each other and trying to

> establish control, and not much real work is being done. What is going on here? Should you be discouraged? What would you do to try to improve things?

Basic Steps in Team Building

Wise managers realize that requiring people to work together does not ensure that a team will result. Instead, a team must be nurtured and developed. Lucile Wilson has delineated the basic steps that managers should follow in setting up successful work teams.

- First, focus on competencies when assigning team members. Look for self-starters and those who take pride in their work.
- Next, establish and communicate clear team goals. Be sure to allow time for the team to invest in the goals and make them their own.
- Establish deadlines and ground rules at the first meeting. Devoting attention at the beginning of the project prevents trouble later on.
- Involve each member of the team in the project. Use individual talents. Take advantage of opportunities for the personal growth of staff members.
- Maintain a results-oriented team structure. Monitor progress to be sure everyone is on track. Frequent feedback reduces miscommunication.
- Provide a collaborative climate and share power. Managers gain, not lose, power when teams share responsibility and authority.
- Strive for consensus. Explore all sides of an issue and get agreement from the group on solutions.
- Keep the group motivated. To meet team goals and fulfill library objectives, a manager needs strong skills in motivating other members of the group.
- Build confidence. Make each team member feel important and essential.
- Build trust and respect. Although team members must earn trust and mutual respect from one another, a manager can set examples of these qualities.
- Be flexible. Both team members and leaders function better if all can adapt to needed change. If a new approach is needed, try it.
- Furnish external support and recognition. Provide recognition for group and individual accomplishments; recognize the team when it reaches major goals.[28]

Employees who have never worked in teams cannot be expected to make an easy transition from an organizational structure in which they always have been told what to do to one in which they are responsible for their own self-management. Libraries that are considering implementing a team approach can learn a great deal from other libraries that already have implemented this type of management system.

The Roles People Play in Teams

Teams are composed of individuals with different temperaments and skills. Teams need to have this diversity in membership to achieve success because different skills are needed at different times. As team members work together, different individuals will assume different roles within the team, dependent upon aspects of their skills and personality. Because teams usually need to accomplish a number of different types of tasks, it is important to have team members who are able to play specific roles in helping the team achieve its objectives. Researchers have done a great deal of work on the roles people play within a team setting and the relationship between these roles and the team's effectiveness.[29] In general, these roles fall into two broad categories. The task management roles are those that facilitate accomplishing the task that needs to be done. The team maintenance roles are focused upon the emotional well-being of the individuals in the group and on the functioning of the group itself, rather than on the task that needs to be done. Some of the major roles in each of these categories can be seen in table 17.3.

Teams need to have individuals play both types of roles. People usually play more than one role in a team, and it is very common to have people who play a variety of roles, depending on what is needed at a particular time. Most people are either stronger at the task management role functions or the more people-centered roles, although some team members may be equally skilled

TABLE 17.3 Useful Roles Played on Teams

Task Management Roles	Team Maintenance Roles
Seeking or giving information or opinions. Initiating ideas or suggesting activities.	Harmonizing to keep conflict and tension at a minimum.
Timekeeping to ensure that the task remains on schedule, that meetings cover the agenda, and that team members' time is used appropriately.	Gatekeeping to ensure that all team members have an opportunity to express their opinions.
Summarizing to help in clarifying and putting parts together. Recording and keeping notes of discussions.	Encouraging others.
Elaborating on the comments or suggestions of others. Clarifying by presenting issues or solutions, providing facts and data, and keeping team members up to date.	Bridge building or negotiating to help bring opposing views together.
Acting as devil's advocate or skeptic to avoid potential problems.	Compromising.

in both types of roles. Teams should try to avoid having members who do not contribute to the set of roles because these individuals contribute little to the success of a team.

What Do You Think?

Think of any type of group meeting that you have attended recently. Did you see people play any of the roles that are described in this section? What type of roles do you typically play in a group or team setting?

Finally, there are some roles that people adopt in groups that impede the work of the team and make it less effective than it could be. These dysfunctional roles, which hinder the work of the team, consist of behavior that is directed toward fulfilling personal rather than team needs. Some of these harmful roles are:

- Blocking other people's suggestions or contributions or the team's attempt to come to closure.
- Being overly aggressive and competitive and always pushing for one's own way.
- Putting down other team members.
- Withdrawing and not participating in the team's activities.
- Disrupting meetings by excessively interrupting, talking excessively, and holding side discussions.
- Acting like a clown and not taking anything seriously.

It is clear from this discussion of roles that all the members of a team are interdependent upon one another. The success of a team depends upon a group of individuals who need to cover a wide range of goals necessary to accomplish a task and to keep a team functioning smoothly. For this reason, teams with a great diversity of personalities and skills often perform better than more homogenous teams.

Role-Play a Situation

You are part of a newly formed cross-functional team that has been implemented to select and purchase a new integrated library system. The team brings together people from many departments of the library and includes many people that you do not know well at all. The first team meeting was last week and the second is scheduled for this morning. You have noticed (it would be hard not to) that one of the team members tends to dominate the discussion. This group member not only talks too much but refuses to let others enter the conversation. You have decided to try to put a stop to this. What type of comment could you make to this group member at the meeting this morning to try to improve group communication?

Team Communication

A team's effectiveness to a large extent depends on communication. Obviously, the ability of team members to understand and to communicate is what enables them to work together collaboratively. All of the factors discussed previously related to improving communication are also applicable to team communication. But in addition to interteam communication, there is communication in any team-based organization that takes place between the managers and the members of the teams.

Managing teams requires different types of managerial skills including a different type of communication, and managers have to learn how to communicate in a fashion that fits this new model. Instead of being a boss, a team leader functions more like a facilitator. The manager goes from being someone who tells employees how to do things to one who facilitates the employees doing it on their own. Coaching is a term that is used often in describing the type of communication that occurs between managers and members of teams. Coaching is defined as "the purposeful and skillful effort by one individual to help another achieve specific performance goals."[30]

If a library has self-directed work teams, coaches can be useful in a number of situations. Sometimes they are needed when goals have to be redefined or clarified, when new skills have to be acquired, or when a team is struggling and appears to have gone off track. Sometimes difficult tasks confronted by a team, such as where to allocate resources, are facilitated by a coach.[31] Managers who are skillful coaches help their organization get the most out of teams.

The Future of Work Teams in Libraries

Some libraries that have switched to a team-based approach have been highly successful. For instance, the professional librarians at Dowling College are organized into a self-managed team, and they report that it has worked very well. The librarians there "work well together, trust each other, value their differences, mentor one another and respect each other, as well as enjoy working, laughing and having fun together."[32] Many other libraries have similar success stories to report about using teams. They have found that teams produce high-quality work and that they are beneficial for the employees because "teaming people up to grapple with challenging service issues, even if the process is inefficient by some standards, gives people a place at the learning table."[33]

Other libraries either have experimented with teams and abandoned them or have decided not even to explore the approach. The team-based organization provides benefits, but to implement it successfully, a library has to be willing to invest considerable time and resources in the effort. For some libraries, the benefits that result from the team approach are not worth the cost. The decision about whether the team approach to management should be implemented will be different for each library, and the decision may change as an organization itself evolves. At the present, there are libraries that are successfully using team-based management and others that are successfully managed without the use of teams. But, in every library, there is more employee participation in management now than in the past, and this participation likely will increase as libraries continue to change in response to the demands of their users and to rapid changes in information technology.

CONTINGENCY APPROACH TO LEADING

Many varying and often contradictory perspectives on leading have been covered in the preceding chapters that have discussed this managerial function. What is clear is that neither behavioral scientists nor experts from any other discipline have been able to provide managers with a specific prescription or universal theory about the most effective way to lead. The factors that constitute this management function are complex and multidimensional, and it therefore demands great skill to perform well. Unlike early theorists in management who relied on general principles to provide the one best way, most modern management theorists are convinced that there are few across-the-board concepts that apply in all instances. The situations with which managers deal are much more complex than originally realized, and different variables require managers to adopt different approaches. Instead of advocating a universal best theory, most contemporary management experts urge managers to be flexible and to adapt to the situation at hand. These experts, if asked how a manager should act, would say, "It all depends."

Managers should not become skeptical about the diversified approaches to management being offered to them. Instead, they should realize that in the case of leading, as in most other instances, one size does not fit all. There is no quick fix or magic solution. But this does not mean that managers should not become familiar with as many of the approaches or tools as possible. All of these new methods are useful, but none of them is guaranteed to be effective in every situation. Instead, managers have to look at the organization and its goals and then adopt a management strategy that will match the overall needs of the organization, its employees, and its customers.

Nor should managers completely deride management fads as useless practices that will go away if only ignored. Reexamination of some recently dismissed fads seems to indicate that they have survived, developed a new life, and remained influential in managerial practices. For instance, although Management by Objectives (MBO) is not being followed in its pure form in many organizations, its principles can still be found in much of our current thinking about goal setting. Even though quality circles and Total Quality Management (TQM) are not as popular as they once were, current interests in continuous quality and team-based initiatives have direct links to those earlier fads.[34] The best parts of these fads have survived and have been recycled, albeit in a different form.

Unfortunately, for those who are looking for one right way to manage, that one right way does not exist. Good management is more complex than that.

Contingency or situational theory, already discussed briefly in chapter 2, provides managers with a way to bring all of the disparate approaches together in an approach that provides the flexibility necessary to manage modern organizations. Contingency theory recognizes that every organization is unique, existing in a unique environment with unique workers and a unique purpose. Contingency theory is used to analyze individual situations and to understand the interrelationships between the variables to help managers determine what specific managerial actions are necessary in particular situations. What is appropriate in one situation may be inappropriate in another. The best techniques can be selected only after one is aware of the particular circumstances of each case. Contingency management suggests there must be a fit between the task, the people, the organization, and the external environment. In each organization, managers must be sure that each unit develops structures, measurement schemes, and reward practices that encourage its members to focus on the appropriate set of activities.

 Try This!

Think about an organization that you know fairly well. This may be either a library or another type of organization. Imagine that this organization is trying to adopt contingency theory management and has hired you as a consultant to help implement this approach. Analyze your organization in terms of the tasks it performs, the people who work there, the structure of the organization, the management style used, and the external environment in which the organization is located.

For an expanded version of this exercise, go to the organizational analysis exercise at http://www.lu.com/management.

Managers who wish to use the contingency approach must understand the complex and interrelated causes of behavior in an organization and then use their intelligence and creative ability to invent a new solution or to judge which existing solutions might best be used.[35] Library managers using this approach might decide that different sections of the library would benefit from different styles of leading. For example, a part of a technical services department that performs highly standardized, repetitive work might benefit from a more task-oriented style of management. In the same library, a more people-oriented style of management might be appropriate for the reference department.

The contingency theory can be used in functions of management other than leading. For instance, as discussed in section 3, there is no one best way for an institution to be organized. There are also no surefire approaches to planning, controlling, or managing human resources. Many variables, such as size, type of organization, and type of tasks being performed, play a role in the choice to be made. In the broadest sense, contingency theory applies to all of the managerial functions and provides managers with a comprehensive model that can be used to achieve maximum effectiveness in all managerial functions. With the contingency approach, the performance of managerial functions is closely tied to an analysis of the total system: the organization, its subsystems, and its environment. Contingency theory offers a flexible approach that is better suited to the complexity of management than are other approaches. "The basic deficiency with earlier approaches is that they did not recognize the variability in tasks and people which produces this complexity. The strength of the contingency approach ... is that it begins to provide a way of thinking about this complexity, rather than ignoring it."[36] Although the contingency approach to management certainly does not provide all of the answers, it provides a way of making sense of a number of disparate approaches.

CONCLUSION

In summary, this section has dealt with the function of leading, which is the most interpersonal aspect of management. The chapters have dealt primarily with how to motivate, lead, and communicate, but other related topics such as ethics and team building have been included. The ultimate aim of leading is to allow the organization to achieve its objectives through the activities of the people employed within it. Leading means getting employees to work efficiently and to produce results that are beneficial to the organization. In short, leading is getting things done through other people for the good of the organization.

Because leading is so complex and multifaceted, managers often find it one of their most challenging and important tasks. The need for managers to excel at leading becomes more pressing as organizations grow larger, as the rate of change in the environment increases, and as demands by employees for a more rewarding work life proliferate. The next section of this book discusses ways that managers coordinate a modern organization. Finally, some of the challenges and rewards of managing in the twenty-first century will be discussed in the last chapter of this book.

NOTES

1. For an overview of the growth in participative management in academic libraries, see Louis Kaplan, "On the Road to Participative Management: The American Academic Library, 1934–1970," *Libri* 38, no. 4 (December 1988): 314–20.

2. Daryl R. Conner, *Managing at the Speed of Change: How Resilient Managers Succeed and Prosper Where Others Fail* (New York: Villard, 1993), 198.

3. Ibid.

4. Nicholas C. Burckel, "Participatory Management in Academic Libraries: A Review," *College and Research Libraries* 45 (January 1984): 32.

5. Conner, *Managing at the Speed of Change.*

6. Fred Luthans, *Organizational Behavior,* 10th ed. (New York: McGraw-Hill-Irwin, 2004).

7. Lorraine Grubbs West, *Lessons in Loyalty: How Southwest Airlines Does It* (Dallas: Cornerstone Leadership Institute, 2005).

8. John Case, *The Open-Book Experience: Lessons from over 100 Companies Who Successfully Transformed Themselves* (New York: Perseus, 1998).

9. Edward E. Lawler III, *Organizing for High Performance: Employee Involvement, TQM, Re-engineering, and Knowledge Management in the Fortune 1,000* (San Francisco: Jossey-Bass, 2001), 149–50.

10. For instance, see Bonnie Horenstein, "Job Satisfaction of Academic Librarians: An Examination of the Relationships between Satisfaction, Faculty Status and Participation," *College and Research Libraries* 54 (1993): 255–69; G. J. Leckie and J. Brett, "Job Satisfaction of Canadian University Librarians: A National Survey," *College and Research Libraries* 58 (1997): 31–47; Aapasia Togia, Athanasios Koustelio, and Nicolas Tsigilis, "Job Satisfaction among Greek Academic Librarians," *Library and Information Science Research* 26, no. 3 (2004): 373–83; Gerrida J. Oosthuizen and Adeline S. A. du Toit, "Participative Management in Academic Library Services," *Library Management* 20, no. 4 (1999): 213–20.

11. Edward E Lawler III, *... From the Ground Up: Six Principles for Building the New Logic Corporation* (San Francisco: Jossey-Bass, 1996), 22.

12. Ibid., 12.

13. Ibid., 30–31.

14. Donald V. Nightingale, "Participation in Decision-Making: An Examination of Style and Structure and Their Effect on Member Outcomes," *Human Relations* 34 (December 1981): 1130.

15. For additional information on this type of team in a library, see Mike Knecht, "Virtual Teams in Libraries," *Library Administration and Management* 18, no. 1 (Winter 2004): 24–29.

16. George Soete, *The Use of Teams in ARL Libraries* (SPEC Kit 232) (Washington, DC: Association of Research Libraries, 1998).

17. Elaine Russo Martin, "Team Effectiveness in Academic Medical Libraries: A Multiple Case Study," *Journal of the Medical Library Association* 94, no. 3 (July 2006): 271–78.

18. See Charles B. Lowry, "Continuous Organizational Development—Teamwork, Learning Leadership, and Measurement," *Portal* 5, no. 1 (January 2005): 1–6; and Shelley Phipps, "The System Design Approach to Organizational Development: The University of Arizona Model," *Library Trends* 53, no. 1 (Summer 2004): 68–112.

19. Rosann Bazirjian and Rebecca Mugridge, *Teams in Library Technical Services* (Lanham, MD: Scarecrow Press, 2006).

20. Knecht, "Virtual Teams in Libraries," 24–29.

21. Betsy A. Bernfeld, "Developing a Team Management Structure in a Public Library," *Library Trends* 53, no. 1 (Summer 2004): 112–28.

22. For an example of how one team-based organization approached this problem, see Michael Ray, "Making Systems Visible," *ARL Bimonthly Report* no. 208–209 (February/April 2000), http://www.arl.org/newsltr/208_209/index.html.

23. Ruth F. Metz, *Coaching in the Library: A Management Strategy for Achieving Excellence* (Chicago: American Library Association, 2001), 46.

24. Ibid., 45.

25. Soete, *Use of Teams in ARL Libraries*.

26. J. Richard Hackman, ed., *Groups that Work (and Those that Don't)* (San Francisco: Jossey-Bass, 1990); Eric Sundstrom, Kenneth P. deMeuse, and David Futrell, "Work Teams: Applications and Effectiveness," *American Psychologist* 45 (1990): 122–24; Dean Tjosvold, *Team Organization: An Enduring Competitive Advantage* (New York: Wiley, 1991).

27. Bruce W. Tuckman and Mary Ann C. Jensen, "Stages of Small Group Development Revisited," *Group and Organizational Studies* 2 (1977): 419–27.

28. Lucile Wilson, *People Skills for Library Managers: A Common Sense Guide for Beginners* (Englewood, CO: Libraries Unlimited, 1996): 50–52.

29. Some of the most interesting research has been done by Belbin. See R. Meredith Belbin, *Management Teams*, 2nd ed. (Burlington, MA: Butterworth-Heinemann, 2004).

30. Metz, *Coaching in the Library*, 7.

31. Ibid., 46–48.

32. Francie C. Davis, "Calling the Shots: A Self-Managed Team in an Academic Library," *Proceedings of the 10th National ACRL Conference* Chicago: ACRL (2001), 240–49, http://www.ala.org/ala/acrl/acrlevents/davis.pdf

33. Metz, *Coaching in the Library*, 47.

34. Jane Whitney Gibson and Dana V. Tesone, "Management Fads: Emergence, Evolution, and Implications for Managers," *Academy of Management Executive* 15 (November 2001): 128–29.

35. Jay W. Lorsch, "Making Behavioral Science More Useful," *Harvard Business Review* 57 (March–April 1979): 174.

36. John J. Morse and Jay W. Lorsch, "Beyond Theory Y," *Harvard Business Review* 48 (May–June 1970): 68.

Coordinating

Quality control requires establishing human and mechanical measures that identify weaknesses, correct those weaknesses, and evaluate the results for continuing development. Assessment and coordination activities are critical for understanding library customers and offering services, spaces, collections, and tools that best meet their needs. They also help establish accountability. Evaluation techniques, such as performance measures, output indicators, program impact indicators and tools are useful in that process. Tools such as unit cost, cost accounting, cost-benefit analysis, and cost-effectiveness and budgeting are examples of techniques and tools employed to measure effectiveness and efficiency. Financial health is a key element in a successful equation of information services. No other element can be successfully developed without strong financial support. However, many elements cannot and should not be measured in strictly monetary terms.

Coordination implies the existence of workable plans with identified and realistic goals. This enhances the development of regulations and focuses organizational activities on those goals and objectives. With that commitment in place, tools and techniques can strengthen accountability and aid progress toward meeting established goals. In order to remain accountable, a library or information center must evaluate its performance to ensure that both the human and the material resources are effectively and efficiently employed toward achieving their goals and those of the larger institution of which it is a part.

Coordination is inextricably tied to the planning process because it is impossible to effectively plan without knowing how success of that plan can be measured. The whole management process can be viewed as a circle, with the evaluation step in the decision-making process being the component that completes the circle and brings the organization back, full circle, to future planning. This is, of course, necessary in the change cycle of organizations. The function of coordinating and controlling in order that good decisions can be made requires accurate and timely information. The budgeting aspect pulls together the various pieces of an organizational plan and relates it to the services plan in monetary terms.

This section addresses the most important tools and techniques necessary for today's information services organizations.

Chapter

18

Measuring, Evaluating, and Coordinating Organizational Performance

Overview

It is time for the annual review of performance of city agencies in this large midwestern city. City Council President Jim Ryan has called an emergency meeting with stern warning that this review session of city agencies might not be a pleasant one because of growing concerns about inflation and out-of-control spending over the last several years. "Some services definitely need to be curtailed or even cut," he states as he concludes his somber opening remarks. The first item on the agenda is the library's budget and how it relates to the needs of the community. Although all city agencies are under scrutiny, Jim relates the gist of a recent conversation he had with a constituent who questioned the continuing almost blind support for the library as a "public good." The phrase that constituent had used in concluding his opposition was that "Large amounts of money are being stuffed down that hole, and for what purpose?" Placed into the context of limited financial resources and that comment, Jim is determined to pursue the need for concrete data to support the escalating costs of the library. What convincing data does the library have; what proof can the library staff provide of their "worth" and need for continuous support at a substantial level? What kind of support is there in the community as to the success, or failure, of programs and use?

A number of tools and techniques have been developed and are employed by library and information services organizations to answer those questions with legitimacy and authority. Some basic ones are quantitative in nature, others are qualitative measures that have been developed to measure outcomes and observe value—how people use and value information accessed through services and systems of the library.

This chapter discusses some of the most important measurement tools and techniques that have been developed to improve information services.

MEASURING AND EVALUATING

During the recent past, with dramatic shifts in the nature of information access and information services, coordinating and control aspects of an information services organization have become more pervasive, committing personnel at all levels to accountability in services quality. The process of reaching this point of accountability has involved development of several levels and types of measures:

1. Input measures, including both:
   a. resources input; that is, budget, staff, facilities, materials, equipment;
   b. activities input; that is, programs developed to fulfill identified goals.

2. Output measures: The various products of program activities, measured by accomplishments (usually counted in numbers: number of books circulated, number of reference questions answered, etc.).

3 Outcomes assessments: The benefits or changes for individuals or populations during or after participating in activities, including, for instance, acquired knowledge or skills, changed attitudes or values, improvement in status or conditions, and so forth. They relate to inputs in order to identify and establish best practices for future services.

The process of measuring, evaluating, and coordinating an organization's performance through identifying and developing output measures and then assessing their success is now, more than ever before, an essential component in the planning process. The concept of measuring user-centered information services through user satisfaction has been incorporated in many strategic planning processes. This has come about through realization that accountability requires assessing outcomes and determination of success in the effort. Management strategies now more stringently address customer needs and satisfaction rather than simply quantifying activities as organizational inputs and tasks. This shift requires understanding user needs, their information-seeking patterns, and ultimate satisfaction, with focus on positive user outcomes.

One major reason for the shift is that users and other stakeholders have become more sophisticated and demands are greater, placing more attention on adaptability and flexibility in services with an information-on-demand attitude. This intense pressure on physical and personnel resources naturally brings with it a greater challenge for quality control. At the same time, it presents opportunities to conduct reality checks along the way—a meaningful process of accountability that helps determine both the effectiveness and the efficiency of programs and services in the context of the organization's stated goals. Various techniques and tools have been developed and/or adopted by information services organizations to achieve this goal. This process of accountability requires greater attention to use of and proof of value of resources as well as a search for greater efficiency of operation and effectiveness in meeting users' needs. It also promotes efforts to measure the institution's worth in terms of user interaction with its resources and services.

 Some Definitions

Performance indicators: An effort to develop decisions and actions in order to guide what an organization does and why it does it.

Input indicators: Measure resources, both human and financial; also can include measures of characteristics of target populations.

Output indicators: Measure the quantity of goods and services produced and the efficiency of production.

Outcomes: Achievement indicator reinforcing an emphasis on a specific performance.

However, this shift does not obviate the need for factual data, which remains one important measure for funding authorities. Traditionally, such statistical data have been collected in input areas, such as expenditures, material resources in analog or digital forms, circulation statistics, cataloging volume, use of catalogs and bibliographic databases, and number of staff, and output areas, such as number of transactions, hours the premises are accessible, and the availability, use, and usability of the material. These statistics also are used for comparative purposes with organizations of similar size and like mission organizations.

Librarians and other information services workers are now also seeking ways of demonstrating deeper quality control along with that quantitative data. Evaluation, accountability, and cost measurement are intertwined in every aspect of the organization's work, and solid performance indicators are required to provide some basis for making some decisions in the strategic planning process.

Qualitative information is gathered from such techniques as focus groups, interviewing, usability studies, and observation, which are but examples of techniques for understanding user behavior and are being utilized to establish value. User satisfaction, coupled with expectations as a performance indicator, is important in the development of such outcome measures as a means of establishing not only user satisfaction but also the impact of library services on communities of users and potential users.

The outcome of those types of tools and techniques enhances efforts to collect more amorphous data from such transactional information sources as library online systems, electronic information sources, consortial use arrangements, and sources available through the Internet, many of them based on technological innovations that now not only enhance but also challenge traditional modes of production and dissemination of information and measurement of information services.

Performance Indicators

In order to improve performance standards, one technique an organization can use is that of establishing measurements; that is, describe the outcome to be achieved. Therefore, performance measurement is not simply concerned with collecting data associated with a predefined performance goal or standard. The process should be quantitative or qualitative or both, with specific measures expressed in order to determine success of that performance over time. Outcomes are the ways in which library users are changed as a result of their contact with the library's resources and programs.[1] Those outcomes have been identified variously as "benefits or changes" for individuals or populations during or after participating in program activities, including new knowledge, increased skills, changed attitudes or values, modified behavior, improved condition, or altered status (e.g., number of students whose grades improved after homework clinics, number of children who maintained reading skills over the summer as a result of the summer reading program, number of people who report being better able to access and use networked information after attending information literacy classes, etc.). This basically incorporates inputs, activities, and outputs, while adding the important element of outcome assessment.[2]

All types of libraries and information services organizations are attempting to take the next important initiative, having instituted input and output measures, to focusing on outcomes assessment. This, of course, requires first identifying those outcomes to be achieved by the organization. This step beyond instituting "quality and outcome measures"[3] is to develop an outcome assessment process to demonstrate the quality and effectiveness of those services and the impact that they have on the lives of the public, the satisfaction, and the value they add. Currently, that is even more challenging because firm standards for outcome assessments have not yet been fully developed.[4] This is evident in the current environment of the virtual library in which electronic visits are combined with physical access and electronic retrieval competes with circulation. Needless to say, the assessment process must be client centered in order to assess changes in the library users themselves, resulting from the services or resources provided.

This gradual shift in the orientation from a preoccupation with input measures, mostly internal in nature and somewhat limited in effectiveness, to a user orientation, with primary emphasis on those output measures, results, and accountability, has tended to balance quantitative and qualitative factors in the coordinating process. Much more emphasis is being placed on the output factors of service performance and assessment. Quality control, quality audit, and quality assessment are common measurement terms. Those types of performance indicators are being examined, not only from the perspective of librarians but also by stakeholders, those customers and funding authorities that often have varying attitudes about what constitutes efficient and effective information services. This introduces the concept of coordinating and controlling what is done and the way it is done.

 What Do You Think?

It is not only what we do, but also what we do not do, for which we are accountable.

Molière's admonition provides opportunity to discuss the kinds of measures that are necessary in the effort of information services organizations to become accountable and remain so. What are some of those measures, or lack thereof, that you can identify in your experiences of information seeking?

COORDINATING AND CONTROLLING

Some distinction must be made between the act of coordinating and the control mechanisms used to accomplish it. The two are obviously interrelated: Effective coordinating within an organization depends on the types of controls that are in place. Coordinating is the act, and controls are the means that provide information for decision making. The former pertains to an end, whereas the latter is the means; the first is concerned with events, and the other with facts; one is analytical and operational, concerned with what was and is, whereas the other deals with expectations.[5] The management of resources requires determination of what resources the organization has at its disposal, or should make available, and how those resources can be employed to achieve the mission of the organization. It requires strong financial planning and feedback mechanisms to ensure success.

Control takes into account any action or process that leads to altered results and involves setting standards, establishing criteria, developing policies and budgets, conducting performance evaluations, scheduling actions to achieve objectives, then monitoring the outcome on a periodic basis, and, finally, providing some type of feedback mechanism to ensure efficiency and effectiveness in the achievement, the latter suggesting corrective measures for adjustments or alternatives to the situation. In a library or information center context, controls relate to physical resources, information resources, and human resources. Although the primary aspect is usually a financial one, because no other element can be effectively developed without money, some things cannot and should not be measured in monetary terms. These include those effective performance-of-services measures and customer-satisfaction measures already mentioned.

Requirements for Control

Control implies the existence of goals and plans and the regulation of the organization's activities toward those goals. Controls are concerned with keeping things on track, successful progress toward meeting specified objectives, identifying operational weakness, and developing corrective action. Whereas plans determine what should be done, controls assure that it is done, acting as the tools and techniques for implementing the planning process. In order to avoid failure, controls are both desirable and, if applied consistently and fairly, necessary. At the operational level, controlling techniques relate to such processes as policies, procedures, task analyses, and job audits. The most effective controls prevent deviations from plans by anticipating that such deviations will occur unless immediate action is taken. However, other types of control are also necessary for feedback, and they naturally emanate from the planning process.

To be effective, controls must be objective and must reflect the job they are to perform. In addition, they should be established and agreed upon before they are needed to minimize conflict and to optimize efforts. At the least, the controls should point out exceptions at critical points. In addition, any control system that does not pose corrective actions after deviations occur is little more than an interesting exercise. In other words, there must be an action plan accompanying the evaluation process. After activities have been initiated, some sort of control mechanism must be established to monitor progress and correct actions, as needed, to achieve goals. Given those guidelines, individuals at all levels are responsible for steering the organization on the right course. Controls, wherever they are found and whatever they control, involve three basic steps:

1. Establishing standards.
2. Measuring performance against standards.
3. Correcting deviations.

The ultimate act of controlling in the library and information services setting is, to some degree, external because most information centers are accountable to higher public- or private-sector authorities that provide primary impetus and funding for the operations of the information services organization. The library or information center usually is legally bound by constitutional provisions, charters, articles of incorporation, and general or special laws applicable to the greater institution as a whole. Ultimate responsibility is coordinated by a president, superintendent, mayor or city manager, executive director, board of overseers, board of directors, and so forth. These external authorities are responsible through their overall institutional or societal charge and because of their funding and fiduciary mandate.

In addition to those bodies directly related to the controlling function of an information services organization, numerous outside groups, some with sanctioning powers, are involved in various aspects of the operation, including standard setting, certification, and accreditation of libraries, librarians, and other information specialists. For example, the North Central Association of College and Secondary Schools, a regional agency in the United States, is a responsible accrediting body that observes and makes recommendations on libraries as a part of its overall review of higher education institutions. The American Library Association influences library support through the establishment of standards for various types of libraries and library services and through its Committee on Accreditation, which is responsible for setting standards for library and information science education and accrediting those institutions that meet the set standards. State departments of education establish guidelines for the certification of school librarians or media specialists and establish standard formulas for the allocation of funds, and specialty-specific interest groups, such as the Medical Library Association, set certification standards and continuing education requirements for their members.

Some groups and agencies exist primarily to regulate activities of organizations and institutions and to measure, to one extent or another, their actions and outputs. Laws, including local, state, national, and international ones, regulate certain activities. For example, planning, constructing, and maintaining library buildings may be controlled through municipal ordinances and regulations, building codes, zoning, and fire regulations, and international copyright agreements or international standards promulgated by the International Standards Organization (ISO) or those that are on the agenda of the World Intellectual Property Organization (WIPO) may direct the services or activities of an information center. Comprehensive legislation, for instance, state and federal funding legislation in the United States, places certain other types of control on the operation of libraries and information centers within their jurisdiction. Such regulatory agencies and their authority vary from one part of the world to another, but their influence remains basically the same.

Other bodies that exert some external control on libraries include unions, special interest groups, and political bodies. Through collective bargaining, unions can influence hiring, salaries, working conditions, fringe benefits, and so forth; political bodies can influence the appointments of individuals, the allocation of monies, and even the disbursal of funds within libraries and information centers. Pressure is sometimes placed on information services by outside bodies in areas of hiring new staff and in issues relating to collection development, censorship and intellectual freedom, and use of library services and facilities. Use of the Internet and access to information through libraries remain heatedly debated topics. Groups such as Friends of the Library are examples of well-meaning supporters that may expect to have some say in the directions libraries will take, sometimes in exchange for their charitable contributions.

 Try This!

Discuss those various outside influences as they relate to curtailment of good information services. Which have positive influence through their promotion of services and which are more controlling in their activities? Suggest possible promotional activities that are not currently apparent in support groups.

TECHNIQUES FOR EVALUATING ACTIVITIES

Developing Standards

Standards are established criteria against which subsequent performance can be compared and evaluations can be made. Most often they are developed, or at least devised, from organizational goals.[6] Standards fall into two basic classes:

1. Those relating to material and performance, including quality, quantity, cost, and time.
2. Those relating to moral aspects, including the organization's value system and ethical criteria that may be used to establish some sort of code of ethics.

Standards may be physical, representing quantities of products, units of service, work hours, and similar things that can be evidenced and measured through time-and-motion studies; they may be stated in monetary terms, such as costs, revenues, or investments, which are evidenced through record keeping, cost analysis, and budget presentation; or they may be expressed in other terms that measure performance, such as performance ratings and appraisal systems. Of course, some other factors are difficult to evaluate and measure, and they require a different approach to measurement. For instance, how does one measure commitment on the part of individuals to organizational goals? Most of the standards are descriptive in nature, prescribe quantitative objectives, are arbitrarily formulated, and are directed toward evaluating the input of the library's resources. General standards, such as those developed by the American Library Association's various units or other national or international associations, are important as guides, but they cannot necessarily provide meaningful evaluation for the individual library or information center for a number of reasons. A good example is those produced by the Reference and Information Services Division of ALA.[7] Some standards are nebulous and almost impossible to measure, some are simply guidelines for proceeding, and others combine qualitative evaluation with quantitative formulas. If a scientific control method is to be used in developing the standard, then it is most likely measurable to some extent. In every case, to be effective, standards should be acceptable to those whose performance is regulated by them. To be accepted and most effective, the process of applying performance standards should be explained and agreed upon by those affected, rather than forced, because it is only human nature that if standards are forced upon individuals, some resistance is likely to occur.

Measuring Performance

Performance measurement is embedded in the strategic planning process and is an essential feedback mechanism to support decision making in libraries and information services. Such measures are expressed in both quantitative and qualitative forms, including measures for economic value and financial adequacy, image value, competency, cost of quality, and so forth. Feedback, or measuring performance, is an important factor in this controlling process. It is particularly important as a technique for establishing the value of information services for the benefit of intended customers or funding authorities.

An important next step is the measurement of performance in relation to standards. After standards have been agreed upon, some sort of analysis must be performed to measure the activity against the standard. Techniques such as cost-benefit analysis and time-and-motion studies commonly are employed to measure the standards of performance for operations. Of course, not everything can be quantified; judgment and flexibility are also necessary. However, great care must be taken because subjective judgment may obviate actual performance.

Some types of performance are more difficult to measure because they are more complex, less regulated, and require greater initiative and thus are less quantifiable. In other words, not all quantitative measures accurately reflect the quality of an activity. For example, a rare books cataloger may perform original cataloging on two items during an eight-hour period. The quality of that activity must be measured delicately, objectively, and with full understanding of all nuances involved.

Increasing attention has been paid to performance measures in libraries and information services, as is particularly evident in international conferences on the topic.[8] There are a number of questions that "outline the different 'hows' of measurement and, in effect, encompass input, output, performance, and outcomes measures. The questions can be used individually or in groups. In fact, some of the 'hows' are calculated by using data derived from other 'hows.'" Simply stated, these questions focus on "How much?" "How many?" "How economical?" "How prompt?" "How valuable?" "How reliable?" "How courteous?" and "How satisfied?"[9] Therefore, measures can be conducted on aspects of extensiveness (i.e., amount of service provided), effectiveness, efficiency, costing (i.e., cost benefit or cost-effectiveness), service quality, satisfaction, or any number of other factors. It is obvious from the large number of reports and studies that measuring performance is a continuous and continuing process, whether it is related to systems measurement or personnel performance.

One continuing challenge among researchers and practitioners is the need to develop a set of representative outcome measures that convey customer expectations from which libraries can choose which ones to use, or modify, for local benchmarking. However, a broad range of methods have been tested in an attempt to prove and substantiate the outcome of information services.[10] It is recognized that performance metrics must be in place, with an infrastructure to collect, filter, analyze, and disseminate them both within and outside the organization. Many groups are working on such activities, particularly the Association of Research Libraries, which, several years ago, began an ARL New Measures Initiative[11] to assess how well libraries meet stakeholder needs and how they use their resources and services. The measures address the issue of impact of the library's resources and services and how this can be evaluated in terms of the difference between the user's expectations and the perception of what is delivered. Quantitative and descriptive statistics are easier to develop and measure than qualitative ones, particularly when benchmarking is used. Such quantitative statistics are compiled by a large number of organizations.

What is important in all measurement activities is to keep accurate records of what is done so that the process can be monitored on an ongoing basis. If records are not kept, if there is lack of control, and if the output cannot be measured objectively, then it is difficult to assess how much actual performance deviates from the planned performance and to determine a measure of success. A number of research reports prove helpful in this activity. Perhaps the most comprehensive is that developed by the International Organization for Standardization, which specifies a set of 29 indicators grouped in three areas:

1. User satisfaction.

2. Public services, which include general indicators as well as specific indicators on providing documents, retrieving documents, lending documents, document delivery from external sources, inquiry and reference services, information searching, and facilities.

3. Technical services, including indicators in the area of acquiring, processing, and cataloging documents.[12]

Besides feedback, the other type of basic control is prevention, which attempts to predict what will happen by setting parameters. Goal setting in the planning process is a good example of this type of control. Goal setting takes information about past performance and introduces it into decisions about adjustments that are needed for future actions. Such a process is just as important to an ordinary control process as it is to a more complex, automated one.

Correcting Deviations

Correcting any deviations from the norm is a vital step in the coordinating process. This correction can be achieved by exercising organizational prerogative, for instance, in the case of personnel, by reassignment or clarification of duties, by additional staffing, by better selection and training of staff, or by some other method of restaffing. Corrections also can be made by adjusting goals, developing new or alternative plans, or altering ways of doing things.

A simplified example of detecting deviations in libraries, which combines elements of goal setting and feedback, is a monthly budget balance sheet that might show, for instance, that by the month of July, three-fourths of the amount budgeted for online access for the year already has been expended and that, unless corrective action is taken, the organization will overrun the budgeted amount in that category well before the end of the calendar year. A decision must be made on how to keep this from happening.

Cybernetics, which has become increasingly important in the control feedback process, studies the interaction of communication and control as fundamental factors in all human activity and now is being applied to many large organizations, including libraries and information centers. Basically, cybernetics is a self-regulating method by which messages that the system sends to itself indicate deviations from the desired course. This may be expressed in a very simplified diagram that shows how the information flow makes possible the self-regulation of the system (see figure 18.1).

Figure 18.1—With Cybernetics, an Organization Can Provide Feedback

Communication is the most important aspect of a feedback control system because it involves transmitting and receiving messages or information—in this case, data used to make the decisions that control the system's behavior. Again, a simplified diagram illustrates the process (see figure 18.2).

Evaluating Efforts

Evaluation and assessment of services is a complex process that attempts to identify areas needing improvement with an aim toward taking corrective action. It is not a one-time thing or even a sometime thing, but rather an ongoing review of operations. This aspect of controlling is inextricably tied to and, indeed, is a major component in the strategic planning process because it is impossible to evaluate unless it is known what is to be evaluated. How effectively and efficiently a library or information center is meeting the goals and objectives identified in the planning process should be measured through such an evaluation. If the whole process is viewed as a circle, the evaluation step in the decision-making process brings the organization to full circle in its planning for change. There are at least three factors to be considered in evaluation:

1. The input to the service or, more specifically, the application of resources necessary for information services to occur, including staff, materials, space, and equipment. They can be measured in terms of the amount or number of resources involved and their cost. Those are all measures of the input one should consider.

2. The output should be considered in terms of the quantities of output of the services and how that can be cost factored, including price, timeliness, availability, and accessibility, all contributing to the value of the services. Quality of output is of primary concern. Measures of use and nonuse of the services require examining the factors that affect use and nonuse and assessment of the importance and satisfaction with specific attributes of those services.

Figure 18.2—Communication Is Key to a Feedback Control System

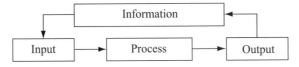

3. The outcomes include such elements as saving time, improving productivity, improving quality of life and work, and enhancing timeliness—adding value. It is the relationship of those measures that begins to illustrate the usefulness and importance of libraries that has some bearing on justifying the budget and resources in the effort to improve both personal and professional lives.

Evaluation requires that several questions will have been answered in the process:

1. Are you now able to make decisions that you wanted to be able to make as a result of your evaluation?
2. Was the primary audience adequately identified and solicited for the results?
3. Was the information needed actually received in the process?
4. Where was that information sought and received, and how?
5. Were resources adequate to get the information, analyze it, and report it?

Those are the same primary questions that will have been identified to begin the process. Evaluation requires careful collection and analysis of that type of data in order to make decisions.

Evaluation can come from a variety of sources. Cost-benefit analysis, budget analysis, performance evaluation, and collection evaluation are examples of techniques used in the evaluation process. Such data provides insight into effectiveness, efficiency, impact, and value of a program, operation, or service.[13] Accountability in libraries has fostered the development of many prescriptive techniques to measure the efficiency of library operations and the effectiveness of library services.

When one thinks of internal controls, mechanical controls come to mind first, including circulation control, automated serials, use of online databases, and the like. These technological controls are only examples of tools that are used to measure library operations. Technology has become an invaluable ubiquitous aid to decision making in all types of library and other information services organizations. It is also being used effectively in establishing models for library operations through decision theory, game theory, graph theory, queuing theory, and simulation exercises, among other applications. Many basic techniques and tools are employed in the control process in the library, particularly as libraries strive for accountability of their operations. These include varying sophisticated tools, including decision support systems and operations research.

 What Would You Do?

You have been asked by the library director of a large academic library to head a committee of staff with the responsibility of developing accountability measures for the library. It is important because the president of the university has dictated the need for value in the peripheral areas of the college's organization—bookstore, computer center, libraries, and so forth—which, according to the board of trustees, seem to be costing disproportionate amounts of budgetary resources. How will you begin to prioritize the kinds of quantitative and qualitative data needed to support arguments for not only continued funding but also for additional resources to meet the goals of information services in the institution?

TOOLS OF COORDINATION

The function of coordinating and controlling so that good decisions can be made requires accurate and timely information for the control and monitoring of specific kinds of data. This process has become heavily dependent upon technology to enhance efficient information gathering. This combination of human expertise within the organization and technology to facilitate its use is what one might identify at the core of discussions about the knowledge management initiative or knowledge networking today. The process of locating, organizing, transferring, and using information and expertise within the organization, made more efficient and effective by the use of technology, fits appropriately in any discussion of tools for decision making. Automated systems have the capacity to crunch enormous amounts of information relating both to input and output of information for decision making in libraries. However, caution always must be exercised in employing some of these tools because, in the hands of amateurs, the quantitative systems and tools frequently produce misleading data or unsubstantiated solutions. In addition, mechanistic formulas for dealing with complex realities are not always appropriate.

Several initiatives can be identified in a library context that lend themselves to adequate measurement tools, and these can prove helpful in meeting goals and objectives as they coordinate and measure performance.

Cost-Benefit Analysis

A cost-benefit evaluation can be conducted to determine whether the potential worth or value of a service is greater than or less than the cost of providing it. In other words, is the service or process justified? Therefore, it is an attempt to identify and express in monetary terms one measure in determining the value. Developing a cost-benefit analysis process need not be an intimidating undertaking. Most people in their daily work lives, in fact, engage in some level of intuitive cost-benefit analysis. In its simplest form, cost-benefit analysis is little more than a formalized approach for identifying and weighing the advantages and drawbacks associated with a decision. In general, cost-benefit analysis provides a useful tool for evaluating the efficiency of a regulation. At its best, it can separate good intentions from good ideas. It is, however, only a tool, and, as with any tool, it can be used effectively or misused. Cost-benefit analysis is flexible and can be adapted to focus on specific functions or aggregated on the costs and benefits of the system as a whole. Some cost-benefit activities appear to have little to do with control—financial reports, status reports, project reports—but they all require some type of monitoring, serving as an overview of what is being done, how it is being done, and if it is being done efficiently.

One of the most difficult aspects for libraries is placing a monetary figure on the benefit of operations, unlike many other organizations that can calculate benefits for service from the financial charge of that service, which somewhat reflects the value of providing that service. In other words, measuring the benefits that users derive rather than just measuring what libraries do.

But cost-benefit analysis is a set of procedures to measure the merit of actions in monetary terms. The process reduces uncertainty by helping make decisions about the best of options available. It is used as a counterpart to private-sector profitability accounting. The difference is that most public actions to improve public well-being, such as those instituted in libraries, do not have well-established private markets that generate price information on which to judge their value or benefits. "Cost-benefit analysis can be defined as a systematic approach which seeks to:

1. Determine whether or not a particular program or proposal is justified,
2. Rank various alternatives appropriate to a given set of objectives, and
3. Ascertain the optimal course of action to attain these objectives."[14]

Cost-benefit analysis is a form of measurement that considers both direct and indirect costs in the allocation of resources. The technique is used to examine both the current budget allocation process and to ascertain the level of financial support required to establish some specified benefits of both new and existing programs. It requires a statement of the problem, accompanied by estimation of costs and benefits associated with each alternative identified in order to compare them with one another and with the benefits that are sought. The objective is to identify that one alternative that offers the greatest benefits at the lowest costs. However, it must be remembered that sometimes the cost of a service may not outweigh its direct benefit, but there may be an intangible benefit that must be considered as well.[15]

Several factors must be identified in the process, including any external constraints that must be built into the mathematical models as parameters. The process also requires identification of input costs and output benefits. Time-factor consideration requires delineation of costs involving research and development, investment, and operations. There must be recognition that there likely will be a time lag between initiation and achievement of the initial benefits. Because the topic is a detailed one, requiring extensive description, it is only mentioned here to give the reader some idea of its approach. The process has been lauded and lambasted, calling it "an infallible means of reaching the new Utopia to a waste of resources in attempting to measure the un-measurable."[16]

The technique of cost-benefit analysis, simply reviewed, involves choosing from alternatives when measurement in monetary or other specific measures may not be enough or even possible. Whenever possible, however, some specific measures should be established. For instance, if the objective is the improvement of referral service at the information desk, effectiveness can be measured by the number of in-person, telephone, or online inquiries answered or unanswered as well as patrons' judgment of staff and satisfaction with the service. As the term suggests, cost-benefit analysis is used to identify not only the cost of a program but also the benefits of the various alternatives that must be considered. The emphasis of cost-effectiveness is on output; each alternative is weighed in terms of effectiveness or costs against the objective that has been set. In some cases, cost models can be developed to show cost estimates for each alternative, or effectiveness models can be developed to show relationships between the alternatives and their effectiveness. Cost-benefit analysis is often confused with cost-effectiveness, but there is a subtle difference.[17] Cost-benefit analysis is concerned with the cost, cost-effectiveness, and value. Cost-benefit analysis asks, "Which is the best (least expensive or efficient) way to perform an operation?" whereas cost-effectiveness asks, "Because this is what the service costs, is it worth it (is it effective)?" which is a measure of quality. The process of cost-benefits analysis has been greatly enhanced by the development of software packages.

Benchmarking

Benchmarking, in its early stages of development, was more commonly identified as a Total Quality Management (TQM) tool used to measure and compare the work processes in one's organization with those in other organizations. It has since come into its own in libraries as they recognize the benefits of using it in measurement of activities. A benchmark is a reference point or standard against which progress or achievements can be assessed.

Benchmarking is information driven and requires libraries to examine their work processes and functions and to measure their productivity against that of others. By monitoring others, they can be encouraged to enhance their own performance by adopting, or adapting, the best practices of others. Benchmarking is an excellent tool to determine how effectively, efficiently, and economically an institution rates against others in its peer group.

The goal of benchmarking is to increase performance by:

1. Identifying libraries with best practices as partners.
2. Measuring and comparing a selected work process against others in the peer group.
3. Emulating, or adapting, the identified best practices for the local library or information center situation.

Of course best practices are not stagnant and are always evolving; therefore, benchmarking is a continuous adjustment process. As a tool, it requires an organization to focus efforts on improving the effectiveness and efficiency of delivery of products and services. Benefits of benchmarking include the possibility of demonstrating the value of a library system and services in numerical terms; in addition, it allows comparison with libraries in the peer group. In many cases a benchmarking study is used to prevent a decrease in services, including financial and systems initiatives. The desired outcomes of benchmarking are efficiency and effectiveness—reduction of costs and improvement in customer service. Several types of benchmarking are being used in libraries: internal benchmarking used to measure similar activities performed by different units; functional benchmarking comparing an organization's practices with those identified as leaders within the same service area; generic benchmarking, which compares an organization's functions or practices that cross different types of organizations; and competitive benchmarking, which compares a unit's performance of a service or process with that of a competitor.[18] Examples can be found in several Web sites, including those of the Association of Research Libraries and the Special Libraries Association.[19]

Five stages have been proposed in the benchmarking process:

1. Measuring services and selecting the aspects to be benchmarked.

2. Identifying benchmarking partners, because the goals, aims, and objectives must be compatible.

3. Identifying the best practice, to be discussed later, because the best practice varies from one group to another.

4. Changing procedures and features of services based upon those best practices identified.

5. Measuring the new approaches to service to determine the impact.[20]

Program Evaluation and Review Techniques (PERT)

Program Evaluation and Review Techniques (PERT) is a commonsense tool that helps remind people of the preparation work needed before an event and helps them check if the tasks will be completed on schedule. PERT is a technique of control in the planning process that is highly applicable to library operations. PERT originally was developed by the U.S. Navy's Special Projects. A method of planning and scheduling work, PERT is sometimes called the Critical Path Method (CPM). It involves identifying all of the key activities in a particular project, devising the sequence of activities and arranging them in a flow diagram, and assigning duration of time for the performance of each phase of the work to be done. This technique consists of enumerating events whose completion can be measured. Most likely times are then calculated for the accomplishment of each event, so that one can see how long it would take for the progression of events to be completed. This model-building network approach is most effectively used for major projects that are one-time events. An example would be the opening of a new library. Activities can be plotted to allow the librarian to determine the most expeditious route—or critical path—that can be taken to carry out the event. As with other techniques discussed, in PERT one must be able to state objectives, then activities must be enumerated and estimates must be given for the time required for each of these activities. The abbreviated, two-path diagram in figure 18.3 illustrates the concept.

Figure 18.3—PERT Diagram Shows the Planned Schedule of a Task, in Graphic Format, of a Two-Path Approach

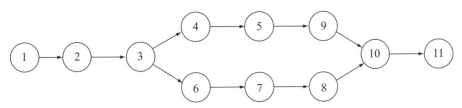

The figure suggests that there are two paths to be taken—say, from the time the idea of a new library is formulated until the building is ready for occupancy (O represents events and → represents activities). Times would be assigned for each activity, say, three weeks between events 4 and 5, one week between 6 and 7. As illustrated, either path 1–2–3–4–5–9–10–11 or path 1–2–3–6–7–8–10–11 can be taken. If time is of the essence, the shorter route might be more desirable. Time is the key element in the critical path schedule. Perhaps a bit more detail, illustrating the CPM concept, can demonstrate the critical issue of time (see figure 18.4). The time required to complete the series is the greatest sum of the combined time requirements. Of the four paths illustrated (1–2–5–8; 1–3–5–8; 1–4–6–8; and 1–2–7–8), the longest path, with work going forth on all four paths simultaneously, is 1–2–7–8. This path takes 5 weeks to complete and is the critical path that controls the schedule, more or less, for the whole project.

The PERT/CPM technique allows one to analyze a project in depth before it is initiated. This not only gives the decision maker an idea of the time frame involved but also aids in identifying potential weaknesses. The biggest disadvantage of PERT is its overemphasis on time at the expense of more detailed attention to cost. This disadvantage has led to the development of PERT/COST, which introduces the cost factor into the process. When the system to be studied is complex and when a number of events are involved, it becomes very expensive to establish a cost for each event. PERT is used mainly in industry, but some library systems have explored its value in the planning process, particularly when the process is a complex and lengthy one.

Figure 18.4—A Four-Path PERT Diagram Can Be Used to Illustrate the Critical Paths of Complex, Multipart Projects

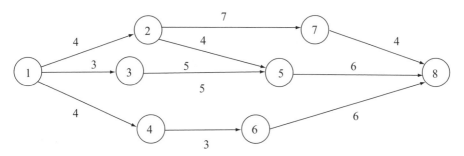

This brief discussion only touches upon the importance or potential of mathematical or statistical controls and does not even begin to present all of their variations. Volumes have been written on each of the topics; interested readers should consult the appropriate headings in the library literature and/or online for a fuller discussion. The possibility of using mathematical or statistical control techniques becomes greater. Expert systems have been developed to monitor performance and are being widely applied in problem-solving activities of information services.

Balanced Scorecard

The Balanced Scorecard process has been adopted by some libraries to integrate financial and nonfinancial measures as well as internal and external performance measures. With a vision in place, the library can decide what it will benchmark and what performance it will measure. Key to the balanced scorecard approach is linking the goals to specific decisions regarding resource allocation. It is now a simple instrument rather than one element of a total planning system.[21] The initial idea was to connect the traditional financial evaluation of an organization with measures concerning customer satisfaction, internal processes, and the ability to innovate.[22] It was built upon some concepts of previously developed management ideas such as TQM, including customer-defined quality, continuous improvement, employee empowerment, and, primarily, measurement-based management and feedback. Performance improvement involves the creation and use of performance measures or indicators, those being measurable characteristics of products, services, processes, and operations. The Balanced Scorecard is a survey instrument that focuses upon a chosen number of measurements identified in a strategic plan process in order to measure the organizational performance. It proposes that those measures or indicators can be selected to best represent the factors that lead to improved customer, operational, and financial performance.

The system consists of the processes:

1. Translating the vision into operational goals.
2. Communicating the vision and link it to individual performance.
3. Develop a service plan.
4. Provide feedback and adjust accordingly.

In other words, identify the most important data elements, those being the most crucial in the mission of the library, and tally them as part of an overall index or scorecard. It allows a library to concentrate on a small number of measures. Most evaluations in this process fall into four areas: users, finance, internal process, and learning and the future. Typically, each of those measures has one or more strategic objectives, and four to eight measurements or metrics are devised for each category. Each metric also has a specific target score. This process provides a quick analysis of the organization's position in relation to its stated objectives and outcomes. At the end of the measurement period, there is a demonstrated score to indicate which measures have met their targets.

LibQUAL+

LibQUAL+[23] is one measurement activity that has been developed to solicit, track, understand, and act upon users' opinions of service quality.[24] It has emerged as both a process and a tool that enables institutions to address service quality gaps between their expectations and the perceived service delivery program. It is an internationally recognized Web-delivered survey that now includes hundreds of libraries of all sizes throughout the world and is pioneering the use of large-scale, Web-based survey applications in a digital library environment.

It is a tool that attempts to measure library users' perceptions of service quality and identifies gaps between desired, perceived, and minimum expectations of service.[25] The survey instrument is designed to be useful to the library administration on several levels: identifying deficits in service performance at an individual library, allowing comparisons with cohort libraries from multiple perspectives, identifying best practices, and responding to pressures for accountability. Basically, it allows the previously mentioned benchmarking to be performed against other institutions as well as obtaining feedback from the institution's own users. The goals of LibQUAL+ are to:

1. Foster a culture of excellence in providing library service.
2. Help libraries better understand user perceptions of library service quality.
3. Collect and interpret library user feedback systematically over time.
4. Provide libraries with comparable assessment information from peer institutions.
5. Identify best practices in library service.
6. Enhance library staff members' analytical skills for interpreting and acting on data.

The LibQUAL+ questions measure customer perceptions of library service across four dimensions:

1. **Affect of service** (nine items): the human side of the enterprise, encompassing traits of empathy, accessibility, and personal competence (e.g., "willingness to help users").
2. **Personal control** (six items): the extent to which users are able to navigate and control the information universe that is provided (e.g., "Web site enabling me to locate information on my own").
3. **Access to information** (five items): an assessment of the adequacy of the collections themselves and the ability to access needed information on a timely basis regardless of the location of the user or the medium of the resource in question (e.g., "comprehensive collections" and "convenient business hours").
4. **Library as place** (five items): comprising, variously, according to the perspective of the user, utilitarian space for study and collaboration, a sanctuary for contemplation and reflection, or an affirmation of the primacy of the life of the mind in university priorities (e.g., "a haven for quiet and solitude").[26]

Along the lines of LibQUAL+ is the ISO 11620, a recently amended international standard on library performance indicators. It specifies a set of 29 indicators grouped in the following areas: (1) user satisfaction; (2) public services, which includes general indicators as well as specific indicators on providing documents, retrieving documents, lending documents, document delivery from external sources, inquiry and reference services, information searching, and facilities; and (3) technical services, including indicators in the area of acquiring, processing, and cataloging documents. Notable points in this proposed standard are its initial emphasis on user satisfaction; its inclusion of cost-effectiveness indicators; its clear and distinct way of describing each indicator, accompanied by suggestions regarding the methodology to be used in collecting the data; and a description indicating how to most accurately interpret each indicator.[27] Work is underway in the area of performance indicators for the electronic library.

Management Information Systems (MIS)

Over the years, several other tools and techniques have been used by libraries to measure the output of services.[28] Such a system, usually consisting of people, procedures, processes, and a data bank, most oftentimes computerized, routinely gathers quantitative and qualitative information on predetermined indicators to measure program progress and impact.

These include techniques relating to operations control. Among the first to be developed was Management Information System (MIS), a system developed to gather internal data, summarize it, and organize it for decision making in the control process. Its biggest failing was that it did not adequately take into account external intelligence.

Management information systems, in general, can be viewed as ways of collecting data to improve efficiency and effectiveness. Well-ordered management information systems can be enhanced through control and evaluation techniques and tools. These include Program Evaluation Review Technique (PERT), the Gantt Chart, On-Line Analytical Processing (OLAP), and the Critical Path Method (CPM). Typically, the systems involve financial information, personnel information, performance information, and user information, all related to the feedback aspect of control. Some of these tools have received and continue to receive criticism over the years from those who believe that management information systems represent simply a process, sometimes with adequate reference to strategic planning, operations planning, or budgets, and that their objectives have no relationship to other developments.

There is no doubt that to be effective, any kind of management information system must be reviewed and, if adopted, have a direct relationship to what is desired as far as information retrieval and outcome for library operations is concerned. Technology has made it easier to standardize procedures and to apply mechanical methods to measure them. Newer techniques, such as expert systems, now offer greater opportunities to manage libraries and have capitalized on the impact that technology provides. Automated systems have made the process of generating process-related statistical data easier.

The primary issue for many information services organizations remains one of identifying the appropriate data and how to utilize it.

Decision Support Systems (DSS)

The Decision Support System (DSS) is an interactive software-based system that is useful for decision makers in the process of compiling useful information from raw data, documents, personal knowledge, and/or business models to identify and solve problems and make decisions. It is an organized method of providing past, present, and projection information related to internal operations and external operations, the latter being related to the environmental scanning process mentioned under the topic of strategic planning. This implies "a structured organized approach with the assistance of some automated mechanism."[29] DSS supports the planning, control, and operational functions of an organization by furnishing information in the proper time frame to assist in the decision-making process. DSS covers a variety of systems, tools, and technologies that incorporate both data and models and that are now being transposed to create a knowledge-based system as state of the art. Newer terms that focus on certain types of decisions, including Executive Support Systems, Executive Information Systems, Intelligent Information Systems, Organizational Support Systems, Controlling Information Systems, and the like, are now prominent. The concept takes advantage of the continuous development in the database management and modeling arena to offer software that supports computerized decision making. It is more interactive in that it can respond to messages and can project alternative approaches upon which decisions can be made. It can simulate situations and project outcomes. This computer-assisted analysis is an effective tool for financial planning, among other activities. It allows for testing assumptions, factoring risks, and exploring alternatives. It is particularly useful when managers are presented with problems that have more than one solution, thereby enhancing the manager's decision-making options, for instance, through time-and-motion study.

Time-and-Motion Studies

Motion studies enable a library system to record in flow chart form the present method of doing things, to analyze the method's effectiveness, and, from this analysis, to improve the method. The new method of doing things can then be timed to report the performance standard. Time studies complement motion studies in determining performance standards. A third element in this quantifying process is cost; that is, attaching a monetary figure to the activities of an individual. Both time and cost vary with the level of expertise of the individual performing the task and the institution in which the work is taking place. Many time-and-motion studies have been and are being done in libraries, particularly relating to routine tasks, such as shelving books, inputting data into online files, checking in periodicals, or preparing items for the bindery.

Operations Research

Two terms that are closely related and often used interchangeably are *operations research* and *systems analysis.* Actually, the latter emerges from the former. Operations research (OR) today is largely identified with specific techniques, such as linear programming, queuing theory analysis, dynamic programming, statistical models, Monte Carlo (randomizing) methods, gaming and game theory, and other computer-simulation models. It attempts to look at and improve the whole organization or system, not just one part of it. It is the scientific methods to study the functions of an organization so as to develop better methods of planning and controlling changes in the organization. "It can be viewed as a branch of management, engineering or science. As part of the field of management, its purpose is to assist decision makers in choosing preferred future courses of action by systematically identifying and examining the alternatives which are available to the manager, and by predicting the possible outcomes for such actions."[30] For libraries, it means making objectives explicit, deriving suitable measures of the extent of meeting them, developing simple quantitative relations between input and output, and identifying constraints that one should strive to remove.[31] It occupies the interest of a number of different groups, particularly statisticians and mathematicians.

From the late 1960s to the present, applied operations research has come into its own in the library decision-making process. This is primarily because in recent years decision making in general has emphasized the mathematical and statistical approach rather than a judgment-based approach. The emphasis of the mathematical approach was facilitated primarily by the application of scientific methods and now technological development, the major impact coming with the development of the computer, which was necessary for the manipulation of complex data. One use to which computers have been put is modeling organizations or systems. Conceptual models used for decision making are simply computer-based attempts at simulating reality. They are powerful means of testing various alternatives without changing the commitments involved in a typical decision. The primary approach of operations research consists of a broad view of the problem by the whole organization. This is succeeded by a team initiative, using personnel with different backgrounds from different departments, with the team addressing the economic-technical aspects of the total system. The key components to the process, then, are application of the scientific method; using a systems approach to problem solving; and employing mathematical, probability, and statistical techniques and computer modeling. Statistical analysis is made easier with the technologies available today: software systems for modeling. However, some types of statistical analysis require a different approach to gathering data that can then be analyzed electronically.

In terms of control, the major contribution of operations research has been in constructing models that can be used in the decision-making process. To accomplish this, a basic knowledge of systems analysis is necessary. Again, the important first step, as in most techniques, is to identify objectives and then to look at variables that might influence the objectives. These are expressed mathematically to determine the best alternative in terms of the objectives set. The system currently in use is described. Based upon this analysis, a series of mathematical models is developed to describe the interrelationships within the organization. Data are then collected to measure the system, or if data are not available, assumptions or speculations are made. This information provides the basis for a working model for a new system. With this information in hand, the librarian is able to make decisions based on the alternatives presented. The analytical statistical technique and the techniques of probability theory are employed.

It has been pointed out that the use of operations research in libraries is based on the application of the scientific approach to practical problems: "It normally operates in four distinctive stages:

1. Description of the system being considered, especially by means of mathematical models and computer simulations;

2. Measurement, using objective data wherever these can be obtained;

3. Evaluation, the presentation of relevant information to the system manager (here the librarian) to aid in making decisions between different courses of action;

4. Operational control, assisting the development of ways and means of achieving the objectives aimed for over a period of time."[32]

Because of the technique's complexity and its use of mathematics, as well as the costs of modeling, librarians have not yet universally applied OR to improving managerial control.

Also, there are limits to this approach. The quantitative method can be no better than the assumptions and estimates used in it. Its greatest limitation to use in libraries is that quantitative analysis is not adaptable to all situations. Some variables in libraries are very difficult to quantify, yet to achieve proper quantitative analysis, all variables must be assigned quantitative weights either through amassed data or through estimates. Therefore, a great deal of judgment is required, first to know when to use the quantitative method and then to know how to estimate costs of activities. In addition, quantitative analysis can become very elaborate and costly. One criticism of the technique is that it does not emphasize human factors enough, because such factors are difficult to model mathematically. Also, this method demands some knowledge of mathematics and statistical concepts, and these are areas in which librarians are thought to be at their weakest; we have relied heavily on nonlibrarians to provide this expertise. Finally, it should be remembered that use of quantitative tools concerns only one phase of the decision-making process. It is a kind of management information that is infrequently used to identify the problem or to develop alternatives.

Knowledge Management

Just as MIS was reinvented in the form of DSS, so has the concept of information resource management been subsumed under the concept of knowledge management, a developing system that attempts to capture the knowledge and expertise of human capital as well as documents, repositories, routines, processes, practices, and norms within and flowing into the organization by creating a computerized system to capture both the implicit and explicit knowledge within the organization. Knowledge management is concerned with developing organizations in such a manner as to derive knowledge from information, Such a systematic process of transferring knowledge within the organization is made easier by technologies, using DSS, statistical analysis software, artificial intelligence, and other developing tools. The question of systematically acquiring outside knowledge, with benchmarking being a good example for identifying best practices, is incorporated in the process. The elements of knowledge management systems include accessing, evaluating, managing, organizing, filtering, and distributing knowledge.

 Try This!

Select one service activity that you feel should be a priority objective in an academic library. Identify one tool or technique that can be used to measure the success in meeting that priority goal. It might relate to both quantitative and qualitative measures. Defend the selection as the best measurement of that service.

MONITORING PROGRAMS FOR RESULTS AND ACCOUNTABILITY

Monitoring is a continuous management function aimed primarily at providing managers with regular feedback and early indications of progress or lack thereof in the achievement of intended results within the organization.

Monitoring

Monitoring tracks the actual performance against what was planned or expected according to predetermined standards. It is that portion of a project or program that involves collecting and analyzing data on processes and results and recommending corrective measures.

The process of monitoring and feedback is the best way of expressing accountability in library and information services in both qualitative and quantitative terms. It provides checks and balances for the service goal. Based on evaluation as part of the reporting mechanism, decision makers decide whether changes are desirable, either in the system or in the strategic goals of the organization. Such reporting mechanisms are not only important to evaluate results and to correct deviations but also as marketing strategies intended for funding authorities, customers, and all staff within the organization.

Monitoring means quality assurance of the programs that have been instituted. Communication tools, which have been used in libraries and information centers that measure performance, include personal observation, focus groups, meetings, e-mail, statistical data, surveys, interviews, oral reports, and written print-on-paper and electronically generated reports. Other publications help facilitate the process of reporting results. When one searches the Internet, it is obvious that the Web is also being used to report to the world, not just to constituents, on activities and on outcomes. This reporting activity is conducted in a number of ways, internally and externally. Sometimes it is on a monthly basis to review results; sometimes it is carried out internally on a daily basis by keeping a scorecard of projects and progress toward their goal accomplishment. Other times, for various audiences, reviews and reports are presented on a less frequent basis. Occasionally, such reports are required at specific intervals, for accrediting or other control purposes, by outside agencies or organizations.

Techniques such as storyboarding, in which goals and objectives are compared with performance to date to identify progress, are sometimes used. Most important, data should be reported and performance explained internally, and performance information should be consolidated and reporting mechanisms consistent across the organization. Results should be shared not only internally but also externally with customers and stakeholders through annual reports. Basically, data from the several techniques available fall into one of three primary categories:

1. Statistics (counting inputs, staff, materials, services).
2. Performance indicators ("How well are we doing?").
3. Economic value ("How much are we worth, in monetary terms?").

In the reporting process, it is important to recognize that there are strong relationships between resource allocation, strategic planning, and performance measurement; each builds upon the other and creates a circle of service. The budget is allocated according to primary goals and objectives that have been identified in the strategic plan, which should have identified some of the measure to be used in terms of output. Because the library is not a static organization, evaluation must be made from that perspective. As the goals and needs of society change, so the library or information center must respond. Therefore, past measures may no longer be important, and new ones may need to be found. A good example is in the area of "access" or "ownership" of materials as a criterion of quality.

Accountability

All types of library information centers must demonstrate a value of service or value-added aspect to the larger organization of which they are a part and to their constituencies. Through accountability, the library and information center is, more than ever before, expected to evaluate the institution's performance to ensure that the human and material resources are effectively and efficiently employed toward achieving its goals and those of the larger institution. In the past, some libraries relied on the public-good view of library services. This is no longer adequate in the current competitive environment.

Accountability measures are intended to provide quality assurance and timeliness of program performance. This requires managing for results through clearly stated expectations and the reporting of results. All three elements also are required to establish clear and effective measure of accountability. It is designed to promote efficiency in monitoring and evaluating performance to demonstrate its added value and effectiveness in improving service. It requires determination of success and understanding of the responsibilities for achieving organizational goals. Accountability is typically a key success factor. Establishing viable performance measures is critical for organizations; making those measures work is even more important. As stated in a previous chapter, performance measurement systems are linked to strategic and operational planning. Employees and managers should understand and work toward the desired outcomes that are at the core of their organization's vision. One motto might be "Focus on the goal of 'customer satisfaction,' measure the end results, and don't focus on the measurements per se."[33]

CONCLUSION

Coordinating functions are created to facilitate the achievement of goals and objectives in libraries and information centers. Those standard-setting activities and evaluation and measurement techniques provide vital feedback information to management and staff as activities are carried out to achieve the mission. Some tools and techniques for developing services are sophisticated yet have great application for information services. They are important parts of the process of accountability and reporting on success.

NOTES

1. *Standards for Libraries in Higher Education* (Chicago: American Library Association, ACRL, 2004).

2. Institute of Museum and Library Services, Washington, D.C., *Perspectives on Outcome Based Evaluation for Libraries and Museums*, 20, http://www.imls.gov/pubs/pdf/pubobe.pdf.

3. Martha Kyrillidou, "From Input and Output Measures to Quality and Outcome Measures, or, from the User in the Life of the Library to the Library in the Life of the User," *Journal of Academic Librarianship* 28, no. 1 (2003): 42.

4. Rowena Cullen, "Does Performance Measurement Improve Organisational Effectiveness? A Postmodern Analysis," *Performance Measurement and Metrics* 1, no. 1 (August 1999): 12.

5. Peter F. Drucker, "Controls, Control and Management," in *Managerial Controls: New Directions in Basic Research*, ed. C. P. Bonini, R. K. Jaedicke, and H. M. Wanger (New York: McGraw-Hill, 1964), 286.

6. George Schreyogg and Horst Steinman, "Strategic Control: A New Perspective," *Academy of Management Review* 12 (January 1987): 91.

7. American Library Association, Reference and User Services Division, "Guidelines for Information Services" (July 2000), http://www.ala.org/ala/rusa/rusaprotools/referenceguide/guidelinesinformation.htm.

8. *Proceedings of the Northumbria International Conference on Performance Measurement in Libraries and Information Services.* 1st ed.–6th ed. (Newcastle, U.K.: University of Northumbria, Information North, 1995–2005).

9. Peter Hernon and Ellen Altman, *Assessing Service Quality: Satisfying the Expectations of Library Customers* (Chicago: American Library Association, 1998), 51–53.

10. Roswitha Poll, "Impact/Outcome Measures for Libraries," LIBER Quarterly (2003), http://webdoc.gwdg.de/edoc/aw/liber/lq-3-03/329–342.pdf.

11. Association of Research Libraries, *ARL New Measures Initiative* (ARL, Washington, DC: Association of Research Libraries, http://www.arl.org/stats/initiatives/.

12. International Organization for Standardization, *ISO 11620, Information and Documentation: Library Performance Indicators* (Geneva, Switzerland: International Organization for Standardization, 1998, amended 2003).

13. Peter Hernon and Ellen Altman, *Service Quality in Academic Libraries* (Norwood, NJ: Ablex, 1996), 15.

14. Alan Walter Steiss, *Strategic Management and Organizational Decision Making* (Lexington, MA: Lexington Books, 1985), 117.

15. St. Louis Public Library, "Development of a Portable Cost Benefit Methodology for Urban Libraries" (n.d.), http://www.slpl.lib.mo.us/libsrc/dev.htm.

16. A. R. Prest and R. Turvey, "Cost Benefit Analysis: A Survey," *The Economic Journal* 85 (March 1965): 583.

17. F. Wilfred Lancaster, "The Evaluation of Library and Information Services," in *Evaluation and Scientific Management of Libraries and Information Centers,* ed. F. W. Lancaster and C. W. Cleverdon (Leyden, Netherlands: Noordhoff, 1977), 4.

18. T. M. Peischel, "Benchmarking: A Process for Improvement," *Library Administration and Management* 9 (Spring 1995): 99–101.

19. http://www.arl.org/stats/newmeas/index.html benchmarking; Special Libraries Association, "Benchmarking: http://units.sla.org/division/dmil/mlw97/gohlke/

20. Claire Creaser, "Performance Measurement and Benchmarking for School Library Services," *Journal of Librarianship and Information Science* 33, no. 3 (2001): 126–32.

21. Robert S. Kaplan and David P. Norton, *Balance Scorecard: Translating Strategy into Action* (Boston: Harvard Business School Press, 1996).

22. Ibid.

23. Association of Research Librarians, "Statistics and Measurement" (2007), http://www.arl.org/stats/.

24. LibQUAL+ (2007), http://www.libqual.org/.

25. Colleen Cook, Fred Heath, and Bruce Thompson, *Users' Hierarchical Perspectives on Library Service Quality: A "LibQUAL+TM" Study* (Washington, DC: Association of Research Librarians, 2001).

26. Fred Heath, Martha Kyrillidou, Duane Webster, Sayeed Choudhury, Ben Hobbs, Mark Lorie, and Nicholas Flores, "Emerging Tools for Evaluating Digital Library Services: Conceptual Adaptations of LibQUAL+ and CAPM," *Journal of Digital Information* 4, no. 2 (June 2003), http://jodi.tamu.edu/Articles/v04/i02/Heath/#top.

27. http://www.niso.org/international/SC8/sc8rpt.html.

28. http://web.syr.edu/~jryan/infopro/stats.htm.

29. Michael E. D. Koenig, *Information Driven Management Concepts and Themes: A Toolkit for Librarians* (IFLA pub. no. 86) (New Providence, NJ: Bowker-Saur, 1998), 49.

30. Ferdinand F. Leimkuhler, "Operations Research and Systems Analysis," in *Evaluation and Scientific Management of Libraries and Information Centers*, ed. F. W. Lancaster and C. W. Cleverdon (Leyden, Netherlands: Noordhoff, 1977), 131.

31. M. Elton and Brian Vicker, "The Scope of Operational Research in the Library and Information Field," *ASLIB Proceedings* 25 (1973): 319.

32. A. Graham Mackenzie and Michael K. Buckland, "Operations Research," in *British Librarianship and Information Science, 1966–1970* (London: Library Association, 1972), 24.

33. Al Gore, "Serving the American Public: Best Practices in Performance Measurement," *National Performance Review* (1997), http://govinfo.library.unt.edu/npr/library/papers/benchmrk/nprbook.html#executie.

Fiscal Responsibility and Control

 Overview

James Fielding, the director of the Avondale Public Library, is facing a budget crisis. Because of increasing costs, the library's budget was overspent before the end of the fiscal year, and Fielding had to make deep cuts in the acquisition budget to avoid laying off staff and decreasing service hours. Now Fielding is pondering a different approach as he prepares for the next budgeting cycle. He is popular and well respected in this affluent town and carries some clout with the board that reviews the libraries' budget. Yet he knows that solving the developing problem without posing a severe challenge to information services will not be easy and that any solution is likely to produce unhappiness in some part of the community. Still, he is resolved that something must be done to ensure that the current year's experience is a one-time fiscal disaster.

Facing that stark fiscal reality, he tries to think of a way to present the new budget to the town's mayor and budgetary committee. Until now, there has been little guidance from the administration as to the type of budgetary presentation that would be most desirable. He knows that in order to solve the problem without harming the library's fine reputation of service delivery he must make a case for supporting a different budgetary approach, one that the funding authorities can buy into but one that will bring the library more funding. Fielding is preparing to present his ideas for discussion next week. This will entail a proposal for a different approach to budget allocation. He has been boning up on various budgetary systems, one or two of which have been used successfully by other libraries in the consortium to which the library system belongs. Because the town has not adopted a specific budgeting model for operations, he is determined to make a case for a best model for information services. But he wonders, "Which is best for this community? Which will garner the necessary support for the library?"

Library managers in every type of library are in charge of budgets that range from those in the thousands of dollars to those in the millions. Often managers face budget shortfalls similar to the one described in this scenario. This chapter discusses the importance of budgetary control and introduces the several applicable budgetary processes.

BUDGETS—PLANNING AND EVALUATION TOOLS

One of the most important of all planning activities is to determine how resources will be allocated among the various alternatives competing with one another within the operation of an organization. Therefore, the budget can be considered a plan set forth in financial terms. Budgets, when viewed as evaluation tools, are commitments or contracts with funding authorities for services and programs to be rendered, and they can facilitate the process of evaluating how successfully the goals and objectives are being addressed. In that sense, it is also a political document, expressing policy decisions about priorities of programs. Budgeting is that part of the total planning equation that assures that resources are obtained and then used effectively and efficiently in accomplishing objectives. The vital link that exists between planned activities and financial outcomes becomes even more important when libraries advance initiatives by employing new tools and techniques.

The budget pulls together the various pieces of the operational plan and relates them to the services plan in monetary terms. This process, having set goals for the organization and priorities for services, ultimately employs a budgetary component in the planning cycle. This tool translates goals into controllable parts and ties performance to financial requirements. The budget, then, is the library's operating plan for a designated fiscal period allowing resources to be allocated, ensuring that programs are successfully delivered.

Budgets, in detail, lay out a direction for allocating and maximizing the use of resources. In addition, the budget gives staff specific directions for achieving identified goals. The budget also is used by management to gauge operational performance. An effective budget establishes criteria that alert management if change is needed or if a course of action should be refined or altered. In that sense it also serves as a necessary monitoring device, because accountability is implied in the budgeting process.

"Which comes first, planning or budgeting?" is a question often asked. "Neither," of course, because they are inextricably tied and neither can proceed without the other. Cost predictions must be based upon a realistic view of service objectives and what financial resources are available to accomplish those service objectives.

Because some objectives already will be in place, and others being newly planned, they must be based upon what monies are likely to be available.

Planning and budgeting also are linked in the preparation and presentation to funding authorities because the adoption of a planning and budgeting framework has to reflect the organization's commitment to effective planning and resource allocation, as well as accountability. This process must be viewed as a whole, with the equally important parts being linked through the goals and objectives of the organization. In essence, the budget is the monetary expression of the strategic plan.

Therefore, in the preliminary stages of developing a strategic plan for the library, each potential goal, when it is financially analyzed, can be assigned a monetary figure based upon projected resources necessary to accomplish it. A preliminary budget for each of those goals should be developed so that benefits can be compared with costs before finally choosing among the various potential goals.

Libraries and information centers usually budget on a yearly cycle, although it is sometimes necessary to construct operational plans that project two or three years into the future. The budget for any current cycle, or even for future ones, inevitably will be affected by past commitments, established standards of service, existing organizational structure, and current methods of operations, as well as future changes. If changes are proposed, consideration must be given to preparing the organization for change and altering the budgetary justification and allocation. The three phases of a budgeting cycle include:

1. Preparation of the budget (some forms are included here; access to others is given on the Web site at http://www.lu.com/management to illustrate this phase).

2. Presentation to funding authorities, with full justification linking inputs (financial) with outputs (results).

3. Implementation of the actual beginning of the phase for which the budget has been allocated.

There are several different types of budgets. For libraries and information centers, the operations budget is the primary type of budget with its focus on revenue and expenses. In addition, a second type of budget, a capital budget, involves capital investments. The capital expense type of budget is developed to reflect expenditures over the estimated period of a project's development. Examples of that capital type of budget requests include major renovations, new buildings, or substantial technology requests or other expensive equipment requirements. The capital budget has less relevance in this discussion because needs are occasional rather than periodic. Capital costs are large-expense items to be planned for in projected future budgets. After capital costs are funded, yearly expenses are calculated and transferred to the operations budget as deposits and are then charged against that budget. For instance, approval and installation of a mainframe computer system would be considered a capital expense, requested separately and budgeted in the capital budget. Expenditure of funds to pay for the mainframe would be reflected, most probably, in a separate account. The two types of budgets discussed here are presented as distinct; however, a combination of budgeting systems often is used.

Some other types of budgets relate primarily to for-profit organizations. Some components, which are typically taught in accounting courses, such as the financial budget, with subsets of cash flow, capital expenditures, and balance sheets, are important, and detailed discussions can be found in textbooks relating specifically to financial accounting.

 What Do You Think?

In many organizations, budgets are prepared by managers with little input from staff on the ground. Do you think it is necessary to involve everyone in the budget planning process? If so, how would you go about doing that as it relates to budgeting in an organization you hope to join? If that involvement is not necessary, how would you convince your colleagues that it is not only unnecessary but also unproductive? Justify your response with specifics.

THE FUNDING PROCESS

The budgetary process is not just a controlling mechanism conducted on the inside by a stereotypical armbanded, green-visored accountant, hovering over huge, figure-laden tomes in a dimly lit back room. Libraries and information centers are accountable for their actions and charged with wisely expending allocated monies. External forces—political, economic, social, and technological—are constant factors that affect the budget and the process of budgeting. In other sections of this volume, factors—including values, organizational culture, commitment, and vision—are discussed, and they also affect the budgetary process. Primarily they influence priorities within the monetary allocations arena.

Funds may come directly to the library or information center or to the parent organization, with designation for library use. Within the income categories for libraries, funds come from a variety of sources: from the larger organization's (university or college, city or town government, school district, company, foundation, or another type of business) operating budget; from local taxes; from local, state, regional, provincial, federal, and/or national government support; from private foundation or other philanthropic organization grants; from Friends of Libraries groups, gifts, fund drives, or endowments; from fees or fines; and so on. Noninstitutional funding is likely to fluctuate more widely than institutional support, and institutional support can depend on the parent organization's commitment to seeking the various types of funds that are then funneled to the library and on the projected fiscal year's budget outlook. Therefore, the budget is not a stable, sure thing, and staffs of many library organizations are deeply involved in fund-raising efforts.

The greatest amount of budgetary support in most institutions comes from the parent body. Determination of the actual amount usually is based on expressed needs, which are justified by services offered or projected and, to a lesser extent, on standards that have been established for particular types of libraries or information centers, such as the American Library Association (ALA) and the International Federation of Library Associations (IFLA) standards for public, school, junior college, college, and university libraries that often are used by accrediting authorities as they consider the quality of institutions. These needs often are defined on budget forms such as those included on this volume's Web site (http://www.lu.com/management).

Fund-Raising Efforts

Financial challenges are steadily compounded by the reality of inflation, reduced budgets, and the information explosion, and some libraries are finding themselves turning to nontraditional sources of funding to supplement their operating budgets. One area of funding, which traditionally has not been thought of as revenue generating but has been part of many library operations for years, is that of fees and fines. Many libraries traditionally have charged fines and fees for services ranging from fines for overdue items to fees for copying services or space rental. Those funds either go directly into the library's budget or into a general fund within the parent institution. In addition, external sources such as gifts and grants are becoming more vital, and sought after, by library staffs as direct financial support sometimes is not adequate to meets new initiatives and continuing needs.

Fund-raising has become a necessary part of many libraries' activities. In recent years, all types of libraries and information centers have engaged in fund-raising activities, tapping nontraditional areas for budgetary support for special projects and for capital expenditures. A new political role, with extensive public relations requirements, is being forced on libraries and librarians. Many types of libraries now depend on private-sector support to expand the monies available for their budgets. Special projects and capital budgets often are supported by outside funding sources. Fund-raising for special projects or for supplementing the budget in specific areas often is done by the library, by friends groups, or via legally established entities such as foundations or endowments. The scope of fund-raising done by or for a library depends upon the need for supplemental funds and the time and effort required for fund-raising activities.

Both such ongoing annual fund-raising activities and major capital campaigns are becoming integral parts of library programs. Fund-raising, through lobbying and direct solicitation, has become a way of life for enhancing budgets. Libraries have become innovative and assertive in seeking funds outside normal budgeting sources and channels. Development and fund-raising are challenges facing management of libraries and have become a major factor in budgeting information services in many library and information services organizations. They recognize the need for seeking supplemental financial support from individuals, governments, corporations, foundations, individuals, and other philanthropic sources.[1] The position of development officer, as part of a management team, is now common in many large library organizations.[2] Friends groups, alumni of educational institutions, community leaders, foundations, and government agencies are funding many library and information services initiatives. Such fund-raising initiatives, seeking new sources of financial support, require clear expression of the goals and objectives of the process, and it should be tied into the broader marketing objectives discussed in chapter 6.

 Try This!

Identify at least one fund-raising activity that would be beneficial for a type of library of your choosing and detail the kind of program that might be presented to an organization you identify as being supportive of libraries for their consideration. What chance does such a proposal have for consideration and what steps will you need to take to justify the request and persuade the funding authority of its worth?

THE BUDGETING PROCESS

The budget is a powerful management and public relations tool and essential for explaining goals and objectives. As a total process, the budgeting concept involves several discrete steps, from the guidelines that are issued by upper management in the larger organization or unit of which the library is a part to the execution of the budget through the fiscal year's appropriation and expenditures to the point when an audit is conducted to determine, in retrospect, how the allocated funds were actually spent. In between are the most important parts of the process: preparation of the budget, with justification for amounts and categories being requested, and review and approval by funding authorities. Preparation, defense, and maintenance of the budget represent a significant part of a management's time. Although planning the budget may be a seasonal activity, its effects are felt throughout the year.

The budget represents one of the most important documents to guide in achieving the library's overall objectives. Justification means convincing funding authorities that a certain development makes sense and that it should be supported. The concept of moving beyond information provision toward one of knowledge management is an example of developments needing justification and requires additional effort to educate funding authorities. The latter step provides the best opportunity for the library to present its case, to enlighten authorities about not only what is being requested but, more importantly, why it is being requested. However, this excellent marketing opportunity is a delicate session in which a balance must be achieved between just the right amount of information and information overload. Some authorities may not understand; others may not really care. To strike that balance and to educate, librarians can employ various public relations gambits to get across their program objectives. Budgets are presented not only in writing but sometimes orally as well, in a variety of settings.

One great danger in budgeting is the problem of disguised needs. Librarians often are accused of asking for more than they actually need and basing current budget justifications on past budgets. Such an incremental approach is no longer valid in the fast-changing environment of today's information services. However, in all fairness, the approach frequently is encouraged by the budgeting technique being employed by the parent institutions in which the incremental mentality can prompt automatic reductions in library budgets by those who hold the purse strings, whether they are city managers, college or company presidents, or school superintendents.

The budgeting process is a time-delayed process. A budget usually is prepared one year or, in a few cases, two or three years in advance. In the latter instances, it is extremely difficult to project what the needs will be even with a strategic-thinking mentality. Still, the budget is expected to forecast realistically expected revenues, support, and expenses for the period of time covered by the budget request. In most cases, a library must follow the budget system and budgeting cycle used by the larger system, whether that is the university, college, city government, school district, corporation, or board. Usually, guidelines for the preparation of the budget come from the school committee, the state or local funding agency, the college or university administration, or the corporation's fiscal officer.

Although many libraries have a separate financial staff concerned primarily with budgets and the accounting process, most involve a number of employees in budget planning. Some larger libraries and information centers have internal budgeting committees composed of representatives from various units of the organization. Budget requests for programs or units frequently originate from the supervisor or a team most familiar with a particular unit, program, project, or other aspect of the operation. A coordinating agent or group—either the director, his or her representative, or a committee—is responsible for pulling the various budget requests together and presenting a comprehensive budget to the funding authority. Timetables for budget preparation, presentation, and overview are essential so that wide support can be gained. Two principles guide the development and presentation of budgets: effectiveness and efficiency, involving what sources of funds will be tapped and how maximum benefit at minimum cost will be accomplished.

The budgetary aspect of control has become more concerted as costs have risen, requiring greater attention to library and information center budgets, with the determination and justification of budget allocations taking on new meaning and urgency. More and more, as greater financial constraint is exercised, librarians find themselves spending more time on budget review, analysis, evaluation, and presentation. With rising costs, librarians are forced to prepare comprehensive reports on the library's financial status so that effective allocation, as well as accurate projections for future funding, can be made. Most often, the librarian is required to make a formal budget presentation that is substantiated by backup documentation, such as an index of inflation for library materials, technological impact, or trends in higher education that affect libraries. The Web site for this textbook (http://www.lu.com/management) includes a number of budgets and budgetary activities.

BUDGETING TECHNIQUES

Budgeting techniques in libraries include traditional approaches used by many types of organizations and several more innovative techniques that recently have found their way into libraries. The former are more fixed in their approach, whereas the latter are more flexible. The shift in focus, just as in the planning process, has taken place as budgets are presented in terms of output, or performance, rather than as input. The most traditional types of budgeting, to be discussed, include line-item allocation, in which expenses are divided into categories such as salaries, benefits, materials, equipment, and so on, and lump-sum allocation, based primarily on an incremental approach in which percentage increases are related to the previous year's budget. An interim view of budgets is represented in such techniques as performance budgeting, in which performance measures are instituted to support justifying input costs as a factor of output measures. The Planning, Programming, and Budgeting System (PPBS) and zero-based budgeting (ZBB) are budgeting approaches that look at programs, objectives, and benchmark costs, respectively. Each approach has advocates who promote advantages of the various approaches. A library or information center considering a switch to another process must be clear about the advantages and disadvantages before it decides to switch from one to another. Every budget system, even rudimentary ones, comprises planning, management, and control processes.[3]

Line-Item Budgeting

The line-item or incremental budget approach is a process whereby categories of the budget are increased or decreased by a percentage. In such a process, the library assumes its prior year's base allocation. Discussion of funding is based upon the amount of the increment, or in some cases decrease, that is to be applied in this next cycle. It basically treats existing services as preapproved, subject only to increases or decreases in financial resources to be allocated. The focus is on the changes anticipated over or under last year's statistics.

This is probably the most common type of budget because of its simplicity. The line-item budget divides objects of expenditure into broad input classes or categories, with further subdivisions within those categories. This classification of expenditures on the basis of categories is called objects of expenditure (personnel services, contractual services, capital outlay, etc.), and within each category are more detailed line items (salaries, travel, telephones, etc.). This type of budget focuses attention on how much money is spent and for what purpose, rather than the activity affected or its outcomes.

It is often referred to as the historical approach, because expenditure requests are based upon historical data, or the lump-sum approach, because the attitude is one of "Here it is, do with it what you will," or incremental, in which funds increases are based upon last year's expenditures and, typically, just a small amount of funding is added each year.

The underlying theory or rationale is that the basic aspects of programs and activities do not change significantly from one year to the next and the change in resources in any given year is probably a small percentage of the base budget. This appears to be a widely practiced model in many large not-for-profit organizations in which the need for efficiency in some administrative areas overrules effectiveness. This system does not involve serious examination of what is being accomplished through the base budget, and it avoids the question of whether there are better uses for some of the resources. With this approach, difficult policy choices are circumvented and planning is relatively unimportant. When resources are allocated through an across-the-board approach, there is no need to identify priorities. Of course, this approach is simple to implement and easier to apply. It certainly minimizes conflict within the larger organization because all institutional components are treated equally.

The budget is a series of lines, each of which represents a different item of expenditure or revenue. This classification of expenditures is on the basis of categories called objects of expenditure (salaries, benefits, materials, etc.) and, within each category, as has already been mentioned, more detailed line items (salaries, travel, telephones, technology, etc.). This type of budget focuses attention on how much money is spent and for what purpose rather than the activity affected or its outcomes; therefore, there is no relationship between that budget request and the priorities of the library. It tends to project the past into the future.

Critics believe this approach is no longer effective because such an incremental approach is based upon maintaining the status quo, with no real review of accomplishments. Its primary disadvantage is that items within those various established categories can be designated to such a degree that it becomes difficult, if not impossible, to shift them, thus being inflexible. For example, within the broad category of materials and supplies, it may become desirable to add subscription money for new online periodicals after the budget has been set. One might wish to accomplish this by transferring money from equipment because it has been determined that the library can do without an additional personal computer, and the subscription can be justified as technology applicable. However, budgeting authorities might frown upon this kind of transfer. If it is not completely discouraged, it is often made very difficult to accomplish because of the paperwork and red tape involved. Line-item budgeting, or incremental budgeting, tends to assume that all currently existing programs are good and necessary. That approach usually requires no evaluation of services and no projection of future accomplishments.

The greatest disadvantage to the line-item approach is that there is almost no relationship between the budget request and the objectives of the organization. Using the line-item approach simply projects the past and present into the future. In recent years, there has been a sharp rise in what is categorized as "other" (i.e., software, contracts, etc.) because of the increased costs of implementing technological innovations, from the purchase of computer equipment to telecommunications and online database searching charges.

There are, however, a few advantages to the line-item approach. For one thing, line-item budgets are easy to prepare. Most are done by projecting current expenditures to the next year, taking cost increases into account. This type of budget is easy to understand and to justify because it can be shown that the allocated funds were spent in the areas for which they were budgeted. The funding authority can understand a request to add a new position or to increase the communication and supplies budgets by 10 percent because that is the average amount that postage, telephone charges, and other supplies rose last year.

A more primitive variation on the traditional line-item approach is the lump-sum approach. In this form of budgeting, a certain dollar amount is allocated to the library, and it becomes the responsibility of the library to decide how that sum is broken into categories that can be identified. These categories are usually the same ones mentioned under line-item budgeting: salaries and wages, materials and supplies, equipment, capital expenditures, and miscellaneous or overhead.

Figure 19.1—The Line-Item Budget, with Expenditures Assigned to Broad Categories

BUDGET REQUEST FORM I				
SUMMARY				
Department or Program: LIBRARY Department No.: 02876 For Fiscal Year: 2008–2009				
Control Number	**Expenditures**	**Actual Prior Year 2006–2007**	**Budget Current Year 2007–2008**	**Budget Request 2008–2000**
	SALARIES			
100	Full-time employees	730,000	784,750	809,500
101	Part-time employees	27,050	27,860	29,200
102	Hourly wages	34,000	35,360	40,000
	STAFF BENEFITS			
103	Social Security	54,750	58,855	60,700
104	Retirement Acct.	65,700	70,625	72,850
105	Unemployment Comp.	4,675	5,025	5,200
106	Worker's Comp.	4,160	4,475	4,600
107	Life Insurance	3,505	3,765	3,900
108	Health Insurance	39,600	42,250	49,175
109	Accident Ins.	400	470	485
110	Disability Ins.	5,250	5,600	6,300
	MATERIALS			
120	Books	120,000	127,200	137,375
121	Serials	180,000	165,500	180,400
122	Binding	36,000	37,800	40,450
123	Media	86,500	92,300	97,650
124	Inst. Materials	17,000	17,850	18,750
125	Technology	90,000	135,000	200,000
150	**OTHER**	39,000	40,150	42,150
151	Utilities	25,500	26,500	27,825
152	Supplies	22,000	22,880	23,950
153	Telephone	19,200	19,975	20,975
154	Travel	9,500	9,975	10,475
155	Postage	8,000	8,450	8,900
156	Insurance	23,700	36,500	38,300
157	Equipment	17,600	18,850	19,800
158	Vehicle cost	15,800	16,600	17,450
159	Service contracts Consultants	3,700	3,850	3,850
	TOTAL	1,682,590	1,818,415	1,970,210

This might seem more flexible than line-item budgeting, but it still does not relate the objectives to services. Libraries using this technique are forced to develop programs within the dollar figure allocated, instead of the other way around.

Formula Budgeting

Formula budgeting uses predetermined standards for allocation of monetary resources. In the past, this approach has been adopted by regional or state library agencies or in school districts and even university systems for appropriating state or regional funds. One reason it is popular among larger funding authorities is that, after the criteria for budget requests has been established, they can be applied across the board to all units within the library system. The popularity of a formula budget is reflected in several factors:

1. A formula budget is mechanical and easy to prepare.
2. The formula budget process applies to all institutions in the political jurisdiction.
3. Governing bodies have a sense of equity because each institution in the system is measured against the same criteria.
4. Fewer budgeting and planning skills are required to prepare and administer a formula budget.

Additional advantages of formula budgets are that they:

1. facilitate interinstitutional comparison;
2. facilitate comparisons from year to year;
3. reduce paperwork in the budgeting process;
4. eliminate extraneous details;
5. provide a systematic, objective allocation technique;
6. connote mathematical infallibility.[4]

The formulas, which usually are expressed in terms of a percentage of the total institutional cost, focus primarily on input rather than activities and, therefore, are more applicable to specific aspects of library operations. For instance, in collection development, percentages of budgets can be allocated, in the case of academic libraries, to the number of programs and number of faculty teaching in each program. This factor determines what the library will get. In that sense, formula budget allocations may be thought of as a combination of the lump-sum and formula approaches.

Such formulas, when used in education institutions, have applied a fixed dollar figure per full-time equivalent student and faculty or have attached collection and staff figures to programs offered. Sometimes formulas are used for programs or faculty numbers. Most libraries have tended to move away from strict formula budgeting, except when outside funding is tied to established formulas or specifically for materials allocation.[5] One distinct disadvantage to formula budgeting is that some functions cannot be related to those formulas and must receive separate justification. Perhaps the biggest fallacy in such an approach is that it assumes a relationship between the quantity being expressed and the quality of service; that is, output measures. There are now attempts to tie in output measures.[6]

Program Budgeting

The program budgeting process is concerned with identifying all of the organization's activities and performance, as opposed to the traditional line-item budget system that allocates resources based on line-item expenses. Every activity in the organization is linked through the all-inclusive programs. Those programs link the activities of the organization to the objectives and financial requirements that can be identified for each program.

The program budget approach identifies the total cost of each service unit/component and sets spending levels and priorities accordingly. In that regard, it is similar to the Planning, Programming, and Budgeting System (PPBS), discussed in a following section, but is somewhat more flexible. Its approach maintains that it is possible to relate programs to the accomplishment of time/action objectives or activities that are stated in output terms in the strategic planning process. Therefore, a program budget displays a series of minibudgets, which then show the cost of each of the activities within the organization. In a way, it can be said that program budgeting developed along with strategic planning because that type of planning process is based upon establishing costs of individual programs, which requires accounting as well as budgeting. Having identified each library's activity unit, monetary figures can be assigned to the various programs or services provided.

For example, if a public library system provides bookmobile service for the community, the total cost of that service (staffing, materials, maintenance, overhead, etc.) can be calculated. In this way, one can see exactly what, for example, the bookmobile service costs. See figure 19.2.

Performance Budgeting

In a way, the performance-budgeting approach could be called "outcome budgeting," because actual performances are measured in terms of service effectiveness and efficiency.

It classifies expenditures on the basis of specific activities, the number of units performed, and their costs. It concentrates attention on what each work unit does, how frequently it does it, and at what cost rather than a simple, line-item accounting of expenditures. It is easiest to build performance-based budgets on the foundation of a program-based budget system. Under performance, or outcome-based budgets, each major program or function is measured using a set of benchmarks. Benchmarks are snapshots of particular activities or functions at a beginning date and time. These benchmarks are used for comparison purposes to measure progress in attaining specific program or functional goals over periods of time (i.e., six months, a year, or several years). Programs, activities, and functions also may be measured quantitatively and qualitatively against other internal and external comparables.

Figure 19.2—Program Budget Sheet

Organization: COUNTY LIBRARY	
Program: BOOKMOBILE SERVICE	
Objective: This service is offered to county residents who reside more than three miles from a public library. Specific services offered include providing basic reference collection of encyclopedias, handbooks, and dictionaries and a rotating collection of circulating materials on a variety of subjects for all levels of readers. Makes two stops per day, covers seven miles, five days per week.	

Costs:	
Personnel Service	
Librarian	$28,500
Driver	20,000
Stocker (to load, unload truck, 4 hrs. per week @ $6.00 x 52 weeks)	1,248
Benefits	9,700
SUBTOTAL	$59,448 (1)
Materials	
Books (2,000 volume collection x $36 average + $10.20 processing costs	$72,000
Periodicals (15 subscriptions @ $40 each)	600
Repairs, binding, etc.	175
SUBTOTAL	$72,775 (2)
Other	
Vehicle depreciation	$1,600
Maintenance, gasoline (30 mi. per week x 52 weeks x 26¢ per mile)	405
Insurance	600
SUBTOTAL	$2,605 (3)
TOTAL (Subtotals 1 + 2 + 3)	$134,828

Recently, measures of performance have been expanded to include more subjective evaluations focused on overall quality of programs and their direct benefits, meaning outcomes. It links revenue to resource allocation and service performance in measurable terms and, as such, serves as an important policy tool. This approach is a combination of program budgeting and performance budgeting.

Based on the cost of a program and its outcome objectives, or benefits, one can decide whether to continue, to modify, or to delete the service. Program budgeting is an effective method of explaining needs to funding authorities. The focus is on consideration of all priorities and alternatives for service.[7] For instance, other than simply withholding funds from the lower-ranked services in a priority list, other alternatives can be explored, including trying to reduce the cost of providing a certain level of services for those already chosen, thereby allowing the next listed priority to be funded. Another alternative might be to increase charges, say for value-added services to individuals and organizations, thereby adding to the pool of nondirect sources of funds, which might in turn support the next level on the priority list.

The upside is that all programs can be identified and valued, whereas the downside is that it is time consuming to establish and maintain the system and programs tend to overlap between departments and units, which can make collecting data difficult.

Performance budgeting measures quantity rather than quality of service offered. The classification of expenditures is based upon specific activities, the number of units performed, and their costs. This type of budget concentrates attention on what a work unit does, how frequently it does it, and at what cost rather than a detailed, line-item accounting of expenditures. Recently, measures of performance have been expanded to include more subjective evaluations focused on overall quality of programs and their direct benefits to users.

This approach requires the careful accumulation of quantitative data over a period of time. Techniques of cost-benefit analysis are required to measure the performance and to establish norms. Performance budgeting has been criticized because the economic aspect overshadows the service aspect. This approach is sometimes called function budgeting because costs are presented in terms of work to be accomplished. A good example of this is processing materials—from submission of an order until the time that the volume is on the shelf and the bibliographic information is in the online or print catalog. All activities involved (verifying the author, title, and so forth; ordering, receiving, cataloging, and classifying; providing book pockets, call number, and catalog cards or electronic data; filing cards in the catalog or the information in the database; and placing the volume on the shelf) can be analyzed as to average time for the activity and average cost per item. Therefore, careful cost and work measurements are applied to each activity. Fixed costs of building maintenance, heating, lights, equipment, and other items that are variable but are directly related to the work being done also must be added to the final cost. With such detailed budgeting activity, benefits of awareness and participation may be overshadowed by the costly time and efforts involved in maintaining the process. Two techniques, Planning, Programming, and Budgeting System (PPBS) and zero-based budgeting (ZBB), are spin-offs of program budgeting.

Planning, Programming, and Budgeting System (PPBS)

Planning, Programming, and Budgeting System (PPBS) was developed by the Rand Corporation and introduced by the U.S. government in 1961. At the height of its popularity, many complex organizations all over the world were, at some point, using PPBS or some modification of it. These include state and local governments, college and university systems, and industry. It is basically a refinement of the program approach discussed previously. Like management by objectives (MBO), which has lost its popularity in recent years, PPBS is not currently as widely promoted as it once was.

PPBS differs from traditional budgeting processes because it focuses less on an existing base, with consideration of annual incremental improvements, but more on objectives and purposes with long-term alternative means for achieving them. As a result, PPBS brings together planning and budgeting by means of programming, a process that defines a procedure for distributing available resources fairly among the competing or possible programs.

The PPBS approach combines the best of both program budgeting and performance budgeting. The emphasis is on planning. Like program budgeting, it begins with the establishment of goals and objectives, but the controlling aspect of measurement, which is paramount in performance budgeting, is also part of PPBS. It emphasizes the cost of accomplishing program goals set by the library instead of stressing objects, which the more traditional budgets highlight. This approach forces one to think of the budget as a tool to allocate resources rather than to control operations. The steps important in PPBS are:

1. Identifying the objectives of the library.
2. Presenting alternative ways to achieve those objectives, with cost-benefit ratios presented for each.
3. Identifying the activities that are necessary for each program.
4. Evaluating the result so that corrective actions can be taken.

In essence, PPBS is a scientific approach to budgeting that improves the decision-making process by calling for a systematic analysis of alternative ways of meeting objectives. The crux of PPBS is the selection of appropriate criteria for evaluating each alternative against relevant objectives; it combines the functions of planning (identifying objectives), translating that to a program (staff and materials), and, finally, stating those requirements in budgetary terms (financing). Headings for a PPBS summary sheet are shown in figure 19.3.

The PPBS approach allows one to enumerate programs and assign costs to those programs. The figures that are the outcome of PPBS are "extremely useful in determining future priorities and direction, in requesting funds, and in justifying the value of libraries and their services."[8] It also allows funding

Figure 19.3—Headings for a PPBS Summary Sheet

County of:	Program Summary
Operating Budget: (Year)	
Program: (Title of program)	
Goal: (Brief operational goal)	
Description: (Brief description of program)	

agencies to place programs into perspective and to evaluate the effects of cutting monies from or adding monies to the budget. As one can imagine, the required detailed examination of every aspect of the operation is not only time consuming but cumbersome as well. It requires goals, objectives, and activities to be stated in measurable terms and then mandates the follow-up activity of measuring the results. Despite these drawbacks, some modification of the intent of this approach is being used in some libraries today.

 Try This!

Develop a budget for a type of library using the information you have identified in the PPBS budgeting, including costs for the major categories of online services, collection development, and staffing, and present the budget, using all appropriate costs for those categories.

Zero-Based Budgeting (ZBB)

The zero-based budgeting (ZBB) approach is not a strict procedural one but rather an approach that annually requires the organization to review and to reevaluate each of their service programs and activities on the basis of both output measures and costs. Each line item or program is examined in its entirety, regardless of prior funding. Detailed measurement of performance and costs of the activity are identified. Those items that cannot be justified are subject to elimination or significant reduction. Efficiency and effectiveness are key considerations, because each program is justified and its priority identified according to its level of importance in achieving the mission of the organization. This process requires stating the reason for the activity as well as the consequences of not implementing the package.

Each activity is expressed in a decision package that is reviewed and ranked in priority order in relation to all other identified decision packages. With all of the decision packages developed and gathered, using objectives as guides, they are ranked in priority order and are presented for approval or rejection, depending upon a package's position in the hierarchy and on affordability. At some level in the hierarchy of priorities is a cutoff level, and decision packages that fall below it are not funded. Because setting priorities at the organization level involves every unit within the organization, clear guidelines for ranking must be established. The process of priority formulation helps the manager rank and, in some cases, delete activities because of obsolescence, inefficiency, or change of policy or objectives.[9]

Ranking decision packages, or setting priorities within each unit of the organization, forces decisions about the most important activities within that unit of the organization. The technique allocates limited resources by forcing decision makers to concentrate on identifying the most important programs and projects to be funded. Each unit of the organization conducts the same process. After each unit identifies its priorities, the priorities of all units are amalgamated into one pool, and the process is repeated in light of the decision packages' importance to the total organization. Each decision package relates to some extent to others, and this interrelationship must be considered in ranking them because related decision packages share costs of personnel and resources. For example, ready reference is dependent upon an up-to-date, fully processed reference collection, which depends upon the selection, acquisition, and processing of materials, and technological access to others, involving staff and materials budgets in those units.

The most important initial steps in ZBB are:

1. Identifying decision packages or units.
2. Ranking of those packages.
3. Determining the cutoff point below which packages cannot be supported.
4. Preparing operating budgets that reflect those units.

In identification of decision packages, a package should be the lowest unit for which a budget can be prepared. A unit may be described along functional lines (e.g., circulation), by smaller units in larger organizations (e.g., reserve function of circulation), or as a special program of the organization (e.g., outreach services to the underserved). However, care must be exercised so that decision units are large enough to reflect major portions of a person's time; smaller distribution probably would be meaningless because it might, for instance, eliminate only a small fraction of a full-time salary. This process of description requires the identification of goals and objectives of the package and how they relate to the mission of the organization, a statement of alternatives, the reason for the activity, consequences of not introducing the package, detailed measurement of performance, projected outcomes in the implementation process, and the costs of the activity. Of course, the size and complexity of the organization determines the number of units that can be identified and supported.

When ZBB budgets are first introduced into an organization, the process of reviewing current activities must be broken into units and placed in a hierarchy of importance. In this examination, duplication of efforts can be more easily detected. Options for reviewing those existing activities include:

1. Should the activity be kept as it is or, perhaps, expanded?
2. Should it be eliminated altogether or, perhaps, reduced in support?
3. Should it be centralized or decentralized?
4. Should it be integrated into other programs or broken down into more finite units?

Analysis in this ranking process of establishing priorities also allows for the selection of the alternatives that have the greatest potential for achieving the objectives in each of the decision packages. Therefore, the process of specifically identifying decision packages also focuses on the best way of doing things, either through cost savings or efficiency of service. The last processes of ZBB, just as should be the case in any budgeting process, are monitoring and evaluation. Adjustments may be essential during the budgeted time period in order to achieve the decision package objectives, and there is a need to know whether the goals of the various packages are being accomplished and at what level. The monitoring and evaluation process of ZBB requires establishing measures of performance and reporting. Specifically relating to costs, quantitative measures must be established to monitor output, which is expressed in financial terms.

ZBB is more concerned with what is required in the future, rather than what happened in the past. In this approach and in its development, ZBB is very similar to PPBS; it requires careful analysis of activities that should take place in the library and requires justification for each unit of work identified. By forcing an organization to identify areas of greater and lesser importance, ZBB emphasizes planning and fosters an understanding, by all units, of the total organization. It helps maintain vitality in the organization by constantly assessing and questioning programs.[10] It forces each unit manager and the unit workers to identify priorities within their unit of the organization. Identifying priorities and stating them in terms of cost force the unit to answer the questions: "Is it really worth it?" and "Are there alternatives to achieving this objective?" The ZBB approach requires that justification for each program start at point zero, and it requires that this be done each year. Of course, after a decision unit has been identified, that particular unit does not need to be reidentified each year; it needs to be further described only if changes occur, although it still must be considered in the list of priorities and costs must be recalculated.

The ZBB process should provide an indication of the real cost of various library activities, an estimate of the minimum cost level necessary to provide each service, a ranking of library functions to facilitate support, a discovery of unnecessary duplication of effort, and a framework for the establishment of criteria for continuous evaluation of performance.

It is assumed in the ZBB model that the sum of those units receiving top priority status is less than the current budgeted amount and that a cutoff will occur at some point. This attitude allows for a reduced level at which activities can be carried out to meet the essential objectives of the organization. Figure 19.4 illustrates, in an abbreviated way, the process involved in establishing a decision package statement and how that package might fit into the priorities of the organization. This approach requires effective communication and efficient training of personnel involved in the approach.

 Try This!

Select one of the budgeting techniques reviewed. Consider its best application to a type of library. Write a justification for selecting it and defend it to a group of colleagues as a best practice.

Figure 19.4—Form for Decision Package Statement

DECISION PACKAGE STATEMENT	Prepared by: Date:
Program Name:	Priority Rank:
Department:	Level:

Statement of Purpose: Goals and Objectives – What is to be accomplished:

Description of Activity:

Benefits Desired Results:

Related Activities:

Alternatives, Other Options (to achieve same or partial results):

Consequences (if activity is not approved/is eliminated):

Cost Resources Required	Prior Period	Budgeting Period
Personnel		
Operations:		
TOTAL		

TECHNIQUES FOR FINANCIAL ALLOCATION

Various techniques have been developed to manage the financial aspects of library and information services organizations. With the application of technology to the budgetary process, many spreadsheet options have been successfully integrated into the accountability process in libraries. A few are mentioned here to give some indication of ongoing accountability measures.

Entrepreneurial Budgeting

Entrepreneurial budgeting is a relatively recently developed attitude toward budgeting that continues to be experimented with in both the public and the private sectors. It differs from traditional techniques in that the ultimate controlling authority decides beforehand what the budget base will be; for example, not more that last year's budget plus 5 percent. Initially, this appears to be the same as an incremental budget, but in fact it is quite different. Simply stated, it allocates a pool of money to the unit or organization that is then responsible for managing it within the program priorities identified. If there are funds left over at the end of the year, they are rolled forward, thus avoiding the usual rush at the end of a fiscal year when the "use it or lose it" mentality takes over. It is reported that this so-called profit-sharing approach improves morale and supposedly management.[11] It decentralizes decision making with incentives to be more innovative.

Allocation Decision Accountability Performance (ADAP)

Allocation Decision Accountability Performance is an innovative technique that is only mentioned because there is little experience with its use in libraries and information service agencies. A budgetary hybrid, it combines aspects of both PPBS and ZBB. It has received awards worldwide and is being adapted by a number of local government agencies. The key aspect is that three budgets must be submitted: the first requesting an increase, the second recognizing a modest decrease, and the third presenting a budget below which the organization cannot function. Administrators are asked to identify whole programs that could be eliminated if necessary. Budgeting authorities can compare the current year's budget with preceding years, and if the same programs are identified as expendable with some frequency, they become candidates for elimination. Despite this pitfall, it is an acceptable way to budget because it allows the administrator to eliminate programs that have relatively poor performance.

Best, Optimistic, and Pessimistic (BOP)

Rolling budgets, variable budgets, contingency budgets, and flexible budgets are all based on varying revenue projections, again applying primarily to for-profit organizations. Sometimes the set of assumptions in this approach are called best, optimistic, and pessimistic (BOP) assumptions. Best assumes normal operating conditions; optimistic assumes there will be problems, but the problems can be surmounted; and pessimistic assumes "if everything goes wrong."[12] By participating in such exercises, management becomes aware of the broad range of possibilities, in both possibilities and coping strategies. In these economic times, that is not a useless exercise.

Responsibility Center Budgeting

Rising costs and tightening budgets have forced greater accountability among institutions of higher education. Responsibility center budgeting is the approach of "each tub on its own bottom" and is being implemented in several large universities, having found its way into higher education through the corporate sector. It forces institutions to identify their units that are capable of self-support, including all academic units with tuition- and fee-paying students; faculty capable of bringing in contracts and grants; and other central administrative units as well as academic support units, including libraries and information centers. Direct institutional support is augmented by other sources of funding: appropriations from governments, contracts, endowments, and contributions. Again, fund-raising on the part of libraries is an important component in this mix. Basically, this approach forces decision making down into all of those units in which costs are directly related to academic priorities. Heated debates revolve around how the central administration allocates funds to units. For example, "how charges for space, libraries, and other services [will] be allocated; and how the hardware and software needed to run the new information systems [will] be configured."[13] It requires that the administration recognize and support units that exist for the "public good—such as the physical plant, technology, and the library [and that they] must receive funding that is adequate, but at taxation levels that the academic units can support financially and intellectually without seriously attenuating RCM's [Responsibility Center Management] underlying incentives."[14]

Bracket Budgeting

Bracket budgeting is an analytical procedure that complements conventional budgeting techniques. It is a combination of modeling and simulation in which the computer performs an integral role. The computer must be programmed to perform various calculations, which requires considerable computer expertise and probably is much too complex to be beneficial in most library situations. It is most useful in for-profit organizations, in which uncertainty can wreak havoc on the profits.

Software Applications

Many libraries use computer software in preparing budgets. Indeed, budgetary control was one of the first functions to make use of computers in libraries. Several financial modeling, budget, financial planning, and data manipulation software packages are applicable to library budgeting. These have been developed both commercially and in-house for specific organizations. Electronic spreadsheet applications are being used to overcome the limitations of manual record-keeping systems. They easily manage numbers and calculations. Electronic spreadsheets are responsive and creative in applying formulas that automatically update data. As the name implies, a spreadsheet is an electronic version of the columnar worksheet used for years. They are available for purchase or license or, sometimes, are in the public domain. Budgeting makes use of electronic spreadsheet software, including, as examples, both Mariner Calc and the Cruncher for Macintosh; Excel 2003, Lotus Improv, Lotus 1-2-3, GS-Calc, SuperCalc, MultiPlan, Perfect-Calc, Context MBA, SAS, Oracle, ClarisWorks, SQL Server, SPSS for Windows, and others. Most are powerful decision tools in the controlling process for libraries.

There are also software packages for forecasting, including Forecast! GFX, Tomorrow, Forecast Pro, and Forecast Plus.[15] Because spreadsheets make number crunching easy, libraries now are able to adjust or revise budgets and projections without expending great amounts in terms of personnel and time. Some libraries even use computer modeling and forecasting to prepare financial plans. However, software tools are only one part of the budgeting process—the mechanical part. Thought and imagination also are needed to prepare successfully and to defend a budget.

ACCOUNTABILITY AND REPORTING

The final aspect of budgeting to be mentioned here is keeping accurate records of what has been disbursed, what has been encumbered, and what remains. Before the budget has been approved by the proper authority, a mechanism for keeping track of both expenditures and encumbrances must be in place to keep track of not only what has been spent but also to set aside funds for items ordered but not yet received so that funds will be reserved and available for their payment when they do arrive. Established account categories and numbers play a vital role in this process to identify such items as salaries, materials acquired or ordered, equipment installed, and so forth. Periodic statements of expenditures and an audit of the expenses at the end of the year provide important feedback to the budgetary process. An accounting process allows for efficient and effective adjustments to the process when and where they are needed. The process has been greatly enhanced by the use of those previously mentioned electronic spreadsheets and other software packages available for financial planning on microcomputers and other equipment. These systems have aided the auditing process, reduced the need for double bookkeeping records, and facilitated reporting by allowing projections of cost activities. Reporting usually is accomplished through monthly records prepared by the accounting office, either of which usually is a part of the library or as a part of the larger organization, such as the city government. Monthly statements, or on-demand electronic reporting, can act as benchmarks to inform the library staff how they are progressing, financially, toward the library's objectives and, at the same time, alert them to potential problem areas (i.e., overexpenditures). This monthly summary statement or balance sheet, electronic or in print form, is typical in most organizations.

Because accounting is an independent function, many large libraries employ budget analysts in staff positions; their primary responsibility is to report facts as they exist or have existed. Such budget officers are not normally responsible for making decisions that affect the operations of the library. However, they are most helpful in collecting relevant cost data for anticipated decisions and in making cost studies that might be keys to decision making.

Along with accounting goes the important element of reporting—reporting to the funding authority, reporting to the staff, and reporting to the public, however that might be defined. Reporting procedures can take a variety of forms: formal written reports, electronically accessed or in printed form, with detailed statistical documentation, or informal reports, such as memos, staff meetings, board meetings, or newspaper articles. In reporting, the librarian's public relations responsibility becomes most evident. Only by conscientiously selling the library and its services can the librarian hope to maintain a high level of activity and funding. The purpose is to be so convincing that support for library activities will increase or, at minimum, remain the same. As detailed in chapter 6, public relations for librarians is an art through which information and persuasion solicit public support for the causes that are set forth in the goals of the library. Public relations is an integral part of the goals and objectives and the budgeting procedure in a library. This is the library's primary means of gaining and holding the support necessary to develop programs. It is also a way of expanding that support through new financial initiatives.

CONCLUSION

Budgeting is the ultimate controlling operation because it is the monetary expression of a plan of information services in libraries and other information centers. Various types and levels of budgeting are used to plan for information services. Some are more applicable to not-for-profit organizations than others, but all are being used, in one form or another, in libraries and information centers. The process of budgeting is important because it is the way organizations remain financially accountable.

NOTES

1. Michigan State University Libraries, "Nonprofit Virtual Libraries" (2006), http://www.lib.msu.edu/harris23/grants/znonprof.htm.

2. Susan K. Martin, ed., "Developing and Fund-Raising Initiatives," *Library Trends* 48, no 3 (Winter 2000): 526.

3. Allen Schick, "The Road to PPB: The Stages of Budget Reform," in *Perspectives on Budgeting,* ed. Allen Schick (Washington, DC: ASPA, 1980), 47.

4. Gary M. Shirk, "Allocation Formulas for Budgeting Library Materials: Science or Procedure?" *Collection Management* 6 (Fall–Winter 1984): 37–38.

5. University of Guelph Library, "Acquisitions of Allocation Mechanism: The Access Model" (1999), http://www.lib.uoguelph.ca/services_for/faculty_and_graduate_students/collections/accessmodel.htm.

6. Denise A. Troll, "How and Why Are Libraries Changing?" (2001), Digital Library Federation, http://www.diglib.org/use/whitepaper.htm.

7. Wisconsin Department of Public Instruction, "Program Budget Guidelines for Public Library System Annual Plans" (2006), http://dpi.state.wi.us/pld/sysbudgetguide.html.

8. Marilyn J. Sharrow, "Budgeting Experience—At the University of Toronto Library," *Canadian Library Journal,* 40 (August 1983), 207.

9. Ching-chih Chen, *Zero Based Budgeting in Library Management* (New York: Gaylord Professional Books, 1980), 36.

10. Ricky W. Griffin, *Management,* 3rd ed. (Boston: Houghton Mifflin, 1990), 697.

11. Dan A. Cothran, "Entrepreneurial Budgeting: An Emerging Reform?" *Budgeting and the Management of Public Spending* (Cheltenham, U.K.: Elgar, 1996), 446.

12. Jay H. Loevy, "The Budget: An Integral Element of Internal Control" in *Handbook of Budgeting*, 5th ed., ed. H.W.A. Sweeney and R. Rachlin (New York: Wiley, 2003), 770.

13. W. W. Wilms, C. Teruya, and M. Walpole, "Fiscal Reform at UCLA: The Clash of Accountability and Academic Freedom," *Change* 29 (September–October 1997): 43.

14. D. L. Slocum and P. M. Rooney, "Responding to Resource Constraints," *Change* 29 (September–October 1997): 56.

15. Jae K. Shim and Joel G. Siegel, *Financial Management for Nonprofits* (New York: McGraw-Hill, 1997), 358–62.

Managing in the Twenty-First Century

Good people in management positions are vital to the existence of library and information services organizations. The internal relations among themselves and staff; the external relations among themselves and stakeholders who are users and supporters of information services; and the temporal relations as "inheritors of the past and ancestors to the future" are all factors to consider as managers and leaders. The future is driven by changing relationships. In order to reinvent the future good managers are required to have a vision of the possible that empowers the future beyond the temporal boundaries of the annual budgets and routine activities. The future is what those leaders create.

Every reader of this textbook, with its focus upon both theory and practice, should take to heart the admonishment to become a manager by beginning to prepare, now, for that eventuality. It requires recognizing that whether a person is a manager or someone being managed, all are involved in the process—team building, strategic planning, motivation, quality control, and evaluation. To be truly committed to information services requires every single member of an organization be dedicated to the vision and mission of the knowledge-based organization, most often called a library. When that happens, society benefits.

This section addresses the challenges facing future leaders and managers of information services organizations.

Chapter 20

Managers: The Next Generation

Overview

Lou has been a reference librarian since she graduated from library school almost forty years ago. She is planning to retire next month. One of her friends asked her, "Lou, did you ever think of doing anything besides being a reference librarian?" Lou replied that she had always enjoyed her position but that she had once considered becoming a manager. This was when the head of the reference department position was available and the director asked her to consider applying for it. "What happened?" asked her friend. "Well," said Lou, "I decided not to apply after all. I thought about it, but decided it was more than I wanted to take on. You know that the head of the department has to do the performance appraisals of everyone who works in the department. The head also has to handle any disciplinary situations. The more I thought about it, the more I knew that I just didn't want the responsibility. What if someone was not doing a good job? I would be the one who would have to write the bad appraisal. What if an employee was consistently late and I had to issue the reprimand? I decided it wasn't worth the hassle."

As Lou's story illustrates, management does not appeal to everyone. There are many students in schools of library and information science who think that they never would want to be managers. Like Lou, they do not want the responsibility. Nonetheless, most LIS graduates become managers if not in their first jobs then soon thereafter. Managers are not born but made (and sometimes reluctantly at that), and libraries need a constant stream of individuals who are willing and able to take on the responsibilities of management. As today's baby boomer managers reach retirement age, there is an even greater need and opportunity for a new generation of library mangers.

This chapter will look first at how the decision to become a manager should be made and then at how individuals who have decided they want to manage can acquire the skills and knowledge necessary to be a successful library manager.

Imagine Melvil Dewey waking from a 100-year-long Rip Van Winkle–like sleep and suddenly being confronted with the twenty-first-century library. He would be astounded at some of the changes he encountered. Where is the card catalog? What about the shelf list? What are these black metal boxes with windows on them? What are those things that people are talking into while walking around? What about library directors? Many directors and high-level managers seem to be women. What are the librarians doing? Librarians no longer deal with books but seem to have been transformed into information navigators, surfing what is called the Internet with zeal and devotion. What is all this talk of metadata and Dublin Core, OCLC, and ARL LibQual+ measurements; outsourcing and customer satisfaction; self-directed teams and flattened organizations; change management and strategic planning? The transformation of the library that has taken place over the past 100 years would, at first, certainly leave Dewey bewildered, but Dewey was always a reformer. It seems likely that after he readjusted to the realities of the twenty-first-century library, he would begin to think like a manager and consider additional innovations that might allow these libraries to serve their users even better.

Stability and continuity are no longer characteristics that can be used to describe the library profession or a library manager's responsibilities. The profession is now best characterized by change, discontinuity, and opportunity. Managers are at the core of all that is happening in libraries today. Perhaps an appropriate slogan for a modern manager might be, "If you sense calm, it's only because you're in the eye of the storm." Few traces of the past remain. Information service has entered a new era, and the only way libraries, under the leadership and initiative of directors, can conserve the good that has been built in the past while performing a more challenging, vital mission in the future is by innovating. The challenge is to achieve a balance between preserving the good aspects of the past while moving toward a new vision of the future.

 Try This!

Interview a manager that you know. Either interview the manager at his or her workplace or perhaps offer to take the manager out for coffee. Ask the person you interview questions that will help you get an insight into what managers actually do and what you should be doing to prepare yourself to be one.

How did he or she become a manager?
What are the most difficult parts of being a manager?

The most frustrating?
The most rewarding?
What has this person learned from being a manager?
How does he or she keep up-to-date?
What ethical dilemmas has that manager faced?
How does that person make decisions?
What difficult decisions has he or she had to make?
What is his or her management style?
What career advice can that manager offer you?

MANAGING IN TODAY'S ORGANIZATIONS

The challenge of managing is one thing that has remained the same from the time of Dewey to the present. The nature of the work being done, the types of technologies employed, the speed with which activities are accomplished, and the way workers think, talk, and react all have been drastically altered. But the managers of the early twenty-first century still face many of the same challenges that confronted their predecessors: How does one motivate workers? How can a realistic budget be developed? How can the organization be both more effective and more efficient? How can library organizations capitalize upon the fact that workers are better educated, more involved in decision making, more motivated to attempt to identify objectives, and more committed to interacting with customers than ever before?

As previously discussed in the introductory chapters of this book, practices and procedures have evolved over the years, drawing upon the theories developed during the last century to cope with developing trends. Management and the techniques used to practice it have changed, but the need for managers remains constant. Many of the interpersonal and organizational skills that made managers successful in the past are still important for modern managers. But, in addition, managers in twenty-first-century organizations require augmented skills and talents to lead new types of organizations. Many of the readers of this textbook will be those new managers of the twenty-first-century library. The future of libraries and information services rests squarely in the hands of this new breed of managers.

THE NEW GENERATION OF MANAGERS

A great deal has been written in the past few years about the graying of the library profession and the need to recruit new librarians. There also will be a need to find replacements for many of today's library managers. The baby boom generation is beginning to reach retirement age, and most library managers fall in this very large age cohort. The vast majority of people working and managing in libraries now are baby boomers born somewhere between 1946 and 1964. The boomers were followed by a much smaller cohort, often called Generation X, born between 1965 and 1978. Individuals belonging to Generation Y (or the millennials) were born between 1979 and 2000 and are just beginning to be part of the library workforce. It is the Generation X and Generation Y librarians (often called NextGen librarians) who will be the managers of the libraries of the twenty-first century.

Because libraries have existed for centuries, they have much experience with successive waves of workers coming into the library workforce, and certainly this is not the first time that there have been librarians who need to interact with colleagues and patrons of different generations.[1] Although libraries are used to welcoming new workers, there is still a need for librarians to realize the unique characteristics of today's entrants to the workplace. The newest entrants, the Generation Y cohort, have been said to have a preference for teamwork, experiential activities, and using technology. They are strong in multitasking, goal orientation, positive attitudes, and a collaborative style.[2] This is the first generation of new workers who come to the library workplace as digital natives and not digital immigrants.

 What Do You Think?

One NextGen librarian was quoted as saying:

> While generational issues do need to be discussed and resolved, I am concerned about making too big an issue out of them. We do not want to draw a line between two generations of librarians and unintentionally alienate them from each other. Instead, we need to learn to work together as we seek to help librarianship evolve with the times to serve the needs of the public. Each librarian, new or experienced, old or young, brings valuable experiences, perspectives, skills, and ideas to the profession. We need to find a way to acknowledge those assets and put them to good use.

How much do you think generational differences affect workers? What differences do you see in baby boomer, Generation X and Generation Y librarians? How can libraries be welcoming work environments for people of all generations?

Unnamed NextGen librarian quoted in Rachel Singer Gordon, "Next Generation Librarianship," *American Libraries* 37, no. 3 (March 2006): 28.

Although many new librarians are from the Generation Y generation, because librarianship often has been a second or third career for many people, there are still new entrants to the library workforce from the baby boomer and Generation X generations. It would be a mistake to focus too much attention on generational differences, but managers need to remember that younger librarians may have different attitudes toward some of the traditional practices in the workplace and may have "changing expectations of work/life balance, a differing view on employer/employee loyalty, and a predisposition toward continuous challenges and lifelong learning."[3] As libraries begin to plan to make the succession from the managers of today to those of the future, the characteristics and strengths of these new managers must be taken into consideration.

DECIDING TO BECOME A MANAGER

Librarianship, like many other service professions, attracts individuals who often do not have a strong desire to manage. In fact, many enter the profession with a strong aversion to being a manager. In librarianship, professionals usually enjoy the tasks traditionally associated with the profession: collecting, organizing, preserving, and disseminating information. People drawn to the library profession like to work with information and people. These are essential tasks for most librarians, but most modern librarians have to combine work on these tasks with managerial responsibilities. In the United States, for example, the proportion of nonprofessional library employees continues to increase, and, as a result, most professional librarians have to serve as managers. The professional librarians customarily supervise the nonprofessionals, and it is common for many librarians to begin to manage on their first job. So individuals who joined the profession so they could perform professional tasks soon find themselves managers, often reluctant managers, because many probably believed in the old adage "managers are born not made" and were convinced they were not born to be one. But managers are not born but made, and, as has been said frequently before, most librarians will need to assume managerial responsibilities at some point in their careers. Almost all librarians will supervise others and engage in some management activities in teams or committees.

However, what if you are interested in going beyond this level of management and want to be a mid- or upper-level manager? Some readers already may have taken initial steps toward such a management career. They have been, perhaps, intrigued by the idea of managing an organization or trying to make things work better. Others may be working in jobs in which the management approach has been poor and believe that they can initiate necessary improvements. Others are intrigued by the idea of putting into practice some of the theories and techniques discussed in this text. The work of a manager, though often difficult, is never dull and is usually rewarding.

Henry Mintzberg, in a seminal study, examined the work that managers do.[4] He actually sat in the offices of managers, followed them around, and recorded their activities. He found that managers work at demanding activities that are characterized by their variety, fragmentation, and brevity. In other words, managers rarely have long stretches of uninterrupted time to spend on any one task. They simultaneously work at a variety of tasks, each for a short period of time. Their days are fragmented, and there are many demands on their time. A manager also performs a great deal of work at a very fast pace and is required to make ultimate decisions after due consideration. For most managers, there is usually more to be done than there is time in which to do it.

Managers are required to assume a great deal of responsibility. They are responsible for other people, their actions, and the success or failure of the enterprise. "The buck stops here!" mentality continues because managers are accountable, at various levels, for the operation of a team, a unit, a division, or a whole organization. With a focus upon customers and their needs, the idea of the library as a knowledge organization whose primary responsibility is knowledge management becomes the most important part of the manager's daily work life. They typically have heavy workloads and often feel stress because of their managerial duties.

Under such circumstances, why would anyone want to be a manager? Although there are many challenges and difficulties associated with management, most competent managers enjoy their jobs. They like the sense of autonomy and the ability to set their own agendas and are proud of being able to make a difference and of performing well. They are challenged by the diversity of the work they do and the diversity of the people—staff, customers, and other stakeholders—with whom they work. Most managers appreciate the higher salaries that accompany managerial positions. Managers are rewarded monetarily because they are accountable for the actions of others and for the achievement of organizational objectives.

The decision about whether to pursue a managerial career deserves thoughtful consideration by all new professionals. Learning to be a manager in a rapidly changing era involves learning about a great many things. The cliché that management is both an art and a skill is an accurate one. Many management skills are developed only through long practice. Through concerted effort, librarians can improve their managerial skills as they acquire experience and advance in management positions. But it takes more than just time to become a good manager.

Before deciding to pursue a managerial track, an individual should decide whether he or she wants to assume the responsibilities of management. Individuals vary greatly in what they hope to achieve from their career. Edgar Schein has developed one of the best-validated and most commonly used models for discovering career interests. His so-called career anchors are composed of a combination of motivation, attitude, and values. Schein states that these anchors are formed early in life and that they both guide and constrain an individual throughout an entire career. These anchors are what an individual holds to—the career values an individual would not give up even in the face of difficulty. Before anyone decides to become a manager, that person should consider what are the characteristics of the type of activities that he or she enjoys most. One of Schein's career anchors is general managerial competence. People who have that as their anchor have the characteristics shown in table 20.1. When an individual's career anchor is general managerial competence, most likely that person will enjoy management and be a success at it.

So if you want to become an upper-level manager, what are the steps that you should take? Getting ahead in management frequently seems to be affected by serendipity. Often, someone just seems to be in the right place at the right time and then moves up the career ladder because of it. Although serendipity and luck sometimes play a role in becoming a manager, it is wise to plan and to prepare for such a move from the start of one's career to be sure to be ready when the opportunity presents itself.

If you are not yet a manger but would like to be one, the first step is to do the best you can at the job you have now. Even entry-level jobs in libraries usually present at least some opportunity to work autonomously and to exercise creativity. But, in addition to working hard, be sure that your manager knows that you are interested in moving up in the organization at some time in the future. Although you may assume that your boss knows this, be explicit about it. One career strategist describes what she called "the good student" syndrome. Many employees use the same behaviors on the job that worked

TABLE 20.1 Schein's General Managerial Competence Anchor

Anchor	Characteristics	Preferred Pay, Benefits, and Rewards
General Managerial Competence	You want to manage or supervise people. You enjoy authority and responsibility. You are ambitious and thrive on analyzing issues, solving problems, and being in charge of something complex. You enjoy the opportunity to make decisions and like directing, coordinating, and influencing others more than perfecting a particular skill or way of doing things.	You measure success by income level and expect to be highly paid. You believe in promotions based on merit, measured performance, and strong results.

For the rest of Schein's career anchors, see http://www.lu.com/management.

for them in school; they do their best and then wait passively for recognition, approval, and promotion. In the workplace, this can lead to frustration when that recognition does not come, and employees often become resentful when others who are newer in the organization or seem to have done less are promoted and given new opportunities.[5]

In every position you hold, begin to think about the skills and the experiences you will need to qualify you for the type of position you desire next. How can they be acquired? Once again, you can enlist your manager's help in finding ways to acquire those skills and experiences. You should also be looking for opportunities on your own. Are there opportunities for you to acquire management experience on committees either in the library or in a professional organization? Are there courses or workshops that you could take to increase your capabilities? More information about obtaining skills needed for management is provided later in this chapter.

Mentoring, which was discussed in chapter 12, is also helpful if a person wants to become a manager. Mentors help protégés advance in an organization by informally teaching them about the job and the organization. Also, as the protégés begin to ascend the organizational ladder, mentors often sponsor them and use their connections to help them advance either in their present organization or in another one.

 What Do You Think?

Mentoring is a complex subject. There are advantages and disadvantages to the practice. Obviously, those in the organization who don't have mentors may resent those who do.... [I]f one wishes to continue to advance, developing a network that includes a mentor greatly enhances the probability of success.

> As the quotation states, there are both advantages and disadvantage to mentoring. What do you think are the primary advantages and disadvantages? If those who do not have mentors resent those who do, is there a way for organizations to provide mentoring for all?
>
> Joseph Berk and Susan Berk, *Managing Effectively: A Handbook for First-Time Managers* (New York: Sterling, 1991), 93–94.

Becoming a manager usually is never accomplished in just one easy step. Although a few new graduates do begin their careers as directors of small libraries or information services units, most managers-in-training have the opportunity to learn about management through a series of positions and promotions.

As has been discussed before, in most large libraries, management is divided into three primary levels: first-line managers (often called supervisors), middle managers, and top-level managers. Many recent graduates immediately become supervisors. They are assigned responsibility for supervising a group of support staff and directing specific services or procedures. Middle managers are in charge of departments or, perhaps, projects or teams. Top management is responsible for the entire organization. This layer of management is made up of directors and their immediate deputies.

If a newly qualified professional begins work in a very small library, he or she may be the only professional and thus becomes the top manager automatically. In these cases, the new manager will need to work with other managers in the larger organization of which the library is a part to develop the expertise needed in the job. However, more frequently, new graduates go to work in larger organizations, in which they have a chance to learn management skills from their supervisors before they themselves become either middle- or top-level managers.

 Try This!

Think about the best manager that you ever had and then think about the worst one. What are three things you learned from each? How do managers shape the behavior of the future managers who have worked for them?

SKILLS NEEDED BY MANAGERS

Managers need different sets of skills at different levels of management. The specific skills needed by most managers were discussed in chapter 1. Many diverse skills, including conceptual, human relations, and technical skills, are required of managers. Skills are needed that will lead to the:

- creation of a vision and a commitment to it, thereby creating a climate conducive to strategic thinking and action;

- coordination of greater team-based initiatives in a knowledge-based learning organization, consultation with funding authorities, within the organization and in the greater environment, and developing fund-raising skills and attitudes;
- communication of ideas and services effectively to constituents—customers, clients, patrons, users, and potential users of information services;
- consolidation of a positive attitude toward change management, with flexibility being the key to success and change being the only constant.

Most people receiving their library and information science (LIS) degrees graduate with a rudimentary knowledge of many of those skills. Some they may have acquired from past job experience, others they have learned during their professional education program, and still others, including analytical and people skills, they either were born with or have acquired in their life experience. But few individuals graduate knowing enough to become a top-level manager. Persons who maintain a lifelong learning attitude can acquire or improve their abilities in all of these skill areas.

ACQUIRING MANAGEMENT SKILLS

If one is interested in learning and acquiring more management skills, where can one acquire that knowledge? If one is already a manager, how can management skills be improved, and how does one keep up-to-date with all the changes in the field?

The first opportunity to learn skills related to management often comes as part of the educational preparation for entering the profession. Management is taught as a part of the curriculum in almost all LIS programs. Most of the schools offer more than one management course, including such offerings as human resource management, strategic planning, marketing, and financial management. The same types of courses are offered not only in North America but also in schools across the world.

Although all LIS schools offer management courses, there are some problems associated with teaching management in programs designed for preparing individuals for their first professional position. One is the short length of most programs. In the United States, where the MLIS is the standard entry-level degree, most programs are still only about a year in duration. In that year, students have to master the skills related to librarianship, and the number of these skills has grown as the knowledge base of the field has expanded in the past twenty years. Many new courses have been added because of the need to prepare students to work in the ever more technologically sophisticated libraries of today. At the same time, learning the traditional skills of librarianship, such as reference, collection development, and cataloging and classification, is still required of new graduates. Because many students do not see themselves as managers, they often do not take the management courses that are offered unless they are required to do so.

On-the-Job Opportunities

When newly minted librarians begin their professional careers, it is then that they see the importance of management. Although a few graduates of LIS schools get jobs as directors of small libraries, most graduates go to work in larger organizations in which they have a chance to learn some management skills before they themselves become middle- or top-level managers. All managers learn from doing. Often mistakes are made when a person is learning to manage, but making mistakes is one way of learning. New managers also learn from other managers in the organization and from professional colleagues outside the organization, through mentoring and networking. Observation and on-the-job training are important aspects of development as a manager. One can learn from other managers who are higher in the management structure as well as from those who are on the same level. New managers can learn a great deal from more experienced managers who already have acquired many of the skills and the characteristics that they would like to emulate. They also can observe bad managers and observe ways not to do things.

What Would You Do?

Duckettville was a medium-size town in the heart of Tennessee. Due to its proximity to a quickly growing city, this historical southern town was experiencing steady population growth while trying to maintain its classic southern charm. The feel of the town was one of the attractions for Meredith, the new assistant manager of the Duckettville Branch Library. After having lived, worked, and studied in the New England area, Meredith was, when she saw the job posting for this position a year ago, excited about the opportunity to experience life in the southern United States and therefore decided to apply for her first managerial position. After a year, however, the excitement had faded, and she was wondering why she remained.

It was a little bit surprising to Meredith that she was selected to fill the position of assistant manager. Although her interview with Pam, the branch manager, went well, Meredith thought that she did not have the experience necessary to obtain the position. When offering the position, Pam explained that it was Meredith's hardworking, dependable, and creative attitude that led to her hiring. If only Meredith had been able to see that these words were the first warning signs of the trials that lay ahead for her.

Soon after she arrived, this new manager was asked to supervise all of the library's full-time employees. She was constantly rushing to get her work accomplished but never felt as though she was caught up. Meredith always had been willing to help wherever she could, but she had reached the point of burnout. She was beginning to feel resentment toward Pam, the branch manager, for the discrepancies she saw in the amount of work they performed.

Meredith has assumed a managerial position but feels that she is in over her head. What is Pam's motive in acting as she does? If you were Meredith, what would you do?

(For the rest of this case study, see http://www.lu.com/management.)

Continuing Education

On-the-job education is rarely enough. Continuing education is an important part of every professional's career development. Most large libraries provide staff development classes to teach the management skills that are needed by many of the managers within the organization. Library organizations, both state and national, provide other opportunities to learn management skills. These organizations often provide preconferences or institutes on specific managerial topics. Library consortia often contract for classes to be given for their members; regional networks such as SOLINET or NELINET provide courses on an ongoing basis. In addition, many library-related organizations provide continuing-education courses. For instance, the Association of Research Libraries offers a number of continuing-education classes. LIS schools also provide continuing-education opportunities. Increasingly, various types of classes are offered online so that managers can learn new techniques and skills without leaving home. As a result of the interest in developing leaders, a number of leadership institutes at both the state level and the national level have been established. There are also programs like the Senior Fellows Institute designed for upper-level academic library administrators as a step on the way to a library directorship.

So aspiring library managers can improve their knowledge by attending a wide variety of educational offerings. Sometimes managers, having recognized that to manage large and complex organizations requires a great deal of advanced management expertise, want a more systematic immersion in the discipline, and so they decide to get an additional degree in the field of management. Today, many library directors have MBA degrees, whereas others have master's degrees in public administration.

 ## What Do You Think?

As one moves up the organizational ladder, matters become less tangible and less predictable. A primary characteristic of managing, particularly at higher levels, is the confrontation of change, ambiguity, and contradiction. Managers spend much of their time living in fields of perceived tensions. They are constantly forced to make trade-offs, and often find that there are no right answers. The higher one goes in an organization, the more exaggerated this phenomenon becomes.

> In the previous quotation, Robert Quinn points out some of the chal-
> lenges facing managers. Why is it so difficult to function in an ambiguous
> environment? How do managers learn to cope with such conditions? How
> do you feel that you would do in circumstances such as these?
>
> ———————————
>
> Robert E. Quinn, *Beyond Rational Management* (San Francisco: Jossey-
> Bass, 1988), 3.

One important component in every manager's continuing-education port-
folio must be keeping up-to-date by reading both LIS management literature
and management literature in general. Most librarians have easy access to
both types of literature, which can provide a quick way to stay abreast of
current trends. In addition, there is a wealth of management information
available at one's fingertips through the Internet. Indeed, there is so much
material available on the Web that individuals are required to use their good
judgment about its accuracy, timeliness, and authenticity.

As was discussed in chapter 12, career development is the responsibility of
each professional. Organizations have a role to play in helping their employees
grow and develop, but the ultimate responsibility to shape a career belongs to
each individual to take responsibility for himself or herself. As Peter Drucker
noted, even today remarkably few Americans are prepared to select jobs for
themselves. "When you ask, 'Do you know what you are good at? Do you know
your limitations?' they look at you with a blank stare. Or they often respond
in terms of subject knowledge, which is the wrong answer. When they prepare
their résumés, they still try to list positions like steps up a ladder. It is time
to give up thinking of jobs or career paths as we once did and think in terms
of taking on assignments one after the other."[6] Twenty-first-century library
and information services managers need to develop their own portfolios of
management skills that will permit them the flexibility to respond to a rapidly
changing environment.

Opportunities for good managers are unlimited. Many organizations are competing for a limited number of talented managers of the twenty-first century.
Those professionals, wearing the two hats of librarians and managers, have
numerous opportunities to assume new, more challenging positions. They are
able to advance in their managerial positions to achieve their professional
goals. They have learned to network effectively, to think strategically, and
to manage skillfully. Consequently, they are given opportunities to advance
through the managerial ranks and to assume top positions at leading institutions. If questioned about their career goals, it is likely that most would describe a plan, a strategy, with at least a ten-year timeline. They have identified
and developed the skills necessary to succeed in the present position while
developing strategies for the next one.

CONCLUSION

Good people in management positions are vital to the existence of library
and information service organizations. The authors hope that every reader of

this textbook considers the option of becoming a manager and begins to prepare for that eventuality. In any case, it should be recognized that, whether a person is a manager or the one being managed, management in successful organizations is a process that involves many individuals, from top-level managers to team leaders. To be committed to customer services requires every employee's total dedication to the vision and mission of the knowledge-based organization.

This chapter began by imagining Melvil Dewey awakening from a long nap, and it will close with him. As a manager, Melvil Dewey had a great impact on the libraries of his day. Because of his efforts, the library profession came of age in the late nineteenth century.[7] Managers like Dewey can have a great influence on their individual organizations and on their professions as a whole.

Due to the efforts of managers such as Dewey, our libraries and information agencies have had an organization and a structure that has worked well in the past. However, at the present time, these institutions are in the process of making a major transition from paper-based to digitally based organizations. They are confronting increasing competition and new challenges. Library managers are needed to prepare libraries to meet the demands of tomorrow. To ensure their continued existence, libraries need managers who will be the Melvil Deweys of the twenty-first century. We hope that the readers of this book will be those managers.

NOTES

1. Rachel Singer Gordon, "Next Generation Librarianship," *American Libraries* 37, no. 3 (March 2006): 36–38.
2. Diane Oblinger, "Understanding the New Students," *Educause Review* 38, no. 3 (2003): 36–42.
3. Gordon, "Next Generation Librarianship," 37.
4. Henry Mintzberg, *The Nature of Managerial Work* (Englewood Cliffs, NJ: Prentice-Hall, 1980).
5. Mary Pergander, "A Tale of Two Librarians," *American Libraries* 37, no. 4 (April 2006): 82.
6. T. George Harris, "The Post-Capitalist Executive: An Interview with Peter F. Drucker," in *Managing in the New Economy*, ed. Joan Margretta (Boston: Harvard Business School, 1999), 163.
7. For more about Dewey as a manager, see Wayne A. Wiegand, *Irrepressible Reformer: A Biography of Melvil Dewey* (Chicago: American Library Association, 1996).

Index

477

About the Authors

Robert D. Stueart is professor and dean emeritus of Simmons College in Boston, where he was dean for twenty years. From 1994 through 1997, he served as professor of information management in the School of Advanced Technologies and as executive director of the Center for Library and Information Resources at the Asian Institute of Technology in Bangkok, Thailand, where he developed both PhD and master's programs in information management. During his career, he also served on faculties of the University of Denver, the University of Wales, and the University of Pittsburgh, as well as on the senior administrative staffs of libraries at both the University of Colorado and Pennsylvania State University.

Dr. Stueart has received many honors, including the American Library Association (ALA) Honorary Member Award, Melvil Dewey medal for creative professional achievement, and the Beta Phi Mu award for service to education nationally and internationally, all presented by the ALA. In 1994, he was presented the Humphrey/OCLC/Forest Press International Award, given for "significant contributions to International Librarianship." He has received outstanding alumni awards from all three of his degree-granting universities.

Professor Stueart has served in leadership roles in many professional organizations, including the executive board and the council of the ALA and the executive board of the International Federation of Library Associations and Institutions. He also has served as president of three library associations: the Association for Library and Information Education; Beta Phi Mu, the international library science society; and the former Library Education Division of the ALA.

He received the John F. Kennedy International Scholar award twice and both a Fulbright fellowship to Thailand and a Fulbright Senior Scholar Award to help develop information management, library, and information science curricula. From 1987 until its dissolution, he chaired the joint U.S.-USSR Commission on Library Cooperation, cosponsored by the American Council on Learned Societies and the USSR Ministry of Culture.

Dr. Stueart has consulted and lectured for the U.S. government, UNESCO, OCLC, foundations, and other governments in many countries in Asia (including China, Hong Kong, India, Indonesia, Japan, South Korea, Laos, Malaysia, Myanmar, Singapore, Thailand, and Vietnam), Europe (Belarus, England, Germany, Russia, Ukraine, and Wales), and Africa (South Africa, Botswana, and Swaziland). In addition, he has conducted many workshops, has facilitated strategic planning exercises, and has completed management evaluations in many of those countries. He recently has worked with a foundation on program development in Vietnam, serving as an expert for UNESCO's project on developing Information and Communication Technology training courses for librarians in developing countries of Asia, and as external examiner for a major university in Malaysia. He is a sought-after facilitator for strategic issue identification and strategic planning.

His books include a two-volume, award-winning work on collection development and the recently published *Guide to International Librarianship.* He has edited or written more than a dozen monographs, including coediting the reference work entitled *World Guide to Library Archive and Information Science Education.* He has written more than fifty refereed articles in journals and has served on the editorial boards of three major international professional journals.

Barbara B. Moran received an AB from Mount Holyoke College, an MLn from Emory University, and a PhD from the State University of New York at Buffalo. Before beginning her PhD studies, she worked as a school and academic librarian. She joined the faculty at the School of Information and Library Science at the University of North Carolina at Chapel Hill in 1981 and became dean there in 1990. In January 1999, she rejoined the faculty. At the present time, she teaches primarily in the management area and has a special interest in human resources management. She has taught and lectured in universities and libraries both in the United States and internationally and received a Fulbright Senior Specialist Award to teach at Charles University in Prague, Czech Republic, in spring 2006. She has served on the editorial boards of four academic journals and presently serves on the Board of Governors of the University of North Carolina Press. She has authored or coauthored seven books and more than seventy articles and is currently engaged in research focusing on new organizational structures in academic libraries and on the individuals working in these new structures.